Studies in the History of Medieval Religion

VOLUME XXXI

A HISTORY OF
THE ABBEY OF BURY ST EDMUNDS
1182–1256

Samson of Tottington to Edmund of Walpole

Studies in the History of Medieval Religion

ISSN 0955–2480

General Editor
Christopher Harper-Bill

Previously published titles in the series
are listed at the back of this volume

A HISTORY OF
THE ABBEY OF BURY ST EDMUNDS
1182–1256

Samson of Tottington to Edmund of Walpole

ANTONIA GRANSDEN

THE BOYDELL PRESS

First published 2007
The Boydell Press, Woodbridge

ISBN 978–1–84383–324–6

The Boydell Press is an imprint of Boydell & Brewer Ltd
PO Box 9, Woodbridge, Suffolk IP12 3DF, UK
and of Boydell & Brewer Inc.
668 Mt Hope Avenue, Rochester, NY 14620, USA
website: www.boydellandbrewer.com

A catalogue record for this book is available
from the British Library

This publication is printed on acid-free paper

Printed in Great Britain by
Antony Rowe Ltd, Chippenham, Wiltshire

This book is dedicated to my two daughters,
Katherine Constable and Deborah Shields, with all my love.

Contents

Part I. SAMSON OF TOTTINGTON, ABBOT 1182–1211

Plates

Full acknowledgement of permission to reproduce illustrations is given in the Acknowledgements below.

Figures

Preface

The Abbey of Bury St Edmunds was one of the wealthiest and most highly privileged Benedictine abbeys in medieval England. It owed its prestige in no small measure to the fact that it contained the shrine of St Edmund, king and martyr, King of East Anglia, who had been killed by the Danes in 869. The abbey was one of the five monasteries in England under the direct authority of the pope and so exempt from metropolitan and diocesan control. In secular affairs it was equally privileged. In its Liberty of the eight and a half hundreds, comprising all west Suffolk, the abbey exercised shrieval jurisdiction and within the town of St Edmunds itself it had regalian rights: no minister or official of the crown could enter without the abbot's express agreement.

An exceptionally rich archive survives from St Edmunds. There are extant about forty registers and cartularies, some of massive size and containing copies of documents and literary pieces relating to all periods of the abbey's history. Besides these, about 270 volumes survive of the monks' library books, though this number is only a small fraction of the original collection which comprised between 1,500 and 2,000 volumes. Despite, or perhaps because of, this abundance of primary sources for the abbey's history, no attempt at a comprehensive study has been made since the publication of Albert Goodwin's *The Abbey of St. Edmundsbury* (Oxford: Basil Blackwell, 1931). This good but short account, now out of print, was the author's Gladstone Memorial Prize Essay, awarded in 1926. For his study Goodwin used what primary sources were available in print at that time, that is, chronicles, public records and documents from the abbey's archives, besides secondary sources. But much relevant material has been published since. New, up-to-date, editions of the Latin texts, with English translations, of its three most important chronicles have appeared in Nelson's, later Oxford, Medieval Texts series: the *Chronicle of Jocelin of Brakelond*, edited by H. E. Butler (1949); the *Chronicle of the Election of Hugh, Abbot of Bury St Edmunds and later Bishop of Ely*, edited by R. M. Thomson; and *The Chronicle of Bury St Edmunds 1212–1301*, which I edited (1964). Concurrently, collections of documents, indispensable for the abbey's history, have appeared: *Feudal Documents from the Abbey of Bury St Edmunds*, edited by D. C. Douglas (Oxford, 1932); *The Kalendar of Abbot Samson and related Documents*, edited by R. H. C. Davis (Camden Society, 1954); and *The Letter-Book of William of Hoo 1280–1294*, edited by me (Suffolk Records Society, 1963). With regard to the abbey's book collection, scholars are indebted to the publication of the monks' extant catalogues by Richard Sharpe in the *Corpus of British Medieval Catalogues*, iv, *English Benedictine Libraries*, edited by him and others (British Library and British Academy, 1996), and to R. H. and M. A. Rouse for a similar edition of Henry of Kirkstead's catalogue in the same series (ix, *Henry of Kirkestede, Catalogue de Libris autenticus et apocrifis* (British Library and British Academy, 2004)). Moreover new light is thrown on

the monks' religious and cultural liturgical life by my edition of the abbey's thir-
teenth-century *Customary* together with other related texts (Henry Bradshaw
Society, xcix, 1973). Besides the publication of these primary sources, there are
numerous monographs relating to particular aspects of the abbey's history. Fore-
most of these secondary sources is M. D. Lobel, *The Borough of Bury St Edmunds*
(Oxford, 1935). Moreover, there are many authoritative articles, notably by
Lobel, W. C. Davis, R. H. C. Davis, V. H. Galbraith, Paul Harvey, R. H. Rouse,
Norman Scarfe, Richard Sharpe and R. M. Thomson.

The scholarly attention which St Edmunds abbey has attracted since
Goodwin wrote must not obscure the fact that our greatest debt is to eight-
eenth- and nineteenth-century antiquaries and historians who, working without
the aid of modern reference books or of modern technology, nevertheless
produced invaluable editions and studies. John Batteley led the way with his
Antiquitates S. Edmundi Burgi ad annum 1272 (Oxford, 1745). He was followed
by John Gage, later John Gage Rokewode, who in 1838 published his definitive *History and Antiquities of Suffolk. Thinghoe Hundred*. He also produced the
earliest edition of Jocelin of Brackland's chronicle, the learned critical apparatus
of which still holds its value (Camden Society, 1840). Then, in 1865, Gordon
M. Hills published a long, two-part article entitled 'The Antiquities of Bury St
Edmunds' in the *Journal of the British Archaeological Association*, xxi. He examines
the abbey's history and topography after research mainly on many of the abbey's
registers and on the few archaeological remains. Among the late nineteenth-
century antiquaries and historians, two are outstanding, Thomas Arnold and M.
R. James. The former, by publishing many of the abbey's chronicles, historical
monographs and documents, some previously unprinted, in his *Memorials of St
Edmund's Abbey* (Rolls Series, 1890–6, 3 volumes), provided a basic source-book
for future historians. M. R. James's monograph *On the Abbey of S. Edmund at
Bury*, I, *The Library*, II, *The Church*, appeared in 1895 (Cambridge Antiquarian
Society, octavo series viii). In it James provided the first list of the monks'
library books, describing each volume in turn, including its binding and physical
appearance, and itemizing the contents. His researches enabled him to discover
much about how and where the books were kept. His interest in the topography
of the abbey's precincts and church is most fully expressed in the second part of
his volume which has a pull-out plan of each. James also had much to say about
the abbey's treasures, almost without exception lost but mentioned in scattered
references in the monastic archives. His work remains an essential source for the
historian today.

Many years ago I conceived the ambition of writing a comprehensive history
of St Edmund's abbey from its origins in the eleventh century to 1539, when the
last abbot, John Reeve, the prior and monks surrendered the abbey, its possessions and its estates to Henry VIII's commissioners. There has been a tendency
of historians of monastic history in general and of those studying individual
houses in particular to concentrate either on the religious aspect of the subject
or on economic affairs. My ambition was to try to bridge the gap, to give a
picture of the whole. However, I soon realized that I would be overwhelmed by
the vast amount of evidence and so resolved to confine myself to the abbey's

history from the late twelfth century, the succession of Samson of Tottington in 1182, to the start of the fourteenth century, the death of John of Northwold in 1301. I chose this period because while the minsters and monasteries of the Anglo-Saxon period have attracted much scholarly attention, as has monasticism in the twelfth century, and likewise in the fourteenth, fifteenth and early sixteenth centuries, monastic history in the thirteenth century has been comparatively speaking neglected. And yet the subject in the thirteenth century is of exceptional interest. It was a period of monastic reform and during it royal, clerical and papal taxation first became a problem for monastic finances. In addition, religious houses had to weather the political crises of the period, notably the Barons' War and its aftermath. St Edmunds, being one of the wealthiest and most highly privileged abbeys in England, was closely affected by national events – its history, indeed, is an integral part of the political, administrative and economic history of England.

The present study attempts to describe a wide range of the preoccupations and activities of the abbot and monks. Included is discussion of the monks' religious life and daily routine, their relations with each other and with the abbot, as well as their cultural and intellectual interests and achievements. Also considered are the abbey's management of its estates and financial problems, and its relations with unfree, free and military tenants, and with nearby neighbours. Where particularly pertinent to St Edmunds' history, parallels are drawn with the situation in other religious houses at that time (St Edmunds had, for instance, especial affinities with St Albans, another highly privileged and wealthy Benedictine abbey with a shrine church). In addition, relations with the king and central government are discussed, and the abbey's contacts with the papacy and episcopacy.

This volume is the first of two which together will cover our prescribed period. It takes the history to 1256, the death of Abbot Edmund of Walpole. It is in two parts. The first part considers the abbacy of Samson, for which the evidence is plentiful: to it belong the earliest register known to survive from St Edmunds as well as numerous charters, and there is of course the renowned chronicle of Jocelin of Brackland, which deservedly holds its place as one of the great medieval Latin classics. The second part discusses the rules of Samson's four successors. Although there is an excellent, contemporary chronicle giving a detailed account of the disputed election in 1212 of Samson's immediate successor, Hugh of Northwold, evidence about the careers of Hugh's three successors is patchy and far from uniformly clear. Nevertheless, although the monks produced no contemporary chronicle in that period, Matthew Paris at St Albans took a close interest in the abbey's affairs, and copies of many charters and other documents survive, mainly scattered through later registers. Of particular interest are the mid-thirteenth-century obedientiary and manorial accounts, the earliest known from St Edmunds. Furthermore, the period is important in the abbey's history because of the involvement of abbot and monks in contemporary ecclesiastical politics, that is with the Church's disputes with King John and Henry III. Whether or not Hugh of Northwold also participated in the baronial opposition is uncertain. Also within this period the papacy embarked on the reform of the

Benedictines order, to tighten observance of the Rule of St Benedict. Its instruments were the episcopacy and papal legates – those *a latera* had the power to
hold visitations of exempt religious houses. And in 1215 Innocent III convened
the Fourth Lateran Council. One of its reforming canons (c. 12) established that
the Benedictines in each province were to hold a General Chapter every three
years, which was to legislate for the reform of houses within its province and to
send out visitors to specific houses. St Edmunds felt the impact of legatine visitations and the abbots played an active role in the work of the General Chapters.

In a study of this kind, which aims at being comprehensive, the problem is to
get the overall balance right. I do not claim to have succeeded in this respect.
The balance is mainly determined by the amount of evidence available, or at
least accessible without too much difficulty, on specific subjects. For example,
the registers and accounts have plenty of information about the abbey's business
affairs but little on the monks' religious life: only Jocelin of Brackland, the Bury
Customary and related documents give us a glimpse of that. The balance is also
influenced by the current preoccupations of historians, and I myself am particularly attracted to some subjects. However, I can claim that I have tried to be fair
and unprejudiced and not to have written anything contrary to the weight of
the evidence as I know it.

Antonia Gransden

Editorial Note

With a view to keeping my book as firmly as possible in its local context I have rendered toponymical surnames in their modern form. For example, I call Jocelin, the chronicler and biographer of Abbot Samson, Jocelin of Brackland, not Jocelin de Brakelond (some of the spellings in the manuscripts are in the index *sub nomine*), unless I have failed to identify the place concerned. Similarly, I use 'of' not 'de' unless this usage might be confusing and misleading and contrary to established practice – thus, Richard earl of Gloucester remains as Richard de Clare and not Richard of Clare. In order to distinguish the abbey from the town I have always referred to the former as St Edmunds (the medieval nomenclature) and the town as Bury St Edmunds or Bury. However, for the sake of brevity I occasionally use 'Bury' as an adjective for the abbey's literary products. For example, I refer to the Bury chronicle.

Year-dates are given below according to modern usage, that is, according to the Gregorian calendar. The day of the week is also given according to modern usage, that is, as Monday, Tuesday and so on, but it must be remembered that in the Christian West in the middle ages a day-date was usually indicated by a saint's day or other church festival or the day nearest to it.[1]

I do not claim that my references in the footnotes are exhaustive. On the contrary, many are intended as pointers, to guide those who wish to pursue the matter further. Nor do I claim that the copies of texts to which I refer are necessarily the only copies. Other copies may well survive in the Public Records or in the abbey's registers, in whose rich resources much remains to be discovered.

---

[1] The varieties and intricacies of medieval dating are best described in A *Handbook of Dates*, ed. C. R. Cheney, new edition revised by Michael Jones (Cambridge, 2000).

This book is produced with the assistance of grants from Isobel Thornley's Bequest to the University of London, and from The Scouloudi Foundation in association with the Institute of Historical Research

Acknowledgements

In the course of writing this book I have incurred many debts of gratitude. Here I shall mention those who have contributed most to my studies. My thanks to others are expressed in footnotes. Foremost are Barbara Harvey, Barrie Dobson, Christopher Brooke, Marjorie Chibnall, Joan Greatrex and John Maddicott, whose advice and encouragement have always been given with generosity and patience. On matters of canon law I am deeply indebted to Mary Cheney and Martin Brett, and on secular law especially to Paul Brand. On economic history I am indebted to a number of scholars, notably to Mark Bailey, Paul Harvey, Sandra Raban and Richard Britnell, and on St Edmunds' mint to Robin Eaglen and Martin Allen. The late Dorothea Oschinsky gave me the benefit of her deep knowledge of the abbey's thirteenth-century registers, and with regard to the monks' library books, I am very grateful to Richard Sharpe for much help and encouragement. I also owe a debt of gratitude to the local historians and archaeologists at Bury St Edmunds and its region, for their unfailing helpfulness and interest, that is, to Margaret Statham, Robert Carr, David Dymond and Norman Scarfe. Their knowledge of the locality saved me from making mistakes and enabled me to fill some gaps in my account of the abbey's history. Nevertheless, despite my debt to these and other scholars, I alone am responsible for all remaining errors and for the opinions expressed.

In addition, I must thank the staff of the following libraries where I have consulted manuscripts: the British Library, where Michelle Brown (now retired) was always helpful and ready to share with me her vast knowledge of manuscripts; the Manuscripts' Department of Cambridge University Library (the present repository of the medieval manuscripts owned by Pembroke College), where I had help and advice from Jayne Ringrose (now retired); the Bodleian Library, Oxford, and especially Duke Humfrey's Library, the staff of which were always helpful and kind. I did not visit Canterbury Cathedral Archives personally but received authoritative and detailed information about the impressions of Abbot Samson's seal held in that repository from the then Archivist, Heather Forbes (a former pupil of mine at Nottingham University).

I must also express my gratitude to the late Nina Coltart (my friend from our days as students at Somerville College, Oxford), who, by lending me her house in Hampstead when she took her six weeks' summer vacation, enabled me to study the abbey's registers and library books in the British Library without undue travel and expense. I am also grateful to Caroline Palmer and her editorial staff at Boydell and Brewer for their efficiency, good-humoured patience and readiness to listen and agree during the progress of this book to publication; and the British Academy for a generous grant for secretarial assistance which paid for the super-efficient services of Denise Bilton and her husband Philip, who were immensely helpful and always a pleasure to work with.

Illustrations

The copyright of the photographs belongs to, and permission to reproduce them was granted by, the institutions and individuals as follows:

Plate I   The Dean and Chapter of Canterbury Cathedral.

Plates II–V, VIIa and b, IX   The Master and Fellows of Pembroke College, Cambridge.

Plate VIII   The Master and Fellows of Gonville and Caius College, Cambridge.

Plates Xa and b, XIa and b   The British Library Board.

Figures VIII and IX   English Heritage.

Fig. 1. Distribution map of St Edmunds' Liberty of the eight and a half hundreds before 1066.

Fig. 2. Distribution map of St Edmunds' Liberty of the eight and a half hundreds, and its manors and other major holdings in 1086.

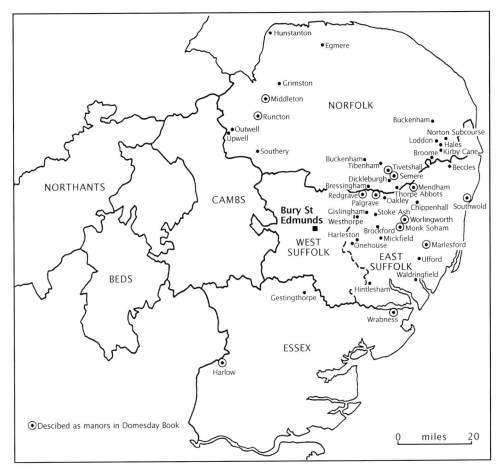

Fig. 3. Distribution map of St Edmunds' holdings outside the Liberty of the eight and a half hundreds before 1066.

Fig. 4. Distribution map of St Edmunds' manors and other major holdings outside the Liberty of the eight and a half hundreds in 1086.

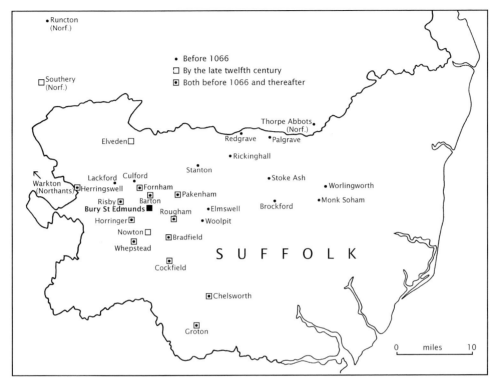

Inside the map:

• Runcton
  (Norf.)

• Before 1066
□ By the late twelfth century
⊡ Both before 1066 and thereafter

□ Southery
  (Norf.)

Thorpe Abbots •
  (Norf.)
Elveden □   Redgrave • Palgrave
                      • Rickinghall
                  Stanton
                              • Stoke Ash
Lackford Culford   • Worlingworth
Warkton ↖ ⊡ Herringswell ⊡ Fornham   • Monk Soham
(Northants)   ⊡ Pakenham
        Risby ⊡ Barton   Brockford
Bury St Edmunds ■ Rougham
                        ⊡
Horringer ⊡   • Elmswell
            Nowton □ • Woolpit
               ⊡
Whepstead   ⊡ Bradfield

                  S U F F O L K
            ⊡
         Cockfield

      ⊡ Chelsworth

      ⊡
   Groton

0   miles   10

Fig. 5. The locations of the food farms: before 1066; by the late twelfth century and in the thirteenth century.

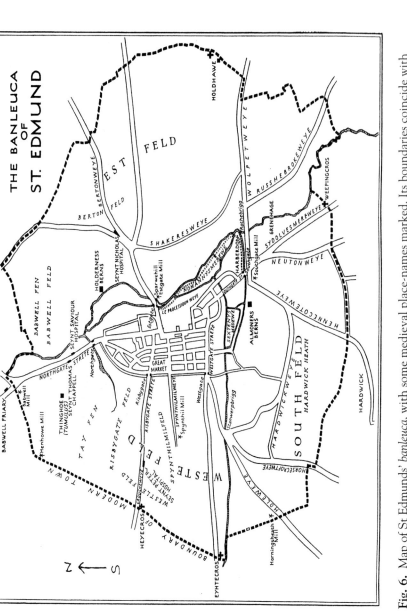

Fig. 6. Map of St Edmunds' *banleuca*, with some medieval place-names marked. Its boundaries coincide with those of the modern borough except that the parishes of Westley and Fornham All Saints, which are now within the borough, were not in the medieval *banleuca*. Reproduced from Lobel, *Bury St Edmunds* (pull-out map at the end of the volume). See esp. Hart, *Early Charters*, pp. 55–8.

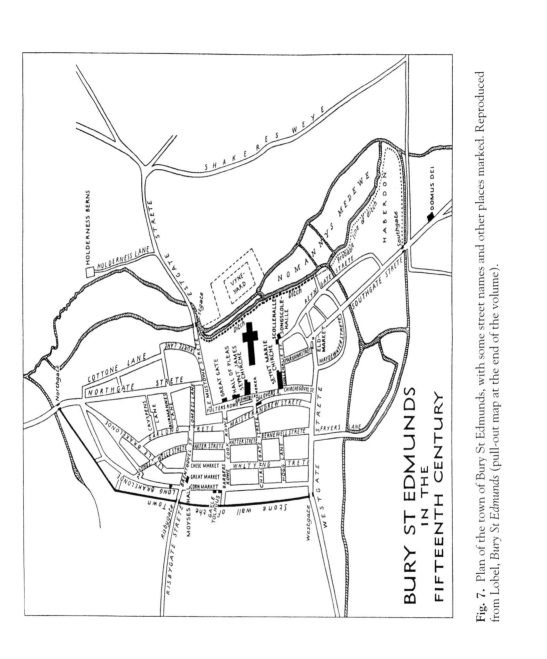

Fig. 7. Plan of the town of Bury St Edmunds, with some street names and other places marked. Reproduced from Lobel, *Bury St Edmunds* (pull-out map at the end of the volume).

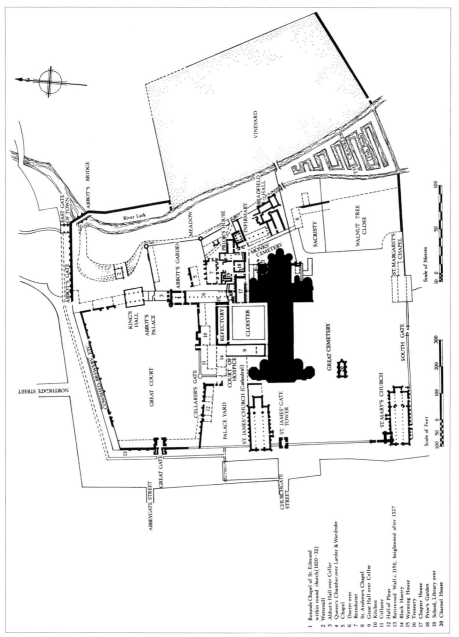

Fig. 8. Conjectural plan of the abbey. Reproduced from A. B. Whittingham, *Bury St Edmunds Abbey* (English Heritage Guidebook, 1992, repr. 2004), pp. 4–5.

1 Rotunda Chapel of St. Edmund within round church (1020–32)
2 Watermill
3 Abbot's Hall over Cellar
4 Queen's Chamber over Larder & Wardrobe
5 Chapel
6 Dorter over
7 Reredorter
8 St Andrew's Chapel
9 Great Hall over Cellar
10 Kitchen
11 Cellarer
12 Hall of Pleas
13 Buttressed Wall c.1150, heightened after 1327
14 Black Hostry
15 Warming House
16 Treasury
17 Chapter House
18 Prior's Garden
19 School, Library over
20 Charnel House

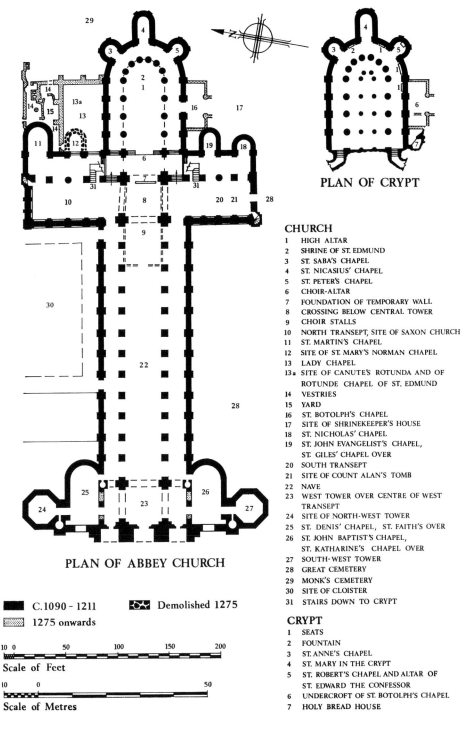

PLAN OF CRYPT

PLAN OF ABBEY CHURCH

■ C.1090 - 1211   ☒ Demolished 1275

▨ 1275 onwards

10 0   50   100   150   200

Scale of Feet

10   0   50

Scale of Metres

CHURCH
1   HIGH ALTAR
2   SHRINE OF ST. EDMUND
3   ST. SABA'S CHAPEL
4   ST. NICASIUS' CHAPEL
5   ST. PETER'S CHAPEL
6   CHOIR-ALTAR
7   FOUNDATION OF TEMPORARY WALL
8   CROSSING BELOW CENTRAL TOWER
9   CHOIR STALLS
10 NORTH TRANSEPT, SITE OF SAXON CHURCH
11 ST. MARTIN'S CHAPEL
12 SITE OF ST. MARY'S NORMAN CHAPEL
13 LADY CHAPEL
13a SITE OF CANUTE'S ROTUNDA AND OF
    ROTUNDE CHAPEL OF ST. EDMUND
14 VESTRIES
15 YARD
16 ST. BOTOLPH'S CHAPEL
17 SITE OF SHRINEKEEPER'S HOUSE
18 ST. NICHOLAS' CHAPEL
19 ST. JOHN EVANGELIST'S CHAPEL,
    ST. GILES' CHAPEL OVER
20 SOUTH TRANSEPT
21 SITE OF COUNT ALAN'S TOMB
22 NAVE
23 WEST TOWER OVER CENTRE OF WEST
    TRANSEPT
24 SITE OF NORTH-WEST TOWER
25 ST. DENIS' CHAPEL, ST. FAITH'S OVER
26 ST. JOHN BAPTIST'S CHAPEL,
    ST. KATHARINE'S CHAPEL OVER
27 SOUTH-WEST TOWER
28 GREAT CEMETERY
29 MONK'S CEMETERY
30 SITE OF CLOISTER
31 STAIRS DOWN TO CRYPT

CRYPT
1   SEATS
2   FOUNTAIN
3   ST. ANNE'S CHAPEL
4   ST. MARY IN THE CRYPT
5   ST. ROBERT'S CHAPEL AND ALTAR OF
    ST. EDWARD THE CONFESSOR
6   UNDERCROFT OF ST. BOTOLPH'S CHAPEL
7   HOLY BREAD HOUSE

Fig. 9. Plan of the abbey church. Reproduced from A. B. Whittingham, *Bury St Edmunds Abbey* (English Heritage Guidebook, 1992, repr. 2004), p. 12.

PART I

SAMSON OF TOTTINGTON, ABBOT 1182–1211

This, the first of two volumes which will cover altogether the years from 1182 to 1256, is longer than the second, despite the fact that it concerns only one abbot, Samson, and his rule, while the second concerns his four successors and their abbacies which cover in total forty-four years. The main reason for this imbalance is that for Samson there is an abundance of evidence, much of it contemporary, but his four successors are comparatively poorly served in that respect. Above all, for Samson there is the superlative work of Jocelin of Brackland. Few medieval abbots were favoured with such lifelike portraits of themselves and such graphic descriptions of the convent under their rule as was Samson. Jocelin's work is more than a biography: in the middle ages it was entitled 'cronica' and it is called a 'chronicle' to this day.[1] It is a literary narrative recounting the history of St Edmunds from 1180 to 1202, with Samson figuring as large as life at its centre.

---

[1] The only known complete text of the chronicle is in the *Liber Albus* of St Edmunds' abbey, BL MS Harley 1005, ff. 127–70 (of modern foliation). The text was copied in the second half of the thirteenth century. Another, rather earlier copy is in BL MS Cotton Vitellius D XV, but it was almost totally destroyed in the fire in Ashburnham House, where the Cottonian manuscripts were kept, in 1731. What can be deciphered of the text shows that it was derived from the exemplar of BL MS Harl. 1005. See R. A. B. Mynors in *JB*, pp. xi–xiii. Two extracts appear in a thirteenth-century hand at the end of Bodl. Lib. MS Bodley 297, a twelfth-century Bury version of John of Worcester's chronicle. The same excerpts and one other are in the fourteenth-century Bury hagiographical collection, Bodl. Lib. MS Bodley 240. These excerpts are discussed by McGuire, 'Collapse of a monastic friendship', pp. 388–91. Besides the edition of Jocelin's chronicle edited and translated by H. E. Butler used here, there is an edition of the Latin text with valuable end-notes ed. John Gage Rokewode (Camden Soc., o.s., xiii, 1840). The edition in *Memorials*, i. 209–336, is largely based on Rokewode's edition. For a recent translation with useful end-notes see *JB*, ed. Greenway and Sayers.

Unfortunately, Jocelin's chronicle does not cover the last decade of Samson's abbacy. Its value as a source for Samson's abbatiate will be very evident in the pages which follow. However, it has been used in conjunction with other literary sources and with record evidence preserved in the abbey's archives[2] and in the Public Record Office. These, of course, are our sole authorities once Jocelin's chronicle ends in 1202. Although nearly all the relevant literary sources extant are thirteenth- and fourteenth-century versions, their authors included earlier material. For example, the *Gesta Sacristarum* has much information on building work in the abbey in Samson's time,[3] and the so-called *Cronica Buriensis* fills in a few gaps in our knowledge of Samson's career.[4] The latter is only known from a copy, incomplete at the end, made in about 1400. It is a history of St Edmunds from 1020 to 1346. Other gaps are filled by the earliest monastic chronicle known to survive from St Edmunds, the so-called *Annales Sancti Edmundi*.[5] This brief chronicle covers the period from the Incarnation to 1212. It ends incomplete in the course of the annal for 1212 owing to the loss of leaves from the only known copy. This last annal is a full, contemporaneous account of national events composed in 1212 or shortly afterwards. The earlier part of the *Annales* is mainly a compilation from various narrative sources. These are all well known until 1199. From then until 1211 one of the sources was a now lost chronicle which was also used by Roger of Wendover.[6] This derivative part of the chronicle includes a few entries not found elsewhere which concern St Edmunds and are of some, though limited, value for the abbey's history and latterly for Samson's

---

[2] Nearly all the charters are discussed and edited by Davis, *Kalendar*, pp. xlvii–lx passim, 74–170.

[3] *Gesta Sacrist.*, pp. 291–2.

[4] The extant text of the *Cronica Buriensis* which (printed *Memorials*, iii. 1–73) is in a composite hagiographic and historical volume from St Edmunds, CUL MS Additional 850, ff. 25v–48v. It records the succession of the abbots and individual important events. It is almost certainly by more than one successive author. Changes of authorship appear to occur in 1327 and 1335. To 1327 it may well have been compiled by the sacrist of St Edmunds, William of Stow, or by some other refugee from St Edmunds while staying along with him in the abbey of St Benet of Hulme (or of 'Holme') during the revolt of the Bury townsmen in 1327. The date when Stow returned to St Edmunds is unknown, but the contents of the *Cronica* show that by 1335 at latest it was at St Edmunds. The compiler, Stow or whoever, used various records probably brought by the refugees in 1327. Many of the *Cronica*'s sources were versions of extant texts, for example the *Annales Sancti Edmundi* (see below and next note) and the Bury Chronicle (below p. 218 and n.3). The sources for the abbatial succession was probably some lost list like that in the abbey's late fourteenth-century register, CUL MS 743, ff. 52–53v (Thomson, *Archives*, p. 129, II.3). Because of the use of variant versions of known sources and now lost sources, the *Cronica* contains some unique information. See Gransden, 'Cronica Buriensis and the abbey of St Benet of Hulme', pp. 77–82 (repr. in eadem, *Legends, Traditions and History*, pp. 239–44), and eadem, *Exhibition Catalogue*, pp. 269–70 and pl. LXXXIII B.

[5] Discussed and printed by Liebermann in *Ungedruckte Anglo-Normannische Geschichtsquellen*, pp. 97–155. The annals from 1032 are printed by Arnold in *Memorials*, ii. vii–viii, 3 and n. a., 4–25; he bases his text on Liebermann's.

[6] Liebermann, ed. cit., pp. 101–3; Vaughan, *Matthew Paris*, p. 24; Gransden, *Historical Writing*, [i]. 359 and n. 24.

abbatiate. The chronicle's detailed last annal, the only one independent of all known narrative sources, relates to the period after Samson's death.[7]

The value of Jocelin of Brackland's chronicle as a source will be amply illustrated in the chapters on Samson and his rule. Therefore, it seems appropriate to start the present book with an account of Jocelin, his career and mentality.

[7] Liebermann, p. 150; *Memorials*, ii. 19–20.

1

Samson's Biographer,
Jocelin of Brackland (de Brakelond),
and his work

Jocelin's toponymic indicates that he was a native of Long Brackland Street or Short Brackland Street in Bury St Edmunds.[1] He reveals in the chronicle that he entered St Edmund's abbey in 1173, when Hugh I was abbot (1157–80), and that Samson was his master during his novitiate.[2] Later he became the prior's chaplain and within four months of Samson's succession to the abbacy he was appointed his chaplain.[3] He held that office for six years, acting as Samson's secretary,[4] 'noting many things and storing them in [his] memory'.[5] After 1188 he seems to have had no official position in the abbey until he was appointed guest-master. The date of his appointment is unknown, but it must have been in 1197 or shortly afterwards.[6] It is also unknown how long he held that office and so is the date of his death. The chronicle itself ends in 1202, with Samson's departure to visit King John in France on the convent's business. This is all that can be learnt about Jocelin's career from the chronicle. However, some scholars have identified him with 'Jocelin the almoner' who occurs as a witness in a charter, datable to between 1206 and 1209,[7] and in the account of the election, 1213–15, of Samson's successor to the abbacy, Hugh of Northwold.[8] This identification entails accepting that the story in the chronicle concerning Henry of Essex,

---

1   Norman Scarfe, *Jocelin of Brakelond* (Grace Guides on British Heritage, Leominster, 1997), p. 5 and facing map. Cf. Statham, 'Medieval town', pp. 4, 5 (map), 8. Some of the following account of Jocelin recapitulates in a revised form a paper I delivered at the Seventeenth Congress of Historical Sciences held in Madrid in 1992. (*Section II. Chronological sessions, Methodology: the Historical Biography*, ed. E. B. Ruano and M. E. Burgos (Madrid, 1992)), pp. 1138–46.
2   JB, pp. 1 and nn. 1, 4.
3   JB, p. 26.
4   JB, pp. 35–6.
5   'plurima notans et memorie commendans', JB, p. 26. In classical Latin *memoria* can mean a memoir. Cf. below p. 11.
6   JB, p. 129.
7   *Kalendar*, ed. Davis, p. 90 no. 26. Cf. JB, ed. Rokewode, p. vi; *Memorials*, i. lix; JB, p. xiii; Thomson, 'Obedientiaries', p. 99.
8   For whom see Thomson in *Electio*, p. 185 and index under 'Jocelin, almoner of St Edmunds'.

recounted to the writer by 'Jocelin, the almoner, a man of great piety, powerful in word and deed', is an interpolation.[9] This is quite possible: it certainly reads like one. Moreover, the description of Jocelin the almoner would fit Jocelin of Brackland nicely. Other scholars have argued that Jocelin was cellarer in the late twelfth and early thirteenth century.[10] In its present form the chronicle was composed in 1202 or 1203. Jocelin, therefore, wrote retrospectively. He used written sources as well as oral testimony and his own recollections. He also worked up some notes or a draft memoir written when he was Samson's chaplain.[11] This must explain the intimate, personal tone of the chronicle.

Jocelin was much more self-revelatory than most medieval biographers and chroniclers. Judging from his chronicle Jocelin was a pious and a good man. He obviously had a deep veneration for the abbey's patron saint, St Edmund. Particularly graphic is his account of the fire which devastated St Edmund's shrine in 1198, its restoration and the martyr's reburial.[12] He describes in moving terms the monks' initial despair and their joy that St Edmund's body and even his cup survived intact. He also describes the grief of those monks whom Samson excluded from the viewing of the body and the community's tearfulness as it sang the 'Te Deum' after the body's translation. Jocelin's personal goodness, his warm heartedness, humility and wisdom appear in a number of passages. Clearly he had a strong personal affection for Samson which survived despite the fact that he came to see much deserving criticism,[13] and he was fond of others besides Samson. He sadly tells how he lost a friend and benefactor: during the discussions which preceded Samson's election as abbot, Jocelin said in private that he did not think that this particular monk was a suitable candidate; unfortunately his remark was repeated to the monk and 'neither words nor gifts' could win back his affection. Jocelin decided that in future he would speak more carefully.[14] He was always ready to learn from adversity. One of his most revealing passages shows how he reconciled himself to one of Samson's most controversial acts, his appointment as prior in 1201, against the convent's wishes, of his chaplain, Herbert, a good-looking, charming, young man but inexperienced and with 'only a smattering of education'. Jocelin sat, he says, 'in the porch of the guest-house hall, dumbfounded', carefully turning over in his mind 'for what qualities such a man was promoted to such a high office'. Gradually, by reflecting on Herbert's merits, his good humour, cheerful disposition and general sociability, and by remembering that 'nothing is entirely perfect',[15] Jocelin came to terms with Samson's choice. He wept for joy and exclaimed 'That God hath visited us [Luke 7.16]: as it hath pleased the Lord, so hath it been done [Job 1.21].'

Jocelin was a learned man. He cites freely from the Bible and from classical

---

9 JB, pp. 68–71.
10 Below pp. 9–10.
11 Above p. 5 and n. 6.
12 JB, pp. 106–16. Below pp. 96–9.
13 Below pp. 7–8.
14 JB, pp. 14–15.
15 See below p. 8 and n.23.

authors, and was knowledgeable in civil and canon law.[16] In his accounts of disputes in the convent between the learned and the unlearned monks, notably before the election of Samson and that of Prior Herbert, Jocelin's sympathies lay with the learned.[17] He apparently preferred the quiet to the active life. Once when he was Samson's chaplain he ventured to ask him, with implied criticism, why he was so uncheerful to his monks. Samson was incensed and upbraided him. He said that Jocelin had no part in, and could not understand, the many worldly cares and difficulties that beset him as abbot, 'things that cause me misery and heartache'. Jocelin's response was to raise his hands to heaven and pray: 'Almighty and merciful God, spare me from such anxieties.'[18]

Jocelin may well have had a reputation as an author, at least with Samson and his intimates. Besides writing the chronicle, he wrote a Life or, more probably, a monograph on the miracles of Little St Robert: having mentioned the (alleged) martyrdom of Robert, his burial in the abbey church and the miracles performed, he adds 'as we have written elsewhere'.[19] Jocelin probably wrote this work while he was Samson's chaplain, perhaps at his request. As will be seen, Samson himself most likely commissioned the revised and much enlarged version of the late eleventh-century work on the miracles of St Edmund (*De Miraculis Sancti Eadmundi*).[20]

The change in Jocelin's circumstances in the late 1180s, from Samson's chaplain to cloister monk and then obedientiary, affected his outlook: the convent replaced Samson as his primary concern; and, since Samson was often in dispute with the convent, Jocelin suffered mental agonies. On the one hand was his loyalty to Samson; on the other hand his sympathy with the convent. This is reflected in his chronicle. The first part concerns his time as Samson's chaplain when, he claims, he 'came to know the merits of his life and the depths of his wisdom in all their fulness'.[21] Here Jocelin shows almost unalloyed admiration for Samson. But in the second part, written when he was a cloister monk and obedientiary, his criticisms of Samson mount although until nearly the end his affection and sympathy for Samson seem not to have wholly deserted him.[22]

---

[16] When the convent objected to Samson's appointment of the town reeves without its consent, Samson asserted his authority to do so as abbot; Jocelin marvelled at his words but 'tandem dubitare coactus, eo quod regula iuris dicit et docet, ut omnia sint in dispositione abbatis' (*JB*, p. 75 and n. 2). Jocelin was referring to Gratian's *Decretum*, pt II, causa 18, quaest. 2, canon 9. Friedberg, *Corpus iuris canonici*, i. 831.

[17] When the monks were discussing candidates for election Jocelin said that he: 'would not agree to any man being made abbot, unless he knew something of dialectic and could distinguish between false argument and true'. *JB*, p. 14. For the issue of learning as a qualification for office at the election of Herbert as prior (*JB*, pp. 125–8) see below p. 41.

[18] *JB*, p. 36.

[19] *JB*, p. 16. For the cult of Little St Robert at St Edmunds see below pp. 117–21.

[20] Below pp. 121ff.

[21] *JB*, pp. 36–7.

[22] E.g. see Jocelin's fair-minded account of the convent's quarrel with Samson over his appointment of one of his clerks to supervise the cellary, and, again, over the convent's gate-keeper, Ralph. *JB*, pp. 79–81, 119–20. Similarly, although Jocelin could not deny the truth of accusations made by 'a certain person' against Samson's encroachments on the convent's rights, he denied that he had ever usurped the convent's pleas 'unless we failed

Finally, Jocelin feels compelled to face up to Samson's faults squarely. 'As the wise man said', he writes, citing Horace, '"no one is entirely perfect" and neither was Abbot Samson.'[23] And he proceeds to mention some of Samson's offences against the cellary.

Jocelin's chronicle is an invaluable source for the history of the convent from 1182 to 1202. It gives a detailed, analytical and authentic account of the monks' relations with Samson. In addition, it throws much light on the abbey's economic problems, particularly on its indebtedness and the measures Samson took to combat it.[24] Lax observance was another problem tackled by Samson, who put the blame for the fire in St Edmund's shrine on the monks' worldliness.[25] One step he took was to demolish 'certain houses of the sacrist in the cemetary', where 'frequent wine-bibbings' had been held.[26] Jocelin reveals many details about the monks' everyday life, their private friendships,[27] and the gossip, chat and serious talk in the infirmary after blood-letting.[28] He mentions the factions which tended to divide the community in times of stress, the unlearned against the learned,[29] the young against the old,[30] the sacrist and his supporters against the cellarer and his followers.[31] The chronicle is much more than a memoir. It is also a record. To provide a business record was clearly one of Jocelin's intentions. He was fully aware of the value of documentary evidence. He cites two documents in full: his own New Year's Gift to Samson comprising a list of abbot's churches and one of convent's churches respectively;[32] and the survey of knights' fees made in 1200.[33] Jocelin himself may well have compiled the long résumé of the cellarer's customs,[34] probably with the intention of strengthening the cellarer's hand in his dispute with Samson – and with the sacrist – which the chronicle describes.[35] Many passages in the chronicle can be checked against

---

to do justice'. *JB*, p. 106. There are a number of examples of Jocelin approving of Samson's acts when he was no longer his chaplain. E.g.: Samson's championing of the cause of the monks of Coventry in 1198 (*JB*, pp. 94–5 and below pp. 71–72); Samson's refusal to strip St Edmund's shrine of gold to help pay King Richard's ransom; his rich gifts to the convent to help pay for the restorations of the shrine after the fire in 1198; the wise precautions he took to prevent a fire in the future (*JB*, pp. 97, 110, 116); Samson's resistance to Richard's attempts to deprive him of the wardship of an heiress in 1198 (*JB*, pp. 98–9); and his defence of St Edmunds' liberties against the bishop of Ely in 1201 (*JB*, pp. 132–6).

[23] *JB*, p. 130. Horace, *Odes*, II. xvi. 27–8.
[24] Below pp. 24–8.
[25] *JB*, pp. 109–10. Below p. 35.
[26] *JB*, p. 31.
[27] See e.g. above p. 6.
[28] *JB*, p. 14.
[29] See above p. 7 and n. 18.
[30] *JB*, pp. 14, 118, 125, 127.
[31] See esp. *JB*, pp. 100–2.
[32] *JB*, pp. 63–4.
[33] *JB*, pp. 120–2.
[34] *JB*, pp. 102–5.
[35] For Samson's quarrels with the cellarer and sacrist see below pp. 32–8 and above n. 31.

evidence in surviving official records.[36] Such cases demonstrate the accuracy of these passages and encourage reliance on Jocelin's testimony in general.

A characteristic of the second part of the chronicle is its interest in and detailed information about the cellary, especially about the concerns of Jocellus, cellarer from 29 September 1197, to 29 September 1199, when he was deposed, and again from his reappointment on 29 September 1200. He was probably the same man who appears as 'Gocelin the cellarer' in the witness list to a charter datable to between 1206 and 1209,[37] and then as 'Joscelinus de altare quondam cellerarius' in the account of the election of Hugh of Northwold.[38] Jocelin of Brackland aligns himself in his chronicle with Jocellus in the latter's disputes with Samson.[39] This has led to the chronicle being described as 'an *ex parte* statement in favour of Jocellus', which in its turn has resulted in the identification of Jocelin of Brackland with Jocellus.[40] It is argued that Jocelin disguised his identity with the pseudonym 'Jocellus', a diminutive of Jocelin, so that he could write favourably about his activities as cellarer without contravening a monk's duty of humility. However, this and other arguments put forward to support the identification are speculative and uncorroborated by concrete evidence. There are reasons for rejecting it. The fact that Jocelin mentions that he was guest-master (*hospitarius*)[41] makes it seem improbable that he would hide behind a pseudonym had he had a term of office as cellarer. If he were the cellarer, the passages in the chronicle which refer directly to Jocellus would appear to be singularly objective (one even borders on the critical).[42] Nor should we infer from the detailed account of the incorrupt body when Samson and a chosen

---

[36] A few examples serve to illustrate Jocelin's use of documents. He describes Samson's dispute with Master Jordan de Ros, parson of Harlow, who claimed land in Harlow as free alms, but Samson claimed it as lay fee: an agreement was reached in the abbot's court, the terms of which Jocelin specifies (*JB*, p. 61); the text of the agreement survives (*Kalendar*, ed. Davis, pp. 163–4) and comparison of it with Jocelin's synopsis shows that he was abstracting from it. Similarly, Jocelin records the terms of the final concord between Samson and Robert de Scales in 1198 concerning the advowson of the church of Wetherden (*JB*, p. 95); the official enrolment survives (Feet of Fines, 9 Richard I, Pipe Roll Soc., xxiii, 1898, pp. 117–18), as does a copy of the notification of the concord (*Kalendar*, ed. Davis, p. 145 and nn. 1, 2) and of the bishop of Norwich's confirmation (CUL MS Mm. iv. 19, f. 222v). Jocelin's account of Samson's dispute with Robert of Cockfield over the manors of Semer and Groton provides another example (see below pp. 54–5).

[37] *Kalendar*, ed. Davis, pp. liv, 90 (no. 26).

[38] *Electio*, p. 8.

[39] *JB*, pp. 114, 118, 122, 123.

[40] The identification is postulated by Davis, *Kalendar*, pp. liv–lvii. It is strongly supported by Norman Scarfe, 'Chronicles of Bury Abbey: the *Chronicle of Jocelin of Brakelond*', in idem, *Suffolk*; idem, 'Jocelin', pp. 1–5. Thomson, 'Obedientiaries', p. 96, and *Electio*, p. 184, accepts the identification, ignoring the problems it entails. I argue the case against the identification in *Historical Writing*, [i]. 383 n. 15. McGuire firmly rejects the identification and supports my opinion in 'Collapse of a monastic friendship', pp. 374–5.

[41] Jocelin was guest-master in 1201 when Herbert was appointed prior. *JB*, p. 129.

[42] In his account of the convent's dispute with Samson over Ralph the gate-keeper Jocelin contrasts the extreme behaviour of Jocellus the cellarer with the moderate course of action advised by the 'older and more prudent' monks ('seniores uero et sapientes de conuentu') – the course actually taken. *JB*, p. 118.

few, including Jocellus the cellarer,[43] viewed it in 1198, that Jocelin himself was present and must, therefore, be identified with the cellarer. Maybe he was one of the many monks who, contrary to expectations, were not invited to the occasion and whose disappointment and annoyance Jocelin vividly records.[44] Assuming that he was not at the viewing, he would have had many possible sources of information; for example, from the monk John of Diss who witnessed the spectacle perched up in the rafters,[45] and from Samson himself who addressed the convent after matins on the next day about the event.[46] The name 'Jocellus' is a diminutive of 'Jocelin', but the fact that Jocelin of Brackland had the same first name as the cellarer does not add weight to the case for the identification since the name was not uncommon among ecclesiastics and the religious in the last half of the twelfth century and in the early thirteenth. Famous examples were Jocelin de Bohun, bishop of Salisbury (1143–84), Jocelin, bishop of Glasgow (1175–99), and Jocelin, bishop of Bath and Wells (1206–42).[47] Similarly, a number of examples could be cited of heads of religious houses called Jocelin. At St Edmunds there were at least two Jocelins among the seventy or so monks – or at least three if Jocelin of Brackland was neither Jocelin the almoner nor Jocelin the cellarer. Moreover, it is unnecessary to identify Jocelin of Brackland with the cellarer in order to explain his interest in the cellary. Jocelin himself demonstrates the dependence of the guest-master on the cellary.[48] His office did not have any share of the convent's property and the cellarer provided the victuals and, if necessary, the fuel for guests.[49]

    The question remains of Jocelin's motive for writing. The chronicle has recently been described as 'very much a personal story'[50] and inspiration must initially have come from Jocelin's admiration for Samson, a man of marked personality and outstanding ability. Samson's influence over Jocelin would have begun when Samson was novice-master and Jocelin a novice, and been confirmed during Jocelin's years as his chaplain. Nevertheless, the question arises whether Jocelin began writing purely from personal choice. It seems more likely that he received some prompting from Samson himself. A man with such a forceful ego might well have liked to have such a biography. In any case, in so far as Jocelin's chronicle celebrated the cult of St Edmund it would have appealed to Samson. He had ordered Jocelin the almoner (possibly the chronicler himself) to record the story of Henry of Essex,[51] and may well have commissioned the new version and continuation of the *De Miraculis Sancti Eadmundi*.[52] Perhaps he asked Jocelin when his chaplain to write his work on the miracles of St Robert.

---

[43] *JB*, p. 114.
[44] *JB*, pp. 113, 115.
[45] *JB*, p. 115.
[46] *JB*, p. 116.
[47] See *Heads*, i. 326 (index).
[48] See *JB*, pp. 6, 35, 39, 88–9.
[49] *Bury Cust.*, p. 25. Cf. *Mon. Angl.*, iii. 156–7.
[50] *JB*, ed. Greenway and Sayers, p. xi.
[51] *JB*, p. 68; above p. 5.
[52] Below pp. 121–30 and nn.

Moreover, Samson was very record conscious. He specifically commissioned the compilation of his *Kalendar*[53] and ordered the monk William of Diss to record the abbey's dispute with Robert of Cockfield over the manors of Semer and Groton.[54] Jocelin would have known that his New Year's Gift to Samson, the list of churches, would have pleased him.

It is not inconceivable, therefore, that Samson encouraged Jocelin to write an account of his rule. It is true that Jocelin wrote retrospectively when he was no longer the abbot's chaplain. But if he used notes or a memoir[55] written earlier, this would explain the eulogistic tendency of the first part of the chronicle which contrasts so starkly with the criticisms of Samson which erupt towards the end. Nor is it inconceivable that after Jocelin became guest-master Jocellus urged him to write in defence of the cellarer's rights and to put on record what those rights were.[56] Jocelin, recognized as a learned man, author of at least two books and experienced in the use of archives, would have been very suitable for such a task. There is nothing improbable in the idea that an obedientiary should want such a chronicle. Indeed, the sacrist's office had kept contemporaneous records of its history in literary form since the late eleventh century. Although the extant *Gesta Sacristarum* (*The Acts of the Sacrists*) was written shortly after 1280 and continued to 1297 when it ends, it was obviously compiled from such early records.[57] If these suggestions are well founded they would lead to the following conclusions: Jocelin wrote notes or a memoir while Samson's chaplain; subsequently, he was encouraged or asked by Jocellus to write a chronicle on behalf of the convent and cellary; he did so, but incorporated into the chronicle his existing material on Samson and, out of loyalty to Samson, left the eulogy intact. Acceptance that both parts of the chronicle are official or semi-official works would explain why Jocelin had access to so many official documents.[58]

---

[53] *JB*, p. 29; below, p. 187 and nn.
[54] *JB*, p. 138; below pp. 54–5.
[55] See above p. 5 n. 5.
[56] Above p. 8 and n. 35.
[57] Printed *Memorials*, ii. 289–296.
[58] Above p. 9 and n. 36.

2

Samson's Early Life and Career

Samson was born in 1135 at Tottington in Norfolk[1] (about nine miles north-east of Thetford). One night he dreamt that he was standing before the gates of the cemetery of St Edmund's abbey and the devil tried to seize him, but he was saved by St Edmund himself who held him in his arms. Therefore, Samson's mother took him to visit St Edmund's shrine. He was nine years old at the time.[2] It would seem that Samson's regard for St Edmund and the abbey originated with this episode. His early education was as a poor clerk in the school of Master William of Diss who admitted him free of charge ('sine pacto et caritative') and whose son, Master Walter of Diss, was a monk of St Edmunds.[3] Samson then studied, again as a poor clerk, at Paris university.[4] He apparently graduated, becoming a 'Master of Arts and Medicine'.[5] At some stage he was 'a well known and respected' schoolmaster apparently in Norfolk.[6]

Samson was probably a clerk in the service of the abbot and monks of St Edmunds when c. 1159–60 he was employed by the monks on an important mission.[7] They sent him to Rome with a letter appealing to Alexander III to restore a pension of 10 marks owed to them from the revenues of the church of Woolpit. The church belonged to the abbot and the pension had lapsed, very likely because pressure from the king had caused the church to be given in free alms to a royal clerk. But c. 1159–60 the church fell vacant and the

---

[1] JB, p. 39 and n. 1, and Cron. Bur., p. 7.
[2] JB, p. 37.
[3] 'Master William of Diss' should not be confused with 'William of Diss', a monk of St Edmunds under Samson mentioned by Jocelin. JB, pp. 113, 138.
[4] JB, p. 44.
[5] JB, pp. 43–4, and Cron. Bur., p. 7.
[6] '... licet liberalibus artibus et scripturis diuinis imbutus esset, utpote uir literatus, in scholis nutritus et rector scholarum, *in sua prouincia notus et approbatus*'. JB, p. 33 and nn. 6, 7. The italics are mine.
[7] JB, pp. 4, 48, 64, 145–7. See: JB, ed. Greenway and Sayers, p. 136 and n. 44 where it is suggested that Samson joined the important ecclesiastics and others to whom Henry II gave permission to go to Rome in 1159/60; see Mary Cheney, 'The recognition of Alexander III: some neglected evidence', EHR, lxxxv (1969), pp. 474–95 (where the possibility that Samson joined this mission is not mentioned). It was probably as a result of Samson's mission that Alexander III included in his bull to St Edmunds dated 12 January 1162, the ruling that when the church of Woolpit fell vacant it was to return to the use of the brethren ('... ecclesiam de Vulpet cum uacauerit in usum fratrum redire statuimus ...': Papsturkunden, iii. 282–3 no. 140; Pinch. Reg., i. 4–6; Memorials, iii. 78–80.

monks saw their chance of recovering the pension. Jocelin describes Samson's journey in dramatic detail. Unfortunately for the mission, there was a schism in the papacy. On the day of Alexander III's election by the majority of cardinals (7 September 1159), supporters of the emperor Frederick Barbarossa had elected Cardinal Octavian as Victor IV. Samson heard that Victor's supporters were liable to capture and mutilate those bearing letters to Alexander. Apparently he (wrongly) believed that the Scots supported Victor and, therefore, he disguised himself for the journey as a Scot. Nevertheless, on the way home he was seized and robbed – but he managed to hide the letter under his drinking cup which he held above his head. For the rest of the journey he had to beg and reached Bury St Edmunds too late to serve the monks' purpose: a royal clerk, Geoffrey Ridel, the future bishop of Ely, had already been presented to the church of Woolpit, presumably in free alms. Abbot Hugh was enraged with Samson, perhaps either because of the failure of the mission or because Samson had acted for the convent against Hugh's wishes – or for both reasons.[8] Fearing the abbot's anger Samson hid under St Edmund's shrine.[9] He was then exiled to 'Acre' (probably to the Cluniac priory of Castle Acre in Norfolk).

Samson professed as a monk of St Edmunds in 1165 or 1166, at the age of about thirty-one.[10] Within a few years he was appointed novice-master. At that time Jocelin of Brackland, then one of the novices, says that Samson was a cloister monk with no desire for office and who feared God more than man.[11] However, this latter trait did not prevent the development during the ten years or so before he became abbot of characteristics which made him unsuited to a contemplative life. His energy, ability in worldly affairs, determination and obstinacy became apparent, and had already won him enemies. His life under Abbot Hugh was far from peaceful. He held a number of offices (and at least once held two at the same time) in quick succession – guest-master, pittancer, third prior and subsacrist.[12] Jocelin explains that he was transferred from one office to another because 'he was often accused',[13] presumably because he aroused hostility and criticism. Abbot Hugh had hoped to win his friendship by appointing him subsacrist, but nevertheless failed to make him more tractable. Jocelin writes: 'unlike the rest of our officials he could never be bent by flattery; the abbot used to say to his

8 When Jocelin was a novice in the care of Samson who was novice-master (see below), he asked him why he did not speak up against Abbot Hugh for allowing St Edmunds' debts to accumulate. Samson replied that he feared imprisonment followed by exile, the fate of those opposing to the abbot's will, and said that he had been first imprisoned and then exiled to 'Acre' 'because we had spoken for the common good against the will of the abbot'. JB, p. 4. Butler believed (ibid., p. 4 n. 3) that Samson went to Rome a second time, in 1173 or 1174, after the pension from the church of Woolpit had again been lost, but there seems to be no evidence supporting this view.

9 For the light this incident throws on the physical structure of St Edmund's shrine see below, p. 95 and nn. 4–8.

10 JB, p. 39 and n. 1, and Ann. S. Edm., p. 5.

11 JB, p. 4.

12 JB, p. 7; Thomson, 'Obedientiaries', pp. 93, 95, 98, 99. Samson witnessed a charter of Abbot Hugh as 'subprior and precentor'. Feudal Docs, p. 140 no. 152.

13 JB, pp. 6–7.

intimates that he had never known a man whom he could not bend to his will, save only Samson, the subsacrist'.

The sacrist at the time of Samson's appointment to the office of subsacrist was William Wiardel. As subsacrist, Samson had charge of the abbey's build-ings, both the abbey church and the other buildings within the precincts. His enthusiasm and competence as a builder and beautifier of the abbey, which were to be marked characteristics of his abbatiate, were already evident. His activity in these respects belongs to the period of the vacancy which followed the death of Abbot Hugh on 14 November 1180.[14] Samson and another monk, Master R. Ruff (*Ruffus*), carried the news to the king in France. Henry gave the custody of the abbot's property and revenues to Robert of Cockfield and Robert de Flam-ville, steward of the Liberty of the eight and a half hundreds.[15] The convent's possessions remained in the monks' control. The vacancy lasted fifteen months and Samson performed his duties as subsacrist with vigour. He tried to keep the goods in his charge in good condition: Jocelin asserts that 'as far as he could, he left nothing broken, cracked, split or unrepaired'.[16] And he embarked on an ambitious building programme. He started work on a new infirmary and on a new chapel of St Andrew in the cemetery, which replaced the chapel of St Andrew built next to the sacristy by Abbot Anselm.[17]

Most important was Samson's determination to make the abbey church itself more beautiful and to continue building work on it. Jocelin records that Samson erected a choir screen 'and arranged the order of the paintings and composed elegiac verses for them'.[18] It is more likely that he compiled the sequence of couplets from existing *exempla* rather than actually composed the verses himself. The verses are probably those preserved in late thirteenth-century copies on the flyleaves of a composite book from St Edmunds, College of Arms MS Arundel 30, ff. 211v–212. These verses are headed 'in choro et circa' and were almost certainly those composed by Samson. They are in fact hexameters, so, if as seems most likely, they are Samson's, Jocelin was wrong to say that they were elegiacs. The verses tell the Genesis story from the Creation of Adam to Jacob's blessing

---

[14] JB, p. 7.

[15] JB, pp. 7–10 passim. For the vacancy and the separation of portions between abbot and convent see also: JB, pp. 72–3, 81, 90; Gransden, 'Separation of portions', p. 368; Chapter 5 below passim. Robert of Cockfield and Robert de Flamville figure in a number of Samson's charters. The former was an important landholder in the Liberty of the eight and a half hundreds and farmed the half-hundred of Cosford. *Kalendar*, ed. Davis, pp. xi, xii and nn. 3–5, xii, xxii, xl, and cf. below p. 62. For Robert of Flamville, steward of the Liberty of the eight and a half hundreds, see ibid., p. li.

[16] JB, pp. 9–10.

[17] *Gesta Sacrist.*, p. 291. Cf. James, *Abbey*, pp. 141, 161, 180, 183. Whittingham marks the location of the chapel of St Andrew as no. 36 in his plan of the abbey with which he concludes his study of the church and monastic buildings. Whittingham, 'Bury St. Edmunds Abbey'. Above fig. 9.

[18] 'In diebus illis chorus noster fuit erectus, Samsone procurante, historias picture ordinate, et uersus elegiacos dictante.' JB, p. 9. See: James, *Abbey*, pp. 119, 131; E. C. Parker and C. T. Little, *The Cloisters Cross. Its Art and Meaning* (London and New York, 1994), p. 55; Sabrina Longland, 'A literary aspect of the Bury St. Edmunds' Cross', *Metropolitan Museum Journal*, ii (1969), pp. 45–9.

of his two sons, in ninety episodes, with a couplet for each. These would have been illustrated by a great cycle of Genesis pictures. The verses and their corresponding pictures were probably painted on the outside of the north and south walls of the choir enclosure. This was the position at Peterborough of a cycle of biblical scenes with verses which were probably painted a little earlier than Samson's cycle.[19] Another comparable cycle is known to have been painted on the walls of the chapter-house at Worcester.[20] However, both the Peterborough cycle and the Worcester one were typological, that is, a type, a scene from the Old Testament, was followed by an antitype, the episode in the New Testament which it was seen to prefigure (often more than one type was included.) Such typological cycles, in fresco, glass and stone, were executed in a number of great churches in late twelfth and early thirteenth-century England. Nevertheless, the Bury cycle comprising scenes from one book of the Bible was not unique. A cycle of scenes from the Book of Maccabees certainly existed at Worcester, though exactly where in the priory it was located is unknown.

The purpose of cycles comprising verses and Biblical scenes is well expressed in the preface to the *Pictor in Carmine*, a massive typological collection composed for the use of artists in the late twelfth century. The author writes that

> being struck with grief that in the sanctuary of God there should be unsuitable pictures, and what are misshapen monstrosities rather than ornament, I wish if possible to occupy the minds and eyes of the faithful in a more becoming and useful fashion. For, since the eyes of people in our time are apt to be attracted by a pleasure that is not only vain but even profane, and since I do not think it would be easy to do away altogether with meaningless paintings in churches, I think it an excusable concession that they should enjoy that class of pictures which, as being the books of the laity, can suggest divine things to the unlearned, and arouse the love of the scriptures in the learned.[21]

Whether Samson employed a professional painter or one of the brothers to execute the Genesis cycle is unknown. If a professional painter were employed he would have required a wage. In any case, the project would have been expensive.

Samson's most expensive project was to continue building the great west tower of the abbey church. Jocelin records that he had 'a great quantity' of stone and sand brought for the work, but that questions were asked about the source of the necessary money. Samson replied that 'certain burgesses' had given it secretly to him for the purpose, but rumour had it that he and one of the guardians of the shrine, Warin, had surreptitiously appropriated some of the oblations to the feretory.[22] Rather than be accused of theft Samson and Warin 'made a box with a hole in the middle of the top, secured with an iron lock; they had it

[19] M. R. James, 'On the paintings formerly in the choir at Peterborough', *Proceedings of the Cambridge Antiquarian Soc.*, ix, n.s. iii (1899 for 1894–8), pp. 178–204.

[20] Idem, 'On two series of paintings formerly at Worcester priory', *Proceedings of the Cambridge Antiquarian Soc.*, x, n.s. iv (1900), pp. 99–110.

[21] Idem, 'Pictor in Carmine', *Archaeologia*, xciv (1951), pp. 141–2.

[22] JB, pp. 9–10.

placed, empty, in the great church near the door from the choir where ordinary folk passed to and fro, so that they might place their alms in it for the building of the tower'.[23] While subsacrist, Samson managed to complete one storey of the tower. But then William Wiardel, the sacrist, and other of Samson's opponents induced the abbey's royal custodians to persuade Henry II to forbid all building and other work on the abbey during the vacancy,[24] which lasted from Abbot Hugh's death on 14 or 15 November 1180 until Samson's election and its confirmation by the king on 28 February 1182.

---

[23] The passage reads: 'Et ut tam felicis furti sui suspicionem tollerent prenominati duo uiro, truncum quendam fecerunt, concauum et perforatum in medio uel in summo, et obseratum sera ferrea; et erigi fecerunt in magna ecclesia, iuxta hostium extra chorum in communi transitu uulgi, ut ibi ponerent homines elemosinam suam ad edificacionem turres'. Scholars do not agree on the exact translation of this passage. See *JB*, p. 10 and n. 1; *JB*, ed. Greenway and Sayers, p. 10.

[24] *JB*, pp. 10–11.

3

Samson's Election to the Abbacy

Late in January or early in February, 1182, Henry II wrote ordering Prior Robert and twelve monks, who were to be unanimously chosen by the monks, to appear before him to elect an abbot. The convent accordingly chose twelve monks.[1] Samson was one of them. These twelve, together with the prior, Robert, were to act as electors, but they knew that the king had control over the appointment: since the abbot, like the head of any great religious house, was a tenant-in-chief, the king could withhold temporalities – the abbot's barony.[2] The monks had to reconcile royal power with the prescriptions of canon law,[3] the Rule of St Benedict and St Edmunds' own privileges. The Rule established that an abbot was to be chosen either unanimously by the whole community, or by some part of the community, however small, which is of 'saner counsel'.[4] In 1158 Pope Adrian IV in his confirmation of St Edmund's privileges added the stipulation that the election of abbots should be by common consent of the brethren or of the 'saner part' of the community 'according to the Rule of the blessed Benedict'.[5] In 1162 Alexander III in his confirmation of St Edmunds' privileges and property reiterated much of Adrian's bull including the passage on abbatial elections.[6] Then, in 1164 Henry II, during his dispute with Archbishop Thomas Becket and his supporters, issued the Constitutions of Clarendon which set out the 'customs, liberties and privileges' enjoyed by his ancestors, notably by Henry I. Clause 12 of the Constitutions concerns the election of archbishops, bishops and the heads of religious houses: it states that the king should summon 'the more important ecclesiastics' ('potentiores personas ecclesie') and that the election should take place in the royal chapel, 'with the assent of the lord king and with the counsel of the clergy of the realm ('assensu domini Regis et consilio personarum regni') summoned for that purpose; the elect should there do homage and fealty to the

---

[1] *JB*, p. 16.
[2] Knowles, MO, pp. 395–403 and nn.; idem, 'Abbatial elections', pp. 252–5, 263–7 and nn.
[3] Canon law ordains that an abbot should not be appointed (*ordinetur*) to a monastery by a bishop or any outsider ('aut per aliquem extraneorum'). *Decretum*, pars 2, cau. xviii, qu. 2, c. 2. The abbot should be the chosen with the common consent of the congregation and no one else. Ibid., c. 3 ('abbatem cuilibet monasterio non alium sed quem … communi consensu congregatio poposcerit').
[4] *Reg. Ben.*, c. 64 § 1.
[5] *Papsturkunden*, iii. 264 no. 121.
[6] Ibid., iii. 283 no. 140.

king as his liege lord for his life, limbs and earthly honour before he is consecrated'.[7]

This clause was a codification of existing procedure which was established by
the compromise agreed between Henry I and Archbishop Anselm in 1103.[8] The
procedure was probably followed in most archiepiscopal and episcopal elections
and in most elections of the heads of religious houses in Henry I's reign and in
that of Henry II, but evidence is scarce. It seems to have been not uncommon
for the king's power over elections to be circumvented with royal connivance
or occasionally despite royal opposition, so that archiepiscopal, episcopal, or
monastic chapters obtained the election of a candidate of their own choice. This
was achieved by the community in question holding an election and choosing
their candidate before an election was held in the royal chapel in the king's presence.[9] And this is what the monks of St Edmunds did in 1182.

Jocelin of Brackland gives a vivid and precise account of how the monks
obtained Samson as their abbot, a man of humble birth, without court connections and unknown to the king, without antagonising King Henry.[10] Having
received Henry's mandate, the monks chose the twelve monks who were to go
with Prior Robert to the king by the second method prescribed by the Rule, that
is, the choice was made by those of 'saner counsel'. The community chose six
senior monks who wrote down the names of three monks whom they considered
the most suitable candidates, and the document was closed and sealed. If the
king allowed a free election, the seal was to be broken in his presence so that he
could choose whichever of the three monks named he preferred. If he did not
allow a free election, the letter was to be brought back to the six seniors with the
seal unbroken, and destroyed. The deputies were to accept the king's nominee,
provided he was a monk of St Edmunds. The monks of St Edmunds had the good
fortune that the king proved amenable. This was partly because of the presence
in the abbey during the period immediately preceding the election of Augustine
(Eystein), 'archbishop of Norway' (that is, of Nidaros, Trondheim). Political
circumstances in Norway had caused him to come to England as an exile in
1180.[11] He stayed in the abbot's lodgings at St Edmunds from 9 August 1181
until 16 February 1182. King Henry ordered that 10s a day be paid to him from
the abbot's revenues, payments which totalled £94 10s, for the twenty-seven
weeks. Jocelin observes: 'he was of great value to us in securing our free election,

---

[7]   C and S, i, pt ii, pp. 868 and n. 4 for further references, 869, 882 (Latin text); Hist. Docs,
      ii. 769–70 (English translation); Knowles, MO, p. 399; idem, 'Abbatial elections', pp.
      264–5.

[8]   See C and S, i, pt ii, 657.

[9]   Ibid., p. 869; Knowles, MO, p. 399; idem, 'Abbatial elections', pp. 265–6. For the detailed
      account of the election in 1175 of Odo, abbot of Battle, which provides an interesting
      parallel to the election of Samson as abbot of Bury, see The Chronicle of Battle Abbey, ed.
      and trans. Eleanor Searle (Oxford, 1980), pp. 278/9–296/7.

[10] JB, pp. 16–23.

[11] JB, pp. 15 and n. 6, 16; JB, ed. Greenway and Sayers, pp. 15, 128; Nideros Cathedral and the
      Archbishops Palace, ed. Øystein Ekroll, Jill I. Løhre and Tove Søreide (Tronheim, 1995),
      esp. pp. 30–1.

testifying to our merits and publicly declaring before the king what he had seen and heard about us'.

The delegates set out from St Edmunds on 21 February to visit the king at Bishop's Waltham, a manor of the bishop of Winchester.[12] Henry received them kindly. The election took place in the bishop's chapel and Henry instructed them through his intermediaries, Richard of Ilchester, bishop of Winchester (1174–88), and Geoffrey, the chancellor (later archbishop of York, 1189–1212), to nominate three of their monks as candidates for election. Accordingly, the deputies opened the sealed letters and found that Samson's was named the first of the three: the second named was Roger, the cellarer, and the third Hugh, the third prior (both of whom were, like Samson, among the convent's delegates). This order, which disregarded seniority, shocked the delegates who thereupon altered it putting Hugh first and Samson last. King Henry, however, objected that he knew none of the three and asked for three more names. So the deputies named three others (all of their number) – Prior Robert, Master William, the sacrist, and Master Denis. But Henry wanted the net spread wider, 'for the honour of the realm', and asked for three more nominations, this time of monks from other houses. The deputies reluctantly put forward three names but with the provision that they would not accept them without consulting the rest of the convent. Perhaps because of this Henry at once eliminated them. He also eliminated five others and William, the sacrist, withdrew. Only Prior Robert and Samson remained. Master Denis, speaking for all the deputies, expatiated on the merits of both, but in particular emphasized Samson's suitability. So Bishop Richard asked the deputies whether they wanted Samson; the majority clearly declared in his favour. Therefore, Henry accepted him.

Thus, the wishes of the majority of the deputies had prevailed and the first preference of the senior six monks, nearly all the cloister monks and most of the obedientiaries were pleased at the choice. It emerges from Jocelin's account of the monks' discussions before the election that they wanted an abbot who was neither very young nor very old.[13] At forty-seven Samson was in his prime. He had already shown powers of leadership. He was articulate, clever and self-confident; he knew his own mind and had the courage to act accordingly, unless he thought restraint the wiser course. Jocelin shows that though all the monks wanted a man of piety and strict life as abbot, some monks insisted that he should be learned, while others emphasized the need for administrative ability. Samson combined both qualities. He was a Master of the schools and, as Master Denis pointed out to the king at the election, he was experienced in a number of administrative offices. His zeal as subsacrist, although obnoxious to the sacrist, had won him much popularity, especially among the cloister monks.

In general, the convent trusted him. In conflicts between it and Abbot Hugh, Samson had bravely supported the convent's cause. In discussion in the cloisters before the election, when monks speculated on which three monks the six seniors would nominate, Jocelin asserts that they agreed that Samson would be

---

12 JB, p. 21 and n. 1.
13 For the pre-election discussions see JB, pp. 11–14.

one of them: they recalled 'his labours and the perils of death that he had faced when he travelled to Rome to defend the possessions of our church, and how he was dragged away and fettered while speaking for the common good'.[14] Samson himself suggested that the monks should all swear that whomever was elected to the abbacy would treat the convent reasonably, and not change obedientiaries without the convent's consent or burden the sacrist or admit any man to be a monk without its approval.[15] Moreover, on the journey to Waltham Samson suggested to the other deputies that they should all swear that the elect should promise on oath to return to the convent the churches taken from it, to pay for hospitality. Prior Robert objected, saying that they had sworn enough oaths. Jocelin comments that this was lucky because 'if such an oath had been sworn it would not have been kept'.

Indeed, Samson's humble bearing when he set out on the journey was deceptive. He walked behind the others, 'his habit hitched over his arm, as if he were the sole servant of the others'. He was carrying the party's money, and had the convent's letters in a wallet (*scrinium*) hanging from his neck.[16] But when Henry announced his election, Samson's bearing was very different. Jocelin writes:

> The elect prostrated himself at the king's feet and kissed them, then he hastily rose and hurried to the altar with the other monks, singing 'Miserere mei, Deus', his head held high and his countenance unchanged. And when the king saw this, he said to those standing nearby, 'By God's eyes, this elect thinks himself worthy to be guardian of his church.'[17]

Samson was blessed by Richard, bishop of Winchester, and Augustine, bishop of Waterford, on Richard's manor of Marwell near Winchester, on 28 February.[18] At the same time Richard placed a mitre on Samson's head and a ring on his finger, saying 'This is the dignity of the abbots of St Edmunds, as I have long known.'[19] Samson returned to St Edmunds on Palm Sunday (21 March). He walked barefoot when he came within sight of the abbey church and was ceremonially received by the monks. After being installed in the abbot's seat in the choir, he entered the chapter-house. There he thanked the convent for his election and asked for their prayers. Then he turned to the assembled crowd of clerks, knights and other laymen; he asked them in future to advise him in his onerous administrative duties. Wimer, the sheriff of Norfolk and Suffolk (1170–87), spoke on behalf of them all, promising to support, advise and assist him in every way, as their 'dear lord, whom God has chosen for His own sake, and for the sake of the holy martyr Edmund'. Afterwards, Samson went to his

---

[14] Above, chapter 2, p. 13 and nn. 8–9.

[15] *JB*, p. 18.

[16] *JB*, p. 19.

[17] *JB*, 23.

[18] *Ann. S. Edm.*, p. 5. Augustine Ua Selbaig was elected bishop of Waterford in 1175 and died in 1182. *Handbook of British Chronology*, p. 376. Jocelin does not mention that Bishop Richard was assisted by the bishop of Waterford.

[19] There is no known papal bull to the abbot of St Edmunds conceding the right to wear a mitre. See below pp. 21–2 and nn.

lodging and held the ceremonial feast customary for such an occasion, with much rejoicing: Jocelin asserts, no doubt with typical medieval exaggeration, that he feasted 1,000 people.[20]

One of Samson's first acts was to summon the prior 'and a few others', to tell them that a new seal must be made and that he should be represented wearing a mitre. Until the new seal was ready he used the prior's seal 'adding at the end of each letter that he had to do this for the time being because he had no seal of his own'.[21] The depiction of Samson wearing a mitre symbolized the episcopal dignity of the abbot of St Edmunds who within the abbey and *banleuca* exercised the powers of a bishop, except that he could not ordain to holy orders or consecrate churches, chapels or altars. Jocelin observes that no previous abbot had been thus represented and cites John 6.6 'he himself knew what he would do'. The incident illustrates Samson's pride in his position as abbot, his determination to make full use of its powers and to increase the abbey's privileges whenever possible. Samson's predecessor, Abbot Hugh, in an endeavour to fortify St Edmunds' position, had obtained numerous papal confirmations and concessions. In 1172 he had obtained confirmation by Alexander III of St Edmund's privilege of exemption from any ecclesiastical authority except that of the pope himself or of a legate *a latere*, a privilege which he again confirmed in 1175.[22] Samson's seal, impressions of which survive, has on the obverse a representation of the abbot in mass vestments, wearing a mitre and holding a book in his left hand and a crosier in his right; the reverse, the counterseal, bears the image of the *Agnus Dei*.[23]

In view of St Edmunds' other extensive privileges, wealth and fame, the claim that the abbot should be mitred, was not unreasonable, especially as Samson would have known that the abbot of St Albans had the privilege of wearing a mitre. This privilege had been granted to the abbot by Pope Adrian IV in a bull of 14 May 1157.[24] Adrian had a close relationship with St Albans because of an exceptional circumstance. He had been born Nicholas Brakespear, in Abbots Langley, south of St Albans. His father was a clerk who, on the succession in 1151 of Abbot Robert de Gorron, had become a monk of St Albans. He had asked Robert to admit Nicholas too, but Robert refused, having found him 'insufficient'. Nicholas, therefore, made his career in the church abroad, finally

---

[20] *JB*, pp. 23–7.

[21] *JB*, pp. 26, 28.

[22] *Papsturkunden*, iii. 322–3 no. 187, 350–1 no. 217.

[23] *JB*, p. 28. Samson's seal is reproduced as the frontispiece to *JB*, ed. Rokewode, from 'an impression preserved in the archives of Christ Church, Canterbury'. However, the reproduction seems to have been engraved with a little artistic licence since it does not exactly match any of the three impressions preserved in the cathedral archives, i.e. L/130, L/132 (both excellent impressions) and L/131. I am indebted for this information to the former cathedral archivist, Dr Heather Forbes. Cf. P. D. A. Harvey and Andrew McGuinnes, *A Guide to British Medieval Seals* (British Library and Record Office, London, 1996), pp. 106–7. Below, pl. I.

[24] *Papsturkunden*, iii. 260 no. 118. See: Michelle Still, *The Abbot and his Rule. Religious Life at St Albans, 1290–1349* (Aldershot, 2002), p. 23 and n. 96; Brenda Bolton and A. J. Duggan, *Adrian IV, the English Pope (1154–1159)* (Aldershot, 2003), p. 95.

joining the papal court in Rome, and in 1154 he was elected pope.[25] Abbot Robert at once made full use of Adrian's connection with St Albans. He visited him personally and later sent envoys, on each occasion giving exceedingly rich gifts to him and to powerful figures at the curia. At his request Adrian granted St Albans numerous privileges, some confirming its exemption from diocesan authority and its direct dependence on the pope, and others concerning the abbot's right to wear episcopal pontificalia, including the mitre.[26] In contrast, St Edmunds had no special relationship with Adrian, though Adrian made two grants in favour of St Edmunds: on 4 May 1155, at the request of Abbot Ording and the sacrist Elias, he confirmed that the borough of St Edmunds belonged to the sacrist and that its income was assigned to St Edmund's altar;[27] and on 7 May 1158 he confirmed St Edmunds' privilege of exemption.[28] Thus, the abbot of St Albans acquired the right to wear a mitre and the abbot of St Edmunds did not.

The question of Adrian's grants to St Albans became an issue at the papal council convened at Tours by Pope Alexander III in 1163. Among the numerous ecclesiastical magnates, heads of religious houses and the like attending were Robert, abbot of St Albans, and Hugh, abbot of St Edmunds. A dispute arose between them and their supporters concerning the precedence of the two abbots. The question of precedence was of the utmost importance because it determined seating arrangements which all could see. Among the arguments used by Robert and his supporters was that St Alban was England's protomartyr – an argument which Hugh and his supports countered by pointing out that St Edmund was England's first *royal* martyr. A disreputable wrangle was only just avoided and Robert won his case by appealing to Adrian's bulls of privilege.[29] Memory and probably record of this dispute must have been preserved at St Edmunds and informed Samson about St Albans' privileges. It could explain why he claimed the right of the abbot of St Edmunds to wear a mitre together with the rest of the episcopal pontificalia. It is commonplace that rivalry between religious houses concerning precedence was a recurrent feature of medieval monasticism; it could raise high passions and sometimes even lead to violence.[30]

[25] For the career of Nicholas Brakespear before his election as pope see Matthew Paris, *GASA*, i. 112–13, 124–5.
[26] Ibid., i. 125–36 passim. Cf.: Still, op. cit., pp. 22–4; Bolton and Duggan, op. cit., pp. 86–95.
[27] *Papsturkunden*, iii. 232 no. 98.
[28] Ibid., iii. 263–4 no. 121.
[29] *GASA*, i. 177–8. See *C and S*, i. pt ii. 847 and nn.
[30] Usually St Edmunds' relations with St Albans were close and friendly.

4

The Early Years of Samson's Abbacy and Reform of Estate Management

Samson inherited a difficult situation from Abbot Hugh. Jocelin, writing of Hugh in his old age, asserts that although the Rule of St Benedict was observed and discipline kept,[1] the abbey's administration was in a bad state and the abbey seriously in debt. He writes:

> Abbot Hugh had grown old and his eyes dim. He was a pious, kindly man, a strict monk and good, but in worldly affairs he was neither good nor prudent. He trusted those about him too much, believed them too readily, always relying on their advice rather than on his own judgement.[2]

Hugh did not control those who had charge of his portion of St Edmunds' property, nor the obedientiaries responsible for the convent's portion. He allowed his vills and hundreds to be leased out, his woods to be destroyed and manors to fall into disrepair. His only remedy to maintain his household's honour was to borrow, and as interest was added to capital, the unpaid debts grew ever larger. Each obedientiary tended to follow suit, and, since each had acquired his own seal,[3] he could transact business without the rest of the convent knowing. Among the examples given by Jocelin is of a debt privately contracted by the sacrist, Master William, to Benedict, the famous Jewish money-lender of Norwich. When the debt had reached £100 King Henry heard of it and informed the abbot and convent. Abbot Hugh was enraged but his intimates dissuaded him from deposing William, who promised that the debt would be repaid. To repay the debt William borrowed again, and finally he borrowed £880, to be paid off at the rate of £80 a year. In all, Jocelin asserts, Benedict was owed £1,200, excluding interest.[4] Later the king remonstrated again at the abbey's indebtedness, and on another occasion (sometime between April 1174 and April 1175) Archbishop Richard did likewise. Thus, debt and maladministration were the main problems facing Samson at the outset of his rule.

---

[1]   JB, p. 4.
[2]   JB, p. 1.
[3]   JB, p. 2. Cf. Harvey and McGuinness, *Guide to British Medieval Seals*, pp. 106–7.
[4]   JB, pp. 2–3 and nn., JB, ed. Greenway and Sayers, p. 124. For Benedict the Jew of Norwich see Roth, *Jews in England*, p. 14; V. D. Lipman, *The Jews of Medieval Norwich* (Jewish Historical Soc. of England, London, 1967), pp. 16 n. 3, 59, 60 and n. 1, 61, 62, 107.

Once abbot, Samson had the canonical duty to care for and protect the abbey's property and to recover any that was lost.[5] Besides his feudal obligation to the king as a tenant-in-chief, he was responsible for the Liberty of St Edmunds, that is, the ancient jurisdictional unit of the Liberty of the eight and a half hundreds, where the abbot exercised the powers of a sheriff, and the even more highly privileged Liberty of the town, the *banleuca*, which no royal official might enter.[6] With regard to property, he had direct responsibility for his own portion, and overall responsibility for the convent's. To protect and promote these interests entailed frequent recourse to the law courts. The justiciar, Ranulf de Glanville, was initially uneasy at Samson's succession because of his lack of administrative experience, but was reassured because Samson soon showed his ability. He acquired the necessary knowledge and skill by study and experience, and chose his advisers, servants and officials wisely. Of those who had served the prior during the vacancy, he kept only those who had proved satisfactory.[7] In appointing new men, he chose only those who would be useful. He applied the same criterion to his own relatives. He resisted their importunity and in the event appointed only one, a knight who 'was eloquent and skilled in the law, not so much on account of his kinship but for his usefulness, since he was accustomed to secular business'.[8] Samson's caution about employing relatives remained with him. This was apparent in 1200, when it was necessary to appoint a new prior. Samson named in chapter those monks whom he considered suitable candidates, specifying his reasons for each choice. One possibility was the third prior, John, his own relative, but Samson objected to him on the ground that, if he were prior, 'the multitude of relatives he had in the neighbourhood would be a weight about his neck'.[9] Jocelin states that Samson 'loved his kin in moderation, not excessively', and that he had heard him claim that he had relatives of high and noble birth whom he would never acknowledge 'because if they knew of the relationship he would find them more of a burden than an honour'.[10]

Samson began his rule with characteristic vigour and determination. In April, he visited all his and the convent's manors and ordered an inquiry to discover the names of tenants, both free and unfree, the location of their holdings, and the rents and services due from them. He had this information written down.[11] That autumn he took back into direct control all except two of his manors from

---

5   See Cheney, Mary [G.], 'Inalienability in mid-twelfth century England', esp. p. 467 n. 1, 472 and n. 18. For a detailed discussion of the problems of enforcing this ruling in England in the face of customary law and common law, royal legislation, and social and political circumstances see: ibid., 467–78; Hudson, *Land, Law and Lordship*, pp. 231–43. See also, for Samson's recovery of Cosford half-hundred, below, pp. 54–5.
6   For the Liberty of the eight and a half hundreds see figs 1 and 2, and for the *banleuca* see fig. 6.
7   JB, pp. 26–8. Ranulf de Glanville was justiciar 1179 or 1180 – Sept. 1189.
8   JB, p. 24.
9   JB, p. 127.
10 JB, p. 43.
11 JB, p. 28.

the tenants to whom they had been farmed.[12] In this context, a farmer was, so to speak, a lessee, that is a tenant who held the property for a fixed rent – though the rent would comprise various 'services' and these might consist solely of cash payments or solely of food-renders, or of some of each, besides a wide range of other services, some variable and/or arduous.[13] In the late eleventh century and until the latter half of the twelfth century landlords had commonly put manors in the hands of farmers. The system was satisfactory as long as prices remained stable. However, the last half of the twelfth century and early thirteenth was a period of sharp inflation: the fixed rents were no longer worth as much as when initially agreed.[14] Some landlords met cash shortages by borrowing, which is what was happening at St Edmunds under Abbot Hugh. However, Samson was averse to this means of meeting the abbey's costs. According to Jocelin, Samson was harassed by 'Jews and Christians demanding payment of debts owed them by St Edmunds'. This so worried and distressed him, that he 'suffered from sleepless-ness and grew thin and pale'. He said that 'his mind would never be at rest until his debts were paid'.[15]

Since most of the abbey's income came from its landed property, to manage it directly and efficiently was obviously the wiser policy rather than farming it out to tenants, some of whom were in any case inefficient, at fixed uneconomic rents.[16] Alternatively, having been resumed, the manor or other property, it might be farmed out again but at a higher rent. For instance a knight offered Samson 30 marks (£20) so that he might hold a carucate of land in Tilney for 'the ancient service of £4' a year: Samson refused and 'that same year he got £25 and the next year £20'.[17] Jocelin explained why Samson allowed two of the farmers to keep their tenancies. One, farmer of Harlow kept his tenancy because Samson was amused at a story he heard about him. Apparently until recently Ernauld had been 'a living devil' to his tenants, but now he treated them better, because 'he fears the new abbot of St Edmunds whom he considers both wise and wiley'.[18] The other farmer left in place was 'a certain Englishman, a free man though tied to the soil'. Samson confirmed his tenancy of the manor of Thorpe; he particu-larly trusted him, Jocelin remarks, 'because he was a good farmer and speaks no French'.[19] Once recovered Samson would put a manor under the management either of a monk or a layman, whom he considered more competent than the dispossessed farmer. Moreover, most importantly, as Jocelin records, 'he restored old halls and buildings through which birds of prey (*milui*) and crows were flying, he built new chapels and lodgings and chambers in many places where there

---

[12] JB, p. 32.
[13] See Miller and Hatcher, *Rural Society*, pp. 204–13.
[14] See ibid., pp. 210–11.
[15] JB, p. 32.
[16] See: Miller and Hatcher, *Rural Society*, pp. 210–11; Harvey, 'Pipe Rolls and the adoption of demesne farming', pp. 345–59.
[17] JB, p. 33.
[18] JB, p. 32.
[19] JB, p. 33.

never had been any buildings except barns'.[20] Samson's activity as a builder of mills, especially windmills, is discussed below in Appendix IV.

Similarly, Samson took back into direct management eight of the eight and a half hundreds – that is most of the Liberty – which Hugh had farmed out. He failed to recover Cosford half-hundred because Robert of Cockfield claimed to hold it by hereditary rights: as will be seen, Samson only succeeded in recovering it several years later.[21] He kept the eight hundreds in his own hands, handing their management to sergeants, members of his own households, but reserving important decisions to himself. Overall control of the Liberty of the eight and a half hundreds belonged to the abbot's deputy, the steward, an office held by hereditary right by the Hastings family. Thomas of Hastings came with his retinue with all St Edmunds' barons, knights and free men to do homage to Samson, their new lord, on 31 March. He brought with him his nephew, a young man not yet a knight, and claimed the stewardship on his behalf. Samson recognized his claim but refused to accept him because he was unfit to exercise the office and asked for a substitute. Later, Samson accepted the substitute offered, Gilbert of Hastings, although an ignorant and foolish young man. Apparently Samson accepted him because the appointment would leave him free to manage the Liberty himself. He observed privately that in case of a default of justice, the king would blame the steward, not him.[22]

Jocelin lists three acts of Samson which 'proved' his goodness (*probitas*). His recovery of the rich manor of Mildenhall heads the list.[23] Mildenhall together with the eight and a half hundreds had been granted to St Edmunds by Edward the Confessor.[24] Abbot Ufi had lent or leased the manor to Stigand when bishop of Elmham (1043–7). The powerful Stigand succeeded to the bishopric of Winchester and subsequently became archbishop of Canterbury. On his disgrace and fall in 1070 his property including Mildenhall passed to the king.[25] It remained in royal possession until 1189 when Samson purchased it from Richard I. The charter is dated 12 November and grants Samson, his successors and the monks the manor and church of Mildenhall which they were to hold on the same terms as St Edmunds had held them by gift of Edward the Confessor.[26] Richard's grant was for 'the salvation of his soul and for the souls of his ancestors and of his successors', but he drove a hard bargain.[27] At this time he was in financial straits and using every possible means to raise money in order to pay off old debts and accumulate funds for the forthcoming crusade. Samson offered

---

[20] JB, p. 28.
[21] JB, pp. 29, 58, and below, pp. 54–5.
[22] JB, pp. 27. For the steward's office and a list of the stewards and their substitutes under Samson see *Kalendar*, ed. Davis, pp. l–li.
[23] JB, p. 45. See below p. 49.
[24] Harmer, *Writs*, pp. 154–5 no. 9, 154–5 n.
[25] DB, *Suffolk*, i. 1, 115.
[26] CUL MS Ff. ii. 33, f. 30 (i.e. a late thirteenth-century or fourteenth-century copy of the charter, in the register of the sacrist, to whom Icklingham was assigned).
[27] JB, pp. 46–7. For Richard's financial problems see Appleby, *England without Richard*, pp. 5–27 passim.

him 500 marks for the manor, saying that it was valued at £70 'in the great roll of Winchester' – he meant Domesday Book, believing it was in roll form.[28] But Richard heard that the manor was worth at least £100 and insisted that Samson pay 1,000 marks. Samson would have had to pay more than this had it not been for the piety of Richard's mother, Queen Eleanor. For he owed her 100 marks, as the 'Queen's Gold', a customary tax of 10% payable to the queen on all the king's financial transactions. To pay this debt she was given a great golden chalice worth 100 marks which, however, she returned as an offering for the 'soul of her Lord King Henry', who had first given it to St Edmunds.[29]

The huge sum for the purchase of Mildenhall was raised with great difficulty by both abbot and convent and then there was the question which of the two should enjoy the income from this rich manor. According to the late eleventh-century author of the *De Miraculis Sancti Eadmundi*, Edward the Confessor had made the grant of the 'royal mansion' (*regia mansio*) and of the eight and a half hundreds after a visit to the shrine of St Edmund 'so that the community of monks dwelling there and serving God and the saints, might support themselves from them in the usual manner' ('ex his usualiter victitet').[30] Traditionally, this was interpreted as meaning that the income from Mildenhall should be used to provision the monks and so the manor was assigned to the cellarer. However, after its purchase from Richard, Samson claimed in chapter part of the income from the manor and the convent agreed. Samson said he should have half because he had raised 400 marks of the purchase price, but would be satisfied with the manor's outlier, Icklingham. The convent 'gladly' granted it to him. Then Samson told the monks that he would not keep Icklingham for himself or give it to a relative, but would give it, for the salvation of his soul and of their souls, to his new hospital at Babwell (that is, to St Saviour's) 'for the sustenance of the poor and the accommodation of travellers'.[31] Unfortunately, further trouble and expense lay in store for St Edmunds before it secured permanent possession of Mildenhall. Already in 1198, when Richard changed his seal, Samson, like other landlords, had to obtain and pay for a charter from Richard to renew the grant.[32] Nor was this the end of the matter. About fifty years later

---

28 Samson must have been using extracts relating to St Edmunds' holdings among the abbey's records. Maybe he mistakenly believed that Domesday Book was in roll form because he knew that some of the original returns were in rolls. For examples of extracts from Domesday Book in the abbey's later registers see BL MS Harley 1005, ff. 38, 38v and *Pinch. Reg.*, i. 410–18. Cf. Thomson, *Archives*, pp. 125, 142.

29 *JB*, p. 46. The chalice was used again in 1193 to help pay for Richard's ransom and Eleanor again redeemed it for St Edmunds. Below pp. 65–6. For the Queen's Gold see Margaret Howell, *EHR*, cii (1987), pp. 373–80.

30 *Memorials*, i. 48. For the story which purports to describe the circumstances prompting Edward the Confessor to give Mildenhall to St Edmunds see below, Appendix II, p. 250. It may well have been a fiction used to strengthen St Edmunds' claim to Mildenhall in the dispute with Richard de Clare, earl of Gloucester, over its right, in the king's court in 1253.

31 For St Saviour's see below.

32 The copy of Richard's charter of 1189 (above n. 26) ends with this note: 'Is erat tenor carte nostre primo sigillo nostro sigillate, quod quia aliquando perditum fuit et dum capti fuimus

St Edmunds had to vindicate its title to the manor by prolonged litigation and at enormous expense.[33]

Added to the great expense of recovering the manor of Mildenhall was the cost of the litigation needed to recover the church of St Mary in Mildenhall. St Edmunds claimed that the church was included in Edward the Confessor's grant of the manor. However, after the fall of Stigand, the church as well as the manor passed into royal hands and William Rufus granted it to Battle abbey. In the course of the twelfth century there were numerous claims and counterclaims to the church, which was a valuable asset. However, before the end of the twelfth century St Edmunds had gained possession of the church. Jocelin of Brackland includes it in his list of c. 1191 of the abbot's churches, and states that it was worth 40 marks, but with a caveat: 'concerning the church of Mildenhall, which is worth forty marks and half the church of Wetherden (see below p. 268) what shall I say?' ('de ecclesia de Mildenhala, quae ualet xl marcae, et de mediatate ecclesie de Wederdena quid dicam?').[34] He also includes Mildenhall in his list of the convent's churches, as one of its three most valuable, all three worth 25 marks. It seems, therefore, that St Edmunds was already holding the church and that more than half of the revenue was assigned to the convent, presumably for the cellarer's use. In 1205 Samson obtained from John de Gray, bishop of Norwich 1200–1214, the appropriation of the church to St Saviour's hospital, saving an annual pension of three marks to Battle abbey and saving a vicarage of twenty marks.[35]

The second of Samson's acts which Jocelin says proved his goodness was the expulsion of the Jews from Bury St Edmunds.[36] Samson petitioned King Richard for letters to this effect. He argued that everyone living within the town or *banleuca* must be St Edmunds' man and that meant that he must be a Christian. Therefore, a Jew must convert or leave. He ordered that anyone henceforth receiving or harbouring a Jew in the town was to be solemnly excommunicated in every church and at every altar, but those who left might take their chattels with them and receive compensation for the value of their houses and lands.

---

in Alem[annia] in aliena potestate constitutum mutatum est. Innouationis autem hii sunt teste [the witness list follows]' dated 18 July 1198, Rock of Andeli. For Richard's change of seal, an expedient for raising money, see Appleby, op. cit., pp. 219–20 and nn. For the Rock of Andeli (Chateau-Gaillard), see Gillingham, *Richard*, pp. 262–5.

[33] See: *Memorials*, ii. xxxi; Gransden, *A History of the Abbey of Bury St Edmunds*, ii, chapter 2 section 2.

[34] *JB*, p. 64. In the assessment for the papal tenth in 1291 the church of Mildenhall was valued among the cellarer's spiritual revenues at 40 marks. *Bury Chron.*, p. 104. See also *Acta, Norwich 1215–43*, ed. Harper-Bill, p. 7 n. For the history of Mildenhall church in the late eleventh and twelfth centuries see *Acta Norwich 1070–1214*, ed. Harper-Bill, pp. 264–5 n.

[35] Ibid., pp. 263–5 no. 332. For the appropriation of the church of Mildenhall to St Edmunds by the legate Pandulph on slightly different terms see below, pp. 171–2 and n. 34.

[36] *JB*, pp. 28–9. For the murder of Little St Robert and the outburst of anti-semitism in England in the late twelfth century see Roth, *The Jews in England*, pp. 20–5. For Jocelin's *miracles* of St Robert see *JB*, p. 16 and above p. 7. For the cult at St Edmunds see below pp. 117–21 and nn.

They were to leave under armed escort. Later, the king's justices ordained that if Jews came to the court of St Edmunds to demand debts owed to them by debtors, they should be allowed to lodge in the town for two nights and on the third day they were to depart in freedom. Samson no doubt had various reasons for expelling the Jews – thus forestalling their general expulsion by Edward I by a century. One of his reasons was the influence of the violent anti-Semitism which burgeoned in the late twelfth century. The outburst was connected with crusading zeal: while the crusaders struggled against the Moslem infidels to recapture Jerusalem and the Holy Sepulchre, Christians in England should not allow Jewish infidels to enjoy their ill-gotten gains. Samson must have remembered that a year before his succession the populace in Bury St Edmunds had attacked the Jews, murdering allegedly fifty-seven of them, because they believed that Jews had murdered a small Christian boy ('little Robert'). This popular uprising must have contributed to another probable reason for Samson's expulsion of the Jews in 1190, that is, the need to keep order in the town; failure to do so could result in the forfeiture of the Liberty of the *banleuca* to the king.

The third of Samson's acts proving his goodness in Jocelin's eyes was the foundation of St Saviour's hospital, but since it did not concern St Edmund's rights but was a charitable act, it will be considered in the appropriate context below. Samson's activities on St Edmund's behalf were accompanied by a flood of documentation. In fact a notable feature of Samson's rule was a marked increase in the production of written records, a notable feature of Samson's rule. Jocelin remarks that the only written record which Samson inherited from his predecessor was 'one small sheet containing the names of the knights of St Edmund, the names of the manors, and the order in which one food farm followed another'.[37] One of Samson's first acts was 'to have an inquiry made concerning the annual rents (*census*) of free men and the names of the peasants, and of their holdings and services, and to have them all written down'.[38] Although no copy of this survey of manors is known to survive, Jocelin's information is particularly interesting because it shows Samson consciously outstripping the position as it existed under Abbot Hugh. He was actually also outstripping the heads of most other great religious and ecclesiastical institutions. The first comprehensive survey of the manors of the archbishopric of Canterbury appears to have been made under Archbishop Stephen Langton (1207–28). Chronologically, parallels to Samson's survey are a survey of the manors of the bishopric of Worcester apparently made under Bishop Roger (1154–79), shortly after his succession, and the survey made by Ralph Diceto of the manors belonging to the chapter of St Paul's almost immediately after his succession as dean in 1180/1.[39] Samson's

---

[37] '… et que firma quam firmam sequi deberet'. *JB*, p. 29. This sentence is incorrectly translated in Butler and also in *JB*, ed. Greenway and Sayers, p. 27. See Cheney, Mary [G.], *Roger, Bishop of Worcester*, p. 111 and n. 92. For the food farms see below pp. 281–87, and fig. 5.

[38] *JB*, pp. 28–9. See *Kalendar*, ed. Davis, pp. xi–xv.

[39] See respectively: F. R. H. Du Boulay, *The Lordship of Canterbury. An Essay on Medieval Society* (London etc., 1966), pp. 10–11 and n. 1; Cheney, op. cit., pp. 107–11. Diceto's survey is printed in *The Domesday of St Paul's of the year MCCXXII*, ed. William Hale,

survey of manors is lost, but another document survives which exemplifies the high quality of records produced in his time. Between c. 1186 and c. 1191 he ordered a survey to be made of the eight and a half hundreds and of all the revenues due from them – revenues which outside the Liberty would normally have been paid to the sheriff: 'this book', Jocelin writes, 'he called his Kalendar and in it were also written down the various debts which he had paid off. He consulted this book almost daily, as though he could see therein the image of his own efficiency as in a mirror.' Jocelin himself made a list of the abbot's churches, with an estimate of the rentable value of each, which he gave to the grateful Samson as a New Year's Gift in 1191.[40] And in 1200 Samson commissioned a survey of St Edmunds' knights' fees.[41]

The principle purpose of these surveys was fiscal. Jocelin claims that because Samson's Kalendar specified the abbot's revenues in writing 'within four years of his election he could not be cheated out of a single penny'.[42] Again, the survey of knights' fees enabled Samson to estimate his income from scutage and other feudal dues. But in so far as both these surveys gave the names of tenants then in possession, their values as records were limited. In fact, the survey of knights' fees was itself an updated version of the survey of the knights' fees in St Edmund's barony returned to the Exchequer in 1166 by Abbot Hugh. This was in response to Henry II's demand for information from all tenants-in-chief about enfeoffments in their honours.[43] Moreover, another version of Samson's survey was made soon afterwards.[44] Only Jocelin's list of churches did not suffer from the disadvantages that it needed periodic updating to maintain its full usefulness.

It was almost certainly Samson who commissioned the earliest surviving register from St Edmunds, the Black Register, a handsome quarto volume now CUL MS Mm. iv. 19.[45] The original core of this volume, which has much additional matter, includes papal and royal privileges, charters of Abbot Ording, Abbot Hugh, and of Samson himself (ff. 52–79v, 83–105v), besides the earliest known copy of Baldwin's Feudal Book (ff. 124–143v).[46] The fact that

Camden Soc., o.s. lxix (1858), pp. 109–17 (see *The Historical Works of Master Ralph de Diceto*, ed. William Stubbs (RS, 1876, 2 vols), i. lvi–lix, and Gransden, *Historical Writing*, [i]. 234 and nn., and for the value of the survey for the history of estate management see C. N. L. Brooke in *A History of St Paul's Cathedral*, ed. W. R. Matthews and W. M. Atkins (London, 1957), pp. 61–2).

40   *JB*, pp. 62–3.
41   *JB*, pp. 120–2.
42   *JB*, p. 29.
43   *Hist. Docs*, ii. 975–7.
44   The list is printed and commented on by Douglas, *Feudal Docs*, pp. lxxxvi and n. 5, lxxxvii. Eight of the thirty-one knights listed are also in the list in *JB* (pp. 120–1): that is, Gilbert Peche, Richard of Ickworth, Audrey de Vere, Robert of Horringer, William Blund, Robert of Hawstead, Geoffrey of Welnetham and William of Bardwell. A few occur in the Kalendar or in Samson's charters.
45   Described: *Feudal Docs*, pp. xx–xxii and nn.; Davis, *Cartularies*, p. 16 no. 118; Thomson, *Archives*, pp. 16, 119–21 no. 1277.
46   For this and later medieval copies of Baldwin's Feudal Book see *Feudal Docs*, pp. xx–xxii and nn.

Celestine III (1191–98) is the last pope whose bulls are included, and that there are no bulls of Innocent III, 1198–1216 (a continuator starts again with bulls of Honorius III, 1216–27) indicates that the register (or its exemplar, if it had one) was compiled in the late twelfth century. The association of the register with Samson seems likely on grounds of probability and is suggested by its late fourteenth-century class-mark, S.40.[47] Other Bury books with the S classification are of sermons or saint's lives; in the case of the Black Register possibly it means that Samson commissioned and owned the original part. The latter is in a beautiful text hand in black ink, with rubrics, some ornamental initials in red and drawings of some of the papal *bullae*. The book's venerable status and respected authority in the abbey is indicated by its preservation in the vestry and by the many thirteenth- and fourteenth-century additions to it. The additions show its continued usefulness, and so do the many borrowings from it in the abbey's later registers.

Archive consciousness was, therefore, a feature of Samson's abbatiate. Although the primary purpose of the documents discussed above was to increase the profitability of St Edmunds' estates, they were intended and served another purpose, as did other records produced of this period. Orderly, accessible archives promoted efficiency in general by making administrative tasks easier. Some records might be compiled primarily for easy reference when defending property and privileges in the law courts: St Edmunds' privileges were valued for reasons of prestige and this had spiritual as well as temporal implications.

---

[47] Entered with a query as to its numerical place in Sharpe, 'Reconstructing the medieval library', p. 214. Cf. Thomson, *Archives*, p. 31.

5

Conflict with the Convent

Under the Rule of St Benedict an abbot's power is absolute. Decision-making lies with him and the monks must obey his commands, however unreasonable, without question and with humility.[1] Nevertheless, the Rule has general injunctions for the abbot's good behaviour: he must always be mindful of the words of St Paul: 'you have received the spirit of the adoption of sons by which we cry Abba, father'.[2] And the abbot should not harass the flock committed to him, nor exercise his power in an arbitrary, unjust way; he should always remember that he must render account to God for all his decisions and acts.[3] Moreover, the Rule states that when an important decision has to be taken, the abbot should call all the monks together, explain the situation and listen to their advice, even to the views of young monks, before deciding what to do.[4] He was also to consult 'God fearing monks' when appointing a prior,[5] and senior monks should be consulted over small matters: the Rule cites the Book of Sirach (*Ecclesiasticus*): 'Do all things with counsel and you will not afterwards repent.'[6] These stipulations in the Rule were advices to the abbot and did not imply rights enjoyed by the monks.

However, in the course of time monks came to claim certain rights which had evolved as customs and received tacit or formal recognition by their abbots. The proliferation of such rights was greatly accelerated by the division of property between abbot and convent in the eleventh and twelfth centuries. As a result, disputes between an abbot and his monks over their respective rights were a constant threat. If an abbot grossly abused his power and violated rights claimed by his monks, the latter could appeal to the local bishop, provided that the monastery in question was not exempt from diocesan authority. St Edmunds, having the privilege of full exemption, could only be visited by the pope himself

---

1   For the 'qualities' of an abbot see *Rule*, ed. Fry, chap. ii. For the obedience owed by the monks see ibid., chap. iv. § 61; chap. v; chap. lxiii. §§ 13–14.
2   Ibid., chap. ii. §§ 2–3, citing Rom. 8.15. Cf. Gransden, 'Democratic movement', pp. 25–39, where some of the issues discussed here are considered in more detail.
3   *Rule*, ed. Fry, chap. lxiii. §§ 2–3; lxv passim.
4   Ibid., chap. iii. §§ 1–4.
5   Ibid, chap. lx. § 15.
6   Ibid, chap. iii. §§ 12–13.

or by a legate *a latere*, that is, one with plenary powers.[7] Jocelin, a novice at the time, realized the danger to the monks of full exemption:

> For if by chance there should be an abbot of ours who wished to dilapidate our property and treat his convent badly, there will be no man to whom the convent can complain of the wrongs done by the abbots, since he will fear neither bishop, archbishop or legate, and his impunity will make him the bolder in wrongdoing.[8]

It is against this background that Samson's disputes with the monks must be seen.

Samson on succeeding to the abbacy at once instituted reform of the convent's administration. As has been seen, debts had risen during the vacancy. The sacrist, William Wiardel, and other officials had raised loans without the consent of the rest of the convent. On his first day in chapter Samson ordained that in future no charter should be sealed with the convent's seal except in chapter,[9] and ordered any monk owning a seal to hand it to him: thirty three seals came to light.[10] Samson returned their seals to the prior and sacrist but kept the rest. Similarly, he called in the keys of all chests, cupboards and hampers (*haneparii*) and forbade any monk to keep anything locked up without his leave, in accordance with the Rule. Each monk was allowed to keep up to 2s from money given to him out of charity, but on condition that he only used it to relieve poor relatives and for pious purposes.[11] The first obedientiary to bear the brunt of Samson's reforming zeal was the sacrist, William Wiardel. William had obstructed his ambition to expedite work on the church's west front during the vacancy. He had also neglected the upkeep of conventual buildings, and as the sacrist's buildings in the cemetery were the scenes of inordinate drinking sessions, Samson had them pulled down.[12] He appointed a subsacrist Hugh, to oversee William's financial transactions.[13] This arrangement was short lived, and within a few days Samson deposed William: he accused him of sealing bonds pledging the church's vestments and other valuables without the convent's consent. To replace William he appointed the precentor, his own namesake, Samson, who seems to have been a likeable man, but nothing is known about his term of office.[14] Samson's energy and determination soon brought him into conflict with the convent. His relations with the monks worsened as he became increasingly autocratic. By the

---

[7]   Above p. 21 and n. 22.

[8]   *JB*, p. 5.

[9]   *JB*, pp. 30–1.

[10] *JB*, p. 38. Noticed Harvey and McGuiness, *A Guide to British Medieval Seals* (above p. 21 and n. 23), pp. 106–7.

[11] *JB*, pp. 38–9. The Rule forbids monks to own anything at all except what is 'given or permitted' by the abbot. *Rule*, ed. Fry, chap. xxxiii passim.

[12] *JB*, p. 31: 'et ita omnia complanari fecit, quod infra annum, ubi steterat nobile edificium, uidimus fabas pullulare, et ubi iacuerant dolia uini, urticas habundare'.

[13] *JB*, p. 30. Hugh the transitory subsacrist is not noticed in the *Gesta Sacristarum* nor listed by Thomson, 'Obedientiaries', p. 94. Possibly he was the same Hugh who later became Samson's sacrist; see below.

[14] *JB*, pp. 30–1.

time Jocelin stopped writing in the early thirteenth century, the disputes had become very bitter indeed.

Samson quarrelled most frequently with the cellarer, the obedientiary who, being responsible for provisioning the monks, held the greatest proportion of the convent's property and was the biggest spender. Samson thought that the monks ate and drank too much. He objected partly because of his desire for strict observance of the Rule, which was the main reason for his destruction of the sacrist's buildings in the cemetery. He himself was of frugal eating habits. After the fall of Jerusalem in 1187 he touched no meat, and he always ate what was placed before him without comment. He hated drunkards and those who complained about food.[15] Another reason for Samson's objection to the cellarer's extravagance was economy. Besides the convent's normal expenses there was the need to liquidate debts and to pay for Samson's ambitious building programme. The cellarer's debts were a recurrent problem, and, as interest was added to capital, they constantly increased. Jocelin writes 'One cellarer succeeded another year by year, and each was deeply in debt.' First £20 and then £50 was added to the cellarer's income, but still the debts grew. Samson then associated a clerk from his own household, Master Ralph, with the cellarer.[16] But even this proved an inadequate remedy and in 1197 Samson resorted to more drastic measures. He again increased the cellarer's income by £50 a year, to be paid to the cellarer in monthly instalments. But the arrangement had to be abandoned in the face of the cellarer's objections. Samson then demanded in chapter to know the cause of the debts. Receiving no reply, he said that it was caused by 'immoderate feasting in the prior's lodging which took place with the consent of the prior and cellarer, and superfluous expense in the guest-house, a result of the guest-master's carelessness'.[17] Since the cellarer's debts continued to grow, Samson took over the management of the cellary himself. He deposed both cellarer and guest-master, and appointed two monks, one to be called subcellarer and the other as guest-master. He also associated one of his own clerks 'Master G.' (probably Master Gilbert of Walsham), to oversee all their expenditure on food and all receipts, and to purchase provisions in the market in place of the convent's old buyers. Samson himself paid outstanding debts, cut all unnecessary expenses and ordered obedientiaries and cloister monks in future to eat in the refectory and nowhere else.[18]

The new economies were unwelcome to many of the monks. This is apparent from the interpretation put by many on a vision experienced 'by a certain great man', whose name Jocelin does not know, and imparted to Samson. This occurred shortly after the fire which devastated St Edmund's shrine in June 1198. Samson was much moved by the vision and narrated it to the monks in chapter, telling them how he interpreted it. St Edmund had appeared to be lying outside his shrine, groaning and saying that he was stripped of clothing and emaciated by

---

[15] *JB*, pp. 39–40.

[16] *JB*, pp. 79–80.

[17] *JB*, pp. 87–8.

[18] *JB*, pp. 88–9. Master Gilbert of Walsham, a clerk who witnessed a number of Samson's charters. See index to *Kalendar*, ed. Davis, p. 178 under 'Gilbert, the master', and p. 192 under 'Walsham-le-Willows, Master Gilbert de'.

hunger and thirst. He also said that his shrine and the porches[19] of his church were carelessly kept. Samson understood this to imply that the monks were withholding their old clothes, and food and drink from the poor, or at best giving them only reluctantly, and that the fire in the shrine was caused by the negligence of the sacrist and his subordinates. Many of the monks, however, interpreted the vision differently. The naked St Edmund represented the convent, despoiled of its ancient customs and liberties: 'we [the monks] are perishing of hunger and thirst, having sustenance only through the abbot's clerk, at his disposition'; and if the keepers of the shrine were negligent, it was Samson's fault, since he appointed them.[20]

The abbot's assumption of the administration of any of the convent's obediences was a serious matter. There was alarm and complaint when Samson associated Master Ralph with the cellarer for the administration of his office. But one monk, 'a very sensible and well educated man', justified Samson saying: 'It is not surprising that the Lord abbot puts his own men in charge of our affairs, since he manages his own portion of the abbey's property well and runs his household wisely, and it is his responsibility to make good any default arising from our carelessness or incompetence.' Nevertheless, this monk admitted the danger of such interference: it eroded the division of property between abbot and convent, which meant that during a vacancy the king might take over the convent's portion as well as the abbot's barony.[21] In 1197 the opposition to his treatment of the cellary was so strong, that about six weeks later Samson promoted the subcellarer to be cellarer and deprived Master G. of his control on grounds of bad behaviour: in future he was to act merely as the cellarer's adviser and as a witness to his transactions. Thus, the cellarer regained his power for the time being.[22]

A document survives which throws much light on Samson's relations with the monks, although the nature and date of the document are problematical. It is a draft for, or an abbreviated version of, a composition (henceforth here referred to as the Composition) agreed between an (unnamed) abbot and the convent, designed to define the respective rights of convent and the abbot. It survives in two late thirteenth-/early fourteenth-century copies.[23] One of them

19 'suum cimiterium et atria ecclesie sue'. Butler notes that here the word *atria* may be used with a general meaning, to include church and cloisters. *JB*, p. 110 and n. 1.
20 *JB*, pp. 110–11.
21 *JB*, p. 81.
22 *JB*, pp. 90–1.
23 The text is described and edited in *Bury Cust.*, pp. xxxix, 100–107, from the late thirteenth- or early fourteenth-century copy in BL MS Harley 1005, ff. 210v–211v (ff. 202v–203v medieval foliation). Additions in the hand of Henry of Kirkstead are in the margin and on a consecutive page: the latter was originally Harley 1005, f. 204 (medieval foliation) but became detached and is now f. 1 in BL MS Harley 743, a later fourteenth-century register of the abbey. A copy of the Composition, incomplete at the end and without the additions, is in Harley 1005, f. 44v and is printed in Lobel, *Bury St. Edmunds*, pp. 189–90. Lobel dates it c. 1190–1210 and cites it (pp. 32, 61–2) as a source of evidence for the history of the borough. For a full discussion of the Composition, see Gransden, 'Democratic movement', pp. 30–6.

is fuller than the other: it has additions and emendations inserted by Henry of Kirkstead probably sometime in the 1360s. Kirkstead states that he copied them from 'a very old roll of the Lord abbot', presumably a copy of the Composition itself. The present texts begin: 'These are the customs which in the past were established between the abbot and convent of St Edmunds, some of which have been observed up to the present time, and some of which have been usurped and quashed by the strength and power of the abbot.' This heading suggests that the Composition became an authorized piece of legislation. Whatever the truth, the original should be dated to before 1234 since the abbey's Customary composed about then[24] contains borrowings from it.[25] Many of the clauses in the Composition relate so closely to the disputes between Samson and the convent as recorded by Jocelin, that it must surely have been drawn up with them in mind. But whether it belongs to Samson's time or rather later is a vexed question. Perhaps it was composed in 1202 when Samson was in an exceptionally weak position, or when he was suffering from the ailments of old age. However, it will be argued below that a stronger case can be made for dating it to early in the abbatiate of Samson's successor, Hugh of Northwold.

In what follows the Composition will be cited when a clause would seem to have been provoked by one of Samson's acts. Thus, the first clause stipulates that the prior, sacrist, cellarer and chamberlain should be appointed 'with the consent of the chapter and in chapter', and that if the abbot 'wishes or ought to appoint other obedientiaries outside chapter, he should do so with the consent of the prior and senior monks'.[26] Another clause states that no clerk or laymen should be associated with a monk in an office; rather the obedientiary should be deposed and a more suitable monk appointed. This clause could well refer to Samson's treatment of the cellarer and his office in 1197, described above.[27] The Composition next states that 'no obedientiary should be deposed so long as he faithfully manages his office because of [the abbot's anger] or someone's accusation, unless there is reasonable cause for his deposition'. Maybe this refers to the deposition of the cellarer Jocellus in 1200 although 'he had carried out his duties well and prudently, and managed the cellary for two years without debt, unlike other cellarers'.[28] Another clause stipulates that the abbot should not give away the convent's serjeanties, that is, of the gate-keeper, two buyers, two butlers, the baker's five master cooks, the guest-house servant and the infirmary servant, except with the consent of the whole convent: and if the recipient pays for any serjeanty, half the money should go to the monks and half to the abbot. Jocelin records among those acts of Samson of which he cannot approve two instances when Samson sold serjeanties belonging to the convent: he sold one belonging to the infirmarer for 100s; and, on the death of one of the convent's

24 See below p. 206.
25 These are listed in *Bury Cust.*, p. xxxi n. 1.
26 *Bury Cust.*, p. 100 and nn.
27 Above p. 34.
28 *Bury Cust.*, p. 100; *JB*, pp. 122–3.

servants, John Ruff, he sold the serjeanty to one of his own servants, reputedly for 10 marks.[29]

The Composition refers to encroachments by the abbot on the management of the convent's manors. One clause states that these should be managed by monks and not by others. Jocelin records that when, shortly after his election, Samson appointed new keepers, both monks and laymen, to manage his manors, he did the same for the convent's manors. He also took two of the cellarer's manors, Bradfield and Rougham, into his own hands.[30] Jocelin, bearing in mind Samson's ability as an administrator, and the inefficiency of the obedientiaries, did not disapprove of this act. However, Samson returned the two manors after hearing that general opposition was so strong that monks complained about his keeping them. The next instance which Jocelin records of Samson's interference with the convent's manors was in 1200.[31] Having heard that the monk, Geoffrey Ruff, keeper of four of the cellarer's manors (Barton, Pakenham, Rougham and Bradfield), though a capable man, was too worldly, Samson had his chests seized, the manors' stock put under guard and Geoffrey imprisoned; he ordered that the great quantity of gold and silver found should be put towards the construction of the new front of St Edmund's shrine. He deposed Jocellus, the cellarer, and made him subcellarer, and ordered that two monks, not one, should manage the convent's manors. One of the new keepers was the monk Roger of Ingham. (Roger had been Samson's companion on the eventful journey to Rome in 1159 and Samson seems to have had an especial regard for him.)[32] Roger offered to take charge of the cellary as well as of the manors. Samson accordingly made him cellarer, although this was against the convent's wishes. Roger soon proved unsatisfactory and Jocellus was reinstated. But all except three of the cellarer's manors (Chippenhall, Southwold and the rich manor of Mildenhall) were separated from the cellary and left under the management of two monks, 'lest the manors be impoverished by the cellary or the cellary by the manors'.

Samson's hostility to Jocellus, who had been cellarer since 1198, could be explained partly by a bitter quarrel he had with the convent, but especially with Jocellus, in 1199.[33] The episode illustrates the kind of conflict which could arise between the abbot, to whom the monks owed obedience, and the convent, which claimed the right to administer its own possessions. Jocelin describes the dispute in graphic detail. It was over Ralph, the gate-keeper, one of the cellar-er's servants. The prior and convent accused him of appearing in suits against their interests. They, therefore, deprived him of certain increments which the cellarer and subcellarer had made to him without consulting the convent. But Ralph was left in possession of the corrody, which he held by virtue of his office, as testified by his charter. Ralph however complained to Samson, apparently making no distinction between the increments and the corrody. Samson seems

---

[29] *Bury Cust.*, p. 101, lines 2–8; *JB*, p. 130. For the dispute over Ralph the gate-keeper see below.
[30] *Bury Cust.*, p. 104 lines 7–9; *JB*, pp. 28–9.
[31] *JB*, pp. 122–3.
[32] *JB*, p. 4. Above pp. 12–13.
[33] *JB*, pp. 117–19.

to have taken the same view and was angry because he considered that the convent acted unreasonably, and in any case without consulting him and to his prejudice. According to the Customary, corrodies and serjeanties were in the abbot's gift and could only be withdrawn in chapter in his presence.[34] The convent defended its action, saying that it was done by the prior in chapter with the convent's consent. Samson, astounded at the opposition, ordered Jocellus to restore the corrody to Ralph in full (that is, to give him the increments). Jocellus was to drink nothing except water until he had done so. But Jocellus was obdurate, refusing to act against the convent's wishes. Samson, therefore, in a fury forbade him both food and drink until he obeyed. He himself left the abbey and stayed away for eight days, communicating with the monks through messengers. He said that he feared to return because the monks plotted to kill him 'with their knives' – but during the final reconciliation he said that it was because he was afraid of what he might have done in his anger. Meanwhile, chapter was in uproar; Jocelin asserts that he had never known such a commotion. Jocellus and his adherents (nearly half the convent) remained obstinate, but 'at length older and wiser monks who had kept a discreet silence, pronounced that the abbot should be obeyed in all things, except in those contrary to God's will'; for the sake of peace they should obey the abbot in this matter 'despite the disgrace'. When Samson eventually returned he summoned the ringleader and, since he was too frightened to come, Samson excommunicated him and had him imprisoned overnight in the infirmary. He also excommunicated three of his adherents. After more ado, an emotional reconciliation took place. Samson, though now behaving humbly, justified his action and said that he had never in his life been so grieved by anything as by this quarrel, especially because rumours of it had spread abroad. Then everyone wept, and Samson absolved those whom he had excommunicated and gave all the monks the kiss of peace. Nevertheless, he secretly returned the whole corrody to Ralph; the monks turned a blind eye, recognising that Samson was, and would be, master.

   This was much the most heated and distressing of Samson's disputes with the convent. Some causes of contention between him and the convent seem to have been peaceably settled. But one recurrent problem was the question of who was responsible for entertaining guests, a costly matter. Jocelin states that under Abbot Hugh all guests were received by the cellarer. He also states that soon after his election Samson promised to restore the 'ancient customs' about hospitality, that is: when at home the abbot should receive all guests except the religious and secular priests who were the cellarer's responsibility; the cellarer was responsible even for bishops if they were monks, unless the abbot wished to do some bishop especial honour; but if the abbot were absent, the cellarer was to receive the abbot's guests as well as his own, unless they came with more than thirteen servants, in which case they were to be received by the abbot's servants and at the abbot's expense.[35] These same regulations appear in the Composition,

---

[34] *Bury Cust.*, pp. 3 line 24 and n. 3, 4 lines 3–6 and nn. 1–2.
[35] *JB*, p. 39.

with a few additional safeguards to ensure that guests were honourably received[36] – a point on which Samson and the monks were agreed. This, indeed, was an obligation imposed on them by the Rule. Chapter 53 begins

> All guests who present themselves are to be welcomed as Christ, for He himself will say. 'I was a stranger, and you took me in' [Matthew 25.35]. Proper honour must be shown 'to all men, especially unto them who are of the household of faith' [Galatians 6.10] and to pilgrims.[37]

Samson did not neglect this duty. Part of his improvements to the monks' buildings was to demolish the old guest-house and to replace it by a better one: at the time when Jocelin wrote the demolition work was nearly completed.[38] Samson himself was a generous host. He dined his guests well, and entertained at least important guests with minstrels and took them hunting in his parks.[39] Nevertheless 'he lost much favour and gratitude with his guests' because of his stern expression which, he said, was the result of the cares of office.[40] The convent on its part accused Samson of often evading his responsibility for guests by staying away from the abbey:

> He lodged in his manors more than any of his predecessors, thus burdening the cellarer with guests whom he should have received, so that at the end of the year he might be called a wise abbot, prosperous and farsighted, while the convent and obedientiaries were thought ignorant and improvident.[41]

---

[36] *Bury Cust.*, p. 104 lines 15–26.

[37] See also *Rule*, ed. Fry, chap. lvi.

[38] JB, p. 96; *Gesta Sacrist.*, pp. 291–2. See Whittingham, 'Bury St. Edmunds Abbey', pp. 176–7.

[39] JB, pp. 26, 28, 42. For the employment of minstrels to entertain guests and monks on important feast days see Legge, *Anglo-Norman in the Cloisters*, p. 117. Payments to minstrels occur in a few of the fourteenth- to sixteenth-century accounts from St Edmunds. Minstrels were hired to entertain distinguished guests, the abbot and monks, on important feast days. Some (partly illegible) accounts of c. 1334, apparently of Abbot Richard of Draughton (1312–35), include many payments to individual minstrels on the feast of All Saints, on Ascension day, at Christmas, on the feast of the Purification and at Easter (BL MS Royal 6 B X, ff. 141, 141v – a flyleaf). The accounts of the sacrist (John Cranewys), 1429–30 include payment of 3s to minstrels on the feast of St Edmund (SRO/BA/6/1/6 (Thomson, *Archives*, p. 69 no. 186)). The accounts of the feretrars (John Finningham and Simon Bardwell, 1520–1, include 3s paid for minstrels of the king, the prince and Lord Curson, on the feast of St Edmund (SRO/B/A/6/1/17) (Thomson, *Archives*, p. 70 no. 200)); see Statham, *Book of Bury St Edmunds*, p. 105. An addition in a late fifteenth- or early sixteenth-century hand to the pittancer's register, compiled c. 1430 (BL MS Harley 27 (Thomson, *Archives*, p. 157), f. 2), lists the contributions owed in the absence of the abbot by each obedientiary for payments to minstrels on the feast of St Edmund. 3s seems to have been the standard charge on the sacrist and feretrar, for here again that was their contribution. It was also the charge on the monastic treasurer (the others paid less). The payments totalled 20s.

[40] JB, pp. 35–6.

[41] JB, p. 35.

At length, in 1198, Samson promised to remain at home more in the future.[42]

Sometimes Samson managed to avoid confrontation with the monks by persuasion. He successfully used this method of getting his own way in a case concerning the church of Woolpit which belonged to the monks.[43] The vicarage was held by a royal nominee, at that time the powerful Walter of Coutances, but it fell vacant in 1183 on Walter's appointment to the bishopric of Lincoln.[44] The position with regard to presentation to a vacant vicarage is stated in the Composition: the abbot should not present anyone to any church or promise anyone any church (presumably, that is, one belonging to the convent) without discussion with most of the monks and with the convent's consent, especially if the church owed a pension.[45] Since the church of Woolpit did in fact owe the convent an annual pension of 10 marks, it fell into this category and it was on account of this pension that Samson had travelled to Rome in 1159.[46] He now summoned the prior and most of the convent and told them the moving story of that journey – of its perils and of the severe and unjust punishment inflicted on him when he returned. All this, he said, he had suffered in order to recover the church for the monks, and so the presentation was rightly his. He added that if the monks agreed he would give the living to a relative of the monk Roger of Ingham, his companion on that dangerous journey. He added that he would restore the church to the monks, but in the event he only restored the pension of 10 marks, 'which,' he said, 'you lost more than sixty years ago'. He explained why it would be unwise to give them the whole income from the church. Jocelin concludes: 'we all rose and thanked him'; they accepted the pension and also Roger of Ingham's brother Hugh as vicar. Jocelin later lists Woolpit among the abbot's churches.[47]

---

42 JB, p. 96.
43 Woolpit was among the churches which Alexander III, in a bull dated 12 Jan. 1162, allowed the monks to appropriate 'for their use'. *Papsturkunden*, p. 282 no. 140, and above p. 12 and n. 7. Alexander had confirmed to Abbot Hugh and the monks the right of presentation to the vicarage. *Papsturkunden*, pp. 353–4 no. 220; *Pinch. Reg.* i. 10–11; *Memorials*, iii. 85.
44 JB, p. 48. Sometime between 1173 and 1180 Henry II, at the request of Abbot Hugh and the monks had granted, in return for their grant of the church of Woolpit to his clerk Master Walter of Coutances, that the church should remain in perpetuity for the use of the sick monks of St Edmunds, on the death or resignation of Master Walter. *Feudal Docs*, pp. 102–3 no. 97. Walter of Coutances, bishop of Lincoln 1183–4, archbishop of Rouen 1184–1207, was one of the most powerful political figures under Henry II and Richard I. He acted as keeper of the seal 1173–89 and as chief justiciar 1191–3, being virtually a regent of England when Richard was on crusade and during his captivity.
45 *Bury Cust.*, p. 104 lines 9–12. The Customary has the same ruling. Ibid., p. 3 lines 21–6 passim and n. 4.
46 JB, pp. 48–50. Above pp. 12–13.
47 JB, p. 64. A charter dated 12 April 1246 of Walter Suffield, bishop of Norwich, assessed the pension owed to St Edmunds from the church of Woolpit at 20 marks, payable at two terms. BL MS Harley 645, f. 229v, and *Memorials*, iii. 81–2. In Edward I's confirmation of the separation of portions between abbot and convent, dated 16 November 1281, 9 marks of the pension from the church of Woolpit was assigned to the infirmarer and 2 marks to the

Samson had much more difficulty in persuading the monks to accept his candidate for the priorate in 1201. The Composition includes the prior with the obedientiaries who were to be appointed with the convent's consent in chapter.[48] It was only with a struggle that Samson managed to keep the form of a free election and yet get his own way. The monks knew that he wanted to appoint his chaplain, Herbert, and this caused much debate among them.[49] Many opposed Herbert's candidature because he was a young man of forty years or less; not learned and inexperienced in the cure of souls, while, on the other hand, there were many mature monks, who were learned and had been Masters of the schools. Herbert's opponents favoured the subprior, Master Hermer, an experienced, mature monk, both learned and eloquent. But the majority were opposed to Hermer because he was bad tempered, quarrelsome and over-anxious. Herbert won some favour because he was good tempered, sociable and tactful, healthy and handsome. On hearing these and other arguments, one monk, unnamed by Jocelin, observed: 'Why multiply words such as these? ... The abbot will do what he wishes in this matter. Perhaps he will seek the advice of each of us in turn, with due solemnity; but in the end by persuasion, plausible arguments and circumlocution, he will achieve his desired end.'[50] And so it turned out. Samson, realising the division and discontent among the monks, said that after chapter he would hear the opinion of each individually. Next day he came to chapter and tearfully said that he had had a sleepless night, worrying lest he appoint a prior displeasing to God. He then nominated four monks, Herbert last, whom he considered worthy, for the monks to choose from, and began expounding their merits. First was the sacrist Walter of Banham, who withdrew, admitting his incapacity. Second was his own relative John, the third prior, but he disqualified him because of his superfluity of relatives in the area. Samson had just begun his disquisition on the third, Maurice, when a senior monk asked the precentor to nominate Herbert. The precentor said 'He is a good man' – which admission Samson at once took as the monks' assent. Indeed, the whole convent cried out 'He is a good man, worthy of our love.' Apparently the learned monks had accepted the inevitable. Nor was it a bad appointment. Jocelin after chapter reflected on Herbert's virtues and merits and decided that he could be called perfect except for his lack of learning. Herbert presumably remedied this defect in so far as he must have acquired a good knowledge of canon law: he occasionally acted as a papal judge delegate between 1201 and early 1208, at first with Samson and later without him.[51]

---

guest-master (hostiller). *Mon. Angl.*, iii. 157. In the fourteenth and early fifteenth century St Edmunds engaged in much litigation with the vicars of Woolpit for their non-payment of the pension. Copies of documents establishing St Edmunds' right to the pension and recording the litigation, in roughly chronological order, are in a tract in the register compiled soon after 1427 by Andrew Aston, guest-master. BL MS Cotton Claudius A XII, ff. 86–99v, printed *Memorials*, iii. 78–112. Cf. Thomson, *Archives*, pp. 155–7 no. 1307.

48 *Bury Cust.*, p. 100 lines 8–11 and nn. 1, 2.
49 *JB*, pp. 125–8.
50 *JB*, p. 126.
51 Prior Herbert held office until his death on 10 September 1220. *Bury Chron.*, p. 4. For

The last episode narrated by Jocelin in his chronicle took place on the eve of Samson's departure to visit King John in Normandy early in 1202.[52] Eustace, bishop of Ely, and he had received a papal mandate to investigate whether there were adequate grounds for absolving Geoffrey Fitz Peter, William de Stuteville and certain other magnates from their crusading vows.[53] King John had asked for their absolution, claiming that they were physically unfit and that in any case he needed their counsel. He now summoned Samson to discuss the matter. This confronted Samson with a dilemma.[54] He would displease the pope if he supported John's request for the absolutions, and the king if he supported the pope by arguing in a favour of the fulfilment of the crusading vows. To add to his troubles Samson was in poor health. The fact that he made his will before departure suggested to Jocelin that he thought he was about to die. These reasons could explain why he was unusually humble and tractable in his dealings with the convent. Using the prior as intermediary, he asked for the convent's advice, which, Jocelin observes, 'he had very rarely done before'. He asked how he was to pay for the journey, and how he could safeguard St Edmunds' liberties and provide for his faithful servants during his absence. The monks said he should raise a loan which they would repay from the convent's resources, for instance from the sacristy and from the fund put aside to pay for pittances. They advised that the abbey be entrusted to the prior and a certain clerk, who could support himself since he had been enriched by Samson, and each servant should be paid a sum proportionate to his previous service. Samson was pleased with the monk's advice: he took it and the day before he left he brought all his books into chapter and gave them to the convent.[55]

Meanwhile, however, there was grumbling in the convent. Some monks said that Samson spoke of the liberties of his barony but not of those belonging to

examples of his service as a papal judge delegate see Cheney and Cheney, *Letters*, pp. 62–3 nos 383–6, 86 no. 527A, 87 no. 530, 93 no. 568, 99 nos 596–7, 129 no. 782. For the use of regulars, among them abbots, priors and obedientiaries of exempt houses, as judges delegate see Sayers, *Papal Judges Delegate*, pp. 120–5. A judge delegate was usually chosen by the litigant who might choose a local person with knowledge of the case. See ibid., p. 113. For a detailed examination of the papal system of delegating cases to local judges see especially Cheney, Mary [G.], *Roger, Bishop of Worcester*, pp. 121–4. However, although the litigant might choose the judge in a case of limited, local importance, the pope would choose the judge in important, difficult cases and if he trusted someone as judge in particular. Ibid., pp. 133–9. Samson seems to have been a judge whom the pope especially trusted. Ibid., p. 137. For Samson's knowledge of canon law see below, p. 68.

[52] JB, p. 135. Ralph Diceto records that at King John's summons, Archbishop Hubert Walter and a number of bishops and abbots, including Bishop Eustace and Abbot Samson, sailed from Shoreham on 14 December 1201. Diceto, *Historical Works*, ii. 173.

[53] Cheney and Cheney, *Letters*, p. 60 no. 364, who date the mandate 1199 x Dec. 1201 and identify it as probably the mandate referred to by Jocelin. Another mandate, ibid., p. 71 no. 439, of 14 Sept. x 28 Oct. 1202, is Innocent's response to the reply of Bishop Eustace and Abbot Samson to the former mandate (no. 364), questioning whether William de Stuteville, Robert de Berkeley and others have valid absolutions from their vows; if not, they must perform their pilgrimages, i.e. go on crusade.

[54] For St Edmunds' dependence on the papacy see below pp. 79–82.

[55] JB, pp. 135–6.

the convent, many of which he had usurped. Three monks, of 'mediocre intelligence' in Jocelin's opinion, supported by others, urged the prior to ask Samson to give some assurance about the usurped liberties before he left. The prior did so; at first Samson was angry, declaring that he would be master as long as he lived. But next day in chapter he relented and allowed discussion of the matters in dispute. He defended his actions, but since he was anxious to leave on good terms with the monks, he promised that when he returned 'he would consult the monks about whatever he did, arrange things justly and return to each man his due'. Jocelin comments that thus 'there was calm, but it was not a great calm', and ends his chronicle on a pessimistic note, citing Ovid's dictum: 'In promises there's none but may be rich.'[56]

---

[56] *JB*, pp. 136–7. Ovid, *Ars Amatoria*, I. 444.

6

Relations with the Town of
Bury St Edmunds

Jocelin's account of the convent's confrontation with Samson in 1202 is probably selective.[1] The monks may well have also complained about other things
about which Jocelin is silent. But the complaints which he does mention as
made on that occasion all concern the administration of the town. They are
matters which figure earlier in his narrative as subjects of dispute and which also
occupy clauses in the Composition.[2] Obviously, the town was a major cause of
dispute between Samson and the convent.

The town of Bury St Edmunds comprised two elements: first the highly privileged Liberty of the *banleuca* where the abbot had regalian rights and ecclesiastical jurisdiction.[3] This was the borough (*burgus*) and the free tenants in it the
burgesses (*burgenses*); secondly, there were the suburbs. However, prosperous free
tenants in the suburbs were numbered among the burgesses, and unfree tenants
in the *banleuca* were not. Certainly, townsmen and burgesses acted together in
attempts to throw off the overriding control of abbot, sacrist and cellarer. They
were unsuccessful and Bury St Edmunds never attained the status of a borough
in the strict sense, with a royal charter. In view of the division of power in the
town's government, it is not surprising that it caused disputes between abbot
and convent. The town belonged to the convent and within the *banleuca* the
abbot's regalian rights and ecclesiastical jurisdiction was exercised on his behalf
by the sacrist: and as the abbot's deputy the sacrist was archdeacon and entitled
to archidiaconal rights and revenues. On the other hand, the cellarer held the
manor in the suburbs with the usual rights and revenues of a manorial lord. But
the abbot had overall responsibilities for the town's good government and in
particular for the *banleuca* for which he was answerable to the king and pope.
Disputes between the sacrist and cellarer over the respective areas of authority
reduced efficiency and could lead to disorder, while the abbot's intervention was
resented by whomever suffered from it.

The day-to-day administration of the town was in the hands of one or two
reeves (until c. 1220–1240 there was usually only one reeve; later there were

---

[1] JB, p. 137; *Bury Cust.*, pp. 101 lines 17–27, 102 lines 1–4; Lobel, *Bury St. Edmunds*, pp.
   189–90.
[2] Ibid., p. 101 lines 17–22. For the Composition see above pp. 35 and n. 23, 35–7.
[3] Ibid., pp. 16–59 passim.

always two).[4] Control of appointments to the reeveship was, therefore, of crucial importance. Abbot Hugh had apparently appointed them at will privately in his lodgings without the convent's consent and despite the monks' complaints. The result was that during the vacancy after his death the royal custodians of the abbey claimed the right to appoint the reeves.[5] The convent was alarmed and probably on this account Samson shortly after his election said that he wished to restore ancient custom whereby matters concerning the reeveship should be settled in the convent's presence and by common consent. Two burgesses, Godfrey and Nicholas, were appointed reeves, and, after debate about who should hand them the moot-horn, the prior did so. They held office for several years but then were said to be lax in the administration of the king's justice. At Samson's order they were deposed and the sacrist, Hugh, took over the management of the town and appointed one reeve, Durand, to replace them. 'But', Jocelin adds, 'in process of time, I know not how, new reeves were appointed elsewhere than in chapter and without the convent's consent.' In his account of the convent's confrontation with Samson in 1202, the first issue Jocelin mentions is that of control of appointments to the reeveship. Samson justified his abrogation of ancient custom by blaming the sacrist: he had had to act to prevent default of the king's justice. However, he promised that when the present reeve, Durand, who was ill, died, the sacrist should take over the reeveship and nominate a new reeve in chapter according to ancient custom – but with the abbot's consent.[6] This last proviso is absent from the Composition: it stipulates that the reeve should be chosen by the convent and sacrist, without the abbot's consent, and should receive the moot-horn and keys annually from the prior and sacrist.[7]

Conflicts between the sacrist and cellarer over their respective rights created serious problems over the custody of prisoners and the administration of justice. One problem concerned the use of the town prison. The prison belonged to the sacrist but the cellarer had the use of it for thieves arrested on his property. The sacrist, however, refused to allow the cellarer to use it, with the result that the cellarer's prisoners escaped and the cellarer was blamed for default of justice.[8] Jocelin does not mention this in his account of the convent's confrontation with Samson in 1202, but a clause of the Composition deals with the matter. It stipulates that thieves captured on the cellarer's fee should be imprisoned in the town prison without opposition from the sacrist or the reeve.[9] An even more serious problem arose from the existence of the sacrist's court, that is the portmann-moot, where the reeve heard pleas concerning the burgesses and held view of frankpledge. The cellarer held his manorial court in Eastgate Barns for

---

4   Ibid., pp. 59–117 passim. See also eadem, 'A list of the aldermen and bailiffs of Bury St Edmunds from the twelfth to the sixteenth century', *PSIANH*, xxii (1936), pp. 17–28.

5   *JB*, pp. 73–4. See Lobel, *Bury St. Edmunds*, p. 33.

6   *JB*, pp. 136–7.

7   *Bury Cust.*, p. 101 lines 27–102 line 2. Cf. Lobel, op. cit., pp. 61–2.

8   *JB*, pp. 100–2. Cf. Lobel, op. cit., 21–3, and eadem, 'The goal of Bury St Edmunds', *PSIA*, xxi (1933) pp. 203–7. Samson had had personal experience of being in the prison under Abbot Hugh. *JB*, pp. 18, 44 and above p. 13.

9   *Bury Cust.*, p. 102 lines 9–14.

his free tenants, which dealt with matters concerning his estates. However, Jocelin records that within living memory by ancient custom the cellarer 'in his court near Scurum's Well' (that is, in Eastgate Barns[10]) had tried robbers and other malefactors, held view of frankpledge and taken the profits, in the same way as the reeve did in the portmann-moot.

Suitors to the cellarer's court did not enjoy the same privilege as those to the portmann-moot. This was unfair on the cellarer's free tenants who lived in the suburbs, outside the town walls (and, therefore, did not owe suit in the portmann-moot), and not within the four crosses of the *banleuca*. An incident occurred in 1198 which gave rise to complaints from the burgesses of injustice to one of the cellarer's suburban tenants, a thief called Ketel. He had been captured, tried in the cellarer's court, forced to defend himself by judicial duel, and was defeated and hanged.[11] The burgesses protested that if he had lived within the town walls and been tried in the portmann-moot he would not have had to do battle but could have cleared himself by compurgation. Jocelin states that Samson and the 'saner part of the convent' agreed that all freemen belonging to St Edmunds, both those with tenements within the *banleuca* and those in the suburbs, should enjoy the same privileges. Samson, therefore, ordered that in future the cellarer's court should sit in the portmann-moot and both courts try cases together, and that the cellarer's free tenants should renew their pledges and pay tithing penny there; half the sum was to go to the cellarer. Jocelin records that at the time when he wrote the cellarer received nothing, and that the arrangement unduly favoured the sacrist.

In the convent's confrontation with Samson in 1202 the monks asked him what would be done about the loss of the cellarer's court, especially about the half pennies which he used to receive from the view of frankpledge. Samson was moved at that and asked by what authority the monks claimed a royal right. They replied that ever since the foundation of their church and even during the first three years of Samson's abbatiate they had had the right to hold the view of frankpledge on all their manors.[12] In the Composition the cellarer's rights are restored almost completely.[13] It stipulates that the cellarer should renew pledges in his court, in the reeve's presence, and have half the tithing pennies and other profits according to ancient custom. It also stipulates that thieves captured on the cellarer's fee should be tried by jury ('by view of legal men'), in his court, either in the guest-house or in Eastgate Barns, in the presence of the reeve and that any forfeited chattels should go to the cellarer, except what was owed to the jailer. The question of the cellarer's revenues predominated in these disputes and sometimes it was the only issue. In 1198 one of the current complaints against Samson was that he appropriated two of the convent's lucrative assets, escheats

---

[10] The cellarer's manor was known as the grange of St Edmund or Eastgate Barns. *JB*, p. 102 and n. 1. Cf. Lobel, *Bury St. Edmunds*, pp. 18–19 and above fig. 6.

[11] *JB*, p. 101. Cf. Lobel, op. cit., pp. 21–2, 34–6. *JB*, ed. Greenway and Sayers, p. 148 n. mistakenly state that Hardwick is a suburb of Bury St Edmund (it lies 2 miles south of Bury).

[12] *JB*, p. 137.

[13] *Bury Cust.*, p. 102 lines 14–17.

of its demesne lands and its right to give in marriage girls and widows who were heiresses to its lands in the town and elsewhere.[14] A clause of the Composition concerns girls and widows who were heiresses to lands held from the convent by free or socage tenure[15] when such lands had escheated. It explains that the heiresses cannot be married without the custodian's permission and payment of *gersuma* (due from free and socage tenants on the marriage of their daughters),[16] and stipulates that they shall be given in marriage by the convent and their custodians without interference by the abbot.

Samson's attitude to the town was more favourable and reasonable than the convent's. He was the last abbot of St Edmunds to ward off conflict between the burgesses and convent by making concessions to them. In 1192 the monks objected that the burgesses by custom paid the convent only £40 a year although the town's prosperity had grown like that of other towns. The monks pointed out that the reeves had leased many shops, booths and stalls in the market-place to burgesses without the convent's consent. They asked Samson to disseize the burgesses concerned, but he told them that this would be contrary to the law of the land, since the burgesses held by prescriptive right, having been in possession 'for a year and a day'. Nevertheless, he urged a compromise for the sake of peace. The burgesses offered the convent 100s so that they might enjoy their holdings as before, but the offer was refused; the monks hoped that they might recover control of the market under a later abbot.[17] The burgesses were alarmed at the monks' attitude and in 1198, when Samson returned from Germany, they persuaded him to confirm the charter of the liberties of the town 'in the same form of words as his predecessors, Anselm, Ording and Hugh had confirmed them'. In return for 60 marks Samson agreed and a charter was dawn up, despite the monks' complaints.[18] Jocelin remarks that after this the burgesses felt so secure that they were reluctant to pay, or even to offer, the 100s to the convent. When Samson tried to insist on payment all the burgesses would offer was to give some precious object for the church worth 100s, on condition that they were quit of tithing penny. Jocelin states that the matter was still unresolved when he wrote, but his account of the convent's confrontation with Samson in 1202 throws more light on the dispute. Samson himself had appropriated the

---

14 *JB*, p. 105.
15 *Bury Cust.*, p. 103 lines 1–6. Socage tenants owned the land they resided on but were subject to specific services to the lord of the hundred. Demesne land on the other hand belonged to the lord who could rent or lease it to whomever he chose. See: *Kalendar*, ed. Davis, pp. xxxi–xxxv, 200 (index); *Feudal Docs*, pp. cxxii–cxxxiii; F. M. Stenton, *Types of Manorial Structure in the Northern Danelaw* (Oxford, 1910), pp. 13–14.
16 *Kalendar*, ed. Davis, pp. xxxvi–xxxvii.
17 *JB*, pp. 77–9. Lobel, *Bury St. Edmunds*, pp. 120–4.
18 Samson's grant to the burgesses of the liberties enjoyed under Edward the Confessor, William I and II and Henry I and under Abbot Baldwin and his successors is printed in *Kalendar*, ed. Davis, pp. 75–6 no. 1. Anselm's charter of privileges to the burgesses is printed in *Feudal Docs*, pp. 114–15 no. 113. Samson's charter is very like Anselm's but the witness list is of course different. *Kalendar*, ed. Davis, p. 75 n. 1, disputes Jocelin's suggestion that the charter was granted in 1193. From the witness list it appears that it should be dated later, 1198 x 1200.

100s. When the convent demanded the restoration of the cellarer's court and of the half the tithing pennies, it accused Samson of receiving 'in private' 100s from the reeve every year in lieu of the profits.[19] The Composition stipulates that the abbot should surrender this 100s to the convent 'to be assigned wherever it pleases'.[20]

One contentious issue was the payment of *repselver*, a penny due every year at the beginning of August in lieu of the labour service of reaping the cellarer's corn. Jocelin explains that originally it was owed by every householder, except knights, chaplains and servants, but in the course of time the cellarer had exempted some of the richer burgesses.[21] This caused discontent among those, some of them very poor, who had to pay, especially as the cellarer's methods of collection were harsh and shameful. Therefore, Samson ordered that in future the burgesses were to pay the cellarer 20s by hand of the reeve in the meeting of the portmann-moot immediately preceding the beginning of August. At the same time the burgesses were to pay 4s in return for exemption from another customary payment, *schorenpeny*,[22] due annually for every head of cattle, except those of the abbot's chaplains and servants, for grazing rights. Samson made the concession about *repselver*, and presumably also about *schorenpeny*, at the unanimous request of the burgesses. There was criticism among the monks, especially by the cellarer, at this erosion of their rights. The date of these negotiations is uncertain but they probably preceded the formal agreement made between Samson, the convent and the burgesses which is datable to sometime before 1200. It commuted the payment of *repselver* and *scarpeni* (Jocelin's *schorenpeny*) for an annual rent of 24s: this rent was to be for a stone building on a site in the market-place bought by the burgesses and built at their expense.[23]

From administrative and economic points of view Samson's policy of commuting these services into money payments was sensible and Jocelin approved: he regarded the peregrinations of the cellarer and his servants collecting *repselver* as oppressive, and describes the collection of *schorenpeny* as very troublesome: the cellarer 'used to place the cows in an enclosure, and had much trouble about the business'. With regard to the abbey's economy it was necessary not to hamper the growing prosperity of the town. It was the abbey's most lucrative asset and income from the market made a substantial contribution to its profitability.[24] Moreover, abbot and convent depended largely on it for supplies. In his account of the ancient customs of the cellarer Jocelin explains that the cellarer and his buyers had

> the right to first purchase in respect of all food required for the convent if the abbot is not resident. The abbot's buyers or the cellarer's, whichever come first to

[19] JB, p. 137.
[20] *Bury Cust.*, p. 102 lines 2–4.
[21] JB, pp. 99–100.
[22] JB, p. 100 and n. 2. In Samson's charter cited below *shorenpeny* is spelt *scarpeni*.
[23] Printed *Kalendar*, ed. Davis, pp. 76 and n. 2, 77; Lobel, *Bury St. Edmunds*, pp. 171–2.
[24] Samson undertook two prolonged and bitter legal disputes, one with the merchants of London and the other with the monks of Ely cathedral priory, St Etheldreda's, to protect the interests of the Bury market. See below pp. 51–2.

the market, should buy first, the former in the absence of the latter, or the latter in the absence of the former, but if both are present, priority should be given to the abbot's buyers. Again, when herring is sold, the abbot's buyers shall buy a hundred herring at a half pence less than others, and so shall the cellarer and his buyers.[25]

However, Samson made a concession to the convent. He

ordered his buyers to give way to the cellarer and his buyers because, as he said, he preferred that he rather than the convent should go short. Therefore, the buyers 'in mutual deference to each other' [Rom. 12.10], if they find something to be bought which is not sufficient for both, should buy it jointly and divide it equally.

But Jocelin is sceptical of the outcome; 'and so betwixt head and limbs and between father and sons "Concord that is no concord still abides."' [Lucan, line 98][26]

Samson made two benefactions to the town which must have met with the approval of monks and townspeople alike. Indeed, Jocelin numbers one of them, the foundation of St Saviour's hospital, as one of Samson's three acts which proved his great goodness.[27] He founded St Saviour's c. 1185; papal protection for the hospital was granted by Urban III on 29 December 1186.[28] It was situated at Babwell just outside Northgate and intended for the relief of 'the infirm and poor'. It was the third of the six hospitals to be founded in Bury St Edmunds in the middle ages and the first intended specifically for poor relief: one of the two earlier hospitals, St Peter's, founded by Abbot Anselm, was for 'infirm brethren',[29] and the other, St Petronilla's, founded in the twelfth century, was for female lepers.[30] And Samson's foundation was much the most generously endowed of all six hospitals in the town. Its first endowment was of revenues from Icklingham, an outlier of Mildenhall. More endowment swiftly followed. The hospital was placed under the authority of the sacrist (who had a manor at Icklingham) but a Master was in immediate control. The purpose of the hospital was to support twelve chaplains, six clerks, twelve poor men and twelve poor

---

25 JB, p. 104.

26 JB, p. 105.

27 JB, p. 45. Cf. above p. 26 and n. 23.

28 For an authoritative account of St Saviour's see Harper-Bill, *Hospitals*, pp. 9–19. Urban III's bull is printed in ibid., p. 120 no. 165. Harper-Bill (*Hospitals*, pp. 9, 120) misdates it 29 January 1186 but Holtzmann, *Papsturkunden*, iii. 492 no. 384 dates it correctly 29 December. For a short, general survey of the hospitals in Bury St Edmunds see Joy Rowe, 'The medieval hospitals of Bury St Edmunds', *Medical History*, ii (1958), pp. 253–63 (*pace* p. 257 line 20; for 1216 read 1252). See also below pp. 80, 193.

29 St Peter's was situated outside Risby Gate on the main road into the town from the west. The earliest information about it is in a final concord made between Abbot Samson and Benedict of Blakenham in the king's court at Michaelmas, 1202, printed Gage, *Thingoe Hundred*, pp. 30–2. See: *Kalendar*, ed. Davis, pp. 87 and n. 1, 88; Harper-Bill, *Hospitals*, pp. 7–8, 94–5 no. 122. For the later history of the hospital, which by the end of the middle ages was a leper house, see: ibid., pp. 8–9, 95–119 nos 123–164A.

30 St Petronilla's was outside Southgate. No charters from it survive. Harper-Bill, *Hospitals*, pp. 5–6 and nn. Cf.: Clay, *Medieval Hospitals*, pp. 119–20, 147, 256; J. C. Cox in *VCH Suffolk*, ii. 135.

women. All were to pray 'in perpetuity' for the soul of the king and the souls of his progeny. Harper-Bill traces the subsequent history of the hospital – the gradual attrition and final loss of its original charitable purpose.

Samson's other important benefaction to the town was the grammar school. This was another of the three acts which Jocelin considered proved Samson's great goodness. As a poor clerk he had studied in the school of Master William of Diss, on his charity.[31] Maybe memory of this was one reason why Samson bought houses in the town to provide free lodgings for poor scholars (previously they had had to pay a penny or halfpenny in rent twice a year).[32] This was probably in the early 1190s and then, in 1198, he came to an agreement with Robert de Scales whereby each party recognized the right of the other to half the advowson of the church of Wetherden (in east Suffolk), but on condition that Robert paid 3 marks a year to the schoolmaster by hand of the sacrist.[33] At the same time Samson ordained in chapter that all scholars, both rich and poor, should be quit of rent for lodgings for ever, and that forty poor clerks should be quit of the customary payment to the schoolmaster for instruction. The forty poor clerks in the first instance should be relatives of Bury monks; the rest of the scholars were to be chosen at the schoolmaster's discretion. The number was to include two clerks and an usher who were to eat in the almonry and come to the school at the three terms of the year, namely at Michaelmas, after Christmas, and after Easter, by the date when the schoolmaster began to lecture and only to leave when he stopped lecturing, except during the Easter vacation, when they must remain until Maundy Thursday.[34] In fact, Samson was one of the earliest benefactors in England to make provision for free education.[35]

---

[31] Above p. 12. Samson, when abbot, expressed his gratitude to Master William by giving his son, Master Walter, the vicarage of the church of Chevington. *JB*, p. 44.

[32] *JB*, p. 45.

[33] *Kalendar*, ed. Davis, p. 145 no. 118 and nn. 1, 2; *Acta Norwich 1070–1214*, ed. Harper-Bill, pp. 139–40 no. 177. Similarly Samson obtained the appropriation of two thirds of the church of [Long] Melford on the death of Hugh, the vicar. Ibid., pp. 140–1 no. 178.

[34] The organization of the school is described in a note in the hand of the scribe of the Bury Customary (see below p. 203 and n. 58); BL MS Harley 1005, ff. 126–126v (modern foliation), 120–120v (medieval foliation). A marginal note by Henry of Kirkstead states that it has been corrected from the almoner's register ('correctum est per registrum elemos[inarii]') which is now lost (Thomson, *Archives*, p. 12). For an English translation of the passage see A. F. Leach in *VCH Suffolk*, ii. 308 (n. 1 refers in error to f. 130).

[35] Orme, *English Schools in the Middle Ages*, p. 184.

7

Samson and Secular Law

On his election to the abbacy Samson took steps to remedy his lack of the legal knowledge necessary in his new office for the protection of St Edmunds' liberties and possessions. He appointed men learned in secular law to advise and instruct him – Jocelin refers to them as his 'private counsellors'[1] – and studied appropriate legal texts. Thus, he soon became a formidable party in the law courts and was regarded as a wise judge.[2] At some stage he was appointed a royal justice in eyre (but is known to have served only once, that was on a circuit in September and October 1194, in Norfolk, Suffolk, Cambridgeshire, Essex, Hertfordshire and Huntingdonshire).[3]

Excellent illustrations of the legal skill of Samson and his lawyers are in Jocelin's chronicle and in the Public Records. Thus, Jocelin relates,[4] the merchants of London desired to be quit of toll in the Bury market, but many nevertheless grudgingly paid it. The citizens of London on this account made a 'great commotion' in their hustings court and sent messengers to Samson informing him that by virtue of a charter of Henry II, Londoners were exempt from toll throughout England. Samson replied that he called the king to warrant that the king had never given them any charter to the prejudice of St Edmunds' liberties, which were granted before the Conquest by Edward the Confessor; furthermore, although the king could grant quittance from toll throughout his own dominions, he could not do so in the town of Bury St Edmunds since within the *banleuca* where the market was situated, the abbot enjoyed regalian rights. The Londoners persisted in the dispute with bitter acrimony and threats of violence. Worst of all, they boycotted the Bury market for two years, 'from which our market suffered great loss, and oblations received by the sacrist were greatly diminished.' So the quarrel dragged on until Samson compromised and persuaded the Londoners to await the king's return so that he might take his advice. Jocelin does not date this episode, but possibly the king in question was Richard I who returned from captivity in Germany in March 1194.

The other dispute which had repercussions on the prosperity of the Bury

---

[1] *JB*, p. 50.
[2] *JB*, pp. 24, 34.
[3] *JB*, p. 34. Crook, *Records*, p. 57. For the employment of abbots as justices in eyre and Grosseteste's anger at the practice see: Knowles, *RO*, i. 276; Grosseteste, *Epistolae*, pp. 105–8 ep. xxvii, 205–34 ep. lxxii*.
[4] *JB*, pp. 75–7 and nn.; *JB*, ed. Greenway and Sayers, pp. 67, 144 nn.

market was between St Edmunds and the monks of St Etheldreda's, that is Ely Cathedral priory. Since before the Conquest the monks of Ely had held the manor of Lakenheath, but it lay within the hundred of Lackford, a hundred within St Edmunds' Liberty of the eight and a half hundreds. In 1201 the monks of Ely, fortified with the assent of king John and a charter from him, established a market at Lakenheath. Samson tried the settle the matter peaceably with the bishop and monks, 'our friends and neighbours', but the monks rejected all over-tures and 'threatening words were bandied two and fro'.[5] Samson, therefore, secured a writ of recognition so that the respective rights of Ely and St Edmunds could be decided by jury. The jurors returned on oath that the Ely market was to St Edmunds' prejudice. This being reported to the king, he caused a search to be made in his register, concerning the nature of the charter he had granted to the monks of Ely; and it was found that he had granted this charter on condition that it should not be 'to the prejudice of neighbouring markets'. St Edmunds then paid 40 marks for a charter stating that no market was to be established within its Liberty without the abbot's consent. The king sent a mandate to the justiciar, Geoffrey Fitz Peter, ordering him to demolish the market; Geoffrey wrote accordingly to the sheriff of Suffolk, 'but he, knowing that he could not enter the liberties of St Edmund nor exercise any power therein', instructed Samson to execute the king's mandate. Samson, therefore, sent the provost of Lackford hundred and a group of freemen as witnesses to Lakenheath market showing the king's and the sheriff's mandates. But the people in the market 'defied and insulted' them. Samson was in London at the time, but on his return, having consulted with 'wise men', ordered his bailiffs to go with a force of well-armed men on horseback to Lakenheath – Jocelin claims, no doubt with exaggeration, that the force comprised six hundred men. They were to seize those in the market and bring them in chains to St Edmunds. They set out about midnight but scouts forewarned those in the market of their approach and everyone scattered. The prior of Ely, suspecting imminent danger from St Edmunds, had come with his bailiffs to protect the traders in the market. But when the men from St Edmunds arrived he refused to leave his house or to give the bailiffs from St Edmunds securities that he would stand trial in the court of St Edmunds. Therefore, having consulted among themselves, the force from St Edmunds destroyed the market and carried off all the goods and drove all the cattle and sheep towards Icklingham. The prior's bailiffs followed and asked for the livestock back for fifteen days in return for pledges. This request was granted. Within this time Samson received a summons to appear at the Exchequer to answer concerning the episode and meanwhile to return the livestock. 'For the bishop of Ely, an eloquent and fluent speaker complained in person to the justiciar and magnates, saying that an act of unprecedented arrogance had been committed on the land of St Etheldreda in time of peace; because of his words

---

5 Jocelin gives a lively account of the dispute. *JB*, pp. 132–3 and nn.; *JB*, ed. Greenway and Sayers, pp. 117–19, 151 nn. Butler correlates the details given by Jocelin with evidence in the Public Records which suggests that Jocelin's account is not entirely accurate. *JB*, pp. 157–60 (Appendix T).

many were stirred with indignation against the abbot'. Jocelin ends his account at this point but we know from the public records that the dispute was ongoing in 1203; after that there is silence.

Another of Samson's disputes concerns conflict of jurisdictions, though in this case the interests of the Bury market was not at issue. Incompatible royal charters were at the root of Samson's disputes with Archbishop Baldwin and the monks of the cathedral priory of Christ Church, Canterbury, over Monks Eleigh. The manor belonged to the Canterbury monks,[6] but it lay within St Edmunds' Liberty of the eight and a half hundreds and St Edmunds had tenants there.[7] In 1186 a man was slain on the manor. Edward the Confessor had granted St Edmunds regalian jurisdiction (sake and soke) over all its men[8] inside and outside the borough[9] and Samson was, therefore, justified in summoning the perpetrators to appear in the court of St Edmunds. But Archbishop Baldwin refused to let them come. Samson accordingly complained to the king, saying that Baldwin was claiming St Edmunds' liberties because of a charter granted by King Henry to Canterbury after the death of Thomas Becket. Henry denied that he had ever granted any charter to Canterbury prejudicial to St Edmunds' ancient rights and had no wish to injure it in such a way. Samson told his counsellors ('consiliarii privati sui') that it would be best to exercise the right and then defend himself in court, since it was preferable that the archbishop should complain of him, rather than Samson of the archbishop. He, therefore, had the culprits seized, bound and imprisoned, with some violence, according to Jocelin.

Baldwin duly complained. Consequently, the justiciar, Ranulf de Glanville, ordered the culprits to be bound by sureties to appear in whichever court was appropriate and Samson was summoned to answer in the king's court for the 'force and injury which it was said he had done to the archbishop'. Finally, early in 1187, both parties appeared before the king in the chapter-house at Canterbury and both had read aloud their charters of privilege granted to their churches by Edward the Confessor. Henry was nonplussed and admitted that the charters were of equal antiquity and mutually incompatible. Samson claimed that St Edmunds always had been and still was in seizin and appealed to the verdict of a jury of men from Norfolk and Suffolk. Baldwin refused, fearing that the jurors would favour St Edmunds. At this Henry lost his temper and left the court in indignation exclaiming 'Let him take who can.'[10] When Jocelin wrote his account the matter was still unresolved,[11] but he notes that the villeins (rustici) at Milden, a hamlet in the same hundred as Monks Eleigh (Babergh double hundred)[12] had attacked certain of Canterbury's men and wounded them 'unto

---

6 Sawyer, *Charters*, pp. 312–13 no. 1047. Cf. F. R. H. Du Boulay, *The Lordship of Canterbury* (London, 1966), pp. 20, 21, 33, 46.
7 *JB*, pp. 50–2. *DB, Suffolk*, i. 14 no. 27.
8 Harmer, *Writs*, pp. 153–9 nos 8–12.
9 For Christ Church's privileges see: Sawyer, *Charters*, p. 324 no. 1088; Harmer, *Writs*, pp. 185 no. 31, 186 no. 33, 187–8 no. 34.
10 Matt. 19.12. See *JB*, p. 52 n. 1.
11 'et adhuc sub indice lis est'. Horace, *Ars Poetica*, 78.
12 *DB, Suffolk*, i. 14 no. 34.

death', but the victims dared not complain to the abbot or to his bailiffs.[13] There survives a copy of a writ allegedly of Henry II (and ostensibly datable to after 1184) which may well have been forged to support St Edmunds' case against Baldwin.[14] It is addressed to three royal justices and states that Henry had never granted to the monks of Canterbury any dignity, custom or right belonging to the church and monks of St Edmunds. He had only granted and confirmed to them what belonged to him; therefore, he ordered that St Edmunds' church and monks should hold their right in peace and that the monks of Canterbury should demand and do nothing against St Edmunds' dignity in pretext of their charter. The form and content of this writ are very suspect, and the statement that the king had no power to grant to anyone else any right already held by St Edmunds resembles the argument used by Samson in his dispute with the London merchants over toll. The writ is almost certainly a forgery, a *pièce justificative*, composed for use against Baldwin or any subsequent archbishop.[15]

The loss of St Edmunds' regalian rights in Monks Eleigh would have made a serious inroad into the abbey's Liberty. But an even more serious threat confronted Samson in 1190, when he was in danger of losing an integral part of the Liberty – Cosford half hundred. At Samson's succession Cosford half hundred was farmed for 100s a year to Robert of Cockfield. When Robert died in 1190, his son and heir Adam of Cockfield claimed the half hundred, and also the manors of Semer and Groton in it, as part of his inheritance. Samson's struggle to prevent him establishing hereditary tenure is well documented in the abbey's archives and, because the case came before royal justices, in the Public Records. Moreover, both Jocelin and William of Diss, in his appendix to Jocelin's chronicle, describe the dispute in some detail.[16] Samson was at first successful in the dispute over Semer and Groton. Adam entered into an agreement with him, c. 1191, accepting a life tenancy of the manors.[17] However, c. 1198, Adam died and his baby daughter, Margaret, inherited his fee. Samson granted the wardship by charter at his own discretion, but then King Richard asked for the wardship for one of his courtiers. Samson replied that he had already given it away and tried to appease Richard's anger with gifts. He remained adamant because he feared otherwise he would set a precedent 'to the prejudice of succeeding abbots'. Suddenly Richard's anger subsided and he wrote a friendly letter to Samson asking for the gift of some of his hounds. These were sent, besides horses and other desirables. In return, Richard thanked him and sent a valuable ring which Innocent III had given him after the coronation.[18] Samson had

13 *JB*, p. 52.

14 *Feudal Docs*, p. 105 no. 101.

15 Douglas notes that the dating of the writ is problematical (*Feudal Docs*, p. 105). Greenway and Sayers regard the writ as of doubtful authenticity and suggest that it was forged by St Edmunds to counter Canterbury's claims (*JB*, ed. Greenway and Sayers, p. 137 n.). J. C. Holt, in a letter to me of 27 March 1996, expressed strong suspicions about the writ and lists five objections. He ends: 'To sum up … I think it *stinks*.'

16 *JB*, pp. 29, 58–9, 138.

17 *Kalendar*, ed. Davis, pp. 127–8 no. 90 and nn.

18 *JB*, pp. 97–9.

had considerable trouble obtaining seizin of Adam's daughter because, as Jocelin says, her grandfather had stolen her away.[19] He at length managed to obtain seizin with the help of Archbishop Hubert Walter,[20] to whom he then sold the wardship for £100. Archbishop Hubert, who did a lucrative trade in wardships, sold it for £500 to Thomas de Burgh, brother of the king's chamberlain, Hubert de Burgh.[21] Thomas, therefore, demanded seizin by hereditary right, as fee-farm, of Adam's estates, including Semer and Groton. In 1201, in the king's court by action of *mort d'ancestor*, his claim was upheld: the settlement of c. 1191 was set aside and the jurors decided that Adam, his father and grandfather had held the manors successively; therefore, the justices decided that long tenure had created hereditary right. Henceforth the manors should be held as fee-farm.

On the other hand, Samson was successful in his defence of St Edmunds' right to Cosford half hundred. The dispute was different from that over Semer and Groton: jurisdiction, not property, was at stake. Samson argued in the king's court that since St Edmunds held the Liberty of the eight and a half hundreds by grant of Edward the Confessor and the confirmations of successive kings, only the king could force him to allow anyone to hold any part of it by hereditary right.[22] He pointed out the danger to the Liberty should this happen: if Adam de Cockfield or any subsequent heir were to hold the half hundred by hereditary right and were disinherited for some offence, the sheriff of Suffolk and the king's bailiffs would seize the half hundred together with the rest of Adam's fee; similarly, if Adam or a subsequent heir were to marry a woman who held land in chief of the king and on his death his heir were a minor, the latter would become the king's ward and the king would seize all his inheritance. Samson's arguments prevailed.

These examples represent a very small proportion of the litigation in which Samson was embroiled. As head of the house he was responsible for defending its privileges and property in court,[23] but he acted in co-operation with the prior or his deputy who defended the convent's interests. After all, much of the property belonging to the convent – for instance the manors of Semer and Groton – were the cellarer's.

---

[19] *JB*, p. 123.

[20] Hubert Walter, archbishop of Canterbury 1193–1205, justiciar 1193–98, chancellor 1199–1205. Jocelin's account of this incident is cited in: Cheney, *Hubert Walter*, p. 114; and esp. J. C. Holt, 'Feudal society and the family in early medieval England, ii, Notions of patrimony', *TRHS*, 5th ser., xxxiii (1983, repr. idem, *Colonial England*, pp. 197–221), pp. 193 and n. 2, 194–8. For the market in wardships, see: Cheney, op. cit., p. 113; Holt, op. cit., iv, 'The heiress and the alien', *TRHS*, 5th ser., xxxv (1985, repr. idem, *Colonial England*, pp. 245–269), pp. 21 et seqq.

[21] Hubert de Burgh (d. 1243) was the king's chamberlain, then justiciar 1215–34.

[22] Ibid., p. 196.

[23] The abbot's obligation to pay the cost of litigation when he sued or was sued in cases concerning the convent's property was among the ancient customs given renewed force by agreement between Abbot John of Northwold and the convent in 1280. Gransden, 'Separation of portions', p. 400 § 9. It was also one of the customs confirmed by Edward I in 1281. *Mon. Angl.*, iii. 158.

8

Samson and the Knights of St Edmund

One of Samson's problems was his relationship with the abbey's military tenants. He had to ensure that they fulfilled their obligations to him and to the king, and that their rights were protected against royal encroachment. The abbot of St Edmunds owed the service of forty knights. But he, like other tenants-in-chief, had enfeoffed knights in excess of his quota, in his case twelve extra. The situation is made clear by the list of knights' fees returned by the abbey to the Exchequer in 1166.[1] The return was in response to the questionnaire sent by Henry II to his tenants-in-chief. He demanded to know: what feudal service each owed and the number of sub-tenants each had enfeoffed both before 1135 (the 'old enfeoffment') and after 1135 (the 'new enfeoffment'); and the names of the knights.[2] The list for St Edmunds names thirty-eight knights of the old enfeoffment and one knight of the new enfeoffment (which shows that sub-infeudation had taken place early on St Edmunds' estates). The list concludes that though the abbey's service was for forty knights, fifty-two and three quarters knights' fees had been created. It adds that Hugh Bigod (earl of Norfolk 1141–77) 'retains and discharges a guard of three knights in the castle of Norwich'. In addition to military service St Edmunds' knights owed castle-guard at Norwich.[3] Jocelin incorporates in his chronicle an up-dated copy of the 1166 list, made in 1200, with the names of the current military tenants and their service.[4] This list omits the distinction between old and new enfeoffments or any mention of castle-guard but adds the locations of the fees. Another list drawn up a little later groups the knights in four sets of ten, each under a constable, each constabulary being responsible in turn for three months' castle-guard at Norwich.[5]

---

[1] *Hist. Docs*, ii. 975–7.
[2] Ibid., pp. 968–9; J. H. Round, *Feudal England* (London, 1895, repr. 1964), p. 200; Chew, *English Ecclesiastical Tenants-in-Chief*, pp. 17–20, 26, 33; J. C. Holt, 'The introduction of knight-service in England', *Anglo-Norman Studies*, vi (1983, repr. idem, *Colonial England 1066–1215* (London, 1997), pp. 81–101), pp. 89 et seqq.
[3] *JB*, pp. 66–8. For the importance of Jocelin's evidence see A. L. Poole, *Obligations of Society in the XII and XIII Centuries* (Oxford, 1946, repr. 1949, 1960), pp. 48–50. Cf.: Chew, op. cit., p. 101; F. M. Stenton, *English Feudalism 1066–1166* (Oxford, 1931), pp. 204–14.
[4] *JB*, pp. 120–2.
[5] BL MS Harley 645, ff. 25, 222. Printed in part by V. H. Galbraith, *EHR*, xliv (1929), p. 371, and discussed and printed complete in *Feudal Docs*, pp. lxxxvi–lxxxvii. Douglas's general conclusions from this text are too sweeping. See: Poole, op. cit., p. 49; Michael Powicke, *Military Obligation in Medieval England* (Oxford, 1962), p. 141.

These were the obligations of St Edmunds' military tenants but they had long been commuted for money payments. Samson's disputes with them and with the king about feudal service usually took the form of haggling over money. A problem arose almost immediately after his succession. When he had received homage from his fifty-two military tenants he demanded an aid.[6] The knights promised him 20s each, but then, after consultation, withdrew £12 in respect of the twelve extra knights; they argued that the twelve ought to help the other forty to pay scutages and aids to the abbot and to discharge castle-guard. Their contention would seem to have had some justification. The king did not demand service from ecclesiastical tenants-in-chiefs for fees of the new enfeoffment.[7] And in 1235 the abbot of St Edmunds (Henry of Rushbrooke), in response to a royal inquiry into the number of fees, returned forty as of old and twelve as of new creation, but denied any liability for the latter; he declared that he had no idea of their number or even where the fees were.[8] In 1182, Samson thought he could do nothing about the knights' refusal to accept that the twelve extra knights owed him feudal service. He was very angry and said to his intimates that 'he would render them like for like, trouble for trouble'.[9]

This Samson did, but it was many years later. Jocelin gives details of his struggle with, and defeat of, the knights in 1196/7.[10] He took action to ensure that all the knights, now calculated as fifty, discharged their feudal obligations in full. He demanded to know why ten should owe him no service but the other forty receive their service instead. The knights replied that it was customary for the ten to assist the forty and that they should not be required to answer to the abbot. The dispute went to the king's court, but the knights were astute and avoided attending together, and those who did attend said that they could only answer if all were present. At length Samson, exasperated at the great delay and expense, appealed to the justiciar, Hubert Walter. Hubert replied 'in full council' that each knight ought to answer individually for himself and his holding, and declared that the abbot had both 'the knowledge and the power' to enforce his church's claim. Samson then managed to persuade or compel each knight separately, to recognize his service in the court of St Edmund. To give the recognitions full authority ('because recognition in the court of St Edmund was not sufficient') he took all the knights and their wives and any heiresses of the fees to London at his own expense to make their recognitions in the king's court. The agreements were enrolled in the Fine Rolls and each knight received a copy of his recognition.[11] He acknowledged his service for his fee with the obligation to pay full scutage and perform castle-guard at Norwich. Samson on his part

6 JB, p. 28.
7 Chew, op. cit., pp. 20–1, 26.
8 Book of Fees (London, 1920–31, 2 vols in 3), i. 584–5. Chew, op. cit., p. 26.
9 JB, p. 28.
10 JB, pp. 65–8.
11 For enrolments see Feet of Fines, 7 and 8 Richard I (Pipe Roll Soc., xxii, 1896), pp. 40–6, 50–3, 86–8, and ibid., 9 Richard I (Pipe Roll Soc., xxiii, 1898), pp. 37–8. Copies of the recognition in a late thirteenth-century hand are in the register of Abbot Thomas of Tottington (1302–12) and Abbot Richard of Draughton (1312–35), a composite volume

pardoned arrears. The recognitions are dated variously from December 1196 to October 1197. Four knights were abroad at the time, but Samson dealt with them later. The last to resist was Audrey de Vere (earl of Oxford 1194–1214), but Samson forced him to come to the king's court and make his recognition like the others by impounding and selling his cattle.

It was undoubtedly to reduce the chance of future conflict that the list of knights, their service and holdings copied by Jocelin was made. The other surviving list arranged under constabularies must have been to clarify the position over castle-guard, which had also been in dispute in 1197.[12] Roger Bigod (earl of Norfolk 1189–1221) had acknowledged his service of three knights, but had been silent about their duty to guard Norwich castle. In fact, none of the knights had been discharging their service in person. Instead, the abbot customarily paid 7s to the king when their turn for service came to make up for their default. Jocelin explains that each knight of the four constabularies used to pay 28d when it was their turn for castle-guard, besides 1d to the marshal who collected the money. They should have paid 3s (36d) but because the ten extra knights contributed they only paid 28d. Moreover, whereas the turn of each of the four constabularies ought to have come round every four months (sixteen weeks), it only did so every twenty weeks. But now Samson made each knight pay his 3s in full. Since the abbot only had to answer for the guard service of forty knights, he made a profit, which he used to recompense himself for the 7s he had to pay because of the default of Roger Bigod's three knights.

Samson's relations with his knights were not always bad. He protected the privilege of Roger Bigod to carry the banner of St Edmund. Roger had carried the banner in 1173 when he and the knights of St Edmund had intercepted and defeated the rebellious Robert, earl of Leicester, and his army just north of Bury, at Fornham St Genevieve.[13] Although in general military service was commuted for money payments, Samson himself, wearing armour and with the banner of St Edmund, had led his knights to the siege of Windsor castle in 1193. The castle was occupied by John, count of Mortain, in rebellion during the captivity in Germany of his brother, King Richard. (Some other abbots also joined the siege.) Jocelin praised Samson's bravery but doubted his wisdom. He and his fellow monks feared he might have set a precedent for the abbot to accompany a military expedition in person.[14]

containing much other material. BL MS Harley 230, ff. 178–182. Cf. Thomson, *Archives*, pp. 22–3, 132–3 no. 1286.

[12] JB, pp. 66–7. Roger's father, Hugh Bigod, had withheld his service at Norwich castle. *Feudal Docs*, p. 99 no. 90. Cf. *Hist. Docs*, ii. 977. Chew, op. cit., pp. 101–3.

[13] JB, pp. 57–8. For the battle of Fornham see e.g. *Ben. Pet.*, ii. 60–1. Cf. Poole, *Domesday Book to Magna Carta*, p. 336. A fifteenth-century illumination depicting the banner is in John Lydgate's *Life and Miracles of St Edmund*, Harley 2278 f. 1v, reproduced in black and white by Rogers, 'Bury artists of Harley 2278', pl. LIVC. For an engraving of the same see JB, ed. Rokewode, p. 104.

[14] JB, p. 55. Jocelin comments that Samson shone in counsel rather than in prowess. This may mean that he did not actually fight. Clerics were forbidden by canon law to fight causing bloodshed. The Council of Westminster in 1175 forbade the bearing of arms by the religious. *C and S*, i, pt ii, p. 988 and n. 1.

Late in 1197 the question of the extent of the knights' duty of corporal military service was put to the test. Richard ordered his tenants-in-chief to send knights to serve him on his French campaign. Jocelin states that he demanded a tenth of the normal quotas. The demand for corporal service overseas aroused immediate and general opposition. Samson, who was to send four knights, summoned the knights of St Edmund, but they said that they had no obligation to serve abroad. They argued that neither they nor their predecessors had ever done so, though they paid scutage. Samson was in a dilemma: on the one hand he was afraid of incurring the king's displeasure and so risking the forfeiture of his barony, but on the other he wished to defend his knights' rights. Therefore, Samson travelled to France apparently to try to persuade Richard to accept scutage instead of corporal service. But 'despite toil, expense and rich gifts' Richard insisted that he wanted knights, not money. Eventually Samson persuaded him to accept four mercenaries. Samson hired the knights for forty days' service for a fixed sum of 36 marks a day. On the advice of 'some of the king's friends' he also paid Richard £100 in order to be quit of further responsibility at the end of the forty days. In this way he won Richard's favour and obtained a royal mandate empowering him to recover from his knights what he had paid to replace the service which they owed the king. On his return Samson summoned his knights but they pleaded poverty and the various recent impositions put on them. They offered two marks on every fee. Samson, knowing that he had already compelled them to pay scutage in full that year and for the sake of their good will, accepted their offer. He probably raised the money from all fifty fees, but even so would have been considerably out of pocket.[15]

---

[15] JB, pp. 85–7. See: C and S, i, pt ii, pp. 1052 and n. 2, 1053; Poole, *Domesday Book to Magna Carta*, pp. 370–1, 375–7; Stenton, *Feudal England*, pp. 42–3; Chew, op. cit., pp. 149–50.

9

Relations with the Angevin Kings

Samson's successful defence of his right as a tenant-in-chief of the crown to the wardship of the infant heiress of one of his military tenants was described above. Similarly, he was constantly on his guard against encroachment by the Angevin kings on St Edmunds' liberties and possessions. When necessary, he acted quickly to protect them. For example, in 1186 or 1187 the royal justices in eyre fined the counties of Norfolk and Suffolk for 'a certain offence' committed within their boundaries: Norfolk was to pay 50 marks and Suffolk 30 marks, and St Edmunds was to pay part of the sum.[1] Samson immediately went with some of his household, including Jocelin of Brackland, to the king at Clarendon.[2] He produced Edward the Confessor's charter which exempted St Edmunds' lands from all royal taxes and impositions.[3] Henry, therefore, instructed that six knights from Norfolk and six from Suffolk should be summoned to recognize before the barons of the Exchequer whether St Edmunds' lands were exempt from common amercements. To save labour and expense only six knights were chosen but they were all landholders in both counties. (Jocelin names only three of them.) They went to London with Samson and his party (Jocelin was again among them). They found in the abbot's favour and their verdict was enrolled by the justices.[4]

Samson's disputes in defence of St Edmunds' rights illustrate the constant interaction of abbatial administration with royal government. Many cases were decided by assize and settled by final concord in the king's court. The enrolment of the settlements ensured permanent, indisputable record. As has been seen, Samson's dispute with the London merchants over toll, the archbishop and monks of Christ Church, Canterbury, over jurisdiction in Monks Eleigh, and with the prior and monks of Ely over Lakenheath market all arose because the parties had incompatible charters: such cases had to be decided in a royal court.[5] Appeal to the king was not usually to him personally but to the justiciar or other regent acting on the king's behalf, since Henry II and John were often,

---

[1] *JB*, pp. 64–5.
[2] That is, Henry was at Clarendon, his palace near Salisbury.
[3] Harmer, *Writs*, pp. 158–9 no. 15; Sawyer, *Charters*, pp. 320–1 no. 1075.
[4] Copies of the enrolments are in BL MS Harley 645, ff. 138v, 167 and Harley 743, f. 74. They are headed 'Irrotulacio Scaccarij de quietanc' communis misericord' et murdr' anno regni Regis H. secundi Aui Regis H. tercij xxxij vel xxxiij vel xxxiiij'.
[5] Above pp. 51–54.

and Richard I was almost always, abroad. An example is a dispute which Samson had with Master Jordan of Ross, parson of the church of Harlow (in Essex).[6] This case was dealt with by the justiciar, Ranulph de Glanville, who held office from 1179 or 1180 until his dismissal in 1189. Jocelin describes the dispute but his account has to be corrected and augmented from other sources.[7] The question was, as Master Jordan claimed, whether a piece of land held by a certain Herard was or was not held of the church of Harlow in free alms, or, as Samson claimed, it was lay fee and owed service to the abbot of St Edmunds. Disputes of this kind had to be determined in a royal court by the assize *utrum*, that is by a jury of recognitors deciding 'whether' a holding was held in free alms or was lay fee. Ranulph de Glanville allowed the twelve recognitors to be summoned and to sit in a hundred court in the cemetery of the church of Harlow.[8] The recognitors returned the verdict that Herard's land had always owed service to the abbot. Later, in the abbot's court of St Edmunds, Master Jordan recognized that the land was lay fee and that he had no claim to it except by grant of the abbot, and it was granted that he should pay 12d a year to the abbot instead of all services.

It was particularly important for St Edmunds' interests that Samson should keep on good terms with Hubert Walter, one of the most powerful Angevin statesmen. Hubert held a number of key offices: he was archbishop of Canterbury (1193–1205), papal legate (1195–1198), justiciar (1193–8) and chancellor (1195–1205). Inevitably, Samson came into close contact with Hubert in the course of secular and ecclesiastical business. Hubert belonged to a large East Anglian family which held land in both Norfolk and Suffolk. He was probably born in West Dereham in Norfolk, where St Edmunds was among the landholders.[9] On one occasion Samson used Hubert's local birth as a means of persuasion. He and Hubert quarrelled in 1197 when the latter proposed to hold a visitation of St Edmunds. Hubert was an assiduous visitor of monasteries and other churches in the interests of reform. As a papal legate he claimed the right to hold visitations even of exempt monasteries.[10] But Samson would not allow him to come to St Edmunds for such a purpose and appealed to the abbey's ancient privilege of exemption. A heated argument ensued. At length the altercation subsided. Jocelin writes: 'the abbot spoke with greater moderation and asked [Hubert] to treat the church of St Edmund more gently, reminding him that, by reason of his place of birth, he was, as it were, born and bred a St Edmunds' man'.[11] Hubert abandoned the attempt and good relations with Samson were restored. Indeed, Samson was one of the abbots to whom Hubert wrote asking for a testimonial

---

6   Master Jordan of Ross, was an Oxford Master; *BRUO*, iii. 1591.

7   *JB*, pp. 62, 149–50; *JB*, ed. Greenway and Sayers, pp. 55, 141 nn.; *Kalendar*, ed. Davis, pp. 163–4 no. 152.

8   King Stephen had in fact granted Harlow half-hundred to Abbot Ording and his successors, but Henry II had not confirmed the grant which had consequently lapsed and was, therefore, irrelevant to the present dispute. For the grant see *Feudal Docs*, pp. clii and n. 9, 90 no. 76.

9   Cheney, *Hubert Walter*, pp. 16–18; *JB*, p. 82.

10   Cheney, op. cit., pp. 67–9, 119–22.

11   *JB*, pp. 84–5.

for him to send to Rome, to clear him of charges brought against him by Geoffrey, archbishop of York: Geoffrey had accused him in the curia of oppression and extortion during his visitations of monasteries. Samson wrote 'and, speaking according to his conscience, testified that the archbishop of Canterbury had not come to our church, and had oppressed neither it nor any other church'.[12]

Hubert's favour was useful to St Edmunds on a number of occasions. Jocelin remarks that Samson would never have gained seizin of Margaret, Adam of Cockfield's heiress, without Hubert's help.[13] Although Samson normally disdained to lean on the counsel of others, he made an exception with regard to Hubert. As mentioned above, he took his advice in 1197 during the dispute with the knights of St Edmund over their service.[14] On another occasion, he asked for, and again took, Hubert's advice. In 1194 a crowd of young noblemen and knights came to St Edmunds after a tournament which had been held nearby contrary to Samson's prohibition. The young men were admitted to the town but on condition that they only left with the abbot's permission. Samson had the town gates locked and entertained the visitors to dinner. But they became intoxicated, made a hullabaloo in the town, keeping Samson and the monks awake all night, and finally escaped by breaking through the town gates. On the advice of Hubert, Samson excommunicated them all.[15] Consequently some of them returned, made amends and received absolution. As will be seen below, Samson's activities as a papal judge delegate led to further contacts with Hubert.[16]

While Samson's relations with the king's regents were of great importance for the abbey's welfare, his relations with the king himself were even more so. The personal nature of monarchy under Henry II, Richard I and John is vividly demonstrated by the spotlights Jocelin casts on royal behaviour in specific instances. There is Henry's spontaneous remark about Samson's deportment on his election to the abbacy,[17] and the sketch of him stamping out of the meeting in the chapter-house at Christ Church, Canterbury, after Samson and the prior and monks of Christ Church failed to come to an agreement over jurisdiction in Monks Eleigh.[18] There is the account of Richard's angry haggling with Samson over the wardship of Margaret of Cockfield and his sudden change of heart.[19] And, as will be seen, there is a telling reference to John's meanness when he came on pilgrimage to St Edmunds immediately after his coronation.[20] It was as necessary for the king to be on close and good terms with the abbot of St Edmunds, as it was for the abbot to be on close and good terms with the king. The abbot was an important tenant-in-chief and had jurisdiction over a third of Suffolk. But ultimate power lay with the king since he could confis-

---

12   JB, p. 85; Cheney, op. cit., p. 119 and n. 3.
13   JB, p. 123. Above p. 54.
14   JB, p. 66. Above, p. 57.
15   JB, pp. 55–6.
16   Below, pp. 69–71, 73–6.
17   JB, p. 23. Above p. 20.
18   JB, p. 52. Above, p. 53.
19   JB, pp. 97–8. Above, p. 54.
20   JB, pp. 116–17. Below, p. 64.

cate the abbot's barony and jurisdictional privileges. Relations between the king and abbot were strengthened by the cult of St Edmund, king and martyr. The Angevin kings had a reverence for St Edmunds only exceeded by their reverence for St Thomas of Canterbury.[21] Shortly after Easter 1177 Henry went on pilgrimage to St Edmunds (and then to Ely, to the shrine of St Etheldreda),[22] and at some stage he gave the abbey a great golden chalice worth 100 marks.[23] St Edmund was regarded especially as a warrior saint. The royalist forces fought the battle of Fornham St Genevieve in 1173 under the banner of St Edmund and won against considerable odds 'with the help of God and His most glorious martyr Edmund'.[24] Henry came to pray at the shrine early in 1188 before setting out on crusade.[25]

Henry died on 6 July 1189 and Richard I reached England from France on 13 August but left again for France and the crusade on 12 December. During this short time in England he visited St Edmunds: he was there on 18 November 1189 until some date between 21 and 25 November;[26] on 18 November he granted to God, St Edmund, Samson and the convent, ten librates of land in Aylsham, the income from which was to provide 'good and suitable lighting for the body of the glorious martyr' and for no other purpose. The grant was confirmed under Richard's new seal on 18 July 1198.[27] Richard obviously believed that St Edmund would help him on his sea crossings and in battle. In 1190 his crusading fleet sailed under the protection of St Thomas, St Nicholas and St Edmund and in 1191 Richard sent the imperial banner ('all woven in gold') of Isaac Comnenus, the defeated prince of Cyprus, 'to the blessed Edmund, king and glorious martyr'.[28] He visited St Edmunds almost immediately after he landed at Sandwich on 13 March 1194, on his return from captivity: he was there from

---

[21] Ralph of Coggeshall, a Suffolk chronicler, equates the two cults: in the annal for 1223 he writes of the multitude of pilgrims which used to flood to Bromholm (in Norfolk) and comments that as great a multitude 'is wont nowadays to go to St Thomas or to St Edmund'. *Radulphi de Coggeshall Chronicon Anglicanum*, ed. Joseph Stevenson (RS, 1875). For Coggeshall's chronicle see Gransden, *Historical Writing*, [i]. 322–31 and nn.

[22] *Ben. Pet.*, i. 61, 159.

[23] *JB*, p. 46.

[24] *Ben. Pet.*, i. 61–2; *Rog. How.*, ii. 55. Cf. Warren, *Henry II*, pp. 130–1 and n.

[25] *JB*, p. 52. Cf. Warren, op. cit., p. 607 and n. 2.

[26] Landon, *Itinerary of Richard I*, p. 16.

[27] For a copy of the charter (which specifies the tenancies granted and the rents) with a record of the confirmation see BL MS Harley 645, f. 206v. For confirmations of charters under Richard's new seal see above p. 27 and n. 32. For the candles at St Edmund's shrine see below pp. 95–6. Aylsham belonged to the king. *DB, Norfolk*, i. 91, 149, 192, 194, 195. The holdings which Richard granted to St Edmunds were assigned to the sacrist, the obedientiary responsible for lighting the church. The Benefactors' List states that Richard gave the 'vill' to St Edmunds, elsewhere referred to as a 'manor', to pay for four candles to burn day and night around the shrine. See: *Bury Chron.*, pp. 42, 109; *Mon. Angl.*, iii. 157; Douai, Bibliothèque Municipale MS 553, f. 7. For the sacrist's hall in Aylsham see *Kalendar*, ed. Davis, pp. 151–2 no. 131. Successive sacrists added to the holdings there in the course of the thirteenth century. See e.g. CUL MS Ff. ii. 33, ff. 67, 83v, 84.

[28] *Ben. Pet.*, ii. 116, 164.

18 March until sometime before 26 March, on his way to besiege Nottingham castle (which was being held by supporters of his brother, John, the count of Mortain).[29] Jocelin does not mention this visit.

Whether or not King John regarded St Edmund as a warrior saint is unknown, but Jocelin leaves no doubt of his veneration for him. He came to St Edmunds immediately after his coronation 'putting all other business aside, drawn by devotion and a vow'. Jocelin records the monks' disappointment that his only offering was 'a silken cloth which his servants borrowed from our sacrist and still have not paid for', and despite the generous hospitality which he had received he only gave 13s at mass on the day he left.[30] On his way back from Northumberland in 1201 John stayed at St Edmunds on 30 March. On the next day he went to Canterbury for a ceremonial crown-wearing on Easter Sunday.[31] When on pilgrimage in 1203 he went to St Edmunds for the feast of St James the Apostle on 21 December: he gave the convent 10 marks to be paid from the Exchequer each year at Easter during his lifetime for repairs to the shrine, but only in return for a life interest in a sapphire and a ruby which he had previously given to the monks.[32] On 24 March 1208 John confiscated St Edmunds' property and revenues, along with those of other ecclesiastical tenants, in retaliation at the papal imposition of an interdict on England. The annals of St Edmunds record that when at Guildford, where he celebrated Easter (on 6 April), John restored all the abbey's liberties 'on account of reverence for St Edmund'.[33] But, as will be seen, this concession was not as generous as might appear from the annalist's words.[34]

Samson's loyalty to the Angevin kings was unswerving and sometimes exhibited by demonstrations of bellicosity. Jocelin was so impressed by Samson's personal bravery that he fills a page or two with examples. However, he writes in such dramatic terms that he raises the suspicion either that he exaggerated or that Samson had a strong sense of theatre. Thus, he relates that when Henry visited St Edmunds early in 1188, Samson asked to be allowed to join him on crusade. He had cut a cross of linen and appeared with needle and thread ready to sew it on. But permission was refused because John, bishop of Norwich, pointed out that 'it would not be expedient for the country nor safe for the counties of Norfolk and Suffolk if both the bishop of Norwich and the abbot of St Edmunds departed at the same time'.[35] The news of Richard's capture reached England early in 1193. Samson attended the meeting of magnates at Oxford, assembled to discuss what to do, and sprang to his feet, offering to go in order to find him and get 'sure knowledge of him' ('et certam notitiam de eo haberet' – that is, to make sure that the prisoner was actually Richard), 'for saying which he won

[29] Landon, *Itinerary of Richard I*, p. 85.
[30] JB, pp. 116–17.
[31] *Ann. S. Edm.*, p. 139. See Warren, *King John*, p. 70.
[32] CUL MS Ff. ii. 33, ff. 31–31v; *Mon. Angl.*, iii. 154; *Ann. S. Edm.*, p. 143. See: JB, ed. Rokewode, p. 154; Warren, *King John*, pp. 139–40.
[33] *Ann. S. Edm.*, p. 146. Warren, *King John*, p. 167.
[34] Below pp. 66–7.
[35] JB, pp. 53 and n. 4, 54.

great praise'.[36] Later in 1193, on the outbreak of John's rebellion, Samson and the monks solemnly excommunicated the rebels 'not fearing Count John, the king's brother, nor anyone else, for which men called the abbot a man of high spirit'.[37] He thereupon led his knights to the siege of Windsor castle. After the castle's surrender he visited the captive Richard at Worms 'bringing him many gifts'.[38] Since Jocelin's chronicle ends early in 1202, there is less information about Samson's relations with John than about those with Henry II and Richard. The annals of St Edmunds give a few facts. Thus, they record that in 1207 Otto, king of the Romans (later emperor), John's ally against Philip Augustus, had a meeting with John in Samson's 'chamber' (in thalamo) on the abbot's manor of Stapleford Abbas (near Chigwell, Essex).[39] The general impression given by Jocelin and the annalist is that the monks of St Edmunds, like most of the religious, were very critical of John. Samson very likely shared the common view.

Obviously Samson expected returns for courting the Angevin kings. Noting Richard's death, Jocelin comments: 'When Abbot [Samson] had purchased the favour and grace of King Richard by gifts and money, so that he thought he could carry out all his affairs just as he wished, King Richard died, and the abbot both lost his money and his labour.'[40] Confirmation of the abbey's charters of privilege by each successive king was the most important, but not the only, concession needed by St Edmunds.[41] Jocelin and documentary sources show that the Angevin kings drove as hard bargains with Samson as they did with their other subjects. A case in point is the recovery of Mildenhall from royal possession in 1189, as described above. Richard insisted that Samson pay him 1,000 marks for it, and Samson would have had to pay again in 1198 when Richard confirmed the grant under his new seal. Another example of financial transactions between Samson and Richard concerns the latter's ransom. Jocelin's brief mention of Samson's visit to the captive Richard at Worms in June 1193 makes it sound like a courtesy call.[42] In fact, he almost certainly went on important business. He was accompanied by Master Roger of St Edmund, probably a clerk in his service. They probably travelled to Worms shortly after the chancellor, William Longchamp, and a number of lay and ecclesiastical magnates who had gone there, in response to summons from Richard, to negotiate about his ransom. The emperor Henry IV demanded 150,000 marks for Richard's release.[43] To raise such a huge sum (not all of which was ever collected) a tax of a quarter was imposed on

---

[36] JB, p. 54. The assembly of magnates met at Oxford, on Sunday, 28 February 1193. It sent two Cistercian abbots, those of Bexley (Kent) and Robertsbridge (Sussex), to discover Richard's whereabouts. Appleby, *England without Richard*, p. 108 and n. 2.

[37] JB, pp. 54–5.

[38] JB, p. 55. The siege began on 29 March 1193. Appleby, op. cit., pp. 109–12.

[39] *Ann. S. Edm.*, p. 146. Poole, *Domesday Book to Magna Carta*, pp. 450–1 and n. 2.

[40] JB, p. 116.

[41] For the confirmation of the charters by William I, William II, Henry I, Stephen and Henry II, see e.g. *Feudal Docs*, pp. 50 no. 6, 57 no. 12, 59 no. 16, 60–61 nos 18, 19, 62–3 nos 21–2, 74–6 nos 44–8, 77 no. 52, 87–8 no. 70, 92–4 nos 79, 80.

[42] JB, p. 55.

[43] Landon, *Itinerary of Richard I*, pp. 72, 76, 77.

revenues and possibly also on movables.[44] Probably it was not unusual for the tax to be compounded for a lump sum. This would seem to be what was done in St Edmunds' case, though Samson apparently paid in kind – with treasure. Jocelin records that 'there was no treasure in all England that was not given or redeemed' in order to pay Richard's ransom.[45] Samson gave all the abbey's treasure with an important exception – the gold on St Edmund's shrine. Jocelin gives an account in rhetorical style of Samson's refusal to allow the barons of the Exchequer to authorize even the partial stripping of the shrine: '"know this for a truth," Samson exclaimed, "it shall never be done as long as I can prevent it, nor can any man force me to agree. But I will open the church doors – let him enter who will, let him approach who dare."' And such was the fear of the martyred saint's wrath that, indeed, no one dared.[46] Both abbot and monks knew that St Edmund's shrine was the heart of the abbey's spiritual glory and those who desecrated such a sacred place suffered terrible fates. But they also knew that it was at the heart of the abbey's worldly splendour and it was the one safe place for its ultimate gold reserve.

Queen Eleanor again, as in 1189, helped Samson in his financial straits. One item of treasure which he relinquished was once more the great golden chalice worth 100 marks. She redeemed it and returned it to St Edmunds in exchange for a charter whereby the monks undertook never to alienate the chalice under any circumstance.[47] Perhaps it was at this time that Queen Eleanor issued a charter concerning a 'great gold chalice': Samson and the convent owed Eleanor 10 marks of gold in respect of a fine which they had made with Richard; they, being short of money, had given her a gold chalice worth 13 marks in satisfaction; she wholly forgave them the 10 marks which was rightly hers and bought the remaining three gold marks with her own money and acquitted them; and she gave them the chalice in free alms, 'prompted by charity and love of the blessed martyr and especially for the salvation of the soul of her dear son, King Richard'. The gift was on condition that the monks never sold or alienated the chalice from the church.[48] Her repeated stipulations that her gifts of treasure should never be alienated was to prevent them being used to raise ready cash, since that would frustrate her pious intention.

King John's impecuniousness and rapacity are notorious, and Samson suffered accordingly. He paid £200 for the confirmation of St Edmunds' royal charters,[49] and 40 marks and two palfreys (commuted for 10 marks) for the charter prohib-

---

[44] *Rog. How.*, iii. 199, 212. See: Mitchell, *Taxation in Medieval England*, pp. 124–6; Harriss, *King, Parliament and Public Finance*, p. 23; Poole, op. cit., pp. 365 and nn. 2, 3, 366; Appleby, op. cit., pp. 112–13.

[45] JB, p. 97. Cf. ibid., pp. 46–7.

[46] JB, p. 97. For Samson's gift to the convent of fifteen gold rings worth, 'it [was] believed', 50 marks, for the repair of the shrine, see ibid., p. 110. For the gold ornaments on the shrine see below pp. 94, 97, 105, 246.

[47] JB, pp. 46–7. Landon, op. cit., p. 76.

[48] CUL MS Ff. ii. 33, f. 29v.

[49] Great Roll of the Pipe, 2 John (1200), publ. *Pipe Roll Soc.*, n.s. xii, ed. D. M. Stenton (1934), p. 148. An estreat like, and following, the one above is in BL MS Harley 743, f. 92.

iting any market or fair to be held within the Liberty to St Edmunds' prejudice.[50] As already mentioned, the annals of St Edmunds note that during the interdict John restored all St Edmunds' liberties about three weeks after their confiscation in 1208.[51] However, the case was not as simple as that. Samson very likely had to pay a great price for the concession.[52] It seems that although St Edmunds soon recovered its rights of jurisdiction and the administration of its estate, it did not recover the full benefit of its property. In 1214, during the dispute over the election of Hugh of Northwold, Samson's successor to the abbacy, one faction of the monks demanded from the royal officials full restitution of what had been extorted from St Edmunds during the interdict. The cellarer, Master Nicholas, reckoned that the losses totalled 4,000 marks 'and gave the place and date of each receipt'.[53] In fact St Edmunds was treated little, if any, better than many other churches, and John's concession 'on account of reverence for St Edmund' was of limited value.

[50] Idem, 4 John (1202), *Pipe Roll Soc.*, n.s. xv, ed. D. M. Stenton (1937), p. 115. *Rot. Chart.* (1837), p. 91.

[51] Above p. 64.

[52] For John's transactions with St Edmunds during the interdict in their context see: Cheney, 'King John's reaction to the interdict', *TRHS*, 4th ser., xxxi (1949 rev. and repr. in idem, *The Papacy and England*, item no. X), pp. 129–50 esp. 131–2; Warren, *King John*, pp. 167–8; Poole, *Domesday Book to Magna Carta*, pp. 447–8.

[53] *Electio*, pp. 138–9, 142–3.

10

Samson and the Papacy

Jocelin writes:

> Seven months had not passed since [Samson's] election when, lo and behold! letters of the pope [Lucius III] were brought to him, appointing him a judge delegate for the hearing of cases, a task for which he had neither the knowledge nor the experience. … Thereupon, he called to himself two clerks learned in [canon] law to be his associates and used their advice in ecclesiastical matters, and he studied the decrees and decretals whenever he had time. Thus, by studying books and hearing cases, he soon became a prudent judge, who proceeded in court according to the forms of law.[1]

The truth of Jocelin's statement is born out by what is known about Samson's career as a papal judge delegate. Twenty-five mandates addressed to him by Innocent III survive or are known to have once existed: they concern judicial or administrative business.[2] Other mandates will have been lost. Although the pope appointed whom he pleased to determine appeals to the curia, it was quite usual for him to appoint the petitioner's nominee or nominees.[3] The frequency with which Samson was employed indicates that Samson's fellow countrymen as well as Innocent himself regarded him as an able judge in ecclesiastical matters. The fact that he would tend to be biased in favour of Benedictine monks must have encouraged them to nominate him as a judge delegate in their disputes.

Conflict between the secular clergy and the religious was a feature of the late twelfth and early thirteenth centuries. It might arise because a secular bishop, fired by reforming zeal, tried to hold a visitation of a highly privileged and wealthy Benedictine monastery, especially if he considered that the administration was lax and the Rule not properly observed. A number of disputes were between secular bishops and their monastic chapters. In general, a secular chapter, composed of prebendary canons, was more useful to a bishop than one composed of monks living communally in the cathedral priory. But, in addition, a bishop might want to reform the priory or simply enrich himself at its

---

[1] *JB*, pp. 33–4.
[2] See the index to Cheney and Cheney, *Letters*, p. 303 under 'St. Edmunds, Bury … abbots of: Samson'. Ibid., pp. 301 under 'Peterborough', and 302 under 'St Albans' indicates that Innocent employed Samson much more often than the abbots of those houses.
[3] See: Cheney, Mary [G.], *Roger Bishop of Worcester*, pp. 133–4; Sayers, *Papal Judges Delegate*, pp. 109–118. Above p. 41 and n. 51.

expense. The latter cause of conflict was exacerbated because often the line dividing a bishop's property from that of his cathedral priory was not clear.[4] The various disputes, whatever their causes, resulted in numerous appeals to Rome by aggrieved parties.[5]

Most of Samson's commissions from the curia were to investigate and settle such disputes. As a judge delegate, he usually served with two others, one of whom was often Eustace, bishop of Ely (1197–1215), as the senior. Eustace was an important political figure under Richard I (he was keeper of the king's seal, 1197/8, and chancellor, 1198/9), and, like Samson, a staunch supporter of the papacy. As explained above,[6] Samson's execution of his abbatial duties not infrequently brought him into close contact with the powerful Hubert Walter, archbishop of Canterbury. The two men must have known each other well and seem to have been on friendly terms. Samson's service for the papacy in the capacity of judge delegate, was another cause of contact with Hubert. Just occasionally Samson served on the same commission,[7] but much more often Hubert was one of the parties to the dispute which Samson and his fellows were commissioned to hear. One such dispute was between the prior and monks of Christ Church cathedral priory, Canterbury, petitioners, and the archbishop, defendant. The dispute arose because Hubert revived a project undertaken by his predecessor, Archbishop Baldwin, to establish a collegiate church at Lambeth, that is, a church served by secular canons. The monks of Christ Church had always opposed the scheme, with constant appeals to the king and to the pope.[8] They objected with reason, because they feared that the archbishop would spend most of his time at Lambeth and seldom visit the cathedral priory. Thus, Christ Church would in effect lose its primatial status. Innocent III gave judgement in the monks' favour and on 20 (or 21) November 1198, ordered Hugh (of Avalon), bishop of Lincoln (1186–1200), Eustace, bishop of Ely, and Samson to enforce the papal judgement against Hubert, who was to destroy the church at Lambeth within thirty days of receiving the mandate.[9]

Hubert did as ordered, but asked for papal permission to found another collegiate church on the site. On 19 May 1199, Innocent instructed the same delegates to try to bring the parties to a settlement: if they failed, they were to compel Hubert to make good any damage to the priory, to inquire into the

---

4   The separation of portions between bishops and their secular or monastic chapters, and disputes arising therefrom in the twelfth century, are discussed in detail in Crosby, *Bishop and Chapter*.

5   For appeals to Rome see: Cheney, Mary [G.], op. cit., pp. 118–20, 155–60; Sayers, op. cit., esp. pp. 96–9.

6   Above, pp. 61–2.

7   See e.g.: *JB*, pp. 94; Cheney and Cheney, *Letters*, p. 90 no. 548.

8   See: Cheney, *Hubert Walter*, pp. 135–57, 187–8; C. R. Young, *Lord of Canterbury and Lord of England* (Durham NC, 1968), pp. 136–40; R. B. Dobson in *A History of Canterbury Cathedral*, ed. Patrick Collinson, Nigel Ramsay and Margaret Sparks (Oxford, 1995), pp. 66–7; Knowles, *MO*, pp. 322, 325–6. Much of the documentation is printed in *Epistolae Cantuarienses* in *Chronicles and Memorials of the Reign of Richard I*, ed. William Stubbs (RS, 1864–5, 2 vols), ii.

9   Cheney and Cheney, *Letters*, p. 12 no. 59. Cheney, *Hubert Walter*, pp. 145–7.

dispute and to settle it if the parties so wished. They were also to hold a visitation of the priory and report to Innocent on its condition.[10] The delegates worked slowly and progress was impeded by appeals to Rome by the monks of Christ Church protesting against certain injuries which Hubert had inflicted on them and their property in the course of the quarrel. On 21 August 1199, Innocent ordered Hubert to restore to the prior and monks the churches on their manors, or to give them adequate satisfaction.[11] This mandate was soon followed by another ordering Hubert to restore the marsh of Appledore, the oblations of the high altar, and other possessions of the priory which he had seized, and to stop obstructing monks as they went about their business.[12] On 11 September Innocent instructed Bishop Hugh, Bishop Eustace and Samson if necessary to compel Hubert to obey the previous mandate.[13] Then, in a mandate of 21 May, 1200, Innocent revoked the commission to the judges delegate and informed them that both parties agreed that the case should be heard in Rome.[14] The monks of Canterbury had obtained this mandate but for some reason never made use of it. Therefore, the case remained in the hands of the judges delegate. They proposed to hear it on 26 October 1200, in Canterbury. But by then the senior judge delegate, Hugh, bishop of Lincoln, was too ill to serve: he appointed the dean of Lincoln, Roger of Rolleston, to take his place. The hearing dragged on fruitlessly apparently for three days. No settlement was reached between the parties.[15] Finally, at the request of both parties, the judges delegate arbitrated between them. Their award was sealed on 6 November and confirmed by Innocent on 31 May 1201, and on 2 June the judges delegate were instructed to enforce it.[16]

Thus, after all the complications and delays of the case, Eustace, bishop of Ely, Samson and Roger, dean of Lincoln, brought the case to a satisfactory conclusion. The award was a compromise. Its centrepiece was permission for Hubert to have a church at Lambeth, but not a collegiate church: it was to be a conventual church served by regular canons of the Premonstratensian order, not by secular canons. Both parties gained a little and lost a little. Actually, Hubert was already a benefactor of the Premonstratensians (in 1188 he had established an abbey of Premonstratensian canons at West Dereham, to pray for his soul and for the souls of his parents, relatives and friends).[17] The foundation at Lambeth provided him with a well-served church when he was staying at Lambeth in order to be near Westminster, the seat of government. But the new church at Lambeth, unlike a collegiate church, would not provide him with prebends to give to his clerks: if

---

[10] Cheney and Cheney, *Letters*, p. 21 no. 115A.
[11] Ibid., p. 29 no. 163.
[12] Ibid., p. 29 no. 164.
[13] Ibid., p. 29 no. 165.
[14] Ibid., p. 40; Cheney, *Hubert Walter*, pp. 148–9.
[15] Gervase of Canterbury, *Historical Works*, ed. William Stubbs (RS, 1879–80, 2 vols), ii. 409–10.
[16] Cheney and Cheney, op. cit., p. 53 nos 322, 324.
[17] Cheney, op. cit., p. 27; H. M. Colvin, *The White Canons in England* (Oxford, 1951), pp. 129–35, 348–9.

he could have provided for them in this way, he could have established a permanent secretariat at Lambeth. This danger removed, the monks of Christ Church had less reason to fear that the archbishop would live more or less permanently at Lambeth. In fact, Hubert seems to have generally been on good terms with the monks and spent much of his time at Canterbury.

The alarm of the Christ Church monks at the Lambeth scheme and at Hubert's behaviour during the dispute must have been heightened by the knowledge of the treatment that the monks of Coventry had received at the hands of the bishop, Hugh of Nonant (elected 1185, consecrated 1188, –1198). Soon after his election Hugh began quarrelling bitterly with the monks of his cathedral priory, and at times seems to have attacked them with bodily violence.[18] By the autumn of 1189 he was striving to replace them by secular canons. He succeeded in his plan with the support of Celestine III: at about Christmas time, 1190, the monks were dispersed and secular canons instituted. It was eight years before the Coventry monks managed to have the cathedral priory restored. Celestine died on 8 January 1198, and it would appear to have been one of his last acts to issue a mandate for the restoration of the cathedral priory, without further appeal to Rome. Samson was one of the three judges delegate instructed to implement Celestine's mandate. Eustace had not yet been consecrated bishop of Ely and in this instance the senior judge was Archbishop Hubert Walter himself. The other judge was Hugh, bishop of Ely. But Samson, though named third in the mandate was the most active in its implementation. The judges summoned the parties to meet at Oxford, but King Richard asked for a delay. Jocelin writes that Hubert and Bishop Hugh 'dissembled and were silent, as if courting the favour of the clerks', that is those occupying the cathedral chapter. Jocelin proceeds:

> Only the abbot [Samson], spoke out, as a monk, on behalf of the monks of Coventry, openly and publicly supporting their cause. And at his instigation proceedings were advanced that day so that simple seizin was given with a book [as a symbol] to one of the monks. But their actual institution as delayed for a time so that the judges would comply with the king's request. Nonetheless the abbot at once received in his lodging fourteen of the Coventry monks who had assembled there. The monks sat at a table in one part of the house, and the masters of the schools who had been invited sat at a table in another part, and the abbot was praised for his generosity and lavish expenditure. Nor at any time of his life did he seem happier than then, such was his zeal for the re-establishment of the monastic order. On the approach of the feast of St Hilary [13 January] he set out with great joy for Coventry, deterred neither by the exertion nor by the expense. He said that if necessary he would be carried in a horse-litter rather than stay behind. On reaching Coventry he had to wait five days for the archbishop's arrival. He gave

---

[18] The affair was well known at Canterbury and aroused indignation elsewhere in monastic circles. See: Gervase, *Hist. Works*, i. 461, 550, 552; Richard of Devizes, *Chronicle*, ed. J. T. Appleby (London, Edinburgh etc., 1963), pp. 69–71; *JB*, p. 94. For the dispute see: Cheney, *Hubert Walter*, pp. 41, 137, 153; Crosby, *Bishop and Chapter*, pp. 126–32; Knowles, *MO*, pp. 322–3; Appleby, *England Without Richard*, pp. 212–13.

honourable accommodation to all the said monks and their servants until a new prior was appointed and the monks formally inducted.[19]

Hugh of Nonant was abroad and terminally ill at the time, and died in March. Although the Coventry monks had regained their priory, they did not recover all their possessions from Hugh's successors for several years.

Samson also served as a judge delegate in another *cause célèbre*, the dispute between the monks of Glastonbury and Savaric, bishop of Bath (elected 1191, consecrated 1192, –1205).[20] The dispute arose because Savaric attempted to move his episcopal see from Bath to Glastonbury. In 1193 Celestine III sanctioned the removal and provided the abbot of Glastonbury, Henry de Soilli, to the bishopric of Worcester. The monks, however, refused to accept the change. Therefore, Savaric made his way into the abbey church, had himself enthroned and took the title of bishop of Bath and Glastonbury. The monks rebelled and violence followed. In 1198, despite a papal prohibition, the monks elected a new abbot, one of their number, Master William Pica. But on 23 June 1200, Innocent III informed Eustace, bishop of Ely, and Samson that he had quashed Pica's election and instructed them to arrange for the abbey's administration.[21] On the same day he informed Savaric, 'bishop of Bath and Glastonbury', of his decision and that Bath and Glastonbury were in future to be joined.[22] Later that year, on 4 September, he ordered Eustace and Samson to divide the revenues between the bishop of Bath and the church of Glastonbury and to settle the matters in dispute.[23] But these attempts at resolving the conflict were unsuccessful. On 7 June 1202, Innocent ordered Eustace and Samson to enforce his ordinance about the monastery.[24] Shortly afterwards Innocent added Geoffrey, prior of Canterbury cathedral priory, to the delegation. The monks of Glastonbury had complained to Rome that Savaric had not complied with the papal judgement concerning the division of the abbey's property, and about acts of violence by Savaric against Master Martin de Summa and others.[25] Therefore, on 28 August, Innocent, ordered Eustace, Samson and Geoffrey to hear the case. And he wrote to them again on 24 September: he recounted the course of the dispute between Savaric and the Glastonbury monks, and informed them that the bishop was to restore any monastic property which he had wrongly taken, and to make restitution for the violence to Master Martin de Summa and the

---

[19] *JB*, pp. 94–5. See Crosby, op. cit., p. 129.
[20] For the dispute see: Adam of Domerham, *Historia de Rebus Gestis Glastoniensibus*, ed. Thomas Hearne (Oxford, 1727, 2 vols), ii. 352–467; J. Armitage Robinson, *Somerset Historical Essays* (Oxford, 1921), pp. 68–70, 142–3, 145–6; Knowles, MO, pp. 328–30; idem, 'Essays in monastic history 1066–1215. v. The cathedral monasteries', *DR*, li (1933), pp. 94–6; Gransden, 'The history of Wells cathedral *c.* 1090–1547', in *Wells Cathedral. A History*, ed. L. S. Colchester (Open Books, West Compton House, nr. Shepton Mallet, 1982), pp. 28–31.
[21] Cheney and Cheney, *Letters*, p. 41 no. 245.
[22] Ibid., p. 41 no. 246.
[23] Ibid., p. 43 no. 257.
[24] Ibid., p. 69 no. 424.
[25] Ibid., p. 70 no. 434.

others. In addition, Innocent ordered Eustace, Samson and Geoffrey to divide the abbey's possessions or revenues between the bishop and monks, to assign to the monks a third part of the patronage, and to remove any prior whom the bishop had instituted without the convent's approval. If the bishop failed to abide by these provisions, the abbey was to be restored to its previous status and the monks could elect an abbot.[26] The dispute dragged on and in a mandate to Savaric of 17 May 1205, Innocent recited and confirmed the ordinance made by Eustace, Samson and Geoffrey.[27] Indeed, in this instance neither Samson and his colleagues nor anyone else brought about a speedy settlement. The dispute was only resolved after Savaric's death (in 1205) by his successor, Jocelin of Wells, who in 1219 finally abandoned any claim to have a see at Glastonbury: he concentrated instead on building the beautiful cathedral at Wells which was served by secular canons.

Another dispute between a secular ecclesiastic and a monastery was between Archbishop Hubert and Abbot Roger and the convent of St Augustine's, Canterbury, one of the other great exempt Benedictine abbeys. Again, Samson was one of the judges delegate appointed to settle it. Innocent addressed numerous mandates concerning the dispute to a commission comprising Bishop Eustace, Samson, and to another judge delegate, often Herbert, prior of St Edmunds. The inclusion of Herbert could well have been on Samson's recommendation: it will be remembered that Samson had procured Herbert's appointment to the priorate in 1201, despite strong opposition from some of the monks.[28] (Herbert hardly ever served as a judge delegate without Samson, and on the rare occasions when he did so, he was the senior but it was to hear cases of merely local importance.[29]) The dispute between Archbishop Hubert and St Augustine's was a complicated one.[30] It began over St Augustine's right to patronage of the parish churches of Faversham and Milton, that is, of its right to present to the livings. It had admitted a royal clerk to the church of Faversham and when in 1201 the church again fell vacant, King John claimed the right to patronage and presented another of his clerks. The dispute grew and covered wider issues – the right of St Augustine's to custody of its parish churches when they were vacant, and to jurisdiction over its clerks and churches in general. Its claims conflicted with the archbishop's jurisdiction in his archdiocese, which was exercised for him by his archdeacons. The ramifications of the dispute were such that both the pope and King John became involved.

Early in February 1202 Innocent, on complaint of the abbot and convent of St Augustine's, ordered Eustace, Samson and Herbert to excommunicate the laymen who had expelled Abbot Roger and the convent from the church of

---

[26] Ibid., p. 71 nos 437–8.

[27] Ibid., p. 104 no. 262.

[28] Above p. 41.

[29] The known occasions were in 1205 and 1208 when Samson was old. See Cheney and Cheney, *Letters*, pp. 99 nos 596–7, 129 no. 782.

[30] See: Cheney, *Hubert Walter*, pp. 58, 85–7; Eric John, 'The litigation of an exempt house, St Augustine's Canterbury, 1182–1237', *Bulletin of the John Rylands Library*, xxxiv (1957), pp. 390–415.

Faversham.[31] He also ordered them to hear the complaint of Abbot Roger and his monks over institutions to the churches of Faversham and Milton, and to deal with the question of the abbey's jurisdiction over its clerks and churches. King John retaliated upon the judges delegate for their disregard for his interests and confiscated the property of St Augustine's churches of Faversham and Milton: on 19 November 1202 Innocent wrote to King John requesting him to restore the property to the abbot and convent.[32] Sometime in November or December Innocent ordered judges delegate, probably Eustace, Mauger, bishop of Worcester, and Samson, on the complaint of Abbot Roger and his monks, to hear the case against Archbishop Hubert and his vice-chancellor for procuring the confiscation of the property of the abbey's church of Faversham, and to send the evidence to the pope in writing: they were also to fix a day for the parties to appear in Rome.[33] And on 3 January 1203 Innocent ordered Eustace, Mauger and Samson to request King John to obey the pope's orders concerning the property of the churches of Faversham and Milton.[34] Sometime in 1203 Innocent ordered Eustace, Samson and this time Herbert once more, to punish those laymen who had occupied the church of Faversham and to reinstate the abbot and monks.[35] Innocent clearly objected to the slow progress of the adjudication and on 1 August 1204 ordered Eustace, Samson and Herbert to settle the dispute quickly.[36] Samson was nearing the end of his service as a judge delegate. On 12 December 1205 Innocent ordered William, bishop of London, Eustace and Samson to give judgement in the dispute between the archdeacon of Canterbury and 'O', a monk of St Augustine's, about the custody of the church of Milton.[37] This is the last datable mandate addressed to a commission which included Samson among the judges delegate.[38]

   The commissions discussed above concerned disputes of more than local importance, and Samson's fellow judges delegate were, with the exception of Prior Herbert, ecclesiastical magnates. Other commissions confirm the conclusion that Samson was high in Innocent's esteem. In 1201 Innocent appointed Eustace and Samson to inquire whether the reasons given by King John would be sufficient to justify the pope in absolving Geoffrey Fitz Peter, Hugh Bardolf, Robert de Berkeley, and Alan and Thomas Basset from their crusading vows.[39] This must have been the papal mandate which, as Jocelin records, reached Samson on 21 January 1202 and faced him with an agonising dilemma, whether to please the king by deciding in his favour, or the pope by deciding against absolution.[40] The reasons given by King John to justify absolution were the men's

[31] Cheney and Cheney, *Letters*, pp. 62–3 nos 383–6.
[32] Ibid., p. 73 no. 444.
[33] Ibid., p. 74 no. 452.
[34] Ibid., p. 74 no. 453.
[35] Ibid., p. 87 no. 530.
[36] Ibid., p. 93 no. 568. Cf. p. 98 no. 590.
[37] Ibid., p. 110 no. 659.
[38] See below p. 78.
[39] Cheney and Cheney, *Letters*, p. 60 no. 364. Cheney, *Hubert Walter*, pp. 125–32.
[40] JB, p. 135. See above p. 59.

bodily infirmity and his own need of their counsel for the preservation of the kingdom. These arguments were not without foundation: Bardolf and Stuteville were old men and died the following year, Fitz Peter, earl of Essex, was justiciar, Bardolf, a justice of the Bench, Briwere was a baron of the Exchequer, and all were important magnates with extensive estates and positions of influence in the localities. There is no evidence that any of them went on the crusade which suggests that Eustace and Samson found in King John's favour.

On two occasions Samson is known to have served on a commission with Archbishop Hubert. One case was of only local importance. A certain Ernald Bil claimed the right to present to the church of Filby in Norfolk, but complained that a clerk, John de Burgo, had obstructed the institution of his nominee.[41] The judges delegate (the abbot of Sibton and two others) ordered to hear the case had decided against John de Burgo, but King John then claimed that the papal mandate to the judges delegate was a forgery. The case seems then to have been referred to Archbishop Hubert, Eustace and Samson, Hubert having received a special mandate to deal with the matter of the authenticity of the mandate. On 17 March 1204 Innocent wrote to him, Eustace and Samson informing them that, having inspected to document in question, which Hubert had sent him, pronounced it genuine and upheld the decision of the original judges delegate that the advowson of the church of Filby belonged to Ernald.[42]

The other occasion when Samson served as a judge delegate with Hubert was a happier one, that is, the process which preceded the canonization of Wulfstan (II) of Worcester. Innocent III had standardized the procedure for canonization and brought it under papal control.[43] The canonization of Wulfstan is a well documented and fairly early example of the process. During Innocent's pontificate two English men were canonized, first Gilbert of Sempringham and then soon afterwards Wulfstan (II) of Worcester.[44] The process for the latter's canonization was put in motion by Mauger, bishop of Worcester (1200–1212), shortly after his succession in 1200. Sometime in the period from May to July 1202 Innocent instructed Archbishop Hubert, Bishop Eustace, Samson, and Peter, abbot of Woburn, to visit the church of Worcester, impose a three-day fast and prayers on the monks and people and to obtain written and oral testimony on the merits and miracles of Wulfstan.[45] Very recently Hubert had been instrumental in obtaining

---

[41] Cheney and Cheney, *Letters*, p. 86 no. 528.

[42] Ibid., p. 90 no. 548. In May 1198 Innocent III issued a warning to archbishops and bishops against forgers of papal bulls and letters. Ibid., p. 4 nos 18, 19. See Cheney, *Hubert Walter*, p. 124 and n. 3.

[43] See: E. W. Kemp, *Canonization and Authority in the Western Church* (Oxford, 1948), pp. 82–106; Nilson, *Cathedral Shrines*, pp. 11–15.

[44] Kemp, op. cit., pp. 104–5; Nilson, op. cit., p. 12.

[45] Cheney and Cheney, *Letters*, p. 70 no. 432. The dates of the mandate are fixed by the Annals of Worcester which mention the inquiry briefly. *Ann. Mon.*, iv. 391. A full account of the inquiry is in the *Miracles and Translation of St Wulfstan* which is printed in *The Vita Wulfstani of William of Malmesbury … and the Miracles and Translation of St. Wulfstan*, ed. R. R. Darlington, Camden Soc., 3rd ser., xl (1928). For the canonization process see ibid., pp. xlvii–xlviii, 115, 116, 120, 148–50, 184.

the canonization of Gilbert of Sempringham which Innocent pronounced on 11 January 1202.[46] Hubert, Eustace, Samson and Peter arrived at Worcester on 1 September and stayed for three days holding the inquiry. A large crowd of the sick, the blind, the deaf, and cripples and paralytics was gathered at Wulfstan's tomb, and came 'now ten, now twelve, now fifteen' to the altar, seeking cure. Besides the delegates, many other ecclesiastical magnates, including abbots, were present. The delegates were 'overwhelmed by the glorious multitude of cures and their witnesses'. It was obviously a deeply emotional, ceremonious and joyful occasion and the delegates left 'rejoicing'. The depositions were written down, sealed with the bishop's seal and the chapter seal, and taken by Bishop Mauger and some of the monks to Rome. They also, at Innocent's request, took the Life of Wulfstan 'written in the English Language a hundred years before'.[47] (This book was undoubtedly the now lost Life of Wulfstan by Coleman, a Worcester monk.) Innocent was convinced, now believing that 'a mute, a leper, a paralytic and a sufferer from dropsy' had actually been cured at Wulfstan's tomb, and many other miracles performed at his intercession. Therefore, on 21 April 1203, he pronounced that Wulfstan should be numbered among the saints. On 14 May he wrote to Mauger and the monks announcing the canonization; he ordered that Wulfstan's feast day be observed and sent an appropriate collect for it.[48]

Another of Samson's cases was of less importance than those so far mentioned but of interest nonetheless. It concerned a dispute between Roger of St Edmund and Master Honorius, a clerk in the service of Geoffrey, archbishop of York (elected 1189, consecrated 1191, –1212), over the archdeaconry of Richmond in the years c. 1198–1202. The interest of the case lies partly in the personal ramification underlying it. Roger of St Edmunds was probably a member of Samson's household. A Master Roger of St Edmund accompanied Samson on his visit to King Richard at Worms in the spring of 1193, and to the royal court at Chahaignes in January 1199.[49] Possibly he was the same man as Master Roger of Walsingham, a member of Samson's household who witnessed a number of his charters and had a holding in Fornham.[50] However, these identifications remain uncertain: Roger is given the title of Master apparently in only one extant papal letter,[51] and perhaps there were both a Master Roger of St Edmunds and a Master Roger of Walsingham. Whatever the truth about his identity, Roger of St

---

[46] Cheney and Cheney, Letters, p. 57 no. 345A; The Book of St Gilbert, ed. and trans. Raymonde Foreville and Gillian Keir (Oxford, 1987), p. xxvi, and see index under 'Innocent III'.

[47] Ibid., pp. viii–ix, xlvii, 149.

[48] Cheney and Cheney, Letters, p. 76 no. 472.

[49] Landon, Itinerary of Richard I, pp. 15 no. 132, 81, 142.

[50] He appears variously as: 'Master Roger' (e.g. Kalendar, ed. Davis, pp. 28, 82 no. 14, 84 no. 18), 'Master Roger of Walsingham' (e.g. ibid., pp. 122 no. 80, 130 no. 93, 163 no. 150), 'Roger clerk of Walsingham' (ibid., pp. 134 no. 102, 141 no. 111), and plain 'Roger of Walsingham' (e.g. ibid., pp. 137 no. 106, 138 no. 107, 168 no. 161). Davis assumes, surely rightly, that the different styles denote the same man. See the index to the Kalendar, pp. 188 under 'Roger the master', 192 under 'Walsingham, Roger de'.

[51] Cheney and Cheney, Letters, p. 50 no. 303.

Edmund was granted the archdeaconry of Richmond by King Richard during the suspension from office of Archbishop Geoffrey by Celestine III.[52]

Roger of St Edmund, having obtained the archdeaconry, met so much opposition to his tenure of the office that sometime in the period from July 1199 to June 1200 Innocent III ordered Samson, Ralph, abbot of St Benet of Holme, and the prior of Toft Monks to enforce obedience to Roger in the archdeaconry, and to ensure that he was compensated for any damage done.[53] Meanwhile, Roger obtained letters from Innocent appointing Samson (Ralph), abbot of Sibton,[54] and Gerard, prior of Norwich, all three chosen by Roger, as judges delegate to hear the case. However, Honorius challenged their conduct of the hearing: he appealed to Innocent, asserting that they had ignored an exception he had brought against Samson. Why Honorius objected to Samson being a judge delegate is not explained. However, if, as seems likely, Samson was Roger's employer, Honorius would not have considered him an impartial judge. Innocent thereupon wrote to Samson (Ralph), abbot of Sibton, and Gerard, prior of Norwich, reciting the course of the action and instructing them to proceed no further with the case and to declare the proceedings null if indeed the latter two judges delegate had ignored Honorius' exception and his appeal to the pope.[55] At about the same time Innocent wrote to the dean (Simon) and chapter of York informing them that Honorius had complained that Archbishop Geoffrey, despite his own faithful service to him, had stirred up Roger of St Edmunds against him, although Honorius had made a composition with Roger: Innocent ordered the dean and chapter to maintain Honorius in his rights.[56] The dispute dragged on until on 1 June 1202 when Innocent announced that he had given judgement in favour of Honorius.[57] He ordered the archbishop and the cathedral chapter respectively to receive Honorius as archdeacon, and Eustace, bishop of Ely, John, bishop of Norwich, and Roger, dean of Lincoln, to enforce his mandates: should Roger dare to keep possession of the archdeaconry, he was to be compelled to abide by the judgement by the withdrawal of his other benefices. Innocent also requested King John not to obstruct the implementation of the judgement.[58] This reversal of Roger's fortunes was probably related to the fact that at about this time Honorius left Archbishop Geoffrey's service and entered that of the archbishop's rival, the powerful Hubert Walter.[59]

By Innocent III's time it was legal for a commission to proceed with a case even if one of the judges delegate was unable to serve. It was also legal by then

[52] *Fasti*, iii. 139.
[53] Cheney and Cheney, op. cit., pp. 41–2 no. 249. Cf. ibid., p. 44 no. 270 datable to July 1199 x June 1200.
[54] For evidence that Ralph was abbot of Sibton at this time see *Sibton Abbey Cartularies and Charters*, ed. Philippa Brown, *Suffolk Charters*, gen. editor R. A. Brown, Suffolk Records Soc., vii–x (Woodbridge, 1985–8, 4 pts), i. 4, iv. 58 no. 1007.
[55] Cheney and Cheney, op. cit., p. 44 no. 270.
[56] Ibid., p. 45 no. 273. Cf. ibid., pp. 47 nos 283–4, 50 nos 303–5.
[57] Ibid., pp. 67 no. 415, 68 nos 417–20.
[58] Ibid., pp. 67–8 no. 416.
[59] Cheney, *Hubert Walter*, p. 165.

for a judge delegate to subdelegate his powers.[60] However, there is no evidence that Samson did not serve personally on the commissions mentioned. Indeed, in most instances there is positive evidence (mostly Jocelin's testimony) that he did so. Thus, his service for the papacy involved him in many journeys. The most distant was to visit King John in France,[61] but he also travelled to Canterbury,[62] Oxford, Coventry and Worcester, and probably to Bath and/or Glastonbury.[63] Possibly he also went to York in the course of hearing the dispute over the archdeaconry of Richmond. The last commission known to include Samson as a judge delegate was to pronounce the papal judgement in the dispute between the archdeacon of Canterbury and 'O', a monk of St Augustine's, is, as has been seen, dated 12 December 1205. The mandate makes it clear that the judges delegate would have to go to Canterbury, since they were ordered to base their decision on the quality (not the numbers) of the witnesses for each side.[64] By that time Samson was about seventy years old, and his advanced age may well have been affecting his performance as a judge delegate, and made him increasingly unwilling to serve in the last few years. In the mandate of 1 August 1204 to Bishop Eustace, Samson and Prior Herbert, Innocent complained of their long delay in settling the dispute over the church of Faversham.[65] And earlier, in 1201, as Jocelin records, Samson had postponed his departure to visit King John in France, to negotiate over the question of the absolution of certain magnates from their crusading vows, because of ill-health; he asserted that he was afflicted by 'bodily weakness'.[66] Samson's age, therefore, could well explain the discontinuance of commissions to him to act as a judge delegate.

The burden of service for the papacy weighed especially heavily on Samson in the 1190s and early 1200s. It must often have distracted his attention from his own convent and quite often necessitated his absence. Possibly the extra exertion and the power which the commissions gave him made him more impatient and high-handed in his treatment of the monks and, therefore, contributed to the deterioration of his relations with them. However, it was essential for the abbey to be on good terms with the papacy. It owed its spiritual privileges to the papacy and depended on it for their protection. Samson obtained confirmation of the abbey's privileges from successive popes: from Lucius III (31 March 1183), Urban III (28 and 29 December 1186 and 17 January, 1187), Clement

---

[60] Sayers, *Papal Judges Delegate*, pp. 135–43. Sub-delegation was rare under Innocent III. Ibid., p. 137.

[61] Above p. 42.

[62] Below.

[63] Above pp. 71–72, 75.

[64] Innocent instructs the judges delegate 'to give judgement for the archdeacon if the witnesses on either side are of equal quality, for the monks if the excellence of their witnesses counts for more than mere numbers'. Cheney and Cheney, *Letters*, p. 110 no. 659.

[65] Ibid., p. 93 no. 568.

[66] JB, p. 135. Above p. 42.

III (20 January 1188), Celestine III (2 May 1192),[67] and Innocent III (at some unknown date during his pontificate).[68]

Particularly close to Samson's heart was St Edmunds' status as a great exempt abbey. Abbot Hugh had acted to protect the abbey's exemption in 1175,[69] but in 1195, when Celestine III granted legatine powers to Archbishop Hubert to hold visitations of monasteries and churches in England, the issue arose again. An added complication was that Hubert besides being a papal legate was justiciar of England. In the course of his visitations, he wrote to Samson and the convent asking if they would receive him at St Edmunds. Samson decided to do so and to treat him honourably, but determined that if he were to attempt to hold a visitation in chapter, Samson would produce the abbey's charters of privilege and appeal to Rome. Hubert thanked him but postponed his visit. Samson, suspecting that Hubert still planned to hold a visitation of the abbey, wrote to Celestine, who responded by writing to Hubert on 9 January 1196 reminding him of St Edmunds' exemption and forbidding him to hold a visitation of it or any other exempt church.[70] Hubert was angry when he heard that Samson had obtained the prohibition and feared that he would not be received at St Edmunds even as justiciar. Samson for his part refused to meet Hubert because he was afraid that a meeting would be construed as an attempt to come to an agreement with the archbishop and so would compromise the abbey's exemption. Finally, in 1197, the two men met 'on the king's highway between Waltham (in Essex) and London'.[71] In the course of the fierce argument which followed, Samson declared that 'he would never, through lack of knowledge or money, allow the Liberty of his church to be overthrown, even if he must die or be condemned to perpetual exile'.[72] At some time during his pontificate Innocent III issued a bull which is now lost but is listed, undated, in thirteenth-century inventories of the abbey's papal bulls, as 'Littera contra visitatores'.[73] Perhaps it was issued after the Fourth Lateran Council of 1215. The Council (decree 12) established trien-

---

67 *Papsturkunden*, iii, nos 347, 382 and 383, 399, 403, 441, respectively. The earliest known copies of St Edmunds' papal privileges from Celestine III (1191–8) are in the Black Register compiled under Samson; CUL MS Mm. iv. 19, ff. 52–77v. Many are printed from CUL MS Ee. iii. 60, ff. 1–22v in *Pinch. Reg.*, i. 24 et seqq. For Samson's promptness in obtaining papal confirmations of the abbey's privileges see *JB*, p. 56.

68 *Pinch. Reg.*, i. 33–4.

69 *Papsturkunden*, iii, nos 217, 218.

70 Ibid., iii, no. 477. Celestine states that the clause in Hubert Walter's commission that he had power to visit 'notwithstanding any commission or privilege' did not include exempt houses subject directly to the apostolic see.

71 *JB*, pp. 81–5. Hubert Walter travelled from Westminster to Norwich in March 1197. He was at Westminster on 18 and 19 March and at Colchester on 23 March. *English Episcopal Acta*, iii, *Canterbury 1193–1205*, ed. C. R. Cheney and Eric John (Oxford, 1986), no. 310. The only copy of the mandate to Hubert cited above, of 9 Jan. 1196, known to Holtzman is in the thirteenth-century cartulary of Waltham abbey (BL MS Harley 391, f. 55). Maybe Samson after the meeting with Hubert stayed at Waltham abbey and gave the canons a copy.

72 *JB*, p. 84.

73 See Cheney and Cheney, *Letters*, p. 187, no. 1140, with references to BL MSS Harley 1005, f. 228, and Harley 638, f. 120 col. 3.

nial General Chapters of the Benedictines and these were to appoint visitors to hold visitations of all houses of the order, including the exempt ones.[74] Thus, St Edmunds' privilege of exemption was out of date and a new bull was needed. Maybe Innocent's bull met this need.

Samson was instrumental in obtaining many other benefits from the papacy for St Edmunds. At his and the convent's request Urban III, on 29 December 1186, issued letters of protection for Samson's new foundation, the hospital of St Saviour,[75] and on 10 May 1192 Celestine III, at the request of the Master and brethren of St Saviour's, granted it protection and confirmed its possessions, which had increased by then.[76] And Innocent III confirmed St Edmunds' rights in the school at Beccles.[77] It was pointed out above that Samson in order to enhance his dignity seems to have appropriated the privilege of wearing a mitre though without papal sanction.[78] There is another example where Samson may have done something similar. Jocelin states that Samson was 'the first of all the abbots of England to obtain the privilege of giving solemn, episcopal benediction wherever he might be and that this privilege was both for him and his successors'.[79] But no bull granting this wide-ranging privilege survives. However, there is a bull of Urban III, dated 17 January 1187, of more limited scope: it grants Samson and his successor the right to give solemn episcopal benedictions within St Edmunds' *banleuca*.[80] It seems not improbable that Samson gave this bull a wider interpretation on purpose. On occasion, Samson apparently asserted his rank excessively. For instance, when the abbot of Cluny visited St Edmunds in 1200, he insisted on his own precedence in the chapter-house and in processions, 'wherefore various people held various opinions and said various things'.[81] However, Samson also sought to raise the dignity of the abbot of St

---

[74] Above p. 31.

[75] *Papsturkunden*, iii, no. 384. Harper-Bill, *Hospitals*, p. 120 no. 165.

[76] *Papsturkunden*, iii, no. 443. Harper-Bill, *Hospitals*, p. 121 no. 166A.

[77] Cheney and Cheney, *Letters*, p. 187 no. 1139. Only known from references in the abbey's inventories of charters and papal bulls (BL MSS Harley 1005, f. 228 and Harley 638, f. 120); among Innocent III's bulls is listed 'Item [confirmatio] de scolis de Beccles'. This seems to be the earliest reference to the school ('schools') at Beccles. The prosperous manor of Beccles had belonged to St Edmunds since before the Conquest (*DB*, *Suffolk*, i. 14. 120) and was assigned to the chamberlain (*Bury Chron.*, pp. 43, 110; *Mon. Angl.*, iii. 157). The church belonged to the abbot (*JB*, p. 64). The Bury Customary states that the appointment of the schoolmaster 'rector scolarum' at Beccles belonged to the abbot, but with the convent's consent, and whoever had custody of the manor (in this case the chamberlain) had the right of collation to the church. *Bury Cust.*, p. 4; *Memorials*, iii. 182–3. The school flourished in the late middle ages. See: *VCH Suffolk*, ii. 37; Nicholas Orme, *English Schools in the Middle Ages* (London, 1973), pp. 95, 104, 118 n. 3, 119 n. 2, 134, 148.

[78] Above p. 21.

[79] *JB*, p. 56.

[80] *Papsturkunden*, iii, no. 399.

[81] *JB*, p. 124 and n. 4. Hugh V abbot of Cluny (d. 1207) was in England as a party in a dispute with Hamelin earl of Warren (d. 1240) over patronage of Lewes priory. Archbishop Hubert, Seffrid bishop of Chichester and Eustace bishop of Ely were the judges delegate commissioned to hear and decide the case. See: Cheney and Cheney, *Letters*, p. 40 no. 240 and Appendix pp. 212–14 no. 202; Cheney, *Hubert Walter*, p. 133 and n. 2;

Edmunds by legitimate means. He obtained from Urban III, on 29 December 1186, the privilege of wearing episcopal vestments, that is, tunicle, dalmatic and sandals, and the right to tonsure monks and clerks of the parishes within his spiritual jurisdiction – the *banleuca* of St Edmunds.[82] Other papal grants gave further spiritual power to the abbot within the *banleuca*: as has been seen, Urban III granted the privilege of giving episcopal blessings there (17 January 1187),[83] and Clement III empowered the abbot to hear and decide matrimonial cases (13 December 1189).[84]

Papal favours entailed obligations and cost money. For instance, Samson, like other patrons of ecclesiastical livings, had to give a benefice to a papal nominee if the pope requested him to do so.[85] Jocelin relates that a certain clerk came to Samson asking for a benefice. Thereupon, Samson took seven papal letters from his document-chest, all requesting benefices for various clerks. He showed them to the man and said that he could only give him a living when he had satisfied all those named in the letters 'for he comes first to the mill ought to have first grind'.[86] The abbot of St Edmunds was patron of sixty parish churches, and the number of benefices required by the pope from St Edmunds would seem to have been in line with what the papacy required from any ecclesiastical institution owning a similar number of churches. In addition, papal concessions had to be paid for in cash, and privileges were the most expensive. Jocelin observes that Samson 'often sent his messengers to Rome, nor did they go empty-handed'.[87] Those seeking a papal letter had to pay fees to the clerks of the papal chancery who wrote and expedited the document. The earliest information about this requirement belongs to Innocent III's pontificate. In 1254–6, Alexander IV tried to regulate the practice by issuing general guidelines for assessing fees and listing those for some kinds of document.[88] In view of the work involved in producing a papal letter, the fees in the late twelfth and early thirteenth centuries were probably not excessive. But *douceurs* also had to be paid to cardinals.[89] When Abbot Hugh's messenger returned from Rome after negotiations for the grant

Diceto, *Historical Works*, ii. 173. Jocelin's seems to be the only known record of Hugh's visit to St Edmunds. The Bury Customary in a passage referring to the 'use of Cluny', seems to betray knowledge of the statutes issued by Hugh for Cluny. *Bury Cust.*, p. 41 line 26 and n. 4. If the author had a text of the statutes perhaps the monks acquired it from Hugh or one of his household during Hugh's visit.

82 *Papsturkunden*, iii, no. 385.
83 Ibid., iii, no. 399.
84 Ibid., iii, no. 416.
85 The papal claim to provide clerks to benefices was strongly resented because it overrode the rights of the patrons. See e.g.: Moorman, *Church Life in England*, pp. 8–9; Sayers, *Honorius III*, pp. 177–80, 184, 189; Lunt, *Fin. Relations*, pp. 211, 213, 224, 526; Matthew Paris, *Chron. Maj.*, iii. 613–14 (translated Lunt, *Papal Revenues*, ii. 218 no. 341); Dunstable chronicle, *Ann. Mon.*, iii. 169–70.
86 *JB*, p. 56.
87 Ibid.
88 Lunt, *Fin. Relations*, pp. 521–3; idem, *Papal Revenues*, i. 125–33, ii. 497–512.
89 For bribes paid to cardinals among others for obtaining confirmation of the election of abbots of St Albans in the thirteenth century see Vaughan, 'The election of Abbots at St Albans', pp. 7–8.

of full exemption for St Edmunds, the monks were alarmed at the huge sums which he had had to promise the pope and cardinals in return for the privilege.[90] They were perplexed how to pay unless they sacrificed the cross above the high altar, and the little image of the Virgin Mary and the image of St John, 'which images Archbishop Stigand had adorned with a great weight of gold and silver, and given to St Edmund'. Some of the monks who where close to Hugh even suggested that the shrine of St Edmunds ought to be stripped 'to pay for such a Liberty'. The shrine certainly was not stripped, nor, it seems, were the cross above the altar and the two images sacrificed.[91] Most likely, the monks borrowed rather than deplete St Edmunds' treasures, thus adding to the pile of debts which faced Samson on his succession to the abbacy.

[90] JB, p. 5.
[91] JB, p. 108. But see James, Abbey, p. 134 n.

11

Samson as a Builder

The repair of derelict buildings and the construction of new ones under Samson have been mentioned above,[1] but his fame as a builder rests primarily on the many building works within the abbey precincts, both ecclesiastical and domestic, which his enthusiasm initiated and his energy pursued. However, of all his projects the completion of the abbey church was paramount in his mind and his overriding ambition was to have the church consecrated. Jocelin ends a passage summarising Samson's merits with these words:

> Samson performed these and similar deeds worthy of eternal record and renown, but he himself said that he would have achieved nothing in his lifetime unless he could bring about the dedication of our church. That done, he asserted, he would die content. He said he was ready to spend 2,000 marks of silver on the ceremony, provided the king was present and all was done with due ceremony.[2]

Samson will have read in the *De Miraculis Sancti Eadmundi* (composed c. 1100) of Abbot Baldwin's failure to obtain permission from William Rufus for the consecration of the new (but unfinished) Romanesque church.[3] He will also have known from his study of canon law that mass should not be celebrated in an unconsecrated place except in cases of 'great necessity', and that if there were any doubt as to whether a church had been consecrated or not, it should be consecrated even at the risk of it being consecrated twice.[4] Doubt arose in the absence of reliable written record or of personal witnesses. There was certainly no written record that the abbey church had been consecrated after Baldwin's time. In Henry II's reign, probably in the late 1170s, a tract was composed recording the consecration of the numerous altars and chapels at St Edmunds and of the

[1] Above pp. 28, 33.
[2] JB, pp. 47–8.
[3] *Memorials*, i. 85–6. Cf. Gransden, 'Question of the consecration', pp. 60–1.
[4] *Decretum*, Pt 3 De consecratione D. 1, canon 1: 'De ecclesiarum consecratione, et missarum celebrationibus non alibi quam in sacris Domino locis absque magna necessitate fieri debere, liquet omnibus, quibus sunt nota noui et ueteris testamenti precepta'; ibid., canon 16: 'Solempnitates dedicationum ecclesiarum, et sacerdotum, per singulos annos sunt celebrandae. De ecclesiarum consecrationibus quociens dubitatur, ut nec certa scriptura, nec testes existunt, a quibus consecratio sciatur, absque ulla dubitatione scitote eas esse sacrandas; nec talis trepidatio facit iterationem, quoniam non monstratur esse iteratum quod nescitur factum.' Friedberg, *Corpus iuris canonici*, i, coll. 1292, 1298. Cf. Gransden, art. cit., pp. 65, 74 and n. 79, 83 and n. 45.

two parish churches (St James's and St Mary's) within the *banleuca*.[5] The object of the tract was to demonstrate that the diocesan, the bishop of Norwich, had never consecrated at St Edmunds and, therefore, had no prescriptive right to do so. The tract was twice continued, first sometime after Samson had built the new infirmary, and then late in Simon of Luton's abbatiate (1257–79).[6] It is clear from it that the abbey church itself had never been consecrated. Perhaps, indeed, the tract had been composed in preparation for the hoped-for consecration, to forestall any attempt by the bishop of Norwich to officiate.

The fire in St Edmund's shrine, the restoration of the shrine and the additions made to its splendour spurred Samson's enthusiasm for the church's consecration.[7] Besides recognising the canonical need for the consecration, he must have wanted the lustre which such a magnificent occasion would shed on St Edmund's church and cult. It seems that as soon as work on the shrine was under way, he began negotiations with Innocent III for licence to consecrate. This was finally issued just a week after the translation of the sacred body to the refurbished shrine. The bull, dated 1 December 1198, gave Samson and the convent licence to dedicate the church without removing the very large crosses and images, and ordered by apostolic authority those bishops who were invited to attend to obey the summons of the abbot and convent.[8]

However, the consecration never took place. The reason for this is unknown, though there are a number of possible explanations. One possibility lies in Innocent's bull. It does not give the abbot and convent permission to choose whichever bishop they liked to officiate at the consecration, and perhaps the then bishop of Norwich, John of Oxford (1175–1200), was pressing his claim as diocesan. It is possible that there was a precedent for a bishop of Norwich consecrating within St Edmund's exempt spiritual jurisdiction. The tract on consecrations, having recorded that Abbot Anselm built the parish church of St James, which lay within the *banleuca*, states that it and the infirmary chapel of St Michael were consecrated at his request by 'William Turbe, archbishop of Canterbury'. Actually, Turbe was bishop of Norwich (1146–74): perhaps the author of the tract made the mistake deliberately in order to suppress the fact that a bishop of Norwich had consecrated a church and a chapel within the *banleuca*.[9] But there are other possible reasons why Samson did not proceed with the consecration. Perhaps he delayed until he could secure the king's attendance

---

5 *Bury Cust.*, pp. xl–xli, 114–21.
6 See ibid., p. 120 and nn. 1, 6, 7.
7 For the fire and the restoration of the shrine see below pp. 96–9.
8 The original, badly damaged, is Lambeth Palace Library Papal doc. 14. See: Cheney and Cheney, *Letters*, p. 13 no. 63; Thomson, *Archives*, p. 47 no. 18; J. E. Sayers, *Original Papal Documents in the Lambeth Palace Library* (London, 1967), pp. 12–13.
9 *Bury Cust.*, p. 119 lines 10–14 and n. 2. However, possibly the author of the tract confused William Turbe with William of Corbeil, archbishop of Canterbury 1123–36. St Edmunds was engaged in defending its exemption against the claims of the diocesan (William Turbe) early in Henry II's reign. At this time St Albans was likewise resisting the claims of its diocesan (the bishop of Lincoln) and produced a tract similar to the St Edmunds' one demonstrating that the abbot of St Albans had always exercised the right to employ whichever bishop he chose to perform episcopal acts, such as the dedication of St Albans'

and there were problems in this respect: Richard I died on 6 April 1199 while John was in France, and John returned to France soon after his coronation. He was in France for most of the first three years of his reign and again for most of 1206. Finally, England was under papal interdict from 1208 to 1214 which would have barred consecration during that period. Another obstacle may have been that the church was still unfinished, and according to canon law a church should be 'perfect' at the time of consecration.[10]

Nevertheless, though Samson's ambition to have the church consecrated remained unfulfilled, he has left his mark in the history of the abbey as a great builder. During the discussions among the monks which preceded Samson's election to the abbacy, one of them said that he had had a dream: he saw St Edmund rise from the shrine and show that his feet and legs were bare as if he were a sick man; when someone approached he told him to stop and, pointing at Samson, said 'There is the man who will cover my feet.' Part of this dream was interpreted to mean that under Samson the towers of the church 'begun a hundred years before' would be completed.[11]

Today, it is hard to visualize the west front as it originally was because it has been stripped of its ashlar, and houses were built into the ruins in the eighteenth and nineteenth centuries. But it was once of great magnificence. It has recently been described as 'perhaps the most complex façade structure ever built in Britain or, indeed, on the continent', one which, moreover, included some most unusual features.[12] In the centre of the west front was a tower. After the

---

altars and churches. *GASA*, i. 146–9. See: Knowles, 'Growth of exemption', pp. 215–17; Gransden, 'Question of the consecration', pp. 62–5.

10 That the church should be complete when consecrated seems implied by *Decretum*, Pt 3 De consecratione D. 1, canon 1 and ibid., canon 16 (above p. 84 n. 4). It is explicitly stated in the first of the thirty-one canons issued at the legatine Council of London in 1237. Canon 1 begins by alluding to the ruling in the *Decretum* that mass should only be celebrated in a consecrated place except in cases of necessity. It continues thus: 'Porro quia vidimus per nosipsos et a plerisque audivimus tam salubre ministerium contempni vel saltem negligi a nonnullis, dum multas invenimus ecclesias et aliquas etiam cathedrales que licet sint ab antiquo constructe nondum tamen sunt oleo sanctificationis consecrate, volentes huic tam periculose negligentie obviare statuimus et statuendo precipimus ut omnes ecclesie cathedrales, conventuales, et parochiales que perfectis parietibus sunt constucte, infra biennium per diocesanos episcopos ad quos pertinet, vel eorum auctoritate per alios, consecrentur. Sicque infra simile tempus fiat in decetero construendis. Et ne tam salubre statutum transeat in contemptum, si loca huiusmodi non fuerint infra biennium a perfectionis tempore dedicata, a missarum solempniis usque ad consecrationem manere statuimus interdicta, nisi aliqua rationabili causa excusentur.' *C and S*, ii, pt 1, p. 246. The legate Ottobuono reiterated Otto's canon 1 in the canons he issued at the legatine council at St Paul's in 1268. See ibid., ii, pt 2, pp. 739, 750–1. In the mid-fourteenth century there was anxiety at St Edmunds concerning the canonical position of St Edmund's church if in fact it had not been consecrated. The question was whether, in view of the relevant canons of Otto and Ottobuono, the church was 'irregular' and 'interdicted'. The matter was referred to a canonist. Among his submissions was the statement that the church could not be consecrated because it was unfinished. He strongly advised that the monks finish it and have it consecrated. Gransden, 'Question of the consecration', pp. 72, 81, 82.

11 *JB*, p. 20.

12 McAleer, 'West front', p. 22.

Conquest until the late middle ages, it was extremely rare for a major church to have a central western tower. Most major churches had twin towers at the west end, as they appear, for example, at Peterborough. The only certain parallel to St Edmunds central western tower is at Ely, where it is still standing. Winchester may also have once had one but no certain evidence survives.[13] The western tower of St Edmunds was flanked by two two-storied apsidal structures: the one on the north contained a chapel dedicated to St Denis below, with a chapel dedicated to St Faith above; the one on the south had a chapel of St John the Baptist below and a chapel of St Katherine above.[14] Each of the apsidal structures was flanked on its northern and southern extremity by an octagon.[15] These octagons were called towers in the middle ages. The northern octagon still stands and is known as 'Samson's Tower'. But whether the octagons deserved to be called towers is unclear because their original height is unknown and there is no evidence to indicate whether they had spires or pitched roofs. 'Samson's Tower' has lost its original appearance because it has been stripped of ashlar and drastically altered in modern times.[16] It seems that the octagons are in fact a unique feature, without precedents or successors. Their practical use is unknown though it has been suggested that the southern octagon was a baptistery and that on the north some kind of memorial chapel.[17]

Another unknown factor is whether or not Abbot Baldwin was responsible for the plan of this remarkable and spectacular west front. On the whole this seems unlikely since building work on it was still in progress in Abbot Samson's time. It seems most likely that the plan developed as building proceeded, especially under Abbot Anselm.[18] At first the west front would have consisted of the central tower and apsidal chapels. The octagons were probably part of the original design, not later additions, but actual work on them proceeded under Samson.[19] The general intention of this magnificent west front was to impress all who saw or heard about it with the majestic grandeur of St Edmund's church. But the inspiration for the unusual features must have been subtler. There seemed to be architectural references to the fact that the church contained the shrine of St Edmund. Ely similarly had a central tower in the west front and it too was a shrine church, and so was Winchester which may also have had a central western tower. It is noteworthy that in all three instances the saint concerned was an Anglo-Saxon saint, and that a central western tower was characteristic of Anglo-Saxon church architecture. Therefore, possibly those who decided to

---

13 Clapham, *English Romanesque Architecture*, ii. 31, 38.

14 For an 'interpretation and reconstruction' of the west front see McAleer, 'West front', pp. 23–7 and nn. and pls. See above fig. 9.

15 For evidence that the Romanesque church had a central western tower see McAleer, art. cit., pp. 24, 28–9 and pl. VI B.

16 Ibid., pp. 24, 28 and pls VII B – VIII B.

17 Ibid., pp. 24–5, 29–30.

18 Ibid., pp. 27–8; Fernie, 'Romanesque church', p. 8.

19 *Gesta Sacrist.*, p. 291; Whittingham, 'Bury St. Edmunds Abbey', p. 172; Fernie, 'Romanesque church', p. 8. McAleer (art. cit., p. 26) produces structural evidence indicating that the octagons were part of the original design. Above art.

construct central western towers in the post-Conquest period were inspired by the desire to stress their churches' Anglo-Saxon past.

At St Edmunds the plan of the abbey church was part of a total design which included the Norman Tower (also called Churchgate) and the town itself. The beautiful free-standing Norman Tower constructed under Abbot Anselm (1121–48), which still stands today, is sited a little to the east of the church of St James (now the cathedral) and was intended both as a grand gateway to the abbey church and as a bell-tower for St James's, then a parish church.[20] The streets of the town itself were laid out on a gridiron plan and a straight line can be drawn down the present-day Churchgate Street, through the gateway of the Norman Tower to the central portal, beneath the great central tower of the west front and so on along the axis of the church to St Edmund's shrine. The symbolism of this total plan is obvious – the shrine was the focal-point of the whole.[21] The value to pre-Conquest foundations of continuity with the past was inestimable, both in terms of prestige and because their lands and privileges originated with pre-Conquest grants. Emphasis on continuity is a feature of the historiography and hagiography of the post-Conquest period.[22] In the present instance architecture seems to have been used for the same purpose.[23] The presence, therefore, of a central western tower is easily explained. But a plausible iconographic reason for the inclusion of the two octagons is harder to find, especially as it is not known what they were used for. Possibly they were intended to recall the round martyrium where St Edmund's body had lain before its translation to the new Romanesque presbytery in 1094. The martyrium was built when the secular community serving St Edmund's shrine was replaced by Benedictine monks in 1020, and dedicated by Archbishop Æthelnoth in 1032.[24] It was in the cemetery just north of the abbey church's north transept and remained standing as a chapel until its destruction in 1275 to make room for Abbot Simon of Luton's new Lady Chapel.[25]

Building work on the west front had slackened or come to a halt after the death of Abbot Anselm in 1148. Under Samson it proceeded apace. Samson's enthusiasm for resuming work on the west tower while he was subsacrist has

20 Whittingham, art. cit., p. 189; Hills, 'Antiquities', pp. 120–1 and pl. 2, fig. 11, 5; Fernie, 'Romanesque church', pp. 1, 5–7 and fig. 6 and pls III A, XXIX A; Statham, 'Medieval town', p. 100; Gauthier, 'Planning the town of Bury St Edmunds', pp. 90–6 and fig. 6.

21 Gauthier, art. cit., pp. 81–90 and figs 1–5, examines the layouts of specific towns in Normandy which were apparently planned to focus on a great church in a similar way as at Bury St Edmunds, and argues for a possible Norman origin of the plan.

22 See: R. W. Southern, 'Aspects of the European tradition of historical writing: 4. The sense of the past', TRHS, 5th ser., xxiii (1973), pp. 246–56; idem, St Anselm and his Biographer, pp. 246–55, 309–13; Gransden, Historical Writing, [i], chapter 7 passim; eadem, 'Traditionalism and continuity during the last century of Anglo-Saxon monasticism', JEH, xl, pt 2 (1989), pp. 298–307.

23 McAleer, 'West front', pp. 28–9.

24 Gem, 'Towards an iconography', pp. 7–12 (p. 9 for the rotunda at St Edmunds); Gem and Keen, 'Late Anglo-Saxon finds', p. 1. Above fig. 9.

25 Bury Chron, p. 58 and n. 3; James, Abbey, pp. 188–9; Hills, 'Antiquities', pp. 51, 112–13.

already been discussed.[26] His efforts had been obstructed by the sacrist William Wiardel and his friends. Soon after his election, Samson deposed Wiardel and appointed his own namesake, Samson, the precentor, 'a man beyond reproach, who pleased us all'.[27] But he did not hold office for long; in 1186 or a little later, he was replaced by Hugh, the subsacrist, who held office until his death in 1200. He was succeeded by Master Walter of Banham, who held office until sometime between 1206 and c. 1210. He was previously the almoner and was also a physician.[28] Sometime before 1211 William of Diss held office for four days. He is known to have been a learned monk and the great responsibilities of the sacristy did not suit him – he could not sleep and realizing his inability, asked Samson to accept his resignation. He was succeeded by Robert of Graveley who, on Samson's death, became one of the two contenders for the abbacy in the prolonged dispute over Hugh of Northwold's election.[29]

Samson used Hugh and Walter of Banham as his instruments in carrying out his building projects. His overall control is expressed in the *Gesta Sacristarium* in its account of Hugh: 'This sacrist wanted no fellow in his acts, receipts and expenses, since the Lord abbot gave him his instructions in full chapter: and [Hugh] on his own faithfully and happily completed what had to be done.'[30] The relationship between Samson and Walter of Banham was probably similar. When Samson named him in 1201 as a suitable candidate for the priorate, Jocelin comments that he was known to be 'weak and unequal to the task', and Walter himself admitted his incapacity on oath.[31] It seems, therefore, that Samson contrived the appointment of malleable sacrists and himself oversaw the building work. By the time Robert of Graveley was sacrist, Samson was an old man and so probably less involved with the sacrist's activities. While Hugh was sacrist the central western tower was completed, Samson himself having 'devoutly' provided the roofing timber.[32] The apsidal chapels of St Faith and St Katherine were newly roofed with lead. Also under Hugh the stonework of the north octagon and the first storey of the southern one was completed. The north octagon was roofed under Walter of Banham and the fabric of the church restored, 'if you do not believe it, open your eyes and see', exclaims Jocelin.[33] For the repairs Samson gave timber which was 'lying in the cemetery', in all 200 tree trunks – 80 from his wood at Worlingworth and 120 from his wood at Melford. The nave was re-roofed under Robert of Graveley.

Samson and the sacrists were equally anxious to add to the splendour and iconographic significance of the church's interior. Hugh built a rood screen in stone (no doubt with elaborate carving on its west face) to divide the nave

[26] Above pp. 15–16.
[27] *JB*, p. 31.
[28] *Gesta Sacrist.*, pp. 291–2; *JB*, p. 96.
[29] Ibid., p. 293. See below pp. 153 et seqq.
[30] *Gesta Sacrist.*, p. 292.
[31] *JB*, p. 127.
[32] *JB*, p. 96; *Gesta Sacrist.*, p. 291.
[33] 'Si non credis, aperi oculos tuos et uide.' *JB*, p. 96. The *Gesta Sacristarum* (p. 292) has a similar passage: 'et ecclesiae fabricam innovavit, ut patet omni transeunti'.

from the choir, presbytery and east end, the most sacred parts of the church. Over the rood screen he erected a rood beam 'with a great crucifix and images of the blessed Mary and St John on either side'; this was the rood beam which, Jocelin asserts, had luckily been temporarily removed before the outbreak of fire in the shrine in 1198.[34] Hugh made the abbot's throne more conspicuous by having it painted, 'by the exertions of Simon the painter'. Hugh also gave rich church vestments – embroidered copes worth 60 marks – and a golden chalice worth 5 marks. Walter of Banham continued the improvement of the church's interior. He built a stone base to carry the panels of the retable behind the choir altar, 'having completely restored and gilded it with gold plate'. For this he used '100 ounces or more of gold-plate and two ounces of gold'.[35] In addition, he 'devoutly' gave 5 silk copes embroidered with gold. Finally, Robert of Graveley had a canopy erected over the shrine of St Edmund and painted with a variety of pictures.[36] Samson himself had had a 'very precious' crest made for the shrine, and earlier, when subsacrist, had had the choir screen painted.[37] Altogether the church must have presented a very colourful, glittering spectacle.

Meanwhile, as work on the building and ornamentation of the work on the abbey church proceeded, Samson undertook an ambitious programme of restoration, improvement and in some cases of replacement of other buildings in the precincts. He completed works begun under William of Wiardel. While Hugh was sacrist, the new infirmary and the chapel of St Andrew in the cemetery were both completed, 'at Samson's procuring'. He 'devoutly' provided beams for the roofs and other timber from his woods.[38] Some of the building work was for the abbot's convenience. Thus, Samson had a new larder built for himself in the great court and gave the old one to the monks for the use of the chamberlain. According to Jocelin, the old one was unsuitable for the abbot's use because it was situated under the monks' dormitory. And the abbot's ancient hall, which was in a ruinous state, was restored and 'completely finished'.[39] However, much of the building work was for the benefit of the monks. When Hugh was sacrist, a new bath-house and a new guest-house for the convent's guests, were built – again, Samson 'generously' provided the necessary roofing timber.[40] Jocelin was guest-master at the time of the demolition of the old guest-house and he notes that construction of a new guest-house had not yet begun. He writes of the project with a mixture of joy and apprehension:

> Behold! The acceptable time, the longed for day is come [cf. 2 Cor. 6.2] of which I write because I have charge of our guests. Behold! At the abbot's command the

---

34 Ibid., p. 291. Cf. *JB*, p. 108.
35 'Centum marcas de plata et eo amplius, et duas marcas auri, ad tabulam faciendam dedicavit.' *Gesta Sacrist.*, p. 292. For goldwork at St Edmunds, see Marian Campbell, 'Medieval metalworking and Bury St Edmunds', in *Bury St Edmunds*, ed. Gransden, pp. 69–70. *JB*, p. 97
36 *Gesta Sacrist.*, p. 293.
37 See below pp. 94, 97, and above p. 15.
38 *Gesta Sacrist.*, p. 291; *JB*, p. 96.
39 *Gesta Sacrist.*, p. 292.
40 Ibid., pp. 291–2.

court resounds with the sound of picks and masons' tools as the guest-house is knocked down – it is now mostly demolished. As for its rebuilding, may the Most High provide![41]

The work on the abbot's hall had taken place under Hugh's successor as sacrist, Walter of Banham. As mentioned above, he had previously been almoner and he was responsible for the construction of a new, stone almonry. Jocelin records that it was high time to replace the old almonry since it was built of wood and was in dilapidated condition. Walter contributed a large sum of money which he had earned as a physician.[42] It was probably because Walter was the monk's physician (who would also have treated other patients) that he began building a wash-place.[43] Although he died before its completion, it is clear from the *Gesta Sacristarum* that construction continued after his death and that he planned the wash-place to be a fine building. The *Gesta* records: 'What we see there, whether completed or in progress, marble or gilded images or masons' work, was all due to him because he paid every kind of expense during his lifetime.' Walter's successor, Robert of Graveley, further improved the monks' amenities. He bought the vineyard on the east bank of the Lark and enclosed it with a stone wall, 'for the recreation of the infirm and those who had been bled'.[44]

Most remarkable of all the building projects undertaken by Samson for the benefit of the convent was the aqueduct constructed under Walter of Banham to supply the monks with water. The aqueduct 'was lined with lead and brought water from a source two miles away, and so underground to the cloisters'.[45] The list of the abbey's benefactors includes in its recital of Samson's merits and acts notice of the aqueduct and wash-place: 'he completed the aqueduct and water conduits and the wash-place, of wonderful workmanship and admirable size'.[46] The aqueduct also figures in the contemporary account of the sack of the claustral buildings by the townspeople and their followers during the revolt in 1327 – the rebels 'broke the aqueduct so that the monks would suffer from shortage

---

[41] *JB*, p. 96.

[42] *JB*, p. 96.

[43] The manuscript reads *Sanatorium* (BL MS Harley 1005, f. 121) and, therefore, so does the printed text (*Gesta Sacrist.*, p. 292). But the reading is probably a scribal error for *Lavatorium*, wash-place. The list of benefactors records that Abbot Samson completed *lavatoria* and makes no mention to a *sanatorium*. Below n. 46.

[44] *Gesta Sacrist.*, p. 293. Cf. the undated statutes drawn up by the prior and convent to promote economy, preserved in an early fourteenth-century text (BL MS Harley 3977, f. 52): 'Et quia sacrista magnos sumptus ad colendam vineam facere consuevit, de cetero assignetur infirmario, qui eam colat et fructus percipiat, ita tamen quod sacrista et subsacrista et conventus habeant ingressum propter solacium.' *Bury Cust.*, pp. xxxiv, 109 lines 11–14. The vineyard was on the east bank of the Lark. Part of the south and east walls survive. Whittingham, 'Bury St. Edmunds Abbey', p. 183 and pl. XXI (plan of the abbey).

[45] 'Aqueductum a capite et fonte duobus miliaribus plumbo inclusit, et usque ad claustrum per occultos terrae meatus derivavit.' *Gesta Sacrist.*, p. 292.

[46] 'Aque ductum et Aquam per riuulos deriuatam et lauatoria opere mirifico et magnitudine admiranda et multa alia bona opere consummauit.' Douai, Bibliothèque Municipale MS 533, f. 8.

of water'.[47] Matthew Paris includes mention of the aqueduct in his *Chronica Majora*, in the notice of Samson's death in 1212. Indeed, the construction of the aqueduct is the only one of Samson's achievements which Matthew specifies: 'he made an aqueduct and did many other good things'.[48] Perhaps Matthew himself or someone else from St Albans had seen the aqueduct. In any case, he was obviously impressed by this engineering feat and regarded Samson as its author.

Robert Carr, of Suffolk County Council Archaeological Service at Bury St Edmunds, has suggested a possible route of the aqueduct. He postulates that it was ducted from the source of the river Linnet in Horringer and followed the river possibly to a cistern above the cloister range: at that point, having travelled about two miles, it would have achieved a drop of about two metres up the slope from the cloisters. The last part of the aqueduct descending to the cloister range would probably have been in an underground conduit. On reaching the cloisters a system of water-pipes and drains would have distributed water to the buildings within the precincts and carried away the waste (presumably to cess-pits and the river Lark). Mr Carr has found archaeological evidence in two places that the water was ducted through Holywater Meadows, to the south of the present Mainwater Lane.[49]

It is unfortunate that our evidence about the aqueduct and waterworks installed by Samson is so sparse and consequently our conclusions about it speculative. However, it probably resembled the system installed nearly half a century earlier at Christ Church, Canterbury, by Prior Wibert (1152/3–1167), of which two contemporary plans survive: one is a diagram of the aqueduct bringing water from a source outside the city walls 'where the springs break out' (about three-quarters of a mile from the abbey). The other is a beautifully drawn plan of the area within the precincts showing in detail the complex network of water-pipes and drains serving the various buildings.[50] This cartographical evidence is supported by archaeological finds of lead pipes, underground conduits and the

---

47 'Et ut penuriam aque paterentur, fregerunt conductum aquae ne ad eos descenderet', *Memorials*, ii. 334–5.

48 'obiitque bonus abbas Sancti Edmundi Sanson, qui aquae ductum et multa alia bona fecit ecclesiae suae', *Chron. Maj.*, ii. 533.

49 I owe my information from Robert Carr to a telephone conversation and to a sketch map which he kindly sent me. The present Mainwater Lane is marked on Thomas Warren's map of the town (Mayne Water Lane). Reproduced in Statham, 'Medieval town', fig. 2 and in eadem, *Book of Bury St Edmunds*, pastedown and flyleaf at the beginning and end of the volume. Statham records that 'in our period it was known as Maydewaterstrete, a name taken from a pool called Maiden Water [which] was corrupted over the centuries to the present Mainwater Lane'. 'Medieval town', pp. 104–5 and fig. 1. However, it seems to me more likely that the name Maydewaterstrete was itself a corruption of the name Mayne Water Lane.

50 These plans, especially the one of the buildings in the precincts, have been often reproduced and extensively written about. See e.g.: William Urry in *Local Maps and Plans from Medieval England*, ed. R. A. Skelton and P. D. A. Harvey (Oxford, 1986), pp. 54–8 and pls 1A, B (in monochrome; 1A reproduced in colour at the end of the volume); Bernard Gille, 'Machines' in *A History of Technology*, ed. Charles Singer, E. J. Holmyard and A. R. Hall (London, 1954–8, 5 vols), ii. 69; Robert Willis, 'The architectural history of the conventual buildings of the monastery of Christ Church in Canterbury', *Archaeologia*

like. How rare it was for a monastery or other institution to have such a system is uncertain in our present state of knowledge.[51] However, methods of controlling the flow and height of water in order to provide the power to turn waterwheels were well known. Unsurprisingly, water-power in a monastery or elsewhere, might be used for industrial as well as domestic purposes. Thus, at Clairvaux in the twelfth century, the water channelled into the precincts was employed in a variety of ways, including fulling cloth and grinding grain.[52] At St Edmunds, before Samson's construction of the aqueduct, the monks presumably relied for their water supply in the precincts on water from the river Lark, probably raised by waterwheel, and/or on rainwater, stored in cisterns. They would not have had the benefit of clear water and constant water-power.

Jocelin and the *Gesta Sacristarum* write about Samson's building achievements from his and the sacrist's point of view. They reveal little about the cost. Jocelin records Walter's contributions towards the expense and the *Gesta* records Samson's gifts of timber, but otherwise nothing is said about funding and the supply of raw materials.[53] Some of the monks must surely have had reservations on grounds of expense about the desirability of such a wide-ranging building programme. There are hints of opposition in the Composition discussed above, between abbot and convent drawn up either late in Samson's abbatiate or early in that of Hugh of Northwold.[54] The sacrists were so closely involved in the building work that it is likely that Samson sometimes used the resources of the sacristy indiscriminately with those of the abbot. A clause in the Composition states that: 'The abbot is to take nothing secretly from the sacristy for any purpose; if he has need of anything, he should have it with the knowledge and consent of the convent'.[55] Other clauses specify exactly what the sacrist's responsibilities were for the abbot's buildings.[56] He was responsible for the care of the plumbing and the furnace belonging to the abbot in the great court, but not for the abbot's 'utensils' and he was responsible for the abbot's 'ancient house', that is, his hall, kitchen, stable, brewery and bake-house. But the abbot, not the sacrist, was responsible for the hall of pleas, the 'oriel' (probably an entrance hall),[57] larder, (new) granary, his house 'next to the garden and similar new buildings'. This division of responsibility was rather severe on the abbot, judging from the abbey's Customary compiled about twenty years later. The Customary

    Cantiana, vii (1869), pp. 158–73; Gies and Gies, *Cathedral, Forge and Waterwheel*, p. 188 (plan reproduced in monochrome on p. 189).

[51] See Barrie Dobson, 'The monks of Canterbury in the later middle ages, 1220–1540', in *A History of Canterbury Cathedral*, ed. Patrick Collinson, Nigel Ramsay and Muriel Sparks (Oxford, 1995), pp. 58–9.

[52] *Vita S. Bernardi*, in *PL*, clxxxv, coll. 570–2, cited in Gille, op. cit., from Singer, Holmyard and Hall, ed. cit., ii. 650. See Gies and Gies, op. cit., pp. 188, 190.

[53] Above p. 88.

[54] Above pp. 35 et seqq.

[55] *Bury Cust.*, p. 103 lines 23–4.

[56] Ibid., pp. 103 lines 26–9, 105 lines 21–7.

[57] At St Albans the building works of Abbot John II (1235–60) included a noble guest-hall and 'adjacit atrium nobilissimum in introitu, quod "porticus", vel "oriolum", appellatur'. *GASA*, i. 314. Cf. *Word-List*, p. 325.

states that care of the hall of pleas ('built at the wish and with the consent of the convent') and 'oriel' belonged to the sacrist.

Nevertheless, the fact that Samson could undertake so much building work testifies to his enterprise, energy and ability, and to his success in improving the abbey's economic position sufficiently to make it possible. In general, the monks, despite anxiety about unwarranted inroads into the convent's resources, must have applauded the improvements to the abbey church and to their domestic quarters.

12

Religious and Intellectual Life
under Samson

The shrine and cult of St Edmund

The shrine of St Edmund, the centre of the martyr's cult and the magnet which drew the pilgrims, was very splendid. It lay behind the high altar and, like all great shrines, consisted of two main parts, the feretory containing the saint's coffin and a base. The feretory was of the normal kind, a rectangular wooden box, a little larger than the coffin, with a gable roof like that of a house. It was covered with silver plates and Samson gave a golden crest to surmount the gable ridge, and Robert of Graveley gave a canopy, with pictures painted on it, to fit over the feretory.[1] The canopy would have been made of wood and usually hung above the feretory, suspended by ropes, but sometimes it would have been lowered to cover the feretory. This was possible because the ropes were attached to pulleys fixed either to the underside of the vault or to beams above it; in the latter case the ropes would have passed through holes in the vault. The actual form of the feretory would not have altered in the course of the middle ages, though the accumulation of precious votive offerings, which were attached to it every now and then, would have altered its superficial appearance. Its general appearance in the late middle ages can be seen from the five miniatures of the shrine illustrating John Lydgate's *Lives of St Edmund and St Fremund* in BL MS Harley 2278 (ff. 4v, 9, 100v, 108v, 109).[2] Henry VIII's commissioners in 1538 described it as 'a rich shrine which was very cumbrous to deface'.[3]

On the other hand, the base of the shrine in Samson's time was the one constructed for Abbot Baldwin's Romanesque church and it was unlike the base depicted in the Lydgate manuscript. Although each of the five miniatures in the manuscript depicts the shrine slightly differently, they all agree about the type

---

[1] *JB*, p. 97; *Gesta Sacrist*, p. 293. For the canopies of feretories see: Nilson, *Cathedral Shrines*, pp. 40–1 and frontispiece; Wall, *Shrines*, pp. 112, 191 and frontispiece.

[2] See: Rogers, 'Bury artists of Harley 2278', pp. 223–4 and pls LVB (f. 9), LVIA (f. 100v), LVIB (ff. 108v, 109).

[3] *Letters and Papers Foreign and Domestic Henry VIII*, ed. James Gairdner, xiii, pt 1 (London, 1896), p. 66 no. 192; *Letters Relating to the Suppression of Monasteries*, ed. Thomas Wright (Camden Soc., 1843), p. 144 no. 67.

of the base – it belonged to a type fashionable in the later middle ages.[4] It was a solid masonry base with nitches in its sides. The architectural details are in the decorated style which suggests that this base was constructed in the first half of the fourteenth century or thereabouts. The nitches enable a crouching pilgrim to lean into the base and so be more or less underneath the sacred body. This close proximity of the saint was believed to give the faithful extra spiritual benefit.[5] But the Romanesque base at St Edmunds was of a different type: it was open and the space was big enough for a pilgrim to crawl right beneath the feretory. This is evident from Jocelin's account of how Samson as a young man hid under the feretory to avoid the anger of Abbot Hugh.[6] Therefore, the base must have been one of two types, both common before the transition to solid bases. Perhaps it was a table type of shrine, with the feretory resting on a stone slab which was on pillars, thus leaving an empty space between the feretory and the masonry foundation. The most famous shrine in England, the shrine of St Thomas at Canterbury, was of this type,[7] and so was the shrine of St Alban at St Albans. Matthew Paris drew a picture of the latter to illustrate his Anglo-Norman *Life of St Alban*: it shows a pilgrim crawling into the space.[8] The other type of shrine with an open space between the feretory and the masonry foundation of the base had masonry walls pierced by openings, like port-holes, large enough to allow a pilgrim to crawl through into the empty space inside. The shrine of Edward the Confessor at Westminster was of this type before it was replaced for St Edward's translation in 1269 by the present shrine with a solid base. Matthew Paris drew it to illustrate his *Estoire de St Aedouard li Rei*, and shows a pilgrim crawling into it through a 'port-hole'.[9] If the base of St Edmund's shrine was of the table type, it presumably had a cloth on the table-top hanging down the sides: otherwise Samson could not have hidden effectively under it. Matthew Paris's picture of St Alban's shrine does in fact have a cloth hanging down from the table-top.

The shrine was lit by four large candles in candlesticks attached to the four corners. The candles burnt perpetually and were paid for by the revenues from the ten librates in Aylsham which Richard I gave to St Edmunds to provide

---

4   For the design of the Romanesque shrine of St Edmund and of the later one see: Rogers, art. cit., pp. 223–4; Crook, 'Architectural setting of the cult of St Edmund', pp. 39–42.

5   Nilson, op. cit., pp. 44–5, 99–100. For examples see: the (reconstructed) shrine of St Alban at St Albans; the (reconstructed) shrine of St Frideswide in Oxford cathedral; and the shrine of Edward the Confessor at Westminster. Wall, op. cit., pp. 41–2 and fig., and pl. XII, 68–9 and pl. XVIII, 229–35 and pls XXVII, XXVIII (sic. for XXVI, XXVII), and in colour on the dust jacket of Nilson, op. cit.

6   JB, p. 49. Above p. 13.

7   Nilson, op. cit., p. 43 and nn. 73, 74, citing William Urry, 'Some notes on two resting places of St Thomas Becket at Canterbury', in *Thomas Becket, Actes de Colloque International de Sédières*, ed. Raymonde Foreville (Paris, 1975), pp. 204–6, and M. H. Caviness, *The Early Stained Glass of Canterbury before the Conquest* (Oxford, 1975), pl. 164.

8   See *Illustrations to the Life of St Alban*, in Trinity College, Dublin, MS. E i 40, ed. in facsimile W. R. L. Lowe and E. F. Jacob, with an introduction by M. R. James (Oxford, 1924). For the manuscript see Vaughan, *Matthew Paris*, pp. 168 et seqq.

9   *La Estoire de Seint Aedward le Rei*, in *Lives of Edward the Confessor*, ed. H. R. Luard (RS, 1858), p. 19 no. LIV; and Wall, op. cit., p. 227 fig.

suitable lighting for the shrine.[10] A wooden platform connected the shrine with the high altar. The space underneath the platform was used for storage by the guardians of the shrine, and the platform was surrounded by iron grilles (called by Jocelin 'iron walls') which had an iron door so that the keepers of the shrine could reach their stores. The platform was covered with a cloth and two candles stood on it.[11] It was here that fire, which badly damaged the shrine, broke out in the night of 22 June 1198.

Most of what is known about the Romanesque shrine is in Jocelin's vivid account of the fire.[12] He asserts that the keepers of the shrine used to cobble candles together, sticking one stump of a candle on top of another. It was thought that on the night of the disaster, while the keepers of the shrine were asleep, part of one of these patched-together candles fell when nearly burnt and set light to the cloth covering the wooden platform. The blaze quickly spread so that the iron grill around the platform 'was white hot with the heat'. The fire was first seen by the vestarer when the clock struck for matins.[13] He 'running with all speed beat upon the board as though to announce a death and shouted at the top of his voice that the feretory was burning'. Jocelin gives a dramatic description of the monks' frenzied alarm and frantic rush to stem the blaze:

> We all ran together and found the flames raging beyond belief, engulfing the whole feretory and reaching nearby to the beams of the church. So the young men among us ran to get water, some to the water cistern, others to the clock, while others, having snatched up various reliquaries, with great difficulty extinguished the flames with their cowls.

Jocelin's account of the damage done is equally graphic:

> When the cold water was poured on the front of the feretory, the gems fell and were reduced almost to dust. The nails which fixed the silver plates to the feretory fell from the wood which was burnt to the thickness of my finger, and the plates hung from each other without any nails to support them. But the golden Majesty in front of the feretory, with certain gems, remained firm and intact, and seemed more beautiful after the fire than before because it was all of gold.

Some of the other sacred objects were also saved. Those on, or hanging from, the rood beam were saved because the beam had been removed. They included a reliquary containing the alleged shirt of St Edmund and some other reliquaries

---

[10] Above p. 63. Rogers, 'Bury artists of Harley 2278', p. 224.

[11] JB, p. 106.

[12] JB, pp. 106–10.

[13] JB, p. 107 and n. 4. This seems to be the earliest dated reference to the existence of a water-clock at St Edmunds. The abbey's customary, compiled c. 1235, mentions the 'keeper of the clock' ('serviens custodiens horologium'); he was to receive seven ells of candle a week in the winter (*Bury Cust.*, p. 59 line 5). Alexander IV's confirmation of St Edmunds' customs in 1256 ordains that the keeper of the clock was to remain on duty day and night. Ibid., p. 63 lines 22–3. For water-clocks see North, *God's Clockmaker*, pp. 147–54. North cites late thirteenth- and early fourteenth-century examples, but the only early thirteenth-century example he cites is from St Albans.

and pyxes, besides the statue of St John and the little statue of the Virgin Mary. Another lucky chance was that the golden crest for the feretory which Samson had commissioned was not yet in place. Once the embers were cold the monks investigated the extent of the damage and found other causes of consolation. They feared that the cup of St Edmund had perished, but

> some of those hunting for gems and silver plates in the cinders and ashes, pulled out the cup quite unharmed. ... They found it wrapped in a linen cloth which was half burnt. The oaken casket in which the cup was kept was burnt to dust and only the iron bands and lock could be found. And seeing this miracle we all wept for joy!

Jocelin also asserts that the monks after thorough investigation of the feretory were convinced that the fire had not penetrated to its interior.[14] Nevertheless, they were appalled at the hideous, burnt appearance of the feretory. Most of the silver plates had fallen off, so they at once sent for a goldsmith to fix them on again, and meanwhile had the traces of burning covered over with wax and disguised by other means. In this way they hoped to remove all visible signs of the fire. But the attempt to deceive pilgrims who arrived with their offerings early next morning failed. Jocelin cites St Luke's gospel: 'Nothing is hidden that shall not be revealed' (Luke 12.2). Rumour of the fire was already abroad. In answer to inquiries, pilgrims were told that a fallen candle had burnt three towels and damaged some of the stones in front of the feretory. 'But lying rumour alleged that the saint's head had been burnt, while some said that it was only his hair.'[15]

Samson was absent when the fire occurred. When he heard of the disaster he was 'much grieved' and was angry with the monks, saying that it was a divine punishment for their sins. Jocelin considered this view unfair and blamed the 'avarice and negligence' of the keepers of the shrine. On his return Samson's immediate reaction was to have the shrine restored and at the same time used the opportunity to speed up the improvements to the shrine which he already had in hand. He wished the front of the feretory to be covered in pure gold and himself gave all the gold in his possession, that is, fifteen gold rings 'worth, it is thought, some 60 marks'.[16] He tried to persuade the monks to forego their pittances, so that the money could be spent on the restoration and improvements. But the sacrist said this was unnecessary because 'St Edmund was well able to restore his own feretory without such help'. The implication is that offerings at the shrine would cover the expense.

Samson's plan was to make the base of the feretory higher, with a masonry foundation of polished marble. The restoration and improvements were completed by late November 1198, and ready to receive the feretory. On Sunday (22 November), Samson announced publicly that the feretory would be moved on to the new base on Monday (23 November). He told the monks to be

---

[14] JB, p. 108.
[15] JB, p. 109.
[16] Above p. 66 and n. 46.

prepared, and meanwhile to put the feretory on the high altar until the masons had completed their work. He also proclaimed a three day fast to the people in preparation for the translation. The 'people' were presumably those living within St Edmund's *banleuca* and in the parishes of churches belonging to the abbey. Thus, he publicized the forthcoming event which was expected to draw a large crowd of pilgrims, since a solemn translation tended to be followed by miracles worked through the saint's intercession. The fast would also have applied to the monks. It was intended to purify all those involved in the translation, especially those who handled the holy body. Fasts had been observed before the translation of St Edmund by Abbot Leofstan and before the translation of 1095 by Abbot Baldwin: both fasts are recorded in Hermann's *De Miraculis Sancti Eadmundi*,[17] a work which, as will be seen, Samson knew well.[18]

Jocelin relates that when the monks came to matins in the early hours of Monday (23 November) they saw the feretory lying on the high altar. It was empty and Jocelin notes that it was fitted throughout with a lining of white (that is, tawed) deer skin fastened with silver nails.[19] One of its panels was propped against a pillar (it must have been detached to allow the removal of the coffin). The coffin was still in its old place. After lauds and discipline in chapter, Samson 'and a few others' vested in albs unwrapped the coffin. It was wrapped in linen fastened with cords tied on top. Under that was a silk cloth and then two more of linen.[20] And then the coffin itself was revealed, and was replaced in the feretory. At this point Jocelin was able to observe the coffin properly. Indeed, he confesses that when, at Samson's command, some of the monks carried it to the high altar in order to replace it in the feretory, 'I placed my sinful hand on it to help them, although the abbot commanded that no one should approach unless summoned'. He gives a precise description of the coffin. It was wooden and had an iron ring at each end 'such as are wont to be found on a Norse chest'.[21] It was bottomless and stood on a wooden tray to protect it from the marble floor of the feretory. Jocelin adds:

> Over the Martyr's breast, fixed to the outside of the coffin, was an angel of gold, about the length of a man's foot, having a sword of gold in one hand and a banner in the other; and beneath it there was a hole in the coffin-lid through which the guardians of the feretory used of old to thrust their hands that they might touch the holy body. And above the angel was written this verse: 'Behold! Michael's image guards the martyr's body.'[22]

In the scriptures the archangel Michael appears as 'one of the chief princes' of the Heavenly Host and the special guardian of the Israelites (Dan. 10.13

---

[17] *JB*, pp. 111–13.

[18] *De Miraculis*, pp. 52, 87.

[19] 'stetit magnum feretrum super altare, uacuum, intus ornatum coriis albis ceruinis sursum et deorsum, et circumcirca, que affigebantur lingo clauis argenteis', *JB*, p. 112.

[20] Below pp. 101 et seqq.

[21] *JB*, p. 113 and n. 2; Butler suggests the possibility that the coffin was a gift from the archbishop of Trondheim who visited the abbey in 1181/2. *JB*, p. 15 and above p. 18.

[22] *JB*, p. 112 and cf. p. 115.

and 12.1), and as the principal fighter in the heavenly battle against the devil (Rev. 12.7–9). In the middle ages Michael was often adopted as patron saint of cemeteries because he was considered to give them special protection.[23] He was, therefore, an appropriate guardian for St Edmund's body.

The coffin was replaced in the feretory and the detached panel re-fixed in its proper place. Jocelin relates that 'we all thought' that Samson intended to display the coffin containing the holy body to the people on the octave of the feast of St Edmund, that is, on Friday 27 November, and then to have it carried to the feretory which stood ready on its new base. In this way all the monks would have witnessed the translation. 'But we were sorely deceived.' Up to this point in the narrative, Jocelin was obviously writing from his own experiences and observations. But, as will be seen, it is not so clear that his description of what followed, of Samson's viewing of the body, was likewise written at first-hand, despite its realistic details.

Jocelin gives the impression that Samson's decision to view the body was the result of pious curiosity. This no doubt was one of his motives but undoubtedly another was to quash the insidious rumours that the sacred body had been scorched in the fire, so that St Edmund no longer lay perfect in his incorruption. So, on Wednesday evening (25 November), while the monks were singing compline, Samson summoned Hugh, the sacrist, and Walter, the physician, and told them that he wished to see 'his patron' and wanted them to accompany him. After consultation, it was decided that Samson should summon twelve monks capable of detaching the panels from the feretory, of carrying them, and of later fixing them back on again. Hugh and Walter were among those chosen. The other ten were Samson's two chaplains (Maurice and Herbert), the two keepers of the shrine, the two masters of the vestry, and four cloister monks (Augustine, William of Diss,[24] Robert and Richard). These twelve, 'while the convent slept', put on albs, removed the coffin from the feretory and placed it on a table near the feretory's previous site. The lid was nailed down by sixteen very long nails and was removed with difficulty. Samson then ordered all the twelve monks except for Hugh and Walter to retire and stand at a distance. Jocelin's famous description of the body follows:

> The coffin was so filled with the holy body, both lengthwise and across, that a needle could scarcely have been placed between the head or feet and the wood. The head lay united with the body and raised a little on a small pillow. The abbot, then looking more closely, found first a silk cloth covering the whole body and after that a linen cloth of wonderful whiteness: and over the head was a small linen cloth and under that a finely woven silk cloth, like a nun's veil. And after that they found the body wrapped in a linen cloth, and then at last the features of the holy body were revealed. Here the abbot stopped, saying that he dared do no further and see the saint's naked flesh. Therefore, taking the head between his

---

23 Binns, *Dedications*, p. 31; Farmer, *Saints*, p. 277.
24 William of Diss wrote the piece on the lands of Robert of Cockfield appended to Jocelin's chronicle. *JB*, pp. 138–9. He occurs as Samson's chaplain 1206 x 1211. Thomson, 'Obedientiaries', p. 100, citing *Kalendar*, ed. Davis, p. 148 no. 124.

hands, he said groaning. 'Glorious martyr, St Edmund, blessed be the hour when you were born! Glorious martyr, do not cast me, a miserable sinner, into perdition for presuming to touch you: you know my devotion, you know my intent.' And he proceeded to touch the eyes and the very large, prominent nose, and then he touched the breast and arms and, raising the left hand, he touched the fingers, and placed his fingers between the fingers of the saint. Proceeding further, he found the feet rigid and upright, as of a man dead that very day, and he touched the toes of the feet, counting them as he touched them.[25]

It was then considered advisable that other monks should be called and should see these wonders.[26] Jocelin states that six monks were summoned. These would seem to have been from among the twelve who had carried the coffin and been told to stand at a distance after the lid was removed. But six monks came uninvited whom Jocelin names. They were Walter of St Albans, Hugh the infirmarer, Gilbert the prior's brother, Richard of Ingham, Jocellus the cellarer and Turstan the little – 'who alone stretched out his hand and touched the saint's feet and knees'. Jocelin continues: 'So that there would be plenty of witnesses, by the disposition of the Most High, one of our brethren, John of Diss, sitting up in the vault with servants of the vestry, had a clear view of everything.'

The body was then re-wrapped so that the wrapping was exactly as before, and the lid of the coffin nailed back with the same sixteen nails. The coffin was put back in its usual place, on the wooden tray on the floor of the feretory. A silk wallet was laid on the coffin near the image of the archangel Michael. Jocelin records that 'a document was placed in it, containing, it is believed, some salutations of the monk Ailwin'. The latter was probably Egelwin, the sacrist of St Edmunds in the eleventh century, who according to legend carried St Edmund's body to London for safety from the Danes and allegedly witnessed the verification of St Edmund's incorruption by Abbot Leofstan.[27] Alternatively, possibly he was Ælfwine, bishop of Elmham, who was responsible for the establishment of the Rule of St Benedict in St Edmund's minster at *Beodericisworth* in 1020.[28] Bishop Ælfwine also most likely attended the dedication of the new church at *Beodericisworth* by Archbishop Aethelnoth and the translation of St Edmund's

[25] *JB*, p. 114.

[26] 'Datumque est consilium, ut ceteri fratres uocarentur et miracula uiderent.' Ibid.

[27] *De Miraculis*, pp. 34–46 passim, 52–4. Gransden, 'Alleged incorruption', pp. 140–2, 160 n. 55.

[28] The earliest record of the establishment of a monastery to replace the secular minster in 1020, and the dedication of the church by Archbishop Æthelnoth and the translation of the body of St Edmund into it, in 1032, is in two marginal notes in Easter Tables in the mid-eleventh-century Bury Psalter (Vatican MS Reg. Lat. 12, f. 16 v). The relevant marginal note reads by the year 1020: 'hinc deniq[ue] presul Ælfwin[us] sub comite Thurkyllo constituit regula[m] monachorum s[an]c[t]i Eadmundi monasterio; et sub voluntate licentiaq[ue] Cnutoni [sic] regis p[er]manet usque in presens'. Printed *New Palaeographical Soc. Facsimiles*, ser. 2, ed. E. M. Thompson et al. (London, 1903–30), ii, commentary to pls 166–8. (The manuscript is described in full in *Codices Reginenses Latini*, ed. André Wilmart (Vatican, 1937–45, 2 vols), i. 30–5.) The *De Miraculis* states that Bishop Ælfwine had been a monk of Ely. *De Miraculis*, p. 47. Cf. Gransden, 'Alleged incorruption', pp. 141, 159 n. 43.

body to it in 1032. Possibly the document was placed in the coffin at that trans-lation but it seems equally likely that Abbot Baldwin had it forged and placed there at the translation in 1095.[29] And now Samson added another document for preservation in the wallet. It read as follows: 'In the eleven hundredth and ninety eighth year of our Lord, Abbot Samson, moved by devotion, saw and touched the body of St Edmund, on the night of the feast of St Katherine, with these witnesses'. Jocelin states that there were eighteen witnesses, but does not name them, no doubt because he had mentioned them in his narrative. The monks then wrapped the coffin in a linen cloth and spread over it 'a new and precious silk cloth which Hubert, archbishop of Canterbury, had given in that same year'. A folded piece of linen was spread over the floor of the feretory to protect the wooden tray holding the coffin from damage by the marble. Finally, the panels of the feretory were fitted back in their proper places.

When the monks came early next morning to matins and saw the re-assem-bled feretory, those monks who had not seen all that had been done in the night said among themselves 'We have been badly misled.' After matins, Jocelin continues,

> the abbot called the monks together before the high altar and told them briefly what had been done and said that he neither ought nor could have summoned everyone to see such things. Having heard this, we tearfully sang the 'Te Deum', and hastened to ring the bells in choir.

The account of the viewing of the body is extremely detailed and graphic. Recent scholars who identify Jocelin with Jocellus, the cellarer, obviously accept that he was an eye-witness. However, it was pointed out above that this iden-tification is not supported by any concrete evidence. The account itself would contain an anomaly if written by Jocelin at first-hand. It would be odd that Jocelin should mention that he personally helped carry the coffin to the high altar and then write of himself as 'Jocellus' in his record of the six witnesses who came unbidden to see the body unwrapped. It seems most likely Jocelin was one of the monks who felt 'sorely deceived' or 'badly misled' in the course of Samson's proceedings. His account is probably based on oral testimony of one or more of the witnesses and from Samson's statement to the monks at the high altar. Possibly it was from the statement that Jocelin obtained the detail that Samson put his fingers between those of the body: this seems unlikely since the body was rigid.

Nevertheless, the details recorded by Jocelin are of great interest. The coffin would seem to have been a late tenth- or eleventh-century one. The fact that the body fitted so tightly in it, so that 'a needle could hardly be placed between the saint's head or feet and the wood', suggests that it was not made for the body it contained in the twelfth century. The body itself would appear to have been embalmed. Jocelin records that the feet were 'rigid and upright, as of a man dead that very day', a detail which could apply to an embalmed body. The nose

---

[29] See ibid., p. 152. For the viewing of the body in 1195 see *De Miraculis*, pp. 87–9. Cf. Gransden, 'Alleged incorruption', pp. 144, 161 n. 82.

was 'very large and prominent': since embalming involves dehydration it tends to accentuate the nose. And the final covering which Samson did not remove was probably bandaging in cere-cloth which would have clung so tightly that it would have been very hard to peel off.[30]

We may accept that the body at the centre of St Edmund's cult at *Beodericis-worth* in the tenth century was embalmed but whether any body embalmed in the middle ages could have remained preserved for three centuries is extremely doubtful.[31] The ancient techniques of long-term embalmment were lost in the west by the late sixth century and it was not until the mid-seventeenth century that reasonably reliable methods were again discovered. However, there were methods for preserving bodies from decay for short periods. If a body could not be buried at once and had to be displayed at a funeral, the chances were that if embalmed by these methods it could be preserved for the necessary period, but how long it remained un-decomposed after burial is in most cases unknown. Occasionally, a coffin was opened several years after burial and the state of the body revealed. For example, Edward the Confessor's coffin was opened thirty-six years after his death, and the body was still recognisable.[32] Abbot Baldwin had been a monk of St Denis in Paris, the burial place of the kings of France. He was a physician and may well have known the current techniques for embalm-ment. The prior of St Edmunds under Abbot Baldwin, Benedict Saxo, who died in 1094, must have been embalmed for when his coffin was opened 'more than thirty years' after his burial, his body was found 'almost incorrupt', and exuded a sweet smell.[33] The last detail is significant because one method of embalmment included stuffing the body after it had been devisced, and packing it around, with aromatic herbs.

There are reasons for suggesting that Baldwin might have used a newly embalmed body for display at the translation of St Edmund in 1095. Quite possibly when he opened the coffin he found only bones and decayed matter which were totally unfit to show to witnesses as proof of St Edmund's incorrup-tion. In that case he might have substituted a newly embalmed body. Such a pious fraud is not inconceivable considering the value placed in the middle ages on the possession of the relics of saints. A church would be prepared to resort to theft or fraud in order to acquire relics or protect the fame of those it owned. Relics drew pilgrims and pilgrims gave offerings, an important source of revenue.[34]

[30] *JB*, p. 114. Cf. Gransden, 'Alleged incorruption', pp. 154, 164 nn. 114–18.

[31] Ibid., pp. 136, 156–7 and nn. 12–14.

[32] 'La vie de S. Édouard le Confesseur par Osbert de Clare', ed. Marc Bloch, *Analecta Bolland-iana*, xli (1923), pp. 121–3. See also *The Life of King Edward the Confessor*, ed. Frank Barlow (London, Edinburgh etc., 1962), pp. 114–15. For this and other examples, including the question of St Cuthbert's incorruption, see, with references, Gransden, 'Alleged incorrup-tion', pp. 135–6, 155–7 nn.

[33] *Memorials*, i. 351.

[34] See Nilson, *Cathedral Shrines*, pp. 26–33, 105–10. Much has been written about the cult of saints and relics. See e.g.: R. C. Finucane, *Miracles and Pilgrims. Popular Beliefs in Medieval England* (London, 1977); P. J. Geary, *Furta Sacra* (Princeton, 1978, revised edn 1990), pp. 23–4; Jonathan Sumption, *Pilgrimage, an Image of Medieval Religion* (London, 1975), pp. 165–7.

The money was often used for the care of shrines and for church-building.[35] In 1095 the cult of St Edmund was of the utmost importance to Baldwin. He was engaged on building the immense Romanesque church of St Edmund and in establishing the abbey as one of the most privileged in England. His ultimate purpose was to make St Edmunds a pre-eminent centre of Christian worship. But meanwhile St Edmund's cult had been threatened by rumours at court that the martyr's incorrupt body did not lie at St Edmunds at all, and the king had frustrated Baldwin's desire to have the completed presbytery of the new church dedicated: Rufus refused to grant a licence for the dedication.[36] It seems possible in these circumstances that Baldwin would have considered himself justified in substituting a newly embalmed body for decayed remains in the coffin. An added justification could have been Abbo's statement that St Edmund's body was incorrupt: if, despite Abbo's testimony, by some unlucky chance, no such body was found in the coffin, Baldwin might well have considered it his duty to supply one and so protect the fame of his church and confirm the belief of the faithful. (In the same way, if a church knew that it owned a certain estate but had no charter to prove it, it might consider itself obliged to forge one.)

Supposing, as seems not improbable, that Baldwin had placed a newly embalmed body in St Edmund's coffin in 1095, this, or its remains, must have been what Samson found when he opened the coffin in 1198. In that case, it seems probable that embalmment had been unusually successful and that this was the body described by Jocelin. On the other hand, if Samson found only decayed remains, he with Hugh, the sacrist, and Walter, the physician, must have substituted a newly embalmed body for display to witnesses. To some extent the circumstances of 1095 were repeated in 1198. Samson was faced with heavy expenses, both for the repair of St Edmund's shrine and for building work on the church. His objective, like Baldwin's, was to have the church conse-crated. He too was vigorously promoting St Edmund's cult. Although there was no rumour that St Edmund did not lie in the shrine, there was one that his body had suffered in the fire and was no longer perfect.[37] Samson's anxiety on this point is reflected in Jocelin's account of Samson's minute inspection of the body before witnesses to prove its perfection. He counted the toes and no doubt also the fingers, probably to assure himself and others that none was missing, perhaps stolen to serve as a precious relic in another church.

The sequence of events recorded by Jocelin as immediately preceding the viewing of the body shows that Samson could have perpetrated the same pious fraud as Baldwin may have done. Perhaps he, Hugh and Walter had the embalmed body of a recently dead man in reserve, ready to put in the coffin if it was found to contain nothing but bones and decayed matter and was quite unfit to show to witnesses. Walter, a physician, must have known how to preserve a body for a

---

[35] See: C. R. Cheney, 'Church-building in the Middle Ages', in idem, *Medieval Texts and Studies* (Oxford, 1973, repr. from *Bulletin of the John Rylands Library*, xxxiv (1951–2), pp. 20–36), pp. 355–8; Geary, op. cit., pp. 23–4; Sumption, op. cit., pp. 158–65.

[36] *De Miraculis*, p. 86.

[37] JB, p. 109. Above pp. 99–100.

funeral, as Baldwin surely did. There are contemporary examples of embalment for this purpose: for instance, when, in 1216, King John died at Newark, Adam, abbot of Croxton, a 'most skilled' physician, embalmed his body for transport to Worcester where it was buried,[38] and in 1235 the body of William, abbot of St Albans, was embalmed in the abbey ready for display at his funeral.[39] St Edmund's coffin could have been opened, the contents inspected and if necessary a newly embalmed body substituted late on Monday night and very early on Tuesday morning, 23–24 November, while the convent slept. The lid of the coffin then would have been nailed down again and the coffin wrapped and bound up as before, ready to be re-opened before witnesses on the Wednesday night.[40]

Whether or not Samson resorted to pious fraud in order to protect the interests of his church cannot be known for certain, but in any event he seems to have achieved his objective. He convinced witnesses of the incorruption and perfection of St Edmund's body. From them the belief would have spread to the faithful at large. The belief seems to have been so well established that no later abbot considered it necessary to inspect the body again.[41] And Samson took

---

[38] 'Abbas igitur canonicorum Crokestoniae peritissimus in phisica, qui medicus regis tunc temporis extiterat facta anathomia de corpore regio, ut honestius portaretur, viscera copioso sale conspersa, in sua domo transportata, honorifice fecit sepeliri.' Matthew Paris, *Chron. Maj.*, ii. 668.

[39] 'Corpus equidem, cum in camera Abbatis ubi obiit … examinaretur, exutum est et lotum, et nisi die antecedenti proxima rasus non extitisset, utique raderetur corona et barba ejus. Deinde intromissis non utique omnibus, sed maturis et discretis fratribus, et uno solo ministro saeculari, videlicet, ministro Sacristae, qui officium anatomiae peracturus erat, incisionne corpus apertum est, a trachea usque ad occiduam corporis partem, et quicquid in corpore repertum est, in quadam cuva repositum est, sale conspersum … Corpus autem, interius aceto lotum, et imbutum, et multo sale respersum, et resutum. Et hoc factum est, circumspecte et prudenter, ne corpus, per triduum et amplius reservandum, tetrum aliquem odorem olfacientibus generaret, et corpus tumulandum contrectantibus aliquod offendiculum praesentaret.' GASA, i. 301–2.

[40] An excellent example of a pious fraud involving the 'invention' of supposititious relics comes from Glastonbury. In 1184 the abbey church and most of the buildings suffered a disastrous fire. To help pay the cost of rebuilding Abbot Henry de Soilly exploited the cult of relics. His efforts culminated in 1191 with the 'discovery' of the skeletons of King Arthur and Queen Guinevere buried in the precincts. See: Gerald of Wales, *Opera*, ed. J. S. Brewer et al. (RS, 1861–91, 8 vols), iv. 47–8; viii. 127; Adam of Damerham, *Historia de rebus gestis Glastoniensibus*, ed. Thomas Hearne (Oxford, 1727, 2 vols), ii. 341–3. For discussion of the episode see e.g.: Gransden, 'The growth of the Glastonbury traditions and legends', *JEH*, xxvi (1976), repr. idem, *Legends, Traditions and History*, pp. 153–74, and *Glastonbury Abbey and the Arthurian Tradition*, ed. J. P. Carley (Cambridge, 2001), pp. 29–53, pp. 349–58; Philip Rahtz, *Glastonbury* (London, 1993), pp. 39, 43–4; Julia Crick, 'The marshalling of Antiquity: Glastonbury's historical dossier', in *The Archaeology and History of Glastonbury Abbey. Essays in Honour of the ninetieth birthday of C. A. Ralegh Radford*, ed. Lesley Abrams and J. P. Carley (Woodbridge, 1991), pp. 217–20. See also *Glastonbury Abbey and the Arthurian Tradition*, ed. Carley, index, under 'Arthur. Exhumation of' (p. 630).

[41] Norman Scarfe rightly pours scorn on the theory put forward by some scholars that St Edmund's body was stolen during the raid on East Anglia in 1216–17, and that the dauphin, Louis, who led the invasion, later presented them to St Sernin's in Toulouse. Scarfe, 'The

practical steps to prevent the recurrence of fire in the future. He deposed the two keepers of the shrine (as well as the keeper of St Botolph's shrine) and appointed new keepers. He issued regulations for the better care of the shrine and had the space under the wooden platform filled with stone and mortar so that inflammable objects could not be stored there.[42]

It remains to consider the financial value of the shrine. The gold and silver and the gems which ornamented it were the abbey's only reserves of capital which were reasonably safe from depredation by an impecunious king – or by robbers. No accounts of offerings to the shrine itself survive, but the valuation of 1292 of St Edmunds' spiritualities estimates the shrine's annual income at £40.[43] This would seem to be an average income for a well-established major shrine like St Edmund's. It was probably slightly more in Samson's day as a result of his energetic promotion of the cult. It was probably rather less than 4% of the abbey's total annual income at this time which was probably rather more than £2,000.[44] But income from the shrine was by no means all profit. It had to cover pay to the shrine keepers and their servants, and for the shrine's upkeep and lighting, besides the cost of hospitality for pilgrims and other visitors, which was a burden on the abbey's finances.[45] Nevertheless, there would have been some profit even after all necessary deductions. The fame of St Edmund's shrine benefited the abbey in more general ways. Pilgrims who came primarily to visit the shrine would make offerings in St Edmund's chapel in the cemetery, where his bier was kept,[46] as well as at other holy places in the precincts.[47] In the abbey

body of St Edmunds. An essay in necrology', *PSIA*, xxxi, pp. 303–17, and idem, *Suffolk*, pp. 65–8. In 1901 a casket containing the supposed relics of St Edmund from St Sernin were donated to the archbishop of Westminster, with the intention that they should be enshrined in the new Westminster cathedral. But such strong doubts were cast on their authenticity that the relics remained, and still remain, in their temporary resting place in the family mausoleum of the dukes of Norfolk in the vault of their chapel in Arundel castle. See Richard Gem, with an appendix by Tony Waldron, 'A scientific examination of the relics of St Edmund at Arundel castle', in *Bury St Edmunds*, ed. Gransden, pp. 45–56. Also: M. R. James's letter to *The Times*, 2 August 1901; Ernest Clark in *The Bury Post*, 31 August 1901 (repr. as a pamphlet).

42 *JB*, p. 116.
43 *Bury Chron.*, p. 112. For comparison with income from other shrines see Nilson, *Cathedral Shrines*, pp. 144–67 passim. Income from the shrine of St Thomas Becket at Canterbury, 1291–3, far exceeded that from other British shrines.
44 See J. C. Cox in *VCH Suffolk*, ii. 68–9.
45 Nilson, pp. 182–7.
46 James, *Abbey*, pp. 188–9. The bier was the cart which reputedly Egelwin used to carry St Edmund's body to London for safety during the Danish raids. It appears in the cycle of thirty-two beautiful miniatures illustrating the Life and Miracles of St Edmund executed at St Edmunds c. 1130, now Pierpont Morgan Library, New York, MS 736 (see ff. 7–22v; ff. 20, 20v for the cart). For the MS see Kauffmann, *Romanesque MSS*, pp. 72–4 no. 34. For a detailed description of the miniatures see McLachlan, *Scriptorium*, pp. 74–104 and pls 22–53 (monochrome); for the cart see pls 48, 49. The miniatures with the cart are also reproduced in Cynthia Hahn, 'Peregrinatio et Natio', the illustrated Life of Edmund, king and martyr', *Gesta*, xxx pt 2 (1991), figs 9, 10 (monochrome).
47 For the numerous chapels, altars etc. in the abbey church and precincts see below Chapter 13 passim.

church itself they would probably put money in the pyx and make offerings at
some at least of the chapels and altars dedicated to the many saints venerated
at St Edmunds. They might also make offerings at the crosses which stood in
the church, and at altars in the crypt, which in total mounted to a considerable sum, as will be seen.[48] Moreover, in a general way, the abbey's spiritual
prestige derived from St Edmund's shrine and to a lesser extent from the other
holy places and objects in the abbey church and precincts, besides helping to
attract testamentary bequests and other kinds of benefactions. It also increased
the abbey's temporal power: fear of the martyr's vengeance on enemies of his
church might even frighten an opponent into compliance.[49]

Secondary cults at St Edmunds

Samson's preoccupation with St Edmund, king and martyr, his shrine and cult,
is reflected in Jocelin who shows practically no interest in the cults of the many
other saints venerated at St Edmunds. And, of course, St Edmund's cult is the
subject of the revised and enlarged version composed under Samson of the late
eleventh-century De Miraculis.[50] Nevertheless, as at most other shrine churches,
numerous secondary cults existed at St Edmunds alongside that of its spiritual
patron. Most of the additional saints venerated were those whose cults were
widespread in Christendom but a few were of local fame and their cults peculiar
to St Edmunds.

Of the secondary cults at St Edmunds, that of the Virgin Mary was pre-
eminent.[51] Indeed, the earliest tenth-century church of Beodericisworth was
dedicated to St Mary and was where the body reputedly of St Edmund was first
translated, perhaps in the reign of King Athelstan (925–39).[52] The evidence is
uncertain, but St Edmund probably still rested in a church dedicated to St Mary
at Beodericisworth, in a shrine served by a community of secular priests, in 1020
when the secular community was replaced by a Benedictine one. A new church
was then built to house the shrine; this church was consecrated in 1032 by Archbishop Æthelnoth and dedicated 'in honour of Christ, St Mary and St Edmund'.
This is stated in one of the notes entered in the margin of the Easter Tables,
opposite years 1032–5, in the mid-eleventh-century Bury psalter, now MS Reg.
Lat. 12 in the Vatican library.[53] The new church was probably the large round
church, part of whose foundations was discovered in 1275 during excavations

---

[48] Below pp. 120–21.
[49] See below pp. 124–5, 128.
[50] Below pp. 126 et seq.
[51] For a fuller discussion of the cult of St Mary at St Edmunds, with further references, see
Gransden, 'Cult of St Mary'.
[52] Three Lives of English Saints, p. 82; De Miraculis, pp. 29–30. Cf. Gem and Keen, 'Late
Anglo-Saxon finds', p. 1, and Ridyard, Royal Saints, pp. 213 and n. 14, 222 and n. 45,
224.
[53] Reg. Lat. 12, f. 17v. The entry is printed in New Pal. Soc. Facs, ed. Thompson and others,
commentary to pls 66–8. See above p. 100 and n. 28.

clearing the site for the spacious new Lady Chapel founded by Simon of Luton.[54] A centrally-planned church would have been equally appropriate to a church dedicated to St Mary and to one dedicated to St Edmund. Some churches so designed were built in honour of St Mary: the prototype was the church allegedly containing her tomb outside Jerusalem. And a centrally-planned church was not uncommonly built as a royal mausoleum or as a martyrium, the prototype of the former being the imperial chapel of Aachen, the burial place of Charlemagne, and of the latter the Holy Sepulchre in Jerusalem: thus, a centrally-planned church was doubly suitable for the tomb of St Edmund who was both a king and a martyr.[55]

It is clear from the Bury psalter that the cult of St Mary thrived at *Beodericisworth* in the mid-eleventh century. Both her Nativity (8 September) and her Assumption (15 August) are entered in the calendar in gold majuscules indicating their status as major feasts.[56] And one of the twenty-two prayers appended to the psalter is a supplication to her, and another is a supplication to the Lord for protection for the church of St Mary, St Edmund and of those peculiarly Bury saints, Botolf and Jurmin, besides Michael the archangel and Gabriel.[57] The psalter's ornament also shows her importance: one of the two full-page illuminations, the Q (the first letter of Psalm 1), encloses a female figure enthroned, holding a sceptre and a palm frond; the image could represent St Mary personifying the Church and/or St Mary as the Queen of Heaven.[58]

Meanwhile, the cult of St Edmund was fostered by abbots Ufi (1020–44) and Leofstan (1044–65), but received its greatest impetus from Abbot Baldwin (1065–97) who was determined that the new Romanesque church should become one of the greatest shrine churches and cult centres in western Europe. When building started on the new church, there was still a church dedicated solely to St Mary standing close to the shrine church which Æthelnoth had dedicated in 1032. But to make space for the southern arm of the new Romanesque church this old St Mary's had to be pulled down.[59] However, under Abbot Anselm (1121–48) it was replaced by another St Mary's to serve as a parish church also within the abbey's precincts – the antecedent of the beautiful, large

---

54 *Bury Chron.*, p. 58; James, *Abbey*, pp. 188–9; Gransden, 'Alleged incorruption', p. 141.
55 See: Gem, 'Towards an iconography', pp. 9–12 passim; Gransden, op. cit., p. 141 and nn. 58–9.
56 *Kalendars*, ed. Wormald, pp. 247, 248.
57 See Wilmart, 'Prayers', pp. 204–5. For prayers to St Mary, including reference to this example, see Clayton, *Cult of the Virgin Mary*, pp. 109–10. For SS Jurmin and Botolf see below pp. 111–13.
58 Reproduced in *New Pal. Soc. Facs.*, ed. Thompson and others (above n. 28), pl. 66. Discussed and also reproduced in Elżbieta Temple, *Anglo-Saxon Manuscripts 900–1066* (*A Survey of Manuscripts Illuminated in the British Isles*, ed. J. J. G. Alexander, ii, London, 1976), p. 100, pl. 262; T. H. Ohlgren, *Anglo-Saxon Textual Illustration* (Kalamazoo, 1992), pp. 44, 265, pl. 3.17. The miniature is noticed in Clayton, *Cult of the Virgin Mary*, p. 169, 170. For St Mary as Queen of Heaven see ibid., pp. 164–5. For the sceptre and the palm frond in Marian iconography see ibid., pp. 158–9, 164, 167–9 passim, 171–2.
59 See *De dedicationibus*, pp. 116 lines 22–3, 117 lines 1–2. Cf. James, *Abbey*, p. 118.

fifteenth-century St Mary's which stands there today.[60] In the new abbey church itself the Lady Chapel was almost certainly the most eastern of the three apsidal chapels in the east end, and an altar dedicated to St Mary was in the crypt.[61] Abbot Anselm had an especial devotion for St Mary, which had already manifested itself in his early monastic career,[62] and her cult flourished at St Edmunds under his rule. His devotion to her found expression in liturgical innovations. According to Henry of Kirkstead, he ordained that a mass for St Mary should be celebrated daily besides 'other observances after the canonical hours'.[63] These 'other observances' were probably the private recitation of the Little Office of St Mary, which became a popular devotion in monastic and secular churches in the later middle ages. Kirkstead also claims that Anselm instituted the observance of the commemoration of St Mary which Hildefonsus, bishop of Toledo (d. 667), had ordered to be observed in his diocese.[64] This was probably the feast of the Annunciation on 18 December, a feast not celebrated on that date anywhere in England except at St Edmunds and in one other (unidentified) church in East Anglia.[65] The accepted date for the feast of the Annunciation was (and is) 25 March. In addition, Kirkstead states that Anselm instituted the observance at St Edmunds of the feast of the Conception of the Virgin Mary (8 December). Indeed, he played a leading role in promoting the spread of the

[60] The parish church of St Mary and its tower were built under Anselm by the two sacrists, Ralph and Hervey, 'men of great prudence', *Gesta Sacrist.*, p. 289. See A. B. Whittingham, 'St Mary's church, Bury St. Edmunds', *JBAA*, xxi (1865), pp. 187–8.

[61] James, *Abbey*, pp. 137–8 and plan of the church at the end of the volume.

[62] R. W. Southern very tentatively suggested that Abbot Anselm was responsible for the compilation of a collection of Marian miracle stories and examined Abbot Anselm's devotion to St Mary evident in his early monastic life. Southern, '"Miracles"', pp. 190–4, 199–202.

[63] For Henry of Kirkstead's account of Anselm's career see BL MS Harley 1005, ff. 217v–218v, printed *Bury Cust.*, pp. 121–2. The daily mass to St Mary was introduced in some other monasteries in the twelfth century. See e.g.: *Registrum Roberti Winchelsey Cantuariensis Archiepiscopi*, ed. Rose Graham (Canterbury and York Soc., li, lii, 1952, 1956), ii. 820; Roger Bowers, 'The liturgy of the cathedral and its music', in *A History of Canterbury Cathedral*, ed. Patrick Collinson, Nigel Ramsey and Margaret Sparks (Oxford, 1995), p. 414; S. E. Roper, *Medieval Benedictine Liturgy: Studies in the Formation, Structure and Content of the Monastic Votive Office c. 950–1450* (New York, 1993), pp. 46–7; Nigel Morgan, 'Texts and images of Marian devotion in English twelfth-century monasticism, and their influence on the secular church', in *Harlaxton Medieval Studies*, iv, *Monasteries and Society in Medieval Britain* (Proceedings of the 1994 Harlaxton Symposium, ed. Benjamin Thompson, Stamford, 1999), pp. 122 and n. 22 for further references, 123.

[64] *Alia Vita S. Hildefonsi per Rodericum Cerratensem scripta*, in *PL*, xcvi. 49–50; Archdale A. King, *Liturgies of the Primatial Sees* (London etc., 1957), pp. 548–52.

[65] There is no certain evidence that the feast was celebrated anywhere in England before the Conquest. See Clayton, *Cult of the Virgin Mary*, pp. 57–60 passim, 100. Nigel Morgan, to whom I am indebted for the following note, told me that of the almost 1,200 British medieval calendars he had examined, only one, twelfth-century calendar (in BL MS Cotton Cleopatra B III) from an unidentified East Anglian house, has the commemoration of St Mary on 18 December. The late medieval ordinal of Barking abbey (University College, Oxford, MS 169) provides evidence of the celebration of the commemoration on 18 December in that house (see King, op. cit., p. 550).

feast in England,[66] in which endeavour his friend, Osbert of Clare, monk of Westminster, was one of his most ardent supporters.[67] In the event, it seems that the feast's protagonists prevailed: according to a late twelfth-century source, the council of London in 1129 confirmed observance of the feast 'in the presence of King Henry and with apostolic authority'.[68]

Nevertheless, despite the importance of the Marian cult at St Edmunds, Jocelin of Brackland throws no light on it beyond providing a little information about the small statue (*Mariola*) of St Mary which stood on one side of the great crucifix on the rood-beam (a statue of St John the Evangelist stood on the other side). Jocelin records the monks' relief that the rood-beam, its ornaments and relics, escaped the fire of 1198 because they had been removed for restoration.[69] He also asserts that the two statues were given and ornamented 'with a great weight of gold' by Archbishop Stigand.[70] However, the *Gesta Sacristarum* records that Hugh, the sacrist under Abbot Anselm, having built the pulpitum, 'erected the great cross flanked by the images of the blessed Mary and St John'.[71] Perhaps Jocelin was reproducing an erroneous legend about the origins of the statues, or perhaps those given by Stigand had been stolen or sold. Whatever the truth, those which stood on the rood-beam in 1175 were obviously of great value. In that year the question arose whether they should be sold to help raise the money to pay Pope Alexander III and the cardinals for a privilege granting the abbey total exemption from any authority except that of the pope himself or of his legate *a latere*. This was the result of the attempt of the archbishop (Richard of Dover) to visit St Edmunds in virtue of his legate powers. (He was a papal legate but not *a latere*.)[72] Jocelin does not say whether the statues were sold or not.

The historiography of the rood-beam exemplifies the difficulty of examining the secondary cults at St Edmunds: the evidence is incomplete and inconclusive. Other iconographic evidence survives from St Edmunds and, though it presents problems, especially chronological ones, it is of considerable interest. There survive copies of many verses inscribed on, or near, individual works of art associated with a specific shrine or sacred object executed in honour of an

66 For Abbot Anselm's promotion of the feast of the Conception see J. A. Robinson in *Letters of Osbert of Clare*, pp. 11–17 passim, and E. W. Williamson in ibid., pp. 65–8 no. 7, 79–80 no. 13.

67 For Abbot Anselm's friendship with Osbert see ibid., pp. 11, 62–72 nos 5–8, and below p. 125.

68 The source for the authorization of the celebration of the feast of the Conception of the Virgin in the council of London of 1129 is the Gloucester copy, made c. 1200, of the chronicle of John of Worcester. See: *Chron. of John of Worcester*, iii. 86/7–88/9; *C and S*, i, pt ii, pp. 751–2 and n. 1 for further references. For the cult of St Mary at Westminster from the twelfth to the fourteenth century see Barbara Harvey, 'The monks of Westminster in the old Lady Chapel', in *Westminster Abbey: the Lady Chapel of Henry VII*, ed. Tim Tatton-Brown and Richard Mortimer (Woodbridge, 2003), pp. 5–31.

69 *JB*, p. 108.

70 *JB*, p. 5.

71 *Gesta Sacrist.*, p. 291.

72 *JB*, p. 5. Cf. *JB*, ed. Greenway and Sayers, p. 125 n. Alexander III granted the desired exemption on 23 April 1175. *Papsturkunden*, iii, no. 217. Cf. Lunt, *Fin. Relations*, pp. 117–18.

individual saint, whether a mural painting, a coloured glass window, a chandelier, a statue or whatever.[73] Some of the verses were engraved on metalwork or
wood, some painted or embroidered on hangings illustrating stories from the
Lives of saints – but some have a more general edificatory purpose and illustrate
stories from the Old and New Testaments and occasionally fables and adages.
These verses are preserved on the flyleaves of a composite volume of miscellaneous items from St Edmunds, now College of Arms MS Arundel 30 and are
in various late thirteenth- and early fourteenth-century hands.[74] None of the
works of art relating to the cult of saints survives, but these verses give an overall
impression of what a colourful and edifying spectacle the abbey church and some
of the chapels in the precincts must have presented in the late thirteenth and
early fourteenth centuries when the inscriptions were copied. Nor would their
general appearance have been much different in Samson's day. He was certainly
aware of the value of visual images to instil Christian beliefs and teach morality,
and to delight and amuse all who saw them. Jocelin records that when Samson
was subcellarer a choir-screen was built under his direction and he 'arranged
the painted stories from the Bible and composed elegiac verses for each'.[75] We
also know that Hugh, the sacrist under Abbot Samson, had the abbot's seat in
the choir 'brightly and painstakingly' painted by Simon 'the painter'.[76] M. R.
James suggests that the five lines of verse which the copyist states were 'on the
abbot's seat' would have been appropriate for a picture of the Wheel of Fortune
or of Hell. If for the latter subject, the picture is likely to have been in brilliant colours. Maybe it was Simon's picture, or at least a restored version of the
original. Similarly, James suggests that the series of ninety lines of verse telling
the Old Testament story from the Creation to the Flight into Egypt, which the
copyist states was 'in and around the choir', were those composed by Samson.[77]
However, as James admits, to make this identification it is necessary to overlook
the fact that these verses are hexameters while, according to Jocelin, Samson's
verses were elegiacs.

A number of verses were for pictures in windows and elsewhere illustrating
the Life and Legend of the Virgin Mary. Many of these were part of the ornamentation of the splendid new Lady chapel founded in 1275 by Abbot Simon
of Luton, as the Bury chronicle records.[78] However, other verses, or earlier
versions of them, could well have been in place in the twelfth century. There
is no indication where many of the verses were inscribed, but verses on the Life
and Legend of St Edmund, stated to be on a hanging, were possibly near his
shrine and perhaps were captions for illustrative pictures painted on the hang-

[73] The verses are discussed, calendared and some printed *in extenso* by James, *Abbey*, pp.
186–203.
[74] Folios 1–10 passim, 208–212v passim. For the verses and the other contents of Arundel 30,
which includes the most authoritative text of the Bury chronicle, see *Cat. Arundel MSS
(College of Arms)*, pp. 44–57.
[75] *JB*, p. 9.
[76] *Gesta Sacrist.*, p. 291; James, *Abbey*, p. 197.
[77] James, *Abbey*, pp. 200–2.
[78] *Bury Chron.*, p. 58; James, *Abbey*, pp. 142–3, 190, 192.

ings.[79] A number of verses relate to secondary cults besides that of St Mary. Six lines of verse were 'at the Relics'.[80] The subject was the story of how St Edmund protected his people from the rapacity of King Swegn and killed him.[81] Verses on the Life of Christ were on a hanging 'over (*ultra*) the door of Relics'.[82] James indicates that the chapel of Relics was the apsidal chapel in the north transept.[83] Verses for twenty-two scenes from the Life of St John the Evangelist were in the windows around his chapel 'at the door of the crypt':[84] the chapel was probably in the south transept.[85] Next to it was apparently a chapel of St Nicholas with a painted window with pictures with appropriate verses illustrating his legend, followed by a few illustrating the Life of Christ.[86] There are verses for a window illustrating scenes from the legend of St Martin of Tours but where his altar or chapel was located puzzled James: he suggests that it was in the choir, on the south-east side.[87] There are also verses illustrating scenes from the life of St Benedict probably in a window and possibly near his altar in the infirmary.[88]

The main interest of this collection of verses is for hagiography and to illustrate the use of art in the service of religion. In that respect they are extremely interesting, but for more precise information about the secondary cults of St Edmunds it is necessary to turn to other written sources. The most reliable information about the pre-Conquest cults of St Edmunds is the mid-eleventh century psalter in the Vatican, discussed above for the value of its evidence concerning the cult of St Mary.[89] For the other secondary cults the calendar and litany are helpful.[90] Of the feast-days entered in the calendar in gold majuscules, indicating that they were major feasts, are a few particularly associated with St Edmunds. Thus, besides the Nativity of St Mary and the dedication of the church at *Beodericisworth* in 1032 to Christ, her and St Edmund, and the Translation of St Edmund on 30 March and his Translation on 31 March by Aelfric the bishop,[91] are two unusual saints, Jurmin and Botolf: the former's cult was

---

[79] Ibid., p. 187.

[80] Ibid., pp. 190–1.

[81] Ibid., p. 137. Below p. 125 and n. 175.

[82] Ibid., p. 202.

[83] Ibid., see plan at the end of the volume and above, fig. 8.

[84] Ibid., p. 191.

[85] Ibid., pp. 140–1 and plan at the end of the volume and above, fig. 8.

[86] Ibid., pp. 140–1, 191–2.

[87] Ibid., pp. 138, 199.

[88] Ibid, pp. 186–7. James points out that it is only by inference that we attribute these verses to St Edmunds.

[89] Above pp. 106–7 and nn.

[90] The litany in Vatican MS Reg. Lat. 12, ff. 159–61, is printed in *Anglo-Saxon Litanies of the Saints*, ed. Michael Lapidge (Henry Bradshaw Soc., cvi, 1991 for 1989–90), pp. 296–9. The feasts of St Peter (29 June), St Benedict (21 March) and All Saints (1 November) are all entered in the calendar in gold majuscules. *Kalendars*, ed. Wormald, pp. 245, 242, 250 respectively.

[91] Ibid., p. 242. The year-dates of the translation on 30 March and that on 31 March 'by Ælfric the bishop', is problematical. Possibly the second was in 967 when 31 March was on a Sunday and Ælfric I was bishop of Elmham. Possibly the translation on 30 March was in 951 (again on a Sunday) when Theodred, a notable benefactor of St Edmunds, was

exclusive to St Edmunds and the latter was venerated in only a very few other churches. The translation of St Jurmin, 'confessor', was celebrated on 24 January and of St Botolf 'bishop of the East Angles' ('Entalium Anglorum Antistis') on 15 February.[92] The importance of their cults in the abbey is highlighted by the psalter's litany. They, St Edmund, St Peter, St Benedict and All Saints are the only ones honoured with a double invocation, an honour especially accorded to Christ. Moreover, as has been seen, one of the prayers in the psalter beseeches the Lord to protect the church of St Mary and St Edmund and of the confessors SS Botolf and Jurmin.[93]

The occurrence of the translations of SS Botolf and Jurmin in the psalter's calendar confirms the statement in a marginal addition to the Bury copy (probably made before 1143) of the chronicle of John of Worcester that the bodies of these two confessors were translated to St Edmunds in the time of Abbot Leofstan.[94] The addition states that Jurmin's body was discovered at Grundisburg (*Grundesburc*) and Botolf's at Blythburg (*Blihteburc*), both vills in east Suffolk. Jurmin's body was found in a lead coffin with a funerary inscription. The epitaph is not in the same hand as the preceding text. It reads 'I, Jurmin, command in the name of the Holy Trinity that no one dares plunder this burial place until the day of the resurrection, otherwise let him know that he is removed from the company of saints.' The translation of St Botolf 'previously a bishop' is described in hagiographic detail: it took place at night and a heavenly beam of light dispelled the darkness and shone upon the tomb. William of Malmesbury, writing in 1125, treats the 'evidence' about Jurmin and Botolf with caution.[95] He visited St Edmunds and says that 'neither there or anywhere else' has he heard anything about their acts, unless the first was the brother of St Etheldreda and the second a bishop, as is asserted. His tentative identifications of Jurmin and Botolf, receives some support from the *De Miraculis Sancti Eadmundi*: it records the translation into the new Romanesque church in 1095 of the 'relics of the gentle bishop and the royal confessor Jurmin'.[96] However, other monasteries claimed to have relics of St Botolf besides St Edmunds. William of Malmesbury records that Folcard, abbot of Thorney (1068–1084/5), had translated the bodies of many saints but that he will not record them because the names sounded so

bishop of London. Cf. D. N. Dumville, *English Caroline Script and Monastic History: Studies in Benedictinism A.D. 950–1030* (Woodbridge, 1993), pp. 42–3, and Gransden, 'Alleged incorruption', pp. 139, 158 nn. 35–7.

92 *Kalendars*, ed. Wormald, pp. 240, 241.

93 '… et sancto Eadmundo uictori ad martyrii nobilitatem, quem celestis priuilegii primiscrinium in alis sanctorum confessorum tuorum Botolfi et Hiurmini hierarchiasti …', Wilmart, 'Prayers', p. 215.

94 *Chron. of John of Worcester*, ii. 316–17. (For the date of Bodl. Lib. MS 297 see ibid., p. xvii.) Also printed *Memorials*, i. 352. See: Norman Scarfe, 'St Botolph, the Iken cross, and the coming of East Anglian Christianity', in idem, *Suffolk* (1986, reprinted from *PSIAH*, xxxi (1984), pp. 279–91), pp. 39–51; Ridyard, *Royal Saints*, p. 233 n. 90; James, *Abbey*, p. 157; Pestell, *Landscapes of Monastic Foundation*, pp. 92 and n. 147, 267 under 'Botolph, St'. For surveys of information about Botolf and Jurmin see Farmer, *Saints*, pp. 51–2, 228.

95 William of Malmesbury, *Gesta Pont.*, p. 156.

96 *De Miraculis*, pp. 88–9.

barbarous; he adds that his reticence was not owing to disbelief but reluctance to expose these saints to ridicule.[97] One of the Lives of saints written by Folcard is the Life of St Botolf, and Thorney's claim is supported by the Anglo-Saxon list of saints' resting-places which states that St Botolf lay at Thorney.[98] According to a tradition at Ely, King Edgar ordered the distribution of St Botolf's relics; the head went to Ely, half the bones to Thorney and the king kept the other half.[99] St Edmunds' pre-Conquest claim, therefore, was not the only one.

However, the evidence of the Bury psalter and twelfth-century tradition demonstrate that Abbot Leofstan added these two saints to the stock of cults at St Edmunds. According to post-Conquest sources, the cult of Jurmin does not seem to have been an important one. After their translation into the new church, he and Botolf shared an altar with St Thomas, apostle and martyr, whose cult was already well-established at St Edmunds (his feast, 21 December, is entered in the calendar in the Bury psalter in blue majuscules).[100] It seems that the cults of all three were fostered in the twelfth century. One story of a vision experienced by an aged and dying monk of St Edmunds, Radulphus, states that when he was a young monk he had been instructed by Abbot Hugh (probably Hugh I, 1157–80) to publicize the altar of St Thomas and of having ornamented the reliquary and the reliquaries of Botolf and Jurmin 'and some others' with gold and gems, in order to display them well.[101] Similarly, the Bury Customary refers to 'the altar of SS. Botolf, Thomas and Jurmin and their reliquaries', which M. R. James tentatively places to the east of St Edmund's shrine.[102] Unlike the cult of St Jurmin, that of St Botolf retained some importance in the thirteenth century and later. On 1 February 1292 Nicholas IV granted an indulgence of a year and four days to those visiting St Edmunds on the feast of St Botolf (17 June), on the Assumption of the Blessed Virgin Mary and on the feast of St Edmund.[103] Furthermore, a document of c. 1300 records that the sacrist had to provide seventeen 'liberal candles' for the circular chandelier (*corona*) at his altar.[104]

Of the post-Conquest sources, the most informative about the progressive increase in the number of secondary cults at St Edmunds in the twelfth century is the tract known as the *De dedicationibus altarum, capellarum etc., apud Sanctum Edmundum*. It was probably originally composed early in Henry II's reign but a monk edited, enlarged and continued it in, or soon after, Abbot Samson's time.

---

97   William of Malmesbury, *Gesta Pont.*, pp. 327 and n. 4, 328.

98   F. Liebermann, *Die Heiligen Englands* (Hanover, 1889), p. 15; Ridyard, *Royal Saints*, p. 108 and n. 43.

99   *Liber Eliensis*, ed. E. O. Blake (Camden Soc., 3rd ser., xcii, 1962), p. 222 and n. 1. See Ridyard, op. cit., p. 203 and n. 120.

100   *Kalendars*, ed. Wormald, p. 251.

101   Horstman, *Nova Legenda*, pp. 655–6; *Memorials*, i. 366–7; James, *Abbey*, p. 157. '... iussuque dompni abbatis Hugonis altare sancti Thome martiris edisset, hac sanctum Botulphum, illac sanctum Jurminum, medioque reliquias Thome et aliorum quamplurium auratis et gemmates feretris preclare collacasset'.

102   *Bury Cust.*, p. 12 line 16. James, *Abbey*, pp. 137, 149, 160.

103   *Les registres de Nicholas IV*, ed. E. Langlois, *Bibliothèque des Écoles françaises d'Athènes et de Rome*, 2nd ser. (Paris, 1886–1905, 2 vols), ii. 875 no. 6551.

104   BL MS Harley 645, f. 50.

Later a final paragraph was added recording the destruction of the ancient church of St Edmund in 1175 and the building by Abbot Simon of the new Lady chapel in its place.[105] The monastic editor of the original tract was a judicious scholar and recognized that much of his evidence was hearsay. For instance, he writes about the provenance of the ancient and much venerated cross which stood in the southernmost of the three apsidal chapels in the east end, the chapel dedicated to St Peter and later to St Cross, with wise caution:

> some believe it had been in St Edmund's church long before the introduction of monks. Others [believe] that when Abbot Leofstan went to Rome, he beheld the sacred cross venerated in the city of Lucca, which so vividly represents the form and size of the Lord's body. On returning home he had a cross made just like it.[106]

The writer goes on to say that he has no idea what has happened to the privilege which Leofstan obtained for the abbey – whether it has perished or, indeed, whether he ever got one. The writer's scepticism is well-founded for it seems unlikely that Leofstan went to Rome, visiting Lucca on the way. On the other hand, the story could well relate to Abbot Baldwin who visited Lucca most probably on his journey to Rome in 1071. He went to Rome in order to obtain the privilege of exemption from Alexander II (1061–73). The latter, then called Anselm, had been bishop of Lucca from 1057–61 and was responsible for building the magnificent new cathedral of St Martin which was consecrated with gorgeous splendour on 6 October.[107] Since Alexander's bull in favour of St Edmunds is dated 27 October in Rome,[108] it is quite possible that Baldwin reached Lucca in time for the consecration ceremony. There is strong evidence indicating that he, not Leofstan, established the cult of St Edmund in St Martin's cathedral. He apparently gave it a copy of Abbo's *Passio Sancti Eadmundi* and probably relics of the saint.[109] Maybe on this visit he was deeply moved and impressed by the

---

[105] Discussed and printed in *Bury Cust.*, pp. xl–xli, 114–21.

[106] Ibid., p. 115 lines 11–20.

[107] For Baldwin's visit to Lucca and the establishment of St Edmund's cult there, see *De miraculis*, pp. 67–8: '[E]x sacri martyrii exuviis pii protectoris [Eadmundi] martyris in diversis mundi partibus vectis … domnus et abbas Baldwinus Romam proficiscens secum de supradictis sancti spoliis tulit, pluribus impertiens, tam sanctae devotionis gratia, quam ut dilataretur sanctus opinione vera. Quibus pignoribus sacris in Italia, in civitate quae Lucas dicitur, quibusdam fidelibus impertitis, et Dei nomine Christique testis [Eadmundi] veneratione in porticu quadam ecclesiae eximii confessoris Christi Martini consecrato altari, provenit gratia Dei invocatione martyris [Eadmundi].' The story of the cure of a young Italian boy through St Edmund's intercession follows. Cf.: Gransden, '"Passio"', pp. 71–8 and nn.; D. M. Webb, 'The holy Face of Lucca', *Anglo-Norman Studies*, ix, *Proceedings of the Battle Conference* (Woodbridge, 1987), pp. 235–7. See also below, p.130 and n. 203.

[108] The bull is printed: *Chron. of John of Worcester*, ii. 647–8 and cf. iii. 309; *Memorials*, i. 345–7; *Pinch. Reg.*, i. 3–4. The papal privilege was a weapon against the claim of the bishop of Elmham, then Thetford, Herfast (1070–84) to move the episcopal see to St Edmunds. See Gransden, 'Baldwin', pp. 69–71 and nn.

[109] For discussion of the copies of Abbo of Fleury's *Passio Sancti Eadmundi* in the two surviving magnificent twelfth-century giant Passionaries in the Biblioteca Capitulare in Lucca (Codd. P+, ff. 180–183v, and F, ff. 101v–107v), and in the giant Lucchese Passionary now

revered cross, had it measured and a replica made at St Edmunds for the new Romanesque church. And maybe he was also responsible for fostering the cult of St Martin in the abbey. However, the feast of St Martin (11 November) was already a major feast at St Edmunds by the mid-eleventh century[110] and it was Abbot Anselm, not Baldwin, who had an altar dedicated to St Martin in the new church.[111] (It was probably the northern apsidal chapel of the two chapels in the north transept.[112]) In any case, the cult of St Martin was widespread and his feast observed in all the pre-Conquest Benedictine monasteries whose calendars are printed by Francis Wormald.

Baldwin had been a monk of St Denis, Paris, which, as the author of *De dedicationibus* explains, was why he built 'a large and beautiful church' dedicated to that saint. There 'he assembled a by no means small community of clerics and established a parish for the town'.[113] This church, however, was pulled down by Anselm to make way for the west end of the great Romanesque church,[114] and the most northerly apsidal chapel in the west end of the new church was dedicated to St Denis.[115] In the course of building works bones were disinterred. Baldwin built a wooden chapel to house them; Anselm replaced it with a stone chapel and had it dedicated to St Stephen the protomartyr,[116] whose feast (26 December) appears as a major feast in the calendar in the Vatican psalter.[117] The fact that Baldwin came from abroad explains the introduction of a new secondary cult at St Edmunds, that of St Denis. Similarly, two subsequent foreign abbots, Alebold and Anselm, added more saints to those already venerated at St Edmunds. Alebold, abbot 1114–1119, had been successively a clerk at Bari, a monk of Bec and then prior of S. Nicaise in Meulun on the river Seine.[118] It was he, no doubt, who introduced the cult of St Nicasius at St Edmunds.

in Rome, in the archives of S. Giovanni Laterano (Cod. 81, ff. 192–196v), see Gransden, '"Passio"', pp. 72–4. The text of these copies of the *Passio* most probably descends from a booklet (*libellus*) comprising a copy of the work which was probably brought to Lucca by Baldwin and his companions.

110 *Kalendars*, ed. Wormald, p. 250.
111 *De dedicationibus*, p. 116 line 1.
112 Whittingham, 'Bury St. Edmunds Abbey', p. 173 and plan. Cf. James, *Abbey*, pp. 138, 140, 192 and plan. Cf. Hills, 'Antiquities', pp. 113–14.
113 *De dedicationibus*, p. 118 lines 8–11 and nn. 1–3. See ibid., pp. 123–4. The text there printed from Harley 3977 should be compared with the earlier, fuller one in Harley 1005, f. 219v.
114 Ibid., p. 119 lines 1–5.
115 Recent excavations appear to confirm the account in *De dedicationibus*: the remains of a church have been uncovered under the north chapel and octagon of the romanesque church. See McAleer, 'West front', p. 27 and n. 33, citing a report by A. R. Dufty and C. A. R. Radford, 'Trial excavations at Bury St Edmunds in [1959]', prepared for the Society of Antiquaries (1960), pp. 4–5. Cf.: Whittingham, op. cit., p. 174 and plan; James, *Abbey*, p. 128 and plan.
116 *De dedicationibus*, p. 119 lines 1–5. James, *Abbey*, pp. 162, 185, 188.
117 *Kalendars*, ed. Wormald, p. 251.
118 *Heads*, i. 32, 242. Whittingham, op. cit., p. 173 and n. 3, misreads Dugdale (*Mon. Angl.*, iii. 155) who states that Alebold was prior of S. Nicaise 'de Molent': Whittingham reads 'Meaux' in error.

However, the cult was a rarity in medieval England and there is only one known reference to it at St Edmunds: Jocelin of Brackland states that Samson made his chaplain, Herbert, subsacrist, in the chapel of St Nicasius, promising to make him prior if he could.[119] The location of the chapel is unknown but M. R. James suggests that possibly it was one of the chapels in the triforium.[120]

Alebold ruled the abbey for little over four years. Anselm ruled for ten years and is a far more important figure in the abbey's history. He introduced two new cults, those of St Saba and St Faith. As the *De dedicationibus* explains, he had previously been abbot of St Saba in Rome. He had an altar constructed and painted in St Saba's honour: the northernmost of the three apsidal chapels in the east end was dedicated to him.[121] The cult seems to have existed nowhere else in England but the many references to St Saba's altar and chapel in St Edmunds' Customary and other records prove its continued importance in the abbey.[122] Similarly, the cult of St Faith gained considerable importance.[123] Moreover, Anselm fostered cults already existing at St Edmunds before his time. His contribution to the cult of St Mary was discussed above: his enthusiasm for it happily conformed with the long-standing veneration of St Mary at St Edmunds. Another pre-existing cult which he promoted was that of St James the apostle, whose cult was widespread in Christendom and already well-established at St Edmunds by 1050: his feast (25 July) is entered in blue letters in the calendar in the Vatican psalter.[124] When Anselm became abbot he planned to go on pilgrimage to the shrine of St James at Compostella. But 'the wise ones of the abbey', while praising his intention, thought it better if instead he built a parish church in honour of St James. This was done and on the same day that the parish church of St James was dedicated, so too was the chapel in the infirmary dedicated to St Michael.[125] Anselm also fostered the cult of St Andrew the apostle and that of St Margaret (of Antioch), both of whose feasts (30 November and 20 July respectively) appear in the calendar of the Vatican psalter though not marked for any distinction. Before Anselm's succession there was already a tiny chapel of St Andrew, which was regarded as exceptionally holy, next to the sacristy, by the south bank of the Lark. This had to be destroyed when the river was widened and Anselm and the sacrist, Hervey, had a new detached chapel built in the great cemetery and painted in St Andrew's honour. In it there were to be daily commemorations, with *Placebo* and *Dirige*, for all those buried in the great cemetery: this was agreed upon both by Anselm and Hervey and by the whole monastic community at that time.[126] On the history of the chapel of St

---

[119] *JB*, p. 125.

[120] James, *Abbey*, pp. 156, 161.

[121] *De dedicationibus*, pp. 116 lines 1–10 passim, 121 line 10. James, *Abbey*, pp. 137, 149, 161, 180.

[122] *Bury Cust.*, pp. 11–12, 55 line 19, 69 note l, 71 line 4, 73 line 11, 83 line 30, 84 line 5, 85 line 15.

[123] Ibid., 46–7 n. *e*, 99. Below pp. 133–5.

[124] *Kalendars*, ed. Wormald, p. 246.

[125] *De dedicationibus*, p. 119 lines 6–11. Above fig. 8.

[126] Ibid., p. 117 lines 3–10. For the procession from the abbey church to St Andrew's chapel

Margaret, *De dedicationibus* records that in the time of Abbot Baldwin a priest called Albold ('Eilbold') built a chapel with Baldwin's permission and dedicated it to St Margaret. 'Afterwards Lang(iua), a virgin devoted to God, was enclosed for many years in it and led an exemplary life. She died and was buried there.'[127] This priest, Albold, was a man of substance: Domesday Book records that he held the manor of Stonham with sixty acres in east Suffolk, which reverted to St Edmunds on his death.[128] His chapel of St Margaret had an attached tower of 'not small' size, but Anselm pulled it down and built another chapel dedicated to St Margaret at the south of the great cemetery.[129]

Abbot Ording (1146–56) added another secondary cult to St Edmunds' collection, that of St Giles, a widely venerated saint. His chapel was in the triforium of the abbey church 'above the chapel of St John the Evangelist' which, as has been seen, may have been the most northern of the chapels in the south transept.[130] The combination of cults of widely venerated saints with those of only local reputation such as existed at St Edmunds was typical of most great churches. But the year before Samson's succession to the abbacy a new, more unusual cult appeared in the town and was soon taken up by the monks and added to their collection of secondary cults. This was the cult of Little St Robert. The earliest reference to it is by Jocelin of Brackland.[131] He states that he had written about Little St Robert, 'a holy boy who had been martyred and was buried in our church'. Jocelin also states that 'marvels and signs were performed among the common folk, as I have set down elsewhere'. This work is lost so we do not know whether Jocelin wrote a Life of Little St Robert or just on his miracles: most probably it was on the latter. The year-date of the alleged martyrdom is supplied by two chroniclers. Gervase, monk of Christ Church, Canterbury, writing a few years after Jocelin, states in his annal for 1181 that 'a boy called Robert was martyred by the Jews at St Edmunds at Easter, who, having been buried with

---

on his feast-day see the Bury Rituale, BL MS Harley 2977, f. 3, cited in James, *Abbey*, p. 183.

127 *De dedicationibus*, p. 117 lines 11–17. A copy, in a fourteenth-century hand, survives in BL MS Harley 230, f. 170, of the reply of an (unnamed) abbot of St Edmunds to the petition of 'dominus L.' to be a recluse. The document is undated. The contents suggest that he was to live in a cell near the abbey church. He was probably an ageing monk seeking peace and quiet in his old age. See Gransden, 'The reply of a fourteenth-century abbot of Bury St. Edmunds to a man's petition to be a recluse', *EHR*, lxxv (1960), pp. 464–7. A number of monasteries had recluses in their precincts and/or on their estates for whose maintenance they were responsible. An early fourteenth-century list is in BL MS 3977, f. 78, names over forty anchorages in the Liberty. It states that the feretrars were to give each recluse on the feast of St Michael 2d or four candles or five *quadrant* (? candles of four-farthing weight). According to a fourteenth-century entry in BL MS 1005, f. 44, some believed that the said allowance to anchorites in the Liberty should be weekly, not only at Michaelmas. For anchorites elsewhere see A. K. Warren, *Anchorites and their Patrons in Medieval England* (University of California Press, 1985), pp. 18, 44, 68–9, 90, 103, 104, 106, 265 n., 266.

128 *DB, Suffolk*, pt 1, 14. 39 (f. 360v); *Feudal Docs*, pp. xcviii, 64 no. 25.

129 See Whittingham, plan, and above, fig. 8. Also Hills, 'Antiquities', pp. 116–17.

130 *De dedicationibus*, p. 119 lines 21–3; James, *Abbey*, p. 141.

131 *JB*, p. 16.

honours in the church of St Edmund, was renowned for many reputed miracles' ('... multis, ut fama fuit, claruit miraculis').[132] The year-date is corroborated by the Bury chronicler, John Taxster, who though writing considerably later, in the 1260s, used early material. But Taxster does not confirm Gervase's day-date – Easter.[133] He records that Robert was 'martyred' by the Jews at St Edmunds on 10 June. William Worcestre, writing in the late 1470s, lends some support to Taxster's day-date: he also dates the 'martyrdom' to June, but leaves a blank for the exact date, but states that Little St Robert's feast-day 'is celebrated in May', again leaving a blank for the exact date.[134]

Easter day in 1181 was on 5 April. But this day-date, that given by Gervase, is surely wrong and more reliance must be placed on the tradition at St Edmunds that the alleged martyrdom happened in June. Gervase's dating conforms with Christian and Hebrew iconography since Easter symbolized the Day of the Resurrection and the Sacrifice of the Paschal Lamb – in this case the death of an innocent little boy. The cult of Little St Robert was more or less paralleled by the cult of Little St William of Norwich, another innocent boy-child allegedly martyred by the Jews. His death took place in 1144 and his anniversary was celebrated at Norwich on Easter day[135] (although it was believed that he died on the previous Wednesday).[136] Both the story of Little St William and that of Little St Robert belong to a genre of anti-semitic literature current in western Christendom in the middle ages and later.[137] At both Norwich and St Edmunds the stories were no doubt travesties of a sad event, such as the accidental death or murder by a person or persons unknown, of a small boy. Possibly at St Edmunds the allegation of ritual murder originated in the town itself and sowed the seeds of a popular cult. Whatever the truth, the cult was promoted by the monks. Jocelin probably wrote his work on Little St Robert when he was Samson's chaplain and at his request.

Samson and the monks may have had more than one motive for fostering the cult, only one of which was anti-semitism. Any cult with popular support attracted pilgrims and so was a potential source of income – and one centred on

---

[132]　Gervase of Canterbury, *Historical Works*, ed. William Stubbs (RS, 1879–80, 2 vols), i. 296.

[133]　'Bury Chron., Critical Edition', ed. Gransden, p. 241, and *Florentii Wigorniensis monachi Chronicon ex Chronicis*, ed. Benjamin Thorpe (English Historical Soc., 1848–9, 2 vols), ii. 155.

[134]　*William Worcestre*, pp. 162/3.

[135]　The calendar in *The Customary of the Cathedral Priory Church of Norwich*, ed. J. B. L. Tolhurst (Henry Bradshaw Soc., lxxxii 1948 for 1945–6), p. 3.

[136]　Thomas of Monmouth, *The Life and Miracles of St William of Norwich*, ed. Augustus Jessop and M. R. James (Cambridge, 1896), p. lxxxix. See also J. McCulloch, 'Jewish ritual murder, William of Norwich, Thomas of Marlborough and the early dissemination of the myth', *Speculum*, lxxii (1997), pp. 3, 698–740.

[137]　See most recently with full bibliographical references A. P. Bale, 'Fictions of Judaism in Medieval England', D.Phil. thesis, University of Oxford, 2001, passim (esp. pp. 244–97 for Little St Robert's cult). For violent outbreaks of anti-semitism in the last half of the twelfth century and early thirteenth century see e.g. Roth, *Jews in England*, pp. 9–25, and R. B. Dobson, *The Jews of Medieval York and the Massacre of March 1190* (Borthwick Paper, xlv, York, 1974, revised with postscript 1996, repr. 2002), passim, esp. pp. 17–21.

a body actually buried in the church was of exceptional value. Therefore, since Little St Robert was buried in St Edmund's church, his cult would have been a welcome addition to the abbey's subsidiary cults. Moreover, in the last half of the twelfth century the monks had extra reasons for valuing his cult. The example of the cult of Little St William at Norwich had shown the power of popular belief in stories of the 'martyrdom' by Jews of innocent young boys, and the success of cults of such 'martyrs'. Little William's body was found in Thorpe wood and was buried there. But it was moved four times in the period between 1144 and 1172. It was first moved to the cathedral priory and buried in the monk's cemetery. Next, it was moved from there into the chapter-house. Thirdly, it was moved to some-where on the south side of the high altar in the cathedral itself, and, finally, to a chapel on the north side of the high altar.[138] The translations of the body to ever more honourable burial places were probably at once a response to, and a means of encouraging the growth of, the flourishing cult centred on the tomb. The cult attracted crowds of pilgrims and generous offerings,[139] and could be seen by the monks of St Edmunds as an example of the benefits accruing from such a cult.

Possibly, the monks of St Edmunds feared damage to the abbey's prestige from the success of the cult of Little St William. But a much more serious rival to the cult of St Edmund was that of Thomas Becket in Canterbury cathedral. Becket was martyred in 1170 and canonized in 1173, and his shrine quickly became the greatest cult centre in England and one famous throughout Christendom. In the latter years of the twelfth century any fall in St Edmunds' income from oblations, which contributed an important part of the revenues needed for building work on, and the ornamentation of, the abbey church, would have been a serious blow:[140] it would have obstructed Samson's ambitious plans for completing the west end and making the church more beautiful. In the event, fear of rivalry from the cult of Little St William proved unnecessary because in the course of the thirteenth century its popularity declined (though it revived somewhat later in the middle ages). The success of the cult of Little St Robert was more moderate than that of Little St William but certainly more enduring: it survived until the end of the middle ages. The Bury Customary (of c. 1234) mentions a chapel dedicated to St Robert in the abbey church: it refers to 'the keepers of the shrine and crypts and of St Robert';[141] and statutes drawn up sometime towards the end of the thirteenth century have an entry 'Memorandum concerning the crypts and St Robert', but it does not expand (the entry probably being a refer-ence to some other record).[142] But there is no evidence that a chapel or altar to St Robert was ever dedicated. Indeed, what the status of the cult was in the abbey is unclear. Robert was not a canonical saint. Possibly this explains why he is not included in the vast compendium of the Lives of saints venerated at St Edmunds in the Bury version of John of Tynemouth's *Legenda Aurea*, compiled

---

138 Thomas of Monmouth, *Life and Miracles*, ed. Jessop and James, pp. lxviii, lxxii, lxxx, 26, 31, 37, 50, 127, 188, 222.
139 Ibid., pp. lxxxii–lxxxviii, and Nilson, *Cathedral Shrines*, pp. 156–8, 170–2.
140 For the problem of the profitability of income from the oblations see below.
141 *Bury Cust.*, p. 46 line 1 and n. 1.
142 Ibid., pp. xxxii, xxxix, 109 line 22.

in the abbey c. 1377, now Bodleian Library MS Bodley 240.[143] However, perhaps the omission of St Robert was because Jocelin's Life and/or Miracles of Little St Robert was already lost and the cult quiescent at that time so that the compilers knew nothing about it. If the latter is true, it must have revived later since there are traces of its existence at St Edmunds in the fifteenth century and later. One of the fourteen verse prayers composed by the poet and monk of St Edmunds, John Lydgate (1371–1449), is addressed to St Robert[144] and the account roll of the keeper of the feretory for 1524–5 records payments to singers in St Robert's chapel on his feast-day.[145] The cult also seems to have had popular support in the town and locality, becoming in fact an element in the personal piety of the late middle ages.[146]

There remains the vexed question of the profitability of the cult of St Robert and other secondary cults at St Edmunds. Since no account of the feretrars survives earlier than 1520,[147] we have to rely on scattered references in other records, which are scrappy and often hard to interpret. In any case, as explained above, income from oblations had to be offset against the cost of caring for the pilgrims. Moreover, offerings to a shrine might take the form of candles or valuables of gold or jewels for its decoration, which cannot easily be evaluated. I have found the following evidence. In some mid-thirteenth-century accounts income from the pyx is entered as £237 7s, from the crypt 73s 4d and from St Robert 55s 4d.[148] In the assessment made in 1275 for the tenth granted by the second Council of Lyons in 1274, the shrines were assessed at 180 marks, the chapel of Relics at 10 marks, the crypts at 12 marks, the altar of St Robert at 5 marks, the prior's chapel at 6 marks, St Michael's chapel at 10s, and St Botolph's at 10s. Unexpectedly, St Leodegar (St Leger, bishop of Autun c. 616–79, sometimes considered a martyr) appears and was assessed at 30s.[149] Although his cult reached England before the Conquest and his feast-day (2 October) is entered in the calendar of the Vatican psalter (but without indication of any particular distinction),[150] he was not one of the saints invoked in St Edmunds' pre-Conquest litany,[151] nor have I found any other reference to his cult at St Edmunds. More information about income from St Edmunds' secondary cults is in the valuation made for the clerical subsidy of a tenth of spiritualities granted to the king by the Provincial Council of Ely in 1290.[152] It is listed under the income assigned to

---

[143]   Printed Horstman, *Nova Legenda*, ii. 573–688 (appendix II).

[144]   Bale, *Fictions of Judaism*, pp. 253–4, 257–9. The prayer is printed in ibid., appendix III. For Lydgate's verse prayers including the one to St Robert see Derek Pearsall, *John Lydgate* (London, 1970), pp. 264–5.

[145]   Bale, op. cit., p. 254 and n. 29 (citing the accounts of the feretrar, PRO SC 6 / Hen. VIII / 3397).

[146]   The cult in the late middle ages is fully discussed by Bale, op. cit., pp. 252–97 passim.

[147]   See Thomson, *Archives*, p. 70.

[148]   BL MS Harley 645, f. 229v.

[149]   *Bury Chron.*, p. 60, and College of Arms MS Arundel 30, ff. 213, 213v. Cf. *Bury Chron.*, p. xxvi and Lunt, *Fin. Relations*, p. 319 and n. 7.

[150]   *Kalendars*, ed. Wormald, p. 249.

[151]   For the printed text in *Anglo-Saxon Litanies*, ed. Lapidge, see above p. 111 n. 90.

[152]   See *C and S*, ii, pt 2, pp. 1091–2, and *Bury Chron.*, p. 95.

the two obedientiaries concerned, the sacrist and the almoner. Thus, the sacrist received: from the black cross, including offerings of candles, £10; the new cross 20s; from oblations to the great cross, for the dead, 30s. He also received alterage from the church of St Mary worth £24 and alterage from the church of St James worth 20 marks. The almoner received: from the pyx 225 marks; from the relics 15 marks; from the crypts 7½ marks; and from St Robert 4 marks.[153]

By the end of the end of the twelfth century the progressive accumulation of new secondary cults at St Edmunds had lost its impetus. The first continuator of the *De dedicationibus*, probably writing in Samson's time, looks back with nostalgia at the distant past:

> There were many other sacred churches or chapels here before the introduction of monks, which at various times were pulled down for new buildings, and other ones constructed [to replace them] or they were totally destroyed. Usually ignorance about them compels us to be silent. For in the place where the new infirmary stands,[154] we saw a great tower dedicated in memory of St Benedict. They said that Abbot Baldwin used to have his chambers next to it and they assert that it was built by Alfric son of Withgar and that a son of his, who was an invalid, was placed there with the permission of the abbots Uvius and Leofstan, and that he gave the manor of Melford with its rents to the church.[155] I say this so that the reader will know that there were many other sacred places here of which there is no memory or trace today.[156]

Indeed, William of Malmesbury had asserted that under Abbot Baldwin nowhere in England equalled St Edmunds in the beauty of its buildings and richness of its ornaments.[157] Nevertheless, much of what had since been lost had been replaced by new buildings and new treasures, and in Samson's day the abbey church was lavishly supplied with side altars, chapels and free-standing crosses, and, besides the two parish churches, St Mary's and St James's, there were the various chapels in the precincts. St Edmunds must have been an immensely impressive and a very interesting and edifying place to visit.

Hagiographical writing at St Edmunds:
the De Miraculis Sancti Eadmundi and other works

Samson's and the monks' concern to promote the cult of St Edmund, which was given such spectacular expression in the restoration of the shrine and the verification of the incorruption of the martyr's body, also appears in literary works

---

153 BL MS Harley 645, f. 240.

154 *Gesta Sacrist.*, p. 291; James, *Abbey*, p. 147.

155 Alfric son of Withgar had administered the eight and a half hundreds, the later Liberty of St Edmunds, for Queen Emma. *Feudal Docs*, pp. cli, clv n. 4, 48 no. 3, 60 no. 18. His gift of the manor of Edmunds and the placing of his son there was apparently transacted 'without any charter'. See the benefactors' list: BL MS Harley 1005, f. 81v; CUL MS Ff. ii. 33, f. 50v. Cf. *Mon. Angl.*, iii. 140.

156 *De dedicationibus*, p. 120.

157 William of Malmesbury, *Gesta Pont.*, p. 156.

produced in the abbey at this time. Most notable is the revised version of the *De Miraculis Sancti Eadmundi*. The original *De Miraculis Sancti Eadmundi* was composed c. 1100 and has been commonly attributed to 'Hermann, the archdeacon', who, however, has never been identified. I have argued elsewhere that the name 'Hermann' in this context is a misreading for a professional hagiographer called 'Bertrann'[158] The much better known and prolific hagiographer Goscelin, originally a monk of St Bertin's in St Omer (who was in England in the last half of the eleventh century, visiting numerous monasteries and writing saints' Lives for them),[159] mentions this Bertrann. He praises his learning and scholarly integrity and states that Bertrann was 'a foreigner, said to be an archdeacon in his own country'.[160] Goscelin also reveals that Bertrann was active at Canterbury in the 1080s and 1090s. It is likely that he was author of the original *De Miraculis* which was written at the command of Abbot Baldwin but completed after his death. The unique text is preserved in BL MS Cotton Tiberius B II (ff. 20–85v) where it is preceded by a copy of Abbo of Fleury's *Passio Sancti Eadmundi* (ff. 2–19v).[161] Tiberius B II is a handsome book and by the late fourteenth century, if not earlier, was kept by the keepers of St Edmund's shrine.[162] All subsequent works composed in the abbey about St Edmund's miracles were indebted, either directly or indirectly, to a greater or lesser extent, to this original *De Miraculis*.

The revised version of the *De Miraculis* composed in Samson's time survives in a composite manuscript, BL MS Cotton Titus A VIII.[163] This is a quarto-sized book with two distinct sections. First, ff. 2–64, is a cartulary containing miscellaneous material of the thirteenth and fourteenth centuries from Westminster abbey.[164] It includes (f. 54) a copy of the confraternity between Hugh [II] abbot of St Edmunds and William [de Humez] abbot of Westminster (1213–22) and their convents. The second section contains an abbreviated copy of Abbo of Fleury's *Passio* (ff. 65–78v) followed by the revised version of the *De Miraculis* (ff. 78v–145v). This section of the manuscript was once a separate book belonging to St Edmunds: it is on separate gatherings from the rest of the volume and has

---

158 Gransden, 'Composition and authorship of the *De Miraculis*', pp. 42–4. See Sharpe, *Handlist*, p. 79.

159 The best account of Goscelin's career and works is in *The Life of King Edward who rests at Westminster attributed to a monk of St Bertin*, ed. Frank Barlow (London, Edinburgh etc., 1962), pp. 91–112 (appendix C).

160 Goscelin refers to Bertrann in his tract *Libellus contra inanes sanctae virginis Mildrethae usurpatores*, printed M. L. Colker, 'A hagiographic polemic', *Mediaeval Studies*, xxxix (1977), pp. 60–108, see p. 77. For the tract see D. W. Rollason, *The Mildreth Legend. A Study in Early Medieval Hagiography in England* (Leicester, 1982), esp. pp. 21–2, 62–4.

161 For a description of Tiberius B II see Gransden, 'Composition and authorship of the *De Miraculis*', pp. 2–4, and eadem, '"Passio"', pp. 65–6 and pls III, IV.

162 Gransden, 'Composition and authorship of the *De Miraculis*', p. 3; eadem, '"Passio"', p. 65 and n. 280 and pl. III; Thomson, 'Library', p. 626 and n. 48.

163 Printed *Memorials*, i. 107–208. See ibid., i. lxvii, and Thomson, 'Two versions of a saint's Life', pp. 387–9.

164 Davis, *Cartularies*, p. 116 no. 1012 (which dates the cartulary to the fourteenth century without mentioning the thirteenth-century material). For the confraternity see below p. 124 and n. 172.

the abbey's class-mark, S. 153. The distinguished antiquary and bibliographer Henry of Kirkstead, monk of St Edmunds, entered the class-mark and wrote many learned notes in the margins.[165] Since he died c. 1379, the book cannot have passed to Westminster until after that date. But the book was copied at St Edmunds much earlier, probably c. 1200. It is written in dark ink and has a few main initials of very good quality in flat colour.[166] This book must have been made for the monks' book collection unless it was done expressly for Abbot Samson, in which case it must subsequently have passed into the convent's possession, perhaps as a gift from Samson himself. The early fifteenth-century list of benefactors includes books among Samson's many gifts to the monks. Jocelin records that before his departure for Normandy in 1202 he presented the monks with 'all his books'.[167]

The version of the *De Miraculis* in Titus A VIII was not the first revision of that work to be produced at St Edmunds in the twelfth century.[168] And instead of using the original *De Miraculis* directly, its author used a revised version composed c. 1125 'at the order of the prelate (Abbot Anselm) and the urging of the brethren'.[169] This important new version survives in the magnificent manuscript, Pierpont Morgan Library, New York, MS 736 (ff. 23–76). It comprises a variant text of the original. The author replaces the latter's 'biblical' style with the rhetorical flowery prose favoured for literary writing in his own day. Moreover, he interpolated historical material in order to place the miracle stories in their appropriate historical setting.[170] This Anselmian version is in two books. Bk I starts with a prologue and has sixteen chapters. Chapter 8, which describes the viewing of St Edmund's body by Abbot Leofstan, has a short prologue of its own. Bk II has a prologue and five chapters. The first two chapters are derived from the original *De Miraculis* and the last three seem to be of the author's own composition: the latest datable miracle would seem to have occurred sometime

---

165 Rouse, 'Bostonus Buriensis', p. 484. Cf. James, *Abbey*, p. 76 no. 201. For examples of Henry of Kirkstead's notes see *Catalogus*, ed. Rouse and Rouse, pp. xl, xli n. 49, lii, liv, 112, 379, and footnotes in *Memorials*, i. 29, 52–3, 172, 180.

166 For the flat-colour style at St Edmunds in the twelfth century see especially McLachlan, *Scriptorium*, pp. 46 50 and fig. A, 262–6 and fig. F. See also Gransden, *Exhibition Catalogue*, p. 231 and pl. LXXc (a colour reproduction of an initial in flat colour).

167 Douai, Bibliothèque Municipale MS 553, f. 8, and *JB*, p. 136 (above p. 42 and n. 55.)

168 The complicated relationship between the twelfth-century versions of the *De Miraculis* is explained by Thomson, 'Two versions of a saint's Life', pp. 385–91.

169 'Nos vero, quos monet Apostolus ne divitias bonitatis Dei contemnamus, quosque hortatur ne in vacuum gratiam ejus recipiamus, licet inculto, veraci tamen stilo, praelativae auctoritatis jussione et fraternae caritatis exhortatione gloriosa miracula gloriosi regis et martyris Ædmundi narranda suscipimus'. *Memorials*, i. 107–8. For Pierpont Morgan 736 see: McLachlan, *Scriptorium*, pp. 74–119 and pls 21–60; Kauffmann, *Romanesque MSS*, pp. 72–4 no. 34; R. M. Thomson, *Manuscripts from St Albans Abbey 1066–1235* (Woodbridge, 1982, 2 vols (i text, ii plates)), i. 25–6, 124 no. 80; Cynthia Hahn, '*Peregrinatio et Natio*. The illustrated Life of Edmund, king and martyr', *Gesta*, xxx pt 2 (1991), pp. 119–39 and figs 1–5, 9–14, 16–19.

170 For the style of the Anselmiam version, preserved in Pierpont Morgan 736, considered in contrast with the late twelfth-century style of the version in Titus A VIII, see Thomson, 'Two versions of a saint's Life', pp. 383–5, 393–408.

between 1096 and 1118.[171] The revised *De Miraculis* in Titus A VIII is, like the Anselmian version, divided into two books. Bk I contains a prologue and sixteen chapters, all except chapter sixteen derived from Bk I of the Anselmian version: chapter sixteen in that version has been moved into Bk II, and its place taken in Bk I by a later miracle, datable to after 1189.[172] The author explains the reason for this transposition and substitution: it is because the subject of the new miracle is related to the subject of the miracle recounted in Bk I, chapter fifteen – they both demonstrate that St Edmund punishes those who wrongfully invade his property.[173]

The new miracle is worth describing because it is a typical example of the kind of story designed to impress readers and listeners with St Edmund's power. Its realistic details would convince them of its truth and its fluent narrative made it entertaining and would hold their attention. The story relates that 'in the time of Henry II, in the fourteenth year of his reign (1167/8), William de Courcy, with the help of Richard (of Ilchester), archdeacon of Poitou (later bishop of Winchester, 1174–88, one of Henry II's *familiaries*), obtained a royal writ restoring to him all the property held by his predecessors. He thereupon claimed Southwold, a manor belonging to St Edmunds, which his ancestor had 'usurped' by violent invasion. He went to St Edmunds and handed the writ to the abbot (Hugh I), who asked for a delay. On his return journey to London, William had hardly reached the hostelry (*hospitium*) at Chelmsford before he fell ill. Although still very ill he proceeded next morning to Colchester where he was received by the monks of St Johns, but he became raving mad. When the abbot heard of this he sent the prior of St Edmunds to the miserable man to persuade him to repent of the injury which he had inflicted on 'the martyr Edmund'. An official of William obtained the latter's promise to make proper amends if through the saint's mercy he could be restored to health. On hearing this, the prior was satisfied and by the next morning William had recovered: he repented, promised to quickly abandon his claim and 'to serve the blessed martyr sedulously all his life'. This substituted miracle in Bk I chapter 16 is preceded in chapter 15 by the miracle described in the original *De Miraculis*, which relates how William's ancestor, Robert de Courcy, had tried to 'invade' Southwold with an armed force, with the consent of the sheriff, Roger Bigod. A terrible storm had broken out before Robert and his men reached Southwold. Robert wisely

171 Thomson, op. cit., p. 386 and n. 3.
172 'Ad beati martyris gloriam ampliandam aliud proximo connectimus miraculum, quod, licet temporis interjectus praecedenti nequaquam sinat continuari, quia tamen ei satis cognatum est et consimile, utpote in pervasoribus jam dicti praedii indebitam puniens presumptionem, et nos illud non indebite proximo continuamus, ut consimilium concors et non interrupta fiat conjunctio'. *Memorials*, i. 148.
173 Ibid., i. 148. I have failed to identify William de Courcy. However, John de Courcy, presumably a member of the same family, was Lord of Ulster under Henry II but was dispossessed of his power and lands there by King John in 1204. See Holt, *Magna Carta*, pp. 82 n. 35, 108, 169, 171 n. 204, 329, and Warren, *King John*, pp. 35, 37, 194. St Edmunds finally parted with Southwold in 1259, under the terms of an agreement between Abbot Simon of Luton and Richard earl of Gloucester. See BL MSS Harley 645, ff. 212, 212v and Additional 14847, ff. 77, 77v; CUL MS Mm.iv.19, ff. 18v–19; *Pinch. Reg.*, i. 432–4.

returned home, but two of his knights went on, occupied the manor – and went mad. 'Thus St Edmund avenges injury and vindicates his right.'[174]

These stories show how successive hagiographers proved that St Edmund's power against his church's and his people's enemies was undiminished by the passing of years. It had been most dramatically demonstrated already in the eleventh century. The original *De Miraculis* relates how Swegn, who ruled England from 1013–1014, tried to impose tribute on *Beodericisworth*, despite the pleadings of the sacrist Egelwin; St Edmund appeared to Egelwin in a vision, threatening Swegn with his lance; shortly afterwards Egelwin heard of Swegn's sudden death; and thus St Edmund saved 'not only the free poor of the vill [of *Beodericisworth*] but also those throughout all England' from the greed of the invader.[175] The same story appears in an elaborated form and beautifully illustrated in the version of the *De Miraculis* in Pierpont Morgan 736,[176] and again in the later twelfth-century versions.[177] It, together with the two 'Southwold' stories, is among the innumerable miracles (otherwise mostly cures) in the vast collection in the Bury version of Bk II of John of Tynemouth's *Legenda Aurea*, compiled c. 1377.[178] The latter also has a story relating that St Edmund appeared in a dream to Edward I during the *quo warranto* proceedings and threatened him with a death like Swegn's unless he restored the liberties of landholders.[179] And among the verses and pictures which adorned the abbey church, apparently on a hanging near St Edmund's shrine, was a series telling the Swegn story.[180]

Book II of the *De Miraculis* in Titus A VIII has a prologue which Henry of Kirkstead attributed in a marginal note to Osbert of Clare 'prior of Westminster'.[181] Osbert, monk of Westminster and a well-known hagiographer, was re-elected prior in 1136.[182] This prologue is followed by a paragraph extolling the merits of St Edmund: Henry of Kirkstead notes in the margin that here 'begins the letter of Osbert prior of Westminster sent to the convent of St Edmund concerning his miracles'.[183] As mentioned above, Osbert was a friend of Abbot Anselm and

---

[174] *De Miraculis*, p. 79. See Gransden, 'Baldwin', p. 67 and n. 4, and D. J. A. Matthew, *The Norman Conquest* (New York, 1966), p. 66.

[175] *De Miraculis*, pp. 34–7. See Gransden, 'Composition and authorship of the *De Miraculis*', pp. 11, 26–7 and nn. 106, 112, where it is suggested that the Swegn story and other elements of the *De Miraculis* belonged to some earlier work on St Edmund's miracles and cult.

[176] Pierpont Morgan Lib. MS 736, ff. 21, 21v. Reproduced McLachlan, *Scriptorium*, pls 50, 51; f. 21v is also reproduced e.g. in O. Pächt, C. R. Dodwell and Francis Wormald, *The St Albans Psalter* (London, 1960), pl. 51.

[177] *Memorials*, i. 114–18.

[178] Horstman, *Nova Legenda*, ii. 600–3. For the Southwold story see ibid., ii. 621, 637–8.

[179] Ibid., ii. 667.

[180] James, *Abbey*, pp. 137, 190, 191. See above p. 111 and n. 81.

[181] *Memorials*, i. 152–3 and n. a. See Thomson, 'Two versions of a saint's Life', pp. 388–9.

[182] Osbert had already been prior for more than two years before his exile. He was again banished shortly after 1139. Henceforth, he devoted himself to writing saints' Lives. See *Letters of Osbert of Clare*, pp. 9, 19.

[183] *Memorials*, i. 153 and n. a, 154. This 'letter' is a florid encomium not a true letter and has no address or subscription. It is noticed but not printed by Williamson (*Letters of Osbert of Clare*, p. 26 and n. 1).

one of his strongest supporters in the struggle to establish observance of the feast of the Conception of the Virgin Mary throughout England.[184] He had apparently stayed at St Edmunds during his exile from Westminster c. 1125 – c. 1134. Following the letter in Titus A VIII are twenty chapters, the last one ending incomplete. The first five chapters derive from the Anselmian version of the *De Miraculis* but, like the other prologue and letter, chapters 8–20 are ascribed to Osbert of Clare in notes by Henry of Kirkstead. This attribution is corroborated by source references in the margins of the section on St Edmund's Life and Miracles in the massive hagiographic collection made at St Edmunds, probably under Kirkstead's supervision, and now Bodley MS 240 in the Bodleian Library.[185] The references in question are to passages borrowed by the compilers from the version of the *De Miraculis* in Titus A VIII. There is no reason to doubt that the attribution is correct.[186] Therefore, it seems that Osbert composed a booklet containing St Edmund's miracles, perhaps as a thank-offering for hospitality in the abbey during his exile from Westminster.[187] The last, unfinished, chapter which follows Osbert's collection is datable to Samson's time. It relates the cure of two people who visited and prayed at St Edmund's shrine: one was Robert Haseley, a canon of Hereford, who was cured of fever through St Edmund's intercession, and the other was his clerk, Roger de Avestane. Robert of Haseley is known to have been active in the last quarter of twelfth century.[188]

The version of the *De Miraculis* in Titus A VIII must be a compilation assembled in the late twelfth century. The fact that it is not the composition of a single author is reflected in the prose style. Bk I is all in simple, straightforward prose except for the new prologue to chapter 8 (the account of Leofstan's viewing of St Edmund's body) which is in the grandiloquent style. In Bk I the prologue, Osbert's letter and chapters 3–20 all attributable to Osbert, and chapter 21, although not by Osbert, are also in inflated prose but chapters 1–2 are in simple prose. This contrast is especially striking because the prologues and chapters derived from the Anselmian version of the *De Miraculis* are in simple prose despite the fact that the Anselmian version itself is in inflated prose. Therefore, the compiler must have drastically pruned the verbal flights of his exemplar – unless he used some now lost intermediate text by an author who had already simplified the prose of the Anselmian version.[189]

It has been argued that Samson himself was the author of the version of the *De Miraculis* in Titus A VIII.[190] It is contended that he was responsible for

---

184 Above pp. 108 and 109, n. 66. For Osbert's contacts with St Edmunds and Abbot Anselm see *Letters of Osbert of Clare*, pp. 11–14.

185 See below.

186 See Williamson in ibid., pp. 26–32, and Thomson, 'Two versions of a saint's Life', pp. 388–9.

187 See *Letters of Osbert of Clare*, p. 11.

188 *Memorials*, i. 207–8 and Horstman, *Nova Legenda*, ii. 664–5. See: *Charters and Records of Hereford Cathedral*, ed. W. W. Capes (Cantilupe Soc., Hereford, 1908), pp. 24–6, 36; Z. N. and C. N. L. Brooke, 'Hereford cathedral dignitaries in the twelfth century', *Cambridge Historical Journal*, viii, no. 1 (1944), pp. 20–1; Thomson, loc. cit., p. 388 and n. 8.

189 *Memorials*, i. 130–1.

190 Both Arnold and Thomson accept that Samson was the author of the version of the *De*

simplifying the prose of the Anselmian version, inserted the Osbert sections unaltered, added chapter 21 to Bk II, again without simplifying the prose. It has also been argued that Samson himself composed Bk I, chapter 16 (the account of the attempt by William de Courcy to acquire the manor of Southwold). This argument is unlikely to be right. The prologue to Bk I states that the author wrote 'at the order of the prelate and urging of the brethren', a statement apparently derived from the Anselmian version, but which nevertheless may be applicable to the new version.[191] In that case Samson cannot have composed it since the miracle story is datable to after 1189, by which time Samson was abbot. However, possibly Samson was the author of the rest of the *De Miraculis* before he became abbot and the story about William de Courcy was added, perhaps at his command, after his succession. The arguments in favour of his authorship deserve examination.

There are two arguments supporting Samson's claim. The first is a justifiable assumption that he liked a simple, direct literary style and not grandiloquent prose. It is most probable that he would have conformed with current literary tastes. He had studied in Paris, and dialectic as taught in the schools demanded clear, forceful language without rhetorical flourishes. Moreover, Samson's judicial and administrative work encouraged a simple prose style. Jocelin provides evidence that Samson favoured simplicity in speech. He hated wordy fellows and was himself 'eloquent in French and Latin, having regard rather to the sense of what he had to say than to ornaments of speech'.[192] He thought that sermons ought to be delivered in simple language so that the audience could readily understand them. 'He condemned highly coloured rhetoric, verbal ornament and elaborate reflections in a sermon, saying that in many churches a sermon is preached to the convent in French or better still in English, for the edification of morals, not for literary ostentation.'

> He read English perfectly, and used to preach in English to the people, but in the speech of Norfolk, where he was born and bred, and to this end he ordered a pulpit to be set up in the church for the benefit of his hearers and as an ornament to the church.

However, the weakness of the argument attributing the version of the *De Miraculis* to Samson on stylistic grounds, is that although it is most likely that Samson would have written simple prose, many of his contemporaries certainly did so. Jocelin himself is a prime example.

The second argument in favour of Samson's authorship is the evidence of Bodley 240. The author of the section on St Edmund in that huge volume names the source of each particular miracle and the like, with the appropriate reference usually written in the margin. One of his many sources was the version of the *De Miraculis* in Titus A VIII, used either directly or through an intermediate text. He ascribes seventeen of these derivative passages variously to 'Sampson',

---

Miraculis in Titus A VIII. *Memorials*, i. xxxix–xli, and (in detail) Thomson, loc. cit., pp. 389–408 passim.

191 *Memorials*, i. xl, 108; Thomson, loc. cit., p. 387.

192 *JB*, pp. 40, 128. See Thomson, loc. cit., pp. 389–90, and below p. 137 n. 260.

'Sampson abbas', 'Sampson abbas sancti Edmundi', 'Ex libros de miraculis eius [i.e. Sancti Edmundi] Sampson', and 'Ex libro primo miraculorum Sampsonis abbatis'.[193] Occasionally Samson is named jointly with another source.[194] This evidence certainly puts beyond doubt that Samson was associated with the miracle collection preserved in Titus A VIII. It belongs, therefore, to Samson's overall plan which involved the completion of the church and the restoration and further beautification of the shrine, and whose final objective was a magnificent consecration ceremony attended by the king and a vast crowd of people of all ranks of society, from the highest to the most lowly. Nevertheless, the evidence connecting Samson with the new version of the De Miraculis does not prove his authorship. It seems quite possible that it went under his name because he commissioned it and owned the master (perhaps the only) copy which he subsequently gave to the convent. If this is the truth, an obvious precedent had been set by Abbot Baldwin who had commissioned the writing of the original De Miraculis,[195] and by Abbot Anselm who had commissioned the revised version of c. 1125.[196]

The intention of the original De Miraculis and its descendants was to steep the minds of readers and listeners in the story of St Edmund's life and merits, and to impress on them his power to cure the sick and to inform and protect his votaries and his property. At the same time it told them about the glorious history of his church and of the community that served it. Most of it was in direct, forceful prose well suited for its purpose in so far as a learned audience was concerned, that is, an audience of clerics and monks. It would primarily have been intended for the monks of St Edmunds. It was especially important that the monks should be thoroughly informed about these matters so that they would be the more ardent in their devotion. In addition, those acting as guides or serving the shrine would be able by word of mouth to stimulate the belief of pilgrims in the martyr's sanctity and power, and the pilgrims in their turn would carry the message to the outside world. Where copies of the De Miraculis were kept in twelfth and thirteenth centuries is unknown. But by the late fourteenth century and probably before, Tiberius B II was kept by the keepers of the shrine.[197] Moreover, Bodley 240, after relating the miraculous cure of Robert of Haseley and his chaplain and

---

[193] Horstman, Nova Legenda, ii. 589 (Memorials, i. 108–12), 593 (Memorials, i. 112–14), 596–9 (cf. Memorials, i. 120–2), 599–600 (Memorials, i. 123–5), 608–9 (Memorials, i. 128–30), 609–10 (Memorials, i. 135–6), 611–13 (Memorials, i. 131–4), 618 (Memorials, i. 137–9), 627–30 (Memorials, i. 166–73), 631–2 (Memorials, i. 173–5), 632 (Memorials, i. 176–8), 632–3 (Memorials, i. 162–4), 633–4 (Memorials, i. 160–2), 637–8 (Memorials, i. 148–51).

[194] See Thomson, art. cit., p. 389 (who counts sixteen miracles as being ascribed to Samson, but seventeen seems to be the correct number). Horstman, Nova Legenda, ii. 600–2 (Memorials, i. 114–19), 603 (Memorials, i. 126–7), 624–5 (Memorials, i. 155).

[195] Memorials, i. 27.

[196] Ibid., i. 108.

[197] See Henry of Kirkstead's note in the top margin of the first page of Abbo of Fleury's dedicatory epistle to Archbishop Dunstan which precedes the text of the Passio Sancti Eadmundi in Tiberius B II (f. 2). Gransden, '"Passio"', p. 65 and n. 280, and pl. III.

noting two other cures, records that they were 'written in an old booklet in the shrine'.[198]

Another manuscript survives which was intended for a different purpose from that of the original *De Miraculis* or from that of later versions. Bodleian Library MS Digby 109 is a booklet written for an unidentified patron for private devotion to St Edmund. Probably it is the sole survivor of other similar booklets written at St Edmunds during Samson's abbacy for various patrons. Booklets of this kind were not uncommon in the middle ages. Usually they contained a saint's Life followed by prayers, a mass, and the like.[199] Two such booklets survive from St Edmunds which were written long before Samson's time, and must be representative of others now lost. The earliest known such booklet is also the earliest known copy of the *Passio*. It is a mid-eleventh-century booklet now Lambeth Palace Library, London, MS 361. In it the text of the *Passio* (ff. 1–11) is marked for eight lessons and is followed by three hymns in honour of St Edmund and a mass, also in his honour.[200] The other early booklet was produced c. 1100 and belonged to the abbey of St Denis, Paris. It is now in the Royal Library in Copenhagen, MS GI. Kgl. 1588.[201] It contains a text (ff. 4v–28) of the *Passio* very closely related to the definitive text written for Abbot Baldwin, and now Tiberius B II.[202] Abbot Baldwin had been a monk of St Denis before his succession to St Edmunds. Therefore, perhaps he was responsible for trans-

---

198 Horstman, *Nova Legenda*, p. 665. Thomson, 'Two versions of a saint's Life', p. 391, postulates that Titus A VIII was 'probably' kept in the refectory. However, it cannot be identified with any of those books prescribed for meal-time reading in the thirteenth- or fourteenth-century list in BL MS Harley 1005. Printed: James, *Abbey*, pp. 111–12; *Shorter Catalogues*, pp. 88–9. See: Henry of Kirkstead, *Catalogus*, ed. Rouse and Rouse, p. xlix and nn. 83–5; Rouse, 'Bostonus Buriensis', p. 489; and in *Shorter Catalogues*, pp. 87–8. Nevertheless, other evidence suggests that by the late fourteenth century, if not earlier, some books were kept in the refectory although perhaps not intended for meal-time reading. Ibid., pp. 87–8.

199 See: P. R. Robinson, '"The Booklet". A self-contained unit in composite manuscripts', *Codicologica*, iii (1980), pp. 46–69; idem, 'Self-contained units in composite manuscripts of the Anglo-Saxon period', *Anglo-Saxon England*, vii (1978), pp. 231–8; Bernhard Bischoff, 'Über gefaltete handschriften, vornehmlich hagiographischen inhalts', *Mittelalterliche Studien*, i (Stuttgart, 1966), pp. 93–100; Francis Wormald, 'Some illustrated manuscripts of the Lives of saints', *Bulletin of the John Rylands Library*, xxxv (1952), pp. 249–50; McLachlan, *Scriptorium*, p. 77. None of these papers mentions the examples from St Edmunds discussed below.

200 See: Gransden, '"Passio"', pp. 63–4 and pl. 1; Winterbottom in Abbo, *Passio*, pp. 8–9. The hymns are printed, with English translations in: J. B. Mackinlay, *Saint Edmund King and Martyr* (London – Leamington, 1893), pp. 343–6 passim; *Carolla Sancti Edmundi*, ed. Francis Hervey (London, 1907), pp. 87–9. For the mass see W. A. Bloor, 'The Proper of the mass for the feast of St. Edmund, king and martyr', *The Douai Magazine*, vii, no. 4 (1933), pp. 226–8.

201 Gransden, '"Passio"', pp. 64–5 and pl. II. Some variant readings are given by Winterbottom; see Abbo, *Passio*, pp. 8–9, 91–2. Gl. Kgl. S. 1588 is described in Ellen Jørgensen, *Catalogus Codicum Latinorum Medii Aevi Bibliothecae Regiae Hafnaiensis* (Copenhagen, 1923–6, 2 fasc.), ii. 190.

202 Tiberius B II was used by Winterbottom as his base text: Abbo, *Passio*, pp. 8–9, 91–2. For the original copy of the *De Miraculis*, which follows the *Passio* in Tiberius B II, see above pp. 121–24. See also Gransden, '"Passio"', pp. 65–6 and pls III, IV.

mission of the booklet to St Denis. The text is marked for twelve lessons and is followed by the office of St Edmund with musical notation. This manuscript illustrates how a booklet might serve to spread St Edmund's cult, since it passed to the royal monastery of St Denis in Paris at an early date. Similarly, a booklet containing the *Passio* had reached Lucca even earlier, possibly taken there with a relic of St Edmund by Abbot Baldwin on his way to Rome in 1071 to obtain the privilege of exemption from Pope Alexander II.[203] Digby 109 belongs, therefore, to a bibliographical genre already well-established at St Edmunds. It is in a good text hand of c. 1200, and its initial letter 'D' is ornament with delicate filigree pen-work, a style of ornamentation which superseded the twelfth-century flat-colour style for some initials.[204] The text begins with six extracts (ff. 14v–32v) from the revised version of the *De Miraculis* exemplified by Titus A VIII. There follows the office of St Edmund with musical notation (ff. 33–50v). There are nine lessons, all based on the Abbo's *Passio* in a text closely related to that in Tiberius B II.[205] Thus, under Samson, a new, definitive text of the *De Miraculis* was produced for monks and clerics, mainly of St Edmunds, and booklets were compiled for private devotion to St Edmund, all designed to stimulate and propagate the cult.

Samson and the monks also promoted the cult in another way. They produced vernacular versions of the St Edmund story, and so, by adding to its entertainment value, adapted it for use when guests, especially noblemen and women, were present. The number of saints' Lives written in Anglo-Norman verse is remarkable. Many were by members of the religious orders and were intended primarily for the instruction and entertainment of secular audiences. But they were probably also sung or read in religious houses for the enjoyment of the religious themselves on the feast-days of the various saints.[206] Versions of the Life and Miracles of St Edmund in Anglo-Norman verse were in circulation in the twelfth and thirteenth centuries.[207] Geoffrey Gaimar includes an account of St Edmund's martyrdom in his *Estoire des Engleis* which he composed shortly before 1140. The account is based on the Anglo-Saxon Chronicle and Abbo's *Passio* but has some slight additions.[208] Then, c. 1200, an Anglo-Norman verse

[203] In the first three quarters of the twelfth century, the *Passio* seems to have been a regular component of the magnificent giant passionaries executed in St Martin's cathedral, Lucca. See Gransden, '"Passio"', pp. 72–4 and nn. For contacts of Abbot Baldwin with Lucca see ibid., pp. 71–8 passim and above, p. 114 and n. 109.
[204] McLachlan, *Scriptorium*, pp. 77, 266.
[205] Abbo, *Passio*, pp. 9, 92; *Memorials*, i. lxiv, lxvii.
[206] Legge, *Anglo-Norman Lit.*, p. 275. A. T. Baker, 'Vie Anglo-Normande de Sainte Foy par Simon de Walsingham', *Romania*, lxvi (1940–1), p. 49 and n. 1.
[207] For the growth of the legend of St Edmund see: Whitelock, 'Fact and fiction', p. 33; Loomis, 'Growth of the St Edmund legend'.
[208] The *Estoire* is edited by T. D. Hardy and C. T. Martin, with an English translation (RS, 1888–9, 2 vols); Alexander Bell (Anglo-Norman Text Soc., xiv–xvi, 1960). These two editions are printed from two different manuscripts and the line references do not correspond. The section about St Edmund in the former is lines 2861–2938 (reprinted Hervey, *Corolla*, pp. 126–33), and in Bell's edition lines 2838–2928. See Legge, *Anglo-Norman Lit.*, p. 29 and n. 2, 30–6.

Plate I. Abbot Samson's seal. Pointed oval, in dark greenish brown wax attached with blue silk cords. Depicted is the abbot, standing, vested and mitred. He holds a crosier in his right hand and a book in his left. The legend (damaged) reads '[SIGNU]M SAMSONIS DEI G[RATIA] ABBATIS SANCTI [EDMUNDI]'. Counterseal, round (complete) see above p. 21 and n. 23. It depicts the Pascal lamb, with a cross, and the legend reads 'SECRETUM SAMSONIS ABBATIS'. Samson appended this seal as one of the arbiters in 1200 of the dispute between Hubert Walter, archbishop of Canterbury, and the prior and convent of Canterbury Cathedral priory over the archbishop's proposal to build a collegiate church at Lambeth. See above pp. 67–9. The document has many other pendant seals. *DCc/Ch Ant/L/130*.

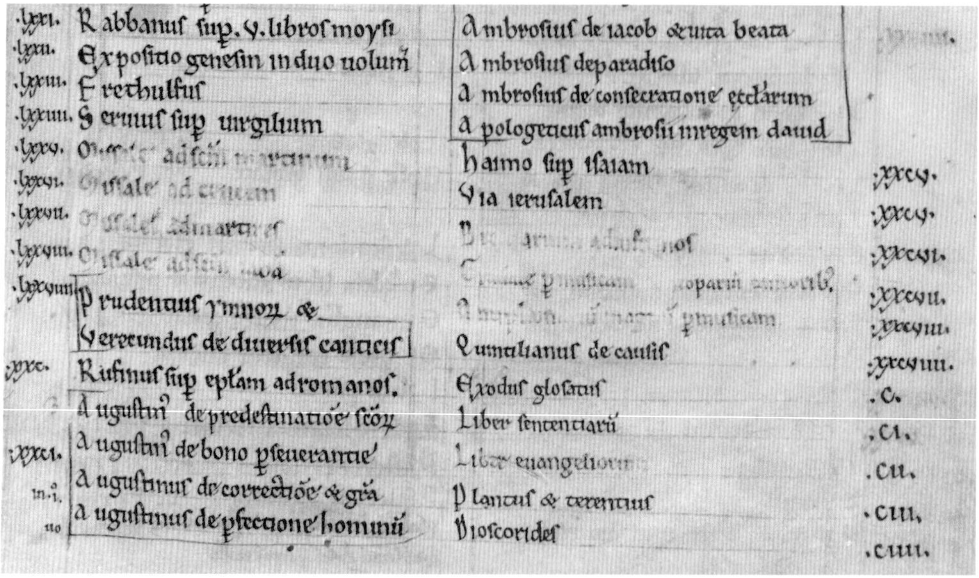

lxxi.	Rabbanus sup .v. libros moysi	Ambrosius de iacob & uita beata	
lxxii.	Expositio genesin in duo uolum	Ambrosius de paradiso	
lxxiii.	Frethulfus	Ambrosius de consecratione ecclarum	
lxxiiii.	Sermus sup uirgilium	Apologeticus ambrosii in regem dauid	
lxxv.	O...c adsci... ...	haimo sup isaiam	xxciii.
lxxvi.	...le ad c...	Uia ierusalem	xxciii.
lxxvii.	...les admart...	...	xxcvi.
lxxviii.	...le ad... ...	...	xxcvii.
	Prudentius ymnoy & ___	...	xxcviii.
	Uerecundus de diuersis canticis	...	xxcviiii.
lxxx.	Rufinus sup eplam ad romanos	Exodus glosatus	.c.
	Augustinus de predestinatioe scoy	Liber sentenciaru	.ci.
lxxxi.	Augustini de bono pseuerantie	Liber euangeliorum	.cii.
iii.i.	Augustinus de correctioe & gra	Plautus & terentius	.ciii.
iio	Augustinus de pfectione hominu	Dioscorides	.ciiii.

Plate II. Part of the late twelfth-century Book-List from St Edmunds, which is a good example of Caroline minuscule script. In the part shown seven titles have been erased, possibly by the scribe who tried to rationalize the Book-List by removing service books (see above p. 136 and nn. 279–80, and below, pl. V). *Pembroke College, Cambridge, MS 47, f. 118. Reduced from folio size.*

Plate III. A historiated initial in a copy of the Forty *Homilies of Gregory*, produced at St Edmunds in the last half of the twelfth century. It illustrates the excellent quality of some of the books in the monks' collection and demonstrates the survival at St Edmunds of the tradition of line drawing in ink with tinted outlines (see also the next plate and above p. 137 and n. 270). Here the initial 'L' of 'Lectio sancti euangelij' is represented as Christ, haloed, seated, and the nobleman (John 4.46–54), crowned, kneeling before Him. The ink outline is tinted with red, green and gold. *Pembroke College, Cambridge, MS 16, f. 70. Enlarged from folio size, double column, detail.*

Plate IV. Detail from a copy of the Gospel of Mark, glossed, produced at St Edmunds in the late twelfth century in a good protogothic minuscule. The historiated initial letter of the prologue, the 'M' of 'MARCVS', is in the form of a monk holding the necks of two serpents, each with a holy wafer in its mouth. The monk is drawn in ink with tinted outlines; one serpent is tinted green and the other red. In the top margin is the early thirteenth-century *ex libris*: 'Liber Sancti Ædmundi', and an inscription by Henry of Kirkstead recording that the book was kept in the monks' book-press or cupboard ('Marcus glossatus de armario sancti Edmundi'). See above pp. 136 and n. 266, 137 and n. 270. The late fourteenth-century class-mark (.B.101.) is at top right. *Pembroke College, Cambridge, MS 72, f. 1. Reduced from folio size.*

Plate V. A historiated initial in an exceptionally beautiful copy of Peter Lombard's *Sentences* (see above p. 139 and nn. 279–80). This book, executed c. 1200, was very likely one of the three copies of the *Sentences* which were among the additional entries made to the Book-List (see above p. 136 and nn. 263–5, and pl. II). The initial 'S' (of 'Samaritanus') is in gold and in vivid body colour and depicts a serpent with four small animals (? lions) disporting in its coils and in acanthus tendrils. The fourteenth-century annotations in the top margin and interlined in the text, in dark ink, and the note in pale ink in the left-hand margin, apparently by the scribe of the Customary (see pl. VI), show that the beauty of the book did not prevent a scholarly monk from studying and annotating it. *Pembroke College, Cambridge, MS 28, f. 160. Reduced from large folio size.*

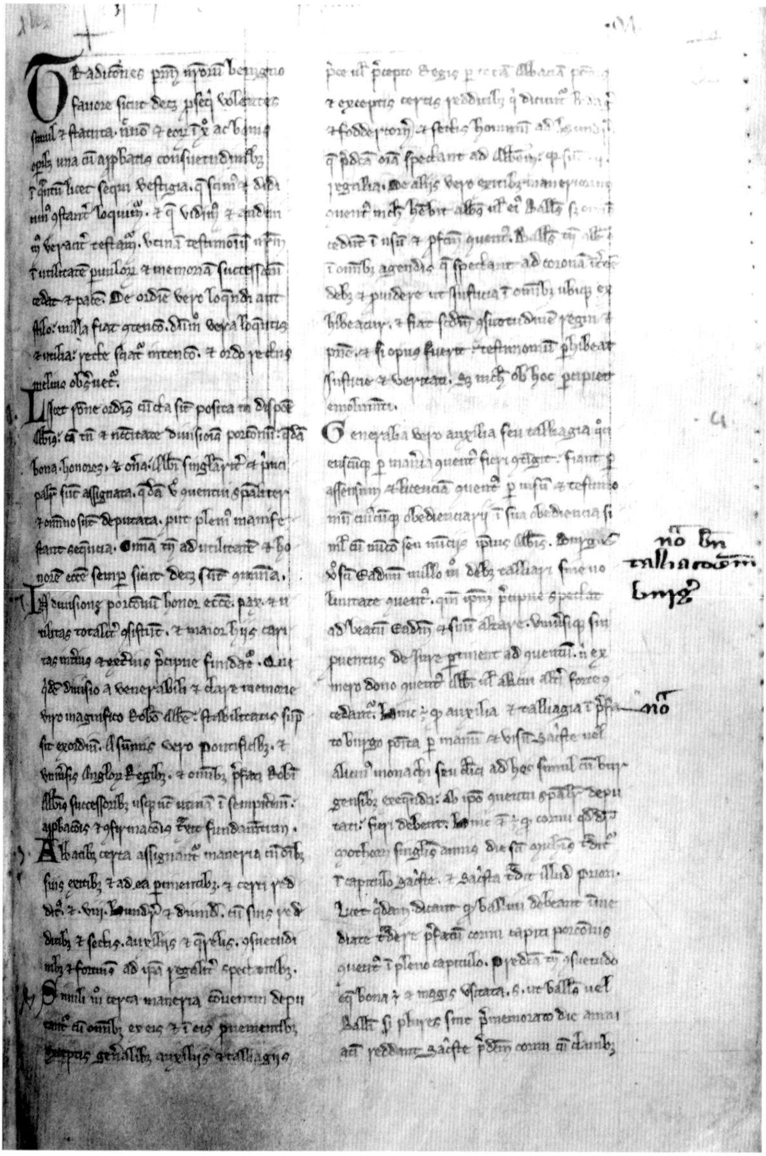

Plate VI. The first page of St Edmunds' Customary of c. 1234. This copy demonstrates the Customary's continued usefulness. It is in pale ink in the cursive script of a scribe writing c. 1260–70 (see above, pl. V and p. 202 and n. 58). The scribe has headed the text 'Incipiunt tradiciones patrum' ('Here begin the traditions of the fathers'). In the right-hand margin Henry of Kirkstead calls attention to the paragraph on the tallaging of the burgesses ('nota bene talliacionem burg") and writes *nota*. By this time in the 1370s, the Customary had been bound in the composite volume, the White Book ('Liber Albus') of St Edmunds, which had the class-mark .C.68. and was paginated in Arabic numerals. Another copy of the Customary, independent of this one, was made in the late thirteenth century (CUL MS Additional 6006, ff. 9, 9v, 16–20v, incomplete owing to the loss of leaves). *BL MS Harley 1005, f. 102 (modern foliation, 67 of Arabic foliation). Reduced from quarto size.*

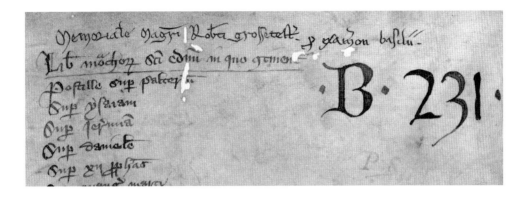

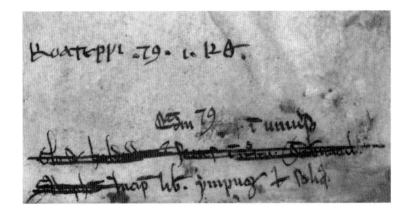

Plate VII. Two inscriptions by Robert Grosseteste, theologian and scientist (bishop of Lincoln 1235–53), who owned this volume of *Glosses* on the Psalms, various Prophets and Mark, before it came to St Edmunds. a. (above) An inscription reading 'Memoriale Magistri Roberti Grossetest' pro exameron basilii' ('Pledge of Master Robert Grosseteste in exchange for the *Hexaëmeron* of Basil'). St Edmunds' late medieval class-mark, .B.231., written alongside the inscription indicates that the volume was never returned to Grosseteste, nor is there evidence that he ever returned the copy of the *Hexaëmeron* to St Edmunds. He himself wrote a *Hexaëmeron* (a treatise on the Six Days of Creation) probably in the early 1230s, borrowing from a Latin translation of Basil's work. See above, p. 000 and nn. 1–3. b. (below) Grosseteste's inscription in Greek, reading 'κματεϱνι.29.i.κθ', which is a transliteration into Greek of the Latin word *quaterni*, that is quires. It records the number of quires in the volume according alternatively to the Arabic and Greek system of numbers. See above p. 217 and nn. 5–11. *Pembroke College, Cambridge, MS 7, front flyleaf verso, and f. 1, respectively.*

Plate VIII. The first page of the *de luxe* copy of the *Canon* of Avicenna in the translation of Gerard of Cremona, possibly given to the monks by their physician, Master Stephen of Caistor. This copy of the *Canon* was executed in Italy, probably at Bologna, in the mid-thirteenth century. In the top margin Henry of Kirkstead has written St Edmunds' *ex libris*, 'Liber mo[na]chorum S[anc]ti Edm[und]i, and the class-mark 'A.200'. See above pp. 220 and nn. 26–8, 221. *Gonville and Caius College, Cambridge, MS 480/476, f. 1. Reduced from large folio size.*

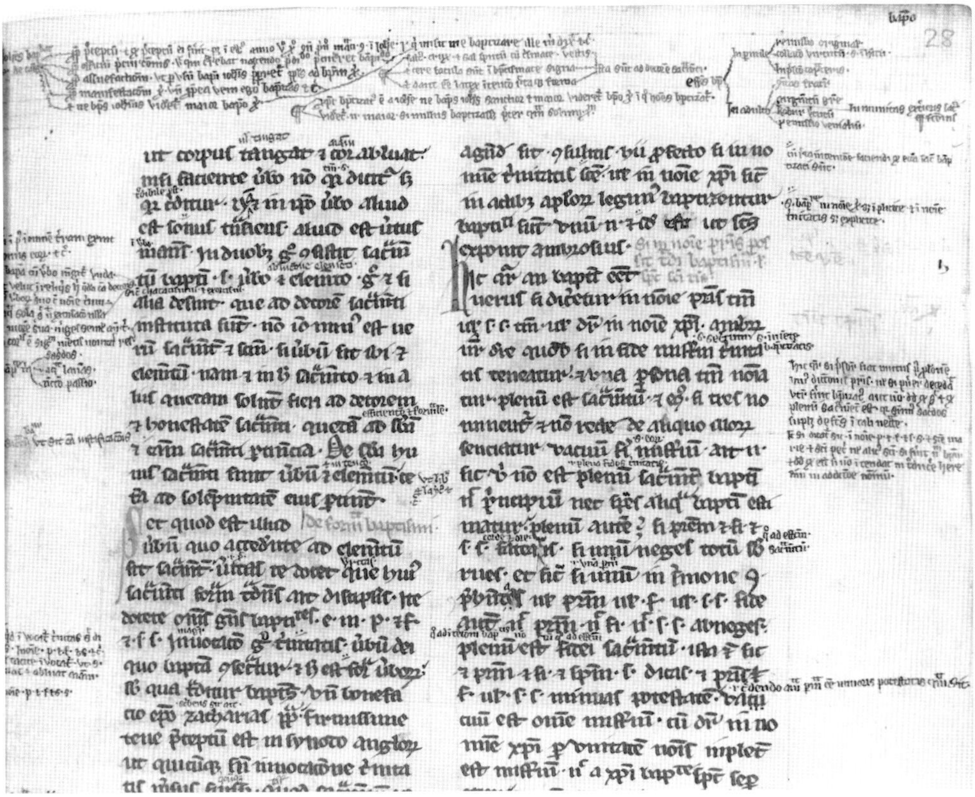

Plate IX. The top half of a page of a workaday copy of Peter Lombard's *Sentences* with copious notes in the margins and interlined in a thirteenth-century hand. (Compare with pl. V.) This copy is preserved in a composite volume of mainly theological and homiletic texts, originally independent booklets, which were bound together at St Edmunds in the late middle ages. See above p. 140 n. 286. *Pembroke College, Cambridge, MS 85, f. 28. Reduced from folio size.*

Plate X. The illuminated initial *E* (of *Et*) at the beginning of the glossed copy of
Joshua. It illustrates Joshua receiving the Word of God for the people. Above, God
holds on the end of a scroll; below, Joshua holds the other end while the Israelites look
up at him. The scroll bears the Lord's words 'Moyses seruus meus mortuus est, surge et
transi jordanum istum, tu et omnis populus tecum' ('Moses my servant is dead; arise
and cross this Jordan, you and all this people with you', Joshua 1, 2). See above p. 138.
Artistically, the initial in gold and body colour, exemplifies a new style of illumination
then gaining currency. Similarly, the bold early gothic text-hand exemplifies a new
kind of text-hand which was replacing Caroline minuscule. The volume may have
been no. 227 in the Book-List. The title ('I[e]h[os]u[e] filii nane') in a early thirteenth-
century hand, and the late fourteenth-century class-mark, .B.54., are in the top margin.
Pembroke College, Cambridge, MS 54, f.1. Reduced from large quarto.

Plate XI. Illustrations from the Luttrell Psalter, executed for Sir Geoffrey Luttrell of Irnham in south-west Lincolnshire (1276–1345), in the second quarter of the fourteenth century. a. (above) A rabbit warren. A dog is about to enter the central burrow. See Appendix III below p. 256 and n. 58). b. (below) An overshot watermill with fish and eel traps in the leat. See above Appendix III pp. 256–7, and Appendix IV, esp. pp. 284–5, 303–5 passim. *BL MS Additional 42130, ff. 176v, 180. Reduced from folio size.*

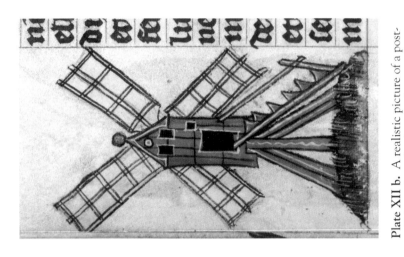

Plate XII b. A realistic picture of a post-mill from the calendar of a fourteenth-century Book of Hours executed in Maastricht or its region in the Netherlands. BL MS Stowe 17, f. 89v. *Reduced from octavo size.*

Plate XII a. An artistic representation of a post-mill in the Luttrell Psalter with a peasant giving a sack of grain to the miller, while a dog stands on guard. See Appendix IV above passim). BL MS Additional 42130, f. 158. *Reduced from large folio size.*

rendering of Abbo's *Passio*, *Le Passiun de seint Edmund*, was composed.[209] It was probably not written at or for St Edmunds since it makes no use of the *De Mirac-ulis* or of the *De Infantia Sancti Edmundi* which Geoffrey of Wells wrote for Abbot Ording (1148–56).[210] The only known copy of *Le Passiun* is a thirteenth-century copy in a manuscript from St Augustine's, Canterbury.[211]

Undoubtedly, a number of Lives of St Edmund in Anglo-Norman verse (and possibly also in English) are lost. The earliest known Life in Anglo-Norman verse actually written at St Edmunds is *La Vie seint Edmund le Rei*, a long Life of St Edmund in two parts composed probably in the 1180s or 1190s.[212] The author names himself Denis Piramus. Nothing is known about him except what he tells us himself.[213] He confesses in the prologue to Part I that he had spent much of his life in frivolity, folly and sin. He had frequented the court (probably Henry II's) and mixed with courtiers. Led astray by the Enemy, he had composed 'satirical verses (*serventeis*), songs, rhymes and messages between lovers'. He considers himself in 'evil plight'. And will never jest again: 'The gay days of my youth are passing and I approach old age, so it is fitting that I should repent; I shall turn my mind to other things.' His early career, therefore, had been as a court poet, and it is almost certain that he later became a monk of St Edmunds. This is indicated by the prologue to Part II, where he states that he 'does not account it a burden or trouble' and asks that the Holy Spirit may grant him grace to perform the task reasonably well and that God, St Edmund and the seniors who commissioned him may bear him goodwill for his pains.[214] It has been suggested that Denis Piramus was Master Denis, the cellarer in the late twelfth century. But among the seventy or so monks of St Edmunds there may have been more than one called Denis.[215] It is hard to reconcile what Denis Piramus reveals of his

---

[209] Ed. Judith Grant (Anglo-Norman Text Soc., xxxvi, 1978).

[210] Printed *Memorials*, i. 93–103; Hervey, *Corolla*, with an English translation, pp. 134/5–160/1.

[211] In a collection of various Latin and French works in various thirteenth- and fourteenth-century hands, now Gonville and Caius College, Cambridge, MS 435, pp. 105–28. For a description of the manuscript see *Le Passiun*, ed. Grant, p. 11 and nn. 2–4, 12–17. Listed Ker, *Libraries*, p. 41.

[212] The best edition of *La Vie seint Edmund le Rei* is by Hilding Kjellman (Göteborg, 1935), who printed from the only manuscript then known (BL MS Cotton Domitian XI). It is also printed in *Memorials*, ii. 137–250 and Hervey, *Corolla*, pp. 224–359. Since Kjellman's edition another text has been discovered and acquired by the John Rylands Library in Manchester (now Rylands French MS 142). It has additions to, and considerable variants from, the Domitian version, and a full collation is given by Harry Rothwell, 'The Life and Miracles of St. Edmund: a recently discovered manuscript', *Bulletin of the John Rylands University Library*, lx (1977–8), pp. 135–80. The text in both Domitian XI and in Rylands French MS 142 are incomplete. The latter lacks 684 lines at the beginning but continues longer than the former but similarly ends incomplete. See Rothwell, art. cit., pp. 135–6.

[213] Lines 1–20. For this passage with a translation see Legge, *Anglo-Norman Lit.*, p. 81.

[214] Lines 3279–86. See Legge, op. cit., pp. 82–3. For this and the previous passage see also eadem, *Anglo-Norman in the Cloisters*, pp. 7–9.

[215] *Kalendar*, ed. Davis, index, p. 176, under 'Denis' ('Deonisius', 'Dionisius') 'the cellarer', 'the chamberlain', 'the chaplain', 'the master' and just 'Denis'. He ('Dionysius', 'Dioni-sius') with Hugo 'chaplains of the abbot' witnessed two extant charters of Abbot Hugh I. *Feudal Docs*, pp. 140 n. 8, 145 n. 2. Thomson, 'Obedientiaries', p. 96, suggests that Denis,

background with Master Denis, a monk banished by Abbot Hugh II and active
in conventual affairs under Samson: he was one of the twelve monks chosen
by the convent to represent it before King John during the abbatial election of
1182, and in 1201 he spoke to Samson on the convent's behalf, objecting to his
gift of a serjeanty belonging to the convent to one of his own servants.[216]

La Vie is in octosyllabic couplets and has literary merit. Denis states that
he has translated from works in English and Latin.[217] No English source has
been traced, but he used Abbo's *Passio*, the *De Miraculis* and Geoffrey of Wells'
De Infantia Sancti Edmundi.[218] Denis also used Anglo-Norman works, certainly
Gaimar and possibly Wace's *Roman de Brut*.[219] In the prologue to Part I, Denis
condemns those writers of verse who tell fanciful, untrue, or even mendacious
fables to please and entertain kings, princes, earls, barons, and their vassals, and
ladies.[220] He cites contemporary examples of such fictional tales in the romance
style. He claims that he on the contrary will tell the truth, and the story will be
both pleasing to the ear and good for the soul. Denis then proceeds with a largely
legendary narrative. He begins with a long account of British history and of the
Anglo-Saxon invasions and settlements, all drawn from the *Brut* tradition, and
in due course fits the legend of St Edmund's childhood and youth, as narrated by
Geoffrey of Wells, into this legendary framework. Denis next tells of St Edmund's
life and martyrdom, and continues with the subsequent conflict between the
Danes and the Anglo-Saxon kings interspersed with miracles occasioned by St
Edmund's intercession and the history of his church up to the reign of Ethelred
the Unready (978–1016). The textual tradition ends incomplete: having related
that the monks of St Edmunds gave thanks at the martyr's tomb for the death of
the Danish king Swegn (in 1014), whom they believed St Edmund killed with
his lance, Denis begins to tell of a miraculous cure of a sick tenant, but then
the manuscript breaks off. Only two manuscripts of *La Vie* are known: both are
incomplete and both thirteenth-century.[221]

The paucity of copies of *La Vie* suggests that it did not have wide circulation, which in addition to its literary mode, suggests the possibility that it was
composed for a royal or aristocratic patron, perhaps a woman. Gaimar had
written the *Estoire des Engleis* for Constance, wife of the Lincolnshire magnate,
Ralph Fitz Gilbert.[222] Matthew Paris composed a number of saint's Lives in
Anglo-Norman verse for ladies: he wrote a Life of St Edward the Confessor for
Henry III's queen, Eleanor of Provence, and a Life of St Edmund of Abingdon

the abbot's chaplain, became cellarer. Thomson does not list Denis in the succession of
chamberlains. Ibid., p. 97. See Legge, *Anglo-Norman in the Cloisters*, pp. 7–8.

216 *JB*, pp. 4, 6, 16, 22, 104, 130.
217 Lines 3256–9, 3279. Legge, *Anglo-Norman in the Cloisters*, p. 7.
218 *De Infantia* is printed in *Memorials*, i. 93–103. For this predominantly fictional account of
St Edmund's early life see Whitelock, 'Fact and fiction', pp. 225–8 passim.
219 Legge, *Anglo-Norman Lit.*, p. 84.
220 Lines 42–78. Legge, op. cit., p. 82. For the contents of *La Vie* and an estimate of its value
as an historical source see Loomis, 'Growth of the St. Edmund legend', pp. 94–6.
221 See above n. 212.
222 *Le estoire des Engleis*, ed. Bell (above n. 208), lines 6430–1. See Gransden, *Historical
Writing*, [i]. 209 and n. 215.

and a Life of St Thomas of Canterbury for Isabel, countess of Arundel.[223] But his Life of St Alban, also in Anglo-Norman verse, seems to have been composed for Matthew's fellow monks and may have been intended for some grand occasion when members of the aristocracy and others of the chivalric class and perhaps royalty would have been present.[224] Similarly, *La Vie seint Edmund le Rei* may have been intended for some special occasion at St Edmunds. Perhaps Abbot Samson and senior monks commissioned it in anticipation of the consecration of the abbey church which they so much desired, an occasion which, they hoped, would be attended by the king and a crowd of noblemen and women. Alternatively, perhaps it was commissioned for one of the royal visits which took place in the last half of the twelfth century: Henry II came as a pilgrim to St Edmunds in 1177[225] and was there again in 1188, after he had taken the crusading Cross;[226] Richard I came as a pilgrim late in November 1189, soon after his return to England consequent on Henry II's death, and again in March 1194 on his return from captivity;[227] and King John visited St Edmunds three times, in 1199, 1201 and 1203.[228] On all these occasions the king and his entourage would have received lavish hospitality and been entertained by minstrels.[229] We can add a yet further speculation, that *La Vie* was composed for presentation to the king on or following a royal visit. Albeit it was over two hundred years later, the poet John Lydgate, monk of St Edmunds, composed the *Lives of SS. Edmund and Fremund* in English verse, at Abbot William Curteys' command, for presentation to Henry VI, following his visit in 1433–4: the *Lives*, a long narrative poem, survives in the beautiful presentation copy (BL MS Harley 2278).[230]

The existence at St Edmunds of many secondary cults alongside that of St Edmunds, king and martyr, was discussed above. Among them was the cult of St Faith, virgin and martyr, who supposedly lived in the third century. Her legend is unhistorical but her cult was very popular in the middle ages, and she was invoked especially by pilgrims, soldiers and prisoners.[231] As already mentioned, one of the chapels which Samson re-roofed in lead was the apsidal chapel dedicated to St Faith in the western transept of the abbey church.[232] Probably a

---

[223] Vaughan, *Matthew Paris*, pp. 168–81; Legge, *Anglo-Norman Lit.*, pp. 268–9; eadem, *Anglo-Norman in the Cloisters*, pp. 30–1; Gransden, *Historical Writing*, [i]. 358–9.

[224] Vaughan, op. cit., p. 181; Legge, *Anglo-Norman Lit.*, p. 268.

[225] *Ben. Pet.*, i. 61, 159.

[226] *JB*, pp. 53 and n. 4, 54.

[227] Landon, *Itinerary of Richard I*, pp. 16, 85; *JB*, p. 116.

[228] *Ann. S. Edm.*, pp. 139, 143.

[229] *JB*, pp. 28, 42.

[230] W. F. Schirmer, *John Lydgate. A Study in the Culture of the Fifteenth Century*, translated by A. E. Keep (London, 1961, first published in German, Tübingen, 1952), p. 163; Derek Pearsall, *John Lydgate* (London, 1970), pp. 281–2; Nicholas Rogers, 'Fitzwilliam Museum MS 3–1979: a Bury St Edmunds Book of Hours and the origins of the Bury style', in *England in the Fifteenth Century: Proceedings of the 1986 Harlaxton Symposium*, ed. Daniel Williams (Woodbridge, 1987), pp. 235–6; idem, 'The Bury artists of Harley 2278', pp. 221–2.

[231] Farmer, *Saints*, pp. 146–7.

[232] *JB*, p. 96; *De dedicationibus*, p. 116. Above, p. 86.

little after Samson's death, shortly before 1216, a monk of St Edmunds, Simon of Walsingham, wrote a Life of St Faith in Anglo-Norman verse.[233] Little is known about Simon beyond his authorship of the *Life*: he was pittancer sometime between 1215 and 1229 and was one of the supporters of the candidature of Hugh of Northwold in the disputed abbatial election of 1213–15.[234] Much more is known about Simon's relative, another monk of St Edmunds, Master Thomas of Walsingham. He was ordained in 1213 and took an active part in the election and was, like Simon, a supporter of Hugh of Northwold.[235] Sometime between 1217 and 1220 he was Master of the hospital of St Saviour's,[236] and then, c. 1220–22, the monks' chamberlain.[237] Possibly it was Master Thomas who asked Simon to write the Life of St Faith. Simon states that he wrote at the request of a fellow monk, 'a man of worth, great learning and understanding, small in stature, but well stocked with virtue'.[238]

   It is not surprising that a monk of St Edmunds should want to know about the Life and miracles of St Faith because her cult, having been established by Abbot Anselm, flourished in the abbey.[239] There was a particular reason for Simon's devotion to St Faith, for, as he himself says, he was born on her anniversary.[240] Moreover, his devotion must surely have owed something to his birthplace: Walsingham is less than fifteen miles from the Benedictine priory of Horsham St Faith, a dependency of the abbey of St Conques, which contains the famous shrine of St Faith,[241] and was well-known as a stopping-place for pilgrims on their way to Santiago de Compostella.[242] Horsham St Faith was dedicated jointly to St Mary and St Faith, which would explain why Simon calls himself 'servant of St Mary and St Faith'.[243] Obviously, Simon must have had contacts with Horsham St Faith before he became a monk of St Edmunds and it is not unlikely that he maintained them thereafter. There is no doubt that St Edmunds was in touch with the prior on at least one occasion: during the abbatial election in 1182, when the king told the monks to nominate three candidates from other monas-

---

[233] Ed. A. T. Baker, 'Vie Anglo-Normande de Sainte Foy par Simon de Walsingham', *Romania*, lxvi (1940–1), pp. 49–84. See: Legge, *Anglo-Norman in the Cloisters*, pp. 9–12.

[234] *Electio*, pp. xviii, xxxvi, 36/7, 74/5, 86/7, 140/1, 188, 193 n. 5. It is uncertain whether or not he is to be identified with 'Simon the painter', who 'painstakingly' painted the abbot's throne in the choir (*Gesta Sacrist.*, p. 291, and above pp. 89, 110). But it would be rash to conclude that the painter was a professional artist and not a monk, as suggested by Thomson; *Electio*, pp. xxxix–xl.

[235] For many references to him see *Electio*, index, p. 207 under 'Thomas of Walsingham'. For the statement that he was a relative (*cognatum*) of Simon of Walsingham see ibid., p. 36 and n. 7. For an outline of his career see ibid., p. 188.

[236] Harper-Bill, *Hospitals*, pp. 22, 127 no. 178.

[237] Thomson, 'Obedientiaries', p. 97.

[238] Baker, ed. cit., p. 63 lines 79–83.

[239] Above p. 116 and n. 123.

[240] Baker, ed. cit., p. 62 lines 52–62.

[241] Binns, *Dedications*, p. 99.

[242] See e.g. Brian and Marcus Tate, *The Pilgrim Route to Santiago* (Oxford, 1987), pp. 25, 48 (map), 52, 138.

[243] Baker, ed. cit., p. 63 line 100. See Pestell, *Landscapes of Monastic Foundation*, p. 155 and nn.

teries for election, one of the three nominated was Bertrand, prior of Horsham St Faith (c. 1163 – c. 1183, later abbot of Chertsey, c. 1183–97).[244]

La Vie de Sainte Foy is known to survive in only one copy which is in a late thirteenth-century hand and is preserved in a collection of thirteen saints' Lives in Anglo-Norman, of various provenances, copied in various thirteenth- and fourteenth-century hands and bound together in one volume.[245] *La Vie*, therefore, probably had limited currency. Simon must have intended it for the instruction and entertainment of his monastic patron. But both he and his patron obviously also had in mind a wider audience. Perhaps they meant it to be read aloud to a gathering of lords and ladies on some special occasion, perhaps for a ceremony held to mark the completion of Samson's re-roofing of the chapel of St faith. The poem is addressed to 'Lords, you who believe in God and are confirmed in the faith'.[246] It is in octosyllabic rhyming couplets which, though correct, are of no literary merit.[247] Simon's information apparently derived from Latin sources which are still extant today, that is from books on St Faith's passion and a book of her miracles. Simon probably used these sources indirectly through an intermediate compilation: he states that he was 'translating' a book sent him by 'Dom Benjamin'.[248]

La Vie seint Edmund le Rei and *La Vie de Sainte Foy* illustrate the vitality of the cult of saints and of Anglo-Norman hagiographical composition in the abbey. Nor are they the last hagiographies in Anglo-Norman verse produced by monks of St Edmunds. The abbey was in fact originally dedicated jointly to St Mary and St Edmund and the cult of St Mary gave rise to Anglo-Norman poems. Two such poems survive but, since one is probably mid-thirteenth century (though it may possibly be earlier) and the other late thirteenth century, they will not be considered here.[249]

Learned monks and the book collection

There were learned monks at St Edmunds in Samson's time. He himself had studied in the schools in Paris and was apparently a Master of Arts and Medicine,[250] and Jocelin refers in passing to monks who were Masters of the schools.[251] The contemporary account of the disputed abbatial election which followed Samson's death gives five of the monks out of the seventy mentioned

[244] JB, p. 22. *Heads*, i. 104.
[245] Welbeck MS ICI from the duke of Portland's collection. For a detailed description of this MS see A. Strong, *Catalogue of the Library of Welbeck Abbey* (London, 1903). See also Baker, ed. cit., p. 1 and n. 1.
[246] Baker, ed. cit., p. 61 lines 1–2. See Legge, *Anglo-Norman in the Cloisters*, pp. 10–11.
[247] Legge, *Anglo-Norman Lit.*, p. 258.
[248] Ibid., p. 257. For the Latin sources see Baker, ed. cit., pp. 53–5.
[249] See Legge, *Anglo-Norman in the Cloisters*.
[250] Above p. 12.
[251] JB, pp. 127, 129.

by name the title of Master.[252] It is not known at what stage in their careers or where they graduated but in most, if not all, cases they would have done so, like Samson, before they took the habit and in Paris.[253] Moreover, by no means all learned monks were Masters. There is no evidence that Jocelin, who was undoubtedly very learned, had ever studied in the schools. Nor apparently had his near contemporary, Simon of Walsingham, author of the Life of St Faith in Anglo-Norman verse.[254] Nor is there good evidence that the learned Denis Piramus, author of *La Vie seint Edmund le Rei*, also in Anglo-Norman verse, was a Master or had at least studied in the schools.[255] Similarly, William of Diss, who sometime between 1206 and 1211 was one of Samson's chaplains, was a learned monk though non-magisterial. He commissioned the production of at least two good-quality books. They still survive: one is a volume of Distinctions (a collection of the various meanings of words occurring in the Scriptures),[256] and the other volume of works by scholastic theologians, that is, the sermons of Peter Comestor (d. c. 1178), the *Liber exceptionum* by Richard of St Victor (d. 1173) and the *De Re Militari* by Ralph Niger (d. c. 1210).[257] The education of novices and monks within the cloister was obviously of high standard.

The presence in the convent of a distinct group of learned monks was recognized at the time and sometimes became an issue in domestic disputes, especially as a good scholar was (and is) not necessarily a good administrator. For example,

---

[252] *Electio*, pp. xxxvi, 86/7, 186–8 passim.

[253] It was rare for a monk in the late twelfth and early thirteenth century to be a Master. Compared with the situation in other religious houses, the number at St Edmunds was very high, almost rivalling the number at Canterbury cathedral priory. According to Greatrex, *Biog. Reg.*, the following monks were Masters in the cathedral priory in the late twelfth- and early thirteenth-centuries: p. 66 (M. Aaron), 69 (M. Alan, prior 1179–86), 155–6 (M. Walter of Evesham, first half of thirteenth century), 206 (M. Humphrey, d. 1188), p. 300 (M. Hamo de Thaneto, d. 1188), 320, 314 (M. Warin, d. 1180), 320 (M. William, occurs 1188 and 1198). In contrast, Greatrex lists one at Bath (p. 22, M. Simon de Cornobia, 1198 x 1223), one at Coventry (p. 360, M. Joybert, occurs 1198, d. 1216), and one at Norwich (p. 556, M. Simon, early thirteenth century).

[254] Above p. 134.

[255] Above, pp. 130–33.

[256] BL MS Royal 7 C V. James, *Abbey*, p. 80, and Sharpe, 'Reconstructing the medieval library', p. 215. Henry of Kirkstead entered the *ex libris* and class-mark, V. 3, on f. 4v. A damaged early thirteenth-century inscription is on f. 1v: '[damage] Willelmus de Dice seruus et monachus sancti Ædmundi ad honorem Sancti Ædmundi [damage] per misericordia [omnium] fidelium defunctorum requiescat in pace amen'. On f. 4v is a copy by Henry of Kirkstead of the inscription before it was damaged: 'Hunc librum scribi fecit frater Willelmus de Dice seruus et monachus sancti Ædmundi ad honorem sancti Edmundi.' William of Diss ('de Dice'), in Norfolk, was Samson's chaplain sometime between 1206 and 1211 (*Kalendar*, ed. Davis, p. liii). He added a passage to Jocelin's chronicle (*JB*, pp. 138–9). He was still alive in 1215 and took part, as a supporter of Hugh of Northwold, in the disputed abbatial election of 1213–15. *Electio*, pp. xiii n. 3, xviii, xxxvi and n. 6, xl, 60/1.

[257] Pembroke College, Cambridge, MS 27. James, *Abbey*, p. 70, and Sharpe, 'Reconstructing the medieval library', p. 214. Henry of Kirkstead wrote the class-mark, P. 25, on f. 1. An early thirteenth-century inscription is on the second flyleaf: 'Hunc librum fecit scribi frater Willelmus de Dice. Anima eius et anime omnium fidelium defuctorum per misericordiam dei requiescant in pace. Amen'. James, *Cat. Pemb.*, p. 30.

William of Diss asked Samson to relieve him of the office of sacrist only four days after his appointment because he could not manage the work properly and worry about it prevented him from sleeping.[258] During the debates among the monks after the death of Abbot Hugh about the election of his successor, the 'literacy' or otherwise of candidates was one of the considerations.[259] Some monks did not think that learning was a necessary qualification: Abbot Ording had been unlearned but 'a good abbot and had ruled the house wisely'. But others said that they did not want a 'dumb image' as abbot, for

> How can a man who has no knowledge of letters preach a sermon in chapter and on feast days to the people?[260] How, since "the rule of souls is the art of arts and the science of sciences," shall he who does not understand the scriptures know how to bind and loose?

Jocelin himself said that he would not agree to any man being elected abbot 'unless he knew something of dialectic and could distinguish between a false and a true argument'. Again, when it was a question of choosing a new prior in 1201, some monks objected to Samson's favoured candidate, Herbert, the sub-sacrist, partly on account of his lack of learning. Herbert humbly confessed that he felt unequal to the task principally because he would not know how to preach a sermon in chapter. Samson 'replied at length for his consolation and said, as if to the prejudice of the literate, that he could easily memorize and inwardly digest the sermons of others, as other people did'.[261]

The learned monks had the benefit of one of the best book collections in England at that time.[262] By the end of the middle ages the collection seems

---

[258] *Gesta Sacrist.*, p. 293.

[259] *JB*, pp. 11–14.

[260] Benedictine monks had the duty of preaching in chapter and occasionally to the people. Samson himself preached to the people in Latin or in English (in the Norfolk dialect) and had a pulpit erected in the church for that purpose: *JB*, p. 40. Above p. 127 and n. 192. Sermons to a mixed congregation of monks and laity usually took place in the afternoon, between dinner and supper, and would be in Latin or English. See: Harvey, *Living and Dying*, pp. 157–8; an important reason for attending university was to equip a monk as a preacher: eadem, 'The monks of Westminster and the University of Oxford', in *The Reign of Richard II. Essays in Honour of May McKisack*, ed. F. R. H. Du Boulay and C. M. Barron (London, 1971), pp. 117–19; J. G. Clark, *A Monastic Renaissance at St Albans. Thomas Walsingham and his Circle c. 1350–1440* (Oxford, 2004), pp. 33, 42, 60–1, 71, 75, 233. See *Chapters*, ed. Pantin, ii. 11–12, 76 art. 4, 120 art. 10, 211 art. 3, 213 art. 11, 214 art. 20. As will be seen, in the disputed abbatial election following Samson's death, the lack of learning of Hugh of Northwold's opponent, Robert of Graveley, became an issue. Below, p. 159. See also: G. R. Owst, *Preaching in Medieval England* (Cambridge, 1926), esp. pp. 48–54; H. Leith Spencer, *English Preaching in the Late Middle Ages* (Oxford, 1993), pp. 60–1, 106; Joan Greatrex, 'Benedictine sermons: preparation and practice in English monastic cathedral cloisters', in *Medieval Monastic Preaching*, ed. Carolyn Muessig, Brill's Studies in Intellectual History, xc (1998), pp. 257–78.

[261] *JB*, pp. 125–7. Spencer, op. cit., p. 106.

[262] See: Sharpe in *Shorter Catalogues*, pp. 44–7; idem, 'Reconstructing the medieval library', pp. 216–17; *Catalogus*, ed. Rouse and Rouse, pp. l–li; Gransden, *Exhibition Catalogue*, pp. 228–9.

to have contained over 3,000 volumes, more even than the libraries of Christ Church and St Augustine's, Canterbury. The growth of St Edmunds' collection had been continuous throughout the middle ages but was especially notable in the twelfth century under abbots Anselm, Ording and Hugh I. By c. 1200 the collection amounted to over 300 volumes.

In the last half of the twelfth century and early thirteenth there was a move to improve the organization of the collection. The earliest serious attempt was made to catalogue the books. The result was the book-list which survives on three leaves at the back of a folio-size copy of Genesis and of the Song of Songs which was copied at St Edmunds in the first half of the twelfth century.[263] Since the leaves containing the list are smaller than those of the preceding volume, the book-list was presumably originally a separate booklet. The list was prob- ably made under Abbot Hugh I. It has 261 entries but a few are repeats: alto- gether 240 titles are included. This number does not comprise the monks' total holding, for the list does not include some 35 books known to have belonged to St Edmunds at that time. The original list was not arranged in any particular order: the scribe numbered the items ii–cxxxviii, but continued with unnum- bered entries – three psalters and then mainly glossed bibles (many of them repeats of earlier numbered entries), ending with a total of 148 entries. At this point a second scribe, probably writing before c. 1175, takes over and adds 26 more books, still with little regard for logical order. Finally, in Samson's time, c. 1200, a third scribe added 185 entries to the book-list and tried to make it more systematic. He adopted the method of grouping entries under authors, sometimes repeating previous entries in order to include them in his author-list. In two instances he gave a cross-reference under the name of one author to a work by that author in a composite volume listed under the name of another author.[264] In the manuscript a few entries have been deleted or erased. Most of these are service books, a few of which had been included by the first scribe.[265] Deletions and erasures cannot be dated but possibly they were part of the third scribe's attempt to rationalize the book-list. About a quarter of the books listed still survive. Some of them have St Edmunds' *ex libris* inscriptions in a single hand datable to the early thirteenth century and, therefore, probably to Samson's time.[266] They are further proof of the monks' efforts to improve the organization of the book collection and to make its rich resources more accessible. It will be remembered that the abbey's archives were also re-organized under Samson and

---

[263] Pembroke College, Cambridge, MS 47, ff. 117–119v. Discussed, printed and annotated by Sharpe in *Shorter Catalogues*, pp. 50–87. See also Thomson, 'Library', pp. 618–19; Gransden, *Exhibition Catalogue*, pp. 230, 258 and pl. LXXIII A.

[264] Sharpe, op. cit., pp. 51, 79 nos 186, 187.

[265] Pl. II, and Gransden, art. cit., pl. LXXIII A.

[266] For an example see the inscription in the top margin of Pembroke College, Cambridge, MS 72, a mid-twelfth-century copy of the gospel of Mark, glossed. Pl. IV and Gransden, art. cit., p. 256 and pl. LXIX B. The *ex libris*, 'Lib[er] S[an]c[t]i Ædm[un]di', is in the early thirteenth-century hand and is followed by an inscription by Henry of Kirkstead recording that this glossed Mark was in the cupboard ('*de armario*') of St Edmunds; he wrote the class-mark, B. 101. The volume is no. 229 in the book-list. Sharpe in *Shorter Catalogues*, p. 84, and idem, 'Reconstructing the medieval library', p. 210.

it is noteworthy that the same scribe who wrote the *ex libris* inscriptions in the monks' books seems to have been involved in the archival re-organization.[267]

It is seldom possible to be certain whether a particular manuscript from St Edmunds was acquired under Samson. But if the handwriting and ornamentation are of that period and it can be identified in the book-list and/or has the characteristic early thirteenth-century *ex libris* inscription, it probably was acquired then. The same is true of a manuscript even in the absence of a relevant entry in the book-list and of the *ex libris* if the contents indicate provenance from St Edmunds. Then there is the question of the attribution of a manuscript to St Edmunds on purely stylistic grounds. Books produced by the monks themselves under Anselm, Ording and Hugh I can be safely attributed to St Edmund because their calligraphy and ornamentation are distinctive. The script is an excellent Caroline minuscule with distinctive features.[268] With regard to book ornamentation, the famous Bury Bible (executed c. 1135–45) with illuminated initials and miniatures by the great artist, Master Hugo, is in a class by itself.[269] Nevertheless, a few books executed in the abbey have very well drawn historiated initials, in pen-outline with the outlines tinted variously in red, blue, yellow and green.[270] These are main initials and show the influence of Master Hugo. Whether Hugo and/or the other artists were monks of St Edmunds or professionals is uncertain, but minor initials were probably by monks. Some are very pretty and are in flat-colour (that is unshaded water-colour) in combinations of red, blue and green with pen-work decoration. But by the time of Samson's succession fashions in general were changing. Early Gothic script was replacing Caroline minuscule. No palaeographer has yet examined manuscripts from St Edmunds in early Gothic to discover whether the script is distinctive. Highly illuminated main initials in gold and bright colours were becoming increasingly popular in high-quality books, while minor initials tended to be ornamented with delicate filigree pen-work, usually in red and blue, rather than in the flat-colour style.[271] As in the case of the early script, it is impossible to decide whether a manuscript was executed by a monk of St Edmunds or by a professional scribe and/or artist, or whether it had been acquired by purchase, exchange or gift. However, there was considerable overlap between the old and the new styles at St Edmunds,

---

[267] Sharpe in *Shorter Catalogues*, p. 47, and Thomson, *Archives*, p. 51 no. 41.

[268] See: McLachlan, *Scriptorium*, passim; eadem, 'The scriptorium of Bury St. Edmunds in the third and fourth decades of the twelfth century: books in three related hands and their decoration', *Mediaeval Studies*, xl (1978), pp. 328–48, with plates. Thomson, 'Library', esp. pp. 629–30; Webber, 'Provision of books', pp. 190–1 and pls XLV A and B, XLVI; Gransden, *Exhibition Catalogue*, pp. 229–31.

[269] See: Kauffmann, *Romanesque MSS*, pp. 88–90; idem, 'The Bury Bible' pp. 60–81; McLachlan, *Scriptorium*, pp. 195–250; Thomson, 'The date of the Bury Bible re-examined', *Viator*, vi (1975), pp. 51–8; Heslop, 'Artistry of the Bury Bible', passim and pls XLI, XLII, XLIII A, B and C, XLIV A and B; Gransden, *Exhibition Catalogue*, pp. 231–2, 245–6 no. 2 and pls LVIII B, LIX A and B.

[270] Pls. III, IV. See: McLachlan, *Scriptorium*, passim and pls; eadem, 'Wake', pp. 216–24; Gransden, *Exhibition Catalogue*, pp. 231, 255–6 nos 9, 10, 11, and pls LXIX A and B, LXX A (Pembroke College, Cambridge, MS 16, 72, 64 respectively).

[271] McLachlan, *Scriptorium*, pp. 262–8.

as elsewhere. Distinctive flat-colour initials occur in a few manuscripts from St Edmunds as late as c. 1200, their pen-work becoming more and more elaborate and imaginative. In such cases it seems fair to conclude that one of the monks was responsible.

A few examples of manuscripts probably or certainly added to the monks' book collection in Samson's time will serve to illustrate the foregoing observations. First, there are three handsome glossed bibles. One is a folio-sized copy of the Book of Kings, with gloss, now Pembroke College, Cambridge, MS 56. The text is in a bold, early Gothic hand in black ink, and each of the four books begins with a pretty initial in flat-colour.[272] Secondly, there is the large quarto-sized copy of the Book of Joshua, with gloss, now Pembroke College, Cambridge, MS 54. This volume is probably no. 227 in the book-list discussed above. Again the script is early Gothic, in black ink, but the ornamentation accords with new fashions.[273] The minor initials are in filigree pen-work and the historiated initial 'E' which opens the text is heavily illuminated in bright body-colour and gold. In the top half of the 'E' God appears arising by the far bank of the Jordan; He points to the right with his left hand and holds the end of a scroll with His right hand. Below, on the right, Joshua supports the middle of the scroll with his right hand, and points to a group of Israelites standing on the left; he and they look upwards at the Lord above. On the scroll, which continues to the bottom of the initial, is written 'Moyses seruus meus mortuus est surge et transi jordanum istum tu et omnis populus tecum'. ('Moses my servant is dead; arise, go over this Jordan, thou, and all this people with you.' Joshua 1.2.) The whole is in a rectangular frame in-filled with russet red. It is not a beautiful picture but its meaning is forcefully expressed.

The third glossed bible to be considered is a small folio-sized gospel of St John, now Pembroke College, Cambridge, MS 76.[274] It has the early thirteenth-century *ex libris* of St Edmund on the front pastedown. It still has its original binding of white tawed skin on bevelled board, with the back pin for the (now missing) clasp and strap. The script is an excellent early Gothic and its ornamentation a good example of the survival of an old style alongside a new one. The minor initials are well executed in the late flat-colour style and the main initial, an 'I', at the beginning of the text is beautifully illuminated in body-colour: the 'I' has a long, thin shaft ornamented with geometrically intertwined leafy tendrils ending in a strap work pattern and finally in a small dragon, all on a gold and blue framed background. A similar initial 'I' is the main initial in

---

[272] McLachlan, op. cit., p. 264 (fig.), 265; Gransden, op. cit., p. 256 and pl. LXX C (in colour).

[273] Pl. X. See McLachlan, op. cit., pp. 267, 297 and pl. 128 (monochrome), and Gransden, op. cit., p. 257 and pl. LXXI B. For comparison, see the account of the new illuminated style in Canterbury cathedral in C. R. Dodwell, *The Canterbury School of Illumination 1066–1200* (Cambridge, 1954), chaps VI–VIII passim and pls 65 a–d.

[274] Pl. IV. See: McLachlan, op. cit., pp. 266–7, 306; Gransden, op. cit., p. 257 and pl. LXI B and C; J. M. Sheppard, 'Some twelfth-century bindings from the library of St Edmunds abbey: preliminary findings. Appendix, Descriptions of four bindings from the Exhibition Catalogue', in *Bury St Edmunds*, ed. Gransden, pp. 199–200 and pl. LII A.

the copy from St Edmunds of the gospel of St Mark, glossed (Pembroke College, Cambridge, MS 71), which like Pembroke 76 has its original binding.[275] The quality of both these illuminated initials is so good that it seems most likely that they were executed by a professional artist, but the style of the minor initials suggests that they were by a monk of St Edmunds.

The survival of the old flat-colour style alongside the new styles is similarly illustrated by two copies of works by scholastic theologians which were added to the monks' book collection c. 1200. Both are high quality folio-sized books. One, now Pembroke College, Cambridge, MS 26, is a copy of Peter Comestor's *Historia Scholastica*.[276] It has the early thirteenth-century *ex libris* of St Edmunds, and is in an excellent early Gothic hand in black ink. The minor initials are in the St Edmunds' late flat-colour style and are very varied, elaborate and imaginative. One initial, an 'M', has a dragon hanging, as it were, from it, in the left hand margin.[277] The dragon is reminiscent of the dragons in two of the beautiful mid-twelfth century (Pembroke College, Cambridge, MSS 16 and 72)[278] glossed bibles from St Edmunds but it is not so well drawn. The other example of a patristic book deserving especial mention is even more attractive than Pembroke 26. It is a copy of the *Sentences* by Peter Lombard (d. 1160 x 1164), Pembroke 28.[279] The *Sentences* were the most widely used text-book of systematic theology in the middle ages.[280] It is probably one of the three copies entered in the contemporary book-list as no. 234, and is an exceptionally beautiful book. It is a large folio and the script is an excellent early Gothic, in black ink. The ornamentation testifies to the growing taste for bright, richly illuminated initials, and both it and the script are of such high quality that they must surely be the work of, respectively, a professional scribe and a professional artist. Each of the four books begins with an illuminated initial but that for Book I has been cut out. Each initial of the remaining three is set on a rectangular background. Thus, the initial 'S' (of 'Samaritanus') of Book IV is on a red background framed by purple.[281] The 'S' encloses coiled acanthus stems, with leaves in various bright colours – blues, pink, red and buff – inhabited by four small prancing lions, and a dragon's head also appears. A very similar book from St Edmunds of another of Peter Lombard's works, his commentaries on the Pauline Epistles, is preserved in St John's College, Oxford, MS 43, and is in the same brightly painted style.[282]

The examples cited above demonstrate that under Samson the monks were adding high quality books to their already impressive collection. They are also representative of some of the categories of books which attracted the monks at

---

[275] McLachlan, op. cit., pp. 266–7; James, *Cat. Pemb.*, p. 62.
[276] McLachlan, op. cit., p. 265 and fig. F; Gransden, op. cit., p. 257 and pl. LXXI A.
[277] Pl. VI.
[278] McLachlan, op. cit., pp. 256–8 and pls 104, 108, 115, 116 (all monochrome) and Gransden, op. cit., pp. 255–6 and pls LXIX A (colour), LXIX B (monochrome).
[279] McLachlan, op. cit., p. 266 and pl. 127 (monochrome); Gransden, op. cit., pp. 257–8 and pl. LXXII B (colour).
[280] See below.
[281] Pl. V.
[282] McLachlan, op. cit., p. 267.

that time. The glossed bibles represent late additions to the magnificent series of glossed bibles acquired principally under abbots Anselm, Ording and Hugh I. Thirty-four glossed bibles, mostly folio-sized, survive and the book-list enters others which have not been found. No other English monastery is known to have had such a good collection.[283] It meant that the monks of St Edmunds were exceptionally well provided with texts for exegetical study, the essential ingredient of monastic learning in the twelfth century.[284] But the copies mentioned above of works by Peter Comestor and Peter Lombard represent a new trend in St Edmunds' book collecting. The acquisition of works by scholastic theologians was necessary in order to keep the collection up-to-date.[285] It is noticeable that these acquisitions were made fairly soon after the publication of the works in question. Scholastic studies were centred mainly in the universities, notably in Paris (where Samson and no doubt some of the other monks had studied) but St Edmunds, like other monasteries at the time, relied mainly on its own school for the education of novices and young monks, besides needing to provide books for the continued studies of scholarly monks. It is remarkable that, however beautiful a book, a scholarly monk might add marginal annotations.[286]

A few more books from St Edmunds deserve mention since they throw light on intellectual activity among the monks under Samson. A unusual theological work, only apparently preserved in the two copies from St Edmunds, one of the late twelfth and the other early thirteenth-century, is a verse rendering of the *De Sacramentis Christianae Fidei* by Hugh of St Victor (d. 1141).[287] The *De Sacramentis* was intended to reveal hidden meanings in the scriptures by use of symbolism and allegory: it was the first comprehensive theological work produced by the Paris schools and became a standard text-book in the middle ages. The versified version may have been for the education of novices and young monks since verse is easier to memorize than prose. Biblical studies at St Edmunds presumably also accounts for the fact that at least one of the monks, or perhaps Samson himself, seems to have had an interest in Hebrew. Knowledge of Hebrew was rare, but not unknown, in medieval English monasteries and it is most unlikely that anyone at St Edmunds had more than a very superficial knowledge of it. However, a twelfth-century Hebrew psalter[288] and two

---

[283] For the collection of glossed Bibles see: Sharpe in *Shorter Catalogues*, p. 46; Thomson, 'Library', esp. pp. 623 and n. 27, 625 and nn. 45, 46, 636–8 and nn.; Gransden, *Exhibition Catalogue*, p. 231 and nn. 17, 18.

[284] See Smalley, *Study of the Bible*, pp. 46–66 and pl. 1.

[285] Thomson, 'Library', p. 638.

[286] The *de luxe* copy of Peter Lombard's *Sentences* in Pembroke 28 has such annotations. See the notes in the top margin of f. 160, pl. V and Gransden, *Exhibition Catalogue*, pl. LXXII A (in colour). For a later example, see the heavily annotated workaday copy of the *Sentences*, Pembroke MS 85, f. 28. Ibid., pl. LXXVI B and pl. IX.

[287] Gonville and Caius College, Cambridge, MS 145 / 195, Pembroke MS 109. Sharpe in *Shorter Catalogues*, p. 72 no. 126 and, for Gonville and Caius MS 145 / 195, Gransden, op. cit., pp. 235, 250–1, and pl. LXII B.

[288] Bodl. Lib., Oxford, MS Laud or 174. See: Smalley, op. cit., pp. 342, 348; Roth, *Jews in England*, pp. 129–30, 280 n. j. For the study of Hebrew in medieval England, espe-

leaves from another Hebrew manuscript, apparently from a liturgy for the Day of Atonement, survive from the abbey.[289] These were probably obtained from Jews in Bury St Edmunds, perhaps when Samson expelled them in 1190.[290]

In view of Samson's known interest in law, it might appear surprising that no law book datable to his time is known to survive from St Edmunds. However, the monks certainly owned the standard texts. The book-list includes a copy of Justinian's *Codex* and a copy of his *Institutes*, besides three copies of Gratian's *Decretum*.[291] Perhaps law books in the monks' possession in the late twelfth and early thirteenth century were among those looted by the townsmen during their revolt against the abbey in 1327.[292] When the monks sued the townsmen after the revolt they included in their list of damages '7 sets (*paria*) of decrees and 10 sets (*paria*) of decretals' besides many other learned books.[293] Nevertheless, traces remain of law books acquired under Samson, and the nature of the evidence shows that in some instances the books do not survive because in a later period the monks themselves destroyed them. The truth of this conclusion is proved by the survival of four double folio-sized leaves from a glossed copy of Justinian's *Digestum vetus* executed in the first half of the twelfth century. These leaves, set sideways, survive as flyleaves and a pastedown in the giant folio-sized copy of the *Digestum vetus* executed in Italy c. 1300, from St Edmunds, now All Souls College, Oxford, MS 49.[294] This magnificent book is probably the sole survivor of a multi-volume copy of the *Corpus iuris*, a collection of Roman law texts, given to the monks by the prior, William of Rockland (1287–1312). It seems that the monks scrapped the twelfth-century copy when they acquired the new copy, salvaging leaves from it for use in the binding of the latter. They probably made this replacement because the new copy was a grander, more beautiful book and also because it had an up-to-date gloss, that by Accursius (d. 1263/4).

Similarly, two leaves from a copy of a *Codex* (another component of any *Corpus iuris*) of c. 1200 are preserved in a late thirteenth-century manuscript from St Edmunds, that is, College of Arms, London, MS Arundel 30, ff. 213–

cially by friars, see Smalley, op. cit., pp. 338–55. Cf. A. S. Abulafia, *Christians and Jews in the Twelfth-Century Renaissance* (London – New York, 1995), pp. 94–7. Exceptionally, later, in the last half of the thirteenth century, Gregory, prior of Ramsey, and Richard of Dodford, a clerk of Ramsey, gave books in Hebrew to the monks. See Sharpe in *Shorter Catalogues*, pp. 330, 337–8 nos 51, 57, 339 no. 70, 403 nos 495–6, 406 nos 527–9, 533.

289   The leaves are now the front pastedown in Pembroke College, Cambridge, MS 59, from St Edmunds.

290   According to Leland, Prior Gregory bought his Hebrew books at an auction in Stamford in 1290, the year when Edward I expelled the Jews from England. Sharpe, op. cit., p. 330, citing John Leland, *Commentarii de Scriptoribus Britannicis* (Oxford, 1709), p. 322.

291   Sharpe, op. cit., pp. 78 no. 174, 75 no. 157, 77 no. 166.

292   The early fourteenth-century tract on the revolt at St Edmunds, the *Depraedatio Abbatiae*, relates that the rebels 'Deinde claustrum ingressi, cistulas, id est carolas, et armariola fregerunt, et libros et omnia in eis inventa similiter asportaverunt.' *Memorials*, ii. 330.

293   *Pinch. Reg.*, i. 150. Cited James, *Abbey*, p. 163, and Sharpe, op. cit., p. 47.

294   See Andrew G. Watson, *A Descriptive Catalogue of the Medieval Manuscripts of All Souls College Oxford* (Oxford, 1997), pp. 103–5 no. 49. Cf. Gransden, *Exhibition Catalogue*, pp. 236–7.

14.[295] Maybe this copy of the *Codex* which was executed and apparently owned by St Edmunds in Samson's time, was dismembered at much the same time as the twelfth-century *Digestum vetus*, probably partly for the same reason, because it was replaced by a copy with an up-to-date gloss, and also perhaps in its case because the replacement was more beautiful. Other flyleaves in Arundel 30 are also fragments of a law book datable on palaeographical evidence to Samson's time: folios 1 and 4 are from a unique decretal collection probably made at St Edmunds.[296] Maybe it too was discarded because it was out-of-date. But a book was not necessarily discarded because it was replaced by another book, more beautiful and/or up-to-date. It might simply be replaced because it was in bad condition or was so cluttered with notes in the margins that it was of no use to scholars who wanted to make their own annotations. Leaves from a workaday thirteenth-century copy of the *Digest*, glossed and heavily annotated, occur as flyleaves and pastedowns in a number of manuscripts from St Edmunds.[297] And one of the abbey's manuscripts has ten flyleaves from a copy of the *Codex* of identical appearance with those from the *Digest* and equally crowded with marginal annotations. This suggests that the monks discarded a thirteenth-century copy of the *Corpus iuris* because it had come to the end of its useful life.

The manuscript evidence surveyed above, patchy though it is, shows that the monks under Samson, despite financial problems and great expenditure on building work, could nevertheless afford to commission or otherwise acquire books of excellent quality. By adding to their book collection they helped to maintain a good standard of education in the cloister, and to provide the scholars among them with the necessary texts for their studies.

---

[295] See C. R. Cheney, 'A fragment of a decretal collection from Bury St Edmunds', *Bulletin of Medieval Canon Law*, n.s. viii (1978), repr. in idem, *The Papacy and England*, VII, pp. 1–7.

[296] Ibid.

[297] Leaves from a workaday thirteenth-century copy of the *Digest*, glossed and copiously annotated, survive as fly-leaves and/or pastedowns in a number of manuscripts: Pembroke College, Cambridge, MSS 62, 69, 85 (for which see Gransden, *Exhibition Catalogue*, pp. 236, 261 no. 25 and cf. pl. LXXVI B), 102, BL Royal MSS 10 B XII, 12 F XV, and Bodl. Lib., Oxford, MS C Mus 8.

13

Samson's Death and Burial

Abbot Samson died at St Edmunds on 30 December 1211.[1] As England was still under an interdict, when no one could be buried in hallowed ground, he was buried in the cloister garth. The interdict was lifted on 2 July 1214 and the prior and some of the senior monks wanted to move Samson's body for re-burial in the abbey church, 'for greater honour'. But at this time the monks were embroiled in a bitter controversy over the election to the abbacy of Hugh of Northwold. His chief opponent was the sacrist, Robert of Graveley, who himself aspired to be abbot and whose candidature was supported by a strong party of monks. Graveley immediately opposed the re-burial of Samson in the church, saying that 'no one, however great his power, ought to be buried there'. Instead it was decided to bury him in the chapter-house where Ording and Hugh I had been buried.[2] Graveley organized the whole proceedings which took place on 12 August in the prior's absence. Samson's coffin was disinterred early in the morning, 'about the hour of matins', and left resting on a tripod in the garth until evening. Then, while the monks were at vespers, he buried the body in the chapter-house in the presence of only one of the monks. Graveley hoped to gain credit for his expedition and efficiency.[3]

Samson's reputation at St Edmunds was high at the time of his death and remained so at least until well into the fifteenth century. This is apparent from the obituary notice in the contemporary *Annales Sancti Edmundi* and the commemoration in the Benefactors' List preserved in the Kitchener's register. The passages are worth quoting, because even though in laudatory style, they show what aspects of Samson's rule the monks prized most. The obituary notice in the *Annales*, freely translated, reads as follows:

> On the sixth day after the Birth of the Lord Samson, of pious memory, the vener-
> able abbot of St Edmunds, died at that place. He had ruled the abbey committed
> to him successfully for thirty years, less two months, and freed it from all kinds
> of debts and extended its very extensive privileges, liberties, possessions and
> buildings, and he had renewed religious observance both inside and outside [the

---

1   *Ann. S. Edm.*, pp. 19–20.
2   For the abbots' burial places see James, *Abbey*, p. 148.
3   *Electio*, pp. 100/101–102/103.

abbey] very sufficiently. He took a final farewell of the brethren by whom, having been blessed in this life, he deserved to be blessed, and they, standing around, all admired his marvellous, not miserable, passing. He rested in peace in the fourth year of the interdict.[4]

The commemoration in the Benefactors' list summarizes the benefactions bestowed by Samson on the convent:

> He recovered the manor of Mildenhall which had been alienated for 127 years, giving King Richard 1,000 marks and the queen 100 marks for it. He discharged the debt of 1,052 marks which burdened the monastery. He recovered certain manors. He appropriated the church of Brooke to the convent for the monks' clothing. He assigned the 60s which his predecessors had received annually from Southery to the convent. He procured for the vestry a golden cross of sumptuous workmanship worth 80 marks, and a cope worked with gold and a precious chasuble and many other adornments. He enriched the monastery with royal and papal privileges, possessions, books and gold and silver vessels. He built in stone a guest-house in the [great] court, a hall of pleas and a school hall and a hall at Redgrave, and many other buildings in the monastery and on the manors. He completed an aquaduct, bringing water from streams, and a wash-place of wonderful workmanship and of admirable magnitude, and many other good works. He built the hospital of St Saviour. He touched the body of St Edmund after the tomb had been opened, and found it incorrupt. Then he renewed the roof (*operimentum*, ? the canopy) of the tomb and adorned it with gems and gold. He ordered his buyers to give precedence to the cellarer's buyers in the market.[5]

Samson's failures are not the concern of the authors of either of these two notices. One of his failures lay in his relations with the convent. His quarrels with the monks revealed divisions among them, for instance between the learned and the unlearned, the young and the old, and between a faction supporting

[4] *Ann. S. Edm.*, p. 20.
[5] Samson 'manerium de Mildenhale per Centum et viginti septem annos alienatum recuperauit, datis ricardo Regi Mille marcis, et regine Centum marcis pro eodem monasterium oneratum debitum millium et quinquaginta et duarum marcarum infra duodecim annos acquietauit. Maneria quedam impignorata recuperauit. Ecclesiam de Brook Conuentui pro vestitu monachorum appropriauit. Item sexaginta solidos quos predecessores sui percipiebant de Sutheree annuatim Conuentui assignauit. Item vnam Crucem de auro et textum su[m]ptuosum precij octoginta marcarum et capam auro textam et casulam preciosam et multa alia ornamenta pro vestiario comparauit. Regum et Paparum priuilegijs, possessionibus, libris, vasis aureis et argenteis Monasterium ditauit. Aulam hospitum in Curia, et Aulam placitorum et Aulam scolarum et Aulam de Redgraue lapideas et multa alia edificia in monasterio et manerijs edificauit. Aque ductum et Aquam per riuulos deriuatam et lauatoria opere mirifico et magnitudine admiranda et multa alia bona opera consummauit. Hospitale sancti Saluatoris edificauit. Corpus sancti Edmundi aperto sepulcro tetigit et reperit incorruptum. Deinde operimentum sepulcri renouauit et auro gemmisque distinctum adornauit. Hic precepit emptoribus suis vt in foro cederent emptoribus Conuentus. Sepultus est in Capitulo secundus ad pedes Ricardi Abbatis sub lapidibus marmoreis quadratis vt superscriptum est de Abbate Ordingo.' Douai, Bibliothèque Municipale MS 553, f. 8. Except for the final notice of the abbots' burial places, the substance of the information is to be found in Jocelin. Comparison of the entry with those for the other abbots shows that few had been as generous to, and active on behalf of, his church as Samson.

the cellarer and another supporting the sacrist. Internal divisions were to seriously disrupt domestic politics once Samson was removed from the scene, as is so vividly described in the contemporary account of the disputed election of his successor, Hugh of Northwold, the *Electio Hugonis Abbatis*. The prolonged vacancy itself was a demoralizing factor. The author of the *Electio* expresses the monks' foreboding at Samson's death. He writes (with an allusion to John 10.12–13): 'His flock, left to the care of hirelings and given over to the ravening of wolves, was greatly distressed at losing so great a shepherd.'[6]

---

6   *Electio*, p. 2/3.

PART II

THE ABBEY 1212–1256

A vacancy of nearly three and a half years followed Samson's death on 30 December 1211, for reasons to be discussed below. In the period which followed until 1256 four abbots ruled in succession, Hugh of Northwold (that is Hugh II, 1213–29); Richard of the Isle (de Insula, de l'Isle, 1229–33); Henry of Rushbrooke (1233–48); and Edmund of Walpole (1248–56). The first three were able men – indeed Hugh of Northwold and Richard of the Isle were of outstanding ability, but with regard to Edmund of Walpole it is hard to form an opinion. Little is known about any of them and none has left a reputation at all equal to that of Samson or even to that of their two successors, Simon of Luton and John of Northwold. This may partly have been because their abbatiates were comparatively short, but it is mainly owing to the lack of sources.

There is nothing to show that any of the four abbots kept a cartulary or register, nor that any prior or obedientiary serving in their time kept one.[1] Similarly, the literary sources are deficient. Jocelin of Brackland had no successor as the biographer of an abbot and a conventual chronicler, and the *Electio Hugonis* is the last piece of top-quality historical narrative produced at St Edmunds.[2] Moreover, the tradition of writing a monastic chronicle dwindled in the abbey until it was revived under Simon of Luton in the late 1260s.[3] Then the monk John Taxster composed a typical monastic chronicle covering the period from the Creation of the World to 1265 (later continued to 1301). But its annals are meagre until the mid-thirteenth century when they become progressively longer and more fluent. In any case, the chronicle is a general history, not a specifically house history and has few details about Abbots Hugh of Northwold (Hugh II), Richard of the Isle, Henry of Rushbrooke and Edmund of Walpole beyond recording the dates of

---

[1] See Thomson, *Archives*, pp.16–19.
[2] For its value see *Bury Chron.*, pp. xvii–xx.
[3] Below pp. 152 and n. 10, 153.

their succession and deaths, nor is it much more informative about other aspects of the abbey's history. Fortunately, the *Gesta Sacristarum* is a valuable source for building achievements under these abbots and for other matters concerning the sacrist's office. Of more general usefulness is the so-called *Cronica Buriensis*, a history of St Edmunds which, although composed at the abbey of St Benet of Hulme in Norfolk, would seem to have been by a monk of St Edmunds.[4] Its author was probably a monk who had taken refuge at St Benet during the revolt of the townspeople against St Edmund's abbey in 1327. It is also noteworthy that Matthew Paris was remarkably well-informed about Abbots Hugh II, Richard, Henry and Edmund and the periods of their rule: he thought highly of all these abbots except for Edmund of Walpole, and shared the monks' concerns.[5] Finally, although no registers appear to have been kept during the period, later registers include verbatim copies and versions of many documents produced then, besides material derived from oral tradition. For example, the information about the four abbots' respective benefactions to the convent in the Book of Benefactors (*Liber Benefactorum*), a list preserved in the early fifteenth-century Kitchener's register, is particularly helpful.[6] In what follows, first, each of the abbots will be considered individually and, secondly, the period will be considered as a whole, thematically under subject headings.

---

[4] Above p. 2 n. 4.
[5] See e.g. pp. 91 above, 159 below.
[6] See e.g. pp. 145, 147 and n. 6 above, 176 below.

14

The Vacancy, 1211–15, and
Election of Hugh of Northwold

Abbot Samson died on 30 December 1211, and Hugh of Northwold, the subcellarer, was elected abbot on 7 August 1213,[1] but did not receive papal confirmation until 10 March 1215.[2] He was blessed by the bishop of Rochester, Benedict of Sawston, on 19 May, 1215,[3] and eventually King John confirmed the election on 10 June.[4] The reason for the long interval between Samson's death and the abbatial election was in the first instance the papal interdict which was pronounced in England on 23 March 1208 and lasted for over six years. It was not finally lifted until 2 July 1214 but negotiations to end it had been in progress for more than a year.[5] For much of this time John was under sentence of excommunication: his excommunication was pronounced in England in November 1209 and he was not absolved until 20 July 1213.[6] During the interdict, until John's absolution, vacant sees and abbeys were not filled.[7] But once absolved John acted quickly. On 25 July he issued a general order for the filling of vacancies:[8] St Edmunds received the mandate on 4 August. The monks immediately began the election procedure and Hugh of Northwold was elected.[9] But then there was a further delay in filling the vacancy: for almost two years John repeatedly refused to confirm the election.

Hugh's election is of exceptional interest because it gave rise to a prolonged dispute within the convent of which a detailed and nearly contemporary

---

1 *Electio*, pp. 2/3, 10/11.
2 *Electio*, pp. 152/3–160/1.
3 *Electio*, pp. 166/7 and n. 4.
4 *Electio*, pp. 170/1.
5 C. R. Cheney, 'King John and the papal interdict', *Bulletin of the John Rylands Library*, xxi (1948), repr. idem, *The Papacy and England*, pp. 295–7.
6 *Selected Letters of Pope Innocent III concerning England* (1198–1216), ed. C. R. Cheney and W. H. Semple (Nelson's Medieval Texts, London – Edinburgh etc., 1953), pp. 123 and n. 2, 154 and n. 2, and Holt, *Magna Carta*, p. 216.
7 For abbatial vacancies during the interdict see: Margaret Howell, 'Abbatial vacancies and the divided "mensa" in medieval England', *JEH*, xxx (1983), pp. 182–7; and Susan Wood, *English Monasteries and their Patrons in the XIIIth Century* (Oxford, 1955), pp. 91, 98 and n. 5, 143.
8 John's mandate to St Edmunds is cited verbatim in the *Electio*. *Electio*, pp. 6/7. See also *Rot. Litt. Claus.*, p. 147.
9 *Electio*, pp. 6/7–10/11.

account survives, the *Cronica de electione Hugonis abbatis postea episcopi Eliensis.*[10]
This has an added interest since detailed, contemporary or near contemporary
accounts of abbatial elections in medieval England are rare. Indeed, the unusually good evidence surviving from St Edmunds is rivalled only by that from St
Albans.[11] Jocelin of Brackland gives a brilliant description of Samson's election in his biographical chronicle, with a lifelike account of the discussions in
the cloister and of Samson's bearing and details of the election process itself.[12]
His account is well known. The *Electio Hugonis* is less well known and deserves
more attention by reason of its rarity, high narrative quality and its content. It
is the earliest chronicle devoted exclusively to an election to survive from St
Edmunds. It is an excellent piece of historical writing, combining fluent narrative with many documents cited verbatim. Comparison with independent, reliable sources indicates that its factual content is in general accurate. As a source
for St Edmunds' domestic history and external relations it is of great value, but it
also has wider implications: the events it relates were part of the national scene
– of King John's conflict with the papacy, with the church in England and with
the barons, on all of which issues the *Electio* casts incidental light. Nevertheless, despite the *Electio*'s excellent historiographical quality and factual value, it
lacks the personal touches and immediacy of Jocelin's writing, and the author,
unlike Jocelin, does not give the impression of writing with complete honesty.
In fact, the *Electio* belongs to a different historiographical genre: it is a *pièce justificative* written in favour of one party in the dispute over Hugh's election. This
in itself adds to its interest because it shows how an abbot elect, his supporters
and opponents might behave in such circumstances.[13] On the other hand, its
partisan approach means that its account should not always be taken at face
value. It was probably written sometime between 1222 and 1229 and the author
was probably Master Nicholas of Dunstable, one of the monks. He figures large
in the *Electio* and appears to have been a canonist and civil lawyer by educa-

---

10 This is the title written by Henry of Kirkstead, monk of St Edmunds, the distinguished
    bibliographer and antiquary (d. c. 1378), at the head of the only known copy (datable
    to the 1260s and 1270s), now BL MS Harley 1005, ff. 171–192v (modern foliation). See
    Electio, p. xlviii. For Kirkstead as an annotator see Rouse, 'Bostonus Buriensis', pp. 481–2;
    and Henry of Kirkestede, *Catalogus*, ed. Rouse and Rouse, p. lxxii–iv. See *Memorials*, iii. 26,
    for part of a variant version of the *Electio* which was incorporated in the *Cronica Buriensis*,
    a fourteenth-century compilation concerning the history of St Edmunds, for which see
    above p. 2 and n. 4.
11 For elections at St Albans see Vaughan, 'The election of abbots at St Albans', pp. 1–12.
    The earliest detailed account known of an abbatial election at St Albans is the account
    of the election of William of Trumpington in 1214. It is not in the version of the *Gesta
    Abbatum* edited by Riley, the edition used for the present article, but in the fuller version
    in the much less accessible edition by William Wats which also includes Matthew Paris's
    Lives of the Offas and is entitled *Vitae duorum Offarum Merciorum regum; et viginti trium
    abbatum S. Albani* (London, 1639), pp. 112–14. Cf. GASA, i. 255, and Vaughan, art. cit.,
    p. 2. Vaughan notes only two disputed elections at St Albans in the period from the
    twelfth to the fourteenth centuries and then the elect was opposed by only one monk who
    had himself aspired to the abbacy. Ibid., pp. 9–10.
12 JB, pp. 15–22.
13 *Electio*, pp. xxi–iv.

tion.[14] The *Electio* was written after the Fourth Lateran Council (1215)[15] and the author wrote with knowledge of its canons.[16] The council had ordained (canons 24 and 25) that prelates should be elected in one of three ways, by scrutiny, compromise or inspiration, and that the election should be conducted free from outside influence.[17] These canons clarified and gave renewed papal authority to existing canonical procedures. Their promulgation underlined the need for careful records to be kept of episcopal and abbatial elections in order to provide written evidence that they had been canonically conducted. And the *Electio* was designed to prove that Hugh's election had been canonical.

Hugh of Northwold was a native of the village of Northwold near Thetford in Norfolk, which lay within the liberty of St Etheldreda, that is, of Ely, and he was of baronial family. It is unlikely that John objected to his election because of his background. Indeed, his initial stated objection to Hugh's election was that the monks had ignored the customary rights of the king in the election process. His mandate had instructed them to choose an abbot 'according to English custom'. In 1164 the Constitutions of Clarendon (clause 12) had ordained that arch-bishops, bishops, abbots and priors should be elected in the king's chapel, with the king's assent and with the advice of those clergy whom he summoned.[18] This merely formulated long-established custom which gave the king virtual control over such appointments.[19] But it conflicted with canon law even before the Fourth Lateran Council. Canon law already stipulated that elections should be conducted free from outside interference,[20] and the Rule of St Benedict assumes that elections were a purely internal affair in a monastery.[21] In the twelfth century many great abbeys acquired papal privileges to bolster their right to free elections. St Edmunds obtained one in 1158.[22] But when at about the same time the monks of St Albans claimed the right to free elections by virtue of a papal privilege, Henry observed that all great monasteries claimed such a privilege but in practice he did what he liked.[23] Innocent III himself recognized the need for compromise. On 31 October 1213, he wrote instructing his legate *a latere* in England, Nicholas, bishop of Tusculum, to arrange for the filling of vacant sees and abbeys and to ensure that those elected were not only distinguished by learning and in their lives, but were also loyal to the king, whose assent must be sought to the electors' choice.[24] John's charter to the church of 21 November, 1214, granted the right to free elections and stated that an election would receive

---

14 See *Electio*, pp. 28/9.
15 *Electio*, pp. xv–xvi.
16 *Electio*, pp. xvi–xxi, and, independently, *Bury Cust.*, pp. xxii and n. 5, xxiii.
17 Printed *Histoire des Conciles*, v, pt 12, pp. 1352–4. For canonical procedure in elections see Gibbs and Lang, *Bishops and Reform*, chapter II.
18 *Hist. Docs*, ii. 769–70.
19 See Knowles, 'Abbatial elections', pp. 252–78 passim.
20 Friedberg, *Corpus iuris canonici*, i. 829. Cf. Knowles, art. cit., p. 254.
21 *Reg. Ben.*, pp. 280/1–284/5, c. 64.
22 *Papsturkunden*, iii. 232 no. 98.
23 GASA, i. 153.
24 Cheney and Cheney, *Letters*, p. 155 no. 938 and cf. p. 161 no. 968.

royal assent provided that it was canonical.[25] But John was not happy with this concession. The *Electio Hugonis* records that he told the monks of St Edmunds in April 1215 that he had written to Innocent III objecting that elections were being conducted 'in derogation of his liberties'.[26] In practice, the king retained his control of appointments throughout the thirteenth century: since he held the temporalities of ecclesiastical and monastic tenants-in-chief during vacancies he had the upper hand.

Hugh of Northwold was elected at St Edmunds by way of compromise, the most usual method in medieval England. After his election Hugh at once went with the prior and six monks to John (who was probably at Corfe) for his assent. But when John heard about the election he angrily refused his assent because he had been given no choice of candidate.[27] Indeed, in 1213 the monks seem to have deviated from normal practice. The election of Samson in 1182 illustrates how the monks' right to free abbatial elections might be reconciled with royal power. Jocelin describes the election.[28] The prior chose twelve of the monks who were to elect an abbot in King Henry's presence. But to avoid discreditable argument among the electors at the election, the monks chose four 'confessors' (that is, monks who had been ordained) and two of the most senior monks. These six were to write the names of three suitable candidates in a document which was enclosed and sealed. The twelve electors were to take this document with them to the king. If Henry allowed a free election, the seal was to be broken in his presence and he was to be offered a choice of one of the three candidates. But if he wanted another monk of St Edmunds, the monks would accept his choice. But if he wanted a monk from another house, the twelve were not to accept his nomination without consulting the monks who had remained at home. In the event, when Henry, who was at Bishop's Waltham (Hants), had been offered the choice of the three candidates named in the document, told the electors to nominate three others. This they did but then Henry told them to nominate three monks from other houses. Again, they obeyed but by degrees tactfully induced Henry to accept Samson as the abbot elect.

Unfortunately, in 1213, the monks of St Edmunds had to negotiate with a less emendable king and at a time when relations between the king, the church in England and the papacy were strained. How King John might bend monks to his will is illustrated by the election of William of Trumpington as abbot of St Albans in 1214.[29] William was a monk of St Albans but not a suitable candidate for the abbacy. A relative of his, Sir William of Trumpington, was the king's 'excellent' knight and John wanted the promotion of Sir William's namesake at St Albans. Matthew Paris leaves no doubt that the monks would have disregarded the king's wishes at their peril. The situation at St Edmunds in 1213 was particularly difficult because the election provoked a bitter dispute

[25] C and S, ii, pt 1, pp. 38–41.
[26] Electio, pp. 164–5. Noticed C and S, ii, pt 1, p. 39 and n. 9.
[27] Electio, pp. 12/13.
[28] JB, pp. 16–23. Cf. Knowles, art. cit., 276–7.
[29] Above p. 152 n. 11. Cf. Knowles, art. cit., p. 261.

in the convent between those monks who supported Hugh's election and those who opposed it. The course of the dispute was complicated and both John and Innocent III became involved, as well as leading magnates and ecclesiastics. John visited St Edmunds himself to try to settle the dispute and sent some of the key figures in his administration and government, for example, the chancellor, Richard Marsh, the treasurer, Peter des Roches, bishop of Winchester, and William Marshal, earl of Pembroke. Innocent III likewise tried to achieve a settlement, commissioning his legate, Nicholas of Tusculum, and judges delegate to hear the case.[30] Nicholas came to St Edmunds on 21 December 1213, for two days[31] and the judges delegate held sessions at St Edmunds and elsewhere on various days between 4 June 1214 and 10 March 1215.[32] The judges delegate were: Henry, abbot of the Cistercian house of Wardon in Bedfordshire;[33] Richard de Morins, prior of Dunstable, a well-known canonist and civil lawyer;[34] and Richard Poore, dean of Salisbury, soon to become bishop of Chichester and later successively bishop of Salisbury and bishop of Durham. Poore was noted for his learning and had been a pupil of Archbishop Stephen Langton[35] who himself intervened in the dispute.[36]

It is noteworthy that two landmarks in the course of the election dispute more or less coincided with landmarks in national history. Thus, King John's visit to St Edmunds took place on 4 November 1214.[37] Soon afterwards, on 21 November in New Temple, London, John sealed the charter granting free elections to the church.[38] Possibly events during his visit to St Edmunds helped convince him that this concession to the church was inevitable. He had demanded that Hugh, the elect, resign, and that the monks should hold a new election, promising to accept whomsoever they elected – even Hugh, provided that the election was canonical and in accordance with English custom. Hugh refused to resign, saying that his election had been canonical and that St Edmunds had the right to free elections by grant of Edward the Confessor, which Henry II, Richard and John had confirmed. Therefore, John had told the convent to divide between

---

[30] *Electio*, pp. 74/5–76/7. Calendared from this text in Cheney and Cheney, *Letters*, p. 161 no. 970.

[31] *Electio*, pp. 26/7–36/7 and nn.

[32] *Electio*, pp. 72/3–74/5, 153/4–158/9 and nn.

[33] Henry, abbot of Wardon (?1213–1215), was elected abbot of Rievaulx on 8 April 1215 (d. 1216). *Heads*, i. 146, 174; *The Chronicle of Melrose from the Cottonian Manuscript, Faustina B.IX in the British Museum … facsimile*, ed. A. O. Anderson and M. O. Anderson (London, 1936), pp. 59 (f. 31), 63 (f. 33).

[34] Richard de Mores (or Morins), prior of Dunstable (1202–42). *Heads*, i. 163. He was the author of an important book on procedure in ecclesiastical courts and served variously as a proctor, arbiter and judge delegate in numerous ecclesiastical cases throughout his long life. Sayers, *Papal Judges Delegate*, esp. pp. 46, 114–18, 296–301 and nn.

[35] Gibbs and Lang, *Bishops and Reform*, pp. 24–7 and nn. He served as arbiter or judge delegate in some important cases in ecclesiastical courts, but in much fewer than did Richard de Mores. See Sayers, op. cit., pp. 105, 116, 125, 133. See also Vincent, *Peter des Roches*, pp. 50–1, 167–8.

[36] Below p. 160 and n. 72.

[37] *Electio*, 116/17–28/9.

[38] See above p. 153 and p. 154 n. 25.

those who supported Hugh's election and those who opposed. He was astounded at the number of Hugh's supporters and the staunchness of their opposition.[39] This episode must surely have helped persuade him of the necessity of making substantial concessions to the church. The second landmark in the election dispute occurred in the following year. John eventually gave his assent to Hugh's election and received him into his favour when he met Hugh 'in the meadow of Staines', that is, at Runnymede, on 10 June 1215.[40] The *Electio* gives a lively description of the reconciliation and incidentally reveals that John was already at Runnymede on that date, where he went to negotiate a settlement with his baronial and ecclesiastical opponents.[41] By 19 June John had agreed on the terms of a settlement, which was to receive statutory authority in Magna Carta. Although on 10 June the matter of Hugh's election was of secondary importance, John's assent can be seen as part of his policy of placating his ecclesiastical opponents. Archbishop Langton was with the king, and, together with other ecclesiastics, was bent on securing recognition of the liberties of the church.[42] He had actively supported Hugh throughout the election dispute[43] and it seems probable that he advised John to give his assent to Hugh's election.

Within the convent during the dispute the monks apparently divided more or less equally between Hugh's supporters and his opponents.[44] The two parties in a general way represented the respective interests of the two most important obediences, the cellary and the sacristy.[45] Hugh's party represented the interests of the cellary and his opponents those of the sacristy. This is apparent from the parties' compositions. At the time of the election Hugh was subcellarer, and his election was supported by the then cellarer, Peter of Worstead. Another supporter was Jocelin of the Altar who had previously been subcellarer and subsequently was cellarer; another was Peter of Lynn, who likewise had once

---

[39] For King John's negotiations with the monks in the chapter-house see *Electio*, pp. 118/9–26/7. For the division of the convent into two separate parties see below and n. 44.

[40] *Electio*, pp. 168/9–70/1.

[41] Holt, *Magna Carta*, pp. 243–4.

[42] Ibid., esp. pp. 241–5, 280–7 (see index for further references).

[43] Langton visited St Edmunds from 19 to 21 November 1213 for the feast of St Edmund, 'led by devotion and veneration'. He attended chapter and, having heard details about the election, urged the monks not to dispute. *Electio*, pp. 20/1. For his part in trying to reach a settlement etc., see ibid., pp. 18/19, 30/1, 36/7, 64/5–66/7, 162/3, 166/7.

[44] *Electio*, pp. 84/5–86/7, 120/1. It is evident from the *Electio* that at St Edmunds at least in the early thirteenth century every monk, regardless of seniority or importance, had a vote in the election of the abbot: choice lay with the numerical majority. Richard Vaughan suggests that at St Albans choice lay with the 'senior and saner' monks. Vaughan, 'The election of abbots at St Albans', p. 12. For the respected and influential position accorded to senior monks by the Rule of St Benedict see *Reg. Ben.*, cc. 3 § 12, 4 § 70, 22 §§ 3, 7, 48 § 17, 56 § 3 and index to Fry, p. 573. On two occasions, if not more, at St Edmunds in the thirteenth century every monk had a vote in the appointment of the prior. See *Bury Chron.*, pp. 18, 89. However, the abbot and prior, with the 'senior and saner' monks, not the whole convent, issued the reforming statute of 16 October, 1280. See Gransden, 'Separation of portions', pp. 388, 397–8.

[45] See *Electio*, pp. xxxiv–xxxv, and, for the offices held by the obedientiaries mentioned below, see Thomson, 'Obedientiaries', pp. 92–101 passim.

been cellarer, and another Richard of Saxham who was to succeed Hugh as subcellarer. The guest-master and refectorar, whose offices depended for supplies on the cellary, also supported Hugh. The leader of the opposition was the sacrist, Robert of Graveley, and his main ally was Richard, the precentor, whose office was dependent on the sacristy for the upkeep of the church, the precentor's sphere of activity. Graveley was also supported by Richard of Newport, who was subsacrist by late 1214 and was later to succeed Graveley as sacrist.[46] The sacrist's party had domestic grievances against Hugh's party. The cellary had run badly into debt under Samson. During the vacancy the subcellarer imposed unpopular economies on the monks' allowance of drink.[47] Another grievance was the cost of Hugh's sustenance as abbot elect, and of his travel and law suits, most of which had to be born by the sacristy.[48] According to the *Electio*, Graveley kept Hugh on short supplies, causing him to suffer from the niggardly allowance.[49] The division in the convent between those whose sympathies lay with the sacristy and those who sympathized with the cellarer existed in Samson's time, if not before. Samson, an ambitious builder and beautifier of the abbey church, had had serious quarrels with the cellarer.[50]

The quarrels under Samson had tended to be heated, and the same is true of the quarrels during the dispute over Hugh's election, which, in fact, could become violent. Hugh left the abbey on 29 January 1214 without the convent's consent. This was mainly to rally outside support for his election, but he may also have feared for his safety at St Edmunds. During his absence, Richard the precentor, allegedly declared, with an oath, to Peter des Roches, bishop of Winchester, that 'heavy blows would be dealt before that fellow Hugh is allowed free entry [to the abbey]'.[51] When Richard of Saxham, the subcellarer, defended Hugh's absence against his opponents' censures, he said: 'It is providential that he did not stay longer, for had he done so you would certainly have strangled him.'[52] Occasionally actual violence broke out in chapter. In the heated arguments that immediately followed the election, one of Hugh's most important

---

46 Either Richard of the Isle (for whom see below pp. 177 et seqq. and nn.), sacrist 1217–20, or Richard of Newport, sacrist 1220 to before 1234, wrote to Robert of Graveley when he was abbot of Thorney (1217–37) inquiring about the customs concerning the sacrist's obligation to provide the abbot with wine and a cart. Graveley replied to 'his special friend, dear R[ichard]', informing him of the customs which he had observed when sacrist, and enjoins him to keep his reply strictly secret. A copy of Graveley's letter survives and is printed in *Memorials*, ii. 133–4. The customs mentioned by Graveley do not correspond to those in the Composition of c. 1215 or to those in the Customary compiled c. 1234. Cf. *Bury Cust.*, pp. 30 lines 2–4, 35 lines 7–10 and n. 2, 104 lines 8–9, 105 lines 1–3, 12–17. See below, p. 166.

47 *Electio*, pp. 70/1–72/3. The monks also objected to the prohibition by the legate, Nicholas, of their meals outside the refectory and of their extra food allowances. Ibid., pp. 28/9, 52/3, and cf. pp. 78/9.

48 *Electio*, pp. 80/1, 100/1, 110/11, 132/3, 152/3. The *Electio* gives the precise sums paid for expenses.

49 *Electio*, pp. 52/3–54/5.

50 *JB*, pp. 79–81, 89, 118–20, 122–3. Above pp. 34–8 passim.

51 *Electio*, pp. 36/7, 50/1.

52 *Electio*, pp. 64/5.

supporters, Master Thomas of Walsingham, stood up and spoke in favour of the elect, but an opponent 'laid hands on him (cf. Mark, 14.46) and pushed him down'. Later, when William Marshal, earl of Pembroke, on his visit to St Edmunds on 28 June 1214, told the monks to divide – Hugh's supporters were to stand on the right side of the chapter-house and his opponents on the left – to increase their number, the sacrist's supporters dragged the reluctant Jocelin of the Altar and John of Lavenham over to their side amidst much shouting.[53] Hugh's time at St Edmunds before the confirmation of his election cannot have been pleasant because of his opponents' hostility. Indeed when, on his return on 31 May, he was ten miles distant from St Edmunds only one monk, Robert, the chamberlain, was there to meet him, though he was warmly welcomed by a group of burgesses and clerks from the town. On his arrival in the abbey his opponents refused to talk or eat with him.[54]

Although Hugh and his supporters always claimed that the election was canonical, the *Electio* betrays signs of irregularity. Before choosing to elect by way of compromise, the monks took the advice of Archbishop Langton 'and of those bishops who feared God and defended the liberties of the holy church', probably Eustace, bishop of Ely, and William de Sainte-Mère Eglise, bishop of London, both papalist bishops.[55] The *Electio* describes the actual election in detail.[56] Three monks were chosen in chapter. They were Albinus, the subprior, Jocelin, the almoner, and Richard, the precentor. They were to choose seven 'trustworthy, virtuous and discrete' brethren to conduct the election and swore not to be influenced in their choice by 'gift, entreaty, love or hate'. All three were later to support Graveley in the dispute which followed. At this point Master Nicholas of Dunstable, seconded by Richard of Saxham, 'brought many charges' against Graveley, 'supporting them with evidence'. The election proceeded and the three electors chose the seven electors in private. But when the prior read out the names in chapter Master Nicholas of Dunstable and Richard of Saxham objected to the inclusion of Graveley as one of the seven. The monks, therefore, replaced Graveley by Robert, the chamberlain, later one of Hugh's supporters. Also among the seven electors were two others, Jocelin of the Altar and John of Lavenham, who both subsequently supported Hugh. And Hugh himself was one of the seven. The electors swore to consider the worth of each monk in turn, and to choose from among themselves or from the rest of the convent a monk suitable for the abbacy, according to the Rule. The convent swore to accept whomsoever they elected from their own community without opposition. The electors consulted in private in the chapel of St Saba, and examined each monk individually, writing down his opinion and nomination. They then asked in chapter for, and obtained from the convent, 'with the assent of all', written

[53] *Electio*, pp. 84/5. A monk might suffer severe punishment for supporting Hugh. See ibid., pp. 44/5–46/7, 60/1, 70/1–72/3.
[54] *Electio*, pp. 76/7.
[55] *Electio*, pp. 6/7.
[56] *Electio*, pp. 8/9–10/11.

confirmation of the monks' oath to accept whomsoever was elected. Finally, they 'joyfully' announced the election of Hugh of Northwold.[57]

At least some of the monks probably disapproved of the electors choosing one of themselves. At the 1182 election another Hugh, the third prior, was one of the electors and was also elected as one of the three internal candidates for the abbacy to be presented to King Henry for his consideration. Jocelin of Brackland remarks that 'all marvelled that Hugh was both elector and elected'.[58] Matthew Paris records that at St Albans the custom (which he said was very unusual) of forbidding electors to elect one of themselves was only finally abolished in 1235 for the election of John of Hertford.[59] But the fact that Hugh of Northwold was both elector and elected was not apparently one of the objections raised by Graveley's party. His supporters objected to the exclusion of Graveley from the electoral panel. They also accused one of Hugh's supporters, Master Thomas of Walsingham, of 'revising in many places without consulting his fellows' the document in which the seven electors had recorded the opinion of each monk. The result was, according to Hugh's opponents, that the person favoured by the majority of the convent could not be chosen.[60] Another thirteenth-century source from St Edmunds, the *Gesta Sacristarum*, does in fact record that some of the monks actually elected Graveley.[61] It probably refers to the stage in the election process when the electors examined each monk individually. In view of the subsequent dispute, it seems obvious that some monks nominated Graveley as their choice. Conceivably, Hugh's party, having packed the electoral board, hoped for the convent's unanimous support for Hugh, and, failing to obtain this objective, they connived at the falsification of the written record of the monks' nominations so that it would appear that Hugh had a clear majority. Possibly it was Graveley who had the majority: some monks were no doubt deterred from declaring their support for him after the election because Albinus, the subprior, pronounced the excommunication of those opposing the electors' choice.[62]

The *Electio* was written to justify Hugh's election and, therefore, is heavily biased in his favour. It seeks to demonstrate not only that the election was canonical but also that Hugh was much more worthy to be abbot than Graveley. It lists Hugh's virtues: he was 'good-humoured, upright, learned in the scriptures, full of grace and compassion, pleasant, absolutely devoid of moroseness, sober and chaste, modest and devout, calm, reliable and prudent' and 'of wonderful simplicity and gentleness'.[63] He always had the interests of the convent, not of himself, at heart. This stereotype of Hugh's character echoes the qualities

---

[57] *Electio*, pp. 10/11, 120/1–22/3.

[58] *JB*, p. 21.

[59] GASA, i. 251.

[60] *Electio*, pp. 122/3.

[61] *Gesta Sacrist.*, p. 293.

[62] *Electio*, pp. 16/17.

[63] *Electio*, pp. 10/11, 24/5. Hugh's character can only be speculated upon from what is known of his acts. For his career see D. M. Owen, 'Northwold, Hugh of (d. 1254)', in *Oxford DNB*, xli. 153–5, and *Electio*, pp. 193/4–195/6 (appendix V). For his building achievements when bishop of Ely see below, chapter 16, pp. 175 and n. 62, 176 and n. 63.

required of an abbot by the Rule.[64] Contrariwise, the *Electio* depicts Graveley as the kind of man whom the Rule would debar from election: he was 'severe, unfeeling, a scoffer and slighter of the brethren, ambitious, a dilapidator of the house and much else',[65] and he was shamefully ignorant of the scriptures.[66] (According to the *Gesta Sacristarum* Graveley was an efficient and successful sacrist.[67]) An ancillary purpose of the *Electio* was to provide a model, to show what kind of man the abbot should be and how he should behave.[68]

The intention of Hugh's party was to obtain papal and royal confirmation of Hugh's election, while Graveley's party wanted the election quashed and a new one held. Naturally, the parties did not base their cases on the respective interests of cellary and sacristy. They argued on a higher plain. On average Hugh's party was the more learned party.[69] It included all five monks of St Edmunds who had the title of Master: at least one of them, Master Nicholas of Dunstable, the putative author of the *Electio*, had probably graduated in canon and civil law at Paris or Bologna.[70] Hugh's party based its case on St Edmunds' right to free elections according to canon law, the Rule of St Benedict, and papal privilege. In addition, his supporters appealed to a charter of privilege allegedly granted by Edward the Confessor to St Edmunds, which included the right to free elections.[71] Archbishop Langton and the papalist bishops supported Hugh because free episcopal and abbatial elections were among the church's liberties for which they were struggling. The *Electio* asserts that when Langton first heard about Abbot Hugh's election, he raised his hands to heaven and exclaimed, 'Glory be to God the Highest! For now in this way the church has triumphed!'[72] Another of the supporters was the French legate, Robert de Courçon, a distinguished theologian and canonist. He had been a contemporary of Langton in the Paris schools where they had both been pre-eminent teachers.[73] He supported Hugh's election from the outset and did much to bring about a reconciliation between him and John.[74] The sacrist's party on its side supported the king's customary rights and a policy of placating the king in general because it was in St Edmunds' temporal interests. A good way of pleasing him was to make financial concessions. Graveley was John's favoured candidate, not only because he defended the king's customary rights but also because he offered the greatest profit to the royal treasury, both during the vacancy[75] and later when Graveley and his party

[64] *Reg. Ben.*, pp. 280/1–284/5, c. 64 passim.
[65] *Electio*, pp. 8/9.
[66] *Electio*, pp. 56/7–58/9. Cf. *Reg. Ben.*, pp. 282/3, c. 64 § 9.
[67] *Gesta Sacrist.*, p. 293.
[68] This is particularly apparent at the end of the *Electio*. See below p. 165.
[69] See *Electio*, pp. xxxvi–xxxviii. Hugh's party was also on average the more youthful party. *Electio*, pp. xxxviii–xl, 6/7, 12/13, 124/5.
[70] *Electio*, pp. 28/9 and n. 5.
[71] For this charter see below, p. 166 and n. 95.
[72] *Electio*, pp. 12/13–14/15. For Langton's involvement in the election dispute see *Electio*, pp. 6/7, 18/19, 20/1, 30/1, 36/7, 162/3, 166/7–168/9.
[73] F. M. Powicke, *Stephen Langton* (Oxford, 1928), pp. 16, 27, 56, 62, 68, 70, 88–91.
[74] *Electio*, pp. 50/1, 64/5, 106/7–112/13, 150/1–152/3, 170/1.
[75] Below p. 162.

argued that the king should be released from the debt of 4,000 marks which he had incurred during the interdict.[76] Hugh's party contended that although the convent could contract a debt during a vacancy, it could not grant a release from one.[77] John at last gave his assent to the election only after 'a certain sum of money' had been paid.[78]

John's reconciliation with Hugh at Runnymede on 10 June 1215 was complete. That day Hugh dined with the king at Windsor. After dinner while they sat together on the royal couch and conversed, Graveley came and knelt before the king and praised God that John had received the abbot into his favour and put the dispute from his mind. But John rounded on Graveley, saying angrily, with an oath, 'but for you I would have received him into my favour and love six months ago'. He then turned to the abbot and said, 'This sacrist, O abbot, has won you many enemies in my court. For when I had returned from overseas I was disposed, because of the petition of the French legate, to receive you into my favour. But those around me, who were working with all their might against you, not only prevented me, but even, by subverting my intention, inflamed my anger against you.' Graveley, abashed and confused, hastily withdrew without the king's leave.[79] Thus, John accused Graveley of nobbling people with influence at court in order to prevent John from giving his assent to Hugh's election. Indeed, it is clear from the *Electio* that the two parties used various methods to gain support both within the abbey and outside it. One way was obviously by secret confabulation. The sacrist's party accused Hugh of holding such a confabulation before the election, although the prior had forbidden the electors to discuss the matter 'apart and in secret' before the election had taken place. Hugh's supporters admitted that Hugh had talked with some men 'who had come by chance to the bake-house, but no mention was made of the election'.[80] (Hugh, as subcellarer, was in charge of the bake-house.) Hugh was accused in general of working for his own promotion.[81] The *Electio* indicates that he certainly did so, but it has much more to say about Graveley's methods of rallying support, and these tended to be unscrupulous.

Bribery played its part as a matter of course. Before the election the prior recited, and the rest of the convent confirmed with 'amen', the excommunication of anyone who during the vacancy attempted to buy promotion to the abbacy or alienate St Edmunds' goods for that purpose.[82] The reference is probably to attempts to bribe the king. The *Electio* expresses strong disapproval of the

---

76 *Electio*, pp. 134/5, 138/9–146/7. This debt was in respect of the king's exactions (*ablata*) from the abbey during the interdict. See C. R. Cheney, 'King John's reaction to the interdict', pp. 131–2. John's confiscations from bishoprics and religious houses and damages to their property during the interdict were the subject of much subsequent bargaining. See *C and S*, ii, pt 1, p. 39.

77 *Electio*, pp. 144/5.

78 *Electio*, pp. 164/5 and see n. 2 for a suggestion as to what the sum of money in question was.

79 *Electio*, pp. 170/1.

80 *Electio*, pp. 150/1.

81 *Electio*, pp. 30/1.

82 *Electio*, pp. 2/3.

bribes given at the outset by Graveley and his supporters to obtain licence from John for a free election to take place. To gain his favour they offered him gold and silver ornaments and utensils, the late abbot's property. John at first rightly refused the bribe. But later he accepted it because, according to the *Electio*, the sacrist lied, alleging that Samson had said that the king was to have these things after his (Samson's) death.[83] Both the sacrist's party and Hugh's were busy at court currying favour shortly after the election. Hugh's supporters there heard that the sacrist was 'maliciously and cunningly, in violation of his oath, corrupting the court with many gifts, and inciting courtiers against Hugh'.[84] For example, at some stage the sacrist gave the chancellor, Richard Marsh, a ruby ring without the convent's consent. When, on 21 December 1214, Marsh with Walter de Grey and the king's proctor, Henry de Vere, attended a session of the judges delegate at St Edmunds, the monks demanded the return of the ring. The *Electio* says that Marsh 'was confused and angry ... and showed the whole chapter the ring hanging around his neck'.[85] But a matter of more importance on this occasion was the debt of 4,000 marks mentioned above.[86] The sacrist's party, anxious for John's favour, wanted him released from the debt, but Hugh's party opposed it. Since a release would have to be made under the convent's seal, Hugh's supporters put the seal under papal protection.[87] However, Marsh and de Vere argued the king's case and finally insisted on a release.[88] Thus, both parties used various forms of bribery to win royal support. No doubt the same methods were employed at the papal curia, but the *Electio* does not record the envoys' proceedings there, presumably because the author was not one of them.[89]

Bribery also played an important part in the conflict within the abbey. The *Electio* accuses the sacrist of inciting his party with gifts and promises, and more specifically of bribing the subprior, Albinus, with gifts in order to undermine his loyalty to Hugh during Hugh's absence.[90] Bribery might take the form of promotion to important obediences within the abbey, and threat of demotion was a powerful weapon. Accordingly, the sacrist visited the legate, Nicholas, at Glastonbury early in 1214 and proposed that he come to St Edmunds, quash the election, and depose the cellarer, Peter of Worstead, and Robert, the chamber-

---

[83] *Electio*, pp. 4/5.

[84] *Electio*, pp. 36/7.

[85] *Electio*, pp. 136/7–138/9.

[86] Above p. 161 and n. 76.

[87] *Electio*, pp. 136/7.

[88] *Electio*, pp. 146/7.

[89] Matthew Paris describes the reception at the papal curia of the proctors sent to obtain the confirmation of John of Hertford, elected abbot of St Albans in 1235, and enlarges on the venality of the curia. GASA, i. 308–9. The cost of visits to the curia rose steadily in the thirteenth century. See Vaughan, 'The election of abbots at St Albans', p. 7. A list survives of the expenses incurred by John de Maryns, abbot of St Albans, when he went to Rome for confirmation of his election in 1302: the expenses were mainly bribes and 'presents' given to the pope, cardinals and others. Cited ibid., pp. 7–8, from G. G. Coulton, *Life in the Middle Ages* (2nd edn, 1928–30, 4 vols), iv. 281–2.

[90] *Electio*, pp. 54/5, 60/1.

lain, another of Hugh's supporters.[91] There seems to be no evidence that this ever happened. But later, in the spring of 1214, the sacrist quarrelled in chapter with Richard of Saxham, the subcellarer, because he had reduced the monks' ale allowance.[92] In retaliation, Richard was rude to the sacrist and, therefore, the prior deposed him and refused to reinstate him, despite intervention by the third prior, the cellarer and chamberlain. In the session of the judges delegate at St Edmunds on 21 December 1214 the king's representatives suggested, on the advice of the sacrist and his supporters, that if Hugh would renounce his election, all the obedientiaries of the sacrist's party would resign their obediences and never seek office again. But Hugh's party at once made the same offer and nothing came of the proposal.[93]

Forgery was probably also used in the dispute but much more rarely. Hugh's opponents accused some of his supporters of forging letters and inventing messages purportedly from Archbishop Langton informing the convent that the election had been confirmed by Innocent III.[94] Another but more doubtful instance of forgery is the charter of privilege allegedly granted by Edward the Confessor to St Edmunds, which includes the right to free elections.[95] The earliest known copy of the charter has been dated to c. 1200, and in its present form it is almost certainly spurious. Even if it is based on an authentic charter, the clause granting the right to free abbatial elections was probably an interpolation. Such a forgery could belong either to Henry II's reign or to 1213: in the latter case it was probably forged to support Hugh in the election dispute. King John certainly seems to have regarded the charter with suspicion. He said that the charter had never been used in the past and so was valueless.[96] If it was actually a genuine charter of Edward the Confessor, it is strange that the earliest confirmation was, according to the monks' own statement, by Henry II.[97]

Once his election had received papal confirmation (10 March 1215), Hugh adopted various measures to establish control and restore peace in the convent. For example, he appointed two monks to take charge of the extrinsic affairs of the cellary, and two others to be in charge of its intrinsic business. Then, on 25 April 1215, he ordered Master Thomas of Walsingham, Philip, John of Diss and Adam to travel around 'and to write down the number of ploughs (*karucas*)

---

[91] *Electio*, pp. 66/7.

[92] *Electio*, pp. 70/1–72/3. The legate, Nicholas of Tusculum, attempted to reform monastic observance at St Edmunds, especially concerning meat-eating and private meals. See *Electio*, 28/9, 50/1–52/3, 62/3–64/5. Cf. pp. xxxix, 78/9.

[93] *Electio*, pp. 140/1–142/3. Another weapon used by Hugh's opponents was to prevent his supporters from being presented for ordination. *Electio*, pp. 102/3–106/7, 138/9–140/1.

[94] *Electio*, pp. 148/9–150/51.

[95] For a list of the many medieval copies of the charter, in both Latin and English versions, with references to printed texts and commentaries, see Sawyer, *Charters*, pp. 311–12 no. 1045. For an easily accessible (Latin) text see *Mon. Angl.*, iii. 138, and for an authoritative commentary see Harmer, *Writs*, p. 141 and n. 2. See also *Electio*, p. 34 n. 1.

[96] *Electio*, pp. 124/5. For another reference to John's alleged confirmation see *Electio*, pp. 88–9.

[97] *Electio*, pp. 34/5.

and the amount of stock on each manor and also which of our lands were sown and which unsown'. This survey extended to the offices of all the obedientiaries so that no one in future would be able to defraud them.[98] Hugh's later methods of promoting peace are discussed in the next chapter.

---

[98] *Electio*, pp. 164/5–166/7.

15

The Abbots 1215–1256

Hugh of Northwold (Hugh II), 1215–1229

Hugh was a native of Northwold in Norfolk, which lay about six and a half miles from Thetford on the road to King's Lynn. It was under the jurisdiction and patronage of St Etheldreda's, that is, of Ely cathedral. People with the toponym 'of Northwold' first appear at St Edmunds' in thirteenth-century records and in a list of c. 1300 a Sir Robert of Northwold appears among St Edmunds' military tenants.[1] Hugh's father, Peter of Northwold, and mother Emma appear in the Book of Benefactors: their respective anniversaries were celebrated with a toll of the bells ('simplici sonitu') and masses recited for their souls. On each occasion the monks received a pittance payable from the cellary.[2] Hugh's family was not only of baronial status but it also included highly educated men, most notably Hugh's nephew, Nicholas of Ely, successively bishop of Worcester (1266–8) and Winchester (1268–80).[3] Another nephew, William of Northwold, witnessed a charter during Hugh's abbacy.[4] A William of Northwold, presumably not the same man, was a monk of St Edmunds, served as Abbot Simon of Luton's chap-

---

1   BL MS Additional 14847, f. 94; *Pinch. Reg.*, i. 281. A useful account of Hugh of North-wold's career is by Thomson, *Electio*, pp. 193–6. Sir Robert of Northwold gave eight acres in Fornham to St Edmunds. BL MS Harley 638, f. 182.
2   The entry in the Book of Benefactors for Emma of Northwold reads: 'Pro Emma matre Hugonis Abbatis Pitancia vnius marce per Cellerarium de molendino de Hennow'; that for Peter of Northwold reads 'Pro Petro de Norwolde patre Hugonis Abbatis pro quo pitancia vnius marce de grangijs Cellerarij sancti Edmundi, et vndecim denarios annui redditus in Bumstede pro pitancia Conventui facienda in die anniversarij sui per Pitanciar'. Simplici Sonitus. Douai, Bibliothèque Municipale MS 553, ff. 16v, 17v–18, respectively. Bump-stead (Steeple) is in north Essex. The cellarer held there. *Mon. Angl.*, iii. 157; *Bury Chron.*, p. 108.
3   CUL MS Ff. ii. 33, f. vᵛ: 'Memorandum quod dominus Elyas de couling capellanus celebrat in capella sancti Edmundi confessoris in capella sancti Roberti pro animabus Hugonis de Nortwold episcopi Elyensis et quondam abbatis sancti Edmundi et Nicholai episcopi Wyncestrie et pro omnibus benefactoribus ecclesie de sancto Edmundo vivis et defunctis.' This memorandum is in the hand of Henry of Kirkstead who apparently copied it from the more or less identical entry in BL MS Harley 1005, f. 42 (cited Thomson, *Electio*, p. 192 n. 6) which adds that for this Bishop Nicholas gave to the high altar of St Edmund for the daily celebration of mass a beautiful enamelled chalice ('unum calicem pulchrum et aumelatum'). Cowlinge/Cooling is in West Suffolk, 6½ miles north-west of Clare. St Edmund, confessor, was of course St Edmund of Abingdon.
4   BL MS Harley 27, f. 76v.

lain c. 1259/60, and was subsequently subcellarer, and then, jointly with 'J'. of Mildenhall, cellarer.[5]

Hugh of Northwold assumed the habit at St Edmunds in 1202[6] and at the time of his election to the abbacy held the office of subcellarer. Once abbot he remained so until his election in 1229 to the bishopric of Ely. Hugh soon proved himself an able and energetic abbot. His first concern was to establish his control and restore peace in the convent. The *Electio* ends with a general paean on his methods, emphasizing his firmness and just dealing and expressing the hope that Hugh will continue with such a wise policy. The author writes

> the worthy Abbot Hugh, adorning his office by the divine will, manfully subdued the tempest of the mighty sea [Acts 27.18] raging against him, vigorously met and overcame the various slanders and deadly perils threatening him, and openly and completely trampled underfoot the perjury and false witnesses employed against him. And he so bore himself towards everybody as not only to show his gratitude to those of the household of faith [Gal. 6.10], who for his sake had honourably borne 'the heat and burden of the day' [Matt. 20.12], but even in the case of others – whom I will not call his enemies although I wish I could say they were his friends – he laboured assiduously to promote to high office and dignity in the church.[7]

Robert of Graveley and some of his supporters probably continued to feel aggrieved at Hugh's election. This would explain why the *Electio* was written several years after the election in order to justify the election process and eulogize Hugh, who possibly commissioned the work. Graveley, according to the *Electio*, had feared that if the election were confirmed Hugh would never pardon him for his 'infinite crimes'.[8] In the event, such fears were partly justified. Hugh certainly may have 'laboured assiduously to promote him to high office and dignity in the church', but, if so, he engineered his removal from St Edmunds. In 1217 Graveley was elected abbot of Thorney. He owed his election to the intervention of the legate, Guala, who forced the resignation of a newly elected abbot of Thorney and secured Graveley's election instead.[9] Very possibly Hugh persuaded Guala that Graveley's removal would be expedient because he was being troublesome, and Graveley himself, from his own self-interest, may have lobbied Guala in order to gain the promotion.

The case with regard to Richard the precentor, Graveley's principal ally during the election dispute, is problematical. He has been identified with Richard of the Isle (de Insula, de l'Isle) who, having succeeded Graveley as sacrist, was appointed prior in 1220.[10] In 1222 he was elected abbot of Burton, but returned to St Edmunds in 1229 on his election to the abbacy in succession to Hugh. However, this identification could well be wrong. On the face of it, it seems

5 BL MSS Harley 645, ff. 254, 262v, and Cotton, Vitellius F. 12, f. 196v.
6 *Ann. S. Edm.*, p. 10.
7 *Electio*, pp. 172/3.
8 Ibid., pp. 70/1.
9 See *Letters and Charters of Cardinal Guala Bicchieri*, ed. Vincent, pp. lvi, 87–9 nos 119–20, 129–33 no. 158.
10 *Gesta Sacrist.*, p. 293.

unlikely that Hugh, having rid himself of Graveley in the sacrist's office, would have replaced him by Graveley's principal ally. The *Electio* describes Richard the precentor's part in the election dispute in denigratory terms[11] but never gives him the toponym 'de Insula' or 'de l'Isle'. In fact, the first appearance of 'Richard de Insula' is in the *Gesta Sacristarum* which records his succession to the sacristy. Perhaps Richard of the Isle was some monk of St Edmunds other than Richard the precentor. However, it is hard to identify him with one of the other Richards known to have been a monk of St Edmunds during the election dispute. Possibly he was a new arrival in the abbey, transferred from another house so that Hugh would have a sacrist with whom he could work in harmony.[12] Bearing in mind the close connections of Hugh of Northwold and the Northwold family with Ely, it seems possible that Richard of the Isle had been a monk of St Etheldreda's. Matthew Paris provides a possible clue to his family background. Describing Richard of the Isle's merits he says that Richard 'called de Insula was distinguished by birth, but even more distinguished in behaviour'.[13] It seems, therefore, that Richard de Insula was of baronial class. More than one baronial family was called 'de Insula' or de l'Isle, but possibly our Richard de Insula was related to Sir Robert (de Insula) who lived in the late twelfth and early thirteenth centuries and appears to have taken his name from the Isle of Ely. He held some of his extensive estates from the bishop of Ely and though most of his holdings were in Cambridgeshire, he held the bishop's manor of Nedging in West Suffolk, in the Liberty of St Edmunds.[14] If this identification is correct, it suggests that Hugh, far from appointing Graveley's ally, Richard the precentor, to the sacristy, chose a man of very similar family background to his own.

Hugh's treatment of less influential monks who had been his opponents during the election dispute was moderate and conciliatory. Within five weeks of receiving papal confirmation of his election, Hugh, on the advice of Prior Herbert, Albinus the subprior and of Graveley himself, appointed two of his previous opponents to oversee the cellary's external affairs, and two more to ensure that funds were sufficient for the monks' sustenance and hospitality.[15] It will be recalled that economy over the monks' ale allowance by the subcellarer,

---

[11] *Electio*, pp. 8/9, 16/17, 26/7–28/9, 44/5, 48/51, 124/5, 158/9. Thomson's identification (Ibid., pp. xxxv, 185 and n. 6) of Richard of the Isle with 'Richard the precentor', who begins to appear in the abbey's records from c. 1186, and Richard the [abbot's] chaplain, who according to the records held that position from c. 1200–1211, is open to the same objection since the name is never qualified with the toponym 'de Insula' or 'de l'Isle'. See e.g. *Kalendar*, ed. Davis, pp. 90, 98, 162, 163, 166, and index p. 187 under 'Richard'. Richard was a very common name at the time (as Davis's index to ibid. illustrates).

[12] For later examples of monks being transferred to other houses with licence of their superiors see Greatrex, *Biog. Reg.*, pp. 181 (Nicholas de Gra[n]tebrigg, 1286), 219 (John Langle III, 1470), 598 (John Cray, 1403), 687–8 (John and Robert de Dureville, 1260). Unlike St Albans, St Edmunds had no dependent priories to which it could send troublesome monks.

[13] *Chron. Maj.*, iii. 239.

[14] G. E. C., *Peerage*, viii. 69 and n.d, 70–1, and William Farrer, *Honors and Knights' Fees ...* (London – Manchester, 1923–5, 3 vols), iii. 171–4.

[15] *Electio*, pp. 70/1–72/3.

one of Hugh's supporters, had been one issue in the dispute. Hugh's conciliatory policy may have gone further than this. It is not unlikely that the (undated) composition between an (unnamed) abbot and the convent discussed above should be attributed to the beginning of Hugh's abbatiate. As was pointed out, much of its content closely relates to acts perpetrated by Samson which the monks considered abuses of his power. Its purpose was clearly to prevent Samson's successors from behaving in the same way.[16]

Compositions (formal agreements) between the head of a house and his convent were not unusual from the last half of the twelfth century onwards. Their content varies: some deal with a wide range of topics, specifying the convent's land holdings, revenues and jurisdictional rights according to their allocation to individual obedientiaries, while others have narrower concerns, perhaps some particular landholding or right claimed by the convent. In general, such compositions were an outcome of the growth of conventual power and a convent's ability to act independently. Thus, in 1206 a large contingent of the monks of Evesham rebelled against their reprobate abbot, Roger Norreys, and left the abbey.[17] They only agreed to return after Norreys had made numerous concessions in writing, in recognition of the abbey's 'ancient customs'. Some of the compositions, for example, the four comprehensive ones between the abbot and monks of Westminster issued in 1225, 1225–6, 1252 and in 1308,[18] appear to have been issued with the willing cooperation of the head of the house, in the interests of both parties, since codification promoted efficient administration and domestic harmony. And, as will be seen, codification helped safeguard a convent's rights and possessions against seizure by the royal custodian during vacancies. But other agreements were intended to settle particular disputes. For example, the monks of the cathedral priory of Worcester after a long struggle reached an agreement in 1224 with William of Blois, bishop and titular abbot, ensuring them a part in the appointment of the prior.[19] If the head of a house was unwilling to grant, or was determinedly opposed to, the convent's requests, the monks might take advantage of an occasion when he was in an exceptionally weak position. A good example is provided by St Albans where a dispute arose centring on one issue, the practice of the abbot, John de Cella (1195–1214), of exiling dissident monks to the abbey's cells and transferring them from one cell to another at will, which he claimed as a right. A group of the monks tried to persuade John on his deathbed (he died on 17 July) to seal a charter forgoing the right in respect of himself and his successors. The dying abbot was too weak to deal with the matter and the monks, choosing to understand his silence as consent, sealed the charter on his behalf. The leader of his opponents, William of Trumpington, was elected on 20 November to succeed John. His arbitrary

---

16 Above pp. 35–41, 44–8.

17 *Chron. abbatiae de Evesham*, pp. 204–23, 234–6. Knowles, MO, pp. 329–45 and nn. For the growth of conventual power and assertiveness see ibid., pp. 412–17.

18 The four compositions are discussed and printed by Barbara Harvey in *Walter de Wenlock*, pp. 4, 217–40.

19 *The Cartulary of Worcester Cathedral Priory*, ed. A. R. Darlington, *Pipe Roll Soc.*, n.s. xxviii (1968), nos 437, 540. Cited Greatrex, *Biog. Reg.*, p. 755.

rule soon aroused opposition and for the sake of peace he promised to abide by the charter. But he broke his word and resumed the practice of banishing dissident monks.[20] The legate, Nicholas of Tusculum, visited St Albans, according to Matthew Paris at William's instigation, later in 1214 and tore up the charter – but that did not end the dispute.

The St Edmunds' Composition must have been written when the abbot was likewise in a weak position. It was suggested above that possibly it should be dated to 1202 when Samson was unwell and about to set out for France for difficult negotiations with King John and was in urgent need of money and support from the convent.[21] But though he promised to make concessions to the monks on his return, Jocelin of Brackland did not believe that he would keep his promise. A stronger case can be made for dating the Composition to the beginning of Hugh of Northwold's rule. In view of the strength of opposition to his election and the length of the dispute it would not be surprising if he promised in the course of negotiations with the convent to rectify the abuses of power of which the monks had accused Samson. Jocelin provides a precedent for such a promise. He records that before the election in 1182 the monks, at Samson's suggestion, had sworn that whosoever was elected would treat the convent reasonably, and neither burden the sacrist, nor charge obedientiaries or admit any man as a monk without the convent's consent.[22] Later, he suggested to those monks travelling to visit King Henry for the election a further oath, but the prior considered that they had sworn enough.[23]

Possibly the opponents of Hugh of Northwold were influenced by the examples set by the dissident monks of Evesham and St Albans. They could well have heard of the Evesham case from the legate, Nicholas of Tusculum, or from one of his entourage. Nicholas had confirmed the Evesham agreement but Norreys did not mend his ways. Therefore, when Nicholas visited Evesham on 22 November 1213 he deposed Norreys.[24] He visited St Edmunds only a month later, to try to settle the election dispute.[25] Again, on 26 July 1214, shortly after the dissident monks of St Albans had tried to compel their dying abbot to seal their charter, the judges delegate who were hearing the case between Hugh of Northwold and his opponents sat in St Peter's church in St Albans: the proctors for both sides were influential monks of St Edmunds.[26]

An important reason why the monks attached such importance to codifying the division between the abbot's portion and the convent's was that during a vacancy the king's custodian of the abbey might take over, or encroach upon, the convent's portion. Jocelin graphically describes the monk's anxiety lest Samson's encroachment would lead to this result.[27] The best method of defence

---

[20] GASA, i. 247–57 passim.
[21] JB, pp. 135–7. Above pp. 42–3.
[22] JB, p. 18.
[23] JB, p. 19.
[24] Chron. Eve., pp. 234–6.
[25] Electio, pp. 26/7 and n. 3, 28/9 and n. 2–36/7 and Bury Chron., p. 2.
[26] Electio, pp. 90/1.
[27] JB, pp. 89–90, and cf. 136–7.

was to banish by codification uncertainty about the exact landholdings, revenues and jurisdictional rights belonging to each respective portion. The *Electio*
has little to say about the vacancy which followed Samson's death and lasted for
nearly three and a half years, treating it as part of the background to the election
dispute. It records that on the sacrist's (Graveley's) advice, King John granted
custody of the abbot's portion as well as the convent's to the monks in return
for fixed payments. The *Electio* states that 'the convent was not consulted and
monks often spoke against it because of the many dangers which would arise
from the mixing of the two portions'.[28] As it happened, the monks fell in arrears
with the fixed payments and early in May 1214 John took the convent's portion
as well as the abbot's into his hands, to maintain it for his own profit, 'allowing
the monks reasonable sustenance'.[29] However, the arrangement can hardly have
been popular with the convent. As Jocelin so graphically describes, the monks
had a perennial objection to a royal custodian taking over their portion of the
abbey's possessions.[30] In fact, the overall concern of the Composition was to
define and codify the convent's portion in particular.

   Therefore, in view of the circumstances it seems reasonable to argue that
the Composition was drawn up sometime during the election dispute or shortly
after Hugh of Northwold's installation as abbot of St Edmunds, and that it was
one of the methods adopted by Hugh and his supporters to pacify opponents.
An early act by one of Hugh's successors could be regarded as adding weight to
this argument.[31] John of Northwold, probably a member of the same family as
Hugh, made a rather similar composition with the prior and convent within a
year of his succession to the abbacy. His election received papal confirmation
on 18 September 1279 and the Composition is dated 16 October 1280. Like
the earlier composition, the document begins by accusing the previous abbot
of usurping the convent's rights. And, as in 1215, the higher echelon of the
conventual hierarchy was replaced by new men. Although there is no evidence
of opposition to John's election, his early acts indicate that he thought that the
means he adopted to establish harmony with his monks, which were very like
those adopted by Hugh, were wise ones.

   Once Hugh had established his control and apparently restored peace in the
abbey, it seems that he did nothing to prevent the sacrist from exercising his
traditional power and to be again foremost of the obedientiaries. Indeed, it is
clear that he gave the sacrist's enterprises his full support. After Richard of the
Isle's short term of office he was succeeded by Richard of Newport, one of the
most successful and active of St Edmunds' sacrists, who is known to have served
as a papal judge delegate at least once.[32] He celebrated his period of office by the

---

[28] *Electio*, pp. 4/5. For this grant the convent initially paid 1,000 marks and then paid at a
      yearly rate of £500. See Howell, 'Abbatial vacancies', p. 186 and n. 73.
[29] *Electio*, pp. 80/1–82/3. For delay in payment see ibid., pp. 22/3, 26/7. In the late summer of
      1214, the king instructed Peter des Roches, bishop of Winchester, to see that the abbey's
      possessions were not plundered while he was in France. Ibid., pp. 108/9, 112/3.
[30] JB, pp. 8, 81.
[31] Gransden, 'Separation of portions', pp. 373–404 passim.
[32] The entry for Richard in *Gesta Sacrist.*, pp. 293–4, is cited below, chapter 19, p. 233 nn.

great bell he had made for 'the major bell-tower at no mean expense', which was called the 'Neweport'. His main achievement was to have the old chapter-house destroyed and a new one built from its foundations. He also had a new fishery made on the sacrist's manor of Icklingham, again 'at great expense', and he constructed a new hall and solar at Manhall, a manor about three miles north of Saffron Walden.[33] Details about Richard's building-work, and about how high-quality stone was transported to St Edmunds from the quarries of Northampton-shire, are in chapter 19.

Apart from the above information about the building activities of the sacrist under Abbot Hugh, little is known about Hugh's rule at St Edmunds itself. The impact on St Edmunds of the movement for monastic reform during his abbacy was presumably reflected in some statutes of reform which Pandulph, bishop of Norwich (1215–26), confirmed, no doubt by his legatine authority, some-time between the summer of 1218 and that of 1221. Possibly the statutes were based on the Composition drawn up between the abbot and monks in c. 1215, but their text does not seem to survive.[34] However, we do have the text for the appropriation to St Edmunds of the church of St Mary, Mildenhall, 'for hospitality, alms and other pious work', by the legate Pandulph, 'bishop elect of Norwich', in 1219. The terms of the appropriation vary slightly from those in the appropriation of that church by Bishop John de Gray in 1205, discussed above. For example, Pandulph's official, Master Alan, and his steward, Alexander of Bassingbourn, assessed the vicarage at 25 marks, while the 1205 appropriation valued it at twenty marks, and there is no mention of an annual pension of three marks to Battle abbey. Thus, St Edmunds fixed its claim to more revenue from the church of Mildenhall.[35]

Abbot Hugh's contribution to the on-going defence, definition and codifi-cation of St Edmunds' privileges in the face of the expansion of royal govern-ment will be considered in wider contexts in chapter 20 below. Here we will outline Hugh's life as a public figure. As was to be expected of the abbot of one

---

20–3. He served as a papal judge delegate with the priors of Ixworth and Thetford for the settlement of a dispute between the rector of Bunwell (south Norfolk) and the monks of Castle Acre priory over tithes. *Acta Norwich 1215–43*, ed. Harper-Bill, pp. 9–10.

[33] Ibid., p. 274. Below p. 233 and n. 20–22. Manhall had been given to St Edmunds by Alan the Red in the late eleventh century. See *Feudal Docs*, pp. xxxvii, 152 no. 169 (also pp. 85–6 no. 67, 168–9 no. 196). D. C. Douglas in *Feudal Docs* misidentified the donor as Alan the Black but corrected his mistake in his *William the Conqueror* (London, 1964), p. 268 and n. 2. Manhall manor was in Chesterford parish and was mainly a region of woodland which became known as Emanuel Wood. See R. H. Reaney, *The Place-Names of Essex* (English Place-Name Soc., xii, Cambridge, 1969), p. 520; see also ibid., p. 503. Abbot Simon of Luton parted with Manhall in 1259 as part of a deal with Richard de Clare, earl of Gloucester. See below p. 193.

[34] Harper-Bill, ed. cit., pp. lxi, 159 no. 6. The statutes of reform confirmed by Alexander IV on 4 August 1256 are unlikely to be the same as those issued under Abbot Hugh of North-wold (*pace* Harper-Bill) since they appear to be a compilation including later statutes among their sources, for example those issued by the papal visitors to St Edmunds in 1234. See below pp. 213–215.

[35] Ibid., pp. 5–9 no. 5. Already in c. 1191 Jocelin of Brackland had given the value of the vicarage as being 25 marks. *JB*, p. 64.

of England's greatest Benedictine houses and a baron of the realm, Hugh was active in the affairs of his order and in national administration and politics. He and the abbot of St Albans (William of Trumpington) were presidents of the first General Chapter of the Benedictines of the province of Canterbury which met at Oxford sometime between late September, 1218, and mid summer, 1219.[36] The chapter was held in obedience to canon 12 of the Fourth Lateran Council which decreed that religious orders should hold general chapters once every three years to legislate for the reform of religious observance.[37] The statutes issued by the General Chapter at Oxford were severe and a second General Chapter met at St Albans on 14 September 1219 which, at the request of the 'weaker brethren' drew up a modified version of the statutes. On this occasion Hugh was not one of the presidents. But the version drawn up at St Albans was not formally issued because of the death of one of the presidents. It was finally published by a General Chapter held at Northampton on 21 September 1225. Again, Hugh was not one of the presidents. In fact, the attendance list records that he arrived only after the chapter had ended ('In recessu de capitulo venit abbas de Sancto Eadmundo').[38] However, the abbot of Westminster (Richard of Barking) and Hugh were chosen to be presidents of a General Chapter to be held in Reading abbey in 1228, but whether it ever met is not known.[39]

Hugh was likewise involved in secular affairs. He sometimes served as an assize judge[40] and in 1228 was appointed a justice in Eyre in Norfolk.[41] In 1218 he was among the many magnates, secular and ecclesiastical, who attended the great Council early in November and witnessed its decisions.[42] Similarly, in 1225 he attended the assembly which re-issued Magna Carta and the Charter of the Forest and again was one of the witnesses.[43] The concession on Henry's part was in exchange for a grant by laity and clergy of a fifteenth on movables.[44] Hugh's attendance at the 1225 assembly and at the great council in 1253 should not be interpreted as indicating that he was a baronial partisan bent on 'constitutional' reform. No doubt his concern for the implementation of Magna Carta was, like that of other churchmen, because he wanted to preserve the liberties of the church. Clause 1 of the 1225 re-issue reaffirmed the commitment in Magna Carta that the church should be free and freely enjoy its rights, and clause 5

---

[36] *Chapters*, ed. Pantin, i. 3–8.
[37] See below p. 200 and n. 24.
[38] *Chapters*, ed. Pantin, i. 18–21.
[39] Ibid., i. 20. Either Hugh when bishop of Ely or his successor William of Kilkenny issued reforming statutes for the diocese of Ely, 1239 x 1256. C and S, ii, pt 1, pp. 515–22.
[40] He was assigned with two others to hear cases in 1221, 1223 and 1225. CPR, *1216–25*, pp. 312, 480, 579.
[41] Crook, *Records*, pp. 82–3.
[42] CPR, *1216–25*, p. 177. See Carpenter, *Minority*, p. 95.
[43] Holt, *Magna Carta*, pp. 510, 517 n. 8. See Carpenter, op. cit., pp. 382–8.
[44] The king granted that Abbot Hugh's bailiffs should collect the fifteenth in the vill. CPR, *1216–25*, p. 571. For the tax see Jurkowski, Smith and Crook, *Lay Taxes in England and Wales*, pp. 12–13.

reaffirmed the sanctions against the despoliation of church property by royal officials during vacancies.[45]

There is every sign of royal favour when Hugh was bishop. According to Matthew Paris, Hugh, having been elected bishop by common consent, was 'received by Henry gladly and invested with all the property of the bishopric'.[46] Along with other ecclesiastics, Hugh served Henry in official capacities on a number of occasions. For example, in 1235 Henry appointed Walter de Gray, archbishop of York, Hugh, bishop of Ely, and other 'trustworthy men' to accompany his brother, Richard of Cornwell, to the congress 'of all great Christian princes of the world' assembled by Emperor Frederick II at Vaucoleurs.[47] In 1236 Henry again appointed Hugh to serve on an embassy, together with Ralph, bishop of Hereford, and other magnates.[48] The embassy was to Raymond Berengar IV, count of Provence, in order to escort his daughter Eleanor to England, for her marriage with Henry; it was received with 'all honour and reverence'. Matthew Paris describes Eleanor's progress to England in colourful terms. The great crowd of princes and magnates and their retinues landed at Sandwich and the marriage was solemnized in Canterbury cathedral by Archbishop Edmund. Hugh was among those present at the splendid ceremony. Matthew elsewhere in his chronicle states that Hugh's journey to Provence was 'laborious and dangerous' and that Hugh 'willingly paid his own expenses'.[49] Hugh seems to have remained in Henry's favour; in 1252, Henry ordered him, with Richard, abbot of Westminster, and Simon, abbot of Waltham, to celebrate the feast of St Edward of Westminster, while he himself was on progress in the north of England. This they did with magnificent ceremony before a large crowd, and afterwards attended the sumptuous banquet in Westminster palace.[50]

Henry declared himself of age in a great council in 1227. Peter, bishop of Winchester, and Hugh, bishop of Ely, wrote to Gregory IX informing him that Henry was of age and reciting the bull of Honorius III, dated 13 April 1223, to confirm the fact and dispel any doubts.[51] In January 1223 Henry, though still in the tutelage of Hubert de Burgh, confirmed Magna Carta and the Charter of the Forest in a council at Westminster, and on 10 December, again at Westminster, gained nominal control of his own seal.[52] The gradual increase in Henry's powers towards the end of his minority was partly the result of pressure from the papacy, the dominant influence on English politics at the time. Bishop Hugh was an obedient servant of the papacy. He acted on a number of occasions as a papal

---

[45] Holt, op. cit., pp. 502, 503.

[46] *Chron. Maj.*, v. 373, 374, 377. C and S, ii, pt 1, pp. 137–8 and n. 8.

[47] *Chron. Maj.*, iii. 393. Powicke, *Henry III and the Lord Edward*, i. 145.

[48] *Chron. Maj.*, iii. 335–6.

[49] Ibid., v. 330. The statement is put in the mouth of Henry III as part of a conversation with Bishop Hugh.

[50] Ibid., iii. 270. Matthew Paris refers with disapproval to the lavish feasts which followed royal and aristocratic marriage ceremonies. Ibid., iii, 168–9.

[51] *Letters Illustrative of the Reign of Henry III*, i. 430–1.

[52] See: Carpenter, *Minority*, pp. 295–7 and n. 5, 301–2, 315, 321–3; Powicke, *Henry III and the Lord Edward*, i. 57–9.

judge-delegate. Thus, in 1231 Gregory commissioned him to assist the sheriff of Cambridgeshire and the chancellor of the university of Cambridge in the repression of the violent disturbances among students and clergy in the city[53] – and to prohibit the charging of exorbitant rents to those students who came in multitudes from abroad to study, since exorbitant rents drive them away.[54] In 1235 Gregory instructed Roger Niger, bishop of London, and Hugh, bishop of Ely, to inquire into the character of John of Hertford, abbot-elect of St Albans, and, if they found nothing amiss, to confirm the election; otherwise they were to quash it. This time Hugh excused himself from serving.[55] Possibly he was reluctant to interfere in the affairs of another great Benedictine monastery, especially one with which St Edmunds was on close and friendly terms.[56] In the event, Bishop Roger (a secular ecclesiastic) acted alone and confirmed John's election. In 1245 both Hugh and Abbot John of Hertford were excused, along with several others, from attending the council of Lyons summoned by Celestine IV.[57] There seems no good reason to doubt the truth of Matthew Paris's explanation that this was on account of illness and old age. Matthew also asserts that their proctors at the curia gained the concession in return for 'precious gifts' to the pope and cardinals.

While Hugh seems never to have incurred the pope's displeasure, there were occasions when he opposed and angered the king. His primary concern when bishop was for the welfare of the cathedral priory of St Etheldreda: if its rights were threatened he was prepared to oppose Henry. For example, he came into conflict with Henry over the fair at Ely.[58] In 1248 Henry suspended the rights of a number of fairs, including that of St Etheldreda, to reduce competition for the new fair which he had established at Westminster. The new fair was to be held in the quindene of the feast of the Translation of St Edward, that is, 13–27 October. Henry had it proclaimed in the city of London and widely elsewhere that during that period all fairs and all trading in London were suspended. The Westminster fair prospered, especially as in any case crowds of people thronged to attend the feast of the Translation. Obviously, the merchants trading in London suffered grave injury and so did Bishop Hugh and his monks because the fair at Ely was held from three days before the feast of the Translation of St Etheldreda on 17 October and for the three days following.[59] Fulk Basset, bishop of London, and Hugh, bishop of Ely, were among the bishops who attended the feast of the

---

[53] *Letters Illustrative of the Reign of Henry III*, i. 552–3, 398. For the migration of students from Paris and elsewhere to Cambridge in 1229 and the riots in Cambridge see e.g.: Rashdall, *Medieval Universities*, iii. 278–9; Cobban, *Medieval English Universities*, pp. 55–8 passim.

[54] *Letters Illustrative of the Reign of Henry III*, i. 398–9.

[55] *Chron. Maj.*, iii. 316–17.

[56] See above, p. 22.

[57] *Chron. Maj.*, iii. 414.

[58] Ibid., v. 28–9, 49, 331–2. See: Rosser, *Medieval Westminster*, pp. 97–9; Wedemeyer Moore, *Fairs*, pp. 20–1; Miller and Hatcher, *Rural Society*, pp. 167, 170.

[59] For the annual cycle of fairs see Wedemeyer Moore, *Fairs*, pp. 10–11. For the coincidence of the date of a fair with a saint's day see Nilson, *Cathedral Shrines*, p. 93. For the date of the Ely fair see ibid., p. 93 and n. 2, citing James Bentham, *The History and Antiquities of the Cathedral Church of Ely* (Norwich, 1812), appendix p. 18.

Translation of St Edward in 1248. They both remonstrated with Henry – Fulk Basset on the damage the suspension of trading did to London's commercial prosperity, and Hugh on the injury to his bishopric and to the monks of Ely – but to no avail.[60] The next year Henry was angry with Hugh because he gave the rich living of East Dereham in Norfolk to Robert Passelewe,[61] on the death of the incumbent, Jeremiah of Caxton, a king's clerk and 'special adviser' ('consiliarius specialis')[62] instead of to Aylmer de Valence – one of Henry's ambitious and much hated Poitevin half-brothers who arrived in England in 1247, intent on making their fortunes.

The building achievements which took place at St Edmunds during Hugh's abbacy have already been referred to. His enthusiasm, energy and enterprise as a builder continued unabated when he was bishop. Since the beautiful arcades of the church of St Andrew in his birthplace, Northwold, are mid-thirteenth century, perhaps Hugh was responsible for having them built. They are the earliest feature of the existing church.[63] But his reputation as a great builder rests primarily on the presbytery of Ely cathedral which he had built in order to extend the pre-existing cathedral eastward. The purpose was to accommodate a magnificent new shrine for the relics of St Etheldreda and make more space for the traffic of pilgrims.[64] Architecturally, the presbytery (or 'retro-choir') is a gem of the late early English style, unsurpassed in the richness of its ornament. St Etheldreda's relics were translated to the new shrine with splendid ceremony in the presence of Henry III in 1252. Hugh's desire to raise the status of Ely as

---

[60] *Chron. Maj.*, v. 29.

[61] For the rich manor of East Dereham in Norfolk see Miller, *Ely*, pp. 31, 133–5 passim, 146, 205. Robert Passelewe (d. 1252) became deputy treasurer in 1232 and a favourite of Henry III though he suffered a temporary fall from favour in 1234. Archbishop Boniface of Savoy quashed his election as bishop of Chichester. Powicke, *Henry III and the Lord Edward*, pp. 104–5.

[62] *Chron. Maj.*, v. 85, 94. Jeremy, *alias* Germanus, of Caxton in Cambridgeshire, had served the king as sheriff of Cambridgeshire and Huntingdon, constable of Norwich castle and as a justice of assize. *CPR, 1225–32*, p. 474, *CPR, 1232–47*, p. 44, *CCR 1237–42*, pp. 58, 133, 233, 238–9, 497, *CCR, 1242–7*, pp. 17, 137, 151, 474, *CCR, 1247–51*, p. 229. In May 1248 Henry gave him a cask (*dolium*) of wine and six oaks for timber, ibid., pp. 51, 160.

[63] Nikolaus Pevsner, *North-West and South Norfolk* (Harmondsworth, 1962, repr. 1970, 1973, 1977), p. 276. There was no church at Northwold before 1066; *DB, Norfolk*, ii, 8, 15 and n. 29.

[64] Pevsner, *Cambridgeshire* (Harmondsworth, 1954, 2nd edn 1970), pp. 346–7; Peter Draper, 'Bishop Northwold and the cult of St Etheldreda', *Medieval Art and Architecture at Ely Cathedral*, BAA CT, ii, 1976 (1979), pp. 8–16 passim; Geoffrey Webb, *Architecture in Britain. The Middle Ages* (Harmondsworth, 1956), pp. 55–60 and pl. XVI; Peter Brieger, *English Art 1216–1307* (Oxford, 1957, repr. with corrections 1968), pp. 187–9; Nilson, *Cathedral Shrines*, pp. 20, 78, 93, 155, and refs. Practically nothing remains of St Etheldreda's shrine. Pevsner, op. cit., p. 366. A representation of the Translation is the last of four scenes illustrating the Life of St Etheldreda painted c. 1425 on two wooden panels, possibly from Ely cathedral and now in the Society of Antiquaries. See: Margaret Rickert, *Painting in Britain: the Middle Ages*, Pelican History of Art, v (Melbourne, London and Baltimore, 1954), p. 134 and n. 16 and pl. 180; Wall, *Shrines*, pl. XVI. All four scenes are reproduced in T. D. Atkinson, *An Architectural History of the Benedictine Monastery of St Etheldreda at Ely* (Cambridge, 1933), frontispiece.

a cult centre is likely to have been stimulated by his intimate knowledge of the cult of St Edmund, its problems and successes. Hugh never lost his veneration for the king and martyr. His tomb in the north aisle of the nave is of the box type with a sumptuously carved canopy and has been described as 'one of the finest of its date in England'.[65] On the lid of the coffin is a nearly life-size image in Purbeck marble of Bishop Hugh in mitre and pontificals with a crozier in his left hand and with his right hand raised in blessing. Below his feet on the end of the coffin three tiny figures are embossed on the side illustrating the martyrdom of St Edmund: the shooting at him with arrows, his decapitation and his head guarded by a wolf.

All in all, Hugh of Northwold deserved the praises of Matthew Paris and the gratitude of the monks of St Edmunds. He died on 6 August 1254 at the bishop's manor of Downham in the Isle of Ely[66] and Matthew Paris awards him a long, laudatory obituary. 'The good bishop of Ely, formerly abbot of St Edmunds, [had] fought for God in both churches in a most praiseworthy manner.' Matthew next expatiated on Hugh's building achievements at Ely before ending with a general encomium:

> Just as he was devout and outstanding at the spiritual table, that is at the altar – 'rivers of water run down mine eyes' [Psalm 119.36] – so also was he bountiful, cheerful and serene at the table of bodily refreshment. With his death died the flower of the Black Monks, for just as he was the abbot of abbots in England, so also did he shine as the bishop of bishops.[67]

Hugh was remembered with gratitude at St Edmunds. He was among the most eminent abbots of St Edmunds to whom was accorded the honour of a 'great ringing' of the bells ('magnus sonitus'[68]) on the anniversary of his death. This is recorded in the Book of Benefactors which states that

> He gave the convent a precious chasuble ornamented with gold and precious stones, and a cope of parti-coloured cloth (de secta), and 37 marks 6s 8d to buy another cope; also 8 large bowls and 6 smaller ones, and 8 silver salt cellars weighing £16 and 12s for the use and service of the convent in the refectory; he also assigned the 60s, which his predecessors took annually from the manor of Ingham, to the convent, besides 50 marks for starting the new cloister; and he gave the convent the first part of a very precious bible and procured many other good things for us. He is buried honourably at Ely at the feet of St Etheldreda. [Finally,] he remitted

---

65 Pevsner, *Cambridgeshire*, p. 366; Thomson in *Electio*, p. 196 n. 7. For the canopy see also Lawrence Stone, *Sculpture in Britain. The Middle Ages* (Harmondsworth, 1955), p. 134.

66 Matthew Paris dated Hugh's death 9 August (v Id. Aug.) but the Bury chronicle gives 6 August (vii Id. Aug.) which is probably right. Hugh was commemorated at Ely on that date. See: *Chron. Maj.*, v. 454; *Bury Chron.*, p. 19; *Fasti, Monastic Cathedrals*, p. 46.

67 *Chron. Maj.*, v. 454–5.

68 There were three grades of bell-ringing at St Edmunds on anniversaries of benefactors, each grade appropriate to the status and generosity of the benefactor concerned: 'simple ringing' ('simplex sonitus'), 'double ringing' ('duplex sonitus') and 'great ringing' ('magnus sonitus'). The latter was a peal of bells (or *classicum*).

to the convent £100 which it owed him for a loan, as appears in the acquittance. Total 267 marks discounting the chasuble and bible.[69]

Ingham, one of the cellarer's manors, provided the pittances for the monks on that day. Presumably Hugh remitted the 60s previously paid annually to the abbot, in order to pay for the pittance. The pittance would have been an extra dish served in the refectory, a charge on the cellarer's resources.

Richard of the Isle (de Insula, de l'Isle), 1229–1233

The question of Richard's identity was discussed above and, as noted, he served as sacrist, then prior of St Edmunds under Abbot Hugh. In 1222 he was elected abbot of Burton (in Staffordshire),[70] but returned to St Edmunds in 1229 on his election to the abbacy on 5 June.[71] His election received royal assent on 20 June[72] and papal confirmation on 28 August[73] which confirmation received royal assent on 12 October.[74] Finally, in 1229, on 20 November, the feast of St Edmund, he was installed in a grand ceremony 'in the presence of Richard Grant, archbishop of Canterbury, Hugh (of Northwold), bishop of Ely, and many other bishops and magnates of England'.[75]

Very little is known about Richard's rule at St Edmunds. The chronicle mentions him only once, besides recording his succession and death. It notes that

---

69 Thomson in *Electio*, p. 194 n. 10 gives a slightly different translation of this entry in the List of Benefactors (Douai, Bibliothèque Municipale MS 553, f. 8v). The entry in the manuscript records that there was a 'great ringing of bells' 'Pro Abbate Hugone secundo et postea Episcopo Eliensi. Hic dedit Conuentui vnam casulam preciosam auro et lapidibus preciosis ornatam et capam de secta et triginta et septem marcas sex solidos et octo denarios pro alia capa emendi. Item octo scutellas magnas et sex minores et octo salsaria de argento ponderis sexdecim librarum et duodecim solidorum ad vsum et seruicium Conuentus in Refectorio. Item sexaginta solidos quos predecessores sui percipiebant annuatim de manerio de Ingham Conuentui assignauit et quinquaginta marcas pro nouo claustro inchoando. Item dedit Conuentui primam partem biblie preciosissima et multa alia bona nobis procurauit. Sepultus est apud Ely honorifice ad pedes sancte Etheldrede. Item remisit Conuentui Centum libras quas Conuentus debuit sibi causa mutui vt patet per acquietanciam. Summa, ducente sexaginta et septem marce preter casulam et bibliam. Pitancia de Ingham.'

70 *Bury Chron.*, p. 5. His election received royal assent on 10 July 1222. *CPR 1216–25*, p. 333.

71 *Bury Chron.*, p. 7. Cf. *Heads*, ii. 25.

72 *CPR, 1225–32*, pp. 253–4.

73 A copy of Gregory IX's confirmation of Richard's election dated 28 August 1229 is one of the four letters (three from Pope Gregory and one from his chaplain Stephen) addressed to the prior and convent concerning the election, in cursive hands, in BL MS Royal 7 C V, f. 2. The latter is a book of distinctions and is one of the two extant volumes commissioned by Abbot Samson's chaplain, William of Diss. Henry of Kirkstead entered the class-mark, V. 3. See: G. F. Warner and J. P. Gilson, *Cat. of Western Manuscripts in the Old Royal and King's Collection* (London, 1921, 4 vols), i. 177–8; James, *Abbey*, p. 80; Sharpe, 'Reconstructing the medieval library', p. 215; and above p. 136 and nn. 256, 257.

74 *CPR, 1225–32*, p. 275.

75 *Burton*, p. 245.

in 1231 when Thomas (Blundeville), bishop of Norwich, came to attend the feast of St Edmund, Abbot Richard 'vested in a secular cope, gave the blessing on the vigil after vespers in the presence of the bishop'.[76] This was probably recorded in the chronicle because Richard's act established an important precedent. It gave effect to the privilege granted by Urban III in 1187 to Abbot Samson and the convent allowing the abbot to give the episcopal blessing within St Edmunds' exempt jurisdiction of the *banleuca*.[77] Here Richard did exactly that, in the presence of the diocesan himself.

In 1232 Gregory IX commissioned Peter des Roches, bishop of Winchester, and Abbot Richard to inquire concerning those who had pillaged the barns of Roman clerics holding benefices in East Anglia; they were to declare the culprits excommunicate until they had been to Rome and obtained papal absolution.[78] Gregory sent a similar mandate to the archbishop of York, the bishop of Durham, and John Romanus; they were to do the same in the metropolitan province of York.[79] These mandates were probably issued on 9 June, which was the date of a mandate addressed to the archbishop of York (the see of Canterbury being vacant at the time) and other prelates of England on the same subject.[80]

It was also on 9 June 1232 that Gregory IX issued a mandate of far reaching importance. He ordered a general visitation of monasteries 'throughout the Christian world'. He appointed special visitors, most of them Cistercian or Premonstratensian abbots, for those monasteries exempt from episcopal authority. They had full powers to reform and correct abuses and lax observance. The visitors for the province of Canterbury were John abbot of the Cistercian abbey of Boxley in Kent, Reginald abbot of the Premonstratensian abbey of Bayham in Sussex, and the precentor of Christ Church, Canterbury.[81] According to Matthew Paris they were 'tactless, harsh men, who carried out the visitation in such an insolent and merciless manner that they exceeded all reasonable bounds in some monasteries, and drove many to resort to the remedy of appeal'.[82] Among those who appealed to Gregory for new visitors were the abbot of Westminster (Richard of Barking), and the abbot of St Edmunds 'called de Insula': Matthew describes him as illustrious by birth but even more illustrious in character ('in moribus'). Matthew Paris states that the appeal was made 'at great labour and expense'. He also notes that Richard was already abroad 'to save expense'.[83] It appears from letters of protection issued by Henry on 8 March 1233 that Richard had left for Rome by that date.[84] Another royal writ, issued on the next day, confirms that Richard was short of money: King Henry states that the abbot has gone to Rome and begs his tenants to grant him a reasonable aid to help pay his

---

[76] *Bury Chron.*, p. 7.
[77] *Papsturkunden*, iii. 500 no. 399; *Pinch. Reg.*, i. 27–8. Above p. 78.
[78] *Chron. Maj.*, iii. 217–18.
[79] *Cal. Papal Letters*, i. 130.
[80] *Burton*, 239–43.
[81] *Cal. Papal Letters*, i. 132–3; *Chron. Maj.*, iii. 234–5; *Dunstable*, p. 133. See below, p. 203.
[82] *Chron. Maj.*, iii. 235.
[83] Ibid., iii. 239.
[84] *CPR, 1232–47*, p. 13.

debts.[85] But probably Richard had not gone abroad only for economy. Another reason was probably to negotiate with Gregory to obtain a bull to protect St Edmunds from the settlement by friars within the *banleuca*. A bull forbidding the erection of any chapel within the *banleuca* without the abbot's consent was eventually issued shortly after Richard's death,[86] but negotiations for it must have begun before and would have added to Richard's indebtedness.

The appeal to Gregory for new visitors was successful and more moderate visitors were appointed. Their visitation of St Edmunds will be considered in a later chapter.[87] Richard never returned home: he died on 29 August 1233, in the Cistercian abbey of Pontigny in Normandy.[88] St Edmunds' Book of Benefactors gives him a generous and moving notice:

> He was prudent and circumspect, very powerful and determined in his labours for the flock committed to him, to such an extent that he was willing to risk death for the liberties of his church. He adorned the vestry with precious copes, silk hangings ('pannis sericis') and other most noble ornaments. He began and would have perfected had he lived a silver and gilt frontal for the high altar and would have done many other good things if he had survived long in the abbacy. He was a monk and greatly loved monks. He is buried in the chapter-house at the feet of Abbot Henry [of Rushbrooke].[89]

His anniversary was marked by a great ringing of the bells and the pittancer provided the monks' pittance.

Henry of Rushbrooke (alias Henry Wodard), 1234–1248

Abbot Henry was presumably a native of Rushbrooke, a vill on the river Lark three miles south east of Bury St Edmunds which owed service to the abbey's manor of Rougham.[90] His family name was Wodard and a memorandum in a hand of c. 1300 notes that 'R. Wodard' paid in rent to the cellarer ½ mark and

85 Ibid.
86 See *Bury Chron.*, pp. 22–3 and n. 3. Gregory IX confirmed St Edmunds' spiritual monopoly within the *banleuca* in 1239. *Cal. Papal Letters*, i. 127; *Pinch Reg.*, i. 39. For the later dispute between St Edmunds and the Friars Minor, 1257–63, see A. G. Little, *Studies in English Franciscan History* (Manchester, 1917).
87 Below pp. 203–205.
88 *Bury Chron.*, p. 8, where the Latin text *Pontiua* or *Pontina* is mistranslated as *Ponthieu*, an error reproduced in *Heads*, i. 26.
89 'Pro Abbate Ricardo primo Qui prudens et circumspectus multum valens et volens pro grege sibi commisso laborare in tantum quod pro libertate ecclesie sue se morti voluit exponere. Hic ornauit vestiarium Capis preciosis pannis sericis et alijs ornamentis tunc nobilissimis Tabulam argenteam et deauratam pro magno altari incepit et perfecisset se vixisset et multa bona fecisset si diu in Abbacia perstitisset. Religiosus erat et religiosos multum diligebat. Sepultus est in Capitulo ad pedes Henrici Abbatis. Pitancia de Pitanciario.' Douai, Bibliothèque Municipale MS 553, f. 8v.
90 *DB, Suffolk*, 14, 67 (f. 363b). See: *JB*, p. 64; *Kalendar*, ed. Davis, pp. xvi, xxxv n. 1, xxxvi, xxxviii.

20s which Abbot Henry assigned to pay for pittances on the anniversaries of his father and mother.[91] The name 'Wodard' is probably a version of 'Woodard' and 'Woodhard', surnames peculiar to East Anglia and probably a corruption of the occupational surname 'Woodherd', that is, someone responsible for animals grazing in woodland pastures.[92] Both Rushbrooke and Rougham had extensive woodlands in the middle ages.[93] Henry first appears in the abbey records as 'Master Henry Wodard',[94] serving Abbot Hugh as his chaplain for an unknown period. Next, he apparently became cellarer. This is assuming that he is to be identified with 'H. de Sancto Eadmundo' who appears as cellarer in the Bury Customary.[95] Again, one can assume that he was the Henry who succeeded Richard of the Isle as prior in 1222[96] and was elected abbot in 1233. His succession to the abbacy following Richard's death on 29 August, 1233, was swift: the licence to elect was issued on 17 September 1233;[97] Henry was elected on 27 September and King Henry informed Gregory IX in a letter dated 10 October that he had given his consent to Henry's election.[98] On 16 December Gregory instructed the bishop of Ely (Hugh of Northwold) to impart the benediction on the prior of St Edmunds, now abbot-elect, a literate man, whose election he confirms on information received by letters and from the envoys of St Edmunds, the monks Nicholas, John and Peter.[99] The mandate to give him seizin of the abbot's temporalities was issued on 1 February 1234,[100] and he was blessed on 2 February by Bishop Hugh in the church of St Etheldreda at Bishop's Hatfield,[101] one of the bishop's manors where Hugh had built a residence.[102]

   Like his predecessors Hugh of Northwold and Richard of the Isle, Abbot Henry was involved in national affairs, and always had the interests of the Church in England in mind. Thus, in 1240 he took an active part in protests against the collection of the subsidy imposed by Gregory IX to help pay for his war against the emperor Frederick II. Otto, the papal legate *a latere* and collector of the subsidy in England, summoned a council of clergy, including abbots and priors who were heads of houses, at Reading in May 1240, followed by another one which met in June.[103] He obtained the king's support: Matthew

---

91 BL MS Harley 645, f. 265.
92 See: McKinley, *Norfolk and Suffolk Surnames*, pp. 34, 60, 61; Rackham, 'Abbey woods', pp. 149–50; *Kalendar*, ed. Davis, pp. 20, 100, 102, 194 (index under 'Wudard (Wdard, Wodard)').
93 Ibid., p. 157.
94 CUL MS Additional 6847, f. 11; Thomson, 'Obedientiaries', p. 101.
95 *Bury Cust.*, p. 40 line 3.
96 CUL MS Additional 6006, f. 51; *Bury Chron.*, pp. 5, 8.
97 *CPR, 1232–47*, pp. 26, 27.
98 Ibid., p. 27.
99 *Les Registres de Grégoire IX*, ed. Lucien Auvray, Bibliothèque des Écoles françaises d'Athènes et de Rome (Paris, 1896–1910, 4 vols), i, col. 895 no. 1621; *Cal. Papal Letters*, i. 137.
100 *CCR, 1231–4*, p. 373.
101 *Bury Chron.*, p. 8.
102 Nikolaus Pevsner, *Hertfordshire* (Harmondsworth, 1953) p. 106; Miller, *Ely*, p. 78.
103 Lunt, *Fin. Relations*, i. 197–8; idem, 'Consent to taxation', pp. 126–32; *C and S*, ii, pt 1, pp. 285–6; *Chron. Maj.*, iv. 10.

Paris alleges, probably with some truth, that King Henry told his councillors, who remonstrated with him for allowing England to be mulcted by the pope, that he dared do no other. Matthew also states that Otto's assistant collector, Pietro Rosso, tried to induce monks in chapter to promise to contribute. Therefore, he continues, the abbots 'tearfully and with bowed heads, went to the king and pleaded that he, their patron, would protect them from papal extortion. ... Those who spoke were the abbot of St Edmunds and the abbot of Battle', that is, Henry of Rushbrooke and Ralph of Coventry.[104]

Abbot Henry again played a significant role in public affairs in 1244. The king summoned the magnates of the realm, both secular and ecclesiastical, to meet him in the refectory of Westminster abbey. He asked for an aid to help pay debts contracted in his last Gascon campaign.[105] The assembly insisted on time to consider the request. Then by common consent, twelve magnates were elected, that is, four ecclesiastics (headed by the archbishop of Canterbury, Boniface of Savoy), four earls and four barons: two of the barons were abbots and those chosen were, as before, Henry, abbot of St Edmunds, and Ralph, abbot of Battle. What the twelve decided was to be reported to the king as the decision of the whole assembly which had elected them. The twelve thereupon asked for certain reforms in exchange for an aid. The king refused the proposals and no aid was granted. The assembly's action was an important step towards establishing the principle that the consent of the community of the realm was necessary for the grant of taxation, the most effective weapon in the community's struggle to gain some control over royal government.[106]

It is impossible to say whether or not Abbot Henry was similarly involved in the work of the General Chapters of the Benedictines of the southern province. The surviving records of the four General Chapters which met while Henry was abbot are scanty and no attendance lists are known. It is quite possible that he was one of the many abbots who failed to attend, giving various reasons for their absence, usually ill-health or the pressing business of their houses. Non-attendance had become such a problem that the General Chapter held at Oxford in 1246 was prorogued because so few abbots were present.[107] However, an exchange of letters survives, one to Abbot Henry from the presidents of the General Chapter which met at Northampton on 11 March 1247, and the other his reply.[108] The letters are of great interest: the first illustrates the work of the presidents of General Chapters between meetings, and the second shows what kind of rejoinder they might expect from the head of a house if they tried to interfere with his authority over his own monks. The matter at issue was the expulsion from St Edmunds sometime earlier in Henry's abbatiate of a delin-

---

104 Ibid., iv, 35–6. This episode is not mentioned by Lunt or in C and S.
105 Jurkowski, Smith and Crook, *Lay Taxes in England and Wales*, p. 17.
106 *Chron. Maj.*, iv. 362–76. See: Harriss, *King, Parliament and Public Finance*, pp. 29–31 passim; Lunt, 'Consent to taxation', pp. 132–3; Powicke, *Henry III and the Lord Edward*, i. 298 n. 2.
107 *Chapters*, ed. Pantin, i. 24–7. For the problem of non-attendance see ibid., i. 20 § 47, 48 § 16.
108 Ibid., i. 28–31.

quent monk, John de Burgo, and Henry's refusal to readmit him. One of the regulations issued by the General Chapter of Northampton concerned fugitive and ejected monks.[109] It ordained that the presidents, having admonished prelates to receive back fugitives and ejected monks, should compel them to do so by ecclesiastical censure, saving regular discipline, in accordance with the decretal of Gregory IX, 'Ne religiosi viri vagandi'.[110] Therefore, the presidents, that is John de Blosmeville, abbot of Abingdon, and Thomas of Gloucester, abbot of Evesham, wrote to Abbot Henry about John de Burgo whom he had refused to readmit into the abbey. They tell him that they have received a letter from Innocent IV, which they recite: Innocent, having addressed them as presidents of the General Chapter, continues,

> John de Burgo, a monk of St Edmunds of the order of St Benedict in the diocese of Norwich, has humbly begged us that we order that he be received [at St Edmunds] (from which, he asserts, he was ejected without reasonable cause) since he wishes to return with humility. Whereas our predecessor, Pope G[regory] of happy memory ordained that in meetings of General Chapters the presidents, whether abbots or priors, should every year solicitously inquire about fugitives and those ejected from the order, so that if they can be received back in their monasteries in accordance with regular discipline, their abbots or priors be urged to receive them. If discipline does not permit this, they, with apostolic authority, provided it can be done without grave scandal, should see that the necessaries of life be ministered to them in suitable places in their own monasteries, or else in other religious houses of the order, there to do their penance. We order you by apostolic prescript that you enforce the statute in respect of the said J[ohn], constraining contradictions with ecclesiastical censures, disregarding any appeal.[111]

Innocent's mandate is dated 23 October 1247. Having cited the mandate, the presidents exhort Abbot Henry in high-flown prose with numerous biblical allusions to obey it:

> We, therefore, affectionately ask your discretion, and by authority of the present mandate, advise and exhort in the Lord, that, opening the bowels of compassion [1 John 3.17] and allowing mercy to triumph over justice [James 2.13, cf. Reg. Ben., c. 64.10], you consent to restore the said J[ohn], a monk of your house, to his former state, saving regular discipline, out of reverence for the apostolic see, remembering that the wine of severity poured on the wounds of the wounded without the oil of compassion harms rather than cures [cf. Luke 10.34]; thus it is that both the rod and the manna are in the golden censer [cf. Hebrews 9.4], and that in Ezekiel the rod which ruled with cruelty withered [cf. Ezekiel 19.11,12]. Knowing that we never can nor wish to deceive with closed eyes, but rather obey the apostolic mandate and also the constitution concerning fugitives and ejected

[109] Ibid., i. 27–8. For the problem of renegade religious, with mainly later examples, see F. D. Logan, *Runaway Religious in Medieval England, c. 1240–1540* (Cambridge, 1996, repr. 2002), pp. 42–50. Cf. R. B. Dobson, *Durham Priory 1400–1450* (Cambridge, 1973), pp. 74–7.
[110] Lib. III, titulus xxx. c. 24. *Chapters*, ed. Pantin, i. 29 n. 17. The mandate is not in Pottast (*Chapters*, ed. Pantin, i. 28 n. 5) nor in *Cal. Papal Letters.*
[111] Part of the mandate cites *Ne religiosi* almost verbatim. *Chapters*, ed. Pantin, i. 29 n. 17.

monks repeated according to the Lord in the last chapter celebrated at Northampton. Farewell.

Abbot Henry's reply is a firm, even what seems to be rather a sarcastic, refusal, repeating the biblical allusions in the presidents' letter. He addresses the 'venerable fathers' and writes:

We have received both the supreme pontif's and your letters, which were delivered to us by the prior of Colne, with due reverence. After they had been examined and carefully considered, it was clear that John de Burgo, formerly our professed monk, had acquired the letters by hiding the truth and by false suggestion, which would never have been acquired had the Lord pope known the truth of the matter, that is, that the said J[ohn] de Burgo to whom he refers, was once one of us but left us, as the Rule permits and after he had been deprived of the monastic habit, on account of his many immoderate and manifest excesses about which it is better for him if we keep silent rather than speak. However, should he wish, we with all our chapter and on the testimony of neighbours, at a convenient place and time, will inform the supreme pontiff and you more fully the reasons for his expulsion and his deprivation of the habit. He himself in fact after his departure from us, openly took the habit of the Cistercian order at Swineshead in the diocese of Lincoln, and wore it publicly for a long time until he was expelled from that monastery just as he had been from ours for his manifest excesses. Moreover, we are greatly amazed and cannot sufficiently wonder why you sent your letters only to us and not to our convent and us together. For you well know that we neither can nor ought to receive monks, nor reject those once received, without the consent of the convent and chapter. You should also know that he is one that in no way can live with us in future without grave scandal. Therefore, if he likes, if you wish to open the bowels of compassion for him, to allow mercy triumph over judgement, and to pour the oil of kindness with the wine of severity on his wounds, we would think it right to provide, if he pleases, in accordance with the papal mandate [that he dwells] in some other religious house, either in yours or in some other, where he can do his penance and receive the necessaries of life, for he can never live in our house with us without scandal or damage. And, moreover, we have no cells such as you and many others in England have. Finally, do not wonder that our convent has not written to you nor impressed its seal along with our seal on the present letter, because you wrote nothing to it. Farewell.

Since the nature of John de Burgo's 'excesses' is unknown, it is impossible to say whether or not Abbot Henry was a strict disciplinarian, or whether John's expulsion was merely for minor breaches of discipline. Nor is the outcome of the affair known.

The other information about Henry's abbatiate mainly concerns his defence of the abbey's rights. In this respect he was energetic and persistent. He continued the battle begun by Richard of the Isle against the Franciscans' attempt to establish a friary in St Edmunds' *banleuca*. On 21 December 1233, when Henry was abbot-elect, Gregory IX issued a bull forbidding the erection of any oratory or chapel within the *banleuca* without the abbot's consent.[112] The Franciscans

---

112 *Memorials*, iii. 27; Auvray, ed. cit., i, col. 923 no. 1676. Matthew Paris notices at some length the Franciscans' attempt to settle within St Edmunds' *banleuca*. GASA, i. 386.

renewed their attempt in 1238, this time joined by the Dominicans. The Bury Chronicle records that when the legate Otho came to St Edmunds in that year,

> the Friars Preacher came to him and earnestly asked him to give them a place to live within the boundaries of that church's Liberty, in spite of the monks' opposition. Otho went personally with a great crowd to inspect the boundaries; after examining the monks' privileges he ruled that the petition of both the Friars Minor and the Friars Preacher had no validity (irritam fore diffinivit).[113]

But on 16 April Abbot Henry obtained a bull confirming St Edmunds' spiritual immunity.[114] However, this did not end the abbey's struggle against the Franciscans.

Henry was an equally assiduous guardian of St Edmunds' temporal interests. He bought back the manors of Semer, Groton and Cockfield which had been lost under Abbot Samson.[115] Nevertheless, St Edmunds' title to Semer and Groton was weak and the two manors were lost again in the late thirteenth century under Abbot John of Northwold – who recovered them at considerable cost. Henry also acted to retain the rights of the abbot's barony. For example, he tried to end the recurrent litigation over a place called *Atburetre* with its chapel, in the parish of Thornham Magna, held by the priory of Eye 'for the use of hospitality and the poor'. The priory owed rent to St Edmunds in recognition of the abbot's overlordship. On 9 March 1243 Abbot Henry, on his manor at Elmeswell, reached an agreement with William, prior of Eye, that the prior should render two 2lb candles every year on the high altar on the feast of St Edmund 'as a symbol and witness of our barony' ('in signum et testimonium baronie nostre'). William Raleigh, bishop of Norwich, confirmed this agreement on 2 May that year.[116] But that did not end the dispute – litigation started again and sometime later in the thirteenth century the annual render of two candles was commuted for two swans on the feast of St Edmund (presumably handed to the kitchener rather than placed on the high altar). On 6 January 1303 Abbot Thomas Tottington issued an acquittance to the prior and convent of Eye for all arrears of the annual render of two swans (*cignorum*) 'over which there had been litigation and controversy'.[117] Henry's actions protecting the integrity of St Edmunds' Liberty against the claims of the bishop of Ely will be discussed later.

Henry was probably nearing the end of his working life by 1245: for on 20 May Innocent IV excused him from attending the Council of Lyons on the grounds that he was suffering from gout. Several other prelates were similarly excused, including Hugh of Northwold, bishop of Ely, as mentioned above.[118]

---

[113] *Bury Chron.*, pp. 9–10. Cf. above p. 179 and n. 85.

[114] Auvray, ed. cit., ii, col. 991 no. 4297; *Cal. Papal Letters*, i. 137, 172.

[115] BL MS Harley 645, f. 104. Above pp. 54–5.

[116] *Eye Priory Cartulary and Charters*, ed. Vivien Brown, Suffolk Records Soc. Suffolk Charters, xii, xiii (2 pts, 1992, 1994), i, 51–2 nos 47–8; *Acta, Norwich, 1215–43*, ed. Harper-Bill, p. 123 no. 134.

[117] BL MS Harley 230, f. 133v.

[118] *Chron. Maj.*, iv. 413–14; *C and S*, ii, i. 405. He was apparently ill in 1238. A mandate dated 18 April 1238 to the sheriff of Suffolk ordered him to adjourn the inquest which

Abbot Henry died on 19 June 1248. The entry for him in the Book of Benefactors, unlike those for Hugh of Northwold and Richard de Insula, makes no
mention of spirituality or moral virtues in his character beyond saying that he
did 'many saintly things'. It concentrates on his contributions to the convent's
well-being but also mentions that he provided alms for the poor on the feast
of St John before the Latin Gate (6 May). Whether the more worldly tone of
the entry indicates a change in the authorship of the Book of Benefactors, or is
symptomatic of a more materialistic attitude in the convent at large, is impossible to say. The entry reads:

> [Henry] recovered the manors of Semer, Groton and Cockfield, which had been
> alienated, paying 500 marks for them and appropriated them to the convent. He
> bought a carucate of land in Great Barton [and] procured the manor of Little
> Barton for the recreation of those who had been bled. He acquired one mark of
> annual rent in Mildenhall for a pittance for the convent on the feast of St John
> before the Latin Gate, thus that the mark would provide 6d for the servants of the
> church and 4d for the poor at the maundy.[119] He was buried in the chapter-house,
> the fourth in number, at the feet of Abbot Edmund. He did many saintly things
> in his lifetime.[120]

There was a great ringing of the bells on his anniversary and the pittancer
provided the monks' pittance.

Edmund of Walpole, 1248–1256

Edmund of Walpole was a native either of Walpole in the marshland of Norfolk
west of King's Lynn,[121] where St Edmunds had a number of holdings, or of
Walpole in east Suffolk. (Later in the thirteenth century Joceus of Walpole,
William of Walpole and Richard of Walpole each served as bailiffs of the town
at various times.[122]) Edmund was a Master, having graduated in canon law.[123] He
was elected abbot on 7 July 1248,[124] the king informed the pope of his assent to

---

was to determine whether the place granted to the friars preacher was within St Edmunds'
Liberty or not, until the abbot of St Edmunds had recovered from his illness. CCR, 1237–
42, p. 127.

119 For almsgiving by Benedictine monks see Harvey, *Living and Dying*, pp. 12, 16 and nn.
120 'Pro Abbate Henrico Qui maneria de Semere, Groten et Cokefeld' alienate, datis pro eis
     quingentis marcis recuperauit et vsibus Conuentus appropriauit. Item emit vnam caru-
     catam terr' in magna Berton'. Item manerium de parua Berton' procurauit pro recrea-
     cione minutorum. Item perquisiuit vnam marcam annui redditus in Mildenhale pro
     pitancia Conuentus in die sancti Johannis (Baptiste *expunct.*) ante portam Latinam ita
     quod illa marca denture sex denarij seruientibus ecclesie et quatuor denarij pauperibus ad
     mandatum. Sepultus est in Capitulo quartus in numero ad pedes Edmundi Abbatis. Hic
     multa bona sanctitatis operatus est in vita sua.' Douai, Bibliothèque Municipale MS 553,
     f. 8v.
121 For St Edmunds' holdings in the Norfolk marshland see above figs 3 and 4.
122 Lobel, 'List of aldermen and bailiffs', pp. 18, 19.
123 *Chron. Buriensis*, p. 29; *Bury Chron.*, p. 15.
124 Ibid., p. 15.

the election on 14 July 1248,[125] and on 17 September, 1248, the keeper of the abbey during the vacancy, Robert Passelewe, was instructed to give him seizin of the temporalities.[126] The Bury chronicler records that Edmund was blessed by the former abbot of St Edmunds, Hugh of Northwold, bishop of Ely, on 27 September,[127] and states that Edmund 'had not been in religion for two years from the day when he received the habit to the day of his election'.[128] Nevertheless, despite his juniority in the abbey he had been one of the two monks to come before the barons of the Exchequer with charters to claim St Edmunds' right to a mint and exchange.[129] Perhaps Abbot Henry had chosen Edmund for this mission because of his legal training, which, moreover, may well have been one reason for his election to the abbacy.

According to Matthew Paris, it had not been a simple matter to obtain confirmation of the election from Innocent IV. The story Matthew tells of transactions at the curia is colourful and dramatic, but since what it relates seems to conform in general with current trends and practices, the gist of it is probably true. Matthew writes:

> When the brothers had elected another to fill the place of the now deceased abbot, [Henry of Rushbrooke], they sent some of the brethren to the Roman curia for his confirmation. After a derisory examination, both the election and the elect was rejected so that the rejected was caught in the merciless net of misery. However, when the sad and shamed monks had left, the pope recalled them and said, 'Since the miserable need mercy, by our grace alone we now grant you the elect, freely and generously conferring on him the abbey of the blessed Edmund, lest you are troubled. All the same, he should compensate us with 800 marks, offering it to the merchant whom we shall assign to him, to whom we owe that sum.[130]

Matthew asserts that the monks were so broken-hearted and upset by their treatment that on the way home they both died, one at Lyons and the other at Dover. The 800 marks which Edmund had to pay for papal confirmation may be an early example of the service tax paid by archbishops, bishops and abbots and those priors who were heads of exempt houses in return for provision or confirmation by the pope. The tax evolved from the giving of gifts to the pope and others on such occasions; such gifts became compulsory payments in the last half of the thirteenth century.[131]

It seems that sometime early in his abbatiate Edmund was given a survey of the convent's estates. This is indicated because of the survival of some remarkable manorial and obedientiary accounts in one of the abbey's registers, BL MS Harley 645, ff. 193–9, 252–3, 261–262v, 265. These accounts provide a rare

---

125 CPR, 1247–58, p. 21.
126 CCR, 1247–51, p. 87.
127 Bury Chron., p. 14.
128 Ibid.
129 PRO, Memoranda Rolls, LTR, 32 Henry III for Michaelmas 1247, membrane 4d. Cited Bury Chron., p. 14 n. 6.
130 Chron. Maj., v. 40; Lunt, Papal Revenues, ii. 237–8.
131 Ibid., ii. 461–3.

insight in the history of accounting because they represent an intermediate stage between early practices and the formal methods adopted later in the thirteenth century. Moreover, they provide invaluable evidence about the administration and management of St Edmunds' estates; they reveal, for example, the survival of the antiquated system of food farms.[132] The accounts fall into two groups; first, those for 1247–50, and, secondly, those for 1256–61. Each group apparently once comprised a separate booklet and both were subsequently bound into the register. Paul Harvey, in a ground-breaking article on the accounts, plausibly suggests that the earlier booklet was compiled for Edmund Walpole and the later one for Simon of Luton, to inform those abbots at the beginning of their respective abbatiates of the state of the convent's holdings.[133] The nature and contents of the accounts will be examined in some detail in appendix III below. There is no evidence that Richard of the Isle or Henry of Rushbrooke had been provided with similar surveys at the beginning of their rules, but it is likely that they were. Samson had commissioned the compilation of his *Kalendar* in his first year,[134] and Hugh of Northwold had appointed four monks 'to travel around and write down the number of ploughs and the amount of stock on each manor' and other information so that in future no obedientiary would be defrauded.[135] As the results of the survey made for Hugh have not come to light, there is no means of judging how detailed it was or of comparing it with the accounts preserved in Harley 645. If the latter accounts are in fact part of surveys made for Edmund of Walpole and Simon of Luton at the outset of their rules they are comparable with surviving surveys made for the prelates of some other churches soon after they took office. Thus, Hugh of Northwold himself commissioned a survey of the estates of the bishopric of Ely immediately after his succession to the see.[136] One of the first acts of Ralph Diceto on his appointment as dean of St Paul's in 1180 had been to compile a survey of chapter property; having completed this by 8 January 1181, he made a survey of the churches belonging to the bishopric.[137] Therefore, it seems very likely that Abbot Edmund commissioned a survey to be made of the convent's property soon after his succession. Assuming that he did so, he probably acted on the advice of his clerks.

Concrete evidence about Edmund's acts is scarce and we have to turn to Matthew Paris who pays him quite a lot of attention but for some unexplained reason is extremely critical of him, whether fairly or unfairly is impossible to say.

---

132 See the essential article by Paul Harvey, 'Some mid-13th-century accounts', pp. 128–38.
133 Ibid., pp. 129–30.
134 *JB*, p. 29. Above pp. 24–25, 29–30.
135 *Electio*, pp. 166/7. Above p. 163.
136 Miller, *Ely*, p. 78 and n. 2. A later example is the survey made for Walter Langton, bishop of Coventry and Lichfield: he was elected bishop on 19 February 1296, granted his temporalities on 16 June and consecrated on 23 December; already in March 1298 he was in possession of a detailed survey of the estates of the bishopric. The survey, dated March 1298, comprises 32 folios in the Stafford Record Office, D(W) 1734/J2268. I owe this reference to Dr Jillian Hughes.
137 W. H. Hale, *Domesday of St Paul's of the year 1222* (Camden Soc., 1858), pp. 109–17, 146–7; *Radulphi de Diceto, Opera Historica*, ed. William Stubbs (RS, 1876, 2 vols), i. lv, lvi–lxi; Gransden, *Historical Writing*, [i]. 234 and nn. 123–4.

He considered that Edmund was too prone to succumb to pressure and over-anxious to have the favour of the powerful – which, indeed, at that time may have been a wise policy. Matthew relates two occasions when he considered that Edmund acted discreditably. The first was in 1250, on 6 March, when Edmund was one of numerous magnates who, following the king's lead, took the cross from Archbishop Boniface. Edmund was the only abbot to take the cross and by doing so 'became the laughing stock of all, set a pernicious example to monks and injured the holy order of St Benedict'. When he became a monk 'he had taken up the cross of Christ which he was committed to carry for ever'. Matthew accuses him of seeking to ingratiate himself with the king and questioned the king's motive for declaring the crusade: he believed that it was not piety but an excuse for raising a tax.[138] In the event Matthew was not far wrong: on 11 April 1250, at the petition of Henry and the English prelates, Innocent IV granted a tax of a tenth of ecclesiastical revenues on the king's domains to pay for the crusade, but in 1255 the proceeds of the tax were diverted to Henry's proposed campaign to win the crown of Sicily for his son Edmund.[139]

The second occasion when in Matthew Paris's opinion Edmund was too compliant arose during the quarrel between Master William Lupus, archdeacon of Lincoln, and Archbishop Boniface. The canons of Lincoln had quarrelled with the archbishop because during the vacancy which followed the death of the bishop, Robert Grosseteste, in October, 1253, Boniface claimed the right to confer prebends and revenues. The dean and chapter objected and Boniface excommunicated his opponents. Matthew continues, 'Only the archdeacon of Lincoln, that is, Master William Lupus, a man learned in the law, an accomplished Latin scholar and great authority,[140] opposed the archbishop to his face, stood firm and appealed to the supreme Pontiff' for the right and liberty of the church. Lupus, therefore, suffered 'miserable tribulations' until his death.[141] The other canons had 'neither the strength nor the wish to oppose such an adversary in such a dubious case', and they gave way and were promised absolution from their excommunication. Meanwhile Lupus had sought somewhere to stay:

> At length, after he had remained under sentence of excommunication for forty days, whether justly or unjustly, and believing that he would have a safe refuge at St Edmunds (for there, as in the territory of St Alban, there is wont to be refuge and protection for the afflicted[142]), betook himself to the protection of St

---

138   *Chron. Maj.*, v. 101–2.

139   Lunt, *Fin. Relations*, i. 255–63.

140   *BRUO*, ii. 1178–9; John le Neve, *Fasti Ecclesiae Anglicanae 1066–1300*, iii, *Lincoln*, compiled by D. E. Greenway (London, 1977), pp. 26, 118.

141   *Chron. Maj.*, v. 412–13. For the quarrel see also: Dunstable, p. 187; *Flores Hist.*, ii. 393, 409.

142   The right of sanctuary in churches is stated in canon law: *Decretum*, D. 87, c. 6, c. 17, q. 4, c. 6. See *C and S*, ii, i. 534 and n. 2. The right of sanctuary of St Edmunds, like that of St Albans and Westminster, extended to the area over which they had ecclesiastical immunity, that is, in St Edmunds' case, the Liberty of the *banleuca*. The Bury Chronicle refers three times to the privilege: it records that Margaret, wife of Hubert de Burgh, took refuge there in 1232 (*Bury Chron.*, p. 8 and n. 1); in 1263 Simon of Walton, bishop of

Edmund's [church] and borough.[143] He was pursued there by the archbishop and found not a safe refuge but harsh imprisonment, for the abbot of St Edmunds was able neither to protect nor to receive the poor, fugitive archdeacon who went as an exile to Rome, seeking at any rate some consolation from the pope.

The pope took up his cause but Lupus died on the way home. In relating this incident Matthew stops short of condemning Edmund for not protecting Lupus but seems to imply that Edmund was more anxious not to offend Boniface than to defend St Edmunds' right of sanctuary. On the other hand, possibly Edmund acted weakly because he was frail after an illness he had suffered not long before. That he had been ill is known from an inventory, taken on 20 August 1253, of his table-linen and table-ware 'when he recovered from illness'.[144]

Maybe Edmund was weak in matters concerning the king or a powerful figure like Archbishop Boniface, but he at least tried to be strong when defending St Edmunds' interests against an aggressive neighbour. The neighbour in question was Richard de Clare, earl of Gloucester, who in 1251 sued the abbot for the manor of Mildenhall and its outlier, Icklingham. Matthew Paris asserts that the earl was 'a known enemy of the abbot and convent' and compares his action in bringing the case to the seizure by Henry III of Ramsey abbey's market at St Ives: 'thus the world turns to robbery and rapine, so that extortion from the religious appears a merit not a demerit'.[145] The dispute culminated in a trial in the king's court, lasting from 1251 to 1253. The earl sued the abbot for the manor of Mildenhall and its outlier, Icklingham.[146] Although Abbot Samson had purchased the manor from Richard I,[147] the manor's complicated descent left even the king's title to it in doubt. Edward the Confessor had given Milden-hall to St Edmund's[148] but the monks parted with it and Icklingham to Arch-

---

Norwich, 'would have found no safe asylum had he not hastily fled to the security of St Edmunds' Liberty' (ibid., p. 27); Edward I's officials violated St Edmunds' sanctuary in 1294, when they ransacked it for money and valuables, 'to the prejudice of ecclesiastical immunity [for] the monastery of St Edmund, king and martyr, together with the adjoining town … had been privileged as a city of refuge from the earliest times and no previous king had dared attack it' (ibid., p. 122).

143 Matthew Paris also compares St Edmunds' right of sanctuary with that of St Albans in the annal for 1173: having recorded the defeat of the rebels at Leicester by the royalist forces he writes: 'Dispersi sunt nobiles civitatis; et quia regem nimis in defensione suae civitatis offenderant, locum tuti refugii quaerebant, ut minas et gravamen regis evaderent. Tunc igitur ad terram Sancti Albani Anglorum prothomartyris, et Sancti Edmundi Regis et martyris, quasi ad sinum protectionis confugerunt. Quia tunc temporis tanta fuit eorum reverentia, ut eorum burgi omnibus transfugis asilium et tutam protectionem ab hostibus praebuerunt.' Chron. Maj., ii. 289.

144 BL MS Harley 230, f. 183v. For the text see below p. 249, Appendix I.

145 Chron. Maj., v. 297.

146 A narrative describing the descent of the manor of Mildenhall, followed by an account of the proceedings in the king's court 1251–3, is in BL MS Additional 14847, ff. 75v–77v.

147 JB, pp. 45, 46. Above pp. 26–28.

148 Harmer, Writs, pp. 154–5 no. 9. The charming but probably fictitious story explaining the reason for Edward's generous gift may have been composed to strengthen St Edmunds' case against Richard de Clare. BL MSS Add. 14847, ff. 65–65v and Harley 1005, f. 126v. See below pp. 250–51, Appendix II.

bishop Stigand, who held it until his deposition in 1070.[149] It then reverted to the crown. Richard de Clare's claim, as stated in the proceedings in the king's court, was based on a grant by William the Conqueror to the founder of the de Clare's fortunes, Richard FitzGilbert, son of Godfrey, count of Brionne, one of the Norman magnates who participated in William's conquest of England. FitzGilbert received extensive lands in Suffolk, most of them within St Edmund's Liberty.[150] The court proceedings state that the grant of Mildenhall was in reward for FitzGilbert's 'strenuous' service in arms and it stipulated that he was to hold the manor until he was provided with forty or fifty librates of land.[151] Domesday Book records that FitzGilbert had two freemen with sixty acres in Mildenhall[152] and that the manor was in the king's hands.[153] Possibly William had previously granted the manor to FitzGilbert who subsequently acquired the two freemen and sixty acres but thereafter the manor returned to the king. Alternatively, William could have granted him the manor sometime between the compilation of Domesday Book in 1086 and his own death on 9 September 1087. Whatever the truth, Earl Richard asserted that successive kings, including most recently Henry III, had confirmed the grant.[154]

The court proceedings were protracted. Simon of Luton, then sacrist and later abbot, and Robert Russel, later prior, often served together as Abbot Edmund's attorneys. The abbot and his attorneys frequently appealed to Edward the Confessor's charter in defence of St Edmund's right. The De Miraculis, written c. 1100, states that Edward gave the monks eight and a half hundreds and 'the royal mansion' of Mildenhall 'by charter'. However, Jocelin of Brackland records that Abbot Samson appealed to Domesday Book for proof of St Edmund's right to Mildenhall: he makes no mention of any charter.[155] Therefore, it seems likely that no charter (either authentic or spurious) recording the grant survived in Samson's day, which raises a strong possibility that the monks forged one in order to support St Edmunds' case against Earl Richard's claim. Be that as it may, the suit was still in progress at the time of Edmund's death. The dispute was finally settled under his successor, Abbot Simon of Luton, in 1259 as part of a complicated property transaction.[156]

The expense of the litigation with Earl Richard would have added to St Edmunds' already considerable burden of debt. Various factors had contributed to a worsening of its financial position. The vacancy following Henry of Rush-

---

[149] DB, Suffolk, i. 1. 115 (ff. 288ᵇ, 289ᵃ).
[150] Ibid., ii. 25. 1–112 passim. Cf. Douglas, William the Conqueror, pp. 232, 269, 270, 286, 288, 298.
[151] Add. 14847, f. 76v.
[152] DB, Suffolk, i. 25. 39 (f. 392ᵃ).
[153] Above and n. 148.
[154] Add. 14847, f. 76v.
[155] De Miraculis, p. 48. JB, pp. 45, 46 and above p.28 and n. 33.
[156] See: BL MSS Harley 645 and Additional 14847, f. 77; CUL MSS Mm. iv. 19, ff. 18ᵛ–19 and Ee. iii. 60, f. 187 (Pinch. Reg., i. 432–4); Bury Chron., p. 24 and n. 3.

brooke's death had only lasted three months[157] but during that time the abbey's resources seem to have been drained to the utmost for the benefit of the royal treasury. Matthew Paris asserts that Henry 'disregarding fear of, and reverence for God and the saintly martyr, took so much money from the vacant abbey that mercy seemed wholly put aside, for 1,200 marks, not counting wages for the royal bailiffs, was brutally extorted from it'.[158] If Matthew's figure of 1,200 marks is correct, it was a very large sum indeed for the king to have taken. When in 1301 Abbot John of Northwold obtained a grant of custody of the abbey for the prior and convent during future vacancies, the sum to be paid to the king in compensation was fixed at 1,000 marks pro rata for every year of the vacancy.[159] St Edmunds' losses during the vacancy and the 800 marks Edmund had to pay for papal confirmation of his election were symptomatic of the growing financial demands made by Henry III and the papacy on the English church. The collection of the triennial tenth granted in 1250 began in July 1254,[160] and in May 1255 Innocent IV authorized Henry to borrow money for the Sicilian project and to pledge suitable English churches for its repayment: St Edmunds was one of the churches pledged, being made liable for 700 marks.[161] The Bury chronicler, no doubt reflecting the views of all those affected, considered their financial expedient outrageous.[162]

One source of the abbey's revenue was the profits of justice from the courts of the king's justices sitting in the Liberty of the eight and a half hundreds or presiding over cases in which tenants on its holdings outside the Liberty were a party. In this context Abbot Edmund may be a significant figure. The entry for him in the Book of Benefactors states that he was 'the first abbot of St Edmunds to 'occupy' the amercements and chattels of felons and [that] the convent [did likewise] on its manors, by virtue of the charter of Henry I which was more explicit than the charter of St Edmund'.[163] It explains that he did this because he realized that up to the time of Richard I the abbot and convent had not obtained amercements from, and the chattels of, felons. His action would have been a result of a change in Exchequer practice in 1233–4. Previously liberty-holders had been allowed the amercements and the chattels of felons on the production at the Exchequer of charters granting them the right of the profits of justice within their liberties. But in 1233–4, at the order of the king's council this practice was disallowed: in future allocations could only be made by special writ. The writ authorized the justices in eyre to allow the liberty-holder to collect,

157 Above pp. 185–7.
158 *Chron. Maj.*, v. 40, cited in English translation in Lunt, *Papal Revenues*, ii. 237.
159 See Gransden, 'Separation of portions', p. 384.
160 Lunt, *Fin. Relations*, i. 255–62.
161 *CPR, 1247–58*, p. 516; Lunt, *Fin. Relations*, i. 264.
162 *Bury Chron.*, p. 20.
163 The reference is to the probably spurious charter of Edmund, king of England 939–46, to the monastery at *Baedericeswirde*. Printed e.g. *Mon. Angl.*, iii. 137 no. 4. See e.g. Sawyer, *Charters*, pp. 191–2 no. 507; Harmer, *Writs*, p. 144 and n. 1. Hart argues that the clause giving the boundary of the privileged area is perhaps derived from pre-Conquest sources. Hart, *Early Charters*, pp. 54–8 no. 74.

that is to 'occupy', the profits of the court himself and no record of them need be sent to the Exchequer.[164] Therefore, the Book of Benefactors' statement means that Abbot Edmund was the first abbot of St Edmunds to obtain the profits of justice directly, by the new procedure. Later, in 1290, the old Exchequer practice was restored. The then abbot of St Edmunds, John of Northwold, successfully led the liberty-holders' struggle to persuade Edward I to recognize their right to the profits of justice specified in their charters.[165] The liberty-holder would present the appropriate charter or charters at the Exchequer; the profits would be allowed to him and the fact entered on the Pipe Rolls.

Nevertheless, the statement in the Book of Benefactors that Edmund was the first abbot of St Edmunds to 'occupy' profits of justice is problematical because it seems to conflict with evidence in the early fifteenth-century Red vestry register. According to it, in 1267–8, Edmund's successor, Simon of Luton, 'occupied the chattels of felons on his eight and a half hundreds and the convent [did so] in its manors. ... And remember that all the said amercements and chattels were not allowed until 1290.'[166] The scribe of this entry remarks on the preceding folio that 'from the time of the separation [of the abbot's and convent's respective portions] no abbot claimed or obtained anything pertaining to the crown until the third year of King Richard, that is during the reigns of nine kings'. There follow copies of St Edmunds' charters of liberties ending with Edward the Confessor's charter. Next there is a heading 'By virtue of which charter Abbot Edmund obtained various allowances, that is as follows': allowances recorded in the Pipe Rolls, for 3 Richard (1191–2) until 1268–9, follow.[167] But none of these allowances are for profits of justice in the Liberty of the eight and a half hundreds or in the convent's manors: they are all for profits of justice from St Edmunds' tenants elsewhere. How these pieces of evidence can be reconciled is hard to see, but it seems possible that the Book of Benefactors wrongly attributed an act of Simon of Luton to Edmund.

However, one notable achievement is certainly attributable to Edmund's abbacy though his personal involvement may have been small. Sometime between 1248 and 1252 he and the convent founded the hospital of St John, the *Domus Dei*, in the town for the temporary relief and recuperation of the begging poor. It was the last of the six hospitals founded by St Edmunds in the

---

[164] See *The Roll and Writ File of the Berkshire Eyre of 1248*, ed. M. T. Clanchy, Selden Soc., xc (London, 1973), pp. xxxvi–xxxvii.

[165] Gransden, 'John de Northwold', pp. 100–2 and refs.

[166] 'Postea anno quinquagesimo 2 Hen. III (1267–8) *Symon abbas occupauit cat[alla] felonum* in octo hundredis suis et dim[idium] et conuentus in maneriis suis vt sequitur. ... Et memorandum quod omnia supradicta amerciamenta et cat[alla] occupabantur sed non allocabantur vsque ad annum 19 [Edward I, 1290].' The italics are mine, to indicate the rubricated heading. CUL MS Ff. ii. 29, f. 2.

[167] '*Cuius carte virtute Abbas Edmundus diuersas allocaciones optinuit vt sequitur.*' It then cites allowances from the Pipe Roll of: 3 Richard (1191–20), for Essex and Herts; 8 Richard (1196–7), for Norfolk and Suffolk; 10 Henry III (1225–6), for Essex and Herts; and amercements from the eyre of Nicholas de Turri (1268–9). The italics are mine, to indicate the rubricated heading. CUL MS Ff. ii. 29, ff. 1v–2.

town, but the first to be intended specifically for temporary poor relief. At least three of the twelfth-century foundations, St Peter's, St Nicholas's and St Petronilla's, were lazar houses (little is known about St Stephen's),[168] while St Saviour's was founded by Abbot Samson for the long-term sustenance of sick and poor men and women.[169] The foundation charter of St John's states categorically that none of the 'brethren or sisters' were to be to be housed permanently; if one fell sick, he or she would be cared for until he recovered but must then 'set forth on Christ's path wheresoever they wish'.[170] The only permanent residents were the two wardens, 'wise and discreet men of good reputation' who were to administer the hospital under the almoner's supervision: when they fell ill or became too old to work, the almoner was to choose two others and present them to the abbot and convent in chapter for approval. If, 'by God's grace', in the future the benefactions conferred on the hospital increased the hospital's resources sufficiently, it might provide more permanent shelter for the poor who are frail or ill. Initially its resources were not great, which may have been a reason why the foundation charter states that mass was not to be celebrated nor an altar set up in the hospital, since this saved the expense of endowing a chaplaincy. Maybe the choice of the insalubrious site in Southgate Street was also dictated by economy. Later, under Abbot Simon, the hospital's resources increased and it was moved to a better site, outside the south gate walls on the royal road. At the same time it was re-organized and a chapel built 'for the praise of God'.[171] The charters which survive from St John's original endowment indicate that its possessions were built up by purchase. It was usually the prior, Richard de Bosco, who acquired the small parcels of land in the town which comprised the hospital's holdings.[172] Although donors were rewarded with confraternity in the abbey, in nearly every instance Richard also paid them.[173] The predominant role played by the prior raises doubts about Abbot Edmund's involvement. Probably the multitude of beggars, many of them needy pilgrims, who crowded the abbey gate for alms, were more of a worry to the convent than to the abbot since he was often absent, staying on his manors or travelling in the execution of his public duties.

Little can be said about Edmund's relations with the convent because of lack of evidence. However, there are indications that he made concessions, perhaps under pressure. The chronicler, having recorded the succession of the priorate of Simon of Luton (the future abbot) after the death of Richard de Bosco on

---

168 The most detailed and authoritative work on these six hospitals is Harper-Bill, *Hospitals*, and for a useful general survey see Joy Rowe, 'The medieval hospitals of Bury St Edmunds', *Medical History*, ii (1958), pp. 253–63.

169 Above pp. 49–50.

170 St John's, the *Domus Dei*, is discussed and the Latin text of the foundation charter, with an English synopsis, is printed in Harper-Bill, *Hospitals*, pp. 3–5, 30–1 no. 1.

171 Listed ibid., p. 21.

172 For a chronological list of benefactors of St John's see Harper-Bill, *Hospitals*, pp. 26–8 passim.

173 See ibid., pp. 3, 30–41 nos 1, 3–21.

23 October 1252, comments: 'This prior, Simon, was the first monk to be elected prior of St Edmund's church by way of scrutiny; it was done by Abbot Edmund and two monks (one chosen by the abbot and the other by the convent) who together with the abbot took the vote orally of each monk.'[174] Obviously the chronicler considered the procedure for the appointment of the prior on this occasion sufficiently remarkable to deserve record and comment. The procedure did not deprive the abbot of all influence over the appointment but must have reduced it. Possibly it also reduced the danger of the monks objecting to whoever was chosen. According to the Rule the abbot should appoint the prior, though he might, if he judged best, be guided by 'a reasonable and humble request' of the community and make the appointment 'with the advice of God-fearing brethren'.[175] However, by the end of the twelfth century monks in some houses had tried to gain control over the appointment of the prior and main obedientiaries.[176] At St Edmunds in 1201 Samson had had to listen to the monks' wishes concerning the appointment of a prior on the death of Prior Robert. Indeed, he went through the forms of the election but contrived the appointment of his own nominee, Herbert.[177] The Composition of c. 1215 specifies that the appointment of the prior, sacrist, cellarer and chamberlain should be with the consent of the convent in chapter or, if outside chapter, with the consent of the prior and senior monks.[178] Possibly the election of Simon of Luton by way of scrutiny in 1252 set a precedent, for in 1287 William of Rockland was elected prior, again by way of scrutiny.[179]

Edmund died on 31 December 1256, and Simon of Luton was elected abbot on 14 January 1257.[180] The obituary notice for Edmund in the Book of Benefactors concentrates almost exclusively on his contributions to the convent's prosperity, thus resembling in tone the entry for Henry of Rushbrooke.

> Abbot Edmund appropriated to the convent the churches of [Great] Barton and Pakenham and a tenement with its appurtenances in Cockfield and a rent of one mark in Whepstead. He, realizing that up to the time of Richard, that is in the time of nine kings – for 503 years – the chattels [of felons] and amercements had been lost, he began to 'occupy' various amercements and chattels in the eight and a half hundreds and in the convent's manors by virtue of the charter of Henry I, which was more explicit than the charter of St Edmund. He was buried in the

---

174 *Bury Chron.*, p. 18. Election by way of scrutiny (the formal taking of individual votes) was one of the three methods of election prescribed by the Fourth Lateran Council. *Histoire des Conciles*, v, pt 2, p. 1353 can. 24.

175 *Rule*, ed. Fry, pp. 284/5–286/7, c. 65.

176 Knowles, MO, pp. 414–15. Gransden, 'Democratic movement', pp. 25–39.

177 JB, pp. 124–8.

178 *Bury Cust.*, p. 100 lines 8–11, and see Alexander IV's confirmation of the customs, ibid., p. 63 lines 28–30.

179 *Bury Chron.*, p. 89.

180 Ibid., p. 21.

chapter-house under square marble stones, at the feet of Abbot Henry, the fifth in number towards the chapter-house door.[181]

His anniversary was marked by a great ringing of the bells[182] and the monks' pittance was 'from Whepstead'.

181 Douai, Bibliothèque Municipale MS 553, f. 9: 'Pro Abbate Edmundo qui appropriauit Conuentui ecclesias de Berton et de Pakenham et vnum tenementum cum suis perti-nenciis in Cokefeld' et vnam marcam annui redditus in Whepstede. Hic perpendens predecessores suos a tempore Regis Canuti vsque ad tempus regis Ricardi nouem scilicet regum temporibus Centum videlicet et quinquaginta ac tribus annis et amplius catallis et amerciamentis caruisse cepit occupare diuersa amerciamenta et catalla infra octo hundra[dis] et dimidium et Conuentus in manerijs suis habentes respectum ad virtutem carte regis Henrici primi que expressius se extendit quam carta Sancti Edwardi. Sepultus est in Capitulo sub lapidibus marmoreis quadratis ad pedes Hugonis Abbatis versus ostium Capituli in numero quintus. Pitancia de Whepstede'. The statement that Edmund was the first abbot of St Edmunds to 'occupy' amercements and the chattels of felons in the eight and a half hundreds, which may be wrong, is discussed above pp. 191–3. For the burial place of Abbot Edmund see James, *Abbey*, pp. 146–8, 181.
182 Douai, Bibliothèque Municipale MS 553, f. 6.

16

Observance of the Rule of St Benedict

Relaxations of the Rule

Observance of the Rule at St Edmunds in the thirteenth century was much the same as that in nearly all other great Benedictine houses at that period. It was moderately lax. The monks lived comfortably but not luxuriously and, so far as we know, gave rise to no scandals. In effect, they enjoyed those relaxations of the Rule which had modified strict observance in previous centuries. To some extent these relaxations were justifiable. St Benedict had intended the Rule to prescribe a monastic life suitable for an ordinary man with a religious vocation, not for one desiring or perhaps even capable of a life of remarkable austerity. But a few of the prescriptions in the Rule, while moderate for monks living in the Italian climate, were severe for those enduring the long, cold winters in northern countries such as England.

Good examples of the kind of relaxations which became common are the Rule's prescriptions concerning the monks' dietary regime and their food and drink. Thus, the Rule prescribes a one-meal-a-day regime for the fasts of Advent and Lent, that is from 13 September until Easter,[1] a period of four or five months coinciding with the coldest part of the year: by the thirteenth century only the few most observant houses observed this restriction strictly.[2] The Rule imposed certain restrictions on what the monks ate, and on the quantity of their food and drink. However, by the thirteenth century, owing to various relaxations of the Rule, the monks' diet in a wealthy monastery such as St Edmunds differed little from that of the lay aristocracy.

Some relaxations were achieved by evasion of, rather than by disobedience to, the Rule. This was the case with regard to meat-eating. The Rule prescribes that 'everyone except the sick who are very weak' ('praeter omnino debiles aegrotas') must abstain entirely from eating the meat of four-footed animals.[3] It also ordains that as soon as a sick monk recovers he must again abstain from meat.[4] Nevertheless, monks in nearly all English Benedictine houses ate a lot of

---

[1] *Rule*, ed Fry, pp. 240/1, c. 41. Cf. ibid., pp. 182/3, c. 4 § 36, which enjoins monks to refrain from over-eating.

[2] See Knowles, *RO*, i. 280–5, and Harvey, *Living and Dying*, pp. 10–12.

[3] *Rule*, ed. Fry, pp. 238/9, c. 39 § 11. For an extended study with documentation of the extent of meat-eating by the English Benedictines see Bishop, 'Fasting and abstinence', pp. 184–237.

[4] *Rule*, ed. Fry, pp. 234/5, c. 36 § 9.

meat in the middle ages. The Rule's prescriptions could be interpreted in ways which allowed considerable latitude. The prohibition of meat-eating was interpreted to apply to meals eaten in the refectory, not to those eaten elsewhere. Therefore, special rooms were built where a rota of monks could eat apart and eat meat.[5] In addition, the Rule stipulates that the abbot (or other monastic superior) should give a ready welcome and hospitality to travellers and pilgrims – 'and monasteries are never without them'.[6] He dined separately with them and if the guest were a layman of high rank, perhaps a benefactor, to entertain him without meat would have been unthinkable. And so meat came to be regularly eaten at the abbot's table. Moreover, the Rule allows the abbot, in the absence of guests, to invite any monks he wished to dine at his table,[7] where they too would eat meat. In practice, monks dined with the abbot whether or not he had guests. The Rule provided yet another loophole. It stipulates that if the monks' work were especially heavy an 'appropriate' extra dish might be added to their normal two-dish-a-day regime.[8] This extra dish might of course be a meaty one. Thus, the Rule obliquely sanctioned the pittances which proliferated over the years. Their proliferation was mainly owing to the increasing number of saints' days – this meant that masses for the saints concerned were added to the monks' liturgical round and so added to 'the burden and heat of the day' (Matt. 20.12).[9]

Again, the Rule's stipulation that 'weak' brethren might eat meat was understood to include all those in the infirmary. Among them were monks who had been bled: each monk underwent blood-letting, the 'seyney', at the intervals determined by the customs of his house; usually the intervals were of six weeks or so for a healthy monk. He would then spend two or three days in the infirmary, enjoying a restful regime and fortifying food – including meat.[10] Yet another way of evading the Rule's intention was in the interpretation of what constituted meat. St Benedict had forbidden the consumption of four-footed animals, but since birds are not quadrupeds, the prohibition did not include chicken, geese and other fowl. More equivocally, the monks distinguished between dishes solely of meat and those in which meat was just one of the ingredients, such as meaty flans. Thus, there were many loop-holes which enabled the monks to eat meat without blatantly flouting the Rule.[11]

Similar relaxation of observance had occurred with regard to drink. The Rule legislated about wine but ale was the usual northern drink, wine being drunk only on special occasions and then only in monasteries that could afford it. The

---

5   See below p. 201 and n. 28.
6   *Rule*, ed. Fry, pp. 254/5–258/9, c. 53.
7   Ibid., pp. 264/5, c. 56.
8   Ibid., pp. 238/9, c. 39 §§ 6–9.
9   Matt. 20.12.
10 For blood-letting at St Edmunds see *Bury Cust.*, pp. xxviii, 50–1, 76 line 20 – 78 line 19, and the ruling of the papal visitors to St Edmunds in 1234 in 'Visitation', ed. Graham, p. 735. See Lanfranc, *Constitutions* (1951 edn), pp. 93–5, 152–3 (appendix C) and (1967 edn), pp. 778 and nn. See also: Harvey, *Living and Dying*, pp. 96–9; L. Gougaud, *Anciennes Coutumes Claustrales* (Ligugé, 1930), pp. 49–68.
11 See: Harvey, *Living and Dying*, pp. 11, 36–40, 62 and n. 88; Bishop, 'Fasting and abstinence', pp. 184–211 and for documentation ibid., pp. 212–37.

Rule states that half a bottle of wine a day should be enough for a monk, 'taking due regard for the infirmities of the sick', but that 'those to whom God gives the strength to abstain must know that they will earn their own reward'.[12] The monastic superior should decide when a more generous measure of wine should be allowed because of 'local conditions, work or summer heat', but he must always be on his guard 'lest excess or drunkenness creep in'. However, there is no doubt that by the thirteenth century monks in general were drinking greater quantities of alcoholic drink than St Benedict would have thought proper. There was, for instance, a marked increase in the number of times a day when the monks were allowed to drink. This increase and the situation with regard to drink at St Edmunds in particular are considered below.

The reform movement

General

A remarkable feature of the thirteenth century was the movement for the reform of the old orders, that is of the Benedictines, with whom we are concerned, and of the Austin canons. The movement covered not only the religious life of monks but also their administrative affairs. The two subjects were inextricably linked. To fulfil the obligation to provide hospitality and to give alms cost money or its equivalent, and the monks' well-being depended on adequate food and clothing, as well as discipline to keep order: lack of both or either tended to result in anxiety, discontent and quarrelling. Therefore, reforming statutes and related documents include administrative reforms alongside those concerning the monks' religious observance.

   Some reforms were the result of spontaneous action within the monasteries themselves and some were the result of papal initiative. Often, it seems, an abbot was bent on at least moderate reform but opposition from the monks, or from a group of them, frustrated his attempts. Sometimes the convent itself was divided between reformers and those opposed to reform. St Edmunds in the early thirteenth century provides good examples of these contending forces. Thus, Abbot Samson tried to reform certain abuses as part of his draconian measures to curb extravagance and to prevent lax administration. He put an end to 'immoderate feasting' in the prior's lodgings[13] and demolished the sacrist's buildings in the cemetery because they were the scene of drinking parties 'and of other things about which it is better to remain silent'.[14] But, on the other hand, he built a new infirmary to provide additional accommodation.[15] Possibly it was intended for those who were not really ill but were weak, having been bled, and for others who were healthy but in the infirmary for a rest and a more comfortable life. This certainly was how it was being used when the papal legate *a latere*, Nicholas

---

[12] *Rule*, ed. Fry, pp. 238/9–240/1, c. 40.
[13] *JB*, p. 88.
[14] *JB*, p. 31.
[15] *Gesta Sacrist.*, p. 291. For customs in the infirmary see *Bury Cust.*, pp. 14–16 line 5, 80–1.

of Tusculum, visited the abbey in 1213. This is apparent from the contemporary account of the dispute over Hugh of Northwold's election, the *Electio Hugonis*.

The *Electio* alludes in several places to the monks' dietary regulations. It shows that the two parties to the dispute, comprising the monks supporting Hugh's election and those opposing it, were also in opposition over dietary reform. Hugh's supporters, among them the cellarer and subcellarer, favoured a stricter regime than did their opponents, who represented the interests of the prior and sacrist. Since Hugh based his case on papal authority and canon law, this no doubt was an incentive to reform observance, but he and his party may also have been moved by the wish to economize – the cellarer and subcellarer were responsible for supplying much of the food and drink. The account in the *Electio* of a dispute over the monks' ale allowance illustrates the conflicting attitudes of the parties. It records that sometime before the time of the election dispute, the ale allowance had been increased by the use of a local measure instead of the less generous king's measure. Some of Hugh's supporters wanted the king's measure restored and the subcellarer, Richard of Saxham, refused to dispense the ale by any other measure. The sacrist, Robert of Graveley, vehemently opposed and a quarrel ensued which led to Richard's deposition from office.[16]

Papal initiatives

The visit of the legate, Nicholas of Tusculum, was St Edmunds' first direct experience of Innocent III's reformist programme.[17] Nicholas arrived in December 1213 and, although his commission was to try to settle the election dispute, he also concerned himself with the reform of lax observance, especially meat-eating by the monks. Again, as in the case of the ale allowance, Hugh's party was in favour of reform. Early in 1214, Nicolas entered the chapter-house and announced that he had forbidden 'everyone' to eat meat and, therefore, the monks of St Edmunds must abstain.[18] He made two general exceptions: the prior and two or three monks chosen to dine with him in his chamber; and those monks in the infirmary who were not making a satisfactory recovery. The prohibition was to last until Easter (that is, during Lent). And in effect it lasted no longer, for 'from that very day, the monks one by one, led by the prior, first eight of them, then ten, then twelve,' left the refectory and went to the infirmary where they resumed their private meals: 'from one side of the choir' only six monks remained in the refectory.[19] The reference is presumably to the prior's side of the choir which included most of Hugh's opponents. Nicholas seems to have referred the matter back to Rome, for on 19 May 1214 he entered chapter

16 *Electio*, pp. 70/1–72/3. Above pp. 157, 163.
17 St Edmunds does not appear to have been among the houses visited in 1206 by Master John of Ferentino, cardinal deacon of Santa Maria in via Lata. See C. R. Cheney, 'The papal legate and English monasteries in 1206', *EHR*, xlvi (1931), pp. 443–52. For his legation and that of Nicholas of Tusculum see Sayers, *Papal Judges Delegate*, pp. 27–9 and nn. passim.
18 *Electio*, pp. 52/3.
19 *Electio*, pp. 62/3–64/5.

with a mandate from Innocent, dated 24 March 1214, addressed to the judges delegate, Henry, abbot of Wardon, Richard de Marins, prior of Dunstable, and Richard Poore, canon (later bishop) of Salisbury: Innocent informs the delegates that he has been notified on behalf of the cellarer and prudent men of St Edmunds that 'certain' wicked customs or rather corruptions' had contaminated that monastery which must be quickly rooted out; he orders the judges delegate to go to St Edmunds, hold an inquiry and enforce regular observance.[20]

The prior and his fellows did as ordered but the statutes they issued do not appear not to have survived. However, something is known about their contents because they were among the sources used by the papal visitors to St Edmunds in 1234 for their own statutes.[21] These later statutes ordain that the abbot shall have copied into the martyrology the statutes of Prior Henry and his colleagues and the statutes of the General Chapter of the Benedictines of the southern province (held in 1219), and they shall be read out to the convent twice a year, once on the day after Epiphany (6 January) and again on the day after the feast of St John the Baptist 24 June. These statutes should be observed 'except in respect of our ordinance concerning fasting and diet'.[22] The 1214 statutes may be the source of a number of clauses in the 1234 statutes but the latter only specifically cite their authority for one clause. This concerns the keeping of accounts.[23] It states that the abbot of Wardon and his fellows ordained that obedientiaries should be of sound judgement, above suspicion and conversant with all receipts and expenses; the sacrist and cellarer were to render accounts of all receipts and expenses and of the livestock on their manors four times a year, in the presence of the abbot and prior and eight monks chosen by the abbot and prior; the other obedientiaries were to render account for their offices twice a year and to keep rolls recording all receipts and expenses for the year 'so that the improvement or deterioration of the monastery from year to year is made clear'.

Of more far-reaching effect than the reforming activities of papal legates and judges delegate was the legislation of the fourth Lateran Council of 1215. No previous council had so profound an influence on the Benedictine order. Previously, each monastery was autonomous, interpreting the Rule in its own way and observing its own customs. There was no central body to impose uniformity and reform observance, and although non-exempt houses were subject to diocesan authority, exempt ones were subject only to the pope and his legates. The Fourth Lateran Council totally altered this situation. Canon 12 decreed that the heads of Benedictine houses in each province should meet together every three years and legislate for the reform of the order.[24] The new organization was modelled on that of the Cistercians and two Cistercian abbots were to attend the first session of the General Chapter and instruct the two presidents on procedure. In addition to legislating, the general Chapters were to appoint visitors who were

---

[20] *Electio*, pp. 72/3, 78/9.
[21] Below pp. 203–213.
[22] 'Visitation', ed. Graham, p. 730 and nn. 10, 11.
[23] Ibid., p. 735. For account keeping at St Edmunds see below, Appendix III passim.
[24] *Histoire des Conciles*, pp. 1342–3; See Knowles, *RO*, i. 9–10.

to visit and reform all houses in their provinces, including those exempt from metropolitan and episcopal authority.

The first General Chapter of the southern province of the English Benedictines met at Oxford sometime between late in 1218 and the summer of 1219.[25] The presidents were William of Trumpington, abbot of St Albans, and Hugh of Northwold, abbot of St Edmunds; the Cistercian abbots in attendance were Roger, abbot of Wardon, and Simon, abbot of Thame. The statutes dealt with a wide variety of topics. A few will be mentioned here because they concerned matters which were of particular concern at St Edmunds. The first six clauses were intended to reduce worldliness and extravagance among abbots. For instance: whenever possible abbots were to attend the conventual chapter, hear the monks' confessions and be with them at the divine office and in the refectory; they were not to alienate the monastery's property or make new customs without the convent's consent; and they were not to have a superfluity of servants or more than twenty vehicles (*vectura*).[26] Other clauses deal with the monks' dietary regime: from the feast of All Saints (1 November) until Ash Wednesday monks were to have only one meal a day, except on feasts in copes, and in the period from Easter until Epiphany, unless the customs of a house imposed greater abstinence.[27] The problem of meat-eating is touched on: the prelate should allow monks who had borne the 'burden and heat of the day' to eat meat privately; a decent (*honestus*) place should be provided for the purpose, if possible near the refectory, and no other monk or any lay person should mingle with them before or after dinner except keepers of the order and servants.[28] Other clauses were aimed at promoting greater economy: the prelate, with the advice of four or more chosen monks, was to cut superfluity in food, drink and other things 'saving the good and approved customs of individual houses'; obedientiaries were not to squander goods committed to their care and were to render account to the prelate, 'aided by the more discerning monks according to the number of brethren'.[29]

Nevertheless, the Oxford statutes emphasize the monks' obligation to give alms: left-overs from all the monks' meals, wherever eaten, should be given to the poor;[30] and when a monk has new clothes, the chamberlain is to give the old ones to the poor on pain of deposition from office. This was in obedience to the Rule which prescribes that when new clothes are given to a monk, the old ones should be immediately returned and stored in the vestry ('in vestiario') for

---

[25] *Chapters*, ed. Pantin, i. 3–14.

[26] Ibid., i. 8–9 §§ 1–9.

[27] Ibid., i. 10 § 12.

[28] Ibid., i. 11–12 § 19. See Bishop, 'Fasting and abstinence', pp. 193–4. For the places outside the refectory at St Edmunds where monks could eat meat see above p. 199, and for those at Westminster, see Harvey, *Living and Dying*, pp. 41–2.

[29] See below p. 215 and n. 105.

[30] *Chapters*, ed. Pantin, pp. 11 §§ 15, 18, 12 § 20. Later, the giving of alms was again enjoined by the General Chapter held at Southwark or Bermondsey in 1249 (ibid., i. 36–7 § 3a, b) and in Alexander IV's confirmation of St Edmunds' customs in 1256 (*Bury Cust.*, p. 65 lines 11–13). For almsgiving by the religious see esp. Harvey, *Living and Dying*, pp. 23–33, 268 (index under 'alms, almsgiving').

the poor.[31] At St Edmunds, Samson had tried to enforce the monks' obligation to give alms. This is illustrated by his interpretation of the man's vision of St Edmund after the terrible fire in the shrine in 1198:[32] the saint appeared to be lying outside his shrine and to say with groans that he was stripped of clothing and emaciated by hunger and thirst. Samson interpreted this to mean that St Edmund attributed his plight to the monks' meanness: they were withholding their clothes from the naked poor, or at least giving them only reluctantly, and treating the poor similarly in respect of food and drink. Moreover, Jocelin records that although Samson himself did not eat meat, he had it placed before him at meals 'so that our alms would be increased'.[33] Again, on the death intestate of Hamo Blund, a rich townsmen of St Edmunds, Samson, to prevent Hamo's brother (his heir) and wife from seizing his whole fortune, took the matter into his own hands: he ordered that all debts owing to him and all his possessions ('worth, it is said, 200 marks') be set down in writing, and a third be given to his brother, a third to his wife and a third to 'his poor relatives and other poor people'.[34] Jocelin also records that, on the death of Abbot Hugh I, his house, bed and body were so pillaged by his servants that 'there was nothing worth a single penny to be distributed to the poor for the benefit of his soul'.[35]

The situation with regard to poor relief was probably fairly typical of a wealthy Benedictine and suggests that a community of monks might be less anxious than their head to fulfil the monastic duty of poor relief.[36] It demonstrates the kind of shortcomings which the Oxford General Chapter intended to reform. But its statutes were condemned as 'burdensome and intolerable' by 'certain weaker spirits' ('quibusdam infirmioribus').[37] One objection was that they overrode the customs of many individual houses. In the long run, such local customs were able to defeat drastic reformist legislation. This fact was already apparent to the author of the Bury Customary, writing c. 1234. With regard to the question of when monks might have two meals a day during the fasting season, he states that the Cistercian, eat twice in one day only on Sundays during that period, and he continues:

> This is not so with the Black Monks, some of whom eat twice more often and some more rarely at that time of year, according to the ancient customs of their houses. Thus it happened that [when] those struggled in the General Chapter to impose unity on the customs of all houses in this matter, individual houses appealed for

[31] *Rule*, ed. Fry, pp. 262/3, c. 55 § 9.

[32] JB, p. 110.

[33] JB, p. 40.

[34] JB, p. 92. Lobel, *Bury St. Edmunds*, p. 44.

[35] JB, p. 7 (see also p. 41).

[36] Later, some of Abbot John of Northwold's reforms were probably the result of opposition in the convent. See Gransden, 'Separation of portions', pp. 392 and n. 106, 401–2 §§ 16–17 and n. 150.

[37] *Chapters*, ed. Pantin, i. 17.

their ancient, approved and observed customs [which had been] justly and holily established by their predecessors.[38]

The severity of the statutes of the Oxford General Chapter was probably the result of the presence of the two Cistercian abbots. No Cistercians oversaw the General Chapter which met at St Albans late in 1219. It was convened at the request of the 'weaker spirits' in order to revise the earlier statutes and reissue them in a modified form. This time neither William, abbot of St Albans, nor Hugh of Northwold, abbot of St Edmunds, were presidents. They were replaced by Ralph, abbot of Evesham, and Alexander, abbot of St Augustine's, Canterbury.[39] Over half of the new decrees reproduce the old ones but the remainder are expanded and/or more moderate versions of them. For example, the new decree on diet omits the injunction for the strict observance of the one-meal-a-day regime during the fasting season, unless a house has a stricter observance. Instead, the new decree stipulates that the Rule of St Benedict should be observed 'save for pious consideration of time and place with regard to juniors, the ailing and infirm, according to the regular customs of individual houses'.[40] Obviously, this left a loophole for lax observance. The statutes did not take immediate effect because Abbot Alexander died before they were formally published, but they were re-issued by a General Chapter held at Northampton on 21 September 1225 together with additional decrees.[41]

The legatine visitation of St Edmunds in 1234

Another important initiative by the papacy for promoting reform followed in 1232. Gregory IX, a zealous reformer, ordered a general visitation of all religious houses in Christendom. He appointed a Cistercian, John, abbot of Boxley, a Premonstratensian canon, Reginald, abbot of Bayham, and a Benedictine, the precentor of the cathedral priory of Christ Church, Canterbury, to visit exempt houses in the province of Canterbury. Their mandate was to reform the 'serious corruptions' in temporal and spiritual matters which had ruined the monasteries in that province 'through malice and neglect'.[42] The visitation was considered excessively severe and drove many heads of houses to appeal to the papal curia against it; Richard of the Isle, abbot of St Edmunds, was one of those who went

---

[38] 'In hac tamen consuetudine non conveniunt albi et nigri. Albi enim ab Exaltacione usque ad Pascham nullo die comedunt bis nisi solis diebus dominicis. Nigri vero non sic sed illorum quidam saepius, quidam rarius bis comedunt praefato tempore anni secundum antiquas consuetudines domorum suarum. Hinc est quod in generali capitulo nitentes omnium locorum consuetudines in hoc casu uniformiter unire, appellatum fuit palam a singulis domibus pro suis antiquis et approbatis et usitatis consuetudinibus a suis praedecessoribus iuste et sancte statutis.' *Bury Cust.*, p. 49 lines 8–16.

[39] *Chapters*, ed. Pantin, i. 15–18.

[40] 'salva pro loco et pro tempore pia consideracione circa iuniores, debiles et infirmos, secundum diversorum monasteriorum regularem consuetudinem', ibid., i. 17 § 14.

[41] Ibid., i. 15–16, 18–21.

[42] For a copy of Gregory's mandate see Matthew Paris, *Chron. Maj.*, iii. 234–5.

to Rome.[43] The opposition by Abbot Richard and by the abbot of Westminster (Richard of Barking) was so strong that they obtained new, more moderate, visitors, that is, a Benedictine, Henry, abbot of Waltham, a Gilbertine, Thomas, prior of Sempringham, and an Augustinian canon, Richard, prior of Holy Trinity, London. They arrived at St Edmunds on 9 July, 1234, and held their visitation on the next day.[44] They issued comprehensive statutes with the overall objective of tightening discipline and promoting economy and efficient administration. They used a variety of sources: besides the Rule of St Benedict, papal decrees and the statutes of the visitation by the abbot of Wardon and his fellows in 1214,[45] they drew heavily on the decrees issued by the General Chapter of 1225;[46] and they specifically cite an ordinance of 'Abbot H.', either Abbot Hugh of North-wold, or Henry of Rushbrooke, and probably used other abbatial ordinances as well.[47] Their statutes, like those of 1214, were copied into the abbey's martyr-ology and were read to the monks in chapter twice a year, at Epiphany and on the feast of St John the Baptist.[48]

The statutes begin by dealing with the abbot's authority and obligations and among the variety of topics which follow is a clause on diet, with a direct refer-ence to meat-eating. The clause begins with a general reference to the decretal of Leo III which ordained that the 'statutes of the Fathers' must not be violated unless it is necessary to alter the law for the use of the church.[49] Next, it copies (without acknowledgement) the clause on diet in the statutes of the 1225 General Chapter,[50] but it omits the reference to local customs; instead it grants reasonable discretion to prelates to allow those who bore 'the burden and heat of the day' to eat meat and have other means of recreation, but he should always have in mind the Rule, the availability of meat and the particular needs of the individual. Another clause tried to check inordinate drinking.[51] Alms owed to the poor are also mentioned.[52] No food was to be taken away from the refectory on pain of the gravest discipline, unless the hostiller or president takes it for a guest; bread and wine not consumed at a meal or otherwise used for the monks' necessities at the disposition of the president, was to be returned to the cellarer to be used for the benefit of the monks or for the profit of the house, 'saving the portion owed to the poor'. The refectorer's servants were to be honest and mature and receive food and pay 'lest they wickedly consume food intended for

[43] Ibid., iii. 238–9. Above pp. 178–9.
[44] Discussed and their statutes printed in 'Visitation', ed. Graham, pp. 728–37.
[45] Ibid., p. 730. Above p. 200.
[46] E.g. 'Visitation', ed. Graham, 733 § 2, 735 § 1.
[47] Ibid., p. 735, last two lines.
[48] Ibid., pp. 736–7.
[49] Ibid., p. 733 and n. 18 citing *Decretum*, i. dist. xiv. 2.
[50] *Chapters*, ed. Pantin, i. 11–12 § 19, 17 § 14. See Bishop, 'Fasting and abstinence', pp. 223 and n. 1, 224, no. 15.
[51] 'Visitation', ed. Graham, p. 732.
[52] Ibid., pp. 731, 732.

alms, and cheat, because it is perilous to turn anything from the patrimony of Christ to evil or superfluous uses'. Among the visitors' priorities was the promotion of efficiency and economy. One clause of the statutes recites the system of accounting by obedientiaries decreed in the statutes issued by the abbot of Wardon and his fellows in 1214.[53] Possibly the earlier statutes were also the source of other clauses on related matters. Thus, a clause decrees that all fixed rents ('certi redditus') of the monastery were to be entered on three rolls, one to be kept by the abbot and one by the 'procurator'; the third was to be preserved in the treasury. Another clause decrees that the cellarer's demesne manors, rents and goods should be valued and then divided into four portions, and each portion should be allocated to support the monastery for part of the year 'lest any part of the year goes short' ('ne una pars anni deficiant'). Those manors at farm should be divided in the same way.[54]

Scattered throughout the statutes are many references to the customs of the house, with regard, for instance, to the enforcement of discipline,[55] the keeping of silence,[56] and the frequency of blood-letting. Thus, for example, the clause about blood-letting states that 'custom and usage should be observed', but adds that licence to be bled should be given only once in any week during Lent and in the weeks of the five solemn feasts; it might be given twice in other weeks, 'saving the prelate's pious consideration for the sick and those clearly needing to be bled'.[57] The visitors were particularly concerned with the growth of new customs in the abbey, unauthorized by long usage, and warn novices not to use them as an excuse for despising the Rule. The statutes, indeed, show that the visitors wished to respect the abbey's ancient, though unwritten, customs, which the abbot and convent were obviously anxious to preserve.

---

[53] Above p. 200 and n. 23.

[54] 'Visitation', ed. Graham, pp. 733–4. A similar system was in place at Christ Church, Canterbury. See R. A. L. Smith, 'The central financial system of Christ Church, Canterbury, 1186–1512', *EHR*, ccxix (1940), esp. pp. 353–5. For Gregory IX's attempts to make monastic obedientiaries present accounts for audit by their superior and senior monks three times a year at least see Snape, *Monastic Finances*, pp. 66–7. For obedientiary and manorial accounts at St Edmunds see below.

[55] 'Visitation', ed. Graham, p. 730.

[56] Ibid., p. 730.

[57] Ibid., p. 735.

St Edmunds' Customary of c. 1234[58]

Any attempt to preserve the abbey's ancient customs made it necessary to know exactly what they were, and with regard to some of the customs this was a problem because there were various opinions about their substance. The need for clarification must have been one reason for the composition of St Edmunds' Customary shortly before, or shortly after, the 1234 visitation. The author states his intention in the prologue:

> Wishing to follow, as is proper, with benign good-will the traditions of our fathers and also their statutes and good deeds in Christ, together with approved customs, as far as it is possible to discern their traces. We will speak of what we know and constantly teach and truthfully testify to what we have seen and heard. May our testimony be useful to the young, a reminder for our successors, and give peace. May there be no dispute over the mode and style of speaking, provided that what is said is true and useful, the intention known to be right, and good order better observed.[59]

There follows a careful and comprehensive account of the respective rights and duties of the abbot, prior and obedientiaries in regard to the administration of the abbey's domestic economy and (to a limited extent) of its estates, with

---

58 The Customary is printed from the best surviving text, a copy in BL MS Harley 1005, ff. 102–119 (modern foliation), in *Bury Cust.*, pp. 1–62. See ibid., pp. xxxvi–xxxvii. The first page is reproduced in ibid., frontispiece, and below pl. VI. This copy is in the small, neat, formal cursive hand dateable to the 1260s and 1270s which copied a number of the many customs and other items, including the tract on dedications (referred to above, pp. 113–17) in Harley 1005. R. M. Thomson contends that the writer of the neat script who copied the Customary and much else in Harley 1005 was the prior, Robert Russel. Thomson, *Archives*, p. 17. Henry of Kirkstead annotated the volume, including a few notes in the margins of the Customary and on an inserted leaf. It has the late fourteenth-century class-mark, C. 68, on f. 1. Two of Kirkstead's notes refer to another copy of the *Traditiones patrum*. Following his list of days when the convent eats twice, he writes 'Haec sumpta sunt de antiquo quaterno consuetudinum cum littera C. 78. intitulato et ex tradicionibus patrum (*interlin*) in custodia T. de Saxham in principio, cum littera C. 64 intitulatis in librario', Harley 1005, f. 115, a leaf inserted between ff. 114 and 116 (ff. 109, 110 of the medieval foliation), *Bury Cust.*, pp. 46–7 n.e. The other reference ends a footnote on the same subject; 'Istud idem scribitur in tradicionibus patrum domini Thom' de Saxham cum antiqua littera et in librario littera C. 64.' Harley 1005, f. 116, *Bury Cust.*, p. 50 n.c. An incomplete text of the Customary in a late thirteenth-century book-hand is in the volume of customs, class-mark C. 63. CUL MS Additional 6006, ff. 9, 9v, 16–20v (medieval foliation) described and collated in *Bury Cust.* Kirkstead annotated the volume apparently in his old age. See *Catalogus*, ed. Rouse and Rouse, p. lxxi n. 187.

59 'Traditiones patrum nostrorum benigno favore, sicut decet, prosequi volentes simul et statuta necnon et eorum in Christo ac bonis operibus una cum approbatis consuetudinibus in quantum licet sequi vestigia, quae scimus et didicimus constanter loquimur, et quae vidimus et audivimus veraciter testamur, utinam testimonium nostrum in utilitatem parvulorum et memoriam successorum cedat et pacem. De ordine vero loquendi aut stilo nulla fiat contencio, dummodo vera loquentis et utilia, recte sciatur intencio, et ordo rectus melius observetur.' *Bury Cust.*, p. 1. This preface is on f. 103 of Harley 1005. At the head of the page a fourteenth-century hand has written in plummet *prolog'* and another fourteenth-century hand has written in ink 'Incipiunt tradiciones patrum'.

particular emphasis on the rights and duties of the sacrist. The Customary also deals with the liturgical life of the monks. The author used a variety of sources. He probably used the statutes of the 1218/19 General Chapter of the Benedictines of the southern province, but he does not acknowledge them.[60] He directly mentions, but does not cite, the customs of St Albans and those of Norwich, the Cluniacs[61] and the Cistercians.[62] Possibly earlier books of St Edmunds' customs once existed and perhaps our author borrowed from them. The first four paragraphs of the Customary, which concern the division of portions between abbot and convent, seem to be partly based on the Composition drawn up between the contending parties c. 1215.[63] The author also cites an ordinance issued in chapter in the presence of Abbot Hugh of Northwold and of the prior, Henry of Rushbrooke (who held that office 1222–33 before succeeding Hugh in the abbacy) and of the whole convent.[64] In addition, he refers to a custom established in the time of Walter of Banham, sacrist under Abbot Samson.[65] But most especially the author drew on his own observation and on oral information, sources which he fully acknowledges in the prologue.

The author was a monk of St Edmunds but nothing seems to be known about him except what he tells us himself, that he was once a keeper of the pyx (the receptacle in which oblations were kept). The sacrist usually had charge of the pyx and its contents but, our author records,

> Sometimes the pyx was taken from the sacrists, that is from Richard of the Isle (sacrist 1217–20, later abbot) and Richard of Newport (1220–?1233), and handed to others; and the oblations were put in the vestry under three keys which were handed to other monks at the order of the convent; at least two of them were cloister monks, as the convent ordered, and the key to the pyx itself was put with the oblations, from which no payment was to be made except at the convent's order and with its assent. I saw this done twice and I was one of the keepers.[66]

The author was obviously an intelligent, thoughtful man. He had researched his subject with meticulous care and weighed the evidence with sensible judgement. It is hard to believe that he was not commissioned to write by a superior, perhaps by Gregory of St Albans, successively sacrist, 1233–4, and prior, 1234–42. Gregory was born in the neighbourhood (*patria*) of St Albans, became

---

[60] See ibid., pp. xxx, 49 lines 12–16.

[61] *Bury Cust.*, p. 41 lines 26–7.

[62] Ibid., p. 49 lines 8–10.

[63] Above pp. 33 et seqq.

[64] *Bury Cust.*, p. 10 lines 18–21.

[65] Ibid., pp. 9 n. 3, 55 and n. 8.

[66] Ibid., xxix, xxxiii. 'Hinc est quod pixis aliquando fuit sacristis scilicet R. de Insula et R. de Nova Porta, et tradita aliis obvencionesque repositae erant in vestiario sub tribus clavibus traditis aliis monachis ad ordinacionem conventus, quorum duo ad minus fuerunt claustrales. Clavisque ipsius pixidis deposita fuit cum obvencionibus, de quibus nichil expensum alicubi fuit, nisi per praeceptum et assensum conventus. Hoc bis vidimus et unus custodum fuimus. Item pluries vidimus idem propter debita ecclesiae solvenda et propter alias causas necessarias.' BL MS Harley 1005, ff. 111–111v; *Bury Cust.*, pp. xxxiii, 35 line 31–36 line 78, and n. 1–3.

a monk of St Edmunds and was a staunch supporter of the sacrist's party in the dispute over the election of Hugh of Northwold.[67] He gained an exceptional reputation for sanctity, and, 'as we saw', miraculous cures were wrought at his tomb.[68] However, even if commissioned and although the Customary reflects the centres of Gregory's loyalty, the sacristy and priorate, our author did not present his work as definitive but rather as advisory. Thus, he gives two or three opinions about a number of questions without necessarily stating categorically which is correct. For example, he states that some say that the abbot was obliged to receive all visiting bishops, both seculars and those of the Benedictine order; others say that the convent should entertain bishops of the Benedictine order; and yet others say that the determining factor is the number of horse accompanying the bishop.[69] In this instance the author tries to distil the correct custom from these three opinions. Usually, if the author gives alternative opinions about a custom, he says which he thinks the 'sanest' and 'most reasonable'. For example, he writes: 'There arises the question who should be blessed first at matins on Sunday – officials for the week (*hebdomadarii*) or monks about to set out on a journey: some wish the officials for the week to be blessed first because they will serve, or have served, the convent and brethren; others say that travellers ought to be first because they are often departing on the church's business and the church prays for travellers; however, the first opinion seems the best to us.'[70] This judicious treatment of his subject suggests the possibility that the author of the Customary also composed the tract on dedications since it too states various opinions on some matters.[71]

The author is careful to distinguish between the abbey's ancient customs and 'new graces' which by frequent usage could acquire similar status to the ancient customs. He points this out, for instance, in his passage on the sacrist's obligation to provide the abbot and his household with candle on the feast of the Purification (Candlemas); the sacrist ought only to do so if the abbot were present; if he did so when the abbot was absent, he must call it a grace lest by usage it is called a custom.[72] However, some new graces were authoritative because they resulted from an authoritative ruling. For example, the author states that whoever sings high mass should receive a pittance 'by a grace newly pronounced (*inventa*) by Prior Henry [Henry of Rushbrooke] and not from ancient custom'.[73]

The Customary is only a reformist document insofar as it clarified and wrote down existing customs, with the general intention of maintaining the *status quo*. It reveals much about the state of the domestic economy and religious observance at St Edmunds. There was obviously no attempt at stringent reform of religious observance. The monks' lives were neither deplorably self-indulgent nor remarkably austere, in fact, they were much the same as in most other

---

[67] *Bury Chron.*, pp. 8, 12, and *Electio*, pp. 84/5, 148/9, 158/9, 184, 185 n. 13, 187 nn. 8, 13.
[68] *Gesta Sacrist.*, p. 294.
[69] *Bury Cust.*, pp. xxix, 5 lines 19–34.
[70] Ibid., pp. 28 line 35 – 29 line 1.
[71] Above pp. 113–17.
[72] Ibid., p. 32 lines 25–30.
[73] Ibid., p. 22 lines 10–12.

Benedictine houses. It is clear that the abbot was often absent and that the main obedientiaries were preoccupied with running their offices, work which was hardly reconcilable with strict religious observance. Moreover, it is clear that there were numerous relaxations in the observance of the Rule. There were, for instance, the usual relaxations in the dietary regime set forth in the Rule, as described above. The Customary is especially informative about the regulations concerning drinking. The Rule assumes that monks would only drink at dinner and supper in the refectory, except in exceptional circumstances. But it also allowed monks who were to read or serve in the refectory to have a preliminary breakfast of bread and a drink. This breakfast (*mixtum*) was also taken by children and sick monks. In the course of the middle ages the proportion of Benedictine monks taking *mixtum* steadily grew until virtually all took it. There is no reason to suppose that the monks of St Edmunds were an exception though the Customary only mentions *mixtum* by name once. But it has a substantial section on another extra drink, the nonal drink. The nonal drink, like the one at *mixtum*, had become normal in Benedictine houses. It was taken after nones (the office which followed dinner) and before the monks sat in the cloister, during the period from Easter until 11 November, except when there was a solemn fast.[74] Reformers objected to this widespread practice on the grounds that drinking led to idle talk.[75] The Customary shows that at St Edmunds the nonal drink was well rooted in the customs of the house.[76] Another drink not prescribed by the Rule, and which became accepted practice at St Edmunds, as in other Benedictine houses, was the *caritas*, a drink taken in the refectory before or after the Saturday maundy, that is the maundy held after vespers every Saturday. This maundy originated because of the prescription in the Rule stipulating that every Saturday the outgoing and incoming servers for the week should wash the brethren's feet.[77] The monks also drank a *caritas* in the refectory before or after the maundy of the poor, which was held after vespers on the Thursday before Good Friday.[78]

Yet another drink not prescribed by the Rule was served in the refectory on all week-days during the fasting season before or after collation (*collatio*), the spiritual reading which preceded compline, the last office of the day. The Rule assumes that all monks would attend compline and prescribes absolute silence afterwards unless guests need attention or the abbot wishes to give a command to someone.[79] However, the discipline of monks at the end of the day was a perennial problem among Benedictines.[80] The Customary has a section regarding

---

[74] The nonal drink was already of general observance in the tenth century. See *Reg. Con.*, ed. Symons, p. 27 and n. 3.

[75] Knowles, *RO*, i. 283.

[76] *Bury Cust.*, pp. 41 lines 4–15, 74 lines 6–7, 77 lines 22–3 and n. 3.

[77] *Rule*, ed. Fry, pp. 232/3, c. 35 § 9; *Reg. Con.*, ed. Symons, pp. xxxi–xxxvii, xl, 22, 63; Lanfranc, *Constitutions*, pp. 35–6, 42; *Bury Cust.*, p. 77 and n. 2; Knowles, *RO*, i. 283; Harvey, *Living and Dying*, pp. 12, 16, 132.

[78] *Bury Cust.*, 45 lines 1–7, 77 lines 22–5 and n. 3, 84 lines 8–11, 85 lines 32–3, and below.

[79] *Rule*, ed. Fry, pp. 242/3, c. 42.

[80] Knowles, *RO*, p. 283.

collation, the collation drink, compline, the subsequent period of silence and related matters, which shows considerable relaxation in the observance of the Rule's injunctions. For instance it says:

> It should be remembered that those who eat in the refectory on that day always ought to attend the collation drink, that is, monks of our order and especially our own monks, if they possibly can. However, those eating with the abbot or prior or in the infirmary or anywhere else outside the refectory need not attend collation or the collation drink, unless it is a common or solemn fast.[81]

Nevertheless, all monks except the sick, wherever they eat, must attend collation during Lent except because of some obvious necessity, 'but it must not be forgotten that those eating outside the refectory are not bound to attend compline with the convent on that day, even if it is a common and solemn fast and presence at collation is necessary, according to the custom of this house'.[82] The author remarks that in many places, such as St Albans, all pray compline together (*simul*) wherever they have eaten. He continues that at St Edmunds, even those who have not attended compline, 'should nevertheless, whatever the day, pray compline (*compleant*) before the *curfu* bell rings, after which no one must presume to eat or drink anywhere except from great necessity and by special licence of his superior and custodian'.[83] The author states in the section on the nonal drink that 'if any monk is thirsty and seeks and obtains leave, he may drink in the Lord, even if necessary at night, provided that the custom does not breed vice'.[84] Overall, these passages show that the monks had plenty of chances to drink and to relax and chat in the evenings. The General Chapters of 1249 and 1277 legislated, but probably with little effect, against this relaxation of the Rule, which seems to have been widespread among the Benedictines.[85]

The Customary mainly consists of precise descriptions such as these of the customs designed to regulate the monks' domestic and liturgical lives. However,

---

[81] *Bury Cust.*, p. 45 lines 1–4: 'Hicque memorandum est quod ad potationes collacionum omnes semper interesse debent, qui illo die comederint in refectorio, monachi suple nostri ordinis et maxime nostrates, si quo modo poterunt. Comedentes vero cum abbate vel priore sive in infirmaria vel alias extra refectorium huiusmodi collacionibus potationibusque non tenentur interesse, nisi fuerit dies ieiunii communis vel solempnis.'

[82] Ibid., p. 45 lines 24–38: 'Sed non est obliviscendum quod comedentium extra refectorium nullus tenetur interesse Completorio cum conventu eodem die, licet etiam fuerit commune et solempne ieiunium et lectioni collacionis necessario interfuerit consuetudinem huius domus. Contraria tamen consuetudo est in aliis locis pluribus sicut apud Sanctum Albanum et alibi, ubi omnes ubicumque comederint simul complent, id est suum simul cantant Completorium. Refectorum vero extra refectorium omnes simul sequantur priorem, cum quo simul compleant. … Unum autem caute provideant omnes omni tempore, ut scilicet compleant ante sonitum curfu appellatum, post quem nullus praesumat alicubi comedere nec eciam bibere nisi ex magna necessitate et licencia speciali a suo superiore et custode.'

[83] BL MS Harley 1005, ff. 112v–113; *Bury Cust.*, pp. 44–6 passim.

[84] Ibid., p. 41 lines 12–15: 'Sed quociens quispiam frater sitierit petita licencia et concessa, bene bibat in nomine Domini eciam de nocte ex necesitate, dummodo consuetudo vicium non pariat.'

[85] *Chapters*, ed. Pantin, i. 37–8 §§ 6–7a and b, 73 § 9, 257 § 19. The prohibitions are among the articles composed for a visitation in the late fourteenth century. Ibid., ii. 86 §§ 24–6.

the first three paragraphs, which concern the relative rights and duties of the principal obedientiaries, are informative about the abbey's temporal organization. Much of the information seems to derive in part from the Composition of c. 1215 between the abbot and convent. It is hard to estimate the extent of the borrowing because, as already mentioned, we appear to have only headings or an abbreviated text of at least the earlier paragraphs of the Composition. However, the Customary is in places fuller than the extant text of the Composition and shows the rational approach characteristic of our author. An example is the account of the appointment of the bailiff or bailiffs of the borough. Their symbol of office was the moot-horn, the horn used to summon burgesses to the portman-moot, and under Abbot Samson there was a debate in chapter as to who should hand the moot-horn to the bailiff (or bailiffs) after his (or their) appointment. Eventually it was decided that the prior, 'who after the abbot is the head of the convent', should do so.[86] The Composition has a short entry on the subject: 'Concerning the appointment of a bailiff by the convent and sacrist and without the assent of the abbot, and the receiving of the horn and keys annually at the hand of the prior and sacrist'.[87]

The Customary explains the procedure in much greater detail. It was an important matter because the procedure was in effect an annual ritual symbolizing the fact that the borough belonged to the convent's portion, that the prior, as head of the convent, had final authority over it, but that the sacrist had day-to-day control. The passage ends with a warning of the danger of the king interfering with the town during a vacancy if the convent's right is not well-known. The passage reads:

> The horn, which is called the *mothorn* is handed in chapter every year at Michaelmas to the sacrist and the sacrist hands it to the prior, although some say that the bailiffs ought immediately to hand the said horn to the head of the convent's portion [i.e. to the prior] in full chapter. However, the aforesaid custom is equally good and more used, that is that the bailiff, or bailiffs if there are more than one, should return the said horn every year to the sacrist with the keys in full chapter and the sacrist in full view of all should hand them to the prior. The prior, indeed, returns them to the sacrist and the sacrist to the bailiff or bailiffs remaining in office, or to the newly appointed bailiff or bailiffs, provided that everything is done with the convent's assent. The annual handing over should be done in this manner so that it is clear to all that the town belongs wholly and principally to the convent and lest during a vacancy of the abbey the king in any way interferes with the said town, from which nothing belongs to the abbot, except the homage of all free tenants of both portions.[88]

---

[86] *JB*, pp. 73–4. See Lobel, *Bury St. Edmunds*, pp. 61–2.

[87] *Bury Cust.*, pp. 101 line 26 – 102 line 2.

[88] Ibid., p. 3 lines 4–19. 'Hinc eciam est quod cornu, quod dicitur mothorn, singulis annis die sancti Michaelis traditur in capitulo sacristae et sacrista tradit illud priori. Licet quidam dicant, quod ballivi debeant immediate tradere praefatum cornu capiti porcionis conventus in pleno capitulo. Praedicta tamen consuetudo aeque bona est et magis usitata, scilicet ut ballivus vel ballivi si plures sint praememorato die annuatim reddant sacristae praedictum cornu cum clavibus in pleno capitulo et sacrista videntibus omnibus tradat ea

The Customary has no passages which point to the reform of the monks' domestic life and liturgical observance during this period. Indeed, the purpose of the only statute it mentions, one issued under Abbot Hugh of Northwold and Prior Henry of Rushbrooke, was to ease any burden on the prior. It states that it was the abbot's duty to celebrate mass on the most important anniversaries, but in his absence the prior had to officiate in his place; therefore, the prior should not be put on the *tabula* except for the feast of St Mary; to include him in the rota of celebrants, as was previously done, was unfair because it meant that he chanted more masses than any two *hebdomedarii*.[89]

The Customary has little to say about administrative reform. It provides only one concrete example, the passage cited above recording the removal of the pyx from the sacrist's charge and the appointment of other monks as custodians.[90] Nevertheless, despite its comparative silence on the matter, other evidence shows that administrative reform was under way. The *Gesta Sacristarum* records that sometime during the sacristy of Nicholas of Warwick (1242 x 1244–1251 or before)[91] the pyx was finally removed from the sacrist's charge and assigned to the treasurer.[92]

Observance and reform under Edmund of Walpole

The rule of Edmund of Walpole marks another important stage in the history of St Edmunds' domestic and administrative customs and liturgical observances. The move to clarify and codify existing customs continued. This is apparent from a tract produced at this time for the instruction of novices, young monks and their masters. Possibly the extant text is a composite work consisting of three short tracts. As it survives it comprises three parts: customs concerning the punishment of monks who committed faults, the severity of the punishment being graded according to the gravity of the fault – serious, light or minor; customs regulating the conduct of novices; and liturgical customs for morning mass and high mass, and customs about bell-ringing and the maundy.[93] The date of the tract is indicated by its opening words: 'In the time of our predecessors and religious men, that is of Abbot Henry [of Rushbrooke], Prior G[regory of

---

priori. Prior vero reddat illa sacristae et sacrista ballivo vel ballivis remansuris vel novis substituendis, dummodo omnia fiant per assensum conventus. Huiusmodi autem tradicio annua fit, ut omnibus fiat notorium villam omnino spectare et praecipue ad conventum et ne rex vacante abbacia aliquatenus intromittat se de praefata villa, de qua nichil spectat ad abbatem, nisi sola homagia sicut et omnium liberorum tenencium utriusque porcionis.'

[89] Ibid., p. 10 lines 18–24 and n. 18. In this context the word *tabula* signifies the notice board on which were inscribed the names of the *hebdomedarii*, the officials for the week.

[90] Ibid., pp. 35 line 31 – 36 line 7. Above p. 207.

[91] Thomson, 'Obedientiaries', p. 94.

[92] *Gesta Sacrist.*, p. 294.

[93] The three parts are printed in *Bury Cust.*, pp. 82–8, 89, 90–95, respectively. The text is printed from BL MS Harley 1005, ff. 212–215v (where it is in the same hand as the Customary), collated with a copy of c. 1300 in BL MS Harley 3977, ff. 6v–11.

St Albans, 1234–42], R. of London and others'.[94] Its clarificatory, codificatory purpose and intended audience are stated at the beginning of last section:

> Because in tracts on customs variations of masses are not sufficiently clear, I propose to resolve doubts and make known what I have learnt from sensible people and have myself often seen and experienced (not, indeed, to search for the peculiar and unusual) for the guidance of novices and especially of ignorant deacons.[95]

The papal confirmation of St Edmunds' customs by Alexander IV also belongs to Edmund of Walpole's abbacy.[96] It was issued on 4 August 1256, at the petition of abbot and convent. Presumably, it was based on a document compiled by Abbot Edmund and senior monks after its details had been settled between them. Those clauses which are mitigations of observance could be the result of insistence by the monks, and those which imposed stricter observance could have been concessions to Abbot Edmund. He, as abbot, would not have had to share any austerities imposed on the convent. However, there may well have been a party among the monks who wanted reform. Nor is it impossible that stricter observance was insisted on at the papal curia, as the price of confirmation.

Abbot Edmund died fairly soon after the issue of the confirmation (on 31 October). But, although the prospect of an approaching vacancy must have been in the monks' minds during that summer and may have impressed on them the desirability of a confirmation of the customs, the actual document is not primarily concerned with protecting the convent's rights while the abbey was in the king's hands. Only part of one clause appears to have had that purpose: it stipulates that obedientiaries should be appointed and removed by abbot and senior monks acting together.[97] Overall, the purpose of the confirmation was to put the abbey's customs on as secure a footing as possible. Parallels to many of the clauses are in the Rule of St Benedict, the decrees of the General Chapter of 1219/20 and in the statutes of the 1234 visitors. It lays particular emphasis on alms-giving and even more on the dietary regime. In most respects the regulations on the latter conformed with those in earlier legislation. One clause reveals a mitigation of strict observance and is apparently merely a codification of existing custom at St Edmunds. It stipulates that:

94 *Bury Cust.*, p. 82 lines 3–4. Perhaps 'R. of London' was the Ralph of London, a cloister monk who was one of Hugh of Northwold's supporters in the election dispute. *Electio*, pp. 64/5, 86/7, 136/7, 187.

95 *Bury Cust.*, p. 90 lines 3–8: 'Quoniam in libellis consuetudinariis de missarum variacione minus sufficienter constat esse distinctum, icirco ad evidenciam noviciorum et maxime rudium diaconorum in rectum statum huiusmodi dubia redigere proposui et certificare, non propria quidem vel inusitata quaerere, sed quae a prudentibus didici et saepius vidi et expertus sum.' The questioning approach of the author resembles that of the author of the Customary, which raises the question whether the present tract was by the same monk.

96 Printed in ibid., pp. 63–7, from the copy in BL MS Harley 1005, ff. 119–20, where it follows, and is in the same hand as, the Customary (see below). Variant readings are given from the text printed from the register of Alexander IV, ed. C. Bourel de la Roncière, J. de Loye and A. Coulon, Bibliothèque des Écoles Françaises d'Athènes et de Rome, 2nd ser., xv (Paris, 1902), pp. 459–60.

97 *Bury Cust.*, p. 63 lines 28–30.

When convenient special monks may, with a licence from a superior, dine privately in the customary designated places and on ordinary food, provided that proper order is kept and left-overs given to the poor; indeed, monks eating outside the precincts for various reasons regularly eat ordinary food, sometimes because of hard work and sometimes for lack of fish, as often happens to those going to various places elsewhere – sometimes when they go to friends with whom fish is not plentiful.[98]

'Ordinary' food, unlike the 'generals' served in the refectory, would have included meat. Indeed, the confirmation makes a direct reference to meat-eating. It states that within the precincts the infirm, the sick and those who had been bled might eat meat in the infirmary.[99] Moreover, meat would be eaten by the abbot and those monks he decided to summon to dine with him in his chambers, and especially if he, or the prior in his absence, were entertaining royalty, a papal legate or others from the Roman curia, when lavish hospitality was necessary 'lest they incur their indignation and their property suffers in consequence'.[100]

In one respect the confirmation prescribed a stricter observance in the monks' dietary regime: it reduced the number of days during the fasting season (from 14 September until Ash Wednesday) when the monks might eat twice. Before the confirmation they had supper as well as dinner during that period, not only on all Sundays, principal feasts and feasts of the second and third grades, but also on feasts of twelve lessons and sometimes even of three. The confirmation, on the other hand, states that they were to fast on all days during that period except on Sundays and solemn feasts (that is, on principal and secondary feasts), when they might eat twice 'both because of the great and protracted labour and for the sustenance of the poor who flock to the monastery especially on those days'.[101] The reduction in the number of days when the monks might eat twice may have been to improve the standard of observance at St Edmunds for religious reasons, but possibly at least one motive was economy, to reduce the cost of the abbey's food supply. At this time papal financial impositions were placing a heavy burden on the church, including religious houses; its impact on St Edmunds aroused the fierce indignation of the Bury chronicler and other chroniclers.[102] Whatever the truth, the restriction was effective, for, in 1280, Abbot John of Northwold agreed with the monks to restore the earlier more lenient regime.[103]

The importance which the compilers of the confirmation attached to the abbey's administration is testified to by the early position which the administra-

---

[98] Ibid., p. 66 lines 25–33. See Bishop, 'Fasting and abstinence', pp. 205, 231–2 (appendix XXIV).

[99] *Bury Cust.*, p. 65 lines 13–15.

[100] Ibid., pp. 65 line 15 – 66 line 11.

[101] Ibid., p. 67 lines 6–12. For the crowds of pilgrims visiting St Edmund's shrine see ibid., p. 63 lines 20–1. Henry of Kirkstead wrote a note on the grades of feasts and lists the days on which the convent had two meals. Ibid., pp. 46–7 n. e, and notes the change as a result of Alexander IV's confirmation. Ibid., p. 50 n. c. For these notes see above p. 206 n. 58.

[102] See esp. *Bury Chron.*, p. 20.

[103] Gransden, 'Separation of portions', pp. 401–2 §§ 15, 16, and nn. 147–9.

tive clauses occupy in the text.[104] The third clause, concerning the appointment and removal of obedientiaries, rules that obedientiaries must render account at least once a year to the abbot and a suitable person chosen by the abbot and convent, and when he leaves office he must take nothing with him, after deducting necessary expenses. This clause is in line with a degree of the General Chapter held at Oxford in 1218/19, which, however, does not specify how often in the year account should be rendered.[105] However, it is less stringent and precise than the statutes issued by visitors to St Edmunds in 1214: they decreed that the principal obedientiaries should render account four times a year and the other obedientiaries twice.[106]

Postscript

Thus, in the period from 1215 to 1256 a body of written customs was assembled. The process of clarifying and codifying unwritten customs continued after Abbot Edmund's death, and reformers later in the thirteenth century built on the achievements of their predecessors. The earliest known text of the Customary and of the tract discussed above, and also of Alexander IV's confirmation, are copies made in the distinctive, small, neat hand of a monk writing in the 1260s and 1270s. The same monk copied numerous tracts and the like on a wide variety of subjects, most of which are preserved in BL MS Harley 1005. He will be called 'A' and discussed in my *Bury St Edmunds Abbey*, vol. ii, in the section on the rule of Abbot Edmund's successor, Simon of Luton. These written customs were regarded as authoritative and of lasting value. An imperfect copy of the Customary survives in a large collection of the abbey's customs, now CUL MS Additional 6006, ff. 9–20v.[107] Abbot John of Northwold almost certainly owned the volume now BL MS 3977 which includes (ff. 6v–11) a copy of the tracts on the punishment of wrong-doers and other matters,[108] and it is very likely that he also owned a copy of the Customary.[109] The latter was certainly well-known to the monks. It is cited by name, the *Traditiones patrum* (the incipit), in the preamble to the Composition drawn up between Abbot John, Stephen of Ixworth, prior (1280–6), and the senior monks dated 16 October 1280, as one of the sources used.[110] Again, it is cited by name ('the book of customs which is called the *Traditiones patrum*') and two passages borrowed from it in a letter which Prior Stephen addressed to Abbot John, probably shortly before the

---

104 *Bury Cust.*, pp. 63 line 30 – 64 line 4.
105 *Chapters*, ed. Pantin, i. 12 § 22: 'omnes obedientiarii hoc maxime observent, sub pena excommunicationis: precaventes ne bona sibi commissa distrahant aut consumant; sed ea in utilitatibus ecclesie fideliter expendant: et secundum receptas et expensas eo modo et ordine quo fiunt fideles prelato reddant rationes, adhibitis ei de discretioribus secundum numerum fratrum'.
106 'Visitation', ed. Graham, p. 735.
107 *Bury Cust.*, pp. xxxviii–xxxix. Thomson, *Archives*, p. 140.
108 *Bury Cust.*, p. xxxviii.
109 For the manuscripts see above 206 n. 58.
110 CUL MS Gg. iv. 4, f. 192. Gransden, 'Separation of portions', pp. 391, 398 § 1.

compilation of the 1280 Composition. In it the prior challenges the abbot's right to commission one of his clerks to hold a visitation of the town, arguing that such a visitation would be contrary to 'the ancient and approved customs of our church' and to apostolic privileges.[111]

Nearly a century later the Customary was studied in depth by Henry of Kirkstead.[112] He made many annotations calling attention to various subjects: the abbot's responsibility to entertain certain categories of guests; on which side of the choir the subprior should be; the sacrist's duty to repair the abbot's old buildings but not his new ones; details of the kitchener's duty to supply the convent with herring; customs about monks' returning to the community from the infirmary; the chandlers' duty to provide a wax candle weighing 5lbs for the feast of Relics; and 'note well' the punishment (of excommunication) to be inflicted on bakers if the bread they supplied fell short in quantity or quality.[113] Much the longest notes are two discussing the customs determining the days on which the convent might have supper as well as dinner during the fasting season.[114] In one of these he cites the authority of some text preceding a copy of the Customary 'in the keeping of Dom. Thomas of Saxham distinguished with the letter C. 64 in the library'. Kirkstead again refers to this lost copy of the Customary in subsequent note on the same subject. The range of Kirkstead's concerns revealed by his annotations strongly suggests that he consulted the Customary when he was prior, from 1361 to sometime before 1375.[115] Previously he had been novice master and armarius, but there is no indication that he used the volume now BL MS Harley 1005 when he held those offices: he did not annotate the copy in it of the tract on novices attributable to Simon de Luton's abbacy, or the copy of the tract which partly concerns novices and is attributable to the abbacy of Edmund of Walpole. The Customary would obviously have been very useful to the prior,[116] but, since it has the class-mark C. 68., it must have belonged to the convent's book collection in the late fourteenth century and no doubt before that.

In conclusion, it is undeniable that the period from 1215 to 1256 marked

111 BL MS Harley 645 f. 242v: 'Qua igitur de zelo vestro presumentes antiquas et approbatas ecclesie nostre consuetudines vos indubitanter velle defendere, protegere et manutenere non ambigimus, verba libri consuetudinarii qui traditionibus patrum dicitur, presentibus duximus inserenda. In capitulo si quidem vbi de talliagiis agitur, sic continetur, Burgum Sancti Eadmundi precipue spectat ad beatum Eadmundum et suum altare vniuersique sui prouentus de iure pertinent ad conuentum. Qui vniuersi dixit nullum excepit, sed et infra eodem capitulo dicitur quod de prouentus ville Sancti Edmundi nichil spectat ad abbatem nisi sola homagia sicut in omnium libe[re] de ecclesia nostra tenentium.' See: Gransden, art. cit., pp. 385–6; Bury Cust., pp. 2 lines 19–22, 3 lines 17–19.
112 See e.g. Kirkstead's marginal notes on f. 102 of BL MS Harley 1005 reproduced Bury Cust., frontispiece and pl. VI.
113 Ibid., pp. 6 n. a, 13 n. a, 34 n. c, 39 n. b, 14 n. a, 55 n. a, 40 n. a, respectively.
114 Above p. 206.
115 See: Catalogus, ed. Rouse and Rouse, pp. xxxv n. 28, xxxix and nn. 43–4, xlvii–xlviii and n. 77, xlix and n. 84, lxix n. 166, lxxiii–lxxiv and nn. 181–5, 372 no. 405.6; Rouse, 'Bostonus Buriensis', p. 482.
116 For this hand see above p. 206 and n. 58.

a crucial stage in the codification of the abbey's customs. Customs prescribing details of observance in St Edmund's church and those defining the rights and duties of specific obedientiaries were clearly stated in writing. The customs thus prescribed would have been observed because they were entrenched in the obedientiary system. An extreme example is the case of the kitchener: he would not have supplied supper as well as dinner unless custom prescribed the extra meal; in face of insistence from the rest of the convent he could hardly fail to do so. In this way the possibility of internal conflict was reduced. This must have been an essential factor contributing to the growth of better relations between abbot and convent. Certainly, by the late thirteenth century, life at St Edmunds was more harmonious than it had been in the late twelfth century.

17

Learning

The problem about studying learning and books at St Edmunds for the period from 1215 to 1257 is the scarcity of datable evidence. The general impression is that in an undistinguished way an élite among the monks continued the tradition of learning established in the twelfth century and fostered under Abbot Samson. Three, if not five, of the Masters active in the convent at the time of Hugh's election were still alive during his abbacy,[1] and Abbot Edmund of Walpole was himself a Master of canon law.[2] There were no doubt other magistral monks in the period from 1215 to 1257, but it should always be born in mind that not all learned monks were necessarily graduates of a university: they could equally have been the products of St Edmunds' monastic school.

The intellectual level reached by a few of the monks can be gauged by reference to their literary productions. The most ambitious of these are: the Chronicle; the *Gesta Sacristarum* (*Acts of the Sacrists*); the Customary; and the tract on the dedication of altars, chapels and churches at St Edmunds. The first two are records, with no literary pretensions but with the virtue of clarity. The Chronicle is a typical monastic chronicle. It forms part of the chronicle of John Taxster[3] who took the habit at St Edmunds in 1244 but wrote his chronicle in the 1260s. He used pre-existing annals, chronicles and documentary records for the earlier period. The annals in the chronicle for 1215–17 are moderately detailed but from 1218 to 1237 they are very scrappy. They comprise brief notices of the succession of popes and bishops – notably those of Ely, Norwich and Lincoln – the obits of a few magnates and so on, besides the succession of the abbots and priors of St Edmunds. From 1237 the annals become more fluent and interesting and are especially useful for the history of the abbey. For example, there is an emotive account under 1238 of the visit to St Edmunds of the papal legate Otto in connection with the attempt by Dominican and Franciscan friars to settle inside St Edmunds' *banleuca*. Some of the subsequent annals are concerned with the crusade and with papal and imperial history, no doubt deriving most or all of their information from news-letters. It is impossible to know whether Taxster

---

[1] I.e. Master Nicholas of Dunstable, Master Thomas of Beccles and Master Thomas of Walsingham. The two other Masters who no doubt were alive during Hugh's abbacy were Master Alan of Walsingham and Master Simon of Walsingham. See *Electio*, pp. 186–8.
[2] Above pp. 185–6.
[3] See *Bury Chron.*, pp. xviii–xxiii, 13 n. *b*.

himself composed these annals or whether they were composed under Edmund of Walpole and merely reproduced by Taxster.

The *Gesta Sacristarum* is a short and precise record of the rules of six sacrists who held office between 1215 and 1257. It would seem that their achievements were few and slight, comparing unfavourably with those of their predecessors under Abbot Samson and their successors under Abbots Simon of Luton and John of Northwold. Only Richard of Newport, sacrist from 1220 until some-time before 1234, was, as will be seen a builder, and he was the only one whose anniversary was celebrated with the ringing of bells.[4] The overall failure of the sacristy to make much mark in this period was undoubtedly partly because on average each successive sacrist held office for only a short time.[5] Richard of Newport held office for just over ten years, but his successor Gregory of St Albans, formerly precentor, was 'not [sacrist] for long' before his election in 1234 to the priorate. Nicholas of Warwick who, it seems, succeeded Gregory, held office until the succession to the sacristy in 1251 of Simon of Luton, but he was elected prior in 1252 and was succeeded as sacrist by Richard of Horringer who resigned sometime before 1257. Most of the entries in the *Gesta* record whatever lands or other sources of revenue the sacrists acquired, but it is more than a dry record. It includes entries reflecting the author's opinions and throwing light on the characters and careers of a few of the sacrists. Gregory of St Albans was notable for his sanctity; cures were miraculously worked at his tomb 'as we saw'.[6] Nicholas of Warwick in his last days was struck by paralysis, voluntarily resigned and spent many years in the infirmary, receiving 40s annually for drugs.[7] His incapacity may explain why the oblations of the pyx were first taken from the sacristy and assigned to the treasurers.[8] The *Gesta* praises Simon of Luton for his wisdom and his ability, but says that Richard of Horringer was an old man and resigned either 'voluntarily or involuntarily': 'he was affected by old age and was a man devoted to agriculture rather than preserving [St Edmunds'] liber-ties'.[9] Nevertheless, despite the lack-lustre history of the sacristy in the period 1215–1257, individual sacrists were proud to hold the office. This is apparent from the *Gesta* which records that three of them had bells cast which commem-orated themselves and/or their office. Thus, it records that Richard of Newport 'had made at no small cost a great bell, which is called "Neweport", for the main bell-tower'. Nicholas of Warwick 'among the many good things he did, had cast ('fundi fecit') the best bell in the choir, which is called the sacrist's bell'. And

---

4   *Gesta Sacrist.*, p. 293.
5   Ibid., pp. 293–4 passim.
6   Ibid., p. 294.
7   'Hic in ultimis diebus suis paralysi percussus sponte cessit, et in infirmaria multos transi-gens annos, de sacristia annuation dum vixit xl.solidos ad species percepit.' *Gesta Sacrist.*, p. 294. *Species* could, alternatively, mean spices.
8   Above p. 207 and n. 66.
9   'cum ibidem aliquanto tempore stetisset, abbate et priore cum conventu hoc volentibus, sponte cessit vel invitus. Erat enim senio affectus, et vir tantum agriculturae et non liber-tatibus servandis deditus.' *Gesta Sacrist.*, p. 294.

Simon of Luton, 'while in office, had cast the bell in the choir which is called "Luyton"'.

Any monk with interest, assiduity and moderate literary skill could have composed the Chronicle or the *Gesta Sacristarum* for the years 1215–1257. The authorship of neither required much learning or deep thought. As demonstrated above, the abbey's Customary belongs to a different intellectual category and to a different literary genre. The author's distinguishing feature is his rationality, his ability to weigh evidence and, if necessary, to confess ignorance. His object was the clarification of past practice to serve as a guide for future generations.[10] A rational approach to his subject is also characteristic of the tract on the dedication of altars, chapels and churches at St Edmunds, the *De dedicationibus altarum, capellarum et ecclesiarum*, which was discussed above for the information it contains about the secondary cults in the abbey.[11] Its central objective was to demonstrate that no bishop of Norwich had ever officiated at a dedication at St Edmunds. The original tract was composed early in Henry II's reign but that tract was edited and continued late in, or soon after, Abbot Samson's time and the final paragraph, which records the foundation by Abbot Simon of Luton in 1275 of the splendid new Lady chapel, was added under that abbot. Examples of the author's rational approach are his judicious treatment of the two opinions about the origins of the much venerated cross which stood in one of the apsidal chapels in the abbey church, and the doubt he expresses whether the papal privilege for St Edmunds, which some believed Abbot Leofstan brought back from Rome but which could not be found, ever existed – or whether it had simply perished. In both instances the author admits that he does not know the truth.[12] Another example is the author's caution with regard to the dedication of the altar of St Peter the apostle: he states that it was dedicated in the time of Prior Baldwin, 'but whoever wishes to know by which bishop must ask someone else because I do not know'.[13]

---

[10] Above pp. 206 et seqq.
[11] Above pp. 113–17.
[12] *De dedicationibus*, p. 115 lines 10–22. See above p. 114.
[13] Ibid., p. 115 lines 8–10.

18

Books

Whether or not the first continuator of the *De dedicatione* had studied at the university is impossible to say but he was certainly a good scholar. An idea of the intellectual level achieved by some of the monks of St Edmunds in this period could to some extent be measured if we knew more about their acquisition of books. Unfortunately, sound evidence about book acquisition is scarce. The problem is to be certain when most of the extant thirteenth-century books were added to the monks' collection. The same is true of some of those earlier ones which have not been identified in the late twelfth-, early thirteenth-century book-list. No other comprehensive book-list survives until c. 1370 when Henry of Kirkstead compiled one. Nor are the extant volumes themselves usually helpful in discovering the date of acquisition. However, there are two manuscripts of exceptional interest which deserve particular mention here. One was certainly acquired by the convent during this period and the other probably was.

The first is Pembroke College, Cambridge, MS 7.[1] It is an early thirteenth-century volume containing reports (*reportationes*) made by students attending a set of lectures (glosses) by Paris masters on the *Gloss* (a work of biblical exegesis which evolved in the late eleventh- and twelfth-centuries and became a standard text-book in the Paris schools).[2] The glosses are on five books of the Old Testament and one of the New Testament – the gospel of St Mark. A note on the front flyleaf in the hand of Robert Grosseteste testifies that he gave the volume as a pledge for the loan of a copy of St Basil's *Hexaëmeron* (a treatise on the Six Days of Creation). The inscription reads: 'Memoriale Magistri Roberti Grossetest, pro exameron basilii'.[3] Although St Edmunds acquired the volume as a pledge, not as a gift, it remained in the monk's library until the dissolution of the abbey in 1539.[4] The late medieval library class-mark, B. 231., is inscribed

---

1   Described in S. H. Thomson, *The Writings of Robert Grosseteste, Bishop of Lincoln* (Cambridge – New York, 1940), pp. 22–7.
2   See Beryl Smalley, 'A collection of Paris lectures of the later twelfth century in the MS. *Pembroke College, Cambridge 7*', *Cambridge Historical Journ.*, vi, no. 1 (1938), pp. 103–13; eadem, *Study of the Bible*, pp. 51–2.
3   Reproduced: S. H. Thomson, op. cit., pl. opposite p. 23; Gransden, *Exhibition Catalogue*, pl. LXXIII B; and pl. VII.
4   See: Smalley, art. cit., p. 104 and n. 3; R. W. Hunt, 'The library of Robert Grosseteste', in *Robert Grosseteste, Scholar and Bishop*, ed. D. A. Callus (Oxford, 1955), p. 129 and n. 11. M. R. James, however, states that Pembroke 7 was acquired in exchange for St Edmunds' copy of the *Hexaëmeron*; James, *Cat. Pemb.*, p. 7.

on the flyleaf alongside Grosseteste's note.[5] Nor is there any evidence that the copy of the *Hexaëmeron* was ever returned to St Edmunds.[6] The most likely date for the transaction with Grosseteste would seem to be sometime in the period c. 1230–1235, before Grosseteste became bishop of Lincoln (1235–53). He was pursuing a scholastic career in Oxford as lecturer to the Franciscans and was probably chancellor of Oxford University. He himself wrote a *Hexaëmeron* apparently in the early 1230s, making extensive use of Basil's work in a Latin translation.[7] Perhaps he had recently borrowed the copy from St Edmunds and used it for his treatise.[8]

Grosseteste would have valued the acquisition because of his growing interest in the works of the Greek Fathers. They had a broader approach to theological problems than that of the scholastics. Their approach conformed with Grosseteste's scientific and historical studies which increasingly influenced his theological writings. At the same time he was gaining a good knowledge of the Greek language.[9] This is illustrated in Pembroke 7: he wrote a note in Greek at the foot of folio 1; it reads, 'κυατεϱνι.29.i.κθ'. The word 'κυατεϱνι' is a transliteration into Greek of the Latin '*quaterni*' (quires); the '.i.' represents 'id est' and 'κθ' is 20 in the Greek numerical system. Thus, the note records the number of quires in the volume.[10] Today it has twenty-nine quires if the final item, the gloss on Mark, is discounted. This item is a self-contained unit of five quires: since it, like the other glosses, has marginal notes by Grosseteste, it must have been added to the other items after he wrote the note but before it went to St Edmunds.[11] There are indications that the volume was bound together in its present form before it left Grosseteste's ownership. Grosseteste obviously did well in the exchange because of his interest in Basil's work. The learned élite at St Edmunds may have parted with it with no reluctance since their approach to biblical exegesis was conservative, still rooted in traditional scholasticism. Nevertheless, the conventual book-collection was already rich in exegetical works and the text in Pembroke 7 is of poor quality although of considerable

---

[5] Sharpe, 'Reconstructing the medieval library', p. 210.

[6] The collection of 121 manuscripts from St Edmunds' preserved in Pembroke College, Cambridge, were nearly all, including MS 7, given in 1599, by William Smart, portreeve of Ipswich. See: James, *Cat. Pemb.*, pp. xi, 7; Sharpe, in *Benedictine Libraries*, p. 48.

[7] R. W. Southern, *Robert Grosseteste. The Growth of an English Mind in Medieval Europe* (Oxford, 1986, repr. 1988, 2nd edn 1992), pp. 137–9, 205–6. Southern states that for his *Hexaëmeron* Grosseteste made use of a Latin translation of Basil's work with occasional references to the Greek text. See ibid., p. 207 and n. 3. Grosseteste's translation of the *Hexaëmeron* is edited by R. C. Dales and Servus Gieben (Oxford: British Academy, 1982), and an English translation is by C. F. J. Martin (Oxford: British Academy, 1996, paperback edn 1999).

[8] Smalley, art. cit., p. 105 and n. 11. However, S. H. Thomson, op. cit., p. 26 and n. *, dates the transaction to 1240–2.

[9] For Grosseteste's knowledge of Greek see Southern, op. cit., pp. 47, 117, 132–3, 181–6.

[10] S. H. Thomson, op. cit., p. 26, and Gransden, *Exhibition Catalogue*, p. 158; see pl. VII.

[11] I owe this suggestion to Mr Timothy Graham. James, *Cat. Pemb.*, p. 7, catalogues the gloss on Mark as a separate component in the volume.

value to modern scholars researching the evolution of the Gloss and its glosses and Grosseteste's intellectual development.

It has been argued that Grosseteste applied to St Edmunds for the loan of the copy of the *Hexaëmeron* because he was on particularly close terms with the abbey. There is, however, no concrete evidence for this. The opinion is mainly based on a letter on monastic life (which cites Basil among other authorities) which Grosseteste addressed 'to the abbot and convent "de Burgo"'.[12] Some scholars have identified 'Burgus' as Bury St Edmunds, others as Peterborough.[13] The latter identification is surely the correct one. St Edmunds is regularly called 'Sanctus Edmundus' (or 'Sanctus Eadmundus' or 'Sanctus Aedmundus'), while Peterborough is referred to as 'Sanctus Petrus de Burgo', or, simply as 'Burgus'.[14] Furthermore, Peterborough was in the diocese of Lincoln, while St Edmunds was not and in any case was exempt from episcopal authority. Grosseteste is known to have had contact with Peterborough on more than one occasion. Matthew Paris records under 1238 that Grosseteste dedicated three 'noble conventual churches in his diocese, that is, of Ramsey, Peterborough and Sawtry'.[15] Grosseteste's concern for the standard of religious life in monasteries under his jurisdiction is well known, and the severity of his visitations aroused resentment and some opposition.[16] In 1243 he convoked Adam, bishop of Connor (a Cistercian, formerly abbot of Wardon) and two Benedictine abbots, that is, the abbot of Ramsey, and the abbot of Peterborough, to meet at Hertford to hear his case against the contumacious William of Hatton, abbot of Bardney.[17] And then in 1249 he had to settle the dispute between the abbot of Peterborough (William de Hotot) and the convent, whom the monks accused of enriching his numerous relatives at their expense.[18] Grosseteste's letter on the religious life should, therefore, be seen as part of his care for the monasteries in his diocese. He may well have sent copies of the letter to other religious houses in his diocese besides Peterborough.

Another piece of evidence which could be adduced to prove that Grosseteste had an especially close relationship with St Edmunds is the existence in the abbey's register, BL MS Harley 1005, ff. 51v–54v, of a copy of the *Rules of Husbandry* which Grosseteste composed for Margaret, countess of Lincoln

---

[12] Grosseteste, *Epistolae*, pp. 173–8 no. LVII.

[13] Luard identified 'Burgus' as Peterborough, while J. H. Srawley, 'Grosseteste's administration of the diocese of Lincoln', in Callus ed. cit., p. 154, and Thomson, op. cit., p. 203, identified it as Bury St Edmunds.

[14] See e.g. Matthew Paris, *Chron. Maj.*, iii. 517, iv. 247, and *Bury Chron.*, pp. 100 n. b., 153.

[15] *Chron. Maj.*, iii. 517.

[16] Ibid., v. 247. For Grosseteste's visitations of monasteries see: C. R. Cheney, *Episcopal Visitation of Monasteries in the Thirteenth Century* (Manchester, 1931, 2nd revised edn 1983), pp. 34–6; *C and S*, ii, pt 1, 261–4; *Ann. Mon.*, iii. 147–8.

[17] *Chron. Maj.*, iv. 247.

[18] Ibid., v. 84. See: Moorman, *Church Life in England*, pp. 252–3; *Heads*, ii. 57–8; and esp. Edmond King, 'Estate Records of the Hotot Family', in *Northamptonshire Miscellany*, ed. idem, Northamptonshire Record Soc., xxxii for 1982 (Northampton, 1983).

1232–43, wife of John de Lacy, earl of Lincoln (1232–40), during her widow-hood.[19] The copy is of the French version, which was probably earlier than the Latin version, and has the usual heading: 'Ici comencent les reules ke le bon Eueske de Nichole [sic] Robert Grosseteste fist a la contesse de Nichole [sic] de garder et gouerner terres et hostel.' It is an exceptionally good copy and is apparently the earliest extant.[20] Moreover, it is unusual because most of the other surviving copies of the *Rules* appear to have belonged to lay lords. Our copy is in the small, neat charter hand of the scribe active in the 1260s and 1270s. Besides the *Rules*, he copied the Customary, two treatises on accounting and auditing,[21] and many customs concerning the management of St Edmunds' estates. Possibly the monks acquired a copy of the *Rules* from Grosseteste himself but it seems more probable that they acquired it from someone connected with Henry de Lacy, nephew of Margaret, the dowager countess of Lincoln. Henry succeeded to the earldom in 1272 and held it until his death in 1311. He became a patron and generous benefactor of St Edmunds[22] but on one issue the interests of both as great landholders conflicted. St Edmunds had tenancies in Wainfleet St Mary in the region of the Wash in Lincolnshire and also claimed to be the rightful owners of the island of Sailholme. These holdings were of particular value to St Edmunds because the salterns clustered around the Wash were the principal source of the monks' salt supply.[23] The earls of Lincoln, however, were lords of the manor of Wainfleet and had over the years appropriated Sailholme. Moreover, from the early thirteenth century at latest the proximity of St Edmunds' property to the earl's manor and confusion of its jurisdictional rights had caused trouble. The matter was apparently resolved by the end of the thirteenth century. Earl Henry had referred the dispute to his steward in Lindsey. Overall, it seems more likely that St Edmunds acquired its early copy of the French version of the Rules through its contacts with Earl Henry, perhaps even from his steward in Lindsey, rather than directly from Grosseteste or one of his household. With regard to Grosseteste's pledge of the book of scriptural glosses in exchange for St Edmunds' copy of the *Hexaëmeron*, it seems unlikely that this was an outcome of close contact between the learned élite at St Edmunds and Grosseteste. Thus, he probably decided to apply to the monks of St Edmunds for the loan simply because of the fame of St Edmunds' magnificent collection of biblical texts.

---

[19] Edited and discussed in Dorothea Oschinsky, *Walter of Henley and other Treatises on Estate Management and Accounting* (Oxford, 1971). See also S. H. Thomson, op. cit., esp. pp. 58–9.

[20] It is used as the base text by Oschinsky, op. cit. (see pp. 191, 192). Oschinsky in her list of the manuscripts of the *Rules* omits an early fourteenth-century copy in another Bury register, BL MS Harley 3977, ff. 67–70v. The exemplar of this copy is not the copy in Harley 1005, where it is preceded (ff. 62v–67) by a copy of Walter of Henley's *Husbandry* (this copy of the latter is not noticed by Oschinsky). See Thomson, *Archives*, p. 146.

[21] See Oschinsky, op. cit., p. 236, and above p. 206 and n. 58. See also Harley 1005, ff. 45–47v, 92v–93v, 73–73v.

[22] Douai, Bibliothèque Municipale MS 553, ff. 15–15v; James, *Abbey*, p 158; *Memorials*, ii. 366–7.

[23] Described in Gransden, *Exhibition Catalogue*, p. 251, 281 nn. 198–200.

While there is no doubt that Pembroke 7 came to St Edmunds sometime during Grosseteste's adult life, fairly certainly while he was studying, writing and teaching before becoming bishop of Lincoln, the evidence that the other manuscript to be discussed here reached St Edmunds within the period 1215–58 is less conclusive. The manuscript, now Gonville and Caius College, Cambridge, MS 480/476, is a high quality folio-sized volume executed in Italy probably in the mid-thirteenth century. The text is the *Canon* by the Arab philosopher, scientist and physician 'Avicenna (d. 1037)' in the Latin translation by Gerard of Cremona (d. 1187). The *Canon*, an encyclopaedia of medical knowledge which, in Latin translation, was for many centuries a standard authority in the medical schools of Christendom, while the Arabic text dominated thought and practice in the Islamic world.[24] A number of manuscripts of the Latin text survive, many of them *de luxe* copies.[25] Caius 480/476 is one of the latter. The text is in two columns and the first page of each of the five Books and of some of the chapters have illuminated initials, some accompanied by decorative partial borders with figures and grotesques and especially dragons. The best of these borders are very lively, with well drawn outlines and clear bright colours. A good example is on folio i. The initial letter, 'I', comprises five historiated medallions arranged one below the other. The little pictures illustrate either study or medical practice: the top one and the fourth each contain a man reading a book, the second and third contain respectively two men or one man holding up a vessel; and the bottom medallion shows a physician feeling a patient's pulse. The illumination of this initial is of mediocre quality[26] but the border surrounding the entire page except the top margin is excellent. Its main decoration comprises five dragons, four with long curly tails. From the mouth of the first emerges the bust of a bearded man with arms raised to support the initial 'I': a similar bust of a man emerges from the mouth of a dragon in the opposite margin; he holds a hunting horn from which emerges the long straight tail of a dragon which reaches nearly to the top of the page.[27] Recent scholars consider that the artistic style of the illumination suggests that the manuscript may have been executed in Bologna, one of the principal medical schools in this period, though a Sicilian provenance is another possibility.[28] The volume shows signs of use but the fact red

[24] C. H. Haskins, *The Renaissance of the Twelfth Century* (Cambridge, Mass. – Oxford, 1927), p. 324; C. H. Talbot, *Medicine in Medieval England* (London, 1967), pp. 30–2; N. G. Siraisi, *Taddeo Alderotti and his pupils: Two Generations of Italian Medical Learning* (Princeton, 1981), pp. 76–7, 105; idem, *Medieval and Early Renaissance Medicine* (Chicago, 1990), pp. 12, 71.

[25] M. T. D'Alverny, 'Avicennisme en Italie', *Convegno Internazionale, 9–15 Aprile 1969, Oriente e Occidente nel Medioevo: Filosofia e Scienze* (Rome, 1971), pp. 124–32. I am indebted for this reference and for those to N. G. Siraisi's two books to Professor Christine Meek.

[26] M. R. James suggested that the manuscript was of Italian provenance but thought that some of the ornamentation was English. James, *Cat. Gonville and Caius*, pp. 550–1. This initial would seem to be English but see the next note.

[27] Reproduced in monochrome in Gransden, *Exhibition Catalogue*, pl. LXIII; and in this volume, pl. VIII.

[28] Professor A. G. Watson and Professor A. C. de la Mare, for whose opinions I am indebted,

silk guards protected at least some of the initials – only one survives (on f. 142) shows that it was valued for its aesthetic quality as well for its practical use. Its binding suggests the same conclusion: it is bound in tawed skin, dyed red, on square boards. The binding was probably done at St Edmunds in the fourteenth or fifteenth century. The red colour would seem to indicate the special value attached to the volume. The spine has no tabs which indicates that the volume was not kept upright on a shelf but preserved in a cupboard or chest.

The earliest indisputable evidence that Caius 480/476 was at St Edmunds is the inscription at the top of folio i by Henry of Kirkstead: 'Liber monachorum sancti edmundi', followed by the late fourteenth-century class-mark, .A.200. My suggestion that it reached St Edmunds in the mid-thirteenth century rests on an entry in the Book of Benefactors in the kitchener's register compiled in 1425. The entry is for Stephen 'physician, monk and infirmarer', whose anniversary was to be celebrated with 'simple bell ringing' ('simplici sonitu'). It records that Stephen: 'acquired 22s annual rent for the office of the infirmary and gave three large and beautiful books on medicine to the convent for treating the sick; from the said 22s a pittance of 15[s] annually should be given annually to the convent by the infirmarer'.[29] Entries in the infirmarer's register provide more information about Stephen. This register, like the kitchener's register, was compiled in 1425. In the relevant entries Stephen appears variously as Stephen of Caistor ('de Castr'') and as Master Stephen. Most useful is the copy of the decree issued unanimously in full chapter on 24 April 1257 establishing Stephen's anniversary; the entry ends with a reference to folio 245 in the abbey's (now lost) martyrology. The gist is that brother Stephen, physician and infirmarer, who had held successively various offices and administered them prudently and faithfully, had thereby increased the abbey's regular income beyond the call of duty: therefore, his earthly labours deserved eternal refreshment; the infirmarer should take 22s from the rents acquired by Stephen in the vill, that is, 20s from a toft in Churchgate Street ('Kyrkgatestrete') and 2s from a toft in Mainwater Lane ('Maydwaterstrete'); when Stephen died 15s of the 22s was to be spent for the recreation of the convent and the monks were to celebrate the full office of the dead, with bells, on the day of his death and on his anniversary; but while he was still alive, the infirmarer was to give the pittance on the feast of St Mark (25 April) and sometime after the feast, on a day convenient to the precentor, the convent was to celebrate the solemn office of the dead for Stephen's father

considered that both the handwriting and all the ornamentation to be Italian. The ornamentation resembles that of manuscripts from Bologna which was famous for its medical school as well as for law. For examples see F. Avril and M.-Th. Gousset, *Manuscrits enluminés d'origine Italienne*: ii, *XIII siècle* (Bibl. Nat., Paris, 1984), pls XXXV no. 59, XLVI no. 97, XLVIII nos 99, 100. However, Professor de la Mare suggested a south Italian provenance, perhaps Naples, where the university also had a medical school.

[29] 'Pro Stephano medico monacho et Infirmario Qui viginti et duos solidos annui redditus pro officio Infirmarie perquisivit, et tres libros magnos et pulcherimus de medicina Conuentui dedit pro infirmis sanandis, de quibus viginti duos solidos fiat pitancia Conuentui de quindecim annuatim per infirmarium', Douai, Bibliothèque Municipale MS 553, f. 17.

and mother.[30] The scribe adds a note that in his time the pittance had been converted into a 'visitation' paid annually by the infirmarer: this probably means that the pittance originally was an extra dish for the monks at meal-time on the anniversary and had been commuted into a money payment. The scribe finally refers the reader to the section in the register where copies of the two charters is to be found. They show that Master Stephen, 'physician and keeper (*custos*) of the infirmary', paid 18s for the toft in Mainwater Lane,[31] and 15 marks for the toft in Churchgate Street.[32] An acquittance by the executors of Henry of Horringer 'deceased' for which Master Stephen paid Henry 40s secured the 20s rent to the abbot and convent: it is dated 24 September 1256, that is, about four months before Stephen's anniversary was agreed in chapter.[33] His acquisition of these two rents for the infirmary were not the only ones he purchased. He also bought rents, totalling 29s, from various other holdings in Churchgate Street, paying Henry of Horringer 11 marks 'in the pennies of St Edmund' for them.[34] Again, John, son of Wido of St Edmunds quitclaimed to the abbot and convent

[30] 'Anniuersarium Stephani medici Quoniam ius dictat equitatis et ordo exigit vt qui bene ministrat fideliter dispensando et prudenter dispensanda ampliando merito referr' debet condignum remuneracionis emolumentum Cum igitur Frater Stephanus medicus Infirmarius noster varijs successiue deputatus officijs commissa sibi fideliter procurauerit et perquisitorum supererogacione eadem multiplicauerit vt ex (vult', *on erasure*) sui temporali sudor[e] eternam recreacionem senciat spiritus [spc] conuentus decretum est in pleno capitulo vnanimique fauor[e] concessum vt quicumque pro tempore fuerit infirmarius sancti Edmundi viginti duos solidatos annui redditus de perquisitis dicti Stephani capiet in villa sancti Edmundi, scilicet viginti solidos de quadam tufta iacente in kyrkgatestrete contra ecclesiam sancti Jacobi et duos alios solidos de alia tufta iacente in Maydwaterstrete, de quibus viginti duobus solidis cum memoratus Stephanus sublatus fuerit de medio quindecim solidos die obitus sui in recreacione Conuentus in perpetuum expendet Dum vero prefatus Stephanus superstes extiterit fiet dicta pitancia plenarie sicut dictum est die Sancti Marci per manum Infirmarij. Ita tamen quod aliquo die post festum dicti sancti cum precentor viderit expedire fiat solempne officium in Conuentu pro animabus patris et matris prenominati Stephani Cum autem vt dictum est prefatus Stephanus in fata decesserit fiet pro eo in Conuentu annuatim die anniuersaria obitus eius cum pulsacione plenarium officium mortuorum quod ante fiebat pro patre suo et matre. Actum in capitulo nostro Anno domini Mill[esi]mo cc^mo lvij° vigilia Sancti Marci in martil' fol. 245. Sed sciendum quod dicta pitancia iam conuersa est in visitacionem per Infirmarium annualim faciendum. Et vide euidencias de supradictis viginti duobus solidis infra littera b verbo Bury in suis locis.' BL MS Landsdowne 416, f. 4.

[31] Henry of Horringer quitclaimed to the abbot and convent 2s quit rent which Walter Wodard was wont to pay Henry annually from a toft in *Maydeswaterstrete* [location given]; for this concession Master Stephen, physician and keeper of the infirmary paid Henry 18s [witness list follows]. Lansdowne 416, f. 15v. This and the following charters are of considerable interest. I have only given the bare substance of them here.

[32] Henry of Horringer quitclaimed to the abbot and convent 20s which Ran[ulph] the moneyer owes him for his toft in *Kyrkegatestrete* by the church of St James [location given]; for this quitclaim Master Stephen physician and keeper of the infirmary paid him 15 marks [witness list follows]. Ibid., f. 20v.

[33] Ibid., f. 21v.

[34] Ibid., f. 21. For St Edmunds' mint see below, chapter 20. One of the rents was from an oven or furnace.

3s 6d rent in Bakers' Street ('in vicu pistorum') in the Baxterstreet area for the infirmary, for which Master Stephen paid 24s sterling.[35]

These charters show that Stephen was an active administrator and, moreover, that he was a Master. Before becoming a monk and physician at St Edmunds, it is likely that he had graduated in medicine at Bologna or Naples (probably at the former). Presumably he would have acquired books on medicine while studying and brought them back to England and to St Edmunds when he took the habit. Perhaps among them were the three 'large and beautiful books on medicine' and the volume now Gonville and Caius MS 480/476 was one of them. However, he may have bought them after returning from Italy. He probably earned a considerable amount from his medical practice outside the monastic commu- nity. (Walter, physician and almoner under Abbot Samson, amassed a large sum through his medical practice and contributed it towards the cost of replacing the wooden almonry by the new stone one.[36]) This fact makes it possible to identify Stephen tentatively as the donor of the early thirteenth-century copy of the Twelve Prophets and Daniel, glossed, now Pembroke College, Cambridge, MS 65. The flyleaf bears an inscription in a thirteenth-century hand, 'Master Stephen gave this book to St Eadmunds: know that if anyone alienates this book from St Eadmunds he incurs the wrath of God and St Edmund'.[37] However, before assuming, if he was the donor, that Master Stephen, besides fulfilling his duties as physician and infirmarer, interested himself in scriptural exegesis, it should be remembered that the Rule of St Benedict forbids monks to own prop- erty, a prohibition reiterated by the reformers.[38] Therefore, money earned by a monastic physician was probably spent as the abbot and convent wanted and for the community's benefit.

---

[35] Ibid., f. 27.
[36] *JB*, pp. 96, 113. Above, pp. 88–90.
[37] 'Dedit magister Stephanus sancto Eadmundo. Si quis hunc librum a sancto Eadmundo alienauerit sciat se iram dei et sancti Eadmundi incurrere.' James, *Abbey*, p. 48.
[38] *Rule*, ed. Fry, pp. 230/1, c. 33, and e.g. *Chapters*, ed. Pantin, i. 18 § 18, lii § 24.

19

Buildings

Of the seven monks who successively held the office of sacrist in the period 1215–57, only the second, Richard of Newport, appears among those benefactors whose acts and merits were recorded in the (now lost) martyrology and in the kitchener's register. He must have been a monk of some seniority already in 1213, since at that time he was subsacrist and took a leading part in opposition to the election of Hugh of Northwold to the abbacy.[1] He was appointed sacrist in 1220 when his predecessor in that office, Richard of the Isle, became prior,[2] and remained sacrist for about fifteen years, until sometime before 1234.[3]

The entry for Richard of Newport in the kitchener's register is in the section for benefactors whose anniversaries were celebrated with 'simple ringing of bells' ('simplici sonitu'). It reads as follows:

> he destroyed the old chapter house and built a new one from the foundations; he bought the fishery at Icklingham at great cost; he had a great bell made for the main bell-tower which is called the 'Newport'; he acquired 40s in annual rents for the recreation of the convent and the poor on the day of his anniversary, that is, two marks for the convent and one for the poor, according to the martyrology; he was a faithful custodian of the monastery's possessions in diverse offices and increased its lands and rents.[4]

The *Gesta Sacristarum* has a similar entry but has an addition after the mention of the bell called Newport. It states that Richard 'having procured timber in the manor of Melford from Abbot Hugh II, constructed buildings of stone at Manhall, except for the hall and solar'.[5] It does not mention Richard's acquisition of 40s rent for the 'recreation' of the convent and the poor, nor does it have the eulogy of his faithful service which ends the entry in the kitchener's register.

---

[1] *Electio*, pp. xxxix, xli, 84/5, 90/1, 92/3.

[2] *Bury Chron.*, pp. 4, 5.

[3] His successor as sacrist, Gregory, became prior in 1234. *Bury Chron.*, p. 8.

[4] 'Pro Sacrista Ricardo Newport Qui vetus Capitulum prostrauit et nouum construxit a fundamentis, Piscariam de Iklyngham magnis sumptibus comparauit. Item vnam magnam campanam in maiori Campanario que dicitur Newport fieri fecit. Item quadraginta solidos annui redditus adquisiuit pro recreacione Conuentus et pauperum in die anniuersarij sui videlicet duas marcas pro Conuentu et vnam marcam pro pauperibus secundum martilogium. Item bona Monasterij in diuersis officijs fideliter custodiuit et in terris et redditibus multiplicauit.' Douai, Bibliothèque Municipale MS 553, f. 17.

[5] *Gesta Sacrist.*, pp. 193–4. Below p. 233.

However, a marginal note apparently by the scribe of the text adds that the 40s rent acquired for 'recreation' comprised '20s annual rent in Manhall and 20s annual rent in Icklingham'. It concludes with the eulogy.[6]

Richard of Newport seems to have inherited the zeal for the sacrist's office characteristic of Samson himself and of the sacrists during his rule. The information cited above shows that he combined concern for the buildings within the abbey precincts with care for those on its estates. There is more evidence about the new chapter-house. It replaced the early twelfth-century chapter-house constructed by Godfrey, sacrist under Abbot Robert II (1102–7), which was a short building with either an apsidal or a polygonal east end.[7] It was probably too small for the community which by the thirteenth century had grown to seventy-five or so monks. The new chapter-house was a large, rectangular building, measuring a hundred feet long and forty feet wide.[8] Its construction was obviously a major undertaking. Central to this project and other building projects was obviously the acquisition of sufficient and suitable stone. The most important sources of supply were the quarries of Northamptonshire, especially the quarry at Barnack in Nassaburgh double hundred (latterly known as the soke of Peterborough).[9] Stone was also brought from the quarry at Alwalton in Huntingdonshire, on the south bank of the Nene, just over the county border and about four miles south-west of Peterborough, where Peterborough abbey held five hides and the right of toll on the river. Barnack 'rag' was a high quality white limestone often referred to as marble in medieval documents. It was the principal stone used for many great churches, for example for the abbeys of Peterborough, Crowland, Thorney and Ramsey, and for the cathedrals of Lincoln, Ely and Norwich.[10] It was also used in many lesser churches, especially in the Holland region in Lincolnshire and in the Marshland in Norfolk. Abbot Baldwin had obtained stone from Barnack for the construction of the magnificent Romanesque abbey church at Bury St Edmunds.[11] It was used again for further building of the church in the twelfth century and, as will be seen, there is charter evidence concerning its use by Hugh of Northwold for Richard of Newport's building projects. Stone from the quarry at Alwalton was also widely used in church building but mainly for decorative work such as effigies and slender ornamental columns. It is often mistaken for Purbeck marble because of its greyish brown colour and exceptional hardness which enables it to take a very high polish.

Evidence concerning St Edmunds' stone supply for building work under Hugh

6   *Gesta Sacrist.*, p. 294 n. a.
7   Ibid., p. 289; Whittingham, 'Bury St. Edmunds Abbey', pp. 170, 176, 178–9; James, *Abbey*, pp. 146–7, 154, 180.
8   *William Worcestre*, pp. 160/1.
9   Nikolaus Pevsner, *Northamptonshire* (Harmondsworth, 1961, 2nd edn extensively revised by Bridget Cherry 1973), pp. 19–20; and esp. J. M. Steane, 'Building materials used in Northamptonshire and the area around', *Northamptonshire Past and Present*, vi, no. 1, Northamptonshire Record Soc. (Northampton 1972), pp. 71–83.
10 See ibid., p. 72.
11 *Feudal Docs*, p. 57 no. 11.

of Northwold is in a charter, copies of which survive in three of the abbey's registers.[12] (A copy of the same charter is in one of the registers of Peterborough abbey.[13]) The charter was issued by Alexander (of Holderness), abbot of Peterborough (1222–6). It relates to the transport of stone and is in two parts. First, Abbot Alexander ratifies the grant by William, son of Reginald, to the abbot and convent of St Edmunds of a rod of his land in 'Castorfields', that is, the area between Castor and the Nene. (Castor lies a mile or so north of the Nene and four miles west of Peterborough.) Secondly, Alexander grants the abbot and convent freedom to transport by public road, without any hindrance or exaction, 'marble, other stone and things, whether already belonging to them or purchased', from Barnack to the river Nene between Alwalton and Peterborough for an annual payment of 6s. The charter's witness list begins with the abbots of three Fenland abbeys, all on or near rivers and, therefore, concerned with water transport: they were Hugh Foliot, abbot of Ramsey (1216–31), Henry de Beauchamp, abbot of Crowland (1191–1236), and Robert III, abbot of Thorney (1217–37).[14] If the route on the waterway taken by barges carrying freight for St Edmunds passed through a region under the jurisdiction of any of these abbots, presumably Abbot Hugh would have had to obtain from him a similar charter granting permission and to have paid him rent.

The charter indicates that stone was taken by cart to 'Castorfields' and hence to a wharf on the Nene at Gunwade Ferry (commonly known as Milton Ferry), a distance from Barnack of six or seven miles. The entrance to St Edmunds' site at Gunwade Ferry was and still is marked by two standing stones of Barnack 'rag'. They are known as the 'St Edmunds' stones' or alternatively called 'Robin

---

[12] 'Notum sit uobis nos ratam et gratam habere concessionem et donationem illius terre in campis de Castr' scilicet unius rode quam Willelmus filius Reginaldi concessit et dedit Abbati et conventui Sancti Edmundi et nos concessisse eisdem liberum caruagium suum per viam publicam de Bernak et per terram illam usque ad aquam sine omni impedimento de nobis et balliuis nostris. Praeterea concessimus eisdem quod liceat eis inperpetuum libere bene et in pace et sine omni exactione et impedimento ducere marmor' et quamlibet aliam petram ad usus suos proprios habeant uel ad usus proprios emptas per aquam que dicitur Nen inter Ale Walton et Burgum prestita securitate per fidei interpositionem proprietatis abbatis et conuentus Sancti Edmundi'; for this grant the abbot and convent of St Edmunds were to pay 6s annual rent. The names of the witnesses follow. CUL MS Mm. iv. 19, ff. 32v–33. For the other copies of the charter in St Edmunds' registers see: CUL MSS Ff. 33, ff. 52v–53 (thirteenth century), and Gg. iv. 4, f. 91 (fifteenth century).

[13] Printed in *Carte Nativorum. A Peterborough Abbey Cartulary of the Fourteenth Century*, ed. C. N. L. Brooke and M. M. Postan, Northamptonshire Record Soc., xx (Oxford, 1960), p. 193 no. 533. Cf. J. E. B. Gover, A. Mawer and F. M. Stenton, *The Place-Names of Northamptonshire*, English Place-Name Soc., x (1933), p. 233. I owe the former reference to Mr T. M. Halliday of Minster Precincts, Peterborough, who generously gave me the benefit of his unrivalled knowledge of the archives of Nassaburgh double hundred. This, together with his knowledge of the locality, has enabled him to trace the route taken by carts conveying stone destined for St Edmunds to Gunwade Ferry, mainly by the then existing public roads.

[14] Barker, *West Suffolk Illustrated*, pp. 53–8; Whittingham, 'Bury St. Edmunds Abbey', pp. 178–9.

Hood' and 'Little John'.[15] These two stones now stand in a small hedged enclosure, between the old A47 road and the river. The A47 has been replaced by the dual carriageway a little to the north, but serves as the access road to Gunwade Ferry. The latter is situated a mile and a half east of Castor, with Alwalton on the opposite bank of the Nene. From Gunwade Ferry stone for St Edmunds would have been loaded onto barges and transported, toll free, up the Nene to Peterborough and so onwards to join the Great Ouse. From there the most likely route taken by the barges is along the Great Ouse until it is joined by the Lark, which the barges would have followed as far as the wharfs at Mildenhall. There the stones would have been unloaded and transported by cart for the last twelve miles to St Edmunds. However, if the Lark were navigable for large barges to Bury St Edmunds itself, the stone might have continued its journey by water. Unfortunately, our knowledge of the actual course of rivers and the existence of canals in this period, as generally for medieval England, is far from complete. It is not impossible that stone for St Edmunds sometimes took different routes. For example, there were wharfs on the Welland at Pilsgate, only a mile north of Barnack. The Welland was the obvious waterway carrying freight destined for Lincolnshire but possibly it was also used for freight going south.[16] If some freight for St Edmunds was transported along the Welland, which joins the Nene at Crowland, this would give the occurrence of the abbot of Crowland in the charter's witness list an added significance.

To return to Richard of Newport's chapter-house. The site was excavated in 1902–3 at the instigation of M. R. James. It was found that the new building was narrower but much longer than the old one. At the east end were remains of a semicircular stone platform a few inches high on which the ambo (*pulpitum*) would have stood. Along the north wall was part of the monks' stone bench and in the centre of the chapter-house, half way from the platform for the ambo and the door, were traces of the base of the lectern; near the lectern were a few tiles, some blue and some yellow. Scattered around were pieces of marble and brightly painted stone and many fragments of coloured glass.[17] The new chapter-house must have been an impressive and colourful building and proved a very suitable place for the burial of abbots: indeed, it became the accepted place for abbatial burials until Simon of Luton built the magnificent new Lady chapel,[18] where he and a number of his successors were buried. The remains of the graves of six abbots in the old chapter-house have been discovered. The graves run in a row from east to west, the first being by the platform for the ambo and the sixth by

[15] I am indebted for this information to Mr Halliday. See also Gover, Mawer and Stenton, op. cit., p. 233, and Steane, art. cit., pp. 73, 74.

[16] For the suggestion that wharfs at Pilsgate were used for freight destined for St Edmunds and interesting comments on the problems posed by the Fenland waterways I am indebted to Dr Paul Bush. Cf.: Darby, *The Medieval Fenland*, pp. 93–106; Parker, *The Making of Kings Lynn*, pp. 5–7; and (mainly for later period), Alistair Robertson 'Rivers and Navigations', in *Historical Atlas of Suffolk*, pp. 130–1, 210–11.

[17] Barker, op. cit., pp. 53, 57–58, with photo of the coffins in their original places after excavation.

[18] James, *Abbey*, pp. 142–3; Whittingham, 'Bury St Edmunds Abbey', p. 174.

the door. The list of benefactors in the kitchener's register makes it possible to identify which abbot was buried in each of these graves since it ends all entries devoted to an abbot by recording the exact location of his grave. Thus, the graves in the chapter-house in order from east to west were as follows: Ording, Samson, Richard of the Isle, Henry of Rushbrooke, Edmund of Walpole, Hugh I.[19] The first five all occur in the register among those benefactors whose anniversaries were marked by a 'great ringing of bells', the highest honour, while Hugh I, lying nearest the door, was among those whose anniversaries were marked by a 'double ringing', the second greatest honour. The graves of Ording, Hugh I and Samson were probably moved from the old chapter-house to the new one. (The burial of Hugh of Northwold elsewhere was, of course, exceptional; having become bishop of Ely he was buried in his cathedral.)

The construction of the new chapter-house was Richard of Newport's main achievement in office. Judging from the entry about him in the kitchener's register and that in the *Gesta Sacristarum*, he was an enterprising, able and energetic man, but information about his building activity on the estates belonging to the sacristy and his maintenance of old and new structures is meagre. The particular reference in the *Gesta* to Richard's building work at Manhall was cited above.[20] Manhall, in Essex, was about two and a half miles north of Saffron Walden, in the parish of Chesterford. Richard's interest in Manhall perhaps had some connection with the fact that he was a native of the same region since presumably he came from Newport which lies on the river Cam about three miles south-west of Saffron Walden. St Edmunds's holding in Manhall originated in a grant, datable to 1089–93, from Alan, count of Brittany, to Abbot Baldwin and the convent of 'the land which Herveus de Hispania' held of him there, for the souls of his father, mother and brother, Count Alan.[21] Manhall and its neighbourhood were rich in woodland – the name survives in old maps in a corrupted form as 'Emanuel wood'.[22] Nevertheless, the *Gesta Sacristarum* states that Richard acquired timber from Hugh of Northwold, from the abbot's manor of Melford. Maybe it was a gift from Abbot Hugh and in any case Manhall was nearer to St Edmunds and Melford than it was to most of the sacristy's other holdings. Its comparative distance from the abbey and proximity to the honour of Clare was probably one reason why Abbot Simon of Luton and the

---

[19] James, *Abbey*, pp. 180–1, citing the list of benefactors in Douai, Bibliothèque Municipale MS 553, ff. 7v–9, 11v.

[20] 'Hic [Richard] vetus capitulum destruxit, et novum a fundamentis contruxit. Piscariam de Ikelingh non modico pretio comparavit; magnam etiam campanam in majori campanario, quae dicitur Neweport, sumptu non mediocri fieri fecit. Hic etiam, meremio ab abbate Hugone secundo in manerio de Meleford comparato, omnia aedificia praeter aulam et solarium de lapide apud Manhale construxit.' *Gesta Sacrist.*, pp. 293–4. The hall and solar were presumably of timber, wattle and daub construction.

[21] *Feudal Docs*, pp. xxxvii, 85–6 no. 67, 152 no. 169. Douglas, ibid., p. cxli and n., identifies the donor as Alan the Black, earl of Richmond, but later corrects this to Alan the Red. See idem, *William the Conqueror* (London, 1964), p. 268 and n. 2.

[22] R. H. Reaney, *The Place-Names of Essex*, English Place-Name Soc., xii (Cambridge, 1969), p. 520.

convent parted with it together with other holdings to Richard de Clare, earl of Gloucester, in 1259.

Both the kitchener's register and the *Gesta Sacristarum* record that Richard of Newport purchased a fishery at Icklingham. The sacrist's manor in the vill was one of the sacristy's most lucrative holdings and included a fishery and a water-mill, both of which would have needed constant maintenance.[23] To discover more about building and repair work during the period 1215–57 it is necessary to turn to documentary sources, notably to the manorial and obedientiary accounts for the years 1247–50 and 1256–61 preserved in BL MS Harley 645. The admittedly scanty evidence they contain about buildings and their maintenance will only be touched on here because it is considered in detail in appendix III below. Very few of the entries for expenses are specific. For example, references to payments to carpenters and those for the purchase of nails do not necessarily imply constructing new buildings or repairing old ones: the carpenters might be making new carts or repairing old ones, and the nails might be for shoeing horses. However, the chamberlain's accounts include the cost of a new building next to the tailor's workshop.[24] Similarly, one of the subcellarer's accounts includes the cost of constructing a new oven 'and for making ovens';[25] another of the subcellarer's accounts records the cost of constructing a wooden wall in the bake-house, and of building a pigsty and a stable for horses.[26] Yet another of his accounts records the cost of repairing a granary and for making a new malt-kiln (*torayll'*).[27] The accounts for the sacrist's manor of Icklingham record the cost of repairing the solar and granary.[28]

St Edmunds' most remarkable building achievement on its estates during this period, and actually from the late twelfth century onwards, was the construction of windmills and, to a lesser degree, of watermills. The spectacular increase in the number of the abbey's mills paralleled similar development on other great estates, for instance on the estates of the bishopric of Ely and of Ramsey abbey. St Edmunds' mills are discussed in some detail below, in appendix IV, but here a few references to them in the Harley accounts will be mentioned to give some idea of their maintenance cost. The accounts for the chamberlain's manor of Hinderclay, which was rich in woodland, reveal that fourteen trees, stripped of their branches and bark, had been sent from there to the mill at Beccles, another of the chamberlain's manors.[29] And one of the subcellarer's accounts records the cost of making new sluices for the watermill at Stowe ('In nouis inclusis ad molendinum de Stowe') and for the construction of a new mill there.[30] These few, isolated examples suggest that the obedientiaries and their officials were trying to keep the buildings on their holdings in repair and to construct new

---

[23] Below, pp. 307–11.
[24] Harley 645, f. 252.
[25] Ibid., f. 262v.
[26] Ibid., f. 265.
[27] Ibid., f. 194.
[28] Ibid., f. 260.
[29] Ibid., f. 252v.
[30] Ibid., f. 262v.

ones when thought necessary. But the evidence is insufficient to prove that there was little or no dilapidation of the monks' agricultural and other buildings – which seems unlikely, especially in view of the abbey's shortage of cash.

Meanwhile, it seems that the abbey church itself was falling into disrepair. Its upkeep, a recurrent and heavy expense, was the sacrist's responsibility, and the *Gesta* states that early in Simon of Luton's abbacy, when Richard of Witham (*alias* of Colchester) was sacrist, the convent decided 'that he should put aside just £12 annually, not more, for repairing dilapidations in the church'. Nevertheless, besides presumably spending this on the church, he 'built a new hall, called the Spanne, for the recreation of the convent'.[31] Thus, it seems that Richard of Newport had allowed dilapidation of the church while not only building the grand new chapter-house but in addition a spacious new hall for the monks' recreation. It could be that an undue proportion of the convent's resources was being used to increase the monks' comfort.

---

[31] *Gesta Sacrist.*, p. 275.

20

St Edmunds' Liberties and the Crown[1]

Jurisdictional liberties

The Liberty of St Edmunds, which comprised both the Liberty of the eight and a half hundreds and the even more highly privileged Liberty of the *banleuca*,[2] was well-established before the Norman Conquest and had been confirmed by the Anglo-Norman kings and their successors. St Edmunds' claim to the Liberty was based primarily on the grants by Edward the Confessor[3] but these were expressed in general terms, and in the twelfth and thirteenth centuries frequent definition and elaboration were necessary in order to accommodate new developments in royal government. For instance, there was the problem of that character-istic feature of the judicial system of the late twelfth and thirteenth centuries, the general eyre. How could the abbot's claim to jurisdiction in the Liberty be reconciled with the visits of itinerant justices? Because of the privilege that no minister of the king could exercise authority within the *banleuca*; thus, the abbot could exclude them from the town of Bury St Edmunds itself and appoint his own justices in eyre. But he could not exclude them from the Liberty of the eight and a half hundreds. For that, the royal justices held special sessions at Cattishall (an open place three and a half miles south-east of Bury). A point of contention between abbot and king was which of them was entitled to the profits of justice accruing from those sessions, notably amercements and the chattels of felons. Such profits normally belonged to the king but the abbot claimed them as part of the regalian rights of the Liberty of the eight and a half-hundreds. Similarly, the convent claimed them in cases involving its manors and tenants within the Liberty. Moreover, the abbot claimed the right to the profits of justice in cases arising in royal or honorial courts outside the Liberty if St Edmunds' holdings or tenants were at issue. The thirteenth-century abbots of St Edmunds, like other liberty-holders, struggled at the Exchequer to establish their right in face of the king's *quo warranto* proceedings, appealing to their charters and to precedents.

---

[1] Part of this section and of the next is based on revised versions of my two articles 'The abbey of Bury St Edmunds and national politics', pp. 67–86, and 'John de Northwold', pp. 91–4.

[2] Harmer, *Writs*, pp. 138–48; Lobel, *Bury St. Edmunds*, pp. 2–7.

[3] Harmer, *Writs*, pp. 154–61 nos 9–19.

This struggle began in the first half of the thirteenth century and culminated in the victory of Abbot John of Northwold in 1290.[4]

Another problem was the procedures in the abbot's court which, compared with those in the royal courts, were antiquated. Steps were taken to bring its procedures up to date, and on 4 May 1231 Henry III granted the abbot the right to use a petty jury.[5] All pleas of the crown involving life and limb brought in the abbot's court by the appeal of an individual accuser and customarily tried by fire and water, 'which has no place nowadays' ('quod modo locum non habet'), might henceforth be determined by an inquisition of legal men of the Liberty. But pleas of the crown where there is no such accuser, but the king brings the suit by means of a jury of presentment, should not be determined in that court, but before the king's itinerant justices. The general eyres themselves made an important contribution to clarifying the abbot's jurisdictional rights, particularly important because the justices' rolls included written record of them and relevant extracts were copied into the abbey's registers. In this way the abbot accumulated a body of precedents. The rolls of the eyre of Martin Pattishall and his fellows in the autumn of 1228 provide an example. On 23 October, when sitting at Cattishall, the justices conceded that rules relating to essoin and distraint in land pleas should be the same in the court of St Edmunds as in a county court. However, unlike a county court it should sit every three weeks, and the portmanmoot (the borough court) be held in the customary way; for this concession the abbot gave the king a palfrey.[6] A jury was also asked how writs of novel disseisin and other pleas of the crown should be determined in the *banleuca*. The jurors said that the abbot should settle them; on the coming of the king's justices he should receive the writs and hold the pleas and assizes in the vill.[7] The same thing was done ('similiter actus fuit') before Robert of Lexington and his fellows in their eyre of Norfolk and Suffolk in 1234, on 22 November at Cattishall.[8] Both judgements were enrolled.

Another example of such codification of rights is supplied by the general eyre of William of York in the spring of 1240.[9] At the session at Ipswich the jurors of Babergh hundred testified on 29 April that Englishry for any dead man is presented by jury in the court of St Edmunds' Liberty in the same way as it is in a county court, and that murder fines fall due in the Liberty as elsewhere. If anyone accuse another for a breach of the king's peace in the court of the Liberty, and both the accuser and the accused are of the Liberty, the plea ought

---

4   Gransden, 'John de Northwold', pp. 100–1.
5   C *Ch. R 1226–57*, pp. 131–2; CUL MS Ff. ii. 33, f. 31v; BL MSS Harley 230, f. 6, and 743, ff. 63v–64.
6   BL MS Harley 645, ff. 81v, 137v. The concession is recorded in the mutilated civil plea roll of the Cattishall session of Martin of Pattishall's Suffolk eyre, 20–9 October 1228: PRO, Just. 1/819, rot. 22 dorso. I owe this reference to Paul Brand. I am also indebted to the late C. A. F. Meekings for relevant observations (see *Letter-Book of William of Hoo*, p. 61 n. 1). Cf. Crook, *Records*, p. 83.
7   *Letter-Book of William of Hoo*, pp. 60–1 no. 87.
8   Ibid., and Crook, *Records*, p. 90, who dates the eyre 24 November – 14 December.
9   Crook, *Records*, p. 101.

to be determined there by duel or in another way. But if the accused cannot be
found, then the court should tell the accuser to go to the county court and sue
him there, until he is summoned or outlawed.[10] In these ways the abbot and
convent constantly pressed St Edmunds' claim to regalian rights. By insistence
they established precedents confirming its liberties and they also won concessions which to some extent brought the procedures in the court of St Edmunds
into line with developments in the royal judicial system.

The mint

One of St Edmunds' highly valued privileges was the right to a mint and exchange.
(An exchange was usually attached to a mint and was the place where old and
foreign coins and bullion were handed in and struck into new coins or simply
exchanged for new coins.) The earliest known grant of this right to mint at St
Edmunds was by Edward the Confessor. He had granted the privilege to Abbot
Leofstan in the mid-eleventh century and towards the end of his life had issued
a writ to Abbot Baldwin giving him the right to a moneyer; a copy of the writ
survives.[11] The evidence that Edward granted the right to a mint and exchange
to Leofstan is numismatic; the earliest surviving coin struck at St Edmunds is of
a type datable to 1048–50 which proves that a mint was active at St Edmunds
at that time. Perhaps the grant of a mint was a response to St Edmunds' growing
importance and prosperity, following Edward's grant to Abbot Ufi of the Liberty
of the eight and a half hundreds in 1042 and 1243.[12] St Edmund's mint was one
of many mints: in the late Anglo-Saxon period there were sixty-five or so ecclesiastical and provincial mints. A reason for the great number was that there was
a recoinage every two or three years; coins became worn and might be debased
by clipping and growing commercial activity constantly increased the need for
a sound, readily available currency.[13] William I and William II continued the
Anglo-Saxon practice of frequent recoinages and the number remained high.
But in the course of the twelfth century the number of mints gradually declined
as recoinages became less frequent and the supply of coins proved adequate
and circulated sufficiently freely to meet the demands of commerce. Henry II
abandoned the practice of frequent recoinages altogether: he allowed Stephen's
last currency to circulate for the first four years of his reign and then in 1158
recoined, introducing the so-called 'Tealby' coins which remained current until
1180 when there was another recoinage;[14] the resultant 'Short Cross' coins

---

[10] CUL MS Ff. iv. 35, f. 1. Presentment of Englishry originated in Anglo-Norman times. It
      offered proof whether the murdered person was of English birth, to escape the fine levied
      on the hundred for the murders of a Norman.
[11] Harmer, *Writs*, pp. 165–6 no. 25, datable to 1 August 1065 x 5 January 1066.
[12] On the early history of the mint see Eaglen, 'The mint at Bury St Edmunds', pp. 111–12,
      114–15; idem, *The Abbey and Mint of Bury St Edmunds to 1279*, pp. 25–8.
[13] Idem, 'The mint at Bury St Edmunds', pp. 111–15. For a useful survey, with maps and
      a graph, of the numerous mints in the late Anglo-Saxon period see David Hill, *Atlas of
      Anglo-Saxon England* (Oxford, 1937), pp. 126–32.

remained current until Henry III's recoinage of 1247. Also under Henry II, the reduction in the number of mints continued. At the end of Stephen's reign there were 40 mints while at the time of the 1180 recoinage the number had fallen to 30. In particular, the ecclesiastical mints of the bishops of Hereford, Lincoln, London and Winchester and the abbot of Reading's mint appear to have been inactive.[15] Even the mint of the bishop of Durham which had started by minting 'Tealby' coins did not continue to do so and remained closed until after Henry's death.[16] Moreover, the mint's output was much greater under Henry II than it had been under Stephen – though, judging from the number of surviving coins, it amounted to only 4.3% of England's total coinage.[17]

The abbacy of Hugh I (1157–80) coincided with the 'Tealby' coinage and Samson's succession in 1182 occurred at about the same time as the introduction of the 'Short Cross' coins. Under Hugh I the mint remained open and productive but, like a number of provincial and other ecclesiastical mints, it took no part in the 1180 recoinage and was inoperative for most of Samson's abbatiate. However, the right to a mint was included in the confirmation of St Edmunds' privileges obtained by Samson in 1189 and 1200.[18] The fact that Samson did not take advantage of the right to a mint was perhaps because the confirmations did not specify the right to an exchange, the source of profit. Then, in 1205, King John had a partial recoinage in an attempt to eliminate clipped and debased coins. It even appears from the Bury chronicler, that at least some 'Tealby' coins were still in circulation, for he states in the annal for 1205 that coins minted in 1158 were 'renewed' in that year.[19] About sixteen provincial mints took part in this partial recoinage and concessions were made to ecclesiastical mints: the bishop of Durham's mint, which had been reopened in 1195, was allowed two dies instead of one, and a die was granted to the bishop of Chichester. St Edmunds' right to a mint was confirmed on 12 June 1205,[20]

14 Eaglen, *The Abbey and Mint of Bury St Edmunds to 1279*, pp. 112–27, 239–53 and pls 4–6.
15 For Henry II's suppression of ecclesiastical mints see: D. F. Allen, *A Catalogue of Coins in the British Museum: The Cross-and-Crosslets ('Tealby') Type of Henry II* (London, 1951), pp. lxxvi–lxxvii, ci; C. E. Blunt, 'Ecclesiastical coinage in England. Pt II. After the Norman Conquest', *Numismatic Chronicle*, 7th ser., i (1961), pp. i–xxi.
16 The Durham mint seems to have been closed in the 1140s and apparently again c. 1220 and c. 1253. Allen, *The Durham Mint*, pp. 167–71.
17 Eaglen, op. cit., p. 198.
18 For a copy of Richard I's confirmation of St Edmunds' liberties, dated 21 November, I Richard, see the sacrist's register, CUL MS Ff. ii. 33, f. 29v, and of John's, dated 15 March 1 John, ibid., f. 30v; *Rot. Chart.*, i. pt 1, p. 38. Abbot Samson paid £200 for the confirmation of St Edmunds' charters in 1200. See above p. 66.
19 'Moneta olim anno Domini M.C.lviij. facta, hoc anno est renouata.' *Bury Chron. Critical Edition*, p. 263; *Ann. S. Edm.*, p. 13. This was not recorded by any other chronicler. Eaglen, op. cit., p. 133, translates 'renovata' as 'withdrawn', and interprets the passage as meaning that coins minted in 1158 were finally withdrawn from circulation in 1205. However, 'renovata' can more accurately be translated as 'renewed' or 'altered'. It seems likely that at least some 'Tealby' coins were still in circulation and that these were melted down and the bullion used to mint coins of the 'Short Cross' type.
20 *Rot. Chart.*, p. 156; BL MSS Harley 645, f. 152v and Harley 743, ff. 11–11v; CUL MS Ff. ii. 33, f. 31.

for which and other concessions Samson paid 500 marks.[21] However, both the Bury mint and the Chichester one, besides about a third of the provincial mints, stopped production in 1207, once the partial recoinage was over. St Edmunds' mint remained inactive until 1215. Thereafter it survived throughout the thirteenth century until towards the middle of the fourteenth. Bearing in mind the demise of nearly all provincial and ecclesiastical mints during this period, the survival of St Edmunds' mint is remarkable.

Although the right to a mint and exchange was one of St Edmunds' regalities, in the thirteenth century and probably earlier it was not under the abbot's control but under the sacrist's.[22] The mint and exchange were a valuable asset of his office: for example, in the two years from 11 April 1246 to 19 April 1258 its profits exceeded £47 9s (equivalent to about £1,000 a year in modern money), and during about five months in some unspecified year between 1268 and 1276 the profit was £10 4s 6d.[23] A contemporary valuation of 1268 which estimated the profit at £3 a year must either represent a dramatic drop in profit or considerable undervaluation.[24] Therefore, it is not surprising that successive sacrists had an interest in the survival and profitability of the mint. Indeed, during the vacancy following Samson's death, it seems to have been the sacrist, Robert of Graveley, the leader of the opposition to the election of Hugh of Northwold, who initiated the negotiations with the king which resulted in the reopening of the mint in 1215. The *Electio Hugonis*, with characteristic disparagement of Robert, states that on 18 January 1214, in the course of the election dispute, the sacrist, 'wishing to carry out some malice which he had plotted, came into chapter and pretended that he was going to visit the legate (Nicholas) on the convent's business, while in reality he went to acquire a die and a sample coin of standard purity'.[25] At the time King John was enraged with the monks because one of them, Master Thomas of Walsingham, had gone to Rome 'to forward the election' on the convent's advice but contrary to the king's liberties. John, therefore, cursed all the monks except the prior and refused to make peace with Robert although the latter protested that he had never ordered anyone to go on such a mission. Having failed to pacify the king, Robert appealed to the powerful Peter des Roches, bishop of Winchester, to intercede on his behalf. But John remained adamant saying, according to the *Electio Hugonis*:

[21] Great Roll of the Pipe, 7 John, ed. Sidney Smith, Pipe Roll Soc., n.s. xix (1941), p. 236. 500 marks was equivalent to £333 6s 8d. See Eaglen, *The Abbey and Mint of Bury St Edmunds to 1279*, p. 134.
[22] Lobel, *Bury St. Edmunds*, p. 53.
[23] See Allen, 'The output, … of the Bury St Edmunds mint', pp. 210, 213.
[24] Lobel, op. cit., p. 59 n. 1; Eaglen, 'The mint at Bury St Edmunds', p. 118.
[25] *Electio*, pp. 36/7. This passage confirms Eaglen's view that the mint and exchange were closed during the vacancy. Eaglen, op. cit., p. 137. The statement in the *Statuta ad relevationem ecclesiae Sancti Edmundi* (BL MS Harley 3977, f. 52), that 'Cuneus maneat in manu conventus, donec aliter ordinetur' (*Bury Cust.*, p. 109 lines 14–15) is unlikely to refer to the 1213–14 vacancy: the extant copy of the statutes is in a late thirteenth-century hand and the statutes are undated.

If the sacrist and convent wish me to attend to their various requests and be restored to my former favour, let them satisfy me with an election conducted in accordance with ancient and well-tried custom; otherwise it is useless for them to come to me again on any matter, however trivial.

As it turned out John did not insist on a new election and on 10 June 1215 he confirmed the election of Hugh and shortly afterwards, on 19 July, he confirmed the abbot's right to a die.[26]

The reopening of the mint may have been the occasion for an inquiry to be held into its organization. The surviving copy of the questions and answers is undated and is in a hand datable to the 1260s or 1270s, but its contents would be appropriate for an inquiry held in preparation for reopening the mint after a ten years' closure. The text is headed 'These things must be inquired about, concerning who have administration in the mint.'[27] It begins with the moneyer's obligations and rights: for example, he gives 100s, but of the new coin ('sed de novo'), to the kings; he pays the profit to the king on whatever day the king chooses, and on the day when he strikes and exchanges; he has jurisdiction over the mint, with power to punish 'by rod, deposition, imprisonment or fine, according to the crime'; he entrusts the profits each day to the exchanger, his second-in-command; the assayer can be removed or deposed at the moneyer's will, and never takes more than 1d for an assay of £31; he is responsible for buying silver bullion; and so on. The text ends with the position of the master craftsmen and labourers: the former are 'always under the moneyer's rule' and the latter 'always in fear and trembling'.

Although St Edmunds' right to a mint seemed secure, its right to an exchange was not. On 21 February 1218 a writ addressed to the officials of the mints at Winchester, London, Durham, York and St Edmunds confirmed them in office but they were instructed to yield their exchanges to William Marshall the junior.[28] It became necessary to defend the right to an exchange. This the abbot and convent of St Edmunds did, for on 13 March 1218 they obtained a writ confirming the abbot's right to have his die and exchange 'in peace'.[29] However, there remained a threat to the full profitability of the exchange. A writ of 1 May 1221 prohibited the abbot, on pain of losing his liberty, to exchange the silver of merchants who would normally have exchanged it at the royal mint in London.[30] A further restriction followed less than two years later: letters patent to the citizens of Ypres, Arras, St Omer and Ghent, dated 10 February 1223, informed them that their silver could only be exchanged in the royal mints of London and Canterbury.[31]

26 Rot. Litt. Claus., p. 221.
27 BL MS Harley 1005, f. 219; Mon. Angl., iii. 164; Allen, 'Ecclesiastical mints', p. 115 and n. 18.
28 CPR, 1216–25, p. 138.
29 Rot. Litt. Claus., p. 354. See Eaglen, op. cit., pp. 147, 150; Allen, 'Ecclesiastical mints', p. 116 and n. 25.
30 Rot. Litt. Claus., p. 479.
31 CPR, 1216–25, p. 366.

It was possibly to prevent further erosion of St Edmunds' right to an exchange that sometime in 1223 Abbot Hugh and the convent farmed the mint and exchange to the king for £20 a year.[32] This is the only time in the history of St Edmunds' mint when it was out of the abbot's control. The terms of the agreement are complicated. The mint and exchange were committed to the keepers of the royal exchange in London until the king (then a minor fifteen or sixteen years old) was of age; the abbot was to receive £20 paid at two terms, Easter and Michaelmas;[33] whenever necessary the abbot and convent were to have coin from their own die while it was in the king's hands; the die was to be kept in St Edmund's church at night, that is, in the sacrist's custody, under the keepers' seals; the abbot and convent granted that there should be no diminution of, or injury to, the king's right to, or dignity or seizin of, his own exchange or mints by reason of the agreement or demission; similarly, the king granted that there should be no diminution of, or injury to, the abbot's right to and seizin of his mint and exchange by reason of the agreement or demission; finally, at the end of the said term everything should be in the same condition as it was when the agreement was made. The penultimate clause in effect confirmed St Edmunds' right to a mint and exchange. The agreement remained in place until late in 1229, although Henry III had it proclaimed in January 1227 that henceforth he would issue charters himself and his twenty-first birthday was on 1 October 1228. Richard of the Isle was elected abbot of St Edmunds on 5 June 1229; he was granted a die and exchange, and control of the mint and exchange on 25 February 1230.[34]

The next important date in the history of St Edmunds' mint and exchange is 1247. In that year Henry III began the recoinage and the Short Cross coinage was replaced by the Long Cross one which remained current until Edward I's recoinage in 1279.[35] For the first year of the recoinage the only mints operative were initially London and Canterbury; St Edmunds' mint joined them later in the year.[36] Sometime in the autumn of 1247 two monks of St Edmunds, Edmund of Walpole (the future abbot) and 'Thomas', had appeared before the barons of the Exchequer bringing St Edmunds' charters of liberties and claiming the abbot's right to a mint and exchange.[37] And on 6 December the treasurer, William of Haverhill (1240–52), and the two men most intimately concerned with the recoinage, Edward of Westminster (a goldsmith often in royal service) and William Hardell (king's clerk and warden of the Exchange), were ordered

---

[32] Ibid., pp. 405–6; *Rot. Litt. Claus.*, p. 544. See: Eaglen, op. cit., p.148, Allen, art. cit., p. 116 and n. 26.

[33] For the king's payment of £10 at Easter and Michaelmas see e.g. *C Lib. R, 1126–40*, pp. 4, 29, 77, 148.

[34] CCR, *1227–31*, p. 299.

[35] See: Lawrence, 'Long-cross coinage', pp. 145–79; Brooke, *English Coins* (1950), pp. 107–9.

[36] The Bury chronicler records in the annal for 1247 'Hoc anno facta est mutacio monete in Anglia. Quo tempore Henricus rex concessit sancto Edmundo unum cuneum noue incisionis ita libere utendum cum excambio, sicut rex utitur suis cuneis.' *Bury Chron.*, p. 12 and n. 6.

[37] PRO Memoranda Rolls LTR, 32 Henry III, for Michaelmas 1247 membrane 4 dorso.

to deliver to the monks of St Edmund a newly cut die so that he could mint his silver 'for the time being' (*interim*), as by right he was accustomed to do.[38] This concession seems to have been a temporary measure because the abbot had not yet returned the old die, a necessary preliminary to the granting of a new one on any but a temporary basis. Finally, on 26 December William of Haverhill, Edward of Westminster and William Hardell were ordered to deliver to Edmund, subsacrist (presumably Edmund of Walpole again), and Simon of Luton, almoner (later successively sacrist, prior and abbot), a new die, 'having first received the old one from them'; so that the abbot and convent could mint money as they did with the old die before the recoinage: this mandate was to be obeyed at once although the Exchequer was not in session. On the same day another mandate instructed the abbot and convent to use the die in the same way as was done in the royal mint in London and in the mints in other towns.[39] In 1248 sixteen provincial mints were opened to help with the recoinage but they were closed in 1250, leaving London, Canterbury and St Edmunds once more with a monopoly.[40]

It is difficult to see why St Edmunds' mint survived when other provincial and ecclesiastical mints closed. Henry III had no need for it since the London and Canterbury mints could have met all England's currency requirements. The proportion of the total currency minted at St Edmunds was very small. For instance, in the period 1217–42 it contributed something in the region of 6% to the Short Cross coinage, and the proportion of its contribution to the Long Cross coinage was even smaller.[41] The mint's survival was undoubtedly owing to the persistence with which the abbot and convent pressed their claim. It is noteworthy that the monks sent to the Exchequer for that purpose in 1247 were of recognized ability – two of the four (Edmund of Walpole and Simon of Luton) were future abbots. Each time such missions succeeded, St Edmunds' right was in effect confirmed. It was also in effect confirmed each time the sacrist presented a newly appointed moneyer at the Exchequer for formal admittance to office, an obligation not imposed on other institutions claiming minting rights; indeed, it gave St Edmunds' mint an advantage over other mints because the presentation of a moneyer was recorded on the Exchequer rolls and so established yet another indisputable precedent. Since Bury was not far from London and the abbot had a residence in the city, the obligation was not a serious inconvenience. Another reason for the mint's survival was probably the cult of St Edmund. Henry III had a deep veneration for the king and martyr. Coins struck at St Edmunds bear the name of the moneyer on the reverse but also the name of the mint, 'St Edmunds'.[42] The association in Henry's mind of the mint with the saint is well illustrated by a mandate issued on 6 December, the same day as the issue of the

[38] *CCR, 1247–51*, p. 12. For Edward of Westminster and William Hardell see Powicke, *Henry III and the Lord Edward*, i. 315 and n. 1, 321, ii. 574–5 and n. 1.

[39] *CCR, 1247–51*, p. 101. For a copy of a similar mandate to the abbot and convent of St Edmunds dated 5 Kal. Jan. (28 December) 1247 see BL MS Harley 645, f. 79v.

[40] Allen, 'Ecclesiastical mints', p. 117; Lawrence, art. cit., pp. 156–7.

[41] Eaglen, 'The mint at Bury St Edmunds', pp. 117–18.

[42] Ibid., pp. 114, 119–20 and pl. XXXI. Only one exception is known, a coin bearing the

mandate to William of Haverhill, Edward of Westminster and William Hardell instructing them to deliver a new die to the abbot and convent. This second mandate was addressed to Edward of Westminster. It instructed him to give the monks who had delivered the die 12 *oboli de musca* 'because the king wishes them to be attached to the shrine of the blessed martyr Edmund as the king had not visited St Edmund's church that year'.[43]

mint inscription 'Beri'. Ibid., p. 119. See also: Lawrence, art. cit., pp. 164–5; Brooke, op. cit., pp. 89, 109.

[43] CCR, *1247–51*, p. 12. For 'oboli de musca' see the next chapter and n. 2.

21

Henry III and the cult of St Edmund

Henry III's veneration for St Edmund seems to have been surpassed only by his veneration for another sainted Anglo-Saxon king, Edward the Confessor, patron saint of Westminster Abbey. Henry's devotion to St Edmund is well attested. He named his second son, Edmund ('Crouchback'), after him. On 18 January 1245, two days after Edmund's birth, Henry wrote to Abbot Henry of Rushbrooke ordering him to tell the monks that his son had been named after 'the glorious king and martyr', their patron saint.[1] And in 1253 he sent 12 *oboli de musca* and 20 measures of wax worth £40 for the feast of the translation of St Edmund (29 April), as votive offerings on account of his and Prince Edmund's infirmity.[2] Henry attended personally the feast of St Edmund (20 November) in 1235 and 1248[3] and nearly always included the abbey in the tours of East Anglian shrines which he was accustomed to make in Lent during the period of his personal rule.[4] When the barons were in power he no longer went on these Lenten pilgrimages. But in the autumn of 1272, when once more in control, he again stayed in the abbey from 2 to 12 September. While there he was afflicted by his final illness, from which he died at Westminster two months later (16 November).[5]

---

[1] *Bury Chron.*, p. 13.

[2] *Oboli de musca* were small gold coins used in thirteenth-century England for oblations and as part of a gold reserve, rather than for currency. They probably took their name from Murcia in southern Spain where gold coins were minted. See: Cook, 'The bezant in Angevin England', pp. 256, 262, 271–3; Carpenter, 'The gold treasure of King Henry III', in idem, *Henry III* (repr. from *Thirteenth Century England I: Proceedings of the Newcastle upon Tyne Conference 1987*, ed. P. R. Coss and S. D. Lloyd (Woodbridge, 1986), pp. 61–88), pp. 109 and n. 10, 111..

[3] CCR, 1234–7, p. 210; ibid., 1247–51, p. 127; Craib, *Itinerary of Henry III*, pp. 122, 204.

[4] For Henry III's Lenten pilgrimages to the East Anglian shrines see Powicke, *Henry III and the Lord Edward*, i. 80–1, 135, 190, 313, ii. 588.

[5] The St Albans' chronicle printed under the name of William Rishanger states that Henry fell gravely ill at St Edmunds: 'Et cum ad abbathiam Sancti Edmundi, regis et martyris, declinasset, gravi languore corripitur, qui eum non deseruit usque ad vitae finem.' *Willelmi Rishanger, quondam monachi S. Albani, et quorundam anonymorum, Chronica et Annales, regnantibus Henrico Tertio et Edwardo primo*, ed. H. T. Riley (RS, 1865), p. 74. Riley wrongly states in a caption in ibid., p. 75, that he died at St Edmunds, but the concluding phrase means that Henry did not forsake St Edmund, king and martyr, to the day he died – that is, his devotion to the saint survived until then. However, possibly the author confused (either deliberately or inadvertently or through ignorance) the fact that Henry died on the

Henry was a generous benefactor of the abbey church and of St Edmund's shrine. When he did not attend the saint's feast he seems regularly to have sent gifts. For example, on 20 November 1236 he ordered the sheriff of Norfolk to buy 8 *oboli de musca* and to offer them at St Edmund's altar on behalf of himself and the queen.[6] His gifts were often given in advance or retrospectively. For example, on 26 December 1238 he gave the sacrist £7 16s for the purchase of wax to make 300 tapers to be placed around the shrine on St Edmund's feast-day.[7] Indeed, gifts of wax to make 300 tapers, or sometimes more, for the feast, seem to have been Henry's usual practice.[8] He also made rich gifts in gold in various forms for the feast, to add to the splendour and glitter of the shrine. On 24 April 1242 he paid Edward of Westminster for acquiring thirty-two pieces of gold, each weighing ten pennyweight, of which the king sent eight pieces to the shrine of St Edmund on his feast-day; he sent the other pieces to Westminster – four at Christmas, four at Epiphany and sixteen on the feast of St Edward.[9] On 1 September 1252 he ordered the treasurer, Philip Lovel, and Edward of Westminster to have 'a fine crown with four flowers on its rim, worth £10 in all', to be hung on the shrine of St Edmund, as a gift from the king, and on 22 November he ordered them to send besides the crown 12 bezants and 12 *oboli de musca* 'to be at St Edmunds on Wednesday the saint's feast-day if possible'.[10] But as the writ was not issued until two days after the feast, Henry was too late. On 7 November 1257 he instructed John Walerand to buy 36 *oboli de musca* and to offer them, or have them offered, to the shrine on the feast-day; they were to be charged on the revenues of the abbey during the vacancy (31 December 1256 to 12 January 1258).[11] Queen Eleanor and the royal children attended the feast personally in that year and gave 30 bezants on the king's behalf.[12] And on 27 October 1262, while Henry was in France, he instructed the treasurer, John of Caux, to send 36 *oboli de musca* and 3 ounces of gold to be attached to the shrine of 'the blessed martyr Edmund' on his feast-day, as an offering from the king.[13]

Sometimes it is not clear from the records whether or not a gift was specifically for St Edmund's feast. For instance, on 8 February 1247 payment of £59 2s 5d was authorized to Henry de Frowik, goldsmith, for a golden communion cup worth 9 marks 10s, which the king had given to the abbey.[14] Similarly, on 3 February 1255 17 marks were allowed for the purchase of two gold buckles, one for St Edward and the other for St Edmund.[15] Henry's generosity was not

feast of St Edmund of Abingdon, and took this as a sign of his lasting devotion to the king and martyr. For Henry's death at Westminster see Powicke, op. cit, ii. 588.

6   C *Lib. R*, 1226–40, p. 246.
7   Ibid., p. 356.
8   See e.g. ibid., 1240–5, pp. 9, 90, 163, 264.
9   Ibid., p. 120.
10 *CCR*, 1251–3, pp. 153–4, 427. Bezants were small gold coins and originated in Byzantium.
11 Ibid., 1256–9, pp. 161–2.
12 C *Lib. R*, 1251–60, p. 428.
13 *CCR*, 1261–4, pp. 162–3.
14 C *Lib. R*, 1245–51, p. 106.
15 Ibid., 1251–60, p. 194.

limited to gifts of gold; he also gave other valuables. For example, on 30 June 1257 the sheriff of Norfolk and Suffolk was instructed to buy a cope of samite worth 10 marks, to be given to the prior and convent for the adornment of St Edmund's shrine.[16] Henry was especially generous when, or after, he had stayed in the abbey, notably during his Lenten tours of the East Anglian shrines. No doubt his gifts were partly intended as recompense for hospitality. A visit was normally preceded by a gift of wax for tapers to light the church and shrine. Thus, in 1242 Henry stayed in the abbey from 17 to 18 March; on 25 March, 1242, the sheriff was allowed on his account 75s for 100 lbs of wax for tapers to be put in St Edmund's church ready for the king's arrival.[17] He also gave, besides the wax, 9 *oboli de musca* (worth 15d each), and 3 bezants (worth 26d each) to be placed on St Edmund's shrine before he arrived.[18] While there, he gave two gold brooches of 14s 4d weight and 12 more *oboli de musca*.[19] In 1251, on 30 March, twelve days after a six-day visit, Henry allowed 44 marks from the issue of the general eyre to pay for four silver candlesticks placed around the shrine, besides 30 marks for the completion of the new altar front, and in addition gave generously to the parish churches and hospitals in Bury.[20] During his visit from 5 to 10 March 1256 Henry gave the abbot £20 to have the picture in front of the high altar finished, under the sheriff's view.[21]

Visits brought substantial temporal benefits as well as gifts to add to the splendour of the church and shrine. For example, shortly after his visit in June 1244, Henry sent the prior a cask of wine,[22] and, more important, while at St Edmunds in March 1251 he granted the sacrist thirty oaks from Inglewood for the repair of the belfry[23] and 40 marks for their transport.[24] Less than a week after his departure from St Edmunds in February 1234 Henry executed business to the abbey's advantage. The abbey had been in his hands from 29 August 1233, when Abbot Richard of the Isle died, until 1 February 1234, when Henry gave his assent to the election of his successor, Henry of Rushbrooke, and restored the temporalities. Shortly afterwards Henry spent two days in the abbey (12 to 14 February) and on 20 February, when at Thetford, he instructed the treasurer to allow £11 19s from the abbey's revenues during the vacancy, to pay for the alms distributed to the poor of Bury at Abbot Richard's funeral.[25] A visit also gave the abbot and convent a chance to impress on the king and whatever great person-

---

[16] Ibid., p. 383.

[17] C *Lib. R, 1240–5*, p. 114. For a similar grant in 1244 see ibid., p. 244.

[18] Ibid., p. 114.

[19] Ibid., p. 113.

[20] Ibid., *1245–51*, pp. 343–4.

[21] Ibid., *1251–60*, p. 275.

[22] CCR, *1242–7*, p. 202.

[23] CCR, *1247–51*, p. 423. Henry had made a similar grant of 20 oaks on 7 August, 1250; ibid., p. 311. See the next note.

[24] C *Lib. R, 1245–51*, p. 343. Later, in a writ of 9 June 1251, Henry gave the abbot and convent permission to use the 40 marks to buy more wood for the repair of the belfry; CCR, *1247–51*, p. 544.

[25] CCR, *1231–4*, p. 379.

ages were with him any immediate issues concerning St Edmunds' interests and rights and the nature of its liberties. On 21 March 1242 at Tivetshall, three days after visiting the abbey (17 to 18 March), Henry made two concessions in explicit recognition of its liberties: he instructed the treasurer to allow the abbot all murder fines and common fines, amercements of vills and tithings, and forfeitures levied by the recent justices in eyre within the Liberty of the eight and a half hundreds and from the abbot's tenants outside the Liberty:[26] and he instructed the justices of assizes to commit a case of novel desseisin concerning a tenement within St Edmund's *banleuca* to the abbot's steward.[27] Besides deferring to old liberties, the king granted new ones. On 19 March 1235, when staying in the abbey, he granted the abbot the right to hold two annual fairs in the suburbs of the town.[28]

Royal visits were costly occasions and disruptive to the religious life. But these disadvantages must have been weighed against the palpable advantages. Provided a visit did not last too long the monks may not have minded, especially as it added excitement to their lives and provided gorgeous spectacles. However, if the visit was a long one, they probably would usually have objected. This certainly seems to have been the case with regard to Henry's visit to St Edmunds in September, 1252. Matthew Paris asserts that the king stayed in the abbey for nearly three weeks 'to the great inconvenience of the house'.[29] Matthew slightly exaggerated the length of the visit – Henry was there for just over two weeks. However, he probably recorded the monks' reaction correctly.

---

[26] CCR, *1237–42*, pp. 404–5.
[27] Ibid., p. 434.
[28] CCR, *1234–7*, p. 61; C Ch. R, *1226–57*, p. 196.
[29] *Chron. Maj.*, v. 304; Craib, *Itinerary of Henry III*, p. 228. Henry had recently spent three days at St Albans, during August (ibid.). Perhaps someone from St Albans had joined the royal entourage.

Appendix I

An Inventory of Edmund of Walpole's Table-linen and Table-ware, date 20 August, 1253[*]

BL MS Harley 230, f. 183v: 'Die mercurii post assumpcionem beate marie fuerunt in panetaria E. abbatis anno suo quinto quando exiuit de langore, de mappis vij, unde due integer, una scilicet ix. ulnarum et alia quatuor et di[midium] sex manuterga integra. Tele iiij. qualibet xviij. ulnarum due saurenapes (*sic.* for *surnapes*) v. (?)portours (ports). Item una mappa noua, unum manutergium nouum.

Eodem die fuerunt in warderoba tres mappe noue (*interlined* una xx^ti ulnas alia xviij. tercia xiiij.) et duo manutergia noua duo surnapes, tria manutergia parua, quinque dupplicia, tria parua, quinque disci argentei, sex salsaria ponderis (*1 in. blank at end of line*) Tres cisti argentei quorum unus est de refectorario, duo petues, argentee cocleares xxiiij. septem pichere noue et vj. veteres ad uinum quatuor barelli ferrei.

In bitiliria (*2 lines deleted*)'

Translation: 'On Wednesday after the Assumption of the blessed Mary there were in the pantry in the fifth year of Abbot Edmund, when he recovered from illness, seven tablecloths, two of them perfect (one of nine ells and the other of four and a half), six towels in perfect condition, four [lengths of] cloth, each of 18 ells, two over-tablecloths, five 'porters' [?trays]. Item, one new tablecloth, one new towel.

On the same day there were in the wardrobe, three new tablecloths (one of twenty ells, of another eighteen, the third of fourteen) and two new towels, two over-tablecloths, three small towels [?napkins], five double [ones], three small, five silver dishes, six saltcellars weighing [blank], three silver cists (one of them is from the refectory), two patens [?], twenty-four silver spoons, seven new pitchers and six old ones for wine, four barrels [bound with] iron.

In the buttery (*entry of 2 lines deleted*)'

[*] Above p. 189.

Appendix II

The Story of Edward the Confessor's Gift of Mildenhall*

Possibly the story purporting to explain what prompted Edward the Confessor to give Mildenhall and the eight and a half hundreds to St Edmunds was a fiction composed to strengthen its claim to Mildenhall in its dispute with Richard de Clare in 1253. It relates that Edward came to St Edmunds, walking the last mile, out of veneration for the king and martyr. He was taken on a tour of the domestic buildings and on visiting the refectory, saw the young monks refreshing themselves on barley bread before their meal (*prandium*). Edward asked why this was and the monks told him that the church's possessions were not sufficient to allow them to have wheaten bread two or three times a day. 'The saintly king then said that, therefore, he gives the blessed Edmund the manor of Mildenhall lest the boys of his relative St Edmund (for thus he calls St Edmund), should in future eat barley-bread'. The story occurs in not quite identical versions in three of the abbey's registers: BL MSS Additional 14847, ff. 65–65v (Thomson, *Archives*, pp. 121–3 no. 1278 item 19)[1] and Harley 1005, f. 126v (ibid., pp. 142–5 no. 1293 cf. item 33); CUL MS Ff. ii. 29, f. 65 (ibid., pp. 130–1 no. 1284). The first two texts are in fourteenth-century hands – the Harley copy is in the hand of Henry of Kirkstead. The text in Ff. ii. 29 was probably written in the early fifteenth century. The story is not in the mid-twelfth century Bury version of the Worcester chronicle, now Bodl. Lib. MS Bodley 297, nor in the mainly hagiographic and historical compilation now Bodley 240 (cf. *Memorials*, i. 363–4, and Horstman, *Nova Legenda*, ii. 607–8). Moreover, the original writ itself granting the land at Mildenhall and the sokes of the eight and a half hundreds survives (Harmer, *Writs*, pp. 145–6, 154–5 no. 9), and contains no clause indicating that the grant was to help victual the monks. However, the *De Miraculis* (p. 48) composed c. 1100, contains what was perhaps the seed of the story. It can be paraphrased as follows. Edward came to St Edmunds, walking the last mile on foot, to venerate the martyred saint, and prayed for the good governance of the realm. Then he honoured the saint with royal revenues; he granted the eight and a half hundreds and he added the royal residence called Mildenhall so that the community of brethren and family serving God and the saint, might be fed as usual. All this was given permanent effect in a charter.[2] This passage

* Above p. 190.
1 This slightly longer version is printed in *Mon. Angl.*, iii. 154.
2 'Qua tunc suffragatorem reditibus imperialibus honorat, centurias *quas anglice hundrez vocant*, octo et semis sibi circum-circa se donat, regiamque mansionem nominee Milden-

in the *De Miraculis* seems to be based on Edward's writ. Apparently the sentence stating that the grant of Mildenhall was to ensure that the monks 'might be fed as usual' was an addition by the author of the *De Miraculis*. Presumably, by the time that work was composed the manor had been assigned to the cellarer.[3] What is especially remarkable about the story is its resemblance to one in the Abingdon chronicle. It relates that when Edward the Confessor came with his mother (Emma) and his wife (Edith) to Abingdon for hospitality, they were shown around the abbey's domestic quarters, and found the young monks in the refectory eating plain bread ('pane … insipientes') before the monks' meal. ('Because of the weakness of their age they needed pre-prandial refreshment.') Queen Edith asked why they had nothing better to eat. On being told that they hardly ever had anything else, she was moved to pious pity at the poverty of their food, and together with Edward, gave the monks her vill of Lewknor.[4] Although the Abingdon chronicle in its present form was compiled in the reign of Henry II it almost certainly used earlier, possibly pre-Conquest material, even perhaps some now lost abbatial history.[5] Therefore, possibly the story of Edward and Edith's gift of Lewknor, with its realistic touches, derived from an early source. If so, the story might have been known at St Edmunds c. 1100, when a copy of a version of the *De Miraculis* reached Abingdon.[6] Possibly Baldwin, abbot of St Edmunds (1065–97), knew Faritius, abbot of Abingdon (1100–17); both were physicians from abroad, the former becoming physician to Edward the Confessor and the latter to Henry I. Perhaps contact between them explains why a copy of the *De Miraculis* reached Abingdon.

hale his adauget, ut coetus fratrum illuc commanentium, Deo sanctoque famulantium, *ex his usualiter victitet.* Quae omnia caractere perpetuo caraxata.' *De Miraculis*, p. 48. The italics are mine. The fact that the author gives an English translation of *centurias* suggests that he used the original writ or a copy of it, in which case the last sentence is an addition. Otherwise he must have used a lost version of it. For the use of charters in the composition of the *De Miraculis* see Gransden, 'Composition and authorship of the *De Miraculis*', p. 22 and n. 173.

3   The separation of the abbot's property from that of the convent existed at St Edmunds before the Conquest and some of the convent's property had already been assigned to individual obedientiaries. See the text printed in D. C. Douglas, 'Fragments of an Anglo-Saxon survey from Bury St Edmunds', *EHR*, xliii (1928), pp. 281–3 passim, and Robertson, *Charters*, pp. 192–9 no. CIV, 221 no. CXIX.

4   *Chronicon Monasterii de Abingdon*, ed. Joseph Stevenson (RS, 1858, 2 vols) i. 461.

5   See Gransden, 'Traditionalism and continuity during the last century of Anglo-Saxon monasticism', *JEH*, xl (1989), pp. 187, 193, 198, repr. eadem, *Legends, Traditions and History*, pp. 59, 65, 70.

6   BN, MS lat. 2621, ff. 84–92v, printed Edmond Martène and Ursin Durand, *Veterum scriptorium et Monumentorum Historicum, Dogmaticorum, Moralium, Amplissima Collectio* (Paris, 1724–33, 9 vols), vi. coll 821–34. Described and collated with the manuscript in Gransden, 'Composition and authorship of the *De Miraculis*', pp. 6–7, 46–8 appendix C.

Appendix III

The Abbey's Economy in the mid-Thirteenth Century: the accounts in BL MS Harley 645 and related documents

1. Introductory

The importance of Edmund of Walpole's abbacy in a number of respects was discussed above. The period is also notable because to it belongs the first detailed information about the convent's system of estate management and financial control. The information is in sixty-six manorial and obedientiary accounts, together with some accounts of the obedientiaries' officials. They survive in copies preserved in the abbey's 'Kempe' register, BL MS Harley 645, ff. 193–9, 252–3, 260–5.[1] The accounts fall into two chronological groups: the first and largest group is of accounts dated variously from 1247 to 50; the second group is of those dated 1256–61. These accounts are far from a complete survey of the abbey's estates in the mid-thirteenth century. They are only of 21 of the 250 or so manors and vills belonging to the convent and, since most of the manors covered were among the most prosperous, the picture they give may not be quite representative of the convent's total holding. Nevertheless, they are an invaluable source for the history of the administration of the abbey's estates and of its economy, and more generally for the history of accounting in the middle ages.[2]

Paul Harvey, in a ground-breaking and learned paper, has subjected the palaeography and codicology of the accounts to exhaustive study, besides speculating about their purpose and establishing their importance in the history of accounting methods.[3] Originally, the accounts were copied on to bifolia, that is, large sheets of parchment which had been folded to form two folio-sized leaves. These bifolia were probably then assembled to form a booklet which by the end of the fourteenth century was bound into the 'Kempe' register, which is an impressive folio-sized volume containing copies of miscellaneous documents of the thirteenth and fourteenth centuries. It appears that the earlier group of accounts (those for 1247–50) was copied by six scribes and the later group (those for 1256–61) by three scribes.[4] A few other documents relating to

---

[1] See also above p. 187.
[2] See below, and n. 17.
[3] Harvey, 'Some mid-13th-century accounts', pp. 128–38. For a numbered list of the sixty-six accounts, with references to the scribe and with the folio numbers, see ibid., pp. 136–8. The top half of f. 194 is reproduced in ibid., pl. XXXII.
[4] Ibid., pp. 129, 136–7.

St Edmunds' financial situation in the mid-thirteenth century were copied into spaces by other scribes: among them is the résumé (f. 199) of the abbey's debts to Florentine merchants and other creditors which provides valuable evidence about the abbey's indebtedness but falls outside Paul Harvey's remit.

Paul Harvey points out that the purpose of the copies of the accounts with which he was concerned is problematical.[5] They are clearly of accounts which had been audited, but memoranda on them show that the audited accounts were later checked through and corrected. Initially, they were compiled from a number of account rolls. The accounts contain references to the cellarer's roll, the prior's roll, and to the roll of some official, apparently the barnkeeper.[6] There are also references to a roll for *metecorn* (the mixed corn allowance given to manorial employees).[7] The account for Whepstead refers to the roll of the previous year and a memorandum, probably by the compiler himself, states that 'all the particulars in the rolls are not specified here but only the major and more noteworthy items'.[8] One of the three accounts for Beccles has a note that it 'was drawn up from details in a certain old roll and a certain new roll written badly and across, but they were rehearsed before Alexander the bedell and Philip and Henry, who all give their agreement, and the details are entered in the rolls in Arabic numerals'.[9]

The accounts provide information about the audit itself and the auditing process. In the earlier group of accounts the auditors are not named or specified by office, but they are in two accounts in the later group: Robert, servant, and Nicholas of Semer rendered account in 1258 for the cellarer's manor of Semer, for the period 20 July 1257 to 15 May 1258, 'before Prior Robert and other monks'; and W. of Northwold ('Northwolde'), subcellarer, rendered account for the year from 22 August 1259 'before the prior and others with him'.[10] The accounts have many details about the auditing process. They reveal the quite frequent use of tallies rather than written evidences. Thus, for the year 1258–9 the cellarer, John of Mildenhall, paid the kitchener, William of Ramsey, £72 by tally.[11] The accounts for the expenses of the subcellarer, 'W.', for six months, 1249–50, for £38 11s 6d were by tally: a memorandum records that although the expenses of Colin, apparently the barnkeeper, exceeded receipts, his expenditure on peas and grain was not allowed because he had no tallies.[12] Again, the expenditure of the reeve, Martin, on malt grout in the year 1247–8 exceeded receipts, but was not allowed because 'he had neither roll nor tallies'.[13] And in the background is evidence for oral transactions. These are especially revealing

5   Harvey, art. cit., pp. 129–30.
6   Harley 645, ff. 193v[b], 260[a], 194[a] respectively. '[a]' here represents the top half of a folio, and '[b]' the bottom half.
7   Harvey, art. cit., p. 32.
8   F. 197[b].
9   F. 252v[b]. Harvey, art. cit., p. 133 and n. 21.
10 Ff. 261[a], 262v[a].
11 F. 262[b].
12 F. 194[b].
13 F. 197v[b].

of the care taken by the auditors to secure for the abbey what was due to it. At Horringer the auditors ordered inquiry to be made concerning fuel owed by Sawbridgeworth in the year 1247–8.[14] The expenses for malt of Colin (? the barnkeeper) in August, 1249, exceeded receipts so that 23¼d was owed to him, but a memorandum records that they had not been witnessed by a monk or a servant'.[15] A memorandum in the accounts for Southery for 1248–9 records that the auditors ordered a diligent inquiry to be made as to how the shortfall of 27s 2d in receipts from fixed rents could be recovered: the names of the defaulting tenants are listed.[16]

These accounts are especially valuable in the history of accounting because they are a rare example of the methods employed on one of England's most extensive and highly privileged liberties. They represent an intermediate stage in accounting history, prior to the introduction of the systematic, formal methods of the late thirteenth century. For example, once methods were formalized, accounts normally ran for a year dating from Michaelmas, but the periods covered by our accounts are by no means uniform: most cover approximately a year, but some are for shorter periods. The kitchener's and subcellarer's accounts in the second (later) group are all for a year and the moneyer's account for approximately two years which suggests a move towards regular annual accounting.[17] Only sixteen of the accounts record the date when the account was rendered and, again, there was no uniformity. The accounts for Chepenhall, Southwold, Barton, Pakenham, Bradfield, Warkton, Hinderclay, Stanton and Beccles, were rendered immediately on, or nearly on,[18] or even just before, the account's closing date, but those for Horringer, Southery and Warkton were rendered early in the following year.[19] The accounts for Chepenhall, Southwold, Barton, Pakenham, Bradfield, Rougham, Hinderclay, Stanton and Beccles were all rendered on dates between 16 and 20 July inclusive.[20]

By the end of the thirteenth century the accepted model for accounts was two sections, charge (receipts) and discharge (expenses) ending with the sum total under each heading. Under these headings the items were arranged in this order – cash, corn and stock: the two sections each end with the total receipts and expenses; the final balance concludes the accounts. Our accounts do not conform rigidly to this systematic arrangement. For example, the accounts for Mildenhall begin the respective sections with the total receipts and expenses.[21] Nor is the factual content of the accounts uniform. The corn accounts provide

---

[14] F. 194v[a], marginal note.

[15] F. 194[a].

[16] F. 197[a]. The shortfall coincided with years of crop failure and famine. See below pp. 285–7.

[17] For the early history of manorial accounts from 1155 to the early thirteenth century see Harvey, 'Pipe Rolls and the adoption of demesne farming in England', pp. 345–52. See also: idem, *Manorial Records*, pp. 3, 25–41; Bailey, *The English Manor*, esp. pp. 105–6.

[18] Harvey, 'Some mid-13th-century accounts', pp. 136–7 nos 15–20, 30–1, 42–4.

[19] Ibid., p. 136 nos 13, 21–2, 29.

[20] Ibid., pp. 136–7 nos 16–20, 42–4.

[21] F. 197v.

examples of considerable variation. The account for Chepenhall lists receipts from the sale of wheat, barley, peas, beans and oat, and from grain for milling, besides the cost of purchasing seed corn, but does not record what was stored in the barn.[22] The accounts for Icklingham record the yield of rye, what was taken from it for seed, and what remained for sale, besides the yield of oats and peas: a memorandum notes the amount stored in the barn for *metecorn*.[23] The accounts for Barton record receipts from the sale of wheat, rye, barley, oats, peas and barley malt respectively, and the cost of purchasing wheat, rye and bean seed: and a memorandum notes the amount stored in the barn to meet the require-ments of the manor's food farm.[24] (The question of the abbey's food farms will be discussed later.) Similarly, the accounts for Pakenham list income from wheat, rye, barley, peas and barley malt while a memorandum notes what was stored in the barn for the food farm.[25]

The stock accounts show even wider variations. Thus, some of the accounts entirely omit stock, and those for Icklingham merely record the total receipt from sale of stock, with no details of what was sold. On the other hand, the accounts for Mildenhall list the animals and related items sold – untanned hides, oxen, pigs, stots (horses or heifers), calves, sheep-skins, lambs and wool: but they do not record the number of each kind of animal or item, and aggre-gate the income from sales.[26] The greatest detail about a manor's stock is in the accounts for Aylsham.[27] The servant and bedell report to the auditors, 1248–9, as follows:

1 bull
2 oxen
11 cows
2 calves aged two and a half years, 1 male
4 calves aged between one and two years (*superannati*), 1 male, 3 female
18 female sheep (*mitonae*)
46 ewes in lamb
30 hogs, 13 male, 17 female
42 lambs, 27 male, 15 female
6 pigs
1 sow
6 cheeses remain
4 old swans
6 cygnets
65 geese

As pointed out above, these accounts are the earliest to survive from St Edmunds. This raises the question why at this time the monks were preserving

[22] F. 195ª.
[23] F. 260ᵇ.
[24] F. 195ᵇ.
[25] Ibid.
[26] F. 197vª.
[27] F. 260vª.

written accounts. In so doing they were in fact abreast of the current movement among greater landowners towards the keeping, auditing and preservation of accounts. These accounts were in roll form. The magnificent series of account rolls surviving from St Swithuns, Winchester, begin in 1208–9 and stray rolls survive from other great landowners from about that time.[28] Similar rolls were the source of our accounts. The development of account keeping was partly the result of landowners' day-to-day experience and common sense, but in the case of the religious orders it was also a response to the reforming initiatives of the papacy – to injunctions issued by papal visitors (for instance to St Edmunds in 1234)[29] and by the General Chapter of the Benedictines of the Southern Province in 1249.[30] More specifically, there is the question why our accounts in particular were extracted from account rolls, copied on to individual pages and probably assembled as a booklet. Paul Harvey's proposed explanation is very plausible. He suggests that what survives is part of drafts of two successive surveys of the abbey's estates and financial position made to inform Edmund of Walpole and Simon of Luton respectively at the beginning of their abbacies.[31] Obviously, it is unlikely that the text of either group of accounts would have been given to the abbot concerned in its present untidy, haphazard form: Harvey postulates that fair copies would have been made based on these drafts. This suggestion is the more convincing because, as we saw earlier, both Samson and Hugh of Northwold had commissioned such surveys to be made shortly after their successions.[32] Although there seems to be no evidence that Richard of Ely and Henry of Rushbrooke did likewise they may well have followed the precedent established by their predecessors. Parallel examples survive from other churches. Roger, bishop of Worcester, had a survey made of the bishopric of Worcester soon after his consecration in 1164.[33] Similarly, one of the first acts of Ralph Diceto on his appointment as dean of St Paul's in 1180 was to compile a survey of the property of the chapter. Having completed this by 8 January 1181, he made a survey of the churches belonging to the bishopric.[34] Later, Walter Langton, who was elected bishop of Coventry and Lichfield on 19 February 1296, granted his temporalities on 16 June and consecrated on 23 December,

---

[28] *The Pipe Rolls of the Bishopric of Winchester*, ed. Hubert Hall (London, 1903), cited Harvey, *Manorial Records*, p. 25 n. 1, and idem, 'Pipe Rolls and the adoption of demesne farming', p. 345.

[29] 'Visitation', ed. Graham, pp. 733–4, 735. See above, p. 205.

[30] *Chapters*, ed. Pantin, i. 36. See above p. 200.

[31] Harvey, 'Some mid-13th-century accounts', pp. 129–30. See above p. 187.

[32] Above, pp. 24–5, 164. In 1251, when Hugh of Northwold (formerly abbot of St Edmunds) was bishop of Ely, he had the obligations of the villeins on nearly all his manors minutely described. Miller, *Ely*, p. 78.

[33] Mary [G.] Cheney, *Roger, Bishop of Worcester*, pp. 107–12, citing *The Red Book of Worcester*, ed. Marjorie Hollings, Worcester Historical Soc. (1934–50, 4 vols with continuous pagination). See also Cheney, *Bishops Chanceries*, pp. 110–19 and n. 2.

[34] See: Diceto, *Historical Works*, i. lv–lxi; W. H. Hale, *Domesday of St Paul's of the Year 1222* (Camden Soc., o.s., 1858); Gransden, *Historical Writing*, [i]. 234 and nn. 123–4.

was already in March 1298 in possession of a survey of the bishopric's estates.[35] These three examples represent others not noticed here, but should suffice to show that practice at St Edmunds conformed with that of similar ecclesiastical institutions at that time.

2. The contents of the accounts

(a) General

The contents of the accounts are so numerous and varied that it is impossible to do justice to them all in the limited space appropriate to the present study. Here, a few subjects will be touched on in order to give as overall an idea of the economy of convent's estates as possible. Then we shall see what light the accounts, considered together with related evidence, throw on three topics: the role of the treasurer/treasurers; the obedientiary system; and the system of food farms. The information on the abbey's watermills and windmills is reserved for a general survey in appendix IV. The section in the accounts on the abbey's debts and that containing the moneyer's accounts were referred to in our main text above. It should be remembered in any discussion of the Harley accounts that the omission of any record of certain receipts or items of expenditure does not prove that record of them never existed; possibly they were recorded in different, now lost, accounts. The Harley accounts, therefore, not only cover just a fraction of St Edmunds' total holdings, but also cannot be trusted to give a full picture of its economy on the estates with which they are concerned.

The accounts relate, of course, to the abbey's secular affairs and information about the monks' religious commitment is not to be expected. However, although the practice of dating days according to the anniversaries of saints on which they fell was so universal in the thirteenth century that it can have had no specific intention,[36] nevertheless, it would have reminded the monks of the liturgical observances of those saints and of the delicious food served on some of the major feast-days, including the pittances served then and on the anniversaries of abbots and of notable monks and benefactors. More particularly, the subcellarer's accounts for 29 April to 29 December 1249 record that 9d was paid to the kitchener for wafers (*wafres*, apparently a kind of sweet biscuit with a savoury topping) for the feasts of St Edmund and St Nicholas, and his accounts for 24 August 1260 to 2 June 1261 that 3s 5½d was paid for *nebulae* (*nebula*, apparently a wafer biscuit, ? an obley) and wafers for the feast of St Edmund and in Lent.[37] The cost of bell-ringing on saints' days is included among minor expenses in the sacrist's accounts for 28 February to 29 September 1249: those

---

35 Staffordshire Record Office, D (W) 1734/J2268. I am indebted for this reference and information about the survey to Dr Jill Hughes.

36 Cheney and Jones, *Handbook*, pp. 59–63.

37 Harley 645, ff. 193v[b], 265[a]. The pittance on the anniversary of Abbot Samson included *nebulae* and *wafres*. *Bury Cust.*, p. 55 line 8. The monks' food, including wafers, is discussed in my *Bury St Edmunds*, ii, appendix II.

for Icklingham for 29 September 1248 to 22 February 1249 record 2s 6d spent buying fish for the feast of Relics, and 7s 9d 'for feasting the servants on the three feasts and for the [servants'] drink on three other days of solemnities, that is for holingsilver' etc. ('In conuiuio seruientum ad tria festa et in potu eorum per tres alios dies solempnes, scilicet in holingsilu' vij. s. 9d.'[38]) Expenditure recorded for the provision of candles in the abbey church and elsewhere is noticed below.

Accounts for the almoner are not included in the Harley collection and, therefore, almsgiving does not figure in what we have. Nevertheless, they illustrate the support St Edmunds gave to the nuns of St George's, Thetford, the nunnery founded by Abbot Hugh I in c. 1160.[39] The monks maintained close links with the nunnery throughout the middle ages. The accounts of the manorial receivers for the year 1249/50 record the payment of 2s to the nuns,[40] and the subcellarer's account for the year 1249/50 records the payment to them of ½ mark 'on the fifteenth days in the past year ('monialibus de Thetford pro liberatione in 15 dierum de anno preterito dimidium marc')'.[41] Other evidence of the abbey's relations with the nunnery is discussed below.

Unsurprisingly, many of the items in the accounts concern agriculture. There is, for example, a reference to marling, a practice which by the end of the thirteenth century was recognized as an excellent way of increasing the productivity of the soil.[42] The accounts for Semer for 20 July 1257 to 15 May 1258 record that 5s 2½d was spent on marling 1 acre, 3 rods of land.[43] The fact that the accounts do not often refer to labour services should not be taken as evidence that their use was becoming outmoded on St Edmunds' estates since, apparently, manorial accounts often omit them.[44] The notices of them in the accounts include references to their sale. The entries are as follows: the accounts for Nowton, 9 April to 1 August 1249, record that the officials had not answered for hens, eggs, geese or labour services (*de operibus*); the accounts for Aylsham for the year from 29 September 1248/9 similarly record that the officials had only answered for labour services 'in bulk' ('de operibus non respondent nisi in grosso'); the accounts for Warkton for the year from 29 September record

---

38 F. 260[a–b].
39 See: *Mon. Angl.*, iv. 475–6; J. C. Cox in *VCH Norfolk*, ii. 355–7; Binns, *Dedications*, p. 87; Thompson, *Women Religious*, p. 64. More will be said about St George's, Thetford, in my *Bury St Edmunds*, ii.
40 F. 199[a].
41 F. 262v[b]. That is, on the quindene, in fact calculated as the fourteenth day after a church festival.
42 Marl (*marla*), a kind of soil consisting of clay mixed with lime. Knowledge of the value of marl as a fertilizer dates back at latest to the end of the eleventh century but its use only began to be at all general, and then only on the largest estates, in the course of the thirteenth century. See: Miller and Hatcher, *Rural Society*, pp. 214–15; Hallam, *Rural England*, pp. 14, 61, 62, 251; R. A. Donkin in *New Historical Geography*, p. 92; R. E. Donkin in ibid., p. 154. Our accounts show that agricultural methods on St Edmunds estates were well up-to-date. Details of the marling of the abbot's manor of Tivetshall, Norfolk, dated 1250, are in Harley 230, f. 184.
43 Harley 645, f. 261[b].
44 Harvey, 'Some mid-13th-century accounts', p. 132 and n. 18.

receipts of £5 19s 5½d, 'sometime more, sometimes less', for the sale of labour services, and those for the period from 29 September 1249 to 5 May 1250 record receipt of £4 2s for their sale.[45] Thus, the accounts indicate that St Edmunds, along with other comparable, contemporary landholders,[46] was moving towards a more money-based economy. To fill any shortfall in its labour force, St Edmunds hired labourers. Our accounts provide examples of this practice, a few of which will be cited here. Thus, the Semer accounts for 20 July 1257 to 15 May 1258 record payment of 9s 10d in wages to two carters, a cowherd, a shepherd, a miller and a 'girl' (*ancilla*), and for the period from 29 September until Pentecost 8s 6d in wages to four ploughmen, a shepherd, a miller and a 'girl'. Similarly, the Icklingham accounts for 22 February to 29 September 1249 record payment of 5½d to 'a certain harrower' (*herciator*), and those for Horringer for 3 July 1257 to 18 May 1258 record payment of 5s 4d for the hire of reapers in the autumn.[47]

The accounts paint an overall picture of the kind of mixed farming typical of medieval husbandry. Nevertheless, they reveal distinctive features in some of the St Edmunds' holdings. Woodland, for example, produced timber for building and firewood, which the monks could either use or sell.[48] This can be illustrated by the accounts for Chelsworth, Hinderclay and Warkton, which record the value of the timber, brushwood and the like produced by the extensive woods at those places. Accounts for Chelsworth for the year from 25 July 1248 to 1 August 1249 record receipt of 38s 6d from the sale of brushwood, bark and loppings from thirty-nine trees felled in the wood.[49] The accounts for Hinderclay manor for the eight months from 29 September 1248 to 17 July 1249 record 48s 6d from the sale of brushwood,[50] besides 39s 4d from the sale of bark and loppings 'from fourteen trees sent to the mill at Beccles, and from trees [felled] in the newly fossed [wood] and in the old hedged [one] to be used for enclosing the wood'.[51] The manor of Warkton, in Northamptonshire, together with the nearby hamlets of Geddlington and Bucton, lay within the royal forest of Rockingham.[52] There-

---

45 Ff. 197^a, 260v^{a-b}, 198^a, 198^b, respectively.

46 See: Miller and Hatcher, *Rural Society*, esp. pp. 124–6, 222–4, 238–9; Bailey, *The English Manor*, esp. pp. 27–31 passim.

47 Ff. 261^a bis, 260^b, 260^a, respectively.

48 For St Edmunds' woodlands see esp. Rackham, 'The abbey woodlands', pp. 139–60 and pls XXXIV A and B. For St Edmunds' woodlands in a national (and international) context see idem, *Ancient Woodland. Its History, Vegetation and Uses in England* (London, 1980, new edn Castlepoint Press, Colvend, 2003), pp. 24–32, 153, 197, 223, 242, 277–8, with many figs.

49 F. 194v^{a-b}.

50 F. 252v^a.

51 Ibid.: 'Et memorandum quod xxxix.s. iiii.d. qui capti fuerunt de cortice et ramuli. xiiii. arboribus missis ad molendinum de Beccles et de arboribus in nouo fossato et ueteri sepe, expon[endis] in claustura bosci.'

52 Later, in 1299, under Abbot John of Northwold, the sacrist, John of Eversden, persuaded the justices of the forest to disafforest Warkton. *Bury Chron.*, pp. 158–9. For an inquisition concerning venison between the men of Warkton and other vills held in 1248 before the justices of the Forest see G. J. Turner, *Select Pleas of the Forest* (Selden Soc., xiii, 1901), p. 89. For the royal forests, with a sketch map showing their extent in Northants. see M. L. Bazeley, 'The extent of the English forest in the thirteenth century', *TRHS*, 4th ser. iv

fore, the timber belonged to the king, but St Edmunds had the right to pannage, that is payments from tenants pasturing pigs in the forest: the account for the manor for 1248/9 records the receipt of 44d from pannage.[53] Another distinctive feature of the Warkton accounts is the reference to socage tenants (*socieresmol*, *socerelesmol*)[54] and socage jurisdiction (*soca forinseca, forinseca socna*).[55] Socage tenants were free tenants who had a right to the land they occupied but owed suit of count and various customary dues, but generally not those of the most burdensome sort, to a lord. Groupings of these free tenancies formed a 'soke' which came to denote a jurisdictional area under one lord.[56] Sokes, sokemen and socage tenure were characteristics of the ancient Danelaw, the region under Danish rule in the eleventh century which included East Anglia and North-amptonshire. In the course of the thirteenth century this ancient system tended to be subsumed into the hundredal and manorial systems, but survived in many places, including on St Edmunds estates. Sokemen and socage tenure appear, for example, in Abbot Samson's charters,[57] and our accounts illustrate their survival in the neighbourhood of Warkton.

Another manor with distinctive features was Mildenhall. It lay on the edge of the Breckland, the sandy region much used in the middle ages and, indeed, continuously until the mid-twentieth century, for rabbit farming. The rabbits usually lived in artificially built mounds enclosed by banks. The landlord leased these warrens or employed a warrener.[58] The ruins of the fifteenth-century warrener's house still stand near Mildenhall.[59] The Mildenhall accounts for the year from 17 October 1247 to 11 October 1248 record receipt of 15s from the warren. The accounts also include Elveden, lying in the Breckland about six and a half miles to the east of Mildenhall; included among Elveden's receipts is a record of 9s 6d from 'Breckland warren' ('war' Brekelnd').[60] Mildenhall lay on the river Lark and was one of the abbey's manors with a watermill and fishery (fisheries often existed as part of the complex of canals, sluices and weirs built

(1921), pp. 40–72. For the rights enjoyed by landholders in the royal forests see C. R. Young, *The Royal Forests of Medieval England* (Leicester, 1979), pp. 74–113.

[53] F. 198$^{a–b}$.

[54] F. 198$^{a, b}$.

[55] F. 198^{a} bis, ^{b}.

[56] Scholars are not agreed about the origin of the system and exact nature of socage tenure, see e.g.: Miller and Hatcher, *Rural Society*, esp. pp. 21–5 passim, 87, 182; Hallam, *Rural England*, esp. pp. 22–3, 29–30, 69, 71–2; Homans, *English Villagers*, pp. 110, 113, 118, 192, 233, 249; Kosminsky, *Agrarian History*, pp. 133, 137–8, 265; Miller, *Ely*, pp. 25–6, 34, 50, 52–3; R. Welldon Finn, *The Eastern Counties* (London, 1967), esp. pp. 139, 189, 199, 205; King, *Peterborough Abbey*, pp. 25–7, 55–8, 117–19. The 'Soke' of Peterborough is a well known example of the survival of the nomenclature and jurisdictional area.

[57] *Kalendar*, ed. Davis, pp. xxxii, xl–xlvii, with refs.

[58] Rosemary Hoppit in *Historical Atlas of Suffolk*, pp. 68–9 with maps, 200–1; Bailey, *The English Manor*, pp. 4–5, 24, 110; idem, 'The rabbit and the medieval East Anglian economy', pp. 1–20; for a lively picture of a warren in the Luttrell Psalter, with a dog hunting the rabbits, see above, pl. Xa. Also reproduced in black and white in Backhouse, *Luttrell Psalter*, p. 32, and in colour in Brown (ed.), *Luttrell Psalter*.

[59] Hoppit, loc. cit., p. 201 n. 10.

[60] F. 197v$^{a–b}$.

to control a mill's supply of water power[61]): the accounts include the purchase of 'one net' among its minor expenses.[62] Icklingham was another manor on the Lark combining mill and fishery and its accounts for 29 September 1258 to 22 February 1249 record payment of 3s to Humfry (*Humfridus*) a fisherman and 12d for buying nets;[63] and the accounts for 22 February to 29 September 1249 record the expenditure of 13s 11d on the fishery, aggregating the cost of nets, stocking the water and the fisherman's/fishermen's wages ('in retibus, stauro et stipendiis piscatoris, viij.s. xi.d.').[64]

The accounts show that the monks' aim in the management of their estates was to prevent dilapidation of buildings, to construct new ones when considered necessary and to maintain, and if possible improve, the fertility of the soil and so increase productivity. Small sums spent on repairs and improvements would have been included in cumulative entries as 'minor expenses', but the accounts contain enough individual entries recording the more important works to illustrate the monks' activity in order to prevent any deterioration in the value of their holdings and to increase the value if possible. For example, the subchamberlain's accounts 1249/50 record a mark spent on a new building next to the taylor's workshop.[65] Similarly, the subsacrist's accounts for 1259/60 and 1260/1 record payment of: 24s 6½d for 'a certain wooden wall in the bake-house' (presumably in the abbey) and 14s for 'a certain stable for horses and a pigsty';[66] and 47s ¾d 'for a furnace and for making furnaces' ('in uno furno et furnenses faciend").[67]

The monks' concern to preserve the productivity of their manors appears in a number of contexts. The number of animals should not be allowed to fall: the official, Colin, having made half a mark for the sale of wool, was ordered to use it to buy more sheep, and auditors of the accounts for Horringer pointed out that the servant and bailiff had received 71s for the sale of stock but only spent 13s on replacing it.[68] Particular concern was for yields of grain and pulses. For example, the accounts for Mildenhall for 1247/8 include a column listing the yield of the year's harvest:

[61] For fishponds see: Darby, *Medieval Fenland*, pp. 14, 21, 23–32, 42, 50, 54–5, 90, 120, 121, 154; J. M. Steane, 'The medieval fish-ponds of Northamptonshire', *Northants Past and Present*, ix no. 5 (1970–1), pp. 299–310. For esp. references to the connection of some with watermills see e.g.: J. McDonnell, *Inland Fisheries*; and the beautiful and precise picture in Luttrell Psalter, reproduced in colour in Backhouse, op. cit., p. 31 pl. 30, and in black and white in Gies and Gies, *Cathedral, Forge, and Waterwheels*, p. 113, and above, pl. Xb.

[62] F. 197v^b. Of course nets would also be used for fishing in the river.

[63] F. 260^a.

[64] F. 260^b.

[65] F. 252 col. 2.

[66] F. 265^a.

[67] Ibid.

[68] Ff. 194^b, 194v^a respectively.

276 loads of wheat
144 loads of rye
30 loads 3 measures of barley
85 loads 3 sieves of peas.[69]

A careful eye was kept on the value of renders in kind and cash. The Mildenhall accounts note that 'a load of grain by the "new measure" was worth to the lord only three sieves as much as the old measure by which the servants took *metecorn*'. ('Et memorandum quod vna sum[ma] de noua mensura non valet domino nisi tres siues quantum ad mensuram ueterem per quam seruientes capiunt metecorn.'[70]) The 'new measure' is mentioned again in a memorandum in the subcellarer's accounts for 1250 which notes that he received wheat and malt according to the new measure.[71] The accounts for Nowton for the year 1259/60 give details of the yields of wheat, rye, barley, oats, peas and beans, recording any increase and the amount sold.[72] As pointed out above, the accounts cover a year beginning in the second year of the 1258/9 famine and note shortfalls in the supply of grain and peas owing to the failure of two of the food farms – Pakenham and Whepstead.[73]

The primary aim of the monks' economic strategy was to supply their own needs; only the surplus produce was sold. Thus, an entry in the accounts for Horringer for 1247/8 records receipt of 14d for the sale of lambs' wool 'without the sheep's wool which the cellarers (sic) took for the use of the convent'.[74] Nevertheless, large quantities of produce were sold and the accounts reflect the monks' concern for its value. This is well illustrated by the subcellarer's corn account for the fourteen months from 29 April 1249 to 29 June 1250. A memorandum lists the price of wheat in successive runs of weeks throughout that period: for the first nine weeks it sold for 3s and more, but less than 4s; for the next six weeks it sold for 4s and more, but less than 5s; for the next 34 weeks it sold for 5s and more, but less than 6s; for nine weeks in the following year it sold for 7s, but for less than 8s.[75] This steady rise in prices suggests that possibly the wheat was released for sale slowly, much being kept in reserve to produce an artificial shortage and so to increase the price. This memorandum follows details of the profit (*commodium*) made from the sale of grain at various periods throughout the year; the total is given as £47 10s 5½d, 'that is for 278½ loads, three bushels'.[76] Profits made from the sale of surplus produce constituted an essential element in the monastic economy. The money was used to reduce the burden of debt and to buy goods which the monks' manors did not produce at all or not in sufficient quantities – nor, perhaps, of good enough quality. As will

---

[69] F. 197v^b.
[70] F. 198^a.
[71] F. 198v^a.
[72] F. 262^a.
[73] Above p. 254 and n. 16.
[74] F. 194v^a.
[75] F. 198v^b.
[76] Ibid.

be seen below, the chamberlain's accounts show that he purchased many items, among them ready-made clothing and footwear, besides cloths and leathers for their manufacture in the chamberlain's own workshops. Likewise, gastronomic delicacies – spices, almonds and rice – were purchased. His deputy, the subchamberlain and his officials travelled widely to markets and fairs to make their various purchases.

I shall discuss the monks' active participation in commercial life in the last half of the thirteenth century more fully in the second volume of my history of St Edmunds abbey, because as the years advanced, so did the commercialization of the abbey's economy. However, it is clear from the Harley accounts that the monks, like other landlords, were already by the middle of the century buying and selling quantities of goods. They sold surplus crops, straw, brushwood and the like, and whatever farm produce not needed for their and their servants' consumption, besides animals – the latter tended to be sold in the autumn to save the cost of feeding them during the winter. Such sales produced considerable income. For example, the subcellarer's accounts for Horringer for 3 July 1257 to 18 May 1258 record receipt of £4 5s 8d from the sale of four oxen, one bull, two cows, twenty-one pigs, four piglets, twenty-five sheep, wool, hens and eggs, and 11s 4¾d from sale of cheese and butter,[77] while those for Nowton for 1 August 1259 to 7 July record receipt of 53s 10¼d from sale of two cows, seven cow-hides, two stots, the hide of one stot, eight pigs, one bullock, three calves, the fleeces of eighty-one sheep, besides cheese, hens and eggs.[78] The Nowton accounts also note that from a total of 125 cheeses produced, seventy-two were sold, four given to the lord and nine paid as tithe.[79] The kitchener's accounts record that he received 18s for the sale of honey and herring.[80]

In the same year as the subcellarer sold livestock from the manor of Semer, he bought an ox and six sheep for 12s 8d. Examples of the purchase of grain, livestock and so forth could be multiplied, but I shall end by mentioning one commodity much needed by the monks, that is wine. Wine served two essential purposes, one was for the post-eucharistic drink and the other was for convivial occasions – to celebrate great feast-days (Christmas, Easter, Pentecost and the Assumption of the Virgin Mary). Pittances on the anniversaries of, for example, Abbot Samson, Abbot Baldwin and King Richard, included wine among the luxuries then enjoyed by the monks, and wine was also served for the entertainment of important guests and it might be used as gifts. The Bury Customary (of c. 1234) has a number of references to the entitlement of the monks to wine on particular occasions[81] and so do other documents in the abbey's archives. There is a list of the eighty-five places in the seven deaneries within St Edmunds Liberty

[77] F. 261v[a–b].
[78] F. 261v[a].
[79] F. 262[a].
[80] F. 262[b].
[81] *Bury Cust.*, pp. 19 lines 15, 24, 30 passim and n. 1, 33 line 1, 44 line 38, 54 § 2, 55 line 7. See also the Compromise (of c. 1214), ibid., p. 105 line 1. The thirteenth-century regulations to promote economy mention muscatel (*muscus*), ibid., p. 109 line 9. For pittances with wine see e.g. BL MS Harley 1005, f. 91. For wine drunk by the Westminster monks

to which the sacrist made allowances of wine, a total of 4½ sesters.[82] Another
list of the wine to which the chaplains in the town, the monks in the refectory,
the choir-boys (cantors) and the prior on certain days ends by recording that the
total wine required was 405 sesters and 'thus 8 casks are enough, counting 55
sesters to each'.[83] The monks, of course, had their own vineyard and made wine,
but not enough to meet the need. Besides, muscatel (*musca*), a strong, sweet
Spanish wine, was sometimes served and this obviously had to be bought. Our
accounts record wine (but do not specify muscatel) among the numerous items
bought by the sacrist in the nine months from 28 February to 29 September
1249: he spent £24 17s buying wine and 57s 7d on the vineyard (*vinea*). This
was a considerable proportion of the total recorded expenditure of £92 19s 4d.
In a concluding memorandum the accountant reports that he has 8 casks of wine
worth £8 in store.[84]

(b) The treasurer/treasurers

The Customary of St Edmunds refers to a 'treasurer',[85] while the Harley accounts
and other records sometimes refer to 'treasurers'.[86] But whether there was one
treasurer or whether there were two or more treasurers, the purpose of the
office was to establish some central control over the abbey's finances and estate
management, in order to prevent extravagance and maladministration by individual obedientiaries and their subordinants. The evidence from St Edmunds
shows that in the thirteenth century the monks took steps similar to those taken
in other major religious houses to achieve these ends. The most thoroughgoing
system was adopted at Christ Church, Canterbury. By the late twelfth century
the monks had more or less completely centralized the priory's finances: the
obedientiaries paid nearly all their revenues into the treasury and the treasurers
disbursed appropriate sums to meet the obedientiaries' current expenses.[87] In the
course of the thirteenth century other houses adopted various systems whereby
treasurers checked extravagance and mismanagement, but generally the limitations they imposed on the financial autonomy of obedientiaries were less
stringent than at Christ Church.[88] A common arrangement was for the obedientiaries to pay a small proportion of their revenues into the treasury, thus creating

see Harvey, *Living and Dying*, pp. 44, 58, 59, 62, 93 and index p. 291 under 'wine' for more
references.
[82] BL MS Harley 645, f. 259.
[83] BL MS Harley 1005, f. 217, and *Pinch. Reg.*, i. 399–400.
[84] F. 260v[b].
[85] *Bury Cust.*, pp. xxx–xxxiii passim, 56–62 passim. See also the Compromise (of c. 1214),
ibid., pp. 108–10 passim.
[86] Often it is impossible to know whether there was just one treasurer because the Latin text
is abbreviated to *thes'* or *thesaur'*. See e.g. the cellarers' accounts for 1283–6, Harley 645,
ff. 230v–231.
[87] R. A. L. Smith, *Canterbury Cathedral Priory* (Cambridge, 1943), pp. 14–25, 27–8; idem,
'The central financial system of Christ Church, Canterbury, 1186–1512', *EHR*, lv (1940),
pp. 353–69.
[88] See Snape, *Monastic Finances*, pp. 37–52. For the treasurer's office at Westminster see

a reserve fund, from which the treasurer or treasurers would disburse sums to obedientiaries to supplement their incomes when necessary.

At St Edmunds the first attempts to prevent extravagance and mismanagement were made by the abbots, notably by Samson who took over management of the cellary.[89] This had aroused fierce opposition from the convent, partly for the reason that by confusing the two portions of property and rights belonging to the abbot and convent respectively, Samson exposed the convent's portion to the risk of royal demands being made on it as if it were part of the abbot's feudal fee. This was an especially alarming prospect in view of future vacancies. The appointment of a monastic treasurer or treasurers helped the convent control expenditure without abbatial intervention. It seems likely that the new office was a result of the reforming statutes issued by the papal visitation of St Edmunds in July 1234: it was, as it were, a corollary to the system of audit ordained by the visitors. The evidence supporting this contention is the fact that the abbey's Customary (of c. 1234) contains the first known references to the treasurer's office. The treasurer is mentioned in connection with his role in the provision of incense and candles for the convent, an obligation which lay mainly on the sacrist. The Customary specifies the days when the sacrist owed the treasurer 'a pyx full' or 'a measure' (or 'measures') of incense. It does this briefly but is much more detailed about the provision of candles, partly because many different kinds were in use and partly because many more people needed to receive them: they were needed not only for the illumination of the abbey church, its altars and chapels throughout the year, but also to provide light for the monks in their daily round, a necessity especially during the dark months.[90] The Customary explains how the sacrist was to provide the treasurer with the appropriate quantity of candles for various occasions, specifying the exact kind and weight of candle required. The treasurer then distributed the candles as occasion demanded. Thus, in the summer months the sacrist had to supply the treasurer every week with ten pounds of small candles (*candela*) and two candles weighing four pounds, and in the winter fifteen pounds of small candles besides the two candles weighing four pounds. In the week of each of the principal feasts the treasurer had to have four candles weighing ten pounds. The Customary continues:

> From the above allowances of small candles the treasurer must answer for all allowances [of small candles], both interior and exterior; and [he must] also supply the prior in his chamber and the brethren eating with him (or the subprior or others in place of prior eating in the prior's chamber) with two torches (*torcatae candelae*) at supper, from the Nativity of St Mary (8 September) until the Purification (2 February) according to some, until Lent according to others, whenever light is lacking, except during the great misericords after Christmas. Indeed, he

Harvey, *Obedientiaries*, pp. 192–5. For that at St Swithun's, Winchester, see *Compotus Rolls of St. Swithun's Priory, Winchester*, ed. Kitchin, pp. 56–8.

89 *JB*, pp. 88–90.
90 *Bury Cust.*, pp. 56–62.

should supply each pair of the other brethren with one torch, so that there is always a torch between every two brethren.[91]

The Customary next details the treasurer's duty to provide servants with candles. For instance, when the prior sat in his chamber after supper, or someone else in his stead sat in the prior's house, or in the proper place where monks ought to eat, the treasurer had to give a candle to the servant who went to the cellary for ale, and one to the cook or keeper of the dishes who served the prior's supper in winter. Details of allowances to obedientiaries and others follow. Marginalia by the scribe of the best surviving text of the Customary (copied in the 1260s) illustrate the lasting importance attached to precision over allowances of candles. For example, he notes that 'the length of an ell must be 16 ins' and that 'formerly [the prior's] candle had to be a torch measuring 14 ins in length [and] of decent thickness'.[92] The Harley accounts supplement this information about the provision of candles for the convent. They record that the sacrist purchased large quantities of wax. For example, in the seven months from 28 February to 29 September, 1249, he bought 1637 lbs of wax, paying £38 9s 1½d for it, but received £55 6s 8d from the treasurer/treasurers (tesaur').[93] Besides buying wax, the sacrist was responsible for the manufacture of candles: a memorandum in the accounts records that he had to pay the servants who made the great Easter candle ('which must always contain 80 lbs of wax') two marks 'for their refection', but this was 'by grace, not ancient custom'.[94]

The system with regard to the distribution of incense and candles described in the Customary was as centralized as the financial system at Christ Church, Canterbury. What prompted the monks of St Edmunds to vest such power in the hands of the treasurer over the distribution of incense and candles in particular is unknown. The most likely explanation is mismanagement of the distribution by the sacrist. Gregory 'of St Albans' was sacrist for a very short time before he was appointed prior early in 1234, that is shortly before the Customary was composed.[95] The Gesta Sacristarum's only comments about him concern his sanctity.[96] He was succeeded as sacrist by Nicholas of Warwick (1234–52). Administration of the sacristy could well have been lax under Gregory and also under Nicholas – at least in his last years when 'he was struck by paralysis and voluntarily resigned and spent many years in the infirmary'. Be that as it may, it was during Nicholas's period in office that, according to the Gesta Sacristarum, treasurers were first given custody of the pyx containing oblations.[97] The problem of maintaining conventual control of oblations was of long standing. Sacrists tended to spend the oblations as they chose. Jocelin of Brackland accuses William, who was sacrist during the vacancy which followed the

---

[91] Ibid., p. 56 § 2.
[92] Ibid., p. 56 nn. c and k.
[93] Harley 645, f. 260v[b].
[94] Ibid., f. 239v; Bury Cust., p. 53 § 3.
[95] Bury Chron., p. 8.
[96] Gesta Sacrist., p. 294.
[97] Ibid.

death of Abbot Hugh I, of 'foolishly squandering oblations and chance income (*subventiones*)'.[98] Samson himself was subsacrist at the time and tried to use oblations for building the tower; he was thwarted by opposition in the convent.[99] The Customary states that the first occasions when the convent assumed control of this source of income were during the successive sacristies of Richard of Ely (1217–20) and Richard of Newport (1220 to before 1234); the oblations were taken and stored under lock and key in the vestry.[100] The Customary makes no mention of the treasurer in this context. This fact would seem to highlight the growing importance of the treasurer's (or treasurers') office towards the mid-thirteenth century.

Treasurers figure prominently in the statutes agreed by the prior and convent 'to relieve the church of St Edmund'. The statutes are undated and the earliest known text is in a hand of c. 1300.[101] Their contents show that they must have been issued after 1234 since they frequently refer to the treasurers; as has been seen the earliest known references to a treasurer at St Edmunds occur in the Customary composed in or shortly after 1234. Moreover, the fact that the statutes stipulate that the sacrist was to have half the oblations suggest a date not much later than 1234 since all the oblations were allocated to the treasurers/treasurer sometime during the sacristy of Nicholas of Warwick. Possibly the statutes were drawn up in response to the papal visitation of St Edmunds in 1234. The abbey would seem to have been in financial straits at that time. According to Matthew Paris, Abbot Richard of the Isle stayed abroad in 1233 after his visit to Rome, in order to save the abbey from expense.[102] Nevertheless, none of these facts amount to concrete evidence and the statutes could belong to later in the thirteenth century when repeated attempts at economy were made to help solve the abbey's financial problems.

The statutes imposed numerous specific economies on the monks and attempted to ensure their implementation by various administrative reforms, some of which involved the treasurers. Thus, the abbot and convent were to choose two 'discreet and faithful' monks to whom were to be committed all the manors and granges of the cellarer, sacrist and chamberlain; these two custodians, under the eye of prior, were to answer to the treasurers for all revenues, from whatever source; the custodians were to have six horses and the prior four but the sacrist was to have 'only' two horses, and they were to provide their own stabling.[103] Other economies follow, among which the treasurers appear again: the nine marks which the infirmarer took from the church of Woolpit were henceforth to be delivered to the treasurers by the vicar of that church; the 100s assigned by the reeve (*prepositus*) of the town of St Edmunds for one cope, in future to be handed by the bailiffs (*baillivi*) to the treasurers; the sacrist was not to 'make misericords' (that is, give 'misericords' – allowances of food) to

98   *Bury Chron.*, p. 9.
99   Ibid., pp. 9–10.
100 *Bury Cust.*, p. 35 line 31–36 line 4.
101 Ibid., pp. 108–10 passim.
102 *Chron. Maj.*, iii. 239.
103 *Bury Cust.*, p. 108 lines 5–11.

the convent nor hand it spices, but they 'should be bought and honourably and handed over by the treasurers';[104] the practice by which wine was formerly handed to the convent by the sacrist on four feast-days, should end and be bought by the treasurers according to the convent's wishes; in future the sacrist was to answer to the treasurers for the 40s which he was wont to pay the infirmarer, refectorer and two guest-masters;[105] and the subcellarer was to answer to the treasurers for the money (de denariis) assigned at collation.[106] Clearly, therefore, the treasurers played a central role in the drive for economy.

However, it seems that an obedientiary's control of his income only devolved on the treasurer/treasurers in exceptional circumstance, especially when an obedientiary failed in his duty. Normally, the principal property-holding obedientiaries managed their own finances. The Harley accounts throw some light on the working of the system at St Edmunds – which resembled that in a number of religious houses. At the time of the accounts there were probably always two treasurers, and obedientiaries made payments to them. Some of these payments appear in our accounts. For example, in the year 1259–60 the subcellarer paid the treasurers £30 11s 8d, and in the year 1260–1, he paid them £60 30s 3¾d.[107] These payments accumulated in a reserve fund from which the treasurers disbursed money to an obedientiary when necessary, to supplement his normal income and to pay heavy, non-current expenses, including the liquidation of debts. In times of exceptional economic crisis the treasurers could disburse substantial sums to relieve struggling obedientiaries. As will be seen, the subsacrist's and kitchener's accounts would seem to provide excellent examples of this kind of intervention in 1257–8, years of crop failure and famine.[108] The accounts indicate that a disbursement from the treasurers might constitute a substantial part of the obedientiary's total receipts. For example, in the winter of 1249–50, the subchamberlain received £16 6s 11d from the treasurers; his total receipts were £20 9s.[109] In the same period the pittancer received £22 7s 3d and his total receipts were £35 3s 2½d.[110]

The treasurer/treasurers remained an important element in the abbey's financial system in the later thirteenth century. Thus, in 1282 Abbot John granted an annuity of 40s to Robert of Bricett, a clerk; it was to be paid by the sacrist until Robert was provided with a serjeanty worth 40s or more; meanwhile the treasurers were to pay that sum to the sacrist, or the latter could deduct it from his annual payments to them.[111] Other evidence from Abbot John's time shows that the two cellarers owed the treasurers large sums of money and that the debts

---

104 Ibid., p. 108 lines 19–23.
105 Ibid., p. 109 lines 15–21.
106 Ibid., p. 110 lines 10–12.
107 F. 262v*b* bis.
108 See below pp. 286–7.
109 Harley 645, f. 252*a/b*.
110 Ibid., f. 252*b*.
111 *Letter-Book of William of Hoo*, pp. 123–4 n. a.

were longstanding.[112] However, despite the limitations in the treasurers' funds and control, the treasurers had clearly kept their position. But whether a treasurer or treasurers held office like the traditionally established obedientiaries or on an *ad hoc* basis is not known.

(c) The obedientiaries, their servants and officials

One advantage of the accounts is that they provide the names and dates of obedientiaries at particular times. Therefore, although they do not provide initial and terminal dates when a named individual held office, they do establish specific periods when they were definitely in post. Obedientiaries are also named in some of the abbey's other records, some of which are dated. Such information helps build up lists of the successions of the various obedientiaries and to revise and to add many new names and dates to the valuable but provisional lists published by R. M. Thomson over twenty years ago.[113] This new information will help date the innumerable undated documents in the abbey's vast archive if they name an obedientiary or, indeed, any of the host of servants, manorial officials and others who appear in the accounts. Thomson's lists are only cited below if the relevant obedientiary is noticed in them. The dates given here are those of the accounts in which the obedientiary is named. The dates are copied from Paul Harvey's list of the accounts; the number in his list is cited thus '(H. …)'.[114]

Sacrists

Nicholas of Warwick, 17 Oct. 1247 – 11 Oct. 1248, f. 197v (H. 28).
29 Sept. 1248 – 22 Feb. 1249, f. 260 (H. 51).
[Also 1240 in BL MS Lansdowne 416, f. 75v.]

Simon of Luton, 22 Feb. – 29 Sept. 1249, f. 260 (H. 52).
28 Feb. – 29 Feb. 1249, f. 260v (H. 54).
Thomson p. 94, states that he occ. 1251 'until shortly after (sic. for before?) 23 Oct. 1252', and cites *Gesta Sacristarum*. See also Chronicle, p. 18.

Richard of Witham (*alias* of Colchester), 11 Apr. 1256 – 19 Apr. 1258, account rendered 17 May 1258, f. 261v (H. 58).[115]

---

112 See the accounts for the joint cellarers Adam of Walsingham and Roger of Chevington for 1283–4, BL MS Harley 645, ff. 230v–232.
113 Thomson, 'Obedientiaries'.
114 Harvey, 'Some mid-13th-century accounts', pp. 136–7.
115 Richard of Witham *alias* of Colchester, probably took name from Colchester Green, a hamlet 1½ miles north of the cellarer's manor of Cockfield, a food farm, 7 miles SE of St Edmunds. He was presumably a native of 'Witham'. There are places of that name in Lincolnshire and one in Essex, 11 miles NE of Chelmsford. The convent committed to Richard the farm of all the cellarer's manors: he was answerable to the cellarer, William of Eccles, for what was owed from them to the kitchener and subcellarer and in alms. He acted as farmer for two years, until he was struck with paralysis. He died soon afterwards. *Gesta Sacrist.*, p. 295. Some undated customs mention an ordinance issued by Richard of Colchester 'cellarer'. This may refer to his time as farmer of the cellary and should not be

Subsacrists

Simon of Leverington, 11 Apr. 1256 – 19 Apr. 1258, account rendered on 17 May 1258, f. 261v (H. 58), notices him as 'formerly subsacrist'.

Alexander of Brandon (Brandun), 11 Apr. 1256 – 19 Apr. 1258, account rendered on 17 May 1258, f. 261v (H. 58).

Cellarers

Richard of Walsingham, 29 Apr. – 29 Dec. 1249, period of office referred to as in the past ('temp. ᵗR. De Walsingham'), f. 193v (H. 3).

Richard of Horringer ('*Horn*' i.e. Horningsheath, the old name of Horringer), 29 Apr. – 29 Dec. 1249, f. 193v (H. 3). Idem, 5 May – 28 July 1250, account rendered 28 July 1250, f. 198 (H. 31).

Subcellarers

Walter of Ramsey, 29 Apr. – 29 Dec. 1249, f. 193v (H. 3). Idem, 2 Mar. – 29 June 1250, f. 198v (H. 32).

Clement, 20 July 1249 – 20 July 1250, f. 193 (H. 1). Idem, 7 July 1257 – 29 May 1258, f. 262. (H. 61).[116]

W[illiam] of Northwold (Northwolde), 22 Aug. 1259 – 24 Aug. 1260, f. 262v (H. 65).[117]

W[alter] of Ramsey, 24 Aug. 1260 – 2 June 1261, f. 262v (H. 66).

Chamberlains

Stephen of Wiggenhall, unknown date to 23 June 1249, f. 252 (H. 37).

Walter de Wich', 23 June 1249 to unknown date, f. 252 (H. 38).[118]

Subchamberlain

S. of Ely, 1 Sept. 1249 – 28 Feb. 1250, account rendered 8 Mar. 1250, f. 252 (H. 39).[119]

---

regarded as evidence that he was ever cellarer. *Pinch Reg.*, i. 399. The date of his death is unknown but his successor, Simon of Kingston, occurs in 1263. Thomson, p. 94.

[116] Clement occurs as almoner, 1250/1 (BL MS Harley 27, f. 112 and cf. ff. 93, 93v, 138), and as refectorer in the undated customs in CUL MS Ee, iii, 60 (*Pinch. Reg.*, i. 368).

[117] W[illiam] of Northwold is probably to be identified as the nephew of Abbot Hugh of Northwold (*Electio*, p. 193 n. 5), and chaplain to the abbot in the early years of Simon of Luton's rule. (BL MS Harley 645, ff. 253v–254). He occurs as cellarer jointly with William of Beccles, 1267/8 (BL MS Harley 638, f. 55 and *Pinch. Reg.*, i. 306).

[118] For Stephen's and Walter's terms of office see below pp. 275–80. Cf. the respective entries in Thomson, p. 97, who notes that 'Richard (sic) of Wicham' occurs 1249 x 1256, citing BL MS Add. 4699, f. 12v.

[119] Below pp. 275–8, 280.

Pittancers

Rad[ulfus], 7 July – 1 Aug. 1249, f. 252v (H. 45). The Beccles account of
Stephen of Caistor (Castre) record that he rendered account from 1 Aug. to
29 Aug. 1249 'post recessum Radulfi pitanciarii', f. 252v (H. 46).

Karolus, 29 Sept. 1249 – 12 Mar. 1250, rendered 8 Mar. 1250, f. 252.
Account struck out. Idem, 29 Sept. 1249 – 7 July 1250, f. 252 (H. 41).

Kitcheners

R. Foliot, 29 Apr. – 29 Dec. 1249, f. 193v (H. 3). Idem, 2 Mar. – 29 June
1250, f. 198v (H. 32).

C. of Chevington (Cheuenī) 2 Mar. – 29 June 1250, f. 198v (H. 32). A
payment to him immediately precedes one to R. Foliot in the subcellarer's
account: they are both described as *coquinarius*.

Wymer is mentioned as a former kitchener in the manorial accounts of 20
July 1249 – 20 July 1250, f. 193 (H. 1).

Besides naming these obedientiaries, the accounts name many sergeants
(*servientes*), bedels, reeves and others employed by the monks. For example,
Colin, perhaps a barnkeeper, rendered five accounts between 21 February 1249
and 8 March 1250 and was reimbursed by the cellarer for deficits.[120] Similarly,
Stephen of Caister, whose office is not specified, rendered account for the chamberlain's manor of Caister St Edmunds in 1249 and, as has been seen, temporarily for the manor of Beccles.[121] Another official who appears is the claviger.
A Galf[ridus], *claviger*, rendered account with Gilbert the bedel, for the chamberlain's manor of Hinderclay.[122] And the Hinderclay accounts record wages
'formerly owed' to 'A.' *claviger*, and the expenses of 'W.' *claviger*. Wages paid to
a claviger also appear on the accounts of each of the cellarer's manors of Semer,
Groton and Horringer.[123] These officials at St Edmunds must have been responsible for security on manors, and in households and other establishments – they
were, as the name implies, 'key bearers'.[124] The thirteenth-century customs of
St Edmunds in BL MS Harley 1005 and the Pinchbeck register (CUL MS Ee.
iii. 60) include a number of allowances to clavigers, sometimes stating where
they were employed. There was a 'claviger grangie', a 'claviger aule hospitum', a

---

120 F. 194 (H. 5–9).
121 Ff. 252v, 253 (H. 46–9).
122 F. 252v (H. 46).
123 Ff. 260v–261v passim. (H. 56–7, 59).
124 One meaning, the most appropriate here, of *claviger*, is 'a keeper of keys'. See R. E.
Latham, *Dictionary of Medieval Latin from British Sources*, fasc. 2 (Oxford, 1981), p. 357
col. 2, 2 (2). The *claviger* at St Swithun's, Winchester seems to resemble the *claviger* at
St Edmunds in function and as a wage-earner. *Compotus Rolls of St. Swithun's Priory,
Winchester*, ed. Kitchin, p. 213 and n. 4. I am indebted to Barbara Harvey for a discussion
concerning the office of the *claviger*.

'claviger de celerario', and a 'claviger infirmarie', and the prior had a claviger.[125] The Semer accounts, 1257–8, record the expense of 'the service of the claviger for the year, 10s'.[126] Thus, it might seem that a claviger was a permanent manorial official. On the other hand, it could be that a claviger was employed only when security was particularly important, for example at harvest time when the granary and mill needed special protection from theft. Or perhaps at such times an additional claviger was employed, or a manorial claviger received extra payment for the extra work involved. The seasonal importance of a claviger is indicated by entries in the Groton and Horringer accounts. The Groton accounts record 'the expenses of a certain claviger and a certain girl (*ancilla*) in the autumn 4s 4d',[127] and the Horringer accounts (1257/8) record 'the expenses in autumn of the reeve and claviger 8s 6½d'.[128] The suggestion that a claviger may have been seasonal official on a manor receives some support from an entry in the Hinderclay accounts for 1249: it records 'the expenses of the claviger and other visitors, minor expenses and wages 42s 4½d.[129]

The convent's manors were not isolated units but integral parts of its overall managerial system. An important obedientiary was responsible for his total holding, exercising supervisory control. The accounts provide evidence of their visits. The cellarer was, of course, the greatest landholder among the obedientiaries: he had charge of fifteen manors besides numerous smaller properties. The Chepenhall accounts for 1248–9 record the cellarer's expenses 'there' (*ibidem*) as 9s 3½d.[130] The manor was about twenty miles from St Edmunds. The manor of Warkton in Northamptonshire was much further away but the cellarer visited fairly often despite the distance, as the accounts testify. His expenses at Easter 1250 were 6s 3½d, and 15s that autumn.[131] Apparently, he stayed in his lodge on the manor on certain feast-days: an entry among the manor's receipts reads 'nothing from the lodge because the lord held the feast there but when he did not hold the feast he should take ½ mark' ('de loc nichil, quia dominus tenuit festum sed quando non tenuit festum capiet dimidium marc").[132] The sacrist frequently visited his manor at Icklingham, only six miles from St Edmund. The accounts record that: in the five months from 29 September 1248 to 22 February 1249 he visited three times and his expenses were 9s 2¾d;[133] and in the seven months from 22 February to 29 September 1249 he visited six times and his expenses were 10s 9d.[134]

Nor did the separation of portions between abbot and convent entail the

[125] *Pinch. Reg.*, i. 364, 369 bis, 397. Clavigers occur among those receiving oblations in the sacristy and cellary at Christmas; see ibid., i. 371, 400.
[126] Harley 645, f. 261[a].
[127] F. 261[b].
[128] F. 261v[b].
[129] F. 252v.
[130] F. 195[a].
[131] F. 198[b].
[132] F. 198[a].
[133] F. 250[a–b].
[134] F. 250[b].

obedientiaries independence from abbatial control. The abbot, as Father of the community, was responsible for its well-being, and also, as tenant-in-chief of the king, was answerable to the central government for good order in the Liberty of St Edmunds. The accounts record a number of occasions when the abbot visited one or other of the convent's manors. The Chepenhall accounts note among expenses 2s 6d 'for the lord [abbot] E[dmund]'.[135] The Mildenhall accounts record: 'For the expenses of the lord abbot on two occasions, [and] of the monks and their prebends £6 10s'.[136] In the Warkton accounts the record of the cellarer's expenses on his visits, ending with the cost of his autumn visit, is immediately followed by the abbot's expenses: 'For the expenses of the abbot and charcoal [*carbon*'] for his use, 20s 7d, and [*siue*] 4 quarters of wheat, 4 quarters of barley, 5 quarters of oats and other stores for the house'.[137] And the abbot stayed on the manor of Beccles at the same time as the chamberlain, Walter de Wich', for two days sometime during the nine months from 29 September 1248. The accounts record: 'For the abbot's expenses for two days 36s 4d, and for W. the chamberlain's expenses 15s 1d.[138] Similarly, the abbot's expenses appear on the Icklingham accounts for the five months from 29 September 1248. They record: 'For the expenses of the abbot and his servants 3s 7¾d'.[139] There was also a payment of 4½d to the abbot's 'boys' (*garciones*) on St James' day (25 July) 1249.[140] Managerial concerns were probably not the only reason for abbatial visits. Sometimes they may only have been an excuse. It saved the abbot the expense of living in the abbey where he had to bear the cost of entertaining guests. Moreover, the convent's manors, like his own, were generally pleasant places to be. Samson aroused criticism because he spent so much time on his manors, leaving the convent with an additional burden of hospitality. Jocelin justified his absences by remarking that Samson was more cheerful and lively away from home.[141] A visit to one of the convent's manors would have served the same purpose. Sometimes an abbot's visit coincided with a feast-day, occasions for conviviality. (The Icklingham accounts reveal that the sacrist feasted the servants on three principal feast-days at the cost of 7s 9d.[142])

The accounts give occasional glimpses of the cost of hospitality to a wide range of visitors. Some of these would have been travelling members of the religious orders and secular clergy, and laymen, especially neighbouring lords and the abbey's benefactors. The total cost of hospitality at Icklingham for the years from 29 September 1248 was £6, a substantial sum.[143] At that time Simon of Luton, the future abbot, was sacrist. If, as the evidence suggests,[144] he belonged

---

135 F. 195[a].
136 F. 197v[a].
137 F. 198[b].
138 F. 252v[b].
139 F. 260[a–b].
140 F. 260[b].
141 JB, p. 35.
142 Harley 645, f. 260[a–b].
143 F. 260[a].
144 Simon may well have been related to Sir Robert of Hoo (or 'Hose', 'Hou'), a knight of St

to an important baronial family, he may have entertained an exceptional number of relatives and friends, and in lavish style. And, if so, his generous hospitality possibly resulted in a rich return: according to one of the abbey's registers, the splendid new Lady Chapel which he constructed when abbot was paid for by his 'relatives and friends'.[145] Another of the sacrist's manors in Simon's care in the year 1248 to 29 September 1249 was Aylsham. The accounts, which were rendered on 18 November 1249, record that the cost of visitors (*venientes*) 'and gifts' was 6s 6½d, besides '8s 11d for two visits by 'Lord Reginald''. This entry is immediately followed by three cryptic ones; the last concerns the cost of hospitality but the first two possibly record payments to corrodians. The entries read: 'For the expenses of '*vic*', 7s 2d; for the expenses of William *de assemne* (?), 10s 4d; and for the expenses of other visitors (*venientes*) and gifts 6s 6½'.[146]

'Lord Reginald' was perhaps the Reginald of Willingham referred to earlier in the Aylsham accounts, which record that an allowance to him of £20 20s was agreed at Norwich[147] – maybe before the royal justices in eyre (Henry of Bath and his fellows) who sat at Norwich from 9 September to 27 October 1249 and again from 18 November 1249 to 2 December 1250.[148] A few other entries in the accounts provide concrete illustrations of the contacts of obedientiaries and the officials of individual manors with the royal courts. The accounts for Horringer for 3 July 1257 to 18 May 1258 record the receipt by the reeve of 22s 6d from 'common amercements' collected from the justices in eyre, Gilbert of Preston and his fellows:[149] they sat at Ipswich from 18 to 25 November and on 9 December in 1257, and from 14 January to 23 February in 1258, and at Cattishall from 25 November to 9 December 1257 and on 14 January 1258.[150] St Edmunds had the right to profits of justice accruing within its Liberty. The respective reeves of Semer and Groton also visited sessions of the justices at Ipswich.[151] This is apparent in the accounts of these manors for the period from 20 July 1257 to 15 May 1258. The expenses of the reeve of Semer for his visit to Ipswich are recorded as 4s, and those of the reeve of Groton as 3s 8d. Presumably they too, like the reeve of Horringer, went to claim the common amercements owed to St Edmunds. However, as there was a long-running dispute concerning St Edmunds' title to both Semer and Groton (which culminated in their temporary loss under Abbot John of Northwold),[152] possibly the dispute itself was heard

Edmunds. Simon's toponymic 'of Luton' suggests a relationship to the Hoo family. One of Sir Robert's numerous and scattered holdings was at Hyde, near Luton (Beds), and the sacrist under Simon's successor, John of Northwold, was called alternatively William of Hoo and William of Luton. See: *Hist. Docs.*, ii. 976; *JB*, p. 120; *Feudal Docs*, p. lxxxvii; Moor, *Knights*, ii. 238; Thomson, 'Obedientiaries', p. 95.

145 Douai, Bibliothèque Municipale MS 553, f. 9.
146 BL MS Harley 645, f. 260v[a].
147 Probably the Willingham in east Suffolk, 3 miles south-east of the chamberlain's manor of Beccles.
148 Crook, *Records*, pp. 115–16.
149 BL MS Harley 645, f. 260v[a–b].
150 Crook, *Records*, pp. 122, 126. For St Edmunds' right to profits of justice see above p. 236.
151 BL MS Harley 645, f. 261[a–b].
152 *Bury Chron.*, p. 189 and n. 7. See: Galbraith, 'Death of a champion', pp. 283–95.

by the justices at Ipswich. Similar expeditions by the chamberlain to the royal courts on cases concerning his manors of Hinderclay and Beccles are noticed in the subchamberlain's accounts, which are discussed in the next section.

(d) The chamberlain's accounts

The accounts of two successive chamberlains, Stephen of Wiggenhall and Walter de Wich' (? Wickham Skeith in east Suffolk),[153] and those of the subchamberlain, S. of Ely, are of exceptional interest because, although the chamberlain was an important obedientiary in any monastery, he is little mentioned in earlier records from St Edmunds.[154] Indeed, it is not known when the execution of his domestic duties devolved upon a subchamberlain: since no such obedientiary is mentioned in the *Electio Hugonis*[155] or in the abbey's Customary, it is not impossible that S. de Ely was the first monk to hold that office. The primary duty of a monastic chamberlain was to provide clothing and footwear for the monks and for certain other individuals. The chamberlain was also responsible for the monks' bathing arrangements, for the bath-house and its attendants, and for the provision of soap and towels.[156] He also had to provide towels for the monks' wash-basin (*lavatorium*) at the entrance of the refectory, and for the foot-washing ceremony at the Saturday maundy and on Maundy Thursday. In addition, he had to provide table-cloths (*mappae*) for the refectory and bedding for the dormitory. Whether or not the chamberlain was responsible for laundering the monks' dirty clothes seems to have varied from one religious house to another house.[157] If the chamberlain was not responsible, each monk had to make his own arrangements for laundering: this may have been the case at St Edmunds since the present accounts make no mention of a laundry, a laundryman or a laundress.

The chamberlain's accounts occupy three quarters of f. 252, comprising in all fifty-two written lines. The text divides into two halves, each half being in

---

153 St Edmunds had a holding valued at 10s in Wickham Skeith, in Hartismere hundred. *DB, Suffolk*, pt 1, 14. 126; listed in Thomson, 'Obedientiaries', p. 97, as 'Richard of Wicham'.

154 The Bury Customary (of c. 1234) states that the chamberlain was to have seven candles, p.a., for his seven servants each weighing 3 quarters. *Bury Cust.*, p. 52 lines 35–6, and see also ibid., p. 79. The Compromise (of c. 1214) numbered the chamberlain among those obedientiaries to be appointed with the consent of chapter and in chapter. Ibid., p. 100 line 7. The regulations for economy in the abbey state that his manors, along with the cellarer's and sacrist's, were to be committed to the care of two 'discreet and faithful monks' chosen by the abbot and convent. For the chamberlain's office in other houses see e.g.: *Eynsham Customary*, ed. Gransden, p. 181 (thirteenth century); Harvey, *Obedientiaries*, pp. 47–8 (Westminster, late thirteenth century); eadem, *Living and Dying*, p. 132 and n. 65; *Barnwell Observances*, ed. Willis Clark, pp. 195–9 (later thirteenth century); Saunders, *Norwich Obedientiary and Manor Rolls*, pp. 114–20 (fourteenth century); *Compotus Rolls of St. Swithun's Priory, Winchester*, ed. Kitchin, pp. 363–80 and index (1416–17).

155 It mentions only Robert the chamberlain. *Electio*, p. 187 and nn. 9–13 for his hypothetical career.

156 For the monks' annual bath see Lanfranc, *Constitutions*, pp. 8–10, 26.

157 See e.g.: Harvey, *Living and Dying*, pp. 133–4, 167, and nn.; Willis Clark, ed. cit., p. 195.

a different hand from the other. The accounts of Stephen of Wiggenhall and Walter de Wich' occupy the first half and are mainly written in two columns.[158] The accounts of S. of Ely occupy the other half and are written in single lines; the latter alone give the dates which they cover, that is, 1 September 1249 – 28 February 1250.[159] Stephen of Wiggenhall's accounts give only the terminal date, 23 June 1249, and Walter's only the initial date, 23 June 1250. Paul Harvey concluded from the contents of Stephen's and Walter's accounts that they covered much less than a year. He was undoubtedly right and comparison of these with the accounts of the manors assigned to the chamberlain, which follow over the leaf in the manuscript (ff. 252v–253), suggest further conclusions. These manorial accounts, which were rendered by the bedels and other officials, are dated thus:[160]

> Hinderclay   29 September 1248 – 17 July 1249
> Stanton   29 September 1248 – 18 July 1249
> Beccles   29 September 1248 – 7 July 1249
> Beccles   7 July – 1 August 1249
> Beccles   1 August – 29 August 1249
> Caister St Edmunds   7 July – 1 August 1249
> Caister St Edmunds   1–29 August 1249
> Caister St Edmunds   29 August – 29 September 1249.

The Hinderclay, Stanton and the first of the three Beccles accounts all cover roughly the same ten months starting on 29 September in 1248 and ending in July 1249, that is, two or three weeks after 23 June. These three accounts include among the expenses incurred by the manorial officials payments made to 'S[tephen] chamberlain' and 'W[alter] chamberlain'. The second Beccles accounts, which cover little more than the last three weeks in July 1249, record the expenses paid to Walter but none to Stephen. The third Beccles accounts and the three for Caister St Edmunds include no expenses of either chamberlain but are so cursory and cover such short periods that they can be disregarded here. If, as seems likely, Walter had replaced Stephen by 23 June 1249, this would explain why only Walter's expenses appear on the second Beccles account. Possibly the replacement of Stephen by Walter as chamberlain had an age-related cause. Since Stephen was cellarer sometime in the period 1234 x 1242, he was probably then already a senior monk. So far as is known he held no other obedience after his term of office as chamberlain ended, nor has he been found in other later contemporary records. Perhaps his health was ailing by 1249 – perhaps he died that summer.

With regard to Walter's accounts, it is observable that unless their terminal date was on or before 1 September 1249, the initial date of S. of Ely's accounts, they would have overlapped with the latter. This seems improbable since Stephen's, Walter's and S. of Ely's accounts all include the same kinds of items

---

[158] Harvey, 'Some mid-13th-century accounts', p. 137 nos 37–8.
[159] Ibid., no. 39.
[160] Ibid., nos 42–9.

needed for providing the monks and others with clothing, footwear and so on, items which the chamberlain was obliged to supply: therefore, if Walter's accounts overlapped with S. of Ely's it would surely have resulted in some duplication. On the other hand, Stephen's and Walter's accounts, but not S. of Ely's, begin by recording income from the chamberlain's manors and churches and then expenditure on the domestic items. S. of Ely's receipts are not from the manors but are entered as follows: £16 6s 11d from the treasurer/treasurers ('de tessaur') and £4 2s 'by hand of Roger 'the ? controller' (cōpot'), 'and so on total receipts £20 9s 1½d (sic)'.[161] This section ends by recording the sum total of expenses, £20 9s 1½d, concluding that 'thus S. owes 6s'. A detailed list of the numerous items of expenditure, with the cost of each, follows.

It was suggested above that S. of Ely was the first subchamberlain. If so, the creation of the new obedience was perhaps part of a major reorganization of the management and funding of the chamberlain's office: in future income from the chamberlain's manors and churches was to be paid to the treasurer/treasurers who would then disburse the necessary sums to the subchamberlain. It is not unlikely that Edmund of Walpole would have instigated this reform in the summer of 1249, less than a year after his succession to the abbacy. Such a reorganization would have included the replacement of Stephen by Walter as chamberlain and also the adoption of the very short accounting periods apparent in the second and third Beccles accounts and of the three Caister St Edmunds accounts, all of which cover only about a month, beginning variously on 7 July, 1 August and 29 August 1249. The motive for this reorganization may partly have been to reduce the burden of work on the chamberlain, but probably the main reason was financial: the expenditure of both Stephen and Walter had exceeded their receipts. The accounts record that Stephen's receipts were £14 8d and his expenses £14 15s 6d 'and thus the chamberlain is owed 14s 10d, besides ancient debts'. Walter's receipts were £54 13s 11d and his expenses £100 55s 10d, 'and thus expenses exceeded receipts [by] £48 23s; a memorandum, however, notes a few sums that he had received from the convent but which did not appear in the accounts. Contrariwise, S. of Ely's total receipts exceeded his expenditure: unlike Stephen and Walter he did not need reimbursement by the convent but himself owed 6s 8½d.

The accounts give an excellent picture of the chamberlain's office. They record the purchase of the wide variety of goods needed to provide the monks' clothing and footwear and to fulfil the other obligations imposed on the office. They also illustrate his share in other conventual expenses and participation in its business affairs. Many of the items in the accounts relate to clothing and footwear. Some items were bought ready-made. For example, Walter paid: £9 for six dozen shirts of lindsey-wolsey (staminae); 52s for quilts (? or mattresses, culcitrae); 18s 8d for two table-cloths (mappae) and twelve towels (manutergae); 1 mark for 'a white tunic in the winter' ('In tunica alba in hieme'); and 46s 8d for 'wages of servants on the manors and for robes (rob') and shoes (sotulares) for the boys'. S. of Ely paid: 13s for tunics for the prior, Wydo and the subchamberlain;

161   Harley 645, f. 252[a-b].

4s for a coverlet for Wydo ('Wido'); 11s 2d for a robe and shoes for R. of Runcton ('Rug'geī); and 4s for quilt covers ('In arra culcitrarum').

However, the accounts show that much of the clothing, footwear and the like were made in the chamberlain's workshops. Furthermore, they indicate that some cloths were dyed and bleached on site and most of the leathers were produced from skins cured in the pelterer's quarters. Both the peltry and the sartry, the tailor's workshop, figure in the accounts: Walter de Wich' paid 1 mark for a 'new building next to the sartry' ('In nova domo facta iuxta sartrinum'), and Stephen of Wiggenhall paid 25s 2d in wages to servants in the sartry ('in stipendiis de sartrino'), while Walter paid them 43s 6d. The latter paid £7 10s 8d to the peltry and, in addition, 60s. Stephen paid 1 mark to Alex[ander] the pelterer in wages ('in stipendiis'), while Walter paid him 40s. Many entries in the accounts, especially those of Walter and S. of Ely, record the purchase of materials needed in the sartry and peltry. Sometimes they specify what they were used for and occasionally where they were bought, and a few entries record expenditure on the manufacturing process. Thus, Walter paid: £23 11s 8d for 140 measures of cloth 'de Warp̄'; 4s 1d for russet for hose; £6 for blanket (*blankettus*, woollen cloth) for tunicles ('ad tunical"); 36s for felt; 34s 4d and, in addition, 8s for blanket for slippers (*pedules*); 30s for 100 ells of serge; 20s for 100 ells of canvas (*canevaz*) £6 6s for 500½ linen cloths (*linea tela*) and for bleaching (*de albatione*); and 30s for dying cloth ('In tincture pannorum'). S. de Ely paid: 33s 4d for 85½ ells of blanket for 30 pairs of slippers for the convent; 26s for six dozen felts bought at Norwich, and, in addition, 14d for felt; 24s for dying 'and moreover still owes 3d'. There are similar entries for the purchase of skins and leather. Stephen paid 3s for soles ('In semellis').[162] Walter paid: £6 6s 1d for 7 hides of cordwain (cured leather from Cordova, used for shoes); 16s 'for white-tawed leather for the peltry and *calberas*', and 15s for cowhide.[163] S. of Ely paid: 38s for 2 dozen hides of cordwain; 2s 8½d for six hides for soles; 25s for ? thread (or binding, 'In ligatura').[164]

Although the accounts of the chamberlain's office make no mention of the manufacture of gloves (*chirothecae* or *cirothecae* in medieval Latin), they reveal their use, as do other records from St Edmunds. This is not surprising considering that the chamberlain, subchamberlain and their servants and dependents when travelling on horseback would almost certainly have worn them, and so would some of the farm labourers, stone-masons and other builders,[165] and gloves

---

162 F. 252ᵃ.
163 F. 252ᵃ⁻ᵇ. I do not know the meaning of *calberas*.
164 F. 252ᵇ.
165 The higher a rider's status the better the quality of his or her gloves. A picture in the Luttrell Psalter (BL MS Additional 42130, first half of the fourteenth century, f. 87v) illustrates the difference in the kind of gloves worn by high class riders and country folk. It depicts the three magi riding to Bethlehem, two of whom wear high quality gloves, and the shepherd pointing to the star: he wears a heavy-duty glove and has its pair tucked in his belt. See Backhouse, *Luttrell Psalter*, p. 16 fig. 14. For farm labourers wearing gloves see: ibid., ff. 170–1, 172; Backhouse, op. cit., pls 17–22, 24. For stone-masons wearing gloves see e.g. Matthew Paris's *Lives of the Offas* (c. 1250, Trinity College, Dublin, MS 177 f. 60v), reproduced e.g. Gies and Gies, *Cathedral, Forge and Waterwheel*, p. 196.

might have been given as gifts to friends and visitors.[166] Thus, our accounts for the chamberlain's manor of Beccles for 1249 include a list aggregating various expenses incurred by the bedell for, among other things, '... [horse-] collars, traces, gloves, [and] sacking ...'.[167] The sacrist's accounts, also for 1249, include 'gloves in the autumn' among his expenses for servants.[168] Possibly it was unusual for an obedientiary to provide servants with actual gloves and the usual practice was to give them money to buy them. There are a number of references in the abbey's registers to 'glovesilver'. For example, besides our accounts in Harley 645 are lists of allowances owed by the sacrist on various feast-days, in a hand apparently of c. 1300; included are allowances of 2d for 'glovesilver' (*glovesylver*, or *gloveselvir*) and 'fortrove' (*fortrove* or *fordrove*).[169] Another register, BL MS Harley 1005 (f. 51), has an entry in a hand of the 1260s, listing the allowances owed by the cellarer to servants 'in preparation for autumn' ('Isti debent habere glovesilver contra autumpnum'). The list begins with the cellarer's clerk and the cellarer's 'esquire' (*armiger*) follows. It then proceeds to list his manorial officials, moving down the social scale to the farm labourers – seven carters, two ploughmen, two stackers (*tassatores*), a cowman and a girl (*ancilla*). The allowance of glovesilver was 2d for all except the cowman and the girl for whom it was 1d. An almost identical list is in the register CUL MS Ee. iii. 60, ff. 1165v–166 compiled by Walter Pinchbeck, the monk who began writing it in 1333. His list ends with the following note: 'Moreover he who has 2d glovesilver ought to have 1d of Lammass silver and whoever has 1d glovesilver ought to have ½d of Lammass silver.'[170] Since Lammass is on 1 August, those receiving the allowance could have bought gloves ready for the harvest season. Probably they could have done so in Bury St Edmunds itself for it is fairly certain that there were gloves sold there – already by 1295 a street was called Glovers' Row.[171]

The accounts of the chamberlain's office allude to many more matters than those so far discussed. For example, Walter's accounts reflect the chamberlain's responsibility for monks' bathing facilities. Thus, Walter paid 7s for soap and 4d to the bath-house attendants (*balneatores*).[172] And then there are miscellaneous

---

166 Saunders, op. cit., p. 81. There were also, of course, liturgical gloves. No medieval English examples survive but there are a few twelfth- and thirteenth-century continental survivals. They are of embroidered fabric or of simple looping technique or are knitted. Some are very ornate and beautiful. I owe this information to Frances Pritchard, Curator of Textiles, Whitworth Art Gallery, Manchester, who, in a letter of 14 October 2003, cited: Dominique Cardon and Sophie Desrosiers, 'Ancient liturgical gloves preserved in France', *The Early Knitting History Group, Newsletter*, ii (June 1997); *Trésors Textiles du moyen âge en Languedoc-Roussillon* (Musée des Beaux-Arts de Carcassonne, 1993), chapter II; and M. Fluny-Lemberg, 'Glove from the burial vestments of Archbishop Rodrigo Ximenez de Rada [d. 1245]', *Textile Conservation and Research*, vii, Schriften der Abegg-Stiftung (Bern, 1988), p. 246 and figs 483–6.

167 F. 252v[b].

168 F. 260[b].

169 Harley 645, ff. 51, 51v.

170 *Pinch Reg.*, i. 372.

171 See L. J. Redstone, 'St Edmunds and town rental for 1295', *PSIA*, xiii (1908), p. 198; Statham, *Book of Bury St Edmunds*, p. 130.

172 For this and the following entries see Harley 645, f. 252[a–b], unless otherwise stated.

entries. For example, on the day of the account itself Walter paid 2 marks for presents of bread, wine and ale. Other entries concern the chamberlain's general conventual obligations. He had to contribute to pittances payable to the monks on feast-days. Stephen paid 40s 'for wine for pittances and presents'. The chamberlain had specific responsibility for the pittance on 16 December (the feast of O.). Walter paid 40s 'in preparation for Christmas' ('In O. contra natale'); this payment was presumably for pittances since S. of Ely paid 26s 11d 'for pittances ad O.' ('In pitanc' ad O.'). Moreover, the pepper, cumin, saffron 'and other spices', and the almonds and rice which Walter bought for 1 mark, were probably for conventual rather than for the chamberlain's particular use. Perhaps the chamberlain, subchamberlain or their servants sometimes made purchases on the convent's behalf as well as on their own when they visited markets and fairs, especially those at a distance from St Edmunds.

S. of Ely's accounts demonstrated that he or his servants, besides buying goods needed for their office at the great winter fair at St Edmunds (which began on the martyr's feast-day), made purchases at a number of other fairs. Indeed, some of the expenses in Stephen's and Walter's accounts relate to travel and to the means of transport – to horses. Thus: Stephen paid 5s for stabling and 11s 12d for provender; Walter paid 32s for stabling, 22s for provender, 6s 8d for harness and 7s for farrier's nails and shoeing. As already mentioned, S. of Ely's accounts record the purchase of felt at Norwich. Even more revealing is the inventory of the cloths, skins and leathers which S. of Ely had in hand at the time of the account. It often records not only what measures of cloth, number of skins and so on had been bought, what they were used for and what remained in hand, but also where they were purchased. For example, the inventory begins by recording that 'he' (the subsacrist) had in hand: 53 measures of black cloth; 40 measures of cloth from the fair at Ely; 40 measures of cloth 'for the feast of St Edmund'; total 133 measures of cloth; from which were made 48½ robes with 114½ measures of cloth; 6½ measures were used for ? hoods (capīī); thus, 12 measures remained. Similarly, 2 dozen skins were bought for day-shoes at the fair at St Edmunds, 23 measures of lindsey-wolsey for shirts from the fair at Ely and 12 measures at St Edmunds, and 100 ells of linen (*linea tela*) for breeches from Ely. In addition, goods were bought at Lynn, the most important commercial centre in East Anglia. The last entry in Walter's accounts records that 'the convent sent £20 to the fair at Lynn for the restoration of the chamber' ('preterea conventus misit ad nundinas de Len. xx. libr' ad restaurandum cameram'). From this entry it is apparent that there were lodgings in Lynn for St Edmunds' monks.

The chamberlain or his representatives also made journeys in connection with the department's external relations. A journey to Reading 'on account of the writ concerning Beccles' ('pro breve de Beccles') cost Walter 15s. The circuit of Suffolk by Roger Thirkleby and his fellow justices in eyre sat at Reading from 15 to 24 July 1248.[173] There must have been some plea before the justices which involved the chamberlain's manor of Beccles. Again, Walter or his representatives travelled to London 'on account of the dower concerning Hilderclay'

---

173 Crook, *Records*, p. 110.

('pro dote de Hildercle'); the journey cost 11s 7d. A case of dower affecting the chamberlain's manor of Hilderclay was presumably in progress in the Court of Common Pleas at Westminster.

(e) The food farms

Most of the sixty-six sets of accounts are for the cellarer and his manors, as opposed to one for the sacrist and two for his manor of Icklingham, and one for the moneyer, an official under the sacrist's jurisdiction. Apart from the one set of accounts for the chamberlain and the one for his manor of Hinderclay, the remaining accounts were for obedientiaries dependent on, or otherwise linked to, the cellary – the kitchener, pittancer and the ? barnkeeper. The main reason for the preponderance of interest in the cellarer's office was obviously because most of the convent's estates was assigned to him and the monks relied on him for most of their supply of food and drink. Mismanagement, therefore, of his estates could have a direct and immediate effect on the monks' sustenance.

An essential element in the management of the cellarer's estates to ensure as far as possible that the convent had the appropriate supply of food was the ancient system of food farms. The system originated before the Conquest, as it did on other great monastic estates, for example at Ely, Ramsey, St Albans and Winchester.[174] The earliest evidence for its existence at St Edmunds is the survey compiled under Abbot Leofstan and continued under Abbot Baldwin. It includes a list of twenty-five manors and vills which singly or in combination had the duty in turn to provide the monks' sustenance in kind for each lunar month throughout the year.[175] They were: Worlingworth[176] with the berewick of Soham in east Suffolk.[177] The rest are in west Suffolk, that is: Palgrave[178] with Thorpe [Abbots];[179] Redgrave; Rickinghall, with Stoke and Brockford; Barton; Rougham; Elmswell, with Woolpit and Groton; Cockfield and Chelsworth; Whepstead with Bradfield; Horringer with Risby; Lackford and Herringswell; Runcton with

---

174 Miller and Hatcher, *Rural Society*, pp. 204–5, 270 nn. 20–5 for further references. See also: Harvey, *Westminster Abbey*, p. 80; King, *Peterborough Abbey*, pp. 140–3; and Miller, *Ely*, pp. 36–41.

175 See: Robertson, *Charters*, pp. 192/193–200/2001 for the text in English translation; Hervey, *King Eadmund*, pp. 4–7, for the OE text with translation; *Kalendar*, ed. Davis, p. 1; and esp. Harvey, 'Some mid-13th-century accounts', pp. 134–5. See above, fig. 5.

176 *DB, Suffolk*, 14. 103.

177 *DB, Suffolk*, 14. 102. A berewick is an outlying estate attached to a manor. Robertson, op. cit., p. 327.

178 *DB, Suffolk*, 14. 45.

179 *DB, Norfolk*, 14. 18. Palgrave is east of Diss and about 5½ miles from Thorpe Abbots, for which see: Whitelock, *Wills*, p. 70/71 no. 25; Robertson, op. cit., pp. 193/194, 197/198. Jocelin of Brackland lists both Palgrave and 'Thorpe' among 'the churches of the manors and socages of the abbot'. However, he lists Morningthorp among the convent's manors. *JB*, pp. 63–4. The latter (*DB, Norfolk*, 14. 40) (about 10 miles south of Norwich) is about 10 miles from Palgrave. Nevertheless, perhaps this is the Thorpe in the list of food farms. Whitelock, *Wills*, p. 180, is non-committal.

Culford and Fornham.[180] These manors and vills together form a group centred on Bury St Edmunds. Most are on the fertile clay soil of that region and were the gifts of generous pre-Conquest benefactors.[181] The system of monthly food renders by the food farms survived the Conquest but from the late eleventh century to the late twelfth it was subject to alteration. First, the frequency of the renders changed; they were now made weekly instead of monthly. The reason for this new arrangement was probably to improve efficiency. The second and third changes were in the choice of food farms; nine of the pre-Conquest food farms were replaced by four others.[182] Thus, Brockford, Culford, Elmswell, Lackford, Palgrave, Redgrave, Rickinghall, Runcton and Stoke were no longer food farms. Thirdly, other manors, previously not food farms, now were so; the new food farms were: Elveden and Pakenham, both near St Edmunds; Southery south of Lynn in west Norfolk; and Warkton in Northamptonshire. St Edmunds had held the first four manors before the Conquest,[183] but Warkton was a post-Conquest acquisition; it was a gift from William the Conqueror's queen, Matilda.[184] Exactly when these changes took place is unknown but it was almost certainly before the end of the twelfth century. The reasons for them are also unknown but the main one was probably efficiency. Although the monks transferred from their portion of property to the abbot's more manors than they gained, Pakenham was a valuable acquisition since it was a very rich manor, second only to the cellarer's manor of Mildenhall which Abbot Samson recovered for the convent from Richard I in 1190.[185] It, Elveden and Nowton lay very close to the abbey, and Warkton, though distant, was productive and, since it was situated on the river Ise, loads, even heavy ones, could be brought from it to St Edmunds by the Fenland waterways.[186] Southery had even better access to the waterways because it was on the river Ouse which, most importantly, had its outflow at Lynn, one of the principal ports for domestic and foreign commerce. Like Runcton, which

---

[180] All these places occur in *DB, Suffolk*. In Jocelin's list some belonged to the abbot and some to the convent.

[181] See index to Whitelock, *Wills*.

[182] See the late twelfth-century list in *Kalendar*, ed. Davis, pl, and compare it with the Anglo-Saxon list in Robertson, *Charters*, pp. 192/193–200/201 (and see above, n. 175). See above, fig. 5.

[183] *DB, Suffolk*, 14. 20, 4, 49 respectively; *DB, Norfolk*, 14. 2.

[184] Abbot Baldwin established that on the anniversary of the death of William I the monks should have 10s and that they should be paid another 10s on the anniversary of the death of Queen Matilda (d. 1083). The 20s was to be paid from the manor of Warkton which William had given for Matilda's soul, and was to pay for better food for the monks on those days. See Robertson, *Charters*, pp. 198/199, and p. 446 for further references. See the thirteenth-century Benefactors' Lists: CUL MS Ff. ii. 33, f. 50v; BL MS Harley 1005, f. 80. Cf. *Bury Chron.*, p. 160; *DB, Northants*, 8. 13; and *Feudal Docs*, p. lxiii n. 4 citing *Cron. Bur.* in *Memorials*, iii. 4.

[185] Above, pp. 26–7 and nn.

[186] See: Parker, 'The making of Kings Lynn', esp. pp. 2, 5–10 and figs; Darby, *The Medieval Fenland*, pp. 92–106; and above pp. 231–32. Transport by waterways will be considered in more detail in my *Bury St Edmunds Abbey*, ii.

it in effect replaced as a food farm, it was a prosperous manor.[187] Moreover, it lay ten miles south of Runcton and so was nearer to St Edmunds.

The convent's need to secure as far as possible a satisfactory provision of food was increased by the policy of the Anglo-Norman kings towards tenants-in-chief. Abbots were among them and on the death of an abbot the king was entitled to take over his fee. William Rufus in particular exploited the assets of deceased tenants-in-chief, and often in the case of monastic fees trespassed on a convent's property.[188] It was essential to establish a clear separation of abbatial from conventual property in order to protect the latter during vacancies. The separation, which existed at St Edmunds for administrative convenience well before the Conquest was confirmed by Henry I in general terms. Perhaps the monks while negotiating for the confirmation also decided to alter the selection of manors chosen to be food farms. However, some of the changes were probably owing to actions by individual abbots. Jocelin records that Samson restored to the convent 60s from Southery 'which his predecessors had unjustly taken for themselves'.[189] He also records the monks' compromise with Samson over Mildenhall. Samson paid 1,000 marks to Richard I for it, which was a 'great sum' and was raised with 'great difficulty'. Therefore, he told the monks in chapter that he could rightly claim half the profit from the manor, but instead he was content with 'a certain portion' of the manor of Icklingham' which he would give to the new hospital of St Saviour's at Babwell.[190]

Abbot Samson, 'in full chapter and with the unanimous assent and at the wish of the convent', made a number of grants relating to the cellarers' food farms. The charters recording these grants throw light on the question whether food renders were paid in kind, or whether they had been commuted for, or were supplemented by, money payments in various forms. The answer seems to be that the obligation to supply the convent was usually fulfilled in a variety of ways. Even the rich manors of Barton and Pakenham (lying two and five miles respectively from St Edmunds), which were largely responsible for renders in kind, accompanied these with monetary payments.[191] Thus, Goda, widow of Simon son of Alfward, baker, and their daughter were granted 12 acres in Barton for 6 loads of oat malt, but they also paid the cellarer and chamberlain 10s for the 'concession'.[192] Again, at Barton, Ralph the porter was granted 27 acres of land in a field for 12 loads of malt 'according to the measure of the court of St Edmund' at two farms, 'that is six after the feast of St Edmund and six after the Purification', and for 2¾d payable at the terms of these farms.[193] At Pakenham, Samson and the convent similarly confirmed to Stephen son of Godfrey of St

187 DB, Norfolk, 14. 1, 4 (Runcton), 14.2 (Southery).
188 See: Howell, 'Abbatial vacancies', pp. 173–92; Gransden, 'Separation of portions', p. 373 and n. 3 for refs.
189 JB, pp. 29–30.
190 JB, pp. 46–7.
191 For the wealth of Pakenham and Barton, see the 1292 assessment for the papal tenth. Bury Chron., p. 108.
192 Kalendar, ed. Davis, p. 95 no. 34.
193 Ibid., p. 92 no. 31.

Edmunds the 25 acres and 3 rods of arable, which his father had held from them, for five loads of oat malt and one load of barley malt at two terms 'that is 2½ loads of oat malt and half a load of barley malt at the first farm after the feast of St Edmund and [the same] at the second farm after the feast of St John the Baptist'.[194] In addition, Stephen paid a money rent totalling 3½d at two terms, that is Easter and Michaelmas.

With regard to the less productive farms of Elveden,[195] Fornham,[196] Groton and Semer,[197] Horringer,[198] Rougham together with Bradfield,[199] Saxham[200] and Whepstead,[201] money rents seem to predominate, but often it is not clear whether a charter which states that the usual farm should be paid at the fixed terms, means that it was to be rendered in kind or partly or wholly in the form of a money rent. However, in a few instances the distinction is definitely made. For example, Hervey of Gedding and Adam son of Margery were granted six tenements in Rougham and Hesset, each of which owed a measure of malt and the same money rent as that paid by the previous tenants. The renders of malt totalled 15 loads and Hervey and Adam were to deliver these in three instalments: 5 loads at the first farm after the feasts of All Saints, the Purification and Pentecost respectively.[202] In some instances it is clear that a money rent had totally replaced a render in kind. For example, Benedict son of Richard of Blakenham was granted a tenement pertaining to the hall at Horringer for a rent of 4s payable at the hall in 12d instalments at each of the four farms owed by Horringer.[203] Again, Solomon of Mucking was granted 30 acres in Whepstead for a rent of 6s payable at the hall at Whepstead in instalments of 18d at each of the four farms owed by the manor.[204]

These examples show that in Samson's time some of the tenants on the manors designated as food farms contributed in cash or kind or both to the quotas owed by those manors for the convent's sustenance. This is not surprising since in the late twelfth century the system of food farming was still practised on other great monastic and ecclesiastical estates.[205] However, it is remarkable that the system was still fully operative in the mid-thirteenth century. This is proved by the Harley accounts which provide invaluable evidence about its administration. By that comparatively late date, when demesne farming was the favoured mode of estate management, a landlord could take what foodstuffs were available from his manors when he needed them, or otherwise he could sell them. That the

---

[194] Ibid., p. 106 no. 55. See also pp. 105–6 no. 54.
[195] Ibid., p. 119 no. 77. Some charters mention that the farm should be paid but do not specify whether it should be in cash or kind.
[196] Ibid., p. 109 no. 59.
[197] Ibid., pp. 127–8 no. 90.
[198] Ibid., pp. 109–10 no. 60.
[199] Ibid., pp. 97–8 no. 40.
[200] Ibid., p. 114 no. 68.
[201] Ibid., p. 111 no. 63.
[202] Ibid., pp. 97–8 no. 40.
[203] Ibid., p. 110 no. 61.
[204] Ibid., pp. 111–12 no. 63.
[205] Hatcher and Miller, *Rural Society*, pp. 205, 270 nn. 20–5.

monks of St Edmund retained the antiquated system illustrates their traditionalism, but also perhaps their good sense since it ensured as far as possible that
they received a regular and adequate supply of food and drink (that is, of ale
which they brewed from the malt).

The Harley accounts give a partial glimpse of the operation of the system as a
whole. They demonstrate that it was administered with the greatest care so that,
despite its obvious complexity, it supplied the daily needs of the monks and their
servants for wheat and other grains, barley malt and oat malt, peas, meat and
straw (for palliasses, floor covering and litter for horses and other animals). The
designated manor or manors made their weekly renders of food stuffs in the first
instance to the cellarer who would deliver them to the kitchener, or they went
directly to the kitchen. The deliveries constituted the 'farm of St Edmund' or
'the small farm of the kitchen' ('firma sancti Edmundi que vocatur parva firma
de coquina').[206] The deliveries were made in regular rotation: the accounts state,
for instance, that Pakenham preceded Horringer in its deliveries, and Elveden
preceded Risby.[207] If one manor's produce was insufficient to meet its quota, the
shortfall would be made up from elsewhere – often from another food farm.
Unfortunately, the accounts do not make clear the extent to which these transactions were only nominally in kind, but whether in fact they were cash transactions: certainly, the accounts often note the money value of wheat and other
components of a manor's quota. Surplus produce was stored in the barn or sold
to another of the food farms or at a market, usually in Bury St Edmunds.

A few examples will illustrate these points. In 1250, in the seventeen weeks
from 2 March to 29 June, Walter of Ramsey, the subcellarer, accounted in turn
for Horringer, Pakenham, Risby and Elveden, and recorded that: the arrears
from the last account were £9 16s ¼d; 77½ loads 3 bushels of wheat were sold
for £24 2s 5¼d; and 'from exchanges' (*de escambiis*) £4 16s 8d, 'that is, from the
sixteen farms'.[208] Paul Harvey plausibly suggests that the phrase *de escambiis* here
and elsewhere in the accounts denotes a cash transaction and postulates that,
if so, possibly it represents the only commutations of renders in kind for cash
taking place on the food farms.[209] Another of Walter's accounts for the same
period records that straw was sold for the farm of Herringswell for 2s ½d and for
the farm of Elveden for 20s.[210] The accounts for Nowton for the eleven months
from 1 August 1259 to 7 July 1260 include the statement that the following
commodities were received for the first farm: '£4 3s 4½d besides (*preter*) 12 loads
of wheat, 10½ loads of barley malt and 29 loads of oat malt, and ½ a load of
wheat and 1½ loads of oat malt [and] 2s 6d for meat (*pro carne*)' for the farm of
St Edmunds; they end with a note that:

---

206   See: *Pinch. Reg.*, i. 389–90, 392–3 (the same lists in a thirteenth-century hand are in BL
      MS Harley 1005, ff. 49, 50); the list of the expenses of the cellarer and other obedien-
      tiaries, Harley 645, ff. 24v, 199v, and the list of pittances owed by the pittancer, ibid.,
      f. 200.
207   Harley 645, f. 198v top. See Harvey, 'Some mid-13th-century accounts', p. 135.
208   Harley 645, f. 198v[b].
209   Harvey, art. cit., p. 135.
210   Harley 645, f. 198v[a].

for the second farm there remained on the manor on the day of the account only half a load of barley malt and half a load of peas and 3½ loads and 2 bushels of oat malt; however, they [?the auditors] must allow in respect of the manor 12 loads of wheat which it had paid because of the default (*defectum*) of Pakenham and 6 loads of wheat it had paid because of the default (*defectum*) of Whepstead.[211]

The accounts for Horringer for the year from 3 July 1257 to 18 May 1258 record receipts for four farms owed by the manor and for the farm of St Edmund as follows: £26 13s 4 ½d besides (*preter*) 23 loads of wheat delivered from the barn and besides 36½ bushels of grout and 248 loads of oat malt. They also record the prices as follows: a load of wheat 11s 4d; a load of malt grout 5s; a load of malt 3s; 'and note that the said prices were lacking' ('quod prec' predicta defecerunt …') from the four farms because of the shortfall (*defectum*) of the manor of 17½ loads and 2 bushels of wheat worth £8 5s 5½d.[212] The reference to the default (*defectum*) of Pakenham in 1257/8 calls to mind that those years were the years of widespread harvest failure and famine.[213] The gravity of the situation is noted by Matthew Paris[214] and the Dunstable chronicler[215] and in particularly graphic terms by the chronicler of Bury St Edmunds, who writes in the annal for 1258:

> There was a great shortage of everything because of the floods in the previous year, and corn, which was very scarce, cost from 15s to as much as 20s a quarter. Famine resulted so that the poor had to eat horsemeat, the bark of trees and worse things; a countless number of people died of hunger. In the same year all kinds of grain grew abundantly on the land but were almost totally ruined by autumn rain and in many places were still standing in the fields after the feast of All Saints [2 February].[216]

Because of the famine the uncompleted business of the royal justices in eyre, who began sitting at Cattishall on 14 January 1258, was postponed until October.[217]

At St Edmunds, as argued above,[218] one result of the shortages resulting from the crop failure would seem to have been to increase the disbursements made by the treasurers to the cellarer and kitchener, in order to supplement the depleted renders from the food farms. Thus, the subcellarer, Clement, records in his accounts for 4 July 1257 to 18 May 1258 that the treasurers allowed the cellarer £93 15s 2½d 'because of the default (*defectum*) of the manor both in wheat and in malt, that is, of 181½ loads and 2 bushels of wheat and of 43 loads of malt and £13 15s 2 ½d …'. The account ends: 'Know that nothing at all is reckoned here about the third farm of Cockfield.'[219] The first of the three kitchener's accounts covers the period from 6 July in one year up until 4 July in the next: the manu-

---

[211] Ff. 261v[b]–262[a].
[212] F. 261v[b].
[213] F. 262[b].
[214] Matthew Paris, *Chron. Maj.*, v. 660, 690, 701–2, 710–12, 728. Cf. Miller and Hatcher, *Rural Society*, p. 57.
[215] *Ann. Mon.*, iii. 208.
[216] *Bury Chron.*, pp. 22–3.
[217] Crook, *Records*, pp. 118, 126.
[218] Above p. 268.
[219] F. 262[b].

script gives the year date as 1259–60. But Paul Harvey points out that in view of the context this year date must be wrong and suggests that it should instead be 1250–1.[220] However, information in the accounts indicates that they should be dated 1257–8 – the famine years. They record that the kitchener received the following from the treasurers: £52 13s 'because of the default (*defectum*) of the convent's manors'; 55s for default of Cockfield; 60s for default of Elveden ...;[221] and £25 16s 6d for default of Mildenhall. The generosity of these disbursements contrasts with the meagre sum of 5s, the amount which according to the accounts, they paid the kitchener in the year 1259/60, a sum representing a small fraction of his total receipts of £259 3s 11d.

Finally, a sidelight on the long-surviving practice of sending renders in kind any distance is provided by the way the nuns of St George's at Thetford, twelve miles from St Edmunds, were provisioned by the monks. Until 1369 they were sent every week thirty-five loaves of bread, ninety-six gallons of ale and also dishes (*fercula*) of cooked food, all conveyed in wagons to the nunnery. But in that year, because of the frequent assault on the servants, the wagons and their loads, the bread, ale and cooked dishes were commuted to an annual render of ten quarters of corn, twenty quarters of barley and 62s in cash.[222] The case also shows the tenacity with which St Edmunds clung to the custom of fulfilling obligations in kind.

---

[220] Harvey, art. cit., p. 137 no. 62 and n. 29.
[221] F. 262v*ᵃ*.
[222] *VCH Norfolk*, ii. 355.

Appendix IV
St Edmunds' Watermills and Windmills

1. Introductory

Mills occupied a predominant position in the medieval economy.[1] They were used initially and primarily for grinding grain, but as techniques developed they were also employed for other purposes, such as pumping water, fulling cloth, smelting metal and sawing wood. The prehistoric method of grinding grain was in a quern: a rounded stone was rubbed up and down on a slightly hollowed lower stone sloping away from the operator. But in the later prehistoric period the rotary quern became the principal tool for grinding grain. This comprised two millstones, the upper (the 'runner') and the lower (the 'bedstone'). The runner had an upright wooden handle inserted in it, which the operator held to rotate it over the bedstone. Handmills of this basic kind survived from ancient times and through the classical and medieval periods into the modern era.[2] Because, although laborious to use, they were cheap, and conducive to social independence and self-sufficiency, they were never totally replaced by technologically sophisticated mills. In the latter the runner stone was rotated by elaborate machinery powered in various ways, occasionally by horses, oxen or even men or women, but most often by water or, alternatively by the wind: as we shall see, in the middle ages wind-power was first harnessed to work the mill machinery rather later than water.

The essential component of a watermill was a waterwheel turned by the force or weight of water. There were various kinds of waterwheel common in medieval England.[3] They were vertical wheels, the most efficient of which was the over-

---

[1] The subject of the following study is mills, an essential part of the medieval economy. Another subject which would merit similar attention is maltings and breweries, equally essential elements in the medieval scene. Nearly every village and, indeed, many households had these manufactories. Evidence about maltings and breweries in Bury St Edmunds itself dates from the early thirteenth century until the twentieth century (see above p. 22) and, indeed, the present Greene King Brewery is one of the twelve independent breweries to survive in England. See: Wilson, *Greene King*; Statham, *Yesterday's Town: Bury St Edmunds*, p. 125; idem, *Book of Bury St Edmunds*, pp. 91, 96 fig.; Robert Malster in *Historical Atlas of Suffolk*, pp. 152, 153 distribution map, 214.

[2] For querns see: Holt, *Mills*, pp. 1, 4, 10, 13, 17, 38–42; Langdon, *Mills*, pp. 18–19, 24–5, 39–40, 127–9, 156, 268; and Watts, *Archaeology of Mills and Milling*, esp. pp. 25–44, and figs 3, 7–16A and colour pls 1, 3–5.

[3] For waterwheels see: Landels, *Engineering in the Ancient World*, pp. 16–25 and figs 2–5; Landers, *Field and Forge*, pp. 51–2; Holt, *Mills*, pp. 1–5, 100, 117–35; Langdon, *Mills*, pp. 74–5, 84–8, 90–7 passim; and Watts, op. cit., pp. 47–102, and figs passim and colour pls 7–15. For a wide ranging and illuminating study of the various kinds of mill which could be used to raise water, grind corn etc., with especial reference to the Islamic world, from

shot wheel. This was turned by water falling on it from a trough just left of dead centre of the top of the wheel which had paddles or buckets on it – if paddles, it was the force of the water which turned the wheel, and if buckets, it was the weight of the water. Another common type of wheel was the breastshot (also the 'half' breastshot and the 'low' breastshot). This was turned by water falling on the wheel at a point level with its axle (or lower). Yet another type was the undershot wheel which was turned by water striking it underneath. Although the overshot wheel was the most efficient, it depended on a fall of water of at least eight feet. In a mainly flat region such as East Anglia this height was rare and, therefore, nearly all watermills were of the breastshot or undershot type.

To function at all a watermill needed a constant water supply. Therefore, an elaborate system of water management was adopted. The system differed from place to place but for an overshot or breastshot mill it was much as follows: the flow of the water of a river or stream was diverted by a sluice into a side-channel, the mill race or leat, leading to a mill-pond above the mill; if the river level rose so that even when the sluice was opened the mill-pond was in danger of overflowing, a sluice in the pond was opened. This canalized excess water into a spillway which led to the mill-pool below the mill. Water from the pond flowed to a chute above the mill-wheel from which it fell; it then entered the mill-pool and so onwards by the tail-race back to the river itself.[4] Both the mill-pond and the mill-pool normally served as fisheries, the pond for eels, carp and pike, and the pool, with its fast running water, for trout and salmon. Nets, to trap fish and eels, were sometimes positioned in the leat.[5]

Examples of watermills occur in England from the eighth century onwards and were relatively common by the time of the Norman Conquest. Their invention had been an epoch-making technological achievement. However, the dependence on a suitable water supply was a serious hindrance to their dissemination. In some areas sites with sufficient water-power were hard to find. Therefore, the discovery that the wind could be harnessed to turn a mill-wheel was of paramount importance. A windmill might even be constructed in places where there was already a watermill. Since it needed no water management system, it was overall cheaper to install, but not necessarily to maintain, than a watermill. Nor does wind-power share the geographical limitations of water-power: the wind blows everywhere, though, of course, always with varying velocity and in some

---

ancient times to the present, see Michael Harverson, *Mills of the Muslim World* (London: SPAB Mills Section, 2000), p. 39. I am very grateful to Michael Harverson for reading this Appendix in typescript and making a number of useful comments which enabled me to emend or modify some of my more general molinological statements.

4 Langdon, *Mills*, pp. 80–92 and figs 3.3–4; and Watts, op. cit., pp. 84, 89–91, 126–8, and figs 32, 36, 58 and colour pl. 21.

5 See the excellent picture of an eel trap in the Luttrell Psalter: BL MS Additional 42130, f. 181. See above, pl. XI b. It is reproduced in colour in Backhouse, *Luttrell Psalter*, p. 31 pl. 30 and in Watts, op. cit., pl. 14 (and in black and white in Holt, *Mills*, p. 130 pl. 3). For the use of mill-ponds and mill-pools as fisheries see: Langdon, *Mills*, p. 206; McDonnell, *Inland Fisheries*, pp. 14, 30, 35. Cases where a miller paid rent in eels suggest the presence of eel traps in the mill-pond. Fisheries associated with mills were, of course, only one way of catching fish.

places more than others. Recent research indicates that the earliest windmills in England are three datable to the 1180s: they were located far apart, in East Yorkshire, Buckinghamshire and Sussex respectively. Fifteen other windmills are known to have existed in the 1190s, but a few of them may have been erected earlier. Of these fifteen, nine were in East Anglia, an exceptionally windy region with extensive dry areas. This East Anglian concentration of early windmills has led to the suggestion that the windmill was an East Anglian invention and spread from there to other parts of England and across the Channel, notably to Flanders. In the thirteenth century windmills were built in many places – the speed of their proliferation was very remarkable.[6]

Only fragments of any medieval watermill or windmill survive in England. The earliest of those restored to working order in modern times date to the late seventeenth century but nearly all are of eighteen- or nineteenth-century construction. The machinery of a medieval mill was made of wood – even when in the late middle ages iron began to be used, wood remained the principal component. Moreover, the housing of a watermill was generally of wood and so was that of a windmill. Almost without exception early windmills were post-mills – timber structures.[7] Medieval pictures of windmills show that the sailyards were made of two lengths of timber crossed and morticed at the centre, to form the arms of four sails. Oak would have been used for long sails. A framework of withies was attached to each sail and when the miller wanted to mill, a strip of canvas was tied to each frame on the windward side. Until cast iron could be used to replace wood for the construction of sailyards, the number of sails was limited to four and their length to about 35 feet; when iron was used the sails could be longer and more numerous.[8] The earliest tower mills, which were built of stone or brick, seem to be datable to the late thirteenth century but only became common later.[9]

Wood is perishable, and millstones wore out, were broken up and discarded. The importance of flour production tended to ensure that a mill, whether a watermill or a windmill, was frequently repaired to keep it in working order, and would, if necessary, be replaced by a new one. Nor would a watermill necessarily remain on the same site: if a mill's source of water-power became inadequate, owing to silting or canalization, it might have to be moved to a new site. But this was an expensive option and rarely adopted. A windmill might also be moved – perhaps a change in land tenure made it possible for the owner to move it to a better site.

Our knowledge of medieval mills depends primarily on documentary, literary and archaeological evidence and on pictures in medieval manuscripts. In addition, there is the evidence of recently restored old mills: although details of

---

[6] For windmills see: Kealey, *Harvesting the Air*, passim; Landers, op. cit., pp. 51–2; Holt, *Mills*, esp. pp. 20–7; Langdon, *Mills*, pp. 6–14, 32–7, 108–9, 141–4, 179; Watts, op. cit., pp. 103–16, and colour pls 18–20, 23, and black and white pls 46–9; *Historical Atlas of Suffolk*, pp. 148–9 no. 67, 213.

[7] Watts, op. cit., pp. 103–110. Above, pl. XII a and b.

[8] See: Holt, *Mills*, pp. 142–3; Langdon, *Mills*, pp. 120–1.

[9] Ibid., pp. 110–13.

their extraordinarily complex and ingenious machinery are the results of post-medieval inventiveness, the basic principles of the gearing, which converted the power of vertical waterwheels or windmill sails into the horizontal power needed to turn runnerstones, and of the mechanism required to operate pulleys and cranes for sackhoists, were well known in the middle ages. There was also expert knowledge of water management by means of dams and sluices. Therefore, much can be learned from restored mills of post-medieval date, especially if one bears in mind that continuity is characteristic of molinary history. Milling was (and is) a highly skilled occupation and a successful miller a man of substance and consequence in his community. Normally, he passed his knowledge and the mill on to a son or sons or to a close relative. In the middle ages many millers were tenants but because of their expertise a landlord was unlikely to dislodge a miller from his holding. This continuity led to localism – a particular mill might be idiosyncratic, a fact which increases the difficulty of generalizing about medieval molinology. Examples of continuity and the practice of keeping a milling business within a family exist today. The twentieth-century history of two mills in West Suffolk, those at Icklingham and Pakenham, both places where St Edmunds once had mills, will now be cited to illustrate this point.

Domesday Book records that St Edmunds held a watermill at Icklingham, a vill on the river Lark. The medieval history of the various mills in the vill, especially of the sacrist's mill, is discussed below.[10] In the post-medieval period there was still a watermill at Icklingham. It was frequently repaired and probably replaced, if necessary, to maintain its milling capacity.[11] It ground grain for flour, and grain and pulses for animal feed. This was to meet the miller's own needs and also those of local bakers and farmers, who brought grain and pulses to the mill for milling, paying the miller a fee. A picture of the late eighteenth-century mill survives; it is of a three storey building with an undershot waterwheel. This building was burnt down in the early nineteenth century and replaced by another one, apparently on a slightly different stretch of the river. In 1910 the water-mill building, the miller's cottage and site with apple orchard were purchased by a miller, Carlos Marston. He and his sons developed the mill, continuing production of flour and animal feed, and adding an extra storey to the watermill building (the window on the second floor of the old mill was moved up accordingly). They supplemented their income by selling eels and trading in timber and coal at their wharf on the Lark: the remains of the eel sluice and wharf can still be seen. (As mentioned above, St Edmunds had had the right to collect toll at Icklingham from merchants using the Lark to transport their goods, and the wharf was an important trading post.) Marston Mill continued to function as a watermill during the First World War but in 1921 it converted to a water turbine

---

10 Below pp. 307–11.
11 I am indebted for the post-medieval history of the flour mill at Icklingham and for information about milling in general to Mr Duncan Marston, Mill Director of Marstons, delivered to me orally when I visited the mill in June, 2003. He also gave me printouts about the mill from http://www.icklingham.com/mills.htm and http://www.icklingham.com/47.jpg and ditto /48.jpg; and *A Short History of Marston Flour Mills* [to 1996] (no date, unpublished).

(of the Francis type) and during the Second World War it adopted power by diesel engine. With the arrival in 1948 of electricity at Icklingham the mill went onto the National Grid: the mill-pool was filled in to provide a car park for the vastly expanded works. Over the years, Marston Mill developed to meet the ever-increasing demand for refined white flour: the mill began producing flour for the commercial market, using grain purchased for milling. Consequently, the building complex was progressively enlarged, modern machinery installed and milling capacity increased. In 1990 C. Marston and Sons Ltd became a division of Tate and Lyle. Further expansion followed and the mill now supplies the total flour requirement of Tate and Lyle for the production of glucose at the works at Greenwich. However, Duncan Marston, a grandson of Carlos Marston, is Mill Director and the old watermill building remains intact, incorporated into the fabric of the modern mill: it houses the dressing machines (which sieve the ground floor to separate the meal from the bran).

Our second example of a mill which remained in the hands of one family throughout the twentieth century and still does so today is Pakenham windmill. The survey of 1279–80 records the existence of two windmills held by St Edmunds at Pakenham,[12] but the present structure was constructed in the nineteenth century. It is a tower mill built of bricks which were made at Woolpit – 'Woolpit whites'. This mill was once at the top of Ixworth Street in Pakenham but at some stage was moved from there to its present site. In 1885 it was purchased by a miller, William John Fordham. His daughter Kate married Sidney John Bryant and their grandson, Michael Bryant, the present miller, owns the windmill, the house and buildings and also a farm. In the twentieth century the Bryants ground grain and pulses for animals on their farm and for local farmers, though during the First World War and the Second World War they also milled flour for bakers and themselves and for local farmers and others. By 1960 the windmill was in need of major repairs: these were paid for by a grant from West Suffolk County Council and by the Bryant family. The windmill continued to function intermittently until 1990. Then, to enable it to resume milling, it needed major restoration. For this purpose £60,000 was raised: three quarters was contributed by the Lottery Fund and the rest was paid by the Bryants themselves and by generous grants from local benefactors; the division of ICI at Stowmarket made a valuable contribution in kind of all the necessary paint. The windmill now grinds grain and pulses, purchased by the Bryants but mostly produced on their own farm, for animal fodder for sale to local farmers and for their own use. Michael Bryant's son and grandson work on the farm and in the mill. It is planned that they will in turn succeed Michael Bryant as owners of the business and as millers.[13]

---

[12] *Pinch. Reg.*, ii. 140–1. For the 1279–80 survey see below.

[13] I owe my information about the nineteenth- and twentieth-century history of Pakenham windmill to the present owner and miller, Mr Michael Bryant and to his informative booklet, Michael Bryant, *A Touch of the Wind* (Thurston: Decroft Ltd, 2006).

2. St Edmunds' watermills

Domesday Book must be the starting point of any discussion of St Edmunds' mills. We are concerned with two forms in which it survives, 'Great' Domesday and 'Little' Domesday. The former was compiled by royal clerks at Winchester. It covers most of England but was never completed. Among the omissions were Essex, Suffolk and Norfolk. These are covered by Little Domesday. It represents an earlier stage than Great Domesday of the editorial process to which the innumerable returns of the local commissioners were subjected.[14] Great Domesday and Little Domesday describe each manor or vill pertaining to an individual or institution, listing its principal components. They record the situation in 1066 and again in 1086, so that any change is apparent. However, only Great Domesday gives the total value of a holding and of a selection of its components in those years. Both books include mills in their descriptions, but since virtually all St Edmunds' estates were in East Anglia we have neither the total value of each holding nor the value of their mills. Because of the early date of the Domesday survey, we can assume that the mills it mentions were watermills, as the use of man- or animal-power to work a mill was extremely rare. For the molinary history of St Edmunds' mills in the twelfth and thirteenth centuries the principal sources are: the chronicle of Jocelin of Brackland; the mid-thirteenth-century obedientiary accounts discussed above; and a few of the abbey's charters and other official documents. Another and especially important source are the hundred rolls of the commission sent out by Edward I in 1279–80 to survey the country, hundred by hundred. This inquiry seems to have aroused surprisingly little attention from contemporaries and not much subsequently, even among recent historians until the authoritative study by Dr Sandra Raban.[15] The rolls cover only some of the southern counties and none of the northern ones. Whether this means that the inquiry was never completed or that the records are lost is unknown. However, fortunately the rolls for West Suffolk survive and these include eight hundreds where St Edmunds had holdings – that is, Babergh double hundred, Blackbourne double hundred, Cosford half hundred, and the hundreds of Hartismere, Lackford, Risbridge, Thedwestry and Thingoe. These sections were copied in the fourteenth century into two of St Edmunds' extant registers.[16]

In discussing the evidence in Domesday Book, I have borrowed its terms which denote the respective situations in 1066 and 1086, or signify that there had been no change – that is, 'then', 'now' and 'always'. Thus, Domesday Book records the existence of a mill 'always' on the following of St Edmunds' manors

---

14   For clear explanations of the making of Domesday Book see esp.: Welldon Finn, *Introduction to Domesday Book*, esp. pp. 9–15; *Hist. Docs*, ii. 858–62; Hallam, *Domesday Book*, pp. 8–31.

15   Raban, *A Second Domesday?*, pp. 78, 108–10, 161 and n. 73, 162.

16   *Pinch. Reg.*, ii. 30–282; BL MS Harley 743 (the Lakenheath register), ff. 149–257v. Sandra Raban argues convincingly that although these transcripts are headed as belonging to the 1286 eyre of Solomon of Rochester and his fellows, their contents virtually prove that they belong to the 1279–80 inquiry. Raban, op. cit., pp. 161–2.

in Suffolk: Nowton,[17] Hengrave,[18] Fornham All Saints,[19] Ickworth,[20] Flempton,[21] Ingham,[22] Stow [Langtoft],[23] Knettishall,[24] Mendham,[25] Semer,[26] Chelsworth,[27] Mildenhall,[28] Icklingham,[29] and Marlesford.[30] Cockfield, Groton and Ricking-hall [Inferior] each had a 'winter-mill':[31] this was probably a watermill which only functioned in the wet winter months when the stream had enough water to turn the waterwheel.[32] In some cases St Edmunds shared lordship of a mill with another lord (or with more than one other lord). Thus, St Edmunds always 'held half a mill' at Saxham[33] and 'two parts of a mill' at Barnwell.[34] Another example of this would come from Southwold, a coastal manor, if we accept that the sea-weirs mentioned in Domesday Book powered waterwheels. Its sea-weirs must have been in the Blyth estuary which was tidal and the water controlled by the weirs used to power waterwheels.[35] Domesday Book records that St Edmunds held 'half of one sea-weir and the fourth part of another half'. Just possibly the 'half sea-weir' was the 'half mill' at Southwold which Samson rented to Henry son of Thurston towards the end of the twelfth century.[36] They may even have been tide-mills. This kind of mill was powered by sea water trapped at high tide through sluice gates in a mill-pond; when the tide had receded sufficiently another sluice was opened to allow the water to rush on to an undershot or low breastshot wheel with enough force to turn it; the mill functioned for about two hours on either side of low tide – for about four hours, that is for about eight hours in the twenty-four.[37]

Moreover, Domesday Book records that St Edmund's held one mill at Herringswell 'then', and 'now' has two,[38] while Pakenham had two mills 'then',

---

[17] *DB, Suffolk*, 14.4.
[18] Ibid., 14.8.
[19] Ibid., 14.9.
[20] Ibid., 14.10.
[21] Ibid., 14.12.
[22] Ibid., 14.69.
[23] Ibid., 14.77.
[24] Ibid., 14.99.
[25] Ibid., 14.106.
[26] Ibid., 14.108.
[27] Ibid., 14.109.
[28] Ibid., 1.115. Mildenhall and Icklingham were in the king's hands at the time of the Domesday survey and so in *DB* they are recorded with his property.
[29] Ibid., 1.115.
[30] Ibid., 14.118.
[31] Ibid., 14.24, 25 and 75. For winter-mills see Welldon Finn, *Introduction to Domesday Book*, pp. 189–90.
[32] *DB, Suffolk*, 14.6.
[33] Ibid., 14.11.
[34] Ibid., 14.82.
[35] Ibid., 14.163.
[36] *Kalendar*, ed. Davis, p. 150 no. 128.
[37] An example of a surviving eighteenth-century tide-mill, restored to working order and open to visitors at fixed times, is at Woodbridge.
[38] *DB, Suffolk*, 14.57.

and 'now' has one,[39] and Wordwell had none 'then', but 'now' has one.[40] Lack-ford, Melford, West Stowe and Bury St Edmunds itself are all recorded as having two mills each,[41] while Fornham St Genevieve (situated on the river Lark about a mile east of Fornham All Saints) had three mills.[42] Domesday Book's coverage of Norfolk records very few mills on St Edmunds' holdings. Runcton and Thorpe [Abbot's] each 'always' had a mill,[43] Kirby [Cane] had half a mill 'then', and 'now' has one and a half mills,[44] while Buckenham had one mill 'then' but none 'now'.[45] St Edmunds held the rich manor of Warkton in Northamptonshire, a gift from Matilda, William I's queen. Great Domesday records the existence there of a mill 'at 12s' ('Ibi molin̄ de xii. solid'), which sum probably denotes the rental income from it.[46]

We have besides the evidence of charters. One charter records that Abbot Anselm (1121–48) constructed a mill in the abbot's court (which would have been powered by the Lark),[47] and others mention mills situated between Wormegay and West Briggs (places situated about six miles south of Lynn on a tributary of the Nar).[48] Of especial interest is the confirmation by Henry II of various holdings which include a mill at Babwell (situated just outside the town walls of Bury St Edmunds, close to Northgate).[49] This was probably the new watermill constructed by Abbot Samson and, if so, dates the mill's origin to early in Samson's rule. More is known about Babwell mill than about St Edmunds' other mills because in its case archaeological excavations and observations have added substantially to what is known from written sources. Our knowledge concerns the mill's water management system. Jocelin of Brackland records that Samson

> so raised the level of the fishpond at Babwell for his new mill that, owing to the holding back of the water, there is no man, rich or poor, having land on the river-side between Tollgate and Eastgate, but that has lost his garden and orchards.[50]

In 1924 Suffolk County Council Archaeological Services explored the land around the present Tollgate public house, near the site of the medieval mill. Interpreting the evidence was not easy because the direction of the Lark was altered in modern times. First, the river from Mildenhall to Fornham St Martin was made navigable in response to the Lark Navigation Act of 1700, and then in the early 1890s the navigation was extended to the town of Bury St Edmunds

[39] Ibid., 14.49.
[40] Ibid., 14.88.
[41] Ibid., 14.7, 23, 71, 167.
[42] Ibid., 14.53.
[43] DB, Norfolk, 14.1, 18.
[44] Ibid., 14.41.
[45] Ibid., 14.6.
[46] DB, Northants, 8.13.
[47] Feudal Docs, p. 113 no. 112.
[48] Kalendar, ed. Davis, pp. 156–7 no. 139.
[49] Feudal Docs, p. 106 no. 102.
[50] JB, p. 131.

itself.[51] Excavation of the locality of Babwell mill was also difficult because it was marshy, but evidence, was discovered of the previous existence of a number of fishponds and of a system of water management, that is, traces of man-made ditches and leats designed to supply the mill with water-power. Moreover, archaeological evidence, interpreted with the help of written records and old maps, showed that there was a dam stretching from the mill apparently as far as 'Tollcote' (the building where toll was collected from traders entering the town), probably near the present Tollgate public house. This dam must have been what held back the water of the Lark and caused the flooding recorded by Jocelin. The abbot's fishpond was obviously the mill-pond of the new mill. More recently, from 1989 to 1994, Suffolk County Council Archaeological Services conducted a comprehensive exploration of the remains and site of St Saviour's hospital. (The latter was founded by Abbot Samson and lay just outside Northgate; his mill was situated a little to the east of the hospital.) In the course of excavations some of the revetments of the mill-pond were discovered. They were of clay and wattle supported by roughly hewn staves, and had been repaired or replaced as they collapsed or became silted up with pond mud. The mill remained in use as a mill at least until the late sixteenth century; in the eighteenth century the mill-house served as an alehouse and by the end of the century the mill itself had become dilapidated. A new one was built on the site.

To return now to St Edmunds' mills in general. According to Domesday Book many of the abbey's manors had no mill, and among them were some of the abbey's most valuable holdings. Seven of the original thirteen food farms had no mill. Thus, Risby, Horringer, Whepstead, Elveden, [Great] Barton, Rougham[52] and Southery[53] were without a mill. Among the other manors which lacked a mill were the convent's rich ones of Redgrave and Hinderclay[54] and the abbot's manors of Elmeswell and Culford[55] – but Ingham, situated less than a mile away from Culford,[56] had a mill which may have served Culford's molinary needs. Among the many other places without a mill were the manors of Chevington, Bradfield [Monachorum], Timworth and Woolpit,[57] all of which will be referred to again below. The reason for the absence of a mill was usually the lack of

51 Alistair Robertson in *Historical Atlas of Suffolk*, pp. 130–1 (sketch map), 210. The following information about the fishponds and system of water management connected with Babwell mill is derived from two reports of Suffolk County Council Archaeological Service. (1) Archaeological Report. St. Saviour's Hospital, Bury St. Edmunds (Bury St Edmunds 013). A Report on the Archaeological Excavations 1989–1994. SCCAS Report no. 97/20. (2) Archaeological Evaluation Report. Tollgate public house Bury St Edmunds 164 … Planning Application no. E/98/1924 – SCCAS Report no. 98/87. I am deeply indebted to Mrs Margaret Statham for drawing my attention to these excavations and for additional information, and to Mr Robert Carr of the SCC Archaeological Service for sending me photocopies of the reports.
52 *DB, Suffolk*, 14.1, 2, 3, 20, 48, 51.
53 *DB, Norfolk*, 14.2.
54 *DB, Suffolk*, 14.42, 74.
55 Ibid., 14.73, 70, respectively.
56 Ibid., 14.69, 70.
57 Ibid., 14.5, 52, 55, 63.

sufficient water-power to turn a mill-wheel. Therefore, the advent of the wind-mill was of the utmost importance to the abbot and convent of St Edmunds as it was to many other landholders. Indeed, windmill-building on St Edmunds' estates kept pace with that elsewhere in East Anglia. The evidence is incomplete but by the late twelfth century St Edmunds certainly had a windmill at Elveden,[58] another at Risby[59] and another at Timworth,[60] all close to the abbey, none of which had had a mill in 1086.

3. Two early examples of windmill-building

An unusual amount of detail survives about the building in the late twelfth century by St Edmunds of a windmill at Hempnall in Norfolk, and of one in Bury St Edmunds by Herbert the dean. Both examples illustrate features of the abbey's molinological history – features, however, which were not peculiar to St Edmunds.

The abbey owed its possession of the Hempnall windmill to a grant from Walter fitz Robert (d. 1198), a knight of St Edmunds (he held one knight's fee),[61] who had inherited extensive estates on the death in 1137 of his father, Robert, son of Richard de Clare.[62] Walter's long and fairly undistinguished career had one moment of glory. That was at the battle of Fornham in 1173. Fornham, lying two miles north of Bury St Edmunds, was attacked by a rebel force led by Robert, earl of Leicester (1168–90). He had invaded Norfolk in support of the young Prince Henry. The royalist force under the command of the constable, Humphrey de Bohun, assembled at St Edmunds.[63] Humphrey was joined by three hundred knights of St Edmund led by Roger Bigod, the future earl of Norfolk (1177–1221), holder of three of St Edmunds' knights' fees. The opposing forces

---

58 In a life-lease dated by Davis c. 1186–1200 (*Kalendar*, pp. 119–21 no. 77), Samson granted Solomon of Whepstead the manors of Ingham and Elveden, specifying stock, equipment etc. At Elveden the lease includes 'a good windmill with all its apparatus' ('molendinum bonum ad ventum cum toto apparatu suo'). Cited Kealey, *Harvesting the Air*, pp. 143, 249.

59 DL 42.5 in PRO, f. 42v: Grant by Ralph le Bretun of Risby (*Reſ*) to God and the church of St Edmund and the monks in free alms of the windmill in Risby which he bought from Richard son of Maurice, and the site (*situs*) and road to it, saving the right of way and drove (*chacia*) on the road to the mill, and his and his men's lands in the same field. Cited by Kealey, op. cit., pp. 134, 251 (*pace* his folio reference) who dates the grant to before 1200.

60 DL 42.5, f. 44v: Grant by Reginald of Groton and Amicia his wife to the abbot and convent in free alms for their souls and the souls of their ancestors, of their windmill with suit owed to it ('cum situ suo secta'). Dated by Kealey (op. cit., pp. 251–2) to c. 1200. Tostock, which is nearby, also had a windmill by c. 1200 (ibid., pp. 252–4).

61 *JB*, p. 121.

62 His family were a branch of the de Clare earls of Gloucester. For Walter's career see Kealey, op. cit., pp. 108–31.

63 The campaign is described in *Chronicle of the Reigns of Henry II and Richard I. A.D. 1169–1192; known commonly under the name of Benedict of Peterborough*, ed. William Stubbs (RS, 1867, 2 vols), i. 60–2.

met at Fornham and the battle was fought under the banner of St Edmund. An especially vivid account of the battle is in the Anglo-Norman verse chronicle by Jordan Fantosme.[64] He expresses a marked admiration for St Edmund's abbey and its knights, and especially for Walter. In referring to the assembling of the royalist forces at St Edmunds he writes: 'For there is no better place on earth for hospitality than St Edmunds'; he describes the knights of St Edmund as 'of the greatest prowess'; and states that at the start of the battle Walter made 'the first tilt' against the enemy and then fought valiantly, laying about him with his axe against fierce resistance. The outcome of the battle was a resounding victory for the royalists.[65] Walter, therefore, as one of St Edmunds' military tenants and, no doubt, a devotee of the king and martyr, had good reason for his generosity to the abbey. However, he was also a benefactor of other religious houses, and among his gifts windmills figure prominently.

The history of St Edmunds' windmill at Hempnall is found in charters. Walter held the manor of Hempnall which, as Little Domesday recorded, had 'always' had a watermill.[66] St Edmunds had no holding in Hempnall until at an unknown date Walter granted it half an acre at Longbridge in the manor of Hempnall, with exclusive milling rights, for the erection of a windmill. That St Edmunds proceeded to do so is proved by the confirmation of Walter's grant by his son and heir, Robert fitz Walter, which mentions the windmill.[67] Walter had already granted to St Edmunds the watermill in Hempnall. It was called Twigrind (or 'Tuigrind'). The miller, called William, was one of Walter's villeins, and Walter quitclaimed him and his heirs to St Edmunds with all William's tenement in Hempnall and 'his mill there called Twigrind'. Robert fitz Walter's confirmation of his father's grant of Twigrind mill also confirms St Edmunds' right to the windmill at Longbridge and to the miller (William), his heirs and his tenement in Hempnall 'with all gifts (*donationes*), liberties, customs, members of his household (*sequela*) and appurtenances'. The value of these gifts was increased by Walter's undertaking that neither he, his heirs nor retainers would build any other watermill or windmill at Hempnall to the detriment of Twigrind watermill or Longbridge windmill. Moreover, it was stipulated that all tenants in Hempnall were to grind their grain at one or other of the two mills unless for some reason this were impossible. In order to free the site for the new windmill, Walter had to move the existing tenant, Adam, and give him instead half an acre at 'Harlslegapp'.

[64] For Jordan Fantosme and the *Chronique de la Guerre entre les Anglois et les Ecossais* see: Legge, *Anglo-Norman Lit.*, pp. 75–81; Gransden, *Historical Writing*, [i]. 236–8. The *Chronique* is ed. and trans. in the *Chronicles of the Reigns of Stephen, Henry II, and Richard I*, ed. Richard Howlett (RS, 1884–9, 4 vols), iii. 202–377.
[65] Howlett, ed. cit., iii. 288–9 lines 1016–17, 291 line 1039. Jordan's eulogy of Walter raises the suspicion that Walter was one of Jordan's patrons and that a copy of the *Cronique* was made for him.
[66] *DB, Norfolk*, 31.6.
[67] CUL MSS Mm. iv. 19, ff. 150v–151 (bis), 163v–164v, and Ff. ii. 33, ff. 56v–57. Kealey, *Harvesting the Air*, pp. 117 and n. 18, 118–20. The windmill would have been a post-mill. For the structure of post-mills see Watts, *Archaeology of Mills and Milling*, pp. 103–10 and pl. 18.

Walter's main motive for these generous grants to St Edmunds (like his other grants to religious houses) was piety. The grants were in free alms and the reciprocal obligations imposed on the monks were spiritual and liturgical. The grant of the plot at Longbridge was for the salvation of his own soul and of the souls of his sons, his wife and parents. The charter granting Twigrind is more specific and seems to imply that Walter's generosity was prompted by his second wife, Matilda de Bohun; the grant was for the salvation of the souls of his father and mother, and of his (first) wife Matilda de Luci, and his other ancestors, besides the souls of himself, his (second) wife Matilda de Bohun, his (eldest) son Robert and all his successors. The spiritual benefits follow: on the deaths of Walter himself and of Robert and Matilda de Bohun, the monks were to enter the names of each in their martyrology and celebrate a full trental of masses – that is, thirty requiem masses and psalms as for one of themselves; every year on the anniversary of the martyrdom of Archbishop Thomas (1170), the monks were to have one silver mark as a pittance, and on the anniversary of Walter's death they were likewise to have one silver mark as a pittance; these pittances were to be paid out of the profits of Twigrind and if, 'from the care (*studio*) and labour or by help of their friends', Twigrind in due course rendered more than two marks, the monks should spend the extra 'as they judge best for the utility of their church'. (As will be seen, the mid-thirteenth-century accounts in the Kempe register, BL MS Harley 645, indicate that the income from Twigrind had much increased by that time.) Matilda de Bohun 'my wife' was first witness to the charter. It should be observed that there was nothing unusual in these spiritual benefits which a donor in free alms might receive in exchange for his gift, nor was it unusual for monks to receive a pittance to compensate them for the extra labour in their liturgical life entailed by additional anniversary masses.

The dating of the grant of Twigrind watermill and of the subsequent grant of the plot at Longbridge for the windmill is problematical. The grant of Twigrind (and, therefore, of the plot in Longbridge) must have been after 1170 since a commemoration of Thomas Becket's martyrdom is included among the new anniversaries to be observed by the monks. Possibly, since Becket is not called a saint, the grant was made before his canonization in 1173. In that case perhaps Walter's grant of Twigrind was a thank-offering for the royalist victory in 1173 at Fornham and in atonement for his slaughter of so many of the enemy. However, there is no hint of this in the charters. It seems most likely that Walter made both grants near the end of his life when his own and Matilda de Bohun's deaths loomed and they were anxious about the salvation of their souls. Therefore, although the grant of the plot at Longbridge could have been made at any time between 1170 and Walter's death in 1198, the windmill was probably built in the late twelfth century. If that dating is accepted and this example is considered alongside the other examples of windmills on St Edmunds' estates mentioned above, it indicates that St Edmunds, like other great East Anglian monasteries, was actively engaged at that time in windmill building.

The other example of the erection of a windmill on St Edmunds' estates of which we have details was in the town of St Edmunds itself, but in this case the windmill did not belong to the abbey but to Herbert the dean, that is, the dean of Christianity, the official who acted as the sacrist's deputy in the exercise of archidiaconal power in the *banleuca* of the town.[68] Herbert erected a windmill in the Haberdun where the sacrist had a watermill. The Haberdun was the area in the town just inside Southgate, between Southgate Street and the Lark, bordering on the parish of Rougham. Herbert can be identified as Herbert, son of Robert, chaplain of Rougham, who was a relative (*consanguineus*) of Abbot Ording, to whom Ording granted land in Rougham, including what Herbert son of Robert held from his uncle, Solomon.[69] The story of the windmill's erection and swift demolition is told by Jocelin of Brackland in his usual precise and lively style. It deserves to be quoted in full because of its literary merit and also because, like the example of the Longbridge windmill, it raises issues to be discussed below. Jocelin writes:

> Herbert the dean erected a windmill in the Haberdun. When Abbot [Samson] heard this he was so enraged that he could hardly bring himself to eat or speak a single word. Next day, after mass, he ordered the sacrist to send his carpenters there without delay to pull it all down and put the timber in safe custody. On hearing this the dean came and said that he had the right to do what he had done on his own free fee and that the benefit of the wind should not be denied to anyone; and he said that he only wished to grind his own grain there, not anyone else's, in case it were thought that what he had done was to the detriment of neighbouring mills. Still angry, the abbot retorted, 'I thank you as I would if you had cut off both my feet. By God's face, I shall not eat until that construction is torn down. You are an old man and ought to know that neither the king nor the justiciar can change or build anything within the *banleuca* without [the consent] of the abbot and convent. Why have you presumed to do such a thing? Nor, as you claim, is it without detriment to my mills because the burgesses would flock to your mill and grind their grain there for their own benefit and I would not legally be able to stop them because they are free men. I would not have allowed even the cellarer's new mill to stand, had it not been built before I was abbot. Go away, go away – before you get home you'll hear what is to happen to your mill.' But the dean, terrified by the abbot's face, on the advice of his son, Master Stephen, forestalled the sacrist's workmen and had the mill which he had erected pulled down by his own men, so that when the sacrist's servants arrived they found nothing to demolish.

4. St Edmunds windmills in the thirteenth century

From the late twelfth century, mill building, especially windmill building, on St Edmunds' estates proceeded apace. This is clear from the survey of West Suffolk in the hundred rolls of the commission of 1279–80.[70] Many of the places noticed in the survey can be disregarded here because, although within the Liberty of the eight and a half hundreds, St Edmunds' holdings in them were minimal. Of

---

[68] See: *JB*, p. 59 and n. 2. See also: *JB*, ed. Greenway and Sayers, p. 140 n.; *JB*, ed. Rokewode, p. 133.
[69] *Feudal Docs*, pp. 131–2 nos 140–1.
[70] Above, p. 293 and nn. 15, 16.

the places which need consideration seventy-one are recorded as having one or more mills: the record always specifies whether a mill is a watermill or windmill. Comparison of its evidence with that in Little Domesday Book is revealing. With regard to the places listed above where Domesday records no mill,[71] we now find a windmill at: [Great] Barton,[72] Bradfield [Monachorum],[73] Chevington,[74] Elmswell,[75] Elvedon,[76] Hawstead,[77] Hinderclay,[78] Horringer,[79] Risby,[80] Rougham,[81] [Great] Saxham,[82] [Little] Saxham,[83] Whepstead[84] and Woolpit,[85] while Brockford had two windmills.[86] In some cases a windmill apparently replaced a watermill: in Nowton[87] and Stow Langtoft[88] each had a watermill in 1066 but in 1279 each had a windmill, while at Cockfield it seems that the winter-mill had been replaced by a windmill.[89] But new watermills were still being built. Thus, Chelsworth[90] and Ingham[91] each had one watermill in 1066, but had two in 1279 besides a windmill. Culford[92] had no mill in 1066 but had a watermill in 1279. If a place had no water-power and wanted a mill, a windmill might be a possibility. However, the Hempnall example illustrates that the presence of a watermill did not preclude the erection of a windmill. The care with which Walter fitz Robert and the monks chose the site for the windmill indicates that Longbridge was a particularly suitable place. Similarly, water-power was available in the Haberdun from the Lark. But the example of Herbert the dean's windmill vividly illustrates other reasons for erecting a windmill despite the presence of water-power: a windmill could be built much more quickly than a watermill and at less cost.

Although the mid-thirteenth-century accounts in BL MS Harley 645 include only eighteen of St Edmunds' two hundred or so holdings covered by Little Domesday, their evidence can be treated as representative of developments elsewhere on St Edmunds' estates. They do not always indicate whether a mill was

[71] Above p. 295.
[72] *Pinch. Reg.*, ii. 115.
[73] Ibid., ii. 102.
[74] Ibid., ii. 155.
[75] Ibid., ii. 209.
[76] Ibid., ii. 259.
[77] Ibid., ii. 163.
[78] Ibid., ii. 211.
[79] Ibid., ii. 167.
[80] Ibid., ii. 180.
[81] Ibid., ii. 124.
[82] Ibid., ii. 190.
[83] Ibid., ii. 185.
[84] Ibid., ii. 195.
[85] Ibid., ii. 151.
[86] Ibid., ii. 32 (*DB, Suffolk*, 14.47).
[87] Ibid., ii. 173 (*DB, Suffolk*, 14.4).
[88] Ibid., ii. 204 (*DB, Suffolk*, 14.77).
[89] Ibid., ii. 173 (*DB, Suffolk*, 14.24).
[90] Ibid., ii. 267–8 (*DB, Suffolk*, 14.109).
[91] Ibid., ii. 222 (*DB, Suffolk*, 14.69).
[92] Ibid., ii. 220 (*DB, Suffolk*, 14.70).

a watermill or a windmill. However, the mills they mention at five of the places where Little Domesday does not record the presence of a mill must surely have been windmills since the 1279–80 survey records the existence of a windmill at each of them. Thus, before the mid-thirteenth century windmills already existed at Great Barton, Bradfield, Hinderclay, Horringer and Whepstead.[93] The accounts include the mill at Nowton but do not indicate whether it was still a watermill or the windmill recorded in the 1279–80 survey.[94] They also include the 'half mill' at Southwold, probably the mill which Abbot Samson leased out.[95]

The above evidence makes it clear that a policy of constructing windmills where expedient on St Edmunds estates was adopted in the late twelfth century and pursued with vigour in the first half of the thirteenth century – the time when the great neighbouring abbeys of Ely, Peterborough and Ramsey were pursuing the same policy.[96]

5. The profitability of mills

The principal reason for this burst of windmill-building activity was economic: mills were seen as a lucrative asset.[97] A mill brought in revenue in one of two ways. First, it might be managed in hand, in demesne; it would be administered by the abbot or by an obedientiary through their servants and/or officials; and the unfree tenants on the manor or in the vill where the mill was situated were obliged to have their grain ground at it, paying multure in cash and/or kind for the facility.[98] Renders in kind were usually of grain or flour. Tenants also had to do labour services for the upkeep of the mill, which the lord might commute for payments in cash or kind. Since the imposition of labour services tended to be sporadic according to immediate need, multure constituted the principal source of income from a mill. A second means of deriving income from a mill was to lease it out. The lessee paid a rent fixed by the lord and sometimes also an entry fine, a *gersuma*. He was probably always responsible for most of the upkeep of the mill. Quite often he was the miller himself. Usually the miller was one of the lord's free tenants but the example cited above concerning Hempnall mill illustrates that he might even be a well-to-do villein: St Edmunds was granted William, miller of Twigrind, and his heirs and tenements.[99] Unfortunately, our sources do not always make it clear whether a mill was held in demesne or was leased. For instance, Great Domesday Book records that the mill at Warkton

---

[93] BL MS Harley 645, ff. 195[a/b], 195v[a], 252v[a], 261[a/b], 197[b] respectively.

[94] F. 197[a] (*Pinch. Reg.*, ii. 173).

[95] F. 195[a]; above p. 294 and n. 36.

[96] Holt, *Mills*, pp. 17–35.

[97] Ibid., pp. 70–89.

[98] Ibid., pp. 80–2; Homans, *English Villagers*, pp. 285–6; Kosminsky, *Agrarian History*, pp. 187–8.

[99] Above p. 298.

in Northamptonshire was worth 12s,[100] but whether this sum was the putative income from multure and other services, or whether it was the yearly fixed rent paid by a leaseholder is not clear. Moreover, the sources are so patchy and often hard to interpret, that they give a very incomplete picture.

The value which was placed on mills in a general way as sources of income appears, for example, in Walter fitz Robert's charter granting Twigrind mill: it estimates the mill's annual value at two marks and foresees the possibility of an increase with careful management.[101] A similar example comes from one of Samson's charters. Early in the thirteenth century Samson granted to Hugh of Thrandeston and his heirs an acre of arable in Palgrave and also conceded that 'our men' in Palgrave should do suit at Roger's mill and grind their corn at it throughout the year.[102] Income from a mill might be assigned by the donor or the monks for a particular purpose. As already explained, Walter fitz Robert's grant of Twigrind mill at Hempnall, the plot for the windmill at Longbridge and the rest, was to pay for the celebration of anniversaries for himself, his wife and other members of his family.[103] Abbot Anselm, in the charter mentioned above, granted the convent the manor of Chippenhall and a number of other properties including two mills: he assigned the income from the 'new mill' in the abbot's court, together with that from three fishponds in Pakenham, Ingham and Stowe respectively, to pay for the 'worthy and festive' ('digne et festive') celebration of the feast of the Conception of St Mary and of the feast of St Saba. He also granted the mill at 'Sidoluesmere' to the convent: it was to be for the infirmary ('dedi infirmis fratribus').[104] The convent assigned two watermills at West Stowe to the precentor to pay for parchment and ink for the monks.[105]

There is no better illustration of the importance attached by the monks to multure as a source of income than Samson's fury with Herbert the dean for constructing a windmill in the Haberdun. He thought that the new windmill would deter tenants from using the sacrist's mill in the Haberdun for grinding their corn, and was unmoved by Herbert's protestation that this was not his intention.[106] If necessary, the abbot would engage in expensive law suits to protect the abbey's right. This was necessary, for example, to secure St Edmunds' right to income from the mill at Wormegay in Norfolk[107] which was disputed by William de Warenne. At length, on 27 April 1186, a final concord was agreed in the king's court at Westminster whereby William recognized that in accordance to the terms of a gift in free alms made by his ancestors to the church of St Edmunds he owed it 60s annually from the mill at Wormegay, payable at four terms, besides 2,000 eels to be rendered annually on 1 August.[108]

100 DB, Northants, 8.13. Cf. Welldon Finn, Introduction to Domesday Book, pp. 225–8.
101 Above p. 299.
102 Kalendar, ed. Davis, p. 148 no. 124.
103 Above pp. 298–9.
104 Feudal Docs, pp. 112–13 no. 112.
105 Mon. Angl., iii. 157; Pinch. Reg., ii. 241.
106 JB, pp. 59–60. Above pp. 299–300.
107 See above p. 295 and n. 48.
108 Feudal Docs, pp. 186–7 no. 229; Kalendar, ed. Davis, p. 156 no. 139; Pinch. Reg., i. 426–7.

The income which a lord might derive from mills could be substantial. A specific example comes from Ely. According to contemporary records, in 1222 the bishop received £37 3s 4d income from his mills; in 1298, after the building of numerous windmills, the income had risen to £192 2s 10d.[109] However, obviously income greatly varied between one mill and another. An important fact was, of course, the number of tenants obliged to use a particular mill. But many other factors have to be considered in determining the profitability of a mill. Income had to be off-set against initial building costs.[110] This varied widely. As most watermills were built before written accounts were kept, the lord's initial costs are unlikely to survive. There is more information about the cost of building a windmill. A rough estimate is about £10, but the mid-thirteenth-century accounts from St Edmunds in BL MS Harley 645 record the cost of building a new windmill at West Stowe as £7 6s 5½d.[111] Obviously, the expense was less if a lord employed only or mainly his own labour-force of unfree tenants to do the building and if he could provide materials, notably wood and stone, from his own estates, or vandalize materials from redundant mills – especially useful were good second-hand millstones.[112]

New millstones were expensive, especially in East Anglia where high-quality stones of basaltic lava were used in preference to the cheaper British stones from quarries of sedimentary rocks in the Pennines and elsewhere.[113] The basaltic stones were quarried in the hills of the mid-Rhine region and were in one piece. They were ferried down the Rhine from Cologne and shipped to ports mainly in East Anglia, notably Ipswich, Yarmouth and Lynn. Stones for St Edmunds' mills seem often to have been bought at Ipswich: from there they would have been transported by cart to the mill in question. Some stones were bought at Yarmouth. But stones imported at Yarmouth were often ferried inland up the Yare to Norwich, or up the Waveney to Beccles: St Edmunds certainly bought stones at Norwich and transported them probably by land to the intended mill, presumably one of its mills in Norfolk. St Edmunds probably also bought stones at Beccles: if so, the stone might have been ferried up the Waveney to Brandon and from there carted to the designated mill. Similarly, stones it bought in Lynn would probably have been ferried up Little Ouse to Brandon and so on by land to its destination. Choosing a good millstone was obviously of prime importance and the miller might well accompany the monastic official who would be responsible for the cost. The whole process was obviously a time consuming, expensive and labour intensive business. Transporting a millstone was undoubtedly an obligation imposed on those unfree tenants who owed service to the mill. Since the German millstones were in one piece, this was an onerous obligation. (As we shall see, the strong objection to transporting millstones of the villeins of St Albans are on record.) Added to the above expenses were the costs of general

[109] Holt, *Mills*, p. 85.
[110] Ibid., pp. 176–7.
[111] BL MS Harley 645, f. 262v^b^.
[112] Holt, *Mills*, pp. 176–7.
[113] Watts, *Archaeology of Mills and Milling*, pp. 98–9; Farmer, 'Millstones for medieval manors', pp. 97–102.

repairs. In the case of a watermill this included ensuring that the leat, the mill-pond and mill-race were kept clear and the water flowing. There were also the wages of the miller and mill servants to pay, and the need to protect flour and corn collected as multure from rats and theft – a serious problem. Multure was stored in chests under lock and key in the mill building and it and the mill-house were also kept locked up.

Much of the information given above about the economics of medieval mills is derived from fourteenth- and fifteenth-century sources. Therefore, the references to mills in the mid-thirteenth-century accounts in the Kempe register, BL MS Harley 645, are especially valuable. They enter the income from a few of St Edmunds' mills and sometimes also the cost of repairs, very occasionally specifying what they were for. These entries deserve attention despite the fact that it is impossible to say how accurate they are in modern terms. Selected examples are cited below, in the order in which they appear in the manuscript. The example of Icklingham will be considered on its own in a section below, because the evidence is particularly detailed. The entries to be cited in the present section are for one year, or approximately one year, unless otherwise noted. If a mill is certainly or probably either managed in hand or leased, this is also noted. First, are accounts dated within the period 1247–50.

6. *Examples where both receipts and expenses are recorded*

[West] Stowe (in hand), *receipts for two months (January and February)* 10s, *expenses for eight months,* 54s 8½d for millstone and board (bord) and repair of 'ball'; *also* 41s 10¾d 'for wall for mill' ('In … pariete molend') *aggregated with many other necessary minor expenses; also* £20 18s 6d 'expenses paid for mill'.[114]

Horringer (*leased*), *receipts* 30s *payable at three terms, expenses* 10s 'for one millstone'.[115]

Chepenhall, *receipts* 15s 4½d 'from grain of mill' ('De blad' molend''), *expenses* 25s 6d.[116]

Southwold, *receipts* 18s 5s, *expenses* 20s 8½d.[117]

Pakenham (2 mills) (*leased*), *receipts* £4, 'but 15s from previous year', *expenses* 33s 'for two millstones'.[118]

Warkton (*leased*), *receipts* 5½ marks *for year,*[119] 52s 1¼d *for six months,*[120] 16s 8d *arrears, expenses* 3s 9d.[121]

Beccles, *receipts* £7, *expenses* 33s 11d 'for two millstones'.[122]

Aylsham, *receipts* 35s 2½d, *expenses* 12s 11¼d.[123]

114 BL MS Harley 645, f. 193v[b] passim.
115 F. 194v[a].
116 F. 195[a].
117 Ibid.
118 F. 195[b].
119 F. 198[a].
120 F. 198[b].
121 Ibid.
122 F. 252v[b].
123 F. 260v[a].

7. Examples where receipts only are recorded

Fornham (*leased*), *receipts* 1 mark.[124]
Bury St Edmunds, *receipts* £5 13s 4d and 60s 'restant', *i.e. remains unpaid*.[125]
Bradfield, *receipts* 2s 8d.[126]
Southery (*leased*), *receipts for six months* 13s 5d, *for year* 12s 2d.[127]
Nowton (*leased*), *receipts for five months* 12s.[128]
Whepstead (*leased*), *receipts* 3s ('Item molend̄ ponebatur ad firmam per annum pro 3s').[129]

Mildenhall (*in hand*), *receipts* £16 9s 3¼d 'except for miller's metecorn and 3 sieves of frumenty ('fr' furmatas') for the hall ('in domo')'.[130]

Barton [Mill] (*in hand*) *receipts* £9 12s; *and* £10 12s 8d 'from new grain, that is wheat, rye, barley and the mill'.[131]

8. Miscellaneous examples

'near **Newebrig'** in Norfolk' (*leased*) 'Pepermilne', ½ mark 'restat', *i.e. remains unpaid*.[132]

Hempnall, *among the pittancer's accounts are three separate entries recording income from Hempnall mill, no doubt to be identified as Twigrind watermill*: 30s 9d 'pittance for Hempnall' ('Hemenhale') (*in deleted paragraph*); 20s 'for Hemehal'; 19s 9d 'pro mol' de Hemehale'.[133] The pittance must have been that provided for in Robert fitz Walter's charter of donation discussed above.[134]

Caister St Edmund, *expenses*, 5d 'for nails for mill' ('pro clauis ad molend").[135]

Moreover, there are a few examples in the miscellaneous obedientiary accounts within the period **1256–1261**.
Cellarer:
Semer (*leased*), *receipts* 50s, *expenses* 2s 'mill's tithe', *and* 9s 10d *for miller's wages for about six months, aggregated with those of carters, shepherd / shepherds and a girl*).[136]

---

[124] F. 193[a].
[125] Ibid.
[126] F. 195v[a].
[127] F. 195v[b].
[128] F. 197[a].
[129] F. 197[b].
[130] F. 197v[a].
[131] F. 197v[b].
[132] F. 193[a]. For the lease of Pepper ('Peper') mill see *Kalendar*, ed. Davis, p. 154 no. 136. Peper occurs as a surname in medieval East Anglia and probably 'Peper mill' took its name from the surname of its miller at some time, possibly one who traded in pepper and other spices as a sideline. Cf. McKinley, *Norfolk and Suffolk Surnames*, p. 49.
[133] F. 252[b].
[134] Above p. 299.
[135] F. 253[a].
[136] F. 261[a].

Groton (*leased*), *receipts* 50s 2d 'from assized rent and mill' ('de redditu assis' et molend'') *and expenses aggregated with other expenses* 7s 10¼d.[137]

Horringer (*leased*), *receipts* 30s.[138]

Nowton (*leased*), *receipts* 38s.[139]

Subcellarer:

[West] Stowe, *receipts* 38s 3d, *expenses* 45s 6d 'for new sluices' ('In nouis inclusis'); *also*, £7 6s 5½d 'for constructing a new mill'.[140]

Great Barton (*leased*), *receipts* 30s 'from watermill'.[141]

? Bury St Edmunds (*in hand*), 24s 8¾d 'for one millstone and other necessaries for the watermill', 13s 6½d 'for wages for the miller and allowances for him'; *also* (*interlined*) 14s 'for one millstone'.[142]

9. Icklingham and its mills

Icklingham was a vill with a number of mills.[143] The village or hamlet of Icklingham was (and is) a long, narrow one with a church at each – St James' in the east and All Saints' in the west. It lies on the right bank of the Lark which flows from the west through Mildenhall and Barton Mills. At Icklingham the Lark is joined by a tributary flowing from the south, closely passing Cavenham. Mildenhall is about four miles from Icklingham and Cavenham about two.[144] The triangular region within these three places roughly coincided with the boundaries of the medieval vill of Icklingham. It is predominantly flat and had (and has) extensive heaths on the sandy, higher ground. Nowadays the lower lying areas in the vicinity of the river beds are of arable or pasture and are intersected by drainage ditches and tracks. In the middle ages they were marshy and dotted with ponds but, as now, had drainage ditches. The vill was greatly valued for its natural resources – for example, the heaths for rabbits, the marshes for reeds and waterfowl, the ponds and rivers for fish. And the rivers provided power to operate watermills.[145]

The vill, being within the Liberty of the eight and a half hundreds, was under the jurisdiction of St Edmunds, but other lords had lands and rights there. Domesday Book records that the king held Icklingham as an outlier of the rich manor of Mildenhall: the latter had been given by Edward the Confessor to St Edmunds which had leased it to Stigand; following the fall of Stigand, the

---

137 F. 261[b]. 'Assized rent' meant a fixed or assessed rent.
138 F. 261v[a/b].
139 F. 261v[b].
140 F. 262v[b]. See above p. 305.
141 F. 262v[b].
142 F. 265[a].
143 See the comprehensive study of medieval Icklingham in Prigg, *Icklingham Papers*.
144 See the map in ibid., [p. ix].
145 Ibid., p. 17.

manor had escheated to the king.[146] Its outlier at Icklingham, Domesday Book records, had a church (in fact, St James'), a mill, and considerable other property. Domesday Book also records that Richard Peverel and Eudo son of Spirwic each held a small manor in Icklingham: both manors had a mill.[147] When in 1190 Samson purchased Mildenhall from Richard I, he also acquired its outlier, Icklingham, then known as the manor of St James. Henceforth this manor belonged to the abbot's portion of St Edmunds' property, but he assigned part of its revenue to his newly founded hospital of St Saviour's at Babwell.[148] In the course of the twelfth century St Edmunds acquired one of the small Domesday manors in Icklingham and this was assigned to the sacrist: it was known as 'Sexten manor' or 'Sacristan manor'. The other small Domesday manor, with mill and a fishery in the mill-pond, soon came into the possession of the Berners family: the church of All Saints was built on it early in the twelfth century. Yet another small estate in the vill was held from St Edmunds by the Twamhill family and became known as 'Twamhill manor': it was administered by the cellarer as part of the manor of Mildenhall.[149] Important among the other landholders were the Knights Templar.[150]

A group of late twelfth- and early thirteenth-century charters adds a few details to this picture, which remains, nevertheless, far from clear. Copies of these charters are in the early thirteenth- and fourteenth-century cartulary, known as the Black register of the vestry (now CUL MS Mm. iv. 19), and in the late thirteenth- and fourteenth-century register of the sacrist's office (CUL MS Ff. ii. 33). Some of these charters name a specific mill. Thus, Abbot Samson granted a lease in heredity to Ralf son of Robert, miller, of 'the mill called Cure-bihinde (or 'Curebehynden' or 'Curebehyndyn'), for 13s 6d annually to be paid at our hall at Herringswell for the three farms owed by that vill, that is 4s 6d for each ferm'; Ralf was also subject to boon work and other servile services 'like one who held fifteen acres in the vill', and was to pay 2d a year to those who mowed the abbot's meadow; if Ralf had many heirs only one was to inherit

146 *DB, Suffolk*, 1.115.
147 Ibid., 34.1; 53.1.
148 *JB*, p. 47 (above p. 49 and n. 28); Prigg, op. cit., pp. vii–viii, 2–3, 54, 80.
149 'Twamhill' manor is mentioned twice in the cellarer's accounts for Mildenhall, 1247–8. BL MS Harley 645, f. 197v.
150 'Temple bridge' is marked on Prigg's map. The inquisition post mortem of Sir Ralph de Berners, of 8 Jan. 1297, records that 12d was owed p.a. to the preceptor of the Temple. *Cal. Inq. P. M.*, iii. 273 no. 411. A late thirteenth-century survey of Icklingham records that the sacrist owed the house of the Templars 1 mark on the feast of St Edmund. 'Item iiij. d. et j. candel' de dimid' libra cere'. BL MS Harley 645, f. 201v. For the Templars' holding in Icklingham see also below and n. 155. There is nothing about the Templars' holdings within St Edmunds' Liberty although there are oblique references to St Edmunds in *Records of the Templars*, ed. Lees. Lord, *Knights Templar*, p. 68, remarks that Templar holdings in Norfolk and Suffolk 'are the least well recorded'. No physical remains of the Templars at Icklingham are mentioned by Tull, *Traces of the Templars*. See below pp. 309 and n. 156, 311 and n. 163.

the holding.[151] Unless, which seems most unlikely, there was another mill also called Curebihinde, this mill was the one bearing that name in Icklingham which appears in other charters. If this identification is correct, Samson's rights in Curebihinde must have been part of his original agreement with the convent concerning Mildenhall and Icklingham, its outlier.[152] It seems that as a result of the agreement the sacrist lost his right to Curebihinde mill. The grant by Gilbert, son of Richard son of Warin, of Icklingham, of a mill for the use of the sacrist, includes a reference to the 'sacrist's mill called Curebehyndyn', in its description of the location of the newly granted mill and its property:[153] the mill now granted was next to the sacrist's manor and the marshy land, with its 'ponds, sluices, watercourses and fisheries', extended from Gilbert's 'said mill to the sacrist's mill called Curebehyndyn and from the said mill to a certain land by the vill of Cavenham'; the marsh also stretched westwards from the other side of the mill up to the pond called 'bȳgrynd'.

Curebihinde mill appears again in two early thirteenth-century charters in the sacrist's register.[154] In the one charter Nicholas, son of Stephen of Cavenham, grants to St Edmunds for the sacrist's use three acres of uncultivated land (*dura terra*) in his heath of Cavenham; in the other he grants one acre of uncultivated land, also in Cavenham heath. Both pieces of land abutted at one end on the mill-pond of 'Curebihinden'. The mill granted by Gilbert, son of Richard son of Warin, is to be identified, I believe, with the sacrist's mill called (like St Edmunds' mill in Hempnall[155]) Twigrind ('Twygrind'). It is mentioned by name in a few thirteenth-century charters. Perhaps it was the mill-pond of this mill which is referred to as the 'pond called bȳgrynd' in Gilbert's grant. Twygrind mill itself appears in a grant made in Samson's time by William, son of Walter son of Warin, of Icklingham, of two acres in Icklingham which 'abut at one head on the mill-race (*aqua*) of T[wy]grind. This mill was assigned to the sacrist. Its mill-pond is mentioned in a chirograph drawn up between Abbot Richard of Draughton (1313–35) and the convent, and Robert of Stamford, Master of the Temple, and the brethren of the Temple[156] – the document reveals that when the mill-pond of Twygrind ('Thwearind' sic MS) overflowed, it flooded the Templars' land, which must, therefore, have been close to the mill-pond. In the thirteenth century, if not earlier, the sacrist held another mill in Icklingham. This was a fulling mill. It is the subject of a chirograph drawn up between the

151 *Kalendar*, ed. Davis, p. 135 no. 104.
152 For the agreement see *JB*, p. 47.
153 CUL MS Ff. ii. 33, f. 114.
154 Ibid., f. 106v bis.
155 See above pp. 298–9.
156 Ff. ii. 33, f. 107. This agreement must be dated to fairly soon after Richard of Draughton's succession to the abbacy which received royal assent on 4 March 1312 (*Heads*, ii. 27), since Clement V issued the bull 'Vox in celso' suppressing the Order of the Temple on 22 March 1312. The bull 'Ad providam Christi' for the transfer of most of the Templars' property to the Hospitallers was issued on 2 May 1312, though its implementation obviously took time. *C and S*, 11, ii. 1351 and nn.; Lord, op cit., pp. 201–3; above p. 308 and n. 150 and below p. 311 and n. 163.

sacrist, William of Hoo, and Robert, the fuller, and his wife Cecilia, in 1282.[157]
According to the terms of the agreement, Hoo granted a life-lease to Robert and
Cecilia of a toft, a mill and buildings for an annual rent of 24 s, payable at two
terms (Michaelmas and Easter) 'for all service and customs': the mill lay opposite the 'exterior gate of the sacrist's manor and one head abutted on St James'
church and the other on the sacrist's fishery'.

The survey of St Edmund's barony made in 1279–80 mentions only one mill
held in chief in Icklingham by the abbot and convent.[158] It immediately follows
the notice of the mill with an entry for 'a toll barrier for merchants passing
through'. That is, St Edmunds had a barrier across the Lark and the right to
collect toll from merchants using the waterway, similar to the barriers at Babwell
and at Barton Mill. The grant of Gilbert, son of Richard son of Warin, included
the right to toll. It is tempting, therefore, to identify the mill granted by Gilbert
as the antecedent of the watermill which has survived, after numerous repairs
and at least two rebuildings, as a working flour mill into the present century.
Today the modern flour mill of C. Marston and Sons stands on the site: it is
powered by electricity but the early nineteenth-century watermill building is
preserved within its structure, as already explained.[159]

The information about the various watermills at Icklingham given above,
although partly speculative, I hope helps interpret the following cryptic entries
about its mills in the sacrist's accounts of 1248–50 in BL MS Harley 645.[160] The
first molinary entry combines receipts from the 'mills' with those from toll and
must surely include Twygrind:

> (*leased*) *receipts from mills* ('de redd' molendinorum') *and toll for five months, from*
> *29 September 1248 to 22 February 1249*, 40s 16d at Michaelmas and 40s 16d at
> Christmas.

> *receipts from the mills* ('mollend'') *and toll for six months, 22 February 1249 to 29*
> *September 1250, at two terms,* [*total*] £4 2s 8d. *Interlined*: 'Item de Tuegrind 16d'.

Another entry, of expenses for the mill 'at the gate' ('ad portam') possibly refers
to the fulling mill mentioned above. The entry notes 'for expenses of the mill
at the gate 5s 1d'. The accounts also record receipt of tithe of half a load of rye
given for the mill' ('In decima data pro molend' dimidium sum[mum] '[siliginis]
…')

Concern to protect the water supply necessary for the abbey's watermills in
Icklingham is apparent in three charters. The information in them compli-
ments the archaeological evidence uncovered in the recent excavations of the
water system serving Babwell mill. The chirograph of 1282, whereby the sacrist,
William of Hoo granted a life-lease to Robert the fuller and Cecilia his wife of the
fulling mill,[161] stipulates that: if ever, owing to defect of the leat (*aqua*) leading

157 *Letter-Book of William of Hoo*, pp. 122–3.
158 *Pinch. Reg.*, ii. 259.
159 Above pp. 291–2.
160 BL MS Harley 645, f. 260[a] and [b].
161 Above, n. 157.

to the sacrist's water mill, the sacrist loses multure, Robert and Cecilia must make amends; and if the leat (*aqua*) to the fulling mill is ever maliciously interfered with by the miller, or the farmer of the sacrist's mill or fishery, so that the fulling mill cannot function, the sacrist must make amends. Similarly, concern to protect the flow of water to a watermill appears in a charter of Nicholas son of Stephen, whose grants of land in Cavenham heath have already been noticed. In the present instance, he granted in free alms to God, the church of St Edmunds and the sacrist that the sacrist and his bailiffs might whenever necessary repair the mill-pond of the sacrist's mill at Icklingham 'within my land next to the river' ('infra terram meam secus aquam') of Cavenham heath, 'saving to me and my heirs the heath and furze'.[162]

The care taken to safeguard the water supply is also illustrated by the chirograph between Abbot Richard of Draughton and the convent, and Robert of Stamford, Master of the Temple and the brethren of the Temple.[163] The opening words of the chirograph announce that its intention was to end the litigation between the parties about the water supply. Details follow. Thus, if by chance, the length, width and depth of the mill-pond of Twygrind having been measured, the water level rose above the agreed measured height, either party could 'without contradiction or delay' make the necessary repairs to reduce the water level to the agreed height; similarly, if floods caused the pond to overflow the Templars might themselves repair the mill-pond; and both parties agreed that neither they or their men would do any damage to the mill-pond. It must be this mill which figures in the sacrist's accounts for 1249–50 in BL MS Harley 645 (f. 260). As will be seen, the accounts enable us to identify with some certainty the mill as Twygrind, the mill which appears in the charters.

To end this section I shall cite a document among the Icklingham archives which provides concrete evidence of the cost of maintaining a mill, in this case a windmill, in working order. The evidence is valuable because it is specific and despite the fact that it does not concern one of the St Edmunds mills and is nearly a century later than the accounts in Harley 645. The bailiff's accounts for the Berners' manor in Icklingham for 1342–3 list the items of expenditure on the mill as follows: wages for a carpenter hired to repair of the foundations of the mill and for mending the wheels, 9d; two oak boards bought for the foundations, 4d; nails bought for fixing the boards, 3d; eight 'Ronwellbordes' [? boards from Runwell, Essex] bought for the netting ('pro retibus') of the mill, 20d; two hundred nails bought for the same, 4d; timber bought for the cog-wheels of the mill, 5d; four and a half days' wages for a carpenter hired to repair the mill wheels and for buying other necessaries for the repair of the mill, 12s; for grease and tallow for greasing the mill, 4d; total expense 5s 1d.[164]

---

[162] Ff. ii. 33, f. 106.
[163] Ibid., f. 107. See above pp. 308 and n. 150, 309 and n. 156.
[164] Prigg, *Icklingham Papers*, pp. 28–9.

10. Disadvantages of demesne management of mills

Managing mills in hand by the monks and their officials usually seems to have been more profitable than leasing them.[165] However, this option had grave disadvantages. It left the monks with the sole responsibility for upkeep. As the example just cited from the Berners' manor in Icklingham shows, the cost of keeping a mill in working order could be substantial. The evidence of the accounts in BL MS Harley 645 corroborates this conclusion. Thus, the accounts for Horringer, Pakenham, Beccles and Bury St Edmunds show that although a millstone could cost 10s, usually one cost more, prices ranging from 14s to nearly 17s – possibly because carriage charges were added but the price was also determined by the quality of the stone and, if it were not a new one, by the amount of wear.[166] As for general maintenance, the cost could be substantial: according to the accounts maintenance costs for the watermill at Southwold and for the one at West Stowe exceeded receipts. Cost for the upkeep of the West Stowe watermill was especially high, amounting to £20 18s 6d in 1249 and 45s 6d in 1260/1;[167] the accounts specify particular items of expenditure; in 1249 a millstone and board, and repair of the *baÞ*, and in 1261 new sluices. In the case of watermills there was the problem of maintaining the water management system, and of protecting it from damage by neighbours: this could involve expensive and time-consuming negotiations and even litigation. Moreover, in any argument with the miller, the landlord was at a disadvantage because of the miller's expertise and day-to-day experience.

A serious problem faced by a lord managing a mill was the enforcement of his rights. The unfree tenants were obliged to use the lord's mill and pay multure for doing so. They also had to perform labour services as need arose in order to keep the mill running; these included the obligation to transport timber, building stone and millstones when required. Such services were especially oppressive because they were sporadic and variable. Specific example of opposition to payment of multure and molinary services by St Edmunds' tenants have not yet come to light, though Jocelin of Brackland mentions opposition by the townsmen to two servile obligations: they accused the cellarer of unjustly exempting some, but not all, of the rich burgesses from the payment of 'repselver' (for the right to reap their own corn) and of exacting payment ruthlessly from the poor; and they objected to paying 'sorpenny' (for the right to graze a cow).[168] When in 1327 many of the townsmen rose in revolt against the abbey, they promised all who joined them freedom from 'all toll and all services' – among the latter would have been service to mills.[169]

---

165   Holt, *Mills*, p. 85.
166   Above p. 304.
167   Harley 645, ff. 195ᵃ, 262vᵇ.
168   *JB*, pp. 99–100.
169   *Depraedatio abbatiae Sancti Edmundi*, in *Memorials*, ii. 334. This near-contemporary monograph will be discussed in vol. ii of the present study.

Excellent examples of the problems associated with enforcing payment of multure and performance of molinary services survive from St Albans. As at St Edmunds, the abbots and monks of St Albans were actively engaged in the thirteenth and fourteenth centuries in repairing old mills and in building new ones, exploiting their potential profitability to the full. Disputes with unfree tenants over payment of multure and labour services begin to appear in the records in the mid-thirteenth century. For instance, the tenants of the manor of Cassio (near Watford) denied that they had the duty of carrying timber and millstones to the mill.[170] Since a millstone might have been bought in London or even further afield, they might have had to transport this heavy load a long way. The tenants of another manor, Abbots Langley (a few miles south of St Albans), frequently disputed the duty of carrying timber for the repair of the mill-house and sluices and also to mudding the bank of the mill-pond and of keeping the dikes and sluices in repair at their own expense.[171] A recurrent problem for St Albans abbey was the tenants' recourse to handmills to avoid using the lord's mill at all. Dispute over this issue came to a head during the revolt in the town in 1327. In the conflict Abbot Richard of Wallingford (1327–36) suppressed the rebels and forced them to surrender their handmills: he used the millstones to pave the entrance of his parlour.[172] Memories were long and resentment at this rough treatment festered in the town. It broke out during the violence of the Peasants' Revolt in 1381: among the rebels' demands in the charter which they compelled the abbot and convent to sign was the right to use handmills.[173] When they stormed the abbey they included in their assault invasion of the abbot's parlour; they ripped up the millstones, broke them into small pieces and distributed the bits to their followers 'as if they were holy relics'.[174]

Although it is not known whether St Edmunds' unfree tenants were as opposed to the payment of multure and the performance of molinary services as were those of St Albans, the obligations cannot have been popular. Even passive resistance, for example delays in paying multure and in performing the labour services, could have been one reason why Abbot Samson often preferred to lease his mills rather than manage them in hand. He did this despite the above mentioned fact that managing mills in hand tended to be more profitable than leasing,[175] and that leasing any property tended in the long run to make serious

---

170 Levett, *Manorial Studies*, p. 204.
171 Ibid., pp. 196–7.
172 GASA, ii. 155–69, esp. pp. 158, 169. For disputes of the abbey with its tenants from the mid-thirteenth century to 1326 over tenants' refusal to pay multure and their insistence on using handmills see: ibid., i. 410–23 passim; Levett, op. cit., p. 204. For Richard of Wallingford's disputes on this matter see: Holt, *Mills*, pp. 40–1; North, *God's Clockmaker*, pp. 119–25 and refs.
173 GASA, iii. 285–371, esp. pp. 271–4, 293, 309, 362–3, 371. See e.g.: R. B. Dobson, *The Peasants' Revolt of 1381* (London, 1970), pp. 269–77. For the revolt at Bury St Edmunds see e.g.: ibid., pp. 42–3, 245–54; Lobel, *Bury St. Edmunds*, pp. 150–5.
174 GASA, iii. 309.
175 Holt, *Mills*, p. 85.

inroads into a lord's seigneurial rights; a leasehold, whether for life, for several lives or in perpetuity (in fee) all too easily became a free tenancy.[176]

11. Abbot Samson's leases of St Edmunds' mills

Abbot Samson renewed existing leases of some mills and also leased out some which had previously been managed in hand. This is noteworthy because it was contrary to his usual policy of recovering alienated properties and returning them to the abbey's demesne. Nine of Samson's printed charters will be cited (omitting some detail) to illustrate the nature of his leases: his lease in heredity of 'Curebehinden' mill, which I identify as the mill of that name in Icklingham was noticed above.[177] The nine others are as follows:

1. **Fornham St Genovieve**, 'the mill called Salmondesforde', with all its arable and meadow land, leased in heredity to William 'of the granary' ('de granario', presumably the miller) for 27s 2d annually, payable at the hall of Fornham. 1186–90.[178]
2. **Fornham St Genovieve**, 'Salmondesforde' mill, with all its arable and meadow land, 'which used to pay at least 27s 2d annually at our hall in Fornham,' leased in heredity to Henry of Thurston for 30s annually. 1196–1206.[179]
3. **Fornham All Saints**, 'the mill called Ailmeres melne' which used to pay 26s annually, leased in heredity to Ailmar (presumably the miller) son of Ailward of Fornham, for 30s annually payable at Fornham hall in four parts, at those times when the vill rendered its four annual food farms. c. 1186–1200.[180]
4. **[West] Stowe**, 'our two mills, which pertain to the scriptorium of the church of St Edmund', leased for life to Gervase son of 'H.' the moneyer, for 60s annually payable at four terms. He is not allowed to mortgage or sell the mills to anyone and on his death they are to be returned to the convent without any claim by Gervase's heirs. c. 1200–11.[181]
5. **Ingham**, two watermills, as part of the manor, leased for life to Solomon of Whepstead. 1186–1200.[182]
6. **Elveden**, the windmill, as part of the manor, leased for life to Solomon of Whepstead. The rent for the manor was to render the food farm it owed to the cellarer twice a year.[183]

[176] See: Harvey, *Westminster Abbey*, pp. 81–3; Holt, *Mills*, pp. 57–8.
[177] Above pp. 308–9.
[178] *Kalendar*, ed. Davis, pp. 107–8 no. 57.
[179] Ibid., pp. 108–9 no. 58.
[180] Ibid., p. 109 no. 59. The place-name 'Fornham' seems to be used indifferently to denote Fornham All Saints and Fornham St Genevieve, the former having one mill and the latter five mills, all on the river Lark.
[181] Ibid., p. 117 no. 74.
[182] Ibid., pp. 119–21 no. 77 and n. 1.
[183] Ibid.

7. **Southwold**, 'half of our mill' leased in heredity to Henry son of Thurstan for 6d annually payable to the cellarer at Michaelmas and an initial entry fine (*gersuma*) of 1 silver mark. c. 1182–1200.[184] It would seem that Henry obtained the lease on exceptionally favourable terms, for in the mid-thirteenth century the half mill was valued at 20s annually.[185]

8. **Unidentified**, 'our part of the small mill' leased in heredity to Reimund son of Reinald of Sudbury for 18s annually payable to the sacrist at two terms for all service. c. 1182–1200.[186]

9. **Unidentified**, 'our mill in Norfolk near Newebrig called Pepirmelne' leased in heredity to Roger of Buckenham for 1 silver mark annually payable to the cellarer.[187]

Seven of the nine leased mills under consideration – the two at Fornham, the two at West Stowe, and those at Ingham and Elveden – were large mills close to St Edmunds in West Suffolk on important manors, two of them food farms (Fornham and Elveden). Two of the lessees of ('Salmondesforde' mill at Fornham and of the mill at Icklingham), are named as the miller, and the lessee of 'Ailmeres melne' at Fornham was probably also the miller. When Samson granted a new lease of 'Salmondesforde' mill and a new lease of 'Ailmeres melne' he raised both rents. The cellarer's two mills of West Stowe and those on his manors of Ingham, and Elveden were granted for life but the other eight leases were in heredity. This in the long run could cause trouble. When Samson granted the leases the fixed rents were good in the current economic situation and the terms imposed by Samson were favourable to the abbey (with the apparent exception of the lease of half the mill at Southwold). But by the end of the twelfth century the economic situation had changed. Owing to inflation the fixed rents were too low and mills held in hand were more profitable than those leased out in heredity. Meanwhile, as pointed out above, leasehold tenancies, both those held in heredity, and even, though less often, those leased for life, tended to become freehold tenancies. Properties thus alienated were hard to recover for the demesne. Attempts to do so in the fourteenth and fifteenth century could involve expensive litigation and might end in failure. For example, while the 1278/9 survey of St Edmunds' barony records five mills at Fornham, none was in the abbey's hands. In order to have a mill in hand there Abbot John of Northwold had to purchase Ailmer's mill which Samson had leased in heredity.[188] Salmondesford's mill, leased out in heredity twice in succession by Samson, was now a free tenancy and remained so: it still existed at least as

---

[184] Ibid., p. 150 no. 128.
[185] *Pinch. Reg.*, i. 346.
[186] *Kalendar*, ed. Davis, p. 131 no. 95.
[187] Ibid., p. 154 no. 136. Newbridge is a common place-name. Buckenham, Old and New, and Buckenham Tofts or Buckenham Parva are Norfolk place-names. For the name Pepper (Peper) mill see above p. 306 n. 132.
[188] *Pinch. Reg.*, ii. 128–9.

late as the mid-fifteenth century.[189] Another of the five mills at Fornham which had belonged to St Edmunds but which Samson had leased out had likewise become a free tenancy: Abbot William of Burnham recovered it after a case in the king's court: he argued successfully that Samson's grant was invalid because it was made without the convent's assent.[190]

---

[189] Holt, *Mills*, p. 62.
[190] Ibid., p. 62, citing the mid-fifteenth-century collection of evidences concerning Fornham, BL MS Additional 34689, f. 15 (Thomson, *Archives*, p. 158 no. 1311).

Abbreviations, and
Select Bibliography with Shortened Titles

Abbreviations

Agric. HR	*Agricultural History Review.*
Ann. Mon.	*Annales Monastici*, ed. H. R. Luard (RS, 1864–9, 5 vols).
Ann. S. Edm.	*Annales Sancti Edmundi*, ed. F. Liebermann, in *Ungedruckte Anglo-Normanische Geschichtsquellen*, ed. idem (Strassburg, 1879), pp. 97–155. The *Annales* are also printed in *Memorials*, ii. 3–25, the edn used here.
BAA CT	*British Archaeological Association Conference Transactions.*
Ben. Pet.	*The Chronicle of the Reigns of Henry II and Richard I, A.D. 1169–1192, known commonly under the name of Benedict of Peterborough*, ed. William Stubbs (RS, 1867, 2 vols).
BL	British Library.
BM	British Museum.
BN	Bibliothèque Nationale, Paris.
BNJ	*British Numismatic Journ.*
Bodl. Lib.	Bodleian Library, Oxford.
BRUO	A. B. Emden, *A Biographical Register of the University of Oxford to A. D. 1500* (Oxford, 1957–9, 3 vols).
Burton	*Chronicle of Burton Abbey*, in *Ann. Mon.*, i. 183–500.
Bury Chron.	*The Chronicle of Bury St Edmunds 1212–1301*, ed. and trans. A. Gransden (Nelson's Medieval Texts, 1964).
Bury Cust.	*The Customary of the Benedictine Abbey of Bury St Edmunds in Suffolk*, ed. A. Gransden, Henry Bradshaw Soc., xcix (1973).
C and S	*Councils and Synods with other Documents relating to the English Church, i, 871–1204*, ed. Dorothy Whitelock, Martin Brett and C. N. L. Brooke (Oxford, 1981, repr. 1986), pt 1, *871–1066*, pt 2, *1066–1204*, ii, ed. F. M. Powicke and C. R. Cheney (Oxford, 1964), pt 1, *1205–1265*, pt 2, *1265–1313*.
C Ch. R	*Calendar of Charter Rolls.*
C Lib. R	*Calendar of Librate Rolls.*
Cal. Inq. P. M.	*Calendar of Inquisitions Post Mortem* (London, HMSO, 1904–55, 19 vols).
Cal. Papal Letters	*Calendar of Entries in the Papal Registers relating to Great Britain and Ireland: Papal Letters (1198–1492)*, ed. W. H. Bliss and J. A. Twemlow (London, HMSO, 1893–1960, 14 vols).
CCR	*Calendar of Close Rolls.*
CPR	*Calendar of Patent Rolls.*
Cron. Bur.	*Cronica Buriensis*, in *Memorials*, iii. 1–73.
CUL	Cambridge University Library.
DB (with shire/county name)	*Domesday Book*, gen. ed. John Morris (Chichester, 1977–92, 38 vols including three final vols of indices).

DB, Norfolk	*DB*, xxxiii, *Norfolk*, ed. Philippa Brown (1984, 2 pts).
DB, Northants	*DB*, xxi, *Northamptonshire*, ed. Frank Thorn and Caroline Thorn (1979).
DB, Suffolk	*DB*, xxxiv, *Suffolk*, ed. Alex Rumble (1986, 2 pts).
De dedicationibus	*De dedicationibus altarum capellarum, etc., apud Sanctum Edmundum*, in *Bury Cust.*, pp. 114–21 (Appendix IX). [Composed c. 1140 with additions to 1275.]
De Miraculis	*Hermanni Archidiaconi Liber de Miraculis Sancti Eadmundi*, in *Memorials*, i. 26–92.
Decretum	*Decretum Gratiani*, ed. Friedberg, i.
DR	*Downside Review.*
Dunstable	*Annals of Dunstable Priory*, in *Ann. Mon.*, iii. 1–408.
Ec. HR	*Economic History Review.*
EHR	*English Historical Review.*
Electio	*The Chronicle of the Election of Hugh Abbot of Bury St Edmunds and Later Bishop of Ely*, ed. and trans. R. M. Thomson (Oxford, 1974). [Composed c. 1222 x 1229.]
Fasti	John le Neve, *Fasti Ecclesiae Anglicanae*, corrected and continued … by T. D. Hardy (Oxford, 1954, 3 vols).
Fasti, Monastic Cathedrals	John le Neve, *Fasti Ecclesiae Anglicanae 1066–1300*, ii. *Monastic Cathedrals*, compiled by D. E. Greenway (London, 1971).
Feudal Docs	*Feudal Documents from the Abbey of Bury St. Edmunds*, ed. D. C. Douglas, British Academy Records of Social and Economic History, viii (Oxford, 1932).
Flores Hist.	*Flores Historiarum*, ed. H. R. Luard (RS, 1890, 3 vols).
GASA	*Gesta Abbatum Monasterii Sancti Albani*, ed. H. T. Riley (RS, 1867–9, 3 vols).
G. E. C., *Peerage*	G. E. C[ockayne], *The Complete Peerage of England, Scotland, Ireland and Great Britain and the United Kingdom*, new edn by Vicary Gibbs et al. (London, 1910–59, 13 vols).
Gesta Sacrist.	*Gesta Sacristarum*, in *Memorials*, ii, pp. 289–96.
Greatrex, *Biog. Reg.*	Joan Greatrex, *Biographical Register of the English Cathedral Priories of the Province of Canterbury c. 1066–1540* (Oxford, 1997).
Heads, i	David Knowles, C. N. L. Brooke and V. C. M. London, *The Heads of Religious Houses: England and Wales, i, 940–1216* (Cambridge, 1972, 2nd edn, 2001).
Heads, ii	D. M. Smith and V. C. M. London, *The Heads of Religious Houses: England and Wales, ii, 1216–1377* (Cambridge, 2001).
Hist. Docs, ii	*English Historical Documents, ii, 1042–1189*, ed. D. C. Douglas and G. W. Greenaway (2nd edn, London, 1981), iii, *1189–1327*, ed. Harry Rothwell (London, 1975).
JB	*The Chronicle of Jocelin of Brakelond*, ed. and trans. H. E. Butler (London – Edinburgh etc., Nelson's Medieval Classics, 1949, repr. 1951).
JB, ed. Greenway and Sayers	*Jocelin of Brakelond, Chronicle of the Abbey of Bury St Edmunds*, in English trans. with introduction and notes by Diana [E.] Greenway and Jane Sayers (Oxford, World's Classics, 1989).
JB, ed. Rokewode	*Chronica Jocelini de Brakelond*, ed. John Gage Rokewode, Camden Soc., 1st ser., xiii (1840), pp. 110, 111, 113.
JBAA	*Journ. of the British Archaeological Association.*

JEH	*Journ. of Ecclesiastical History.*
Knowles, *MO*	David Knowles, *The Monastic Order in England* (Cambridge, 1940, repr. with corrections 1949, 2nd edn, 1963).
Knowles, *RO*, i	David Knowles, *The Religious Orders in England*, i, *1216–1340* (Cambridge, 1956).
Memorials	*Memorials of St. Edmund's Abbey*, ed. Thomas Arnold (RS, 1890–6, 3 vols).
Mon. Angl.	W. Dugdale, *Monasticon Anglicanum*, ed. J. Caley, H. Ellis and B. Bandinel (London, Record Commission, 1817–30, 6 vols in 8 pts).
Papsturkunden	W. Holtzmann, *Papsturkunden in England*, 3 vols, Abhandlungen der Gesellschaft der Wissenschaften zu Göttingen, Phil.-Hist. Klasse, new series, xxv (1931), 3rd series, xiv (1935) and xxx (1952).
Parl. Writs	*Parliamentary Writs and Writs of Military Summons*, ed. Francis Palgrave (London, Record Commission, 1827–34, 2 vols in 4 pts).
Pinch. Reg.	*The Pinchbeck Register Relating to the Abbey of Bury St. Edmunds, etc.*, ed. Francis Hervey (Brighton – London, 1925, 2 vols).
Potthast	August Potthast, *Regesta Pontificum Romanorum ... 1198–1304* (Berlin, 1874–5, 2 vols).
PRO	Public Record Office (Kew, Surrey).
PSIA	*Proceedings of the Suffolk Institute of Archaeology.*
PSIAH	*Proceedings of the Suffolk Institute of Archaeology and History.*
PSIANH	*Proceedings of the Suffolk Institute of Archaeology and Natural History.*
Rog. How.	*Chronica Magistri Rogeri de Houedene*, ed. William Stubbs (RS, 1868–71, 4 vols).
Rot. Chart.	*Rotuli Chartarum in Turri Londinensi Asservati, 1199–1216*, ed. T. D. Hardy (London, Record Commission, 1837).
Rot. Litt. Claus.	*Rotuli Litterarum Clausarum in Turri Londinensi Asservati, 1204–1227*, ed. T. D. Hardy (London, Record Commission, 1833–44, 2 vols).
RS	Rolls Series.
SOED	*Shorter Oxford English Dictionary.*
SRO/B	Suffolk Record Office, Bury St Edmunds Branch.
SRO/I	Suffolk Record Office, Ipswich Branch.
TRHS	*Transactions of the Royal Historical Soc.*
VCH Norfolk	*Victoria History of the Counties of England. Norfolk* (London, 1901–6, 2 vols).
VCH Suffolk	*Victoria History of the Counties of England. Suffolk* (London, 1907, 1911, 2 vols).
Word-List	*Revised Medieval Latin Word-List from British and Irish Sources*, prepared by R. E. Latham (London, 1965).

Select Bibliography

Further titles are to be found in the list of abbreviations.

Primary sources

For manuscript sources see below, *index*, under Bury St Edmunds, Abbey, manuscripts

Abbo, *Passio*	Abbo of Fleury, *Passio Sancti Eadmundi*, in *Three Lives of English Saints*, ed. Michael Winterbottom, Toronto Medieval Latin Texts (Toronto, 1972), pp. 67–87, 91–92. The *Passio* is also printed in *Memorials*, i. 3–25. [Composed 985–87.]
Acta. Norwich 1070–1214, ed. Harper-Bill	*English Episcopal Acta, 6. Norwich 1070–1214*, ed. Christopher Harper-Bill (Oxford: British Academy, 1990).
Acta. Norwich 1215–43, ed. Harper-Bill	*English Episcopal Acta, 21. Norwich 1215–43*, ed. Christopher Harper-Bill (Oxford: British Academy, 2000).
Backhouse, *Luttrell Psalter*	Janet Backhouse, *The Luttrell Psalter* (London: British Library Board, 1989). See also below under 'Brown'.
Barnwell *Observances*, ed. Willis Clark	*The Observances in Use at the Augustinian Priory of S. Giles and S. Andrew at Barnwell, Cambridgeshire*, ed. John Willis Clark (Cambridge, 1897).
Brown (ed.), *Luttrell Psalter*	*The Luttrell Psalter*, facsimile edition by M. P. Brown (London: British Library Board, 2006).
'Bury Chron., Critical Edition', ed. Gransden	'A Critical Edition of the Bury St Edmunds Chronicle in Arundel 30 in the College of Arms, [Creation to 1301]', ed. A. Gransden, Ph.D. thesis, University of London, 1956.
Catalogus, ed. Rouse and Rouse	Henry of Kirkestede, '*Catalogus de Libris Autenticis et Apocrifis*', ed. R. H. Rouse and M. A. Rouse, Corpus of British Medieval Library Catalogues, xi (London, 2004).
Chapters, ed. Pantin	*Documents Illustrating the Activities of the General and Provincial Chapters of the English Black Monks 1215–1540*, ed. W. A. Pantin, Camden Soc., 3rd ser., xlv, xlvii, liv (London, 1931–7, 3 vols).
Cheney and Cheney, *Letters*	*The Letters of Pope Innocent III concerning England and Wales*, cal. C. R. Cheney and M[ary] G. Cheney (Oxford, 1967).
Chron. abbatiae de Evesham	*Chronicon abbatiae de Evesham ad annum 1418*, ed. W. D. Macray (RS, 1863).
Chron. of John of Worcester	*The Chronicle of John of Worcester*, ii, ed. R. R. Darlington † and Patrick McGurk, trans. Jennifer Bray † and Patrick McGurk (Oxford, 1995), iii, ed. Patrick McGurk (Oxford, 1998; vol. i forthcoming).
Compotus Rolls of St. Swithun's Priory, Winchester, ed. Kitchin	*Compotus Rolls of the Obedientiaries of St. Swithun's Priory, Winchester*, ed. G. W. Kitchin (Hants Record Soc., 1892).
Crook, *Records*	David Crook, *Records of the General Eyre*, Public Record Office Handbooks no. 20 (London, 1982).
Diceto, *Historical Works*	*The Historical Works of Master Ralph de Diceto, Dean of London*, ed. William Stubbs (RS, 1876, 2 vols).

Eynsham Customary, ed. Gransden	The Customary of the Benedictine Abbey of Eynsham in Oxford-shire, ed. Antonia Gransden. Corpus Consuetudinum Monasticarum, ii (Siegburg, 1963).
Friedberg, Corpus iuris canonici	Corpus iuris canonici, ed. Emil Friedberg (Leipzig, 1879–81, repr. 1922–8, 2 vols).
Grosseteste, Epistolae	Roberti Grosseteste Epistolae, ed. H. R. Luard (RS, 1861).
Harmer, Writs	F. E. Harmer, Anglo-Saxon Writs (Manchester, 1952, 1959, 2nd edn with an addition, Stamford, 1989).
Harper-Bill, Hospitals	Charters of the Medieval Hospitals of Bury St Edmunds, ed. Christopher Harper-Bill, Suffolk Records Soc., xiv (Woodbridge, 1994).
Hart, Early Charters	C. R. Hart, The Early Charters of Eastern England (Leicester, 1966).
Harvey, Obedientiaries	Barbara [F.] Harvey, The Obedientiaries of Westminster Abbey and their Financial Records c.1275 to 1540, Westminster Abbey Record Ser. iii (Woodbridge, 2002).
Harvey, Walter de Wenlock	Barbara [F.] Harvey, Documents Illustrating the Rule of Walter de Wenlock, Abbot of Westminster, 1283–1307, Camden Soc., 4th ser., ii (1965).
Hervey, Corolla	Corolla Sancti Eadmundi. The Garland of Saint Edmund King and Martyr, ed. Francis Hervey (London, 1907).
Hervey, King Eadmund	The History of King Eadmund the Martyr and of the Early Years of his Abbey, ed. Francis Hervey (Oxford, 1929).
Histoire des Conciles	C.-J. von Hefele, Conciliengeschichte (2nd edn, Freiburg, 1873–90, 6 vols), corrected and greatly enlarged, with French translation, by Henri Leclercq, Histoire des Conciles après des documents originaux (Paris, 1907–38, 20 vols), the text used here.
Historical Atlas of Suffolk	An Historical Atlas of Suffolk, ed. David Dymond and Edward Martin (revised and enlarged edn, Ipswich, 1999).
Horstman, Nova Legenda	Nova Legenda Anglie, as Collected by John of Tynemouth, John Capgrave and others, ed. Carl Horstman (Oxford, 1901, 2 vols).
Kalendar, ed. Davis	The Kalendar of Abbot Samson of Bury St. Edmunds and Related Documents, ed. R. H. C. Davis, Camden Soc., 3rd ser., lxxxiv (1954).
Kalendars, ed. Wormald	English Kalendars before A.D. 1100, ed. Francis Wormald, Henry Bradshaw Soc., lxxii (1934, repr. Woodbridge, 1988).
Lanfranc, Constitutions	The Monastic Constitutions of Lanfranc, ed. and trans. [M.] David Knowles (London – Edinburgh etc., 1951) (the edition used here), repr., Latin text only, with a few additions to the footnotes, and a full index, Decreta Lanfranci Monachis Cantuariensibus transmissa, Corpus Consuetudinum Monasticarum, iii (Siegburg, 1967).
Letter-Book of William of Hoo	The Letter-Book of William of Hoo sacrist of Bury St Edmunds 1280–1294, ed. A. Gransden, Suffolk Records Soc., v (Ipswich, 1963).
Letters and Charters of Cardinal Guala Bicchieri	The Letters and Charters of Cardinal Guala Bicchieri papal legate in England 1216–1218, ed. Nicholas Vincent (Canterbury and York Soc., lxxxiii, 1996).

Letters Illustrative of the Reign of Henry III	*Royal and other Historical Letters Illustrative of the Reign of Henry III from the Originals in the Public Record Office*, ed. W. W. Shirley (RS, 1862–6, 2 vols).
Letters of Osbert of Clare	*The Letters of Osbert of Clare, Prior of Westminster*, ed. E. W. Williamson, with a biography by J. A. Robinson (Oxford, 1929).
Matthew Paris, *Chron. Maj.*	*Matthaei Parisiensis, monachi Sancti Albani, Chronica Majora*, ed. H. R. Luard (RS, 1872–83, 7 vols).
Matthew Paris, *Hist. Anglorum*	*Matthaei Parisiensis, monachi Sancti Albani, Historia Anglorum sive historia minor*, ed. Frederic Madden (RS, 1866–9, 3 vols).
Records of the Templars, ed. Lees	*Records of the Templars in England in the Twelfth Century. The Inquest of 1185 with Illustrative Documents*, ed. B. A. Lees (Oxford, 1935).
Reg. Con., ed. Symons	*Regularis Concordia. The Monastic Agreement of the Monks and Nuns of the English Nation*, ed. and trans. Thomas Symons (London – Edinburgh etc., 1953).
Robertson, *Charters*	*Anglo-Saxon Charters*, ed. and trans. A. J. Robertson (Cambridge, 1939).
Rule, ed. Fry	*The Rule of St. Benedict*, ed. and trans. Timothy Fry (Collegeville, Minnesota, USA, 1981).
Saunders, *Norwich Obedientiary and Manor Rolls*	H. W. Saunders, *An Introduction to the Obedientiary and Manor Rolls of Norwich Cathedral Priory* (Norwich, 1930).
Sawyer, *Charters*	P. H. Sawyer, *Anglo-Saxon Charters. An Annotated List and Bibliography* (London, 1968).
'Visitation', ed. Graham	'A papal visitation of Bury St Edmunds and Westminster in 1234', ed. Rose Graham, *EHR*, xxvii (1912), pp. 728–39.
Whitelock, *Wills*	*Anglo-Saxon Wills*, ed. and trans. Dorothy Whitelock, Cambridge Studies in English Legal History (Cambridge, 1930).
William of Malmesbury, *Gesta Pont.*	*Willelmi Malmesbiriensis Monachi de Gestis Pontificum Anglorum Libri Quinque*, ed. N. E. S. A. Hamilton (RS, 1870).
William Worcestre	*William Worcestre, Itineraries*, ed. and trans. J. H. Harvey (Oxford: Oxford Medieval Texts, 1969).

Secondary sources

Allen, *The Durham Mint*	Martin Allen, *The Durham Mint*, British Numismatic Soc. Special Publication, iv (London, 2003).
Allen, 'Ecclesiastical mints'	Martin Allen, 'Ecclesiastical mints in thirteenth-century England', in *Thirteenth Century England, Proceedings of the Durham Conference 1999*, ed. Michael Prestwich, Richard Britnell and Robin Frame (Woodbridge, 2001), pp. 113–22.
Allen, 'Mint output … 1247–50'	Martin Allen, 'Mint output in the English recoinage of 1247–1250', *BNJ*, lxix (1999), pp. 207–10.
Allen, 'The output, … of the Bury St Edmunds mint'	Martin Allen, 'Documentary evidence for the output, profits and expenditure of the Bury St Edmunds mint', *BNJ*, lxix (1999), pp. 210–13.

Altschul, *A Baronial Family* — Michael Altschul, *A Baronial Family in Medieval England: The Clares, 1217–1314* (Baltimore, [USA], 1965).

Appleby, *England without Richard* — J. T. Appleby, *England without Richard 1189–1199* (London, 1965).

Bailey, *The English Manor* — Mark Bailey, *The English Manor c. 1200–c. 1500. Selected sources translated and annotated* (Manchester – New York, 2002).

Bailey, 'The rabbit and the medieval East Anglian economy' — Mark Bailey, 'The rabbit and the medieval East Anglian economy', *Agric. HR*, xxxvi, pt 1 (1988), pp. 1–20.

Barker, *West Suffolk Illustrated* — H. R. Barker, *West Suffolk Illustrated* (Bury St Edmunds, 1907).

Binns, *Dedications* — Alison Binns, *Dedications of Monastic Houses in England and Wales* (Woodbridge, 1989).

Bishop, 'Fasting and abstinence' — Edmund Bishop, 'The method and degree of fasting and abstinence of the Black Monks in England before the Reformation', *DR*, xliii (1925), pp. 184–237.

Brooke, *English Coins* (1950) — G. C. Brooke, *English Coins from the Seventh Century to the Present Day* (3rd edn, London, 1950).

Bryant, *A Touch of the Wind* — Michael Bryant, *A Touch of the Wind* (Thurston: Decroft Ltd, 2006). [About Pakenham windmill, its history and restoration.]

Bury St Edmunds, ed. Gransden — *Bury St Edmunds. Medieval Art, Architecture, Archaeology and Economy*, ed. A. Gransden, *BAA CT*, xx (1998 for 1994).

Cam, *The Hundred and the Hundred Rolls* — H. M. Cam, *The Hundred and the Hundred Rolls* (London, 1930).

Cam, 'The King's government as administered by the greater abbots of East Anglia' — H. M. Cam, 'The King's government as administered by the greater abbots of East Anglia', *Cambridge Antiquarian Soc. Communications*, xxix (1928), repr. eadem, *Liberties and Communities*, pp. 183–204.

Cam, *Liberties and Communities* — H. M. Cam, *Liberties and Communities in Medieval England. Collected Studies in Local Administration and Topography* (Cambridge, 1944).

Cam, 'Quo Warranto proceedings' — H. M. Cam, 'The Quo Warranto proceedings under Edward I', *History*, xi (1926), pp. 143–8, repr. eadem, *Liberties and Communities*, pp. 173–82.

Carpenter, *Henry III* — D. A. Carpenter, *The Reign of Henry III* (London – Rio Grande, 1996).

Carpenter, *Minority* — D. A. Carpenter, *The Minority of Henry III* (Berkeley – Los Angeles, 1990).

Cat. Arundel MSS (College of Arms) — [W. H. Black], *Catalogue of the Arundel Manuscripts in the Library of the College of Arms* (London, 1829, not published).

Cautley, *Suffolk Churches* — H. M. Cautley, *Suffolk Churches and their Treasures* (5th edn, Ipswich, 1982).

Cheney, *Bishops Chanceries* — C. R. Cheney, *English Bishops Chanceries 1100–1250* (Manchester, 1950).

Cheney, *Hubert Walter* — C. R. Cheney, *Hubert Walter* (London etc., 1967).

Cheney, 'King John's reaction to the interdict' — Cheney, 'King John's reaction to the interdict on England', *TRHS*, xlix (4th series, 1949), repr. idem, *The Papacy and England*, item X.

Cheney, *The Papacy and England*
C. R. Cheney, *The Papacy and England 12th–14th Centuries* (London, 1982).

Cheney and Jones, *Handbook*
C. R. Cheney, *Handbook of Dates for Students of English History* (London, 1945, rev. edn. 1970, revised by Michael Jones, Cambridge, 2000).

Cheney, Mary [G.], 'Inalienability in mid-twelfth-century England'
Mary [G.] Cheney, 'Inalienability in mid-twelfth-century England: Enforcement and consequences', *Monumenta Iuris Canonici, ser. C: subsidia*, vii (Vatican, 1985), pp. 467–78.

Cheney, Mary [G.], 'The litigation between John Marshal and Archbishop Thomas Becket in 1164'
Mary [G.] Cheney, 'The litigation between John Marshal and Archbishop Thomas Becket in 1164: A pointer to the origin of novel disseisin?', in *Law and Social Change in British History. Papers presented to the British Legal History Conference, 14–17 July 1981*, ed. J. A. Guy and H. G. Beale (London: Royal Hist. Soc. – New Jersey: Humanities Press, 1984), pp. 9–26.

Cheney, Mary [G.], *Roger, Bishop of Worcester*
Mary [G.] Cheney, *Roger, Bishop of Worcester 1164–1179. An English Bishop of the Age of Becket* (Oxford, 1980).

Chew, *Ecclesiastical Tenants-in-Chief*
H. M. Chew, *The English Ecclesiastical Tenants-in-Chief and Knight Service* (Oxford, 1932).

Clapham, *English Romanesque Architecture*
A. W. Clapham, *English Romanesque Architecture* (Oxford, 1930–4, repr. 1965), i, *Before the Conquest*, ii, *After the Conquest*.

Clay, *Mediaeval Hospitals*
R. M. Clay, *The Mediaeval Hospitals of England* (London, 1909, repr. 1966).

Clayton, *Cult of the Virgin Mary*
Mary Clayton, *The Cult of the Virgin Mary in Anglo-Saxon England*, Cambridge Studies in Anglo-Saxon England, ii (Cambridge, 1990).

Cobban, *Medieval English Universities*
A. B. Cobban, *The Medieval English Universities: Oxford and Cambridge to c. 1500* (Aldershot: Scolar Press, 1988).

Cook, 'The bezant in Angevin England'
B. J. Cook, 'The bezant in Angevin England', *The Numismatic Chronicle*, clix (1999), pp. 255–75.

Craib, *Itinerary of Henry IIII*
MS itinerary in the PRO compiled by Theodore Craib and other PRO officers.

Crook, 'Architectural setting of the cult of St Edmund'
John Crook, 'The architectural setting of the cult of St Edmund at Bury 1095–1539', in *Bury St Edmunds*, ed. Gransden, pp. 34–44 and pls XII A and B, XIII A and B, and XIV A and B.

Crook, *Records*
David Crook, *Records of the General Eyre*, Public Record Office Handbooks, xx (London, 1982).

Crosby, *Bishop and Chapter*
E. U. Crosby, *Bishop and Chapter in Twelfth-Century England. A Study of the 'Mensa Episcopalis'* (Cambridge, 1994).

Darby, *The Medieval Fenland*
H. C. Darby, *The Medieval Fenland* (Cambridge, 1940).

Davis, *Cartularies*
G. R. C. Davis, *Medieval Cartularies of Great Britain. A Short Catalogue* (London, New York and Toronto, 1958).

de Hamel, *Glossed Books*
C. F. R. de Hamel, *Glossed Books of the Bible and the Beginnings of the Paris Booktrade* (Woodbridge, 1984).

Douglas, *William the Conqueror* — D. C. Douglas, *William the Conqueror* (London, 1964).

Eaglen, *The Abbey and Mint of Bury St Edmunds to 1279* — R. J. Eaglen, *The Abbey and Mint of Bury St Edmunds to 1279*, British Numismatic Soc. Special Publication, vi (2006).

Eaglen, 'The mint at Bury St Edmunds' — R. J. Eaglen, 'The mint at Bury St Edmunds', in *Bury St Edmunds*, ed. Gransden, pp. 111–121.

Farmer, 'Millstones for medieval manors' — D. L. Farmer, 'Millstones for medieval manors', *Agricultural History Review*, xl, pt 2 (1992).

Farmer, *Saints* — D. H. Farmer, *The Oxford Dictionary of Saints* (Oxford, 1978).

Fernie, 'Romanesque church' — E. C. Fernie, 'The Romanesque church of Bury St Edmunds abbey', in *Bury St Edmunds*, ed. Gransden, pp. 1–15.

Gage, *Thingoe Hundred* — John Gage [Rokewode], *The History and Antiquities of Suffolk. Thingoe Hundred* (London, 1838).

Galbraith, 'Death of a champion' — V. H. Galbraith, 'The death of a champion (1287)', in *Studies in Medieval History Presented to F. M. Powicke*, ed. R. W. Hunt, W. A. Pantin, and R. W. Southern (Oxford, 1948, repr. 1969), pp. 283–95.

Galbraith, 'East Anglian see' — V. H. Galbraith, 'The East Anglian see and the abbey of Bury St Edmunds', *EHR*, xl (1925), pp. 222–8.

Gauthiez, 'Planning of the town of Bury St Edmunds' — Bernard Gauthiez, 'The planning of the town of Bury St Edmunds: a probable Norman origin', in *Bury St Edmunds*, ed. Gransden, pp. 81–97.

Gem, 'Towards an iconography' — Richard Gem, 'Towards an iconography of Anglo-Saxon architecture', *Journ. of the Warburg and Courtauld Institutes*, xlvi (1983), pp. 1–18.

Gem and Keen, 'Late Anglo-Saxon finds' — Richard Gem and Lawrence Keen, 'Late Anglo-Saxon finds from the site of St Edmund's abbey', *PSIAH*, xxxv, pt 1 (1981), pp. 1–30.

Gibbs and Lang, *Bishops and Reform* — Marion Gibbs and Jane Lang, *Bishops and Reform 1215–1272* (Oxford, 1934, repr. London, 1962).

Gies and Gies, *Cathedral, Forge and Waterwheel* — Francis and Joseph Gies, *Cathedral, Forge and Waterwheel. Technology and Invention in the Middle Ages* (New York, 1994).

Gillingham, *Richard* — John Gillingham, *Richard the Lionheart* (London, 1978).

Gilyard-Beer, 'Eastern arm' — R. Gilyard-Beer, 'The eastern arm of the abbey church at Bury St Edmunds', *PSIA*, xxxi, pt 3 (1969), pp. 256–62.

Gransden, 'The abbey of Bury St Edmunds and national politics' — A. Gransden, 'The abbey of Bury St Edmunds and national politics in the reigns of King John and Henry III', in *Monastic Studies*, ii, ed. Judith Loades (Bangor, 1991), pp. 67–86.

Gransden, 'Alleged incorruption' — A. Gransden, 'The alleged incorruption of the body of St Edmund, king and martyr', *The Antiquaries Journ.*, lxxiv (1994), pp. 135–68.

Gransden, 'Baldwin' — A. Gransden, 'Baldwin, abbot of Bury St Edmunds, 1065–1097', *Anglo-Norman Studies*, iv, *Proceedings of the Battle Conference, 1981* (Woodbridge, 1982), pp. 69–71 and nn.

Gransden, *Bury St Edmunds Abbey*, ii — A. Gransden, ~~A History of Bury St Edmunds Abbey, ii, 1257–1301~~: *Simon of Luton and John of Northwold* (Woodbridge, forthcoming).

Gransden, 'Composition and authorship of the *De Miraculis*' — A. Gransden, 'The composition and authorship of the *De Miraculis Sancti Eadmundi* attributed to "Hermann the Archdeacon"', *Journ. of Medieval Latin*, v (1995), pp. 1–52.

Gransden, 'Cronica Buriensis and the abbey of St Benet of Hulme' — A. Gransden, 'The Cronica Buriensis and the abbey of St Benet of Hulme', *Bulletin of the Institute of Historical Research*, xxxvi (1963), pp. 77–82 (repr. in eadem, *Legends, Traditions and History*, pp. 239–44).

Gransden, 'Cult of St Mary' — A. Gransden, 'The cult of St Mary at Beodericisworth and then in Bury St Edmunds abbey to c. 1150', *JEH*, lv, pt 4 (2004), pp. 627–53.

Gransden, 'Democratic movement' — A. Gransden, 'A democratic movement in the abbey of Bury St. Edmunds in the late twelfth and early thirteenth centuries', *JEH*, xxvi (1975), pp. 25–39.

Gransden, *Exhibition Catalogue* — A. Gransden, 'Some manuscripts in Cambridge from Bury St Edmunds abbey: Exhibition catalogue', in *Bury St Edmunds*, ed. Gransden, pp. 228–85 and pls LVII A – LXXXIV B.

Gransden, *Historical Writing*, [i] — A. Gransden, *Historical Writing in England*, [i], *c. 550–c. 1307* (London, 1974, repr. 1998).

Gransden, 'John de Northwold' — A. Gransden, 'John de Northwold, abbot of Bury St. Edmunds (1279–1301), and his defence of its Liberties', in *Thirteenth-Century England. Proceedings of the 1989 Newcastle Conference*, ed. Simon Lloyd and P. R. Cross (Woodbridge, 1991), pp. 91–112.

Gransden, *Legends, Traditions and History* — A. Gransden, *Legends, Traditions and History in Medieval England* (London, 1992).

Gransden, '"Passio"' — A. Gransden, 'Abbo of Fleury's "Passio Sancti Eadmundi"', *Revue Bénédictine*, cv (Maredsous, 1995), pp. 20–78 and pls I–V.

Gransden, 'Question of the consecration' — A. Gransden, 'The question of the consecration of St Edmund's Church', in *Church and Chronicle in the Middle Ages. Essays presented to John Taylor*, ed. Ian Wood and G. A. Loud (London, 1991), pp. 59–86.

Gransden, 'Separation of portions' — A. Gransden, 'The separation of portions between abbot and convent at Bury St Edmunds: The decisive years, 1278–1281', *EHR*, cxix (2004), pp. 373–406.

Hagiography, ed. Head — *Medieval Hagiography*, ed. Thomas Head (New York – London, 2001).

Hallam, *Domesday Book* — E. M. Hallam, *Domesday Book through Nine Centuries* (London, 1986).

Hallam, *Rural England* — H. E. Hallam, *Rural England (1066–1348)* (Brighton: Harvester Press Ltd – New Jersey: Humanities Press Inc., 1981).

Handbook of British Chronology — *Handbook of British Chronology*, 3rd edn by E. B. Fryde, D. E. Greenway, S. Porter and I. Roy (London, 1986).

Harriss, *King, Parliament and Public Finance*
G. L. Harriss, *King, Parliament and Public Finance in Medieval England to 1369* (Oxford, 1975).

Harvey, *Living and Dying*
Barbara [F.] Harvey, *Living and Dying in England 1100–1540. The Monastic Experience* (Oxford, 1993).

Harvey, *Westminster Abbey*
Barbara [F.] Harvey, *Westminster Abbey and its Estates in the Middle Ages* (Oxford, 1977).

Harvey, *Manorial Records*
P. D. A. Harvey, *Manorial Records*, British Records Assoc., Archives and the User, no. 5 (1984).

Harvey, 'Pipe Rolls and the adoption of demesne farming'
P. D. A. Harvey, 'The Pipe Rolls and the adoption of demesne farming in England', *Ec. HR*, 2nd ser., xxvii, no. 3 (1974), pp. 345–59.

Harvey, 'Some mid-13th-century accounts'
P. D. A. Harvey, 'Some mid-13th-century accounts from Bury St Edmunds Abbey', in *Bury St Edmunds*, ed. Gransden, pp. 128–38.

Heslop, 'Artistry of the Bury Bible'
T. A. Heslop, 'The production and artistry of the Bury Bible', in *Bury St Edmunds*, ed. Gransden, pp. 172–85.

Hills, 'Antiquities'
G. M. Hills, 'The Antiquities of Bury St. Edmunds', in *JBAA*, xxi (1865), pp. 32–56, 104–40.

Historical Atlas of Suffolk
An Historical Atlas of Suffolk, ed. David Dymond and Edward Martin (revised and enlarged edn, Ipswich, 1999).

Holt, *Colonial England*
J. C. Holt, *Colonial England, 1066–1215* (London, 1997).

Holt, *Magna Carta*
J. C. Holt, *Magna Carta* (Cambridge, 1965, 2nd edn with additions, Cambridge, 1992, repr. 1994, 1995).

Holt, *Mills*
Richard Holt, *The Mills of Medieval England* (Oxford, Blackwells, 1988).

Homans, *English Villagers*
G. C. Homans, *English Villagers of the Thirteenth Century* (Cambridge, Mass., 1942, repr. paperback New York 1970).

Howell, 'Abbatial vacancies'
Margaret Howell, 'Abbatial vacancies and the divided "Mensa" in medieval England', *JEH*, xxxiii (1982).

Howell, 'The resources of Eleanor of Provence'
Margaret Howell, 'The resources of Eleanor of Provence as queen consort', *EHR*, cii (1987), pp. 372–93.

Howell, *Regalian Right*
Margaret Howell, *Regalian Right in Medieval England* (London, 1962).

Hudson, *Land, Law and Lordship*
John Hudson, *Land, Law and Lordship in Anglo-Norman England* (Oxford, 1994).

James, *Abbey*
M. R. James, *On the Abbey of S. Edmund at Bury*, I. *The Library*, II. *The Church*, Publication of the Cambridge Antiquarian Soc., octavo ser. viii (Cambridge, 1895).

James, *Cat. Corpus*
M. R. James, *A Descriptive Catalogue of the Manuscripts in the Library of Corpus Christi College, Cambridge* (Cambridge, 1909, 2 vols).

James, *Cat. Gonville and Caius*
M. R. James, *A Descriptive Catalogue of the Manuscripts in the Library of Gonville and Caius College, Cambridge* (Cambridge, 1907–14, 3 vols).

James, *Cat. Pemb.*
M. R. James, *A Descriptive Catalogue of the Manuscripts in the Library of Pembroke College, Cambridge* (Cambridge, 1905).

James, *Cat. St John's*
M. R. James, *A Descriptive Catalogue of the Manuscripts in the Library of St John's College, Cambridge* (Cambridge, 1913).

James, *Verses formerly inscribed on Twelve Windows in the Choir of Canterbury Cathedral* M. R. James, *The Verses formerly inscribed on Twelve Windows in the Choir of Canterbury Cathedral*, Publication of the Cambridge Antiquarian Soc., octavo ser. xxxviii (Cambridge, 1901), pp. 1–42.

Jurkowski, Smith and Crook, *Lay Taxes in England and Wales* M. Jurkowski, C. L. Smith and D. Crook, *Lay Taxes in England and Wales 1188–1688* (London: PRO Publications, Public Record Office Handbook no. 31, 1998).

Kauffmann, 'Bury Bible' C. M. Kauffmann, 'The Bury Bible (Cambridge, Corpus Christi College, MS 2)', *Journ. of the Warburg and Courtauld Institutes*, xxix (1966), pp. 60–81.

Kauffmann, *Romanesque MSS* C. M. Kauffmann, *Romanesque Manuscripts 1066–1190. A Survey of Manuscripts illuminated in the British Isles*, ed. J. J. G. Alexander, iii (London, 1975).

Kealey, *Harvesting the Air* E. J. Kealey, *Harvesting the Air: Windmill Pioneers in Twelfth-Century England* (Berkeley: University of California Press, 1987).

Ker, *Libraries* N. R. Ker, *Medieval Libraries of Great Britain: A List of Surviving Books* (2nd edn, London, 1964).

King, *Peterborough Abbey* Edmund King, *Peterborough Abbey 1086–1310. A Study in the Land Market* (Cambridge, 1973).

Knowles, 'Abbatial elections' David Knowles, 'Essays in monastic history 1066–1215. i. Abbatial elections', *DR*, xlix (1931).

Knowles, 'Growth of exemption' M. D. Knowles, 'Essays in monastic history. iv. The growth of exemption', *DR*, l (1932), pp. 201–31, 396–436.

Kosminsky, *Agrarian History* E. A. Kosminsky, *Studies in the Agrarian History of England in the Thirteenth Century*, ed. R. H. Hilton, trans. from the Russian by Ruth Kisch (Oxford, 1956).

Landels, *Engineering in the Ancient World* J. G. Landels, *Engineering in the Ancient World* (Berkeley – Los Angeles: University of California Press, 1978).

Landers, *Field and Forge* John Landers, *The Field and the Forge: Population, Production, and Power in the Pre-Industrial West* (Oxford, 2003).

Landon, *Itinerary of Richard I* Lionel Landon, *The Itinerary of King Richard I*, Pipe Roll Soc., n.s. xiii (1935).

Langdon, *Mills* John Langdon, *Mills in the Medieval Economy. England 1300–1540* (Oxford, 2004).

Lawrence, 'Long-cross coinage' L. A. Lawrence, 'The long-cross coinage of Henry III and Edward I', *BNJ*, ix (1912), pp. 145–79.

Legge, *Anglo-Norman in the Cloisters* M. D. Legge, *Anglo-Norman in the Cloisters. The Influence of the Orders upon Anglo-Norman Literature* (Edinburgh, 1950).

Legge, *Anglo-Norman Lit.* M. D. Legge, *Anglo-Norman Literature and its Background* (Oxford, 1963).

Levett, *Manorial Studies* A. E. Levett, *Studies in Manorial History*, ed. H. M. Cam, Mary Coate and L. S. Sutherland (Oxford, 1938).

Lobel, *Bury St. Edmunds* M. D. Lobel, *The Borough of Bury St. Edmunds: A Study in the Government and Development of a Monastic Town* (Oxford, 1935).

Lobel, 'List of aldermen and bailiffs' M. D. Lobel, 'A list of the aldermen and bailiffs of Bury St. Edmunds from the twelfth to the sixteenth century', *PSIANH*, xxii (1936), pp. 17–28.

Loomis, 'Growth of the St Edmund legend' — Grant Loomis, 'The growth of the Saint Edmund legend', *Harvard Studies in Philology and Literature*, xiv (1932), pp. 83–113.

Lord, *Knights Templar* — Evelyn Lord, *The Knights Templar in Britain* (Harlow – London, 2002).

Lunt, 'Consent to taxation' — W. E. Lunt, 'The consent of the English lower clergy to taxation during the reign of Henry III', in *Persecution and Liberty. Essays in Honour of George Lincoln Burr* (New York, 1931), pp. 117–69.

Lunt, *Fin. Relations* — W. E. Lunt, *Financial Relations of the Papacy with England to 1327* (Cambridge, Mass., 1939).

Lunt, *Papal Revenues* — W. E. Lunt, *Papal Revenues in the Middle Ages* (Columbia UP, 1934, repr. Octagon Books, New York, 1965, 2 vols).

McAleer, 'West front' — J. B. McAleer, 'The west front of the abbey church', in *Bury St Edmunds*, ed. Gransden, pp. 22–33 and pls VI A and B – XI B.

McDonnell, *Inland Fisheries* — J. McDonnell, *Inland Fisheries in Medieval Yorkshire 1066–1300*, Borthwick Papers no. xl (York, 1981).

McGuire, 'Collapse of a monastic friendship' — P. B. McGuire, 'The collapse of a monastic friendship: The case of Jocelin and Samson of Bury', *Journ. of Medieval History*, iv (1978), pp. 369–97.

McKinley, *Norfolk and Suffolk Surnames* — Richard McKinley, *Norfolk and Suffolk Surnames in the Middle Ages*, English Surnames Series, ii (London – Chichester: Phillimore, 1975).

McLachlan, *Scriptorium* — E. P. McLachlan, *The Scriptorium of Bury St Edmunds in the Twelfth Century* (New York – London: Garland Publishing, Inc., 1986).

McLachlan, 'Wake' — E. P. McLachlan, 'In the Wake of the Bury Bible: Followers of Master Hugo at Bury St. Edmunds', *Journ. of the Warburg and Courtauld Institutes*, xlii (1979), 216–24.

Miller, *Ely* — Edward Miller, *The Abbey and Bishopric of Ely. A Social History of an Ecclesiastical Estate from the tenth century to the early fourteenth century* (Cambridge, 1951).

Miller and Hatcher, *Rural Society* — Edward Miller and John Hatcher, *Medieval England: Rural Society and Economic Change 1086–1348* (London – New York, 1978).

Miller and Hatcher, *Towns, Commerce and Crafts* — Edward Miller and John Hatcher, *Medieval England: Towns, Commerce and Crafts 1086–1348* (London – New York, 1995).

Mills, *British Place-Names* — A. D. Mills, *A Dictionary of English Place-Names* (Oxford, 2003 edn).

Mitchell, *Taxation in Medieval England* — S. K. Mitchell, *Taxation in Medieval England*, ed. Sidney Painter (New Haven, [USA], 1951).

Mitchell, *Taxation under John and Henry III* — S. K. Mitchell, *Studies in Taxation under John and Henry III* (New Haven, [USA], 1914).

Moorman, *Church Life in England* — J. R. H. Moorman, *Church Life in England in the Thirteenth Century* (Cambridge, 1955).

New Historical Geography — *A New Historical Geography of England before 1600*, ed. H. C. Darby (Cambridge, 1976, repr. 1980).

A New History of the Royal Mint	*A New History of the Royal Mint*, ed. C. E. Challis (Cambridge, 1992).
Nilson, *Cathedral Shrines*	Ben[jamin John] Nilson, *Cathedral Shrines of Medieval England* (Woodbridge – New York, 1998).
North, *God's Clockmaker*	John North, *God's Clockmaker. Richard of Wallingford and the Invention of Time* (London – New York, 2005).
Norwich Cathedral	*Norwich Cathedral. Church, City and Diocese, 1096–1996*, ed. Ian Atherton, Eric Fernie, Christopher Harper-Bill and Hassell Smith (London – Rio Grande, 1996).
Parker, *The Making of Kings Lynn*	Vanessa Parker, *The Making of Kings Lynn. Secular Buildings from the 11th to the 17th century*, Kings Lynn Archaeological Survey, i (London – Chichester, 1971).
Pestell, *Landscapes of Monastic Foundation*	Tim Pestell, *Landscapes of Monastic Foundation* (Woodbridge, 2004).
Pestell, 'Monastic foundation strategies'	Tim Pestell, 'Monastic foundation strategies in the early Norman diocese of Norwich', *Anglo-Norman Studies*, xxiii, *Proceedings of the Battle Conference, 2000* (Woodbridge, 2001), pp. 199–229.
Pluck, *The River Waveney*	D. F. Pluck, *The River Waveney. Its Navigation and Watermills* (Bungay, Suffolk, 1940).
Poole, *Domesday Book to Magna Carta*	A. L. Poole, *From Domesday Book to Magna Carta 1087–1216* (Oxford, 1951).
Powicke, *Henry III and the Lord Edward*	F. M[aurice] Powicke, *Henry III and the Lord Edward* (Oxford, 1947, 2 vols).
Prigg, *Icklingham Papers*	Henry Prigg, *Icklingham Papers. Manors, Churches, Town-Lands and Antiquities of Icklingham together with the text and translation of the Berners' Manorial Accounts, 1342–3*, with notes and addenda by V. B. Redstone (Woodbridge, 1901).
Raban, *A Second Domesday?*	Sandra Raban, *A Second Domesday? The Hundred Rolls of 1279–80* (Oxford, 2004).
Rackham, 'Abbey woods'	Oliver Rackham, 'The abbey woods', in *Bury St Edmunds*, ed. Gransden, pp. 139–60.
Rashdall, *Medieval Universities*	Hastings Rashdall, *The Universities of Europe in the Middle Ages* (Oxford, 1895, 3 vols, new edn by F. M. Powicke and A. B. Emden, Oxford, 1936, 3 vols).
Ridyard, *Royal Saints*	S. J. Ridyard, *The Royal Saints of Anglo-Saxon England*, Cambridge Studies of Medieval Life and Thought, 4th ser., ix (Cambridge, 1988).
Rogers, 'Bury artists of Harley 2278'	Nicholas Rogers, 'The Bury artists of Harley 2278 and the origins of topographical awareness in English art', in *Bury St Edmunds*, ed. Gransden, pp. 219–27 and pls LIII A and B – LVII.
Rosser, *Medieval Westminster*	Gervase Rosser, *Medieval Westminster 1200–1540* (Oxford, 1989).
Roth, *Jews in England*	Cecil Roth, *A History of the Jews in England* (Oxford, 1941, 3rd edn 1964).
Rouse, 'Bostonus Buriensis'	R. H. Rouse, 'Bostonus Buriensis and the author of the *Catalogus Scriptorum Ecclesiae*', *Speculum*, xli (1966), pp. 471–99.
Sayers, *Honorius III*	J. E. Sayers, *Papal Government and England during the Pontificate of Honorius III (1216–1227)* (Cambridge, 1984).

Sayers, *Papal Judges Delegate* — J. E. Sayers, *Papal Judges Delegate in the Province of Canterbury 1198–1254. A Study in Ecclesiastical Jurisdiction and Administration* (Oxford, 1971).

Scarfe, 'Jocelin' — Norman Scarfe, 'Jocelin of Brakelond's identity: A review of the evidence', *PSIAH*, xxxix, pt 1 (1997), pp. 1–5.

Scarfe, *Suffolk* — Norman Scarfe, *Suffolk in the Middle Ages* (Woodbridge, 1986).

Sharpe, *Handlist* — Richard Sharpe, *A Handlist of the Latin Writers of Great Britain and Ireland before 1540* (Turnhout: Brepols, Publication of the Journ. of Medieval Latin, 1997).

Sharpe, 'Reconstructing the medieval library' — Richard Sharpe, 'Reconstructing the medieval library of Bury St Edmunds abbey: The lost catalogue of Henry of Kirkstead', in *Bury St Edmunds*, ed. Gransden, pp. 204–18.

Shorter Catalogues — *English Benedictine Libraries. The Shorter Catalogues*, ed. Richard Sharpe, J. B. Carley, R. M. Thomson and A. G. Watson, *Corpus of British Medieval Library Catalogues*, iv (London: The British Library in association with the British Academy, 1996).

Smalley, *Study of the Bible* — Beryl Smalley, *The Study of the Bible in the Middle Ages* (Oxford, 1941, 2nd edn Oxford – New York, 1952).

Snape, *Monastic Finances* — R. H. Snape, *English Monastic Finances in the Later Middle Ages* (Cambridge, 1926, pr. New York, 1926 and repr. 1968).

Southern, '"Miracles"' — R. W. Southern, 'The English origins of the "Miracles of the Virgin"', *Medieval and Renaissance Studies*, iv (1958), pp. 176–216.

Southern, *St Anselm and his Biographer* — R. W. Southern, *Saint Anselm and his Biographer* (Cambridge, 1963).

Statham, *Book of Bury St Edmunds* — Margaret Statham, *The Book of Bury St Edmunds* (Baron Birch, 1988, revised edn, privately printed, Frome, 1996).

Statham, 'Medieval town' — Margaret Statham, 'The medieval town of Bury St Edmunds', in *Bury St Edmunds*, ed. Gransden, pp. 98–110.

Statham, *Yesterday's Town: Bury St Edmunds* — Margaret Statham, *Yesterday's Town: Bury St Edmunds* (Baron Birch, 1992).

Thompson, *Women Religious* — Sally Thompson, *Women Religious. The Founding of English Nunneries after the Norman Conquest* (Oxford, 1991, special edn for Sandpiper Books Ltd, 1996).

Thomson, *Archives* — *The Archives of the Abbey of Bury St Edmunds*, ed. R. M. Thomson, Suffolk Records Soc., xxi (Woodbridge, 1980).

Thomson, 'Library' — R. M. Thomson, 'The Library of Bury St Edmunds Abbey in the Eleventh and Twelfth Centuries', *Speculum*, xlvii (1972), pp. 617–45.

Thomson, 'Obedientiaries' — R. M. Thomson, 'Obedientiaries of St Edmund's Abbey', *PSIAH*, xxxv, pt 2 (1982), pp. 91–103.

Thomson, 'Two versions of a saint's Life' — R. M. Thomson, 'Two versions of a saint's Life from St Edmund's abbey. Changing currents in twelfth-century monastic style', *Revue Bénédictine*, lxxxv (1974), pp. 387–9.

Tull, *Traces of the Templars* — G. F. Tull, *Traces of the Templars* (Rotherham: The King's England Press, 2000).

Vaughan, 'The election of abbots at St Albans' — Richard Vaughan, 'The election of abbots at St Albans in the thirteenth and fourteenth centuries', *Proceedings of the Cambridge Antiquarian Soc.*, xlvii (1953), pp. 1–12.

Vaughan, *Matthew Paris*   Richard Vaughan, *Matthew Paris* (Cambridge, 1958).

Vincent, *Peter des Roches*   Nicholas Vincent, *Peter des Roches* (Cambridge, 1977).

Wall, *Shrines*   J. C. Wall, *Shrines of British Saints* (London, 1905).

Warren, *Henry II*   W. L. Warren, *Henry II* (London, 1973).

Warren, *King John*   W. L. Warren, *King John* (London, 1961, 2nd edn, 1978).

Watts, *Archaeology of Mills and Milling*   Martin Watts, *The Archaeology of Mills and Milling* (Stroud: Tempus, 2002).

Webber, 'Provision of books'   Teresa Webber, 'The provision of books for Bury St Edmunds abbey in the eleventh and twelfth centuries', in *Bury St Edmunds*, ed. Gransden, pp. 186–93.

Wedemeyer Moore, *Fairs*   Ellen Wedemeyer Moore, *The Fairs of Medieval England*, Pontifical Institute of Medieval Studies; Studies and Texts, lxxii (Toronto, 1985).

Weiler, *Henry III of England and the Staufen Empire*   B. K. U. Weiler, *Henry III of England and the Staufen Empire, 1216–1272* (London: Royal Historical Soc., Studies in History).

Welldon Finn, *Introduction to Domesday Book*   R. Welldon Finn, *An Introduction to Domesday Book* (London etc., 1963).

Whitelock, 'Fact and fiction'   Dorothy Whitelock, 'Fact and fiction in the legend of St Edmund', *PSIA*, xxxi, pt 3 (1969), pp. 217–33.

Whittingham, 'Bury St. Edmunds Abbey'   A. B. Whittingham, 'Bury St. Edmunds abbey. The plan, design and development of the church and monastic buildings', *Archaeological Journ.*, cviii (1952 for 1951), pp. 173–83.

Whittingham, *Bury St Edmunds Abbey*   A. B. Whittingham, *Bury St Edmunds Abbey* (London: English Heritage, 1992).

Wilmart, 'Prayers'   André Wilmart, 'The prayers of the Bury Psalter', *DR*, xlviii (1930), pp. 198–216.

Wilson, *Greene King*   R. G. Wilson, *Greene King: A Business and Family History* (London, 1983). [About the present-day brewery at Bury St Edmunds]

Yarrow, *Saints and their Communities*   Simon Yarrow, *Saints and their Communities. Miracle Stories in Twelfth-Century England* (Oxford, 2006).

Index

Names in small capitals denote nineteenth-century and later contributors to monastic and manuscript studies and/or local history.

no ref to Coggeshall

Other Volumes in
Studies in the History of Medieval Religion